Cover

HMCS *Drumheller* entering harbour at St. John's, Newfoundland, early in 1945, painted by Tom Wood (1913-), a Canadian war artist. Fifty years ago, the small ships of the Royal Canadian Navy, such as this corvette, played a major part in defeating the German submarine threat in the Battle of the Atlantic, a battle fought from the very first to the very last day of the war.
(Courtesy Canadian War Museum, no. 10554)

Couverture

Dans ce tableau à l'huile par Tom Wood (1913-), un peintre canadien de guerre, le *Drumheller* entre dans le port de St. John's (Terre-Neuve), au début de l'année 1945. Il y a cinquante ans, les petits vaisseaux de la Marine royale canadienne, comme cette corvette, ont joué un rôle majeur dans l'élimination de la menace que constituaient les sous-marins allemands dans la bataille de l'Atlantique qui aura duré du premier jour de la guerre jusqu'au tout dernier.
(gracieuseté du Musée canadien de la guerre, no 10554)

DEPARTMENT OF NATIONAL DEFENCE
DIRECTORATE OF
HISTORY AND HERITAGE

Monograph Series No. 2

THIRD EDITION

Published by authority of the Minister
of National Defence

DIRECTION — HISTOIRE ET PATRIMOINE DU MINISTÈRE DE LA DÉFENSE NATIONALE

Monographie n° 2

TROISIÈME ÉDITION

Publication autorisée par le ministre
de la Défense nationale

O.A. COOKE

The Canadian Military Experience 1867-1995: A Bibliography

THIRD EDITION

Directorate of History and Heritage
Department of National Defence
Ottawa, Canada
1997

O.A. COOKE

Bibliographie de
la vie militaire au Canada
1867-1995

TROISIÈME ÉDITION

Direction — Histoire et patrimoine
Ministère de la Défense nationale
Ottawa, Canada
1997

Foreword to the Third Edition

Between 1989 and 1995 we have witnessed a wealth of 50th anniversaries of events related to the Second World War. Some have marked episodes well-known in Canadian military history, such as the Normandy landings, the strategic bombing offensive or the Battle of the Atlantic, while others, such as the construction of the Alaska Highway, are less famous. All have, however, provided occasions for research in greater depth and scope based upon sources which, with the passage of time, have become more accessible, including recently published memoirs of the war years from many of the participants, now long retired. But, since the second edition of this bibliography in 1984, new works on Canadian military history and thought have not been limited simply to revision of Second World War history. The end of the Cold War, diminishing resources for defence, the changing nature of Canada's security problems and Canada's part in an alliance structure have all prompted re-examination of Canada's defence policy. The roles of the Canadian Armed Forces in the Oka crisis and in the Persian Gulf have resulted in new books, as has the changing nature of peacekeeping in the former Yugoslavia, in Somalia, in Haiti and in Rwanda.

The end of the Cold War has also meant that many previously inaccessible records are now being opened to study, resulting in new scholarship on the post-war era: on the Cuban missile crisis, the air defence of North America, the Avro Arrow and Canadian involvement in chemical and biological warfare research, to name only a few areas.

Since 1984 the number of titles cited in *The Canadian Military Experience* has increased by about one-third. These new works deal not only with the Second World War and the years 1945-1995, but they also include growth in all aspects of Canadian military history since 1867 and bring us a better understanding of the military aspect of our history.

We believe that this third edition of the bibliography will be an indispensable tool both for scholars beginning further research and as a guide to the reader in Canadian military history. This excellent bibliography has been a labour of love for

Avant-propos de la troisième édition

Entre 1989 et 1995, nous avons vécu une panoplie de 50e anniversaires d'événements reliés à la Seconde Guerre mondiale. Certains marquaient des épisodes bien connus de l'histoire militaire canadienne, comme le débarquement en Normandie, le bombardement stratégique ou la bataille de l'Atlantique, alors que d'autres étaient moins bien connus, comme la construction de la route de l'Alaska. Tous ont cependant fourni l'occasion de recherches plus poussées fondées sur des sources que le passage du temps a rendu récemment accessibles, dont des réflexions et des témoignages révélateurs sur les années 1939-1945 fournis par de nombreux acteurs de l'époque, aujourd'hui à la retraite. Mais, depuis la deuxième édition de cette bibliographie, en 1984, la préparation d'ouvrages sur la pensée et l'histoire militaires canadiennes a été bien plus qu'une simple révision du déroulement de la Seconde Guerre mondiale. La fin de la guerre Froide, la diminution des ressources allouées à la défense, la nature changeante des problèmes reliés à la sécurité du pays et la participation canadienne à des alliances sont toutes des situations qui ont conduit à réviser notre politique de défense. Les rôles des Forces armées canadiennes à Oka et dans le golfe Persique ont abouti à des livres alors que les changements vécus dans le cadre d'opérations de maintien de la paix en Yougoslavie, en Somalie, en Haïti ou au Rwanda, sont étudiés en ce moment même.

La fin de la guerre Froide a donné accès à plusieurs fonds d'archives restés jusque-là inaccessibles. Leur ouverture a permis la parution d'ouvrages sur l'après-1945: la crise des missiles à Cuba, la défense de l'espace aérien nord-américain, l'avion Avro Arrow et l'implication du pays dans la recherche sur la guerre chimique et bactériologique sont quelques-uns des exemples de cette nature.

Depuis 1984, la *Bibliographie de la vie militaire au Canada* a vu son nombre de titres s'accroître d'environ un tiers. Ces nouveaux ouvrages, qui ne traitent pas que de la Seconde Guerre mondiale ou des années 1945-1995, aboutissent au total à un approfondissement et à un élargissement de tous les aspects de l'histoire militaire canadienne depuis 1867 et permettent une meilleure compréhension de cette partie de notre histoire.

Nous sommes assuré que cette troisième édition de la bibliographie sera un outil indispensable à tous les chercheurs entreprenant une nouvelle recherche en histoire militaire canadienne ainsi qu'à tout amateur de ce type d'histoire. Ce merveilleux instrument est dû, d'abord et avant tout, au travail acharné et à l'amour

Owen Cooke since its inception. In the name of all those who use it and personally, I thank him for it.

Serge Bernier
Director
Directorate of History and Heritage
National Defence

March 1997

que porte Owen Cooke à cette bibliographie qui est restée son enfant chéri depuis sa conception. Au nom de tous les utilisateurs et en mon nom personnel, je tiens à l'en remercier.

Serge Bernier
Directeur
Histoire et patrimoine
Défense nationale

Mars 1997

Foreword to the First Edition

Occasional papers are published by the Directorate of History at National Defence Headquarters in Ottawa. They contain information that, although it is of great interest, is too detailed for inclusion in the official histories of the Canadian armed forces. The first such book was T.W. Melnyk's *Canadian Flying Operations in South East Asia, 1941-1945*, published in 1976.

Occasional Paper No. 2, O.A. Cooke's *The Canadian Military Experience, 1867-1967: a Bibliography* represents years of patient investigation to fill a serious gap in our knowledge about published sources of Canadian military history. The extraordinary number of books and pamphlets in this field tends to belie the popular impression that Canadians are an unmilitary people. To be sure, careful examination will show that there are relatively few works of great substance, but that is not the point. What is important is that for the first hundred years after Confederation there was sufficient public interest to warrant the efforts required to write and publish over 2000 books and pamphlets purely on military affairs. They all need to be consulted by historians of Canada's military past, and we can say with some assurance from this evidence that the subject has enjoyed a continuing and dynamic interest in the nation.

The editor would have had to expand this bibliography significantly had he included titles dealing with political and social affairs that also touched on military topics. Such titles have therefore been omitted. They are readily found in standard Canadian bibliographies such as those mentioned in Part A of the text. The purpose of this book is to guide readers to purely military titles that are often left out of all the listings now in print.

The Canadian military experience is of course bound up in geography. The 3000-mile border with the United States, the transatlantic economic and political ties with European nations, the coastline that includes our polar regions as well as two very long seaboards on the Atlantic and Pacific oceans, have on the one hand placed Canada in a position of some strategic importance and on the other have always rendered it vulnerable to military threats from powerful neighbours. The entries that deal adequately with such questions should be fairly self-evident, even though no attempt has been made to provide annotations for the list. But the military experience is also bound up in personalities and outlooks formed by the various backgrounds of the authors here represented. Whether they had military experience themselves or not, on land, sea or air, they were all formed by the

Avant-propos de la première édition

Le Service historique de la Défense nationale, à Ottawa, publie parfois des ouvrages qui, même s'ils sont d'un grand intérêt, sont trop détaillés pour paraître dans les histoires officielles des Forces armées du Canada. Le premier de ces ouvrages, *Les opérations aériennes du Canada dans le Sud-Est asiatique, 1941-1945,* de T.W. Melnyk, a été publié en 1976.

Le deuxième, *Bibliographie de la vie militaire au Canada, 1867-1967,* édité par O.A. Cooke, représente plusieurs années de travail acharné pour combler une profonde lacune dans nos connaissances des documents publiés sur l'histoire militaire du Canada. Le nombre incroyable de volumes et de brochures dans ce domaine tend à démentir l'impression générale voulant que les Canadiens ne soient pas un peuple militaire dans l'âme. Bien sûr, un examen attentif montrera qu'il y a relativement peu de travaux de grande valeur, mais là n'est pas la question. Ce qui importe c'est qu'au cours des cent années qui ont suivi la Confédération le grand public a montré suffisamment d'intérêt pour qu'on fasse l'effort d'écrire et de publier plus de 2 000 livres et brochures sur des sujets purement militaires. Les historiens s'intéressant au passé militaire du Canada se doivent de les consulter et nous pouvons dire avec quelque assurance à partir de ces chiffres que le sujet a connu et continue de connaître une grande vogue au pays.

Le rédacteur aurait pu augmenter considérablement cette bibliographie s'il y avait inclus les titres des ouvrages portant sur des questions politiques et sociales qui touchent également à des sujets militaires. Il les a donc laissés de côté. On peut néanmoins facilement trouver ces titres dans d'autres bibliographies sur le Canada comme celles mentionnées dans la partie A du texte. Cet ouvrage vise plutôt à orienter les lecteurs vers les volumes purement militaires, qu'on ne retrouve pas dans les listes imprimées actuelles.

L'expérience militaire du Canada est évidemment reliée à la géographie du pays. Sa frontière de 3 000 milles avec les États-Unis, ses liens politiques et économiques avec les pays d'Europe, son littoral qui comprend les régions polaires et les rives des océans Atlantique et Pacifique ont, d'une part, placé le Canada dans une position importante sur le plan stratégique et d'autre part, l'ont toujours rendu vulnérable à la menace militaire de ses puissants voisins. Il suffit de lire les titres des ouvrages pour savoir lesquels sont consacrés à ces questions, même si l'on n'a pas jugé bon d'ajouter des notes explicatives à la liste. Mais la vie militaire est aussi liée à certaines personnalités et à la perspective que nous donnent les origines

circumstances of their lives, by such things as education, religion, political leanings and climate. Understanding the Canadian military means understanding these people, and in that respect the present bibliography is unique, containing information that in some cases has never been tapped. We hope therefore that this Occasional Paper will be of use to the scholar, the military buff and the general reader alike. And we hope it will lay the basis for a continuing and complete record of writings in this field.

W.A.B. Douglas
Director
Directorate of History

November 1979

des divers auteurs ici répresentés. Qu'ils aient ou non servi dans l'infanterie, la marine ou l'aviation, ils ont tous été formés par les expériences qu'ils ont vécues, par l'éducation qu'ils ont reçue, par leur religion, leurs tendances politiques et le climat politique. Comprendre la vie militaire au Canada, c'est comprendre ces auteurs; à cet égard, cette bibliographie est unique, car elle contient des sources de renseignements qui parfois n'ont jamais encore été utilisées. Nous souhaitons que cet ouvrage soit de quelque utilité à l'érudit, au mordu de la chose militaire et au public en général. Nous espérons en outre qu'il constitue le point de départ d'un dossier complet et sans cesse renouvelé des ouvrages publiés dans ce domaine.

W. A. B. Douglas
Directeur
Service historique de la Défense nationale

Novembre 1979

Table of Contents

		Page
	Introduction	xvi
A.	Bibliography	1
B.	Defence Policy and General Works	5
C.	Naval Forces	
	1867-1914	63
	1914-1918	67
	1919-1945	76
	1946-1967	98
D.	Land Forces	
	1867-1914	113
	1914-1918	155
	1919-1945	218
	1946-1967	280
E.	Air Forces	
	1867-1918	305
	1919-1945	317
	1946-1967	353
F.	The Unified Canadian Forces since 1968	371
	Index	
	Subjects	410
	Persons	476

Table des matières

		Page
Introduction	. . . .	xvii
A.	Bibliographie	1
B.	Les politiques de la défense et généralités	5
C.	Les forces maritimes	
	1867-1914	63
	1914-1918	67
	1919-1945	76
	1946-1967	98
D.	Les forces terrestres	
	1867-1914	113
	1914-1918	155
	1919-1945	218
	1946-l967	280
F.	Les forces aériennes	
	1867-1918	305
	1919-1945	317
	1946-1967	353
F.	Les Forces canadiennes unifiées depuis 1968	371
	Index	
	Sujets	411
	Personnes	476

Introduction

Canadian military history and military matters have not been well represented in general in retrospective bibliographies of Canadiana or in international military bibliographies. Although a small number of very useful listings of some aspects of Canadian military history, such as those on unit histories or of the writings of such prolific military authors as C.P. Stacey or G.F.G. Stanley, have been produced, no comprehensive list of references to guide the researcher interested in Canada's military past has been published.

What has been attempted here is a bibliography of published primary sources and secondary works on Canadian military topics, excluding poetry and fiction, covering the period from Confederation to the present.

Entries in the bibliography represent printed monographs, books and pamphlets (from a minimum of ten pages), and serial titles. The prime criteria for inclusion were that the work be chiefly or uniquely both Canadian and military in its contents.

Many in-house publications, of the training pamphlet or regulations type, have been included, but only insofar as they tell us something of the armed forces themselves, rather than details of tactical doctrine or of pieces of equipment. Works by or about Canadians serving with the armed forces of other countries have been included, as well as materials relating to the military history of Newfoundland since 1867.

In order to keep the bibliography to a reasonable size, periodical articles are not listed individually. Instead, serial titles of mainly Canadian and military content have been included, interfiled with monograph titles in the appropriate sections of the bibliography. Newspapers and newsletters have been excluded, but unit magazines and yearbooks regularly containing material of historical interest about the unit are found here.

Materials on soldiers' rehabilitation have not been considered. Veterans' publications and works about veterans have been included only if they deal directly with the wartime activities of individuals or units.

Introduction

En général, peu d'ouvrages sur l'histoire et la vie militaire au Canada figuraient dans les recueils rétrospectifs de publications sur le Canada ou dans les bibliographies militaires internationales. Même si l'on a constitué quelques listes très utiles d'oeuvres consacrées à certains aspects de l'histoire militaire canadienne, notamment à l'histoire des unités, ou à des écrits d'auteurs militaires aussi prolifiques que C.P. Stacey ou G.F.G. Stanley, il n'existe aucune liste complète sur laquelle peut se fonder le chercheur qui s'intéresse au passé militaire du Canada.

Nous avons donc tenté de dresser ici la liste des sources premières publiées et des oeuvres secondaires, hormis la poésie et la fiction, consacrées à la vie militaire canadienne depuis la Confédération jusqu'à l'époque actuelle.

La bibliographie regroupe des monographies, des livres et des brochures d'au moins dix pages, ainsi que des titres de périodiques. Notre choix des oeuvres s'est fondé sur le critère primordial suivant: le sujet devrait être uniquement ou principalement canadien et militaire à la fois.

Plusieurs publications internes du Ministère, telles les manuels d'instruction ou de règlements, ont été retenues, mais seulement dans la mesure ou elles nous renseignent sur les forces armées en plus de donner des détails de pièces d'équipement ou d'ordre tactique. Les ouvrages de Canadiens servant au sein de forces armées d'autres pays ou consacrés à ceux-ci, ainsi que ceux touchant l'histoire militaire de Terre-Neuve depuis 1867, ont également été catalogués.

Afin d'éviter de surcharger la bibliographie, les articles de périodiques ne sont pas repertoriés séparement. Nous avons plutôt retenu les titres des périodiques à fonds principalement militaire et canadien, que nous avons insérés avec les monographies dans les sections appropriées de la bibliographie. Les journaux et les lettres au rédacteur ont été laissés de côté, mais les revues et les livrets annuels des unités contenant régulièrement des articles d'intérêt historique ont été catalogués.

Les ouvrages portant sur la réadaptation des soldats ont été rejetés. Les publications des anciens combattants et les ouvrages qui leur sont consacrés n'ont été retenus que s'ils portaient directement sur les activités de temps de guerre des soldats ou des unités.

It is obvious from these criteria that a certain amount of subjective judgement has had to be exercised on the inclusion of individual items. This is most obvious in Part B, "Defence Policy and General Works," in which the criteria of mainly or uniquely Canadian and military content have been most difficult to apply.

In general, first editions of books have been listed. Later editions have been included only if they have been greatly enlarged or are much different in their bibliographic description. An effort was made to inspect each work to verify its bibliographic description and subject relevance. Some works were unobtainable, but have been included on the basis of entries in reliable bibliographies.

In compiling this bibliography, I have relied heavily on the holdings of the National Library of Canada and the major military and academic libraries of the Ottawa, Kingston and Toronto areas. No critical evaluation or selection has been made, for what may seem a weak book to the compiler might well provide vital information to a researcher working from a different viewpoint.

Materials have been arranged so that individual entries are sometimes repeated in several different sections of the bibliography. For example, a regimental history of an infantry regiment raised in 1885 and existing to the present day appears in all four time-periods of the land forces section. A work on some aspect of the Royal Canadian Air Force and the Canadian Army in the Second World War would appear in the 1939-1945 parts of both the land and air forces sections.

I wish to express my thanks to present and former historians and staff of the Directorate of History and Heritage who contributed to this project, particularly to John Armstrong, Vince Bezeau, Bob Caldwell, Isabel Campbell, Jon Caven, Ted Chambers, Phil Chaplin, Carl Christie, Elizabeth Chenier, John Dendy, Ron Dodds, Jean Durocher, Jean-Pierre Gagnon, Richard Gimblett, Liliane Grantham, Don Graves, Ben Greenhous, Hugh Halliday, Steve Harris, Fred Hatch, Norman Hillmer, Bill Johnston, David Kealy, Réal Laurin, Bill McAndrew, Winston MacIntosh, Michael McNorgan, Morris Mason, Terry Melnyk, Marc Milner, Jean Morin, Faye Nicholson, Jean Pariseau, Donna Porter, Gabriel Proulx, Bill Rawling, Roger Sarty, Andrea Schlecht, Bob Stokely, Mike Whitby and Glenn Wright for their expertise in collecting many entries and for their assistance with the editing and publishing processes. I am grateful to the staffs of the military, academic and public libraries of Ottawa, Kingston and Toronto for their assistance, and particularly to the Royal Canadian Military Institute, Toronto, for making its library freely available. I am also indebted to Tom LaRue, Herb Slaght and Joe Harper for details of works in their collections. My wife, Atsuko, proofread countless entries and provided encouragement through all three editions of this work. Last, I wish to thank

Comme vous le voyez, une bonne part de subjectivité a régi le choix des ouvrages. La chose est encore plus évidente dans la partie B intitulée «Les politiques sur la défense et généralités» ou le caractère principalement ou uniquement canadien et militaire des ouvrages a été très difficile à cerner.

En général, nous avons retenu les premières éditions des livres. Les éditions ultérieures n'ont été repertoriées que si leur contenu a été considérablement augmenté ou si leur description bibliographique a été largement modifiée. Nous nous sommes efforcé de vérifier la description bibliographique et la pertinence de chaque ouvrage. Il nous a été impossible de nous procurer certains d'entre eux, mais nous les avons quand même catalogués parce qu'ils figuraient dans des bibliographies fiables.

Pour dresser cette bibliographie, nous nous sommes considérablement fondé sur les ouvrages détenus par la Bibliothèque nationale du Canada et les principales bibliothèques universitaires et militaires des régions d'Ottawa, de Kingston et de Toronto. Il n'y a pas eu d'évaluation ou de choix critiques, car l'ouvrage qui peut nous avoir semblé de peu d'importance pourrait fournir des renseignements inestimables au chercheur qui a un autre point de vue.

Les ouvrages ont été classés de façon que le même titre figure parfois dans plusieurs sections de la bibliographie. Par exemple, l'histoire d'un régiment d'infanterie formé en 1885 et existant encore aujourd'hui paraît dans chacune des quatre grandes époques de la section consacrée aux forces terrestres. Un ouvrage portant sur certains aspects de l'Aviation royale du Canada et de l'Armée canadienne pendant la seconde Guerre mondiale figurerait dans la partie 1939-1945 de la section des forces terrestres et de la section des forces aériennes.

Je tiens à exprimer ma reconnaissance aux historiens, actuels et passés, ainsi qu'aux membres de la Direction – Histoire et patrimoine qui ont contribué à la réalisation de ce projet et notamment Mmes Isabel Campbell, Elizabeth Chenier, Liliane Grantham, Faye Nicholson, Donna Porter et Andrea Schlecht, et MM. John Armstrong, Vince Bezeau, Bob Caldwell, Jon Caven, Ted Chambers, Phil Chaplin, Carl Christie, John Dendy, Ron Dodds, Jean Durocher, Jean-Pierre Gagnon, Richard Gimblett, Don Graves, Ben Greenhous, Hugh Halliday, Steve Harris, Fred Hatch, Norman Hillmer, Bill Johnston, David Kealy, Réal Laurin, Bill McAndrew, Winston MacIntosh, Michael McNorgan, Morris Mason, Terry Melnyk, Marc Milner, Jean Morin, Jean Pariseau, Gabriel Proulx, Bill Rawling, Roger Sarty, Bob Stokely, Mike Whitby et Glenn Wright, dont le précieux concours nous à permis de relever bon nombre de titres, et pour l'aide que ces personnes nous ont fournie relativement à la mise au point et à la publication de cet ouvrage. Je remercie également le personnel des bibliothèques militaires, universitaires et publiques d'Ottawa, de Kingston et de Toronto pour l'aide qu'il nous a apportée, et notamment le Royal Canadian Military Institute de Toronto qui nous a permis de consulter sa bibliothèque. Je suis également reconnaissant à MM. Tom LaRue, Herb

Dr. W.A.B. Douglas, former Director of History, and Dr. Serge Bernier, the present Director of History and Heritage who have made this publication possible.

O.A. Cooke

An asterisk (*) opposite an item indicates that it has also been published in the other official language and is so listed in the bibliography.

Slaght et Joe Harper pour les renseignements qu'ils nous ont fournis sur les oeuvres de leurs collections. Mon épouse, Atsuko, a fait la correction d'épreuves et vérifié un nombre considérable d'entrées; elle et m'a aussi prodigué ses encouragements pour chacune des trois éditions de cet ouvrage. Enfin, je tiens à remercier M. W.A.B. Douglas, ancien directeur du Service historique, et M. Serge Bernier, l'actuel Directeur, Histoire et patrimoine, dont les bons offices ont rendu cette publication possible.

O.A. Cooke

Un astérisque (*) dénote un ouvrage qui figure également dans la bibliographie presentée dans l'autre langue officielle.

A. BIBLIOGRAPHY — BIBLIOGRAPHIE

In addition to the works listed below, other bibliographies, not primarily both Canadian and military, are relevant. General Canadian historical bibliographies, such as *Canadian History: a Reader's Guide*, Volume 1: *Beginnings to Confederation*, M. Brook Taylor, ed., Volume 2: *Confederation to the Present*, Doug Owram, ed. (Toronto: Univ. of Toronto Press, 1994) list many works on the Canadian military experience among references to other facets of our history. More specialized references will be found in regional bibliographies, such as Jacques Rouillard, dir., *Guide d'histoire du Québec; du Régime français à nos jours: bibliographie commentée* (Montréal: Méridien, 1991), [368] pp., or Agnes C. O'Dea, comp., *Bibliography of Newfoundland*, Anne Alexander, ed. (Toronto: Univ. of Toronto Press, 1986), 2 vols.

Similarly, international military bibliographies also contain Canadian materials. General works, like Commission international d'histoire militaire, Comité de bibliographie, *Bulletin de bibliographie*, No 1- (Lausanne, Suisse: Centre d'histoire, 1978-   ), or such specific topical bibliographies as Roger Perkins, comp., *Regiments; Regiments and Corps of the British Empire and Commonwealth, 1758-1993; a Critical Bibliography of their Published Histories* (Newton Abbot, Eng.: privately printed, 1994), 806 pp., are useful.

———————

En plus des oeuvres citées on devra consulter d'autres bibliographies dont l'intérêt primordial est ni canadien, ni militaire. Certaines bibliographies générales portant sur l'histoire du Canada citent des ouvrages à caractère militaire parmi les nombreuses études sur divers aspects de notre histoire, telles que les *Canadian History: a Reader's Guide*, Volume 1: *Beginnings to Confederation*, M. Brook Taylor, ed., Volume 2: *Confederation to the Present*, Doug Owram, ed. (Toronto: Univ. of Toronto Press, 1994). On trouvera aussi des études plus spécialisées à même les bibliographies régionales, telles que celle de Jacques Rouillard, dir., *Guide d'histoire du Québec; du Régime français à nos jours: bibliographie commentée* (Montréal: Méridien, 1991), [368] pp., ou celle d'Agnes C. O'Dea, comp., *Bibliography of Newfoundland*, Anne Alexander, ed. (Toronto: Univ. of Toronto Press, 1986), 2 vols.

Quelques travaux canadiens sont aussi publiés dans des bibliographies militaires à caractère international. Des études générales sont utiles, telles que celle de la Commission internationale d'histoire militaire, Comité de bibliographie, *Bulletin de bibliographie,* No 1- (Lausanne, Suisse: Centre d'histoire, 1978-), ou encore celle de Roger Perkins, comp., *Regiments; Regiments and Corps of the British Empire and Commonwealth, 1758-1993; a Critical Bibliography of their Published Histories* (Newton Abbot, Eng.: imprimé privé, 1994), 806 pp., qui traite évidemment d'un aspect bibliographique particulier.

Bell, Sandra M. *Victory Bonding; Wartime Messages from Canada's Government, 1939-1945; a Bibliography./Victoire oblige: les messages du Gouvernement canadien pendant la guerre, 1939-1945; une bibliographie*. Ottawa: National Library of Canada, National Archives of Canada/ Bibliothèque nationale du Canada, Archives nationales du Canada, 1995. 15 pp.

Canada. Committee on the Defences of Canada. *The Defences of Canada, 1st January, 1886*. Ottawa: Queen's Printer, 1886. 171 pp.
Caption title: Report, by the Secretary, upon the Correspondence Submitted to the Committee.

[Canada. Dept. of Militia and Defence.] *List of Military Books Issuable to (a) Permanent Force (b) Active Militia*. n.p.: n.d. 13 pp.

Canada. Dept. of National Defence. Directorate of Strategic and Air Defence Operational Research. *A Selected Bibliography of Peacekeeping (Revised)(U)*. Gordon S. Smith, comp. (ORD Report no. 66/R14.) Ottawa: Queen's Printer, 1966. 35 pp.

Canada. Director of Public Information. *Selected List of Wartime Pamphlets*. No. 1-2? Ottawa: King's Printer, 1941-?

Canada. Public Archives. Manuscript Division. *Preliminary Inventory; Record Group 9; Department of Militia and Defence, 1776-1922*. Ottawa: Queen's Printer, 1957. 36 pp.

Canadian Institute of International Affairs. Toronto Men's Branch. Defence Study Group. *Problems of National Defence; a Study Guide and Bibliography*, by Brian A. Crane, Sydney Peck, and Tom Wickett. Toronto: Canadian Institute of International Affairs, 1962. 14 pp.

Cross, Michael, and Robert Bothwell, eds. *Policy by Other Means; Essays in Honour of C.P. Stacey*. Toronto: Clarke, Irwin, 1972. 258 pp.

Dhand, H., L. Hunt and L. Goshawk. *Louis Riel; an Annotated Bibliography*. Saskatoon, Sask.: Univ. of Saskatchewan, 1972. 41 pp.

Dornbusch, C.E., comp. *The Canadian Army, 1855-1958; Regimental Histories and a Guide to the Regiments*. Cornwallville, N.Y.: Hope Farm Press, 1959. 216 pp.

_____. *The Canadian Army, 1855-1955; Regimental Histories and a Guide to the Regiments*. Cornwallville, N.Y.: n.p., 1957. 162 1.

_____. *The Canadian Army, 1855-1965; Lineages; Regimental Histories*. Cornwallville, N.Y.: Hope Farm Press, 1966. 179 pp.

_____. *Preliminary List of Canadian Regimental Histories*. Cornwallville, N.Y.: n.p., 1955. 49 pp.

Dubé, Timothy D., comp. *Canada at War, 1939-1945; a Survey of the Archival Holdings of the Second World War at the National Archives of Canada*. Waterloo, Ont.: Laurier Centre for Military Strategic and Disarmament Studies, Wilfred Laurier Univ., 1996. 52 pp.

Evonic, I.N. *An Annotated Bibliography of CFPARU Publications: 1948-1976*. (Report 76-8.) Toronto: Canadian Forces Personnel Applied Research Unit, [1976]. 35 pp.

Fancy, Margaret, comp. *A Bibliography of the Works of George Francis Gillman Stanley*. (Bibliography Series, no. 1.) Sackville, N.B.: Ralph Pickard Bell Library, Mount Allison Univ., 1976. 52 pp.

Graves, Donald E., and Anne E. MacLeod, comps. *Nova Scotia Military History: a Resource Guide*. Halifax: The Army Museum, 1982. 106 pp.

Kerr, W.B. *Canada's Part in the Great War; Reprints of Bibliographies*. Toronto: Canadian Historical Review, n.d. v.p.

Kerr, W.K. *Bibliography of Canadian Reports in Aviation Medicine, 1939-1945*. n.p.: Defence Research Board, 1962. v.p.

O'Brien, Jerome W., and/et Glenn T. Wright. *Sources for the Study of the Second World War./Documents sur la Deuxième Guerre mondiale*. (Public Archives of Canada Public Records Division Special Publications Series./Archives publiques du Canada, Division des archives fédérales, collection de publications spéciales.) Ottawa: Supply and Services Canada/ Approvisionnements et Services Canada, 1979. 22/24 pp.
Bilingual text./Texte bilingue.

Saskatchewan. Provincial Library. Bibliographic Services. *Louis Riel; a Bibliography*. Ved Parkash Arora, comp. Regina: Queen's Printer, 1972. 66 pp.

Stewart, Charles Herbert. *The Service of British Regiments in Canada and North America; a Resume, with a Chronological List of Uniforms Portrayed in Sources Consulted; Based on Regimental Histories Held in Department of National Defence Library*. (Department of National Defence Library Publication no. 1.) Ottawa: Queen's Printer, 1962. v.p.

B. DEFENCE POLICY AND GENERAL WORKS
— LES POLITIQUES SUR LA DÉFENSE ET
GÉNÉRALITÉS

Adams, E.G. *Disarmament and Prosperity for Canada.* Toronto: Canadian Peace Congress, [1962?]. 34 pp.

Agreement Amending and Extending the British Commonwealth Air Training Plan Agreement of December 17, 1939, Relating to Training of Pilots and Aircraft Crews in Canada and their Subsequent Service, between the United Kingdom, Canada, Australia and New Zealand, Dated at Ottawa, June 5, 1942. Ottawa: King's Printer, 1942. 28 pp.

Agreement Relating to Training of Pilots and Aircraft Crews in Canada and their Subsequent Service between the United Kingdom, Canada, Australia and New Zealand, Signed at Ottawa, December 17, 1939. Ottawa: King's Printer, 1941. 19 pp.

Air Force College Journal. Toronto: privately printed, 1956-64. 9 vols.
Title varies.

Aitchison, J.H. *Canada at War; Report of Two Round Tables of the Annual Conference of the Canadian Institute of International Affairs, London, Ontario, May, 1940.* Toronto: Canadian Institute of International Affairs, 1940. 19 pp.

The Alaska Highway Today; a Brief History and Guide to Those Seeking New Scenic Thrills in North America's Last Frontier ... that Rugged, Vast Hinterland Now Traversed by the Famous Alaska Highway ... Linking Bustling Cities of Canada and the United States of America to the Awe-Inspiring Land of the Midnight Sun. Edmonton: printed by Douglas Print. Co., [1951]. 1 vol., unpaged.

*Allard, Jean V. *Mémoires du général Jean V. Allard.* Collaboration spéciale de Serge Bernier. s.l.: Editions de Mortagne, 1985. 533 pp.

*_____. *The Memoirs of General Jean V. Allard,* written in cooperation with Serge Bernier. Vancouver: Univ. of British Columbia Press, 1988. 366 pp.

Amery, L.S. *Canadian Citizenship and Imperial Defence.* Toronto: privately printed, [1910]. 11 pp.

Andrew, G.C. *Canada at War; a Report of a Round Table Held by the Canadian Institute of International Affairs at its Eighth Annual Conference, Kingston, Ontario, May 1941.* Toronto: Canadian Institute of International Affairs, 1941. 11 pp.

Angers, François-Albert. *Le bilan canadien d'un conflit.* (Actualités, no 12.) Montréal: Editions de l'Action nationale, [1946?]. 46 pp.

_____. *Est-ce ainsi qu'on fait la guerre sainte? Conscription des femmes, moralité dans l'armée; "C'est non encore une fois!"* (Actualités, no 9.) Montréal: Editions de l'Action nationale, [1943?]. 21 pp.

_____. *Pourquoi nous n'accepterons "jamais" la conscription pour service outre-mer.* (Actualités, no 8.) Montréal: Editions de l'Action nationale, [1942]. 22 pp.

Anglin, Douglas G. *The St. Pierre and Miquelon Affaire of 1941; a Study in Diplomacy in the North Atlantic Quadrangle.* [Toronto]: Univ. of Toronto Press, 1966. 219 pp.

Armstrong, Elizabeth H. *The Crisis of Quebec, 1914-18.* New York: Columbia Univ. Press, 1937. 270 pp.

_____. *French Canadian Opinion on the War, January, 1940 — June, 1941.* (Contemporary Affairs, no. 12.) Toronto: Ryerson Press, 1942. 44 pp.

The Art of War, 1914-18 1939-45; an Exhibition of Paintings and Drawings by Canadian and British Artists Produced during the Two Great Wars, 19 May — 19 August 1994, Canadian High Commission, Canada House, Trafalgar Square, London SW1 5BJ. n.p.: 1994. 24 pp.

Asselin, Olivar. *Pourquoi je m'enrôle.* Montréal: s.i., 1916. 50 pp.

_____. *Trois textes sur la liberté.* (Collection Reconnaissances HMH.) Montréal: Editions HMH, 1970. 195 pp.

Atherton, W.H. *A Report of the First National Unity and Win the War Convention, Held in Montreal, May 21-25, 1917./Rapport de la première Convention de l'unité nationale et pour gagner la guerre, tenue à Montréal, du 21 au 25 mai 1917.* Montreal: Canadian Unity and Win the War League, n.d./s.d. 49 pp.
Bilingual text./Texte bilingue.

Bailey, W.J. *Canadian Military Postmarks.* Ottawa: The British Commonwealth Stamp Exchange, 1978. 72 pp.

Bailey, W.J., and E.R. Toop. *Canadian Military Post Offices to 1986.* Toronto: Unitrade Press, 1987. 95 pp.

Bailey, W.J., and E.R. Toop. *The Canadian Military Posts.* Edward B. Proud, ed. n.p.: 1984-90. 3 vols.
Canadian Postal Corps and postal markings.

Barlow, Maude, in collaboration with Shannon Selin. *Women and Arms Control in Canada.* (Issue Brief no. 8.) Ottawa: Canadian Centre for Arms Control and Disarmament, 1987. 24 pp.

Barratt, Glynn. *Russian Shadows on the British Northwest Coast of North America, 1810-1890; a Study of Rejection of Defence Responsibilities.* (University of British Columbia Press Pacific Maritime Studies, [no. 3.]) Vancouver: Univ. of British Columbia Press, 1983. 196 pp.

Barris, Ted, and Alex Barris. *Days of Victory; Canadians Remember: 1939-1945.* Toronto: Macmillan Canada, 1995. 304 pp.

Bélanger, Yves, et Pierre Fournier. *Le Québec militaire; les dessous de l'industrie militaire québécoise.* (Collection paix.) Montréal: Editions Québec/Amérique, 1989. 202 pp.

Bell, K., and Desmond Morton. *Royal Canadian Military Institute; 100 Years 1890-1990.* Toronto: Royal Canadian Military Institute, 1990. 208 pp.

Bercuson, David J. *True Patriot; the Life of Brooke Claxton, 1899-1960.* Toronto: Univ. of Toronto Press, 1993. 363 pp.

Bercuson, David J., and J.L. Granatstein. *Dictionary of Canadian Military History.* Toronto: Oxford Univ. Press, 1992. 248 pp.

Bernard, Yves, et Caroline Bergeron. *Trop loin de Berlin; des prisonniers allemands au Canada (1939-1946).* Sillery (Qué.): Septentrion, 1995. [359] pp.

*Bernier, Serge, and Jean Pariseau. *French Canadians and Bilingualism in the Canadian Armed Forces.* Volume II: *1969-1987: Official Languages: National Defence's Response to the Federal Policy.* (Socio-Military Series, no. 4.) Ottawa: Directorate of History, Dept. of National Defence, 1994. 843 pp.

Bernier, Serge, *et al. La participation des Canadiens français à la Deuxième Guerre mondiale: mythes et réalités; actes du colloque du 6 au 9 octobre 1994.* Numéro spécial du <u>Bulletin d'histoire politique</u>, III(Printemps/Eté, 1995). Montréal: AQHP/Septentrion, 1995. 408 pp.

*Bernier, Serge, et Jean Pariseau. *Les Canadiens français et le bilinguisme dans les Forces armées canadiennes.* Tome II: *1969-1987: Langues officielles: la volonté gouvernementale et 'a réponse de la Défense nationale.* (Collection d'histoire socio-militair ?, no 4.) Ottawa: [Service historique de la Défense nationale], 1991. 871 pp.

Bishop, William A. *Winged Peace.* New York: Viking Press, 1944. 175 pp.

Bishop, William Arthur. *Our Bravest and our Best; the Stories of Canada's Victoria Cross Winners.* Toronto: McGraw-Hill Ryerson, 1995. 211 pp.

Bland, Douglas. *The Administration of Defence Policy in Canada, 1947 to 1985.* Kingston, Ont.: R.P. Frye, 1987. 252 pp.

_____. *Chiefs of Defence; Government and the Unified Command of the Canadian Armed Forces.* Toronto: [Canadian Institute of Strategic Studies], 1995. 314 pp.

Blatherwick, F.J. *Canadian Orders, Decorations and Medals.* Toronto: Unitrade Press, 1983. 123 pp.

_____. *1000 Brave Canadians; the Canadian Gallantry Awards, 1854-1989.* Toronto: Unitrade Press, 1991. 415 pp.

Borden, (Sir) Robert L. *Canada at War; Speeches Delivered by Rt. Hon. Sir Robert Laird Borden, K.C., P.C., G.C.M.G., before Canadian Clubs, Toronto, Montreal, Halifax, Winnipeg, December 1914.* n.p.: n.d. 31 pp.

_____. *Canada at War; Speeches Delivered by Rt. Hon. Sir Robert Laird Borden, K.C., P.C., G.C.M.G., in Canada and the United Kingdom, June-September, 1918.* n.p.: n.d. 31 pp.

_____. *Canada at War; Speeches Delivered by Rt. Hon. Sir Robert Laird Borden, K.C., P.C., G.C.M.G., in Canada and the United Kingdom, December, 1916 — May, 1917.* n.p.: n.d. 28 pp.

_____. *Canada at War; Speeches Delivered by Rt. Hon. Sir Robert Laird Borden, K.C., P.C., G.C.M.G., in England, Canada, and the United States, July-December, 1915.* n.p.: n.d. 58 pp.

_____. *Manifestos, 1916-17.* Ottawa: King's Printer, 1918. 16 pp.

_____. *The Naval Aid Bill; Speech Delivered by Right Honourable R.L. Borden.* Ottawa: King's Printer, 1912. 31 pp.

_____. *Robert Laird Borden; his Memoirs.* Henry Borden, ed. Toronto: Macmillan, 1938. 2 vols.

_____. *The War and the Future.* Percy Hurt, comp. London: Hodder and Stoughton, 1917. 162 pp.

Bourassa, Henri. *Canadian Nationalism and the War.* Montreal: n.p., 1916. 31 pp.

*_____. *La conscription.* Montréal: Editions du Devoir, 1917. 46 pp.

*_____. *Conscription.* Montreal: Le Devoir, 1917. 46 pp.

_____. *Le Devoir et la guerre; le conflit des races; discours prononcé au banquet des amis du DEVOIR, le 12 janvier 1916.* Montréal: Imprimerie du Devoir, [1916]. 45 pp.

Bourassa, Henri. *The Duty of Canada at the Present Hour; an Address Meant to be Delivered at Ottawa, in November and December, 1914, but Twice Suppressed in the Name of "Loyalty and Patriotism".* Montreal: Le Devoir, [1915?]. 43 pp.

————. *Henri Bourassa expose une des conséquences de la guerre totale en répondant à la question "Que seront nos enfants?"; texte sténographié de la conférence que M. Henri Bourassa a prononcée au Plateau, à Montréal, le 10 février 1943.* Montréal: La Ligue pour Défense du Canada, s.d. 39 pp.

————. *La mission Jellicoe; nouvelle poussée d'impérialisme.* [Montréal]: Editions du Devoir, 1920. 37 pp.

————. *La prochaine guerre impériale; en serons-nous?* Montréal: Imprimeur du Devoir, 1920. 32 pp.

————. *Le projet de loi navale; sa nature, ses conséquences; discours prononcé au monument national le 20 janvier 1910.* Montréal: Le Devoir, [1910]. 37 pp.

————. *Que devons-nous à l'Angleterre? La défense nationale; la révolution impérialiste; le tribut à l'empire.* Montréal: [Le Devoir], 1915. 420 pp.

————. *Why the Navy Act Should be Repealed; Imperial Problems.* Montreal: Le Devoir, 1912. 62 pp.

————. *"Win the War" and Lose Canada.* (The Case Against Conscription, 1.) Montreal: Le Devoir, 1917. 14 pp.

Boyd, John. *The Naval Question; in the Light of Canada's National Interests.* Montreal: n.p., 1912. 24 pp.

Brewin, Andrew. *Stand on Guard; the Search for a Canadian Defence Policy.* Toronto: McClelland & Stewart, 1965. 140 pp.

Brewin, Andrew, and Kenneth McNaught. *Debate on Defence; Two Viewpoints on Canadian Foreign Policy.* Toronto: Ontario Woodsworth Memorial Foundation, 1960. 27 pp.

Bricker, Calvin. *Canada's Reserves and Peacekeeping; a Workshop Report.* n.p.: York Centre for International and Strategic Studies, [1988]. 62 pp.

British Columbia War Memorials; an Index of Names. Richmond, B.C.: British Columbia Genealogical Society, 1990. 84 pp.

*Brouillette, Benoit. *Canada's Strategic Position.* (Current Affairs for the Canadian Forces, vol. II, no. 2.) Ottawa: King's Printer, 1952. 22 pp.

*————. *La position stratégique du Canada.* (Actualités; revue destinée aux Forces canadiennes, vol II, no 2.) Ottawa: Imprimeur du Roi, 1952. 22 pp.

Brown, George A. *Canadian Welcome Home Medals, 1899-1945.* Langley, B.C.: Western Canadian Distributors, 1991. 155 pp.

Bruce, Jean. *Back the Attack! Canadian Women during the Second World War — at Home and Abroad.* Toronto: Macmillan, 1985. 182 pp.

Bryden, John. *Best-Kept Secret; Canadian Secret Intelligence in the Second World War.* Toronto: Lester Pub., 1993. 390 pp.

Buchan, John, *see* Tweedsmuir, John Buchan, baron.

Buchan, Susan Charlotte (Grosvenor), *see* Tweedsmuir, Susan Charlotte (Grosvenor) Buchan, baroness.

Buchner, W.R. *Canada, Ours to Defend.* London, Ont.: privately printed, [1961]. 99 pp.

Buck, Tim. *Canada in the Coming Offensive.* Toronto: privately printed, 1943. 40 pp.

_____. *Fight for Peace — as for Life! Report to the 4th National Convention, Labor-Progressive Party.* Toronto: privately printed, [1951]. 48 pp.

_____. *For Victory in the War and Prosperity in the Peace; Speech Delivered at Spadina Riding Labor Nominating Convention, Feb. 5, 1943.* Toronto: privately printed, [1943?]. 15 pp.

_____. *A National Front for Victory.* n.p.: [1941?]. 22 pp.

_____. *Organize Canada for Total War! The Decisive Year of the War, 1942.* n.p.: [1942?]. 64 pp.

_____. *The Way Forward to Total War; Lessons of the Plebiscite; Smash the Fascists in Quebec.* Toronto: privately printed, [1942]. 20 pp.

The Bulletin. No. 1-60? Montreal: Canadian Ordnance Association, 1948-69? *Frequency varies. Canadian Ordnance Association became Canadian Industrial Preparedness Association in 1948.*

Burns, E.L.M. *Between Arab and Israeli.* Toronto: Clarke, Irwin, 1962. 336 pp.

_____. *Defence in the Nuclear Age; an Introduction for Canadians.* Toronto: Clarke, Irwin, 1976. 133 pp.

_____. *Megamurder.* Toronto: Clarke, Irwin, 1966. 288 pp.

_____. *A Seat at the Table; the Struggle for Disarmament.* Toronto: Clarke, Irwin, 1972. 268 pp.

Business Council on National Issues. *Canada's Defence Policy: Capabilities Versus Commitments; a Posistion Paper of the Business Council on National Issues.* [Ottawa]: n.p., 1984. 62 pp.

Byers, R.B. *Canadian Security and Defence: the Legacy and the Challenges.* (Adelphi Papers, 214.) London: International Institute for Strategic Studies, 1986. 88 pp.

Byers, R.B., and Colin S. Gray, eds. *Canadian Military Professionalism; the Search for Identity.* (Wellesley Paper 2.) [Toronto]: Canadian Institute of International Affairs, 1973. 84 pp.

Byers, R.B., and Michael Slack, eds. *Canada and Peacekeeping: Prospects for the Future.* Downsview, Ont.: York Univ. Research Programme in Strategic Studies, 1984. 56 pp.

_____. *Strategy and the Arctic.* (The Polaris Papers, 4.) Toronto: Canadian Institute of Strategic Studies, 1986. 117 pp.

Byers, R.B., and others. *Canada and Defence Industrial Preparedness: Options and Prospects.* n.p.: Centre for International and Strategic Studies, York Univ., 1987. 201 pp.

Byers, R.B., John Hamre, and G.R. Lindsey. *Aerospace Defence: Canada's Future Role?* (Wellesley Papers 9/1985.) Toronto: Canadian Institute of International Affairs, 1985. 56 pp.

Caldwell, Nathaniel French. *Arctic Leverage; Canadian Sovereignty and Security.* New York: Praeger, 1990. 123 pp.

Campagna, Palmiro. *Storms of Controversy; the Secret Avro Arrow Files Revealed.* Toronto: Stoddart, 1992. 228 pp.

Campbell, John P. *Dieppe Revisited; a Documentary Investigation.* London: F. Cass, 1993. 247 pp.

Canada. Army Headquarters. *A Brief History of the Canada-United States Permanent Joint Board on Defence, 1940-1960.* Ottawa: Queen's Printer, 1960. 16 pp.

*Canada. Canadian Forces Headquarters. Directorate of History. *The Armed Forces of Canada, 1867-1967; a Century of Achievement.* D.J. Goodspeed, ed. Ottawa: Queen's Printer, 1967. 289 pp.

Canada. Defence Construction (1951) Limited. *Annual Report.* n.p.: 1951- .

*Canada. Département [*sic*] du Secrétaire d'Etat. *Documents relatifs aux incursions des rebelles sudistes sur la frontière des Etats-Unis et à l'invasion du Canada par les Féniens.* Ottawa: Imprimeur de la Reine, 1869. 176 pp.

Canada. Dept. of Defence Production. *Canada-United States Defence Development Sharing.* Ottawa: Queen's Printer, 1962. 68 pp.

_____. *Canada-United States Defence Production Sharing.* Ottawa: Queen's Printer, 1960. 122 pp.

*Canada. Dept. of Defence Production. ***Canadian Defence Products.*** Ottawa: Queen's Printer, 1964. 345 pp.

*_____. ***Report.*** Ottawa: King's Printer, 1952-69.

*Canada. Dept. of External Affairs. ***Canada and NATO.*** (Current Affairs for the Canadian Forces, vol. III, no. 1.) Ottawa: Queen's Printer, 1952. 22 pp.

*_____. ***Canada and the Korean Crisis.*** Ottawa: King's Printer, 1950. 36 pp.

Canada. Dept. of Justice. Military Service Branch. ***Report of the Director of the Military Service Branch to the Honourable the Minister of Justice on the Operation of the Military Service Act, 1917.*** Ottawa: King's Printer, 1919. 162 pp.

Canada. Dept. of Justice. Military Sub-Committee. ***Military Service Act, 1917; Pamphlet of Information and Instructions for Local Military Representatives.*** n.p.: n.d. 18 pp.

*Canada. Dept. of Militia and Defence. ***Annual Report.*** Ottawa: Queen's Printer, 1867-1922.
Title varies. Until 1883 was State of the Militia of the Dominion of Canada, *with further variation in some years.*

_____. ***Minutes of the Militia Council.*** Ottawa: King's Printer, 1905-21. 23 vols.

Canada. Dept. of National Defence. ***The Battle of Brains; Canadian Citizenship and the Issues of the War.*** Ottawa: King's Printer, 1943. 182 pp.

_____. ***Canadian Defence Policy./La politique de défense du Canada,*** [par le ministère de la Défense nationale.] n.p./s.l.: National Defence/Défense nationale, 1992. 38/44 pp.
Bilingual text./Texte bilingue.

_____. ***Challenge and Commitment; a Defence Policy for Canada; a Synopsis of the Defence White Paper./Défis et engagements; une politique de défense pour le Canada; synopsis du livre blanc sur la défense,*** [par le ministère de la Défense nationale.] Ottawa: Supply and Services Canada/Approvisionnements et Services Canada, 1987. 22 pp.
Bilingual text./Texte bilingue.

*_____. ***Challenge and Commitment; a Defence Policy for Canada.*** Ottawa: Supply and Services Canada, 1987. 89 pp.

_____. ***Defence/Défense, 1971-90,*** [par le] ministère de la Défense nationale. Ottawa: Dept. of National Defence/Ministère de la Défense nationale, 1972-91.
Annual. Bilingual text./Annuel. Texte bilingue.

Canada. Dept. of National Defence. *1994 Defence White Paper./Le livre blanc sur la défense de 1994*, [par le ministère de la] Défense nationale. Ottawa: Minister of Supply and Services Canada/Ministre des Approvisionnements et Services Canada, 1994. 50/55 pp.
Bilingual text./Texte bilingue.

        _____. *Rationale for Canadian Defence Forces.* (CFP 243.) n.p.: [1968?] 83 pp.
Originally Confidential.

*_____. *Report.* Ottawa: King's Printer, 1923-59.
Title varies. Annual, most years.

        _____. *Statement on Defence Policy, Ottawa, Canada./Déclaration sur la politique de défense, Ottawa; Canada*, [par le ministère de la Défense nationale.] n.p./s.l.: s.i., 1991. 24/23 pp.
Bilingual text./Texte bilingue.

        _____. *Where Do We Go from Here? Facts for the Guidance of Canadian Army Personnel.* n.p.: [1945]. 28 pp.

*_____. *White Paper on Defence.* Ottawa: Information Canada, 1971. 50 pp.
Cover title: Defence in the 70s.

*_____. *White Paper on Defence.* Ottawa: Queen's Printer, 1964. 30 pp.

Canada. Dept. of National Defence. Operational Research Division. *Some Problems Met in the Allocation of Defence Resources in Canada*, by G.R. Lindsey. (ORD Informal Paper, no. 67/P4.) Ottawa: n.p., 1967. 41 pp.

Canada. Dept. of National Defence. Special Commission on the Restructuring of the Reserves. *Report./Rapport* de la Commission spéciale sur le Restructuration des Réserves, ministère de la Défense nationale. Ottawa: Dept. of National Defence/Ministère de la Défense nationale, 1995. 124/133 pp.
Bilingual text./Texte bilingue.

Canada. Dept. of National War Services. *Annual Report.* Ottawa: King's Printer, 1945. 3 vols.

Canada. Dept. of the Secretary of State. *Copies of Proclamations, Orders in Council and Documents Relating to the European War.* Ottawa: King's Printer, 1915. 5 vols.

*_____. *Correspondence Relating to the Fenian Invasion, and the Rebellion of the Southern States.* Ottawa: Queen's Printer, 1869. 176 pp.

*Canada. Directeur de l'Information publique. *L'effort du Canada pour la Guerre, 1914-1918.* Ottawa: Imprimeur du Roi, 1918. 31 pp.

*Canada. Director of Public Information. *Canada at War.* No. 1-45. Ottawa: King's Printer, 1941-45.

Canada. Director of Public Information. *Canada's Part in the Great War.* Ottawa: n.p., 1919. 64 pp.
Also issued by Information Branch, Dept. of External Affairs.

*_____. *Canada's War Effort, 1914-1918.* Ottawa: King's Printer, 1918. 31 pp.

Canada. Emergency Planning Canada. *Symposium 1983; Civil Mobilization Planning.* n.p.: [1983?]. 293 pp.

*Canada. Forces armées. Quartier général des Forces canadiennes. Direction des services historiques. *Les Forces armées du Canada; un siècle de grandes réalisations.* D.J. Goodspeed, rédacteur. Ottawa: Imprimeur de la Reine, 1967. 289 pp.

*Canada. Ministère de la Défense nationale. *Défis et engagements; une politique de défense pour le Canada.* Ottawa: Approvisionnements et Services Canada, 1987. 89 pp.

*_____. *Livre blanc sur la défense.* Ottawa: Imprimeur de la Reine, 1964. 34 pp.

*_____. *Livre blanc sur la politique de défense.* Ottawa: Information Canada, 1971. 54 pp.
Titre de la couverture: La défense dans les années 70.

*_____. *Rapport.* Ottawa: Imprimeur du Roi, 1923-59.
Divergence du titre. Annuel, la plupart des années.

*Canada. Ministère de la Milice et de la Défense. *Rapport annuel.* Ottawa: Imprimeur de la Reine, 1867-1922.
Divergence du titre. Jusqu'à 1883 le titre était Rapport annuel sur l'état de la Milice de la Puissance du Canada, divers titres suivirent pendant quelques années.

*Canada. Ministère de la Production de Défense. *Matériels de défense du Canada.* Ottawa: Imprimeur de la Reine, 1966. 396 pp.

*_____. *Rapport.* Ottawa: Imprimeur de la Reine, 1952-69.

*Canada. Ministère des Affaires extérieures. *Le Canada et la crise coréenne.* Ottawa: Imprimeur du Roi, 1950. 40 pp.

*_____. *Le Canada et l'OTAN.* (Actualités; revue destinée aux Forces canadiennes, vol III, no 1.) Ottawa: Imprimeur de la Reine, 1952. 22 pp.

Canada. Munition Resources Commission. *Final Report of the Work of the Commission, November, 1915, to March, 1919, Inclusive.* Toronto: Industrial and Technical Press, 1920. 260 pp.

Canada. National Defence Headquarters. Defence Industrial Preparedness Task Force. *Defence Industrial Preparedness; a Foundation for Defence: Executive Version of the Final Report of the Defence Industrial Preparedness Task Force./L'état de préparation de l'industrie de défense: une assise de la défense; résumé à la direction du rapport final*, préparé par le Groupe de travail sur l'état de la préparation industrielle de défense. Ottawa: National Defence Headquarters/Quartier général de la Défense nationale, 1987. v.p./pagination mutiple.
Bilingual text./Texte bilingue.

Canada. National Defence Headquarters. Director General Public Affairs. *Defence Matters./Questions de défense*, [par le Directeur général – Affairs publiques, Quartier général de la Défense nationale.] Vol. I- . Ottawa: Dept. of National Defence/Ministère de la Défense nationale, 1995- .
First pilot issue was 1 December 1995. Bilingual text./La première édition-pilote était le 1 décembre 1995. Texte bilingue.

*Canada. Parcs Canada. Section de Recherche historique. *Les travailleurs de l'Arsenal de Québec, 1879-1964*. s.l.: Parcs Canada, 1980. 46 pp.

*Canada. Parks Canada. Québec Region. Historical Research Branch. *The Workers of the Québec Arsenal, 1879-1964*. n.p.: Parks Canada, 1980. 45 pp.

*Canada. Parlement. *Conférence de la limitation des armements tenue à Washington du 12 novembre 1922, au 6 février 1922, rapport du délégué du Canada comprenant les traités et résolutions*. (Document parlementaire, no 47.) Ottawa: Imprimeur du Roi, 1923. 236 pp.

*_____. *Copies des décrets du conseil, correspondance, etc., échangés entre le gouvernement impérial et le gouvernement canadien touchant l'organisation d'un état-major général impérial*. (Document parlementaire, no 99.) Ottawa: Imprimeur du Roi, 1909. 23 pp.

*_____. *Copies du décret en conseil nommant le major général comte de Dundonald commandant de la milice canadienne, 20 mai 1902, et du décret en conseil relevant le comte de Dundonald du commandement de la milice canadienne, 14 juin 1904, ainsi que de la correspondance et des autres documents s'y rattachant*. (Document de la session, no 113, 113a.) Ottawa: Imprimeur du Roi, 1904. 42 pp.

*_____. *Correspondance concernant la discontinuation de l'usage de la carabine Ross dans l'armée canadienne*. (Document parlementaire, no 44.) Ottawa: Imprimeur du Roi, 1917. 12 pp.

*_____. *Correspondance relative à l'envoi de contingents militaires coloniaux dans le sud Africain*. (Document de la session, no 20, 20a.) Ottawa: Imprimeur de la Reine, 1900. 54 pp.

*Canada. Parlement. *Mémoire des membres militaires du Conseil de la Milice au ministre de la Milice et de la Défense; et aussi mémoire du Membre financier du dit Conseil concernant le budget de milice pour l'exercice 1905-1906.* (Document de la session, no 130.) Ottawa: Imprimeur du Roi, 1905. 25 pp.

*_____. *Réponse à une adresse de la Chambre des Communes en date du 29 novembre 1911, demandant copie de toute la correspondance échangée à la suite de la Conférence impériale entre le gouvernement du Canada et le gouvernement de Sa Majesté au sujet du Service naval du Canada ou d'une manière quelconque y afferant.* (Document parlementaire, no 40d.) Ottawa: Imprimeur du Roi, 1912. 19 pp.

*Canada. Parlement. Chambre des Communes. Comité permanent de la défense nationale. *Procès-verbaux et témoignages.* Ottawa: Imprimeur de la Reine, 1966-68.

*Canada. Parlement. Chambre des Communes. Comité permanent des Affaires extérieures et de la Défense nationale. *Huitième rapport du Comité permanent des Affaires extérieures et de la Défense nationale au sujet des Nations unies et du maintien de la paix.* Ottawa: Imprimeur de la Reine, 1970. 103 pp.

*Canada. Parlement. Chambre des Communes. Comité spécial chargé d'étudier le bill no 133. *Procès-verbaux et témoignages.* No 1-8. Ottawa: Imprimeur du Roi, 1950.

*Canada. Parlement. Chambre des Communes. Comité spécial de la défense. *Etudes spéciales à l'intention du Comité spécial de la Chambre des Communes concernant les questions relatives à la défense.* Ottawa: Imprimeur de la Reine, 1965. 196 pp.

*_____. *Procès-verbaux et témoignages.* Ottawa: Imprimeur de la Reine, 1963-65.

*Canada. Parlement. Chambre des Communes. Comité spécial de la défense nationale. *Procès-verbaux et témoignages.* Ottawa: Imprimeur du Roi, 1950.

*Canada. Parlement. Chambre des Communes. Comité spécial de la loi sur les mesures de guerre. *Procès-verbaux et témoignages.* Ottawa: Imprimeur de la Reine, 1960-61. 53 pp.

*Canada. Parlement. Chambre des Communes. Comité spécial d'enquête sur les dépenses de guerre. *Procès-verbaux et témoignages.* Ottawa: Imprimeur du Roi, 1940-45.

*Canada. Parlement. Chambre des Communes. Comité spécial d'enquête sur les règlements concernant la défense du Canada. *Procès-verbaux et témoignages.* No 1-2. Ottawa: Imprimeur du Roi, 1944.

*Canada. Parlement. Chambre des Communes. Comité spécial des dépenses aux fins de la défense. *Procès-verbaux et témoignages.* Ottawa: Imprimeur du Roi, 1951-60.

*Canada. Parlement. Chambre des Communes. Comité spécial des dépenses et économies de guerre. *Procès-verbaux et témoignages.* Ottawa: Imprimeur du Roi, 1945-46.

*Canada. Parliament. *Conference on the Limitation of Armament Held at Washington, November 12, 1921, to February 6, 1922; Report of the Canadian Delegate Including Treaties and Resolutions.* (Sessional Paper, no. 47.) Ottawa: King's Printer, 1922. 222 pp.

*_____. *Copies of Orders in Council, Correspondence, &c., between the Imperial and Canadian Governments, Relating to the Organization of an Imperial General Staff.* (Sessional Paper, no. 99.) Ottawa: King's Printer, 1909. 22 pp.

*_____. *Copies of the Order in Council Appointing Major General, the Earl of Dundonald, to the Command of the Canadian Militia, 20th May, 1902, and the Order in Council Relieving from the Command of the Canadian Militia, 14th June, 1904, and also, Correspondence and Other Papers Connected Therewith.* (Sessional Paper, no. 113, 113a.) Ottawa: King's Printer, 1904. 41 pp.

*_____. *Correspondence Relating to the Despatch of Colonial Military Contingents to South Africa.* (Sessional Paper, no. 20, 20a.) Ottawa: Queen's Printer, 1900. 51 pp.

*_____. *Correspondence Relating to the Withdrawal of the Ross Rifle from the Canadian Army Corps.* (Sessional Paper, no. 44.) Ottawa: King's Printer, 1917. 12 pp.

*_____. *Memorandum from the Military Members of the Militia Council to the Minister of Militia and Defence; and also Memorandum of the Finance Member of the Militia Council Relating to the Militia Estimates for 1905-1906.* (Sessional Paper, no. 130.) Ottawa: King's Printer, 1905. 24 pp.

_____. *Report of the Delegates to England of their Correspondence with Her Majesty's Government on the Subject of Fortifications, Defence, Arms, etc.* Ottawa: Queen's Printer, 1869. 15 pp.

*_____. *Return to an Address of the House of Commons, Dated November 29, 1911, for a Copy of All Correspondence between the Government of Canada and His Majesty's Government Subsequent to the Last Imperial Conference, Concerning the Naval Service of Canada and in Any Way Connected with It.* (Sessional Paper, no. 40d.) Ottawa: King's Printer, 1912. 18 pp.

*Canada. Parliament. House of Commons. Special Committee on Bill No. 133. *Minutes of Proceedings and Evidence.* No. 1-8. Ottawa: Queen's Printer, 1950.

Canada. Parliament. House of Commons. Special Committee on Boot Inquiry. *Proceedings and Evidence.* Ottawa: King's Printer, 1915.

Canada. Parliament. House of Commons. Special Committee on Defence. *Interim Report./Rapport intérimaire.* Ottawa: Queen's Printer/Imprimeur de la Reine, 1963. 24 pp.
Bilingual text./Texte bilingue.

*_____. *Minutes of Proceedings and Evidence.* Ottawa: Queen's Printer, 1963-65.

*_____. *Special Studies Prepared for the Special Committee on Matters Relating to Defence.* Ottawa: Queen's Printer, 1965. 179 pp.

*Canada. Parliament. House of Commons. Special Committee on Defence Expenditure. *Minutes of Proceedings and Evidence.* Ottawa: King's Printer, 1951-60.

*Canada. Parliament. House of Commons. Special Committee on Defence of Canada Regulations. *Minutes of Proceedings and Evidence.* No. 1-2. Ottawa: King's Printer, 1944.

*Canada. Parliament. House of Commons. Special Committee on National Defence. *Minutes of Proceedings and Evidence.* Ottawa: King's Printer, 1950.

*Canada. Parliament. House of Commons. Special Committee on the War Measures Act. *Minutes of Proceedings and Evidence.* Ottawa: Queen's Printer, 1960-61. 48 pp.

*Canada. Parliament. House of Commons. Special Committee on War Expenditure. *Minutes of Proceedings and Evidence.* Ottawa: King's Printer, 1940-45.

*Canada. Parliament. House of Commons. Special Committee on War Expenditures and Economics. *Minutes of Proceedings and Evidence.* Ottawa: King's Printer, 1945-46.

*Canada. Parliament. House of Commons. Standing Committee on External Affairs and National Defence. *Eighth Report of the Standing Committee of External Affairs and National Defence Respecting United Nations and Peacekeeping.* Ottawa: Queen's Printer, 1970. 96 pp.

_____. *Minutes of Proceedings and Evidence./Procès-verbaux et témoignages* du Comité permanent des Affaires extérieures et de la Défense nationale, Chambre des Communes. Ottawa: Supply and Services Canada/Approvisionnements et services Canada, 1968-86.
Bilingual text./Texte bilingue.

Canada. Parliament. House of Commons. Standing Committee on National Defence. *The Canadian Submarine Acqusition Project./Le programme canadien d'acquisition de sous-marins*, un rapport du Comité permanent de la Défense nationale, [Chambre des Communes]. Ottawa: Queen's Printer/ Imprimeur de la Reine, 1988. 65/77 pp.
Bilingual text./Text bilingue.

*_____. *Minutes of Proceedings and Evidence.* Ottawa: Queen's Printer, 1966-68.

_____. *Minutes of Proceedings and Evidence./Procès-verbaux et témoignages* du Comité permanent de la Défense nationale, Chambre des Communes. Ottawa: Queen's Printer/Imprimeur de la Reine, 1986-88.
Bilingual text./Texte bilingue.

_____. *The Reserves./La Réserve*, un rapport du Comité permanent de la Défense nationale, Chambre des Communes. Ottawa: Queen's Printer/ Imprimeur de la Reine, 1988. 38/42 pp.
Bilingual text./Texte bilingue.

Canada. Parliament. House of Commons. Standing Committee on National Defence and Veterans Affairs. *Canada and European Security./Le Canada et la sécurité en Europe*, rapport du Comité permanent de la Défense nationale et des Affaires des anciens combattants, [Chambre des Communes]. Ottawa: Queen's Printer/Imprimeur de la Reine, 1992. 38/42 pp.
Bilingual text./Texte bilingue.

_____. *The Dilemmas of a Committed Peacekeeper: Canada and the Renewal of Peacekeeping./Les dilemmes d'un gardien de la paix motivé: le Canada et le renouvellement du maintien de la paix*, rapport du Comité permanent de la Défense nationale et des Affaires des anciens combattants, [Chambre des Communes]. Ottawa: Queen's Printer/Imprimeur de la Reine, 1993. 46/48 pp.
Bilingual text./Texte bilingue.

_____. *Maritime Sovereignty./La souveraineté maritime*, rapport du Comité permanent de la Défense nationale et des Affaires des anciens combattants, [Chambre des Communes]. Ottawa: Queen's Printer/Imprimeur de la Reine, 1990. 88/92 pp.
Bilingual text./Texte bilingue.

_____. *Minutes of Proceedings and Evidence./Procès-verbaux et témoignages* du Comité permanent de la Défense nationale et des Affaires des anciens combattants, Chambre des Communes. Ottawa: Queen's Printer/Imprimeur de la Reine, 1989- .
Bilingual text./Texte bilingue.

Canada. Parliament. Senate. Special Committee on National Defence. *Canada's Land Forces./Les forces terrestres du Canada*, rapport du Comité spécial du Sénat sur la Défense nationale. Ottawa: Supply and Services Canada/ Approvisionnements et services Canada, 1989. 141/155 pp.
Bilingual text./Texte bilingue.

_____. *Canada's Territorial Air Defence./La défense aérienne du territoire canadien*, rapport du Comité spécial du Sénat sur la Défense nationale. Ottawa: Supply and Services Canada/Approvisionnements et services Canada, 1985. 70/78 pp.
Bilingual text./Texte bilingue.

_____. *Military Air Transport./Le transport militaire aérien*, rapport du Comité spécial du Sénat sur la Défence nationale. Ottawa: Supply and Services Canada/Approvisionnements et services Canada, 1986. 83/91 pp.
Bilingual text./Texte bilingue.

_____. *Proceedings./Délibérations* du Comité spécial du Sénat sur la Défense nationale. Ottawa: Queen's Printer/Imprimeur de la Reine, 1984-89.
Bilingual text./Texte bilingue.

Canada. Parliament. Senate. Standing Committee on Foreign Affairs. *Meeting New Challenges: Canada's Response to a New Generation of Peacekeeping./Le Canada, force au défi du maintien de la paix dan une ère nouvelle*, rapport du Comité sénatorial permanent des Affaires étrangères. n.p./s.l.: s.i., 1993. 94/103 pp.
Bilingual text./Texte bilingue.

Canada. Parliament. Senate. Standing Committee on Foreign Affairs. Subcommittee on National Defence. *Canada's Maritime Defence./La défense maritime du Canada*,[par le]Sous-comité sur la Défense nationale, [Sénat]. Ottawa: Supply and Services Canada/Approvisionnements et services Canada, 1983. 129/142 pp.
Bilingual text./Texte bilingue.

_____. *Manpower in Canada's Armed Forces./Les effectifs des Forces armées canadiennes*, premier rapport du sous-comité sur la Défense nationale du Comité sénatorial permanent des Affaires extérieures. Ottawa: Supply and Services Canada/Approvisionnements et services Canada, 1982. 48/46 pp.
Bilingual text./Texte bilingue.

_____. *Proceedings./Délibérations* du Sous-comité sur la Défense nationale du Comité sénatorial permanent des Affaires étrangères. Ottawa: Queen's Printer/Imprimeur de la Reine, 1980-83.
Bilingual text./Texte bilingue.

Canada. Parliament. Senate. Standing Committee on Foreign Affairs. Subcommittee on Security and National Defence. *Proceedings./Délibérations*, du Sous-comité de la Sécurité et de la Défense nationale, Comité sénatorial permanent des Affaires étrangères. Ottawa: Queen's Printer/Imprimeur de la Reine, 1992- . *Bilingual text./Texte bilingue.*

Canada. Parliament. Senate. Standing Committee on Social Affairs, Science and Technology. *The Valour and the Horror; Report of the Standing Senate Committee on Social Affairs, Science and Technology.* n.p.: 1993. v.p.

Canada. Parliament. Special Joint Committee on Canada's Defence Policy. *Minutes of Proceedings and Evidence./Procès-verbaux et témoignages* [du Comité mixte spécial du Parlement sur la politique de défense du Canada.] Ottawa: Queen's Printer/Imprimeur de la Reine, 1994. *Bilingual text./Texte bilingue.*

_____. *Security in a Changing World./La sécurité dans un monde en évolution*, rapport du Comité mixte spécial [du Parlement] sur la politique de défense du Canada. Ottawa: Canada Communication Group – Publishing, Public Works and Government Services Canada/Groupe Communication Canada – Edition, Travaux publics et Services gouvernementaux Canada, 1994. 2 vols./tomes. *Bilingual text./Text bilingue.*

Canada. Privy Council. *Proclamations and Orders in Council Passed under the Authority of the War Measures Act; R.S.C. (1927) Chap. 206.* Ottawa: King's Printer, 1940-42. 8 vols. *Vols. IV-VIII titled: Proclamations and Orders in Council Relating to the War.*

Canada. Royal Commission Concerning Purchase of War Supplies and Sale of Small Arms Ammunition. *Evidence.* The Honourable Sir Charles Davidson, Commissioner. Ottawa: King's Printer, 1917. 3 vols.

Canada. Royal Commission on Purchase of Surgical Field Dressings and Other Surgical Supplies. *Report of the Commissioner.* The Honourable Sir Charles Davidson, Commissioner. Ottawa: King's Printer, 1917. 28 pp.

Canada. Royal Commission on Shell Contracts. *Minutes of Evidence.* Ottawa: King's Printer, 1916. 2 vols.

Canada. Royal Commission on the Bren Machine Gun Contract. *Report.* Henry Hague Davis, Commissioner. Ottawa: King's Printer, 1939. 52 pp.

[Canada. Royal Commission to Inquire into the Purchase by and on Behalf of the Government of the Dominion of Canada, of Arms, Munitions, Implements, Materials, Horses, Supplies, and Other Things for the Purpose of the Present War.] *Report of the Commissioner Concerning Sale of Small Arms Ammunition.* Sir Charles Davidson, Commissioner. Ottawa: King's Printer, 1917. 56 pp.

*Canada. Service de l'Information. *Le Canada en guerre.* No 1-45. Ottawa: Imprimeur du Roi, 1941-45.

Canada. War Purchasing Commission. [*Report.*] A.E. Kemp, Chairman. Ottawa: King's Printer, 1916-19. 6 vols.

Canada and Western Security; the Search for New Options. Toronto: Atlantic Council of Canada, 1982. 39 pp.

* *Le Canada arme ses troupes.* (Actualités; revue destinée aux Forces canadiennes, vol VII, no 11.) Ottawa: Imprimeur de la Reine, 1954. 27 pp.

* *Canada Arms Her Forces.* (Current Affairs for the Canadian Forces, vol. VII, no. 11.) Ottawa: Queen's Printer, 1954. 31 pp.

Le Canada français et les conflits contemporains; actes du colloque tenu à l'Université du Québec à Montréal, le 27 août 1995, sous la direction de Claude Beauregard, Robert Comeau et Jean-Pierre Gagnon. (Cahiers d'histoire politique, no 2, hiver 1996.) s.l.: Société historique du Canada; Association québécoise d'histoire politique; Service historique, Défense nationale, 1996. 288 pp.

Canada; Neighbor at War; a University of Chicago Round Table Broadcast. (Univ. of Chicago Round Table, no. 195.) Chicago: Univ. of Chicago, 1941. 29 pp.

Canada, the Arms Race and Disarmament. Ottawa: United Nations Association in Canada, [1981?]. 47 pp.

Canada's Effort in the Great War to March, 1917. Moose Jaw, Sask.: privately printed, [1917]. 79 pp.

Canadian Broadcasting Corporation. Publications Branch. *We have been There; Authoritative Reports by Qualified Observers who have Returned from the War Zones, as Presented over the CBC National Network.* Toronto: Canadian Broadcasting Corporation, 1941-42. 2 vols.

Canadian Defence League. *The Canadian Defence League, Organized May 5th, 1909.* Toronto: n.p., 1913. 48 pp.

Canadian Defence Quarterly. Vol. I-XVI. Ottawa: privately printed, 1923-39.

Canadian Defence Quarterly./Revue canadienne de défense. Vol. I- . Toronto: Baxter Pub., 1971- .

Canadian Institute of International Affairs. Toronto Men's Branch. Defence Study Group. *Problems of National Defence; a Study Guide and Bibliography,* by Brian A. Crane, Sydney Peck, and Tom Wickett. Toronto: Canadian Institute of International Affairs, 1962. 14 pp.

Canadian Institute of Strategic Studies. *Canadian Defence Policies for the Future.* Michael A. Stevenson, ed. (Spring Seminar 1980, Vol. 1-6.) Toronto: Canadian Institute of Strategic Studies, n.d. 56 pp.

Canadian Liberal Party. Central Information Office. *Canada and the Navy; Australia and New Zealand; Methods of Naval Defence; the Policies of Other Self-Governing British Dominions and their Bearing upon the Naval Controversy in Canada.* (Publication no. 9.) Ottawa; privately printed, 1913. 23 pp.

_____. *Canada and the Navy; Canada's Position in Military and Naval Defence; an Outline of Important Events.* (Publication no. 7.) Ottawa: privately printed, 1913. 16 pp.

_____. *Canada and the Navy; Is There an Emergency? Conflicting Opinions Examined in the Light of Facts.* (Publication no. 6.) Ottawa: privately printed, 1913. 24 pp.

_____. *Canada and the Navy; the Memorandum Prepared by the Board of Admiralty on the General Naval Situation.* (Publication no. 5.) Ottawa: privately printed, 1913. 16 pp.

_____. *Canada and the Navy; the Real Emergency; the Nationalist-Conservative Alliance and Some of its Consequences; How British Interests have been Sacrificed to Serve Party Ends.* (Publication no. 8.) Ottawa: privately printed, 1913. 20 pp.

_____. *Canada and the Navy; the Two Policies; 100 Reasons Why the Laurier is Better than the Borden Policy!* (Publication no. 12.) Ottawa: privately printed, 1913. 15 pp.

_____. *Canadian Defence and the Navy Question.* Ottawa: privately printed, 1915. 80 pp.

_____. *Correspondence of General Sir Sam Hughes, ex-Minister of Militia, and the Right Hon. Sir Robert Borden, G.C.M.G., at the Time Sir Sam Resigned; Sir Sam Accused of Insubordination but Dismissed for Writing the Premier an Insulting Letter; Read the "Charges and Accusations".* (Publication no. 52.) Ottawa; privately printed, [1917]. 16 pp.

Canadian Liberal Party. Central Information Office. *A Series of Pamphlets and Leaflets on Canada and the Navy Issued by the Liberal Information Office during the 1912-13 Session of Parliament.* Ottawa: privately printed, n.d. v.p.

_____. *Shell and Fuse Contracts; a Million Dollar Rake-off; Taken from Government Records.* (Publication no. 49.) Ottawa: privately printed, 1917]. 12 pp.

_____. *War Contract Scandals, as Investigated by the Public Accounts Committee of the House of Commons, 1915; also the Purchase of Boots, as Investigated by the Special "Boot Committee" Appointed by the House of Commons, Ottawa, 1915.* Ottawa: privately printed, 1915. 47 pp.

Canadian Military Biography. Vol. I. Hinton, Alta.: Military Archives & Records Service, 1989.

The Canadian Military Gazette. Vol. I-LXIII. Ottawa: privately printed, 1885-1948.

Canadian Military History. Vol. I- . Waterloo, Ont.: Laurier Centre for Military, Strategic and Disarmament Studies, Wilfrid Laurier Univ., 1992- .

The Canadian Military Journal. Vol. I- . Beauceville, P.Q.; Montreal: privately printed, 1934- .
Title 1934-1943. Salute.

Canadian Military Medals and Insignia Journal. Vol I- . Guelph, Ont.: privately printed, 1965- .
Title varies.

Canadian Military Review./Revue militaire canadienne. Vol. I-II. Quebec, P.Q.: privately printed/imprimé privé, 1880-81?

Canadian National Railways. *Canada's National Railways; their Part in the War.* Toronto: privately printed, n.d. 167 pp.

The Canadian Navy in Peace and War in the 1990's [sic]. (The Niobe Papers, Volume 3.) Halifax: Naval Officers' Association of Canada, 1991. 90 pp.

The Canadian Strategic Review. Vol. I- . Toronto: Canadian Institute of Strategic Studies, 1982- .
Annual.

The Canadian War. No. 1-12. Toronto: n.p., 1914-15.

Canadian War Museum./Musée canadien de la guerre. [Ottawa: National Museums of Canada/Musées nationaux du Canada, 1987.] 21 pp.
Bilingual text./Texte bilingue.

Canadian War Museum./Musée canadien de la guerre. Ottawa: Queen's Printer/Imprimeur de la Reine, 1969. 1 vol., unpaged./l tome, non paginé. *Bilingual text./Text bilingue.*

Capon, Alan R. *His Faults Lie Gently; the Incredible Sam Hughes.* Lindsay, Ont.: F.W. Hall, 1969. 159 pp.

Carnegie, David. *The History of Munitions Supply in Canada, 1914-1918.* London: Longmans, Green, 1925. 336 pp.

Caron, Serge. *The Economic Impact of Canadian Defence Expenditures.* (Occasional Paper 1-94). Kingston, Ont.: Centre for Studies in Defence Resources Management, National Defence College of Canada, 1994. v.p.

Carter, David J. *Behind Canadian Barbed Wire; Alien, Refugee and Prisoner of War Camps in Canada, 1914-1946.* Calgary: Tumbleweed Press, 1980. 334 pp.

Carter, G. *The British Commonwealth and International Security; the Role of the Dominions, 1919-1939.* Toronto: Ryerson Press, 1947. 326 pp.

Carter, H. Dyson. *Sea of Destiny; the Story of Hudson Bay — our Undefended Back Door.* New York: Greenberg, 1940. 236 pp.

Challenge and Commitment: Comments on the Defence White Paper. (Behind the Headlines, vol. XLV, no. 1) [Toronto]: Canadian Institute of International Affairs, 1987. 22 pp.

Chapman, Harry. *Dartmouth's Day of Anguish; ... the Explosion, December 6, 1917 ....* Dartmouth, N.S.: Dartmouth Museum Society, 1992. 45 pp.

Charters, David A. *Armed Forces and Political Purpose: Airborne Forces and the Canadian Army in the 1980s.* Fredericton, N.B.: Univ. of New Brunswick Centre for Conflict Studies, 1984. 145 pp.

Chase-Casgrain, T. *Address by Hon. T. Chase-Casgrain, K.C., M.P., Postmaster General, Delivered at a Luncheon Given in His Honour by the Canadian Club, Vancouver, B.C., on the 16th of August, 1915.* n.p.: [1915]. 23 pp.

Chassé, Noël. *Avant la poussée finale.* Québec, P.Q.: Imprimerie "L'événement", 1918. 98 pp.

*Choko, Marc H. *Affiches de guerre canadiennes, 1914-1918, 1939-1945.* Laval, Qué.: Méridien/Canada Communication Group, 1994. 199 pp.

*_____. *Canadian War Posters, 1914-1918, 1939-1945.* Laval, Qué.: Méridien/Canada Communication Group, 1994. 199 pp.

Churchill, (Sir) Winston Leonard Spencer. *Churchill in Ottawa.* [Ottawa: King's Printer, n.d.] 1 vol., unpaged.

Citizens' Inquiry into Peace and Security. *Transformation Moment: a Canadian Vision of Common Security.* n.p.: Project Ploughshares and the Canadian Peace Alliance for the Citizens' Inquiry into Peace and Security, 1992. 105 pp.

Climo, Percy L. *Cobourg 1914-1919; a Magnificent Sacrifice.* Cobourg, Ont.: privately printed, 1986. 110 pp.

Coates, Kenneth, ed. *The Alaska Highway; Papers of 40th Anniversary Symposium.* Vancouver: Univ. of British Columbiea Press, 1985. 208 pp.

Coates, Kenneth, and W.R. Morrison. *The Alaska Highway in World War II; the U.S. Army of Occupation in Canada's Northwest.* Toronto: Univ. of Toronto Press, 1992. 309 pp.

Code, David E., and Caroline Ursulak, eds. *Leaner and Meaner: Armed Forces in the Post Gulf War Era.* Ottawa: Conference of Defence Associations Institute, 1992. 131 pp.
Conference of Defence Associations Institute Annual Seminar, January 1992.

Code, David E., and Ian Cameron, eds. *Canadian Forces and the Modern World.* Ottawa: Conference of Defence Associations Institute, 1993. 142 pp.
Conference of Defence Associations Institute Ninth Annual Seminar, January 1993.

[Coffin, W.F.] *Thoughts on Defence; from a Canadian Point of View*, by a Canadian. Montreal: J. Lovell, 1870. 55 pp.

Colombo, John Robert, and Michael Richardson, comps. *We Stand on Guard; Poems and Songs of Canadians in Battle.* n.p.: 1985. 210 pp.

Comeau, Paul-André, Claude Beauregard et Edwidge Munn. *La démocratie en veilleuse; rapport sur la censure; récit de l'organisation, des activités et de la démobilisation de la censure pendant la guerre de 1939-45.* (Dossiers documents.) Montréal: Editions Québec/Amérique, 1995. 301 pp.

Comité des 13/Committee of 13. *Rapport sur la révision de la politique de défense du Canada./Report on the Review of Canadian Defense Policy.* Saint-Foy (Qué.): Centre québécois de relations internationales, Univ. Laval, 1994. 95/93 pp.
Texte bilingue./Bilingual text.

Comments on the Senate's Rejection of the Naval Aid Bill. Ottawa: Ottawa Print. Co., [1913]. 27 pp.

Communauté urbaine de Montréal. Service de planification du territoire. *Architecture militaire.* (Répertoire d'architecture traditionnelle sur le territoire de la Communauté urbaine de Montréal.) Montréal: Communauté urbaine de Montréal, 1982. 63 pp.

Conant, Melvin. *The Long Polar Watch; Canada and the Defence of North America.* New York: Harper, 1962. 204 pp.

————. *A Perspective on Defence: the Canada-United States Compact.* (Behind the Headlines, vol. XXXIII, no. 4.) Toronto: Canadian Institute of International Affairs, 1974. 36 pp.

Conn, Stetson, and Byron Fairchild. *The Western Hemisphere; the Framework of Hemisphere Defense.* (United States Army in World War II.) Washington: U.S. Govt. Print. Off., 1960. 470 pp.

Conscription 1917. Essays by A.M. Willms and others. (Canadian Historical Readings, 8.) Toronto: Univ. of Toronto Press, n.d. 77 pp.

*Le Conseil du service militaire. *Pour la défense du Canada.* Ottawa: imprimé privé, 1917. 29 pp.

[Conservative Party (Canada).] *Imperial Defence; the Record of the Liberal Party; Persistent Opposition to any Proposals which would Bind Canada Closer to the Motherland; Refused to Share the Burden.* Ottawa: Federal Press Agency, 1915. 16 pp.

————. *Imperial Naval Defence; the Record of the Liberal Party.* Ottawa: Federal Press Agency, 1915. 32 pp.

————. *The Collapse of the "Boot Scandal"; Liberal Campaign of Falsehood a Total Failure; but It has Robbed the Canadian Workingman of Millions of Dollars.* Ottawa: Federal Press Agency, n.d. 11 pp.

Co-operative Commonwealth Federation. National Office. *A New Order shall Arise; Statements on the Policy of the Co-operative Commonwealth Federation (C.C.F.) in the Present Struggle against the Nazis and Fascists, Consisting of an Address by M.J. Coldwell, M.P., C.C.F. National Chairman, Policy Resolutions Adopted by the 1940 National Convention of the C.C.F., Cables of Greetings Exchanged by the C.C.F. with the British Labour Party.* Ottawa: privately printed, n.d. 24 pp.

Coulon, Jocelyn. *En première ligne; grandeurs et misères du système militaire canadien.* s.l.: Le Jour, 1991. 277 pp.

Coulon, Jocelyn, et Yvan Cliche. *La dernière croisade; la guerre du Golfe et le rôle caché du Canada.* Montréal: Méridien, 1992. [226] pp.

Cowan, John Scott. *See No Evil; a Study of the Chaos in Canadian Defence Policy.* Toronto: Annex Pub., 1963. 35 pp.

Cox, David. *Canada and NORAD, 1958-1978; a Cautionary Retrospective.* (Aurora Papers 1.) Ottawa: Canadian Centre for Arms Control and Disarmament, 1985. 48 pp.

Cox, David. *Canadian Defence Policy; the Dilemmas of a Middle Power.* (Behind the Headlines, vol. XXVII, no. 5.) Toronto: Canadian Institute of International Affairs, 1968. 43 pp.

*_____. *La défense continentale: analyse des tendances et perspective canadienne.* (Les cahiers de l'Institut, numéro 2.) Ottawa: Institut canadien pour la paix et la sécurité internationales, 1986. 55 pp.

*_____. *Trends in Continental Defence: a Canadian Perspective.* (Occasional Papers, number 2.) Ottawa: Canadian Institute for International Peace and Security, 1986. 50 pp.

Crane, Brian. *An Introduction to Canadian Defence Policy.* Toronto: Canadian Institute of International Affairs, 1964. 75 pp.

Crickard, Fred W., Peter T. Haydon and Douglas A. Ross. *Canadian Perspectives on Maritime Strategy.* (Issue Brief 11.) Ottawa: Canadian Centre for Arms Control and Disarmament, 1990. 32 pp.

Cross, Michael, and Robert Bothwell, eds. *Policy by Other Means; Essays in Honour of C.P. Stacey.* Toronto: Clarke, Irwin, 1972. 258 pp.

Cuff, R.D., and J.L. Granatstein. *Canadian-American Relations in Wartime; from the Great War to the Cold War.* Toronto: Hakkert, 1975. 205 pp.

Culhane, Claire. *Why is Canada in Vietman? The Truth about our Foreign Aid.* Toronto: NC Press, 1972. 125 pp.

Cuthbertson, Brian. *Canadian Military Independence in the Age of the Superpowers.* Toronto: Fitzhenry & Whiteside, 1977. 282 pp.

Dafoe, John W. *The Voice of Dafoe; a Selection of Editorials on Collective Security, 1931-1944.* W.L. Morton, ed. Toronto: Macmillan, 1945. 293 pp.

Dafoe, John W., ed. *Canada Fights; an American Democracy at War.* New York: Farrar & Rinehart, 1941. 280 pp.

Datta, Shabnam K., and Fred W. Crickard, eds. *Canadian Military Aviation in the Year 2000; Proceedings of a Conference Held in Halifax, N.S., May 1990.* Halifax: Centre for Foreign Policy Studies, Dalhousie Univ., 1991. 127 pp.

Davidson, (Sir) Charles, *see* Canada. Royal Commission ...

Davies, Raymond Arthur. *This is our Land; Ukranian Canadians against Hitler.* Toronto: Progress Books, 1943. 158 pp.

Davis, Henry Hague, *see* Canada. Royal Commission on the Bren Gun Contract.

Dawson, R. MacGregor. *The Conscription Crisis of 1944.* Toronto: Univ. of Toronto Press, 1961. 136 pp.

Defence in the 70s: Comments on the White Paper. (Behind the Headlines, vol. XXX.) Toronto: Canadian Institute of International Affairs, 1970. 21 pp.

*****Defence of Canada Regulations.*** Ottawa: King's Printer, 1939. 57 pp. *Reprinted and expanded 1940, 1941, 1942.*

Defence Research and Education Centre. ***Towards a World without War; Next Steps in Canadian Defence Policy.*** Halifax: Veterans Against Nuclear Arms, 1987. 15 pp.

De Malijay, Paul. ***Le Colonel d'Orsonnens; considérations sur l'organisation militaire de la Confédération canadienne; observations critiques.*** Montréal: Les Presses à vapeur du Franc-Parleur, 1874. 58 pp.

Denison, George T. ***Naval Defence; St. Andrew's Society Banquet; Colonel George T. Denison's Reply to the Toast of Army and Navy, 30th November, 1909.*** n.p.: [1909]. 14 pp.

*Desjardins, L.G. ***L'Angleterre, le Canada et la Grande Guerre.*** Québec, P.Q.: s.i., 1917. 460 pp.

*_____. ***England, Canada and the Great War.*** Quebec, P.Q.: Chronicle Print., 1918. 422 pp.

*Deschamps, Gaston. ***Canada's Effort.*** (Publications of the Committee "The Effort of France and her Allies".) Paris: Bloud & Gay, 1917. 27 pp.

*_____. ***L'effort canadien.*** (Publication du comité "L'effort de la France et de ses alliés".) Paris: Bloud & Gay, 1916. 30 pp.

Dewitt, David B., and David Leyton-Brown, [eds.] ***Canada's International Security Policy.*** Scarborough, Ont.: Prentice Hall Canada, 1995. 504 pp.

De Wolfe, J.H., comp. ***Our Heroes in the Great World War; Giving Facts and Details on Canada's Part in the Greatest War in History.*** Ottawa: Patriotic Pub. Co., 1919. 415 pp.

Dillon, G.M. ***Canadian Naval Forces since World War II; a Decision-Making Analysis***, with comments by Dr. G.R. Lindsey and Professor Jonathan Wouk, with a reply from the author. (Dalhousie Univ. Center for Foreign Policy Studies Occasional Paper.) Halifax: Dalhousie Univ., 1972. 79 pp.

Diubaldo, R.J., and S.J. Scheinberg. ***A Study of Canadian-American Defence Policy (1945-1975); Northern Issues and Strategic Resources.*** (Operational Research and Analysis Establishment ORAE Extra-Mural Paper no. 6.) Ottawa: Dept. of National Defence, 1978. 115 pp.

Donneur, André, et Jean Pariseau, éds. ***Regards sur le système de défense du Canada.*** (Centre d'Etudes et de Recherche sur l'Armée série: Bilan et perspectives.) Toulouse, France: Presses de l'Institut d'Etudes politiques de Toulouse, 1989. 238 pp.

Dose, Daniel C. *NORAD: a New Look.* (National Security Series, no. 1/83.) Kingston, Ont.: Queen's Univ. Centre for International Relations, 1983. 93 pp.

*Douglas, W.A.B. *La création d'une aviation militaire nationale.* Responsable de l'édition française: Jean Pariseau. (Histoire officielle de l'Aviation royale du Canada, Tome II.) s.l.: Ministère de la Défense nationale et le Centre d'édition du gouvernement du Canada, Approvisionements et Services Canada, 1987. 881 pp.

* _____. *The Creation of a National Air Force.* (The Official History of the Royal Canadian Air Force, Volume II.) n.p.: Univ. of Toronto Press in co-operation with the Dept. of National Defence and Canadian Government Pub. Centre, Supply and Services Canada, 1986. 797 pp.

Douglas, W.A.B., ed. *The RCN in Transition, 1910-1985.* Vancouver: Univ. of British Columbia Press, 1988. 411 pp.

Douglas, W.A.B., and Brereton Greenhous. *Out of the Shadows; Canada in the Second World War.* Toronto: Oxford Univ. Press, 1977. 288 pp.
Rev. ed. Toronto: Dundurn Press, 1995. 304 pp.

Dow, James. *The Arrow.* Toronto: J. Lorimer, 1979. 160 pp.

Dowe, Francis S. *The Canadian Military Register of Foreign Awards.* Ottawa: privately printed, 1979. 236 pp.

"Du Guesclin" [*pseud.*] *voir Notre marine de guerre.*

Dunbar, Francis J., and Joseph H. Harper. *Old Colours Never Die; a Record of Colours and Military Flags in Canada.* Toronto: privately printed, 1992. 294 pp.

Dundonald, Douglas Mackinnon Baillie Hamilton Cochrane, 12th earl. *My Army Life.* London: E. Arnold, 1926. 342 pp.

Dunmore, Spencer. *Wings for Victory; the Remarkable Story of the British Commonwealth Air Training Plan in Canada.* Toronto: McClelland & Stewart, 1994. 399 pp.

Dyer, Gwynne, and Tina Viljoen. *The Defence of Canada; in the Arms of the Empire.* Toronto: McClelland & Stewart, 1990. 375 pp.

Dziuban, Stanley W. *Military Relations between the United States and Canada, 1939-1945.* (United States Army in World War II; Special Studies.) Washington: U.S. Govt. Print. Off., 1959. 432 pp.

_____. *U.S. Military Collaboration with Canada, World War II.* [Washington]: Office of the Chief of Military History, Dept. of the Army, 1954. 830 pp.

Eayrs, James. *Future Roles for the Armed Forces of Canada.* (Behind the Headlines, vol. XXVIII.) Toronto: Canadian Institute of International Affairs, 1969. 16 pp.

_____. *In Defence of Canada.* (Studies in the Structure of Power; Decision Making in Canada.) Toronto: Univ. of Toronto Press, 1964-83. 5 vols.

_____. *Northern Approaches; Canada and the Search for Peace.* Toronto: Macmillan, 1961. 195 pp.

Edgar, Alistair D., and David G. Haglund. *The Canadian Defence Industry in the New Global Environment.* Montreal: McGill-Queen's Univ. Press, 1995. 229 pp.

Eggleston, Wilfrid. *Canada's Nuclear Story.* Toronto: Clarke, Irwin, 1965. 368 pp.

_____. *Scientists at War.* London: Oxford Univ. Press, 1950. 291 pp.

Ehrhart, Hans-Georg, and David G. Haglund, eds. *The "New Peacekeeping" and European Security: German and Canadian Interests and Issues.* (Demokratie, Sicherheit, Frieden ... DSF Band 93.) Baden-Baden, Germany: Nomos Verlagsgesellschaft, 1994. 286 pp.

Epps, Ken. *The Defence Industry Productivity Program; Contributions 1969 through 1990.* (Ploughshares Working Paper 91-2.) Waterloo, Ont.: Project Ploughshares, 1991. 29 pp.

Eustace, Marilyn. *Canada's Commitment to Europe. I: The European Force 1964-1971.* (National Security Series, no. 1/79.) Kingston, Ont.: Queen's Univ. Centre for International Relations, 1979. 166 pp.

Evans, W. Sanford. *The Canadian Contingents and Canadian Imperialism; a Story and a Study.* Toronto: Publishers' Syndicate, 1901. 352 pp.

Ewart, John S. *Canada and British Wars.* n.p.: n.d. 88 pp.

Fédération libérale nationale. *Complot et crise; novembre-décembre 1944.* Ottawa: s.i., s.d. 27 pp.

_____. *Deux guerres, 1914-1918 — 1939-1944; parallèle entre la conduite du parti conservateur-nationaliste-unioniste et celle du parti libéral, au cours de deux guerres mondiales.* Ottawa: s.i., [1944?]. 24 pp.

_____. *Je fais la guerre.* Ottawa: s.i., [1944?]. 17 pp.

A Few Words on Canada, by a Canadian. Ottawa: Hunter-Rose, 1871. 72 pp.

Finnie, Richard. *Canol; the Sub-Arctic Pipeline and Refinery Project Constructed by Bechtel-Price-Callahan for the Corps of Engineers, United States Army, 1942-1944.* San Francisco, Calif.: privately printed, 1945. 210 pp.

Fletcher, [Henry Charles]. *A Lecture Delivered at the Literary and Scientific Institute, Ottawa, by Col. Fletcher, Scots Fusilier Guards, Military Secretary, February, 1875.* Ottawa: n.p., n.d. 19 pp.

_____. *Memorandum on the Militia System of Canada.* Ottawa: Citizen Print. Co., 1873. 20 pp.

For King and Country; Alberta in the Second World War. Edmonton: Provincial Museum of Alberta; Reidmore Books, 1995. 364 pp.

Fortmann, Michel. *La politique de défense canadienne de Mackenzie King à Trudeau (1945-1979).* (Département de science politique notes de recherche, no 20.) Montréal: Département de science politique, Université de Montréal, [1988?]. 90 pp.

Forum; Conference of Defence Associations. Vol. II- . Ottawa: Conference of Defence Associations, 1987- .

Foulkes, Charles. *Canadian Defence Policy in a Nuclear Age.* (Behind the Headlines, vol. XXI, no. 1.) Toronto: Canadian Institute of International Affairs, 1961. 20 pp.

_____. *Canadian Response to United States Strategy.* [(Carleton Univ. School of International Affairs Occasional Papers, 2.) Ottawa: Carleton Univ., 1968?]. 20 pp.

French, John Denton Pinkstone French, 1st earl. *Report by General Sir John French, G.C.B., G.C.V.O., K.C.M.G., Inspector General of the Imperial Forces, upon his Inspection of the Canadian Military Forces.* (Sessional Paper, no. 35a.) Ottawa: King's Printer, 1910. 38 pp.

Gaffen, Fred. *In the Eye of the Storm; a History of Canadian Peacekeeping.* Toronto: Deneau & Wayne, 1987. 302 pp.

Gaffen, Fred, ed./rédacteur. *The Road to Victory: a History of Canada in the Second World War./La route de la victoire: la participation du Canada à la Deuxième Guerre mondiale.* French translation/Traduction en français: Jean Pariseau. n.p./s.l.: Canadian War Museum/Musée canadien de la guerre; Esprit de Corps, 1995. 84 pp.
Bilingual text./Texte bilingue.

Gardam, John. *The Legacy./Mon héritage.* (A-PD-007-007/JD-001.) n.p.: Dept. of National Defence/s.l.: Ministère de la Défense nationale, 1988. v.p./p.m.
Bilingual text./Texte bilingue.

Gellner, John. *Canada in NATO.* Toronto: Ryerson Press, 1970. 117 pp.

_____. *The Defence of Canada: Requirements, Capabilities and the National Will.* (Behind the Headlines, vol. XVII, no. 3.) Toronto: Canadian Institute of International Affairs, 1958. 16 pp.

Gellner, John. *Problems of Canadian Defence.* (Behind the Headlines, vol. XVIII, no. 5.) Toronto: Canadian Institute of International Affairs, 1958. 16 pp.

Giangrande, Carole. *The Nuclear North; the People, the Regions, and the Arms Race.* Toronto: Anansi, 1983. 231 pp.

Gibson, Colin. *"Air Power in Canada"; an Address by Col. the Hon. Colin Gibson, M.C., M.A., Minister of National Defence for Air, to the Empire Club of Toronto, February 28, 1946.* n.p.: n.d. 11 pp.

[Gillis, Clarence.] *Letter from Home.* Toronto: Canadian Forum, 1943. 32 pp.

Glazebrook, G. de T., and Winslow Benson. *Canada's Defence Policy; Report of Round Tables of the Fourth Annual Conference of the Canadian Institute of International Affairs.* Toronto: [Canadian Institute of International Affairs], 1937. 16 pp.

Godsell, Philip H. *The Romance of the Alaska Highway.* Toronto: Ryerson Press, 1944. 235 pp.

Gold, Lorne W. *The Canadian Habbakuk Project; a Project of the National Research Council of Canada.* Cambridge, Eng.: International Glaciological Society, 1990 [*i.e.* 1993]. 323 pp.

[Golden, L.L.L.] *Conscription*, by "Politicus" [*pseud.*] (Macmillan War Pamphlets, Canadian Series.) Toronto: Macmillan, 1941. 32 pp.

Goldie, Mary L., and Douglas A. Ross, eds. *Pacific Security 2010; Canadian Perspectives on Pacific Security into the 21st Century.* (Aurora Papers 10.) Ottawa: Canadian Centre for Arms Control and Disarmament, 1991. 84 pp.

Good, Mabel Tinkiss. *Men of Valour.* Toronto: Macmillan, 1948. 137 pp. *Reprinted 1973, titled: The Bridge at Dieppe and Other Canadian War Stories.*

Granatstein, J.L. *Canada's War; the Politics of the Mackenzie King Government, 1939-1945.* Toronto: Oxford Univ. Press, 1975. 436 pp.

_____. *Conscription in the Second World War, 1939-1945; a Study in Political Management.* (The Frontenac Library, Number 1.) Toronto: Ryerson Press, 1969. 85 pp.

Granatstein, J.L., and Desmond Morton. *A Nation Forged in Fire; Canadians and the Second World War 1939-1945.* Toronto: Lester & Orpen Dennys, 1989. 287 pp.

Granatstein, J.L., and J.M. Hitsman. *Broken Promises; a History of Conscription in Canada.* Toronto: Oxford Univ. Press, 1977. 281 pp.

Granatstein, J.L., and Peter Neary, eds. *The Good Fight; Canadians and World War II.* Toronto: Copp Clark, 1995. 466 pp.

Granatstein, J.L., and R.D. Cuff, eds. *War and Society in North America.* Toronto: T. Nelson, 1971. 199 pp.

Grant, Shelagh D. *Sovereignty or Security? Government Policy in the Canadian North, 1936-1950.* Vancouver: Univ. of British Columbia Press, 1988. 385 pp.

Gravel, Jean-Yves, *L'armée au Québec; un portrait social, 1868-1900.* Montréal: Les Éditions du Boréal Express, 1974. 157 pp.

Gravel, Jean-Yves, éd. *Le Québec et la guerre, 1867-1960.* Montréal: Les Editions du Boréal Express, 1974. 173 pp.

Gray, Colin S. *Canada and NORAD; a Study in Strategy.* (Behind the Headlines, vol. XXXI, nos. 3-4.) [Toronto]: Canadian Institute of International Affairs, 1972. 20 pp.

_____. *Canada's Maritime Forces.* (Wellesley Paper 1.) Toronto: Canadian Institute of International Affairs, 1973. 79 pp.

_____. *Canadian Defence Priorities; a Question of Relevance.* Toronto: Clarke, Irwin, 1972. 293 pp.

_____. *Canadians in a Dangerous World.* Toronto: Atlantic Council of Canada, 1994. 32 pp.

The Great War and Canadian Society; an Oral History. Daphne Read, ed. Toronto: New Hogtown Press, 1978. 223 pp.

Greenhous, Brereton, and others. *The Crucible of War, 1939-1945.* (The Official History of the Royal Canadian Air Force, Volume III.) n.p.: Univ. of Toronto Press in cooperation with the Dept. of National Defence and the Canadian Government Pub. Centre, Supply and Services Canada, 1994. 1096 pp.

Gunning, C. *Eyes Right! The Cadet Story; Three-Quarters of a Century of North Bay's Cadet Corps.* North Bay, Ont.: printed by Bond Print. & Graphics, 1993. 199 pp.

Haddow, Robert. *More Planes to Smash Fascism.* [Montreal?: n.p., n.d.] 18 pp.

Haglund, David G., ed. *Canada's Defence Industrial Base; the Political Economy of Preparedness and Procurement.* Kingston, Ont.: R.P. Frye, 1988. 261 pp.

Haglund, David G., and Joel J. Sokolsky, eds. *The U.S.-Canada Security Relationship; the Politics, Strategy and Technology of Defense.* (Studies in Global Security.) Boulder, Col.: Westview Press, 1989. 306 pp.

Hall, H. Duncan. *North American Supply.* (History of the Second World War; United Kingdom Civil Series.) London: H.M. Stationery Office and Longmans, Green, 1955. 559 pp.

Halliday, H.A. *Through Artists' Eyes: War Art in Canada./L'art militaire du Canada.* (Canada's Visual History/Histoire du Canada en images, volume 59.) n.p.: National Museum of Man and National Film Board of Canada, n.d./s.l.: Musée national de l'Homme et Office national du film du Canada, s.d. 28/30 pp.
Bilingual text./Texte bilingue.

The Halship Saga; the War Effort of Halifax Shipyards, Limited; "An Illustrious War Achievement". [Halifax: n.p., n.d.] 1 vol., unpaged.

Halstead, John. *Canada's Security in the 1980s: Options and Pitfalls.* (Behind the Headlines, vol. XLI, no. 1.) Toronto: Canadian Institute of International Affairs, 1983. 18 pp.

_____. *A Defence Policy for Canada: the White Paper Two Years On.* (Behind the Headlines, vol. XLVII, no. 1.) n.p.: Canadian Institute of International Affairs, 1989. 17 pp.

Hannon, Leslie F. *Canada at War.* (The Canadian Illustrated Library.) Toronto: McClelland and Stewart, 1968. 127 pp.

Harris, Stephen. *Canadian Brass: the Making of a Professional Army, 1860-1939.* Toronto: Univ. of Toronto Press, 1988. 271 pp.

Harrison, W.E.C., and others. *Canada, the War and After.* (Live and Learn Books.) Toronto: Ryerson Press, 1942. 78 pp.

Harvey, Jean-Charles. *French Canada at War.* (Macmillan War Pamphlets, Canadian Series.) Toronto: Macmillan, 1941. 26 pp.

Hasek, John. *The Disarming of Canada.* Toronto: Key Porter Books, 1987. 248 pp.

Hattersley-Smith, G. *North of Latitude Eighty; the Defence Research Board in Ellesmere Island.* Ottawa: Defence Research Board, 1974. 121 pp.

Haycock, Ronald G. *The Evolution of Canadian National Security Policy.* (Distinguished Lectures 1-94.) Kingston, Ont.: Centre for National Security Studies, National Defence College, 1994. 17 pp.
Notes for remarks to the National Security Studies Course 10.

_____. *Sam Hughes; the Public Career of a Controversial Canadian, 1885-1916.* (Canadian War Museum Historical Publication no. 21.) n.p.: Wilfrid Laurier Univ. Press in collaboration with Canadian War Museum, 1986. 355 pp.

Haycock, Ronald G., with/avec Serge Bernier. *Teaching Military History; Clio and Mars in Canada./L'enseignement de l'histoire militaire; Clio et Mars au Canada.* (Teaching History./L'enseignement de l'histoire.) Athabasca, Alta.: Athabasca Univ., 1995. 152 pp.

Haydon, Peter T. *The 1962 Cuban Missile Crisis: Canadian Involvement Reconsidered.* Toronto: Canadian Institute of Strategic Studies, 1993. 297 pp.

Haydon, Walter. *Canada and the War.* Bristol, Eng.: J.W. Arrowsmith, 1915. 90 pp.

Hayward, Daniel. *The Air Defence Initiative.* (Issue Brief no. 9.) Ottawa: Canadian Centre for Arms Control and Disarmament, 1988. 32 pp.

Heal, S.C. *Conceived in War, Born in Peace; Canada's Deep Sea Merchant Marine.* Vancouver: Cordillera Pub. Co., 1992. 234 pp.

Hellyer, Paul. *Damn the Torpedoes; My Fight to Unify Canada's Armed Forces.* Toronto: McClelland & Stewart, 1990. 306 pp.

Hertzman, Lewis, John W. Warnock and Thomas A. Hockin. *Alliances and Illusions; Canada and the NATO-NORAD Question.* Edmonton: Hurtig, 1969. 154 pp.

Hicks, Bob. *They Stand on Guard; a Defence Direction for Canada.* Ottawa: Conference of Defence Associations Institute, 1991. 153 pp.

Hill, Roger. *Framework for a New Canadian Defence Policy.* (Working Paper 35.) Ottawa: Canadian Institute for International Peace and Security, 1991. 60 pp.

Hill, Roger, ed. *The NORAD Renewal Issue; Report of the Special Panel to the Sub-Committee of the House of Commons Standing Committee on External Affairs and International Trade Considering the Question of Renewing in May 1991 the North American Aerospace Defence Agreement.* (Working Paper 33.) Ottawa: Canadian Institute for International Peace and Security, 1991. 65 pp.

Hillmer, Norman, Bohdan Kordan and Lubomyr Luciuk, eds. *On Guard for Thee: War, Ethnicity and the Canadian State, 1939-1945.* Ottawa: Canadian Committee for the History of the Second World War, 1988. 282 pp.

Hitchins, F.H. *Air Board, Canadian Air Force and Royal Canadian Air Force.* (National Museum of Man Mercury Series; Canadian War Museum Paper no. 2.) Ottawa: Queen's Printer, 1972. 475 pp.

Hitsman, J. Mackay. *Canadian Naval Policy.* Kingston, Ont.: Queen's Univ., 1940. 208 pp.

_____. *Military Inspection Services in Canada, 1855-1950.* Ottawa: [Queen's Printer, 1962]. 122 pp.

_____. *Safeguarding Canada, 1763-1871.* Toronto: Univ. of Toronto Press, 1968. 240 pp.

Hodgins, J. Herbert, and others, comps. *Women at War.* Montreal: MacLean Pub., 1943. 190 pp.

Holmes, John W., Malcolm N. Bow and John G.H. Halstead. *Canada, NATO and Arms Control.* Edited by Shannon Selin. (Issue Brief no. 6.) Ottawa: Canadian Centre for Arms Control and Disarmament, 1987. 27 pp.

Hopkins, J. Castell. *The Province of Ontario in the War; a Record of Government and People.* Toronto: Warwick Bros. & Rutter, 1919. 123 pp.

Hornung, Rick. *One Nation under the Sun.* Toronto: Stoddart, 1991. 294 pp. *Mohawk Crisis, 1990.*

Hughes, J. Paul. *Military Proof Strikes of Canada.* (Proof Strikes of Canada, volume XXVI.) Kelowna, B.C.: R.A. Lee Philatelist, 1993. 148 pp.

Hunt, B.D., and R.G. Haycock, eds. *Canada's Defence; Perspectives on Policy in the Twentieth Century.* (New Canadian Readings.) Toronto: Copp Clark Pitman, 1993. [277] pp.

Hunt, M.S., comp. *Nova Scotia's Part in the Great War.* Halifax: Veteran Pub., 1920. 466 pp.

Hurst, Alan M. *The Canadian Y.M.C.A. in World War II.* n.p.: n.d. 398 pp.

Hyde, H. Montgomery. *The Quiet Canadian; the Secret Service Story of Sir William Stephenson.* London: H. Hamilton, 1962. 255 pp.

Independent Research Associates Ltd. *The Continuing Search for a Realistic Canadian Defence Policy.* (Canadian Business Papers, vol. 1.) Toronto: Independent Research Associates Ltd., 1972. 15 pp.

Ing, Stanley, and Theodore Olson. *Seeking Common Ground on the Defence of Canada.* (Occasional Paper, no. 1.) Downsview, Ont.: York Univ. Research Programme in Strategic Studies, 1983. 25 pp. *Report of a colloquy between strategic analysts and peace activists, 12 April 1983, York Univ.*

Irwin, Ross W., comp. *A Guide to the War Medals and Decorations of Canada.* [Guelph, Ont.: privately printed], 1969. 114 pp.

Irwin, Ross W., and Edward E. Denby. *Orders, Decorations and Medals to Canadians.* n.p.: 1976. 63 pp.

Ito, Roy. *Stories of my People; a Japanese Canadian Journal.* Hamilton, Ont.: S-20 and Nisei Veterans Association, 1994. 497 pp.

Jackson, H.M. *Canadian Prime Ministers and the Canadian Militia.* n.p.: 1958. 11 pp.

James, F. Cyril. *The Impact and Aftermath of War; an Address Delivered before a Meeting of the Canadian Club at Toronto, Canada, on Monday, December 14, 1942.* Toronto: privately printed, [1942?]. 19 pp.

Japanese Canadian Centennial Society. Hamilton Chapter. *Proceedings of the War Measures Act Conference, in Hamilton, Canada, April 23, 1977.* London, Ont.: P. Anas Pub., 1978. 99 pp.

*Jellicoe, John Rushworth Jellicoe, 1st earl. *Report of Admiral of the Fleet, Viscount Jellicoe of Scapa, G.C.B., O.M., G.C.V.O. on Mission to the Dominion of Canada, November-December, 1919.* Ottawa: n.p., n.d. 3 vols. *Vol. I also printed as Sessional Paper no. 61, 1920. Vol. II-III originally Secret.*

*Jellicoe, John Rushworth Jellicoe, 1er earl. *Rapport de l'Amiral de la Flotte le Vicomte Jellicoe de Scapa, G.C.B., O.M., G.C.V.O., sur la mission navale au Canada en novembre et décembre 1919.* (Document de la session, no 61.) Ottawa: Imprimeur du Roi, 1920. 59 pp.

Jockel, Joseph T. *Canada and International Peacekeeping.* (Significant Issues Series, Volume XVI, Number 3.) Toronto: Canadian Institute of Strategic Studies; Center for Strategic and International Studies, 1994. 83 pp.

_____. *Canada and NATO's Northern Flank.* n.p.: York Centre for International and Strategic Studies, 1986. 58 pp.

_____. *No Boundaries Upstairs; Canada, the United States, and the Origins of North American Air Defence, 1945-1958.* Vancouver: Univ. of British Columbia Press, 1987. 160 pp.

_____. *Security to the North; Canada-U.S. Defense Relations in the 1990s.* (Canadian Series #1.) East Lansing, Mich.: Michigan State Univ. Press, 1991. 217 pp.

Jockel, Joseph T., and Joel J. Sokolsky. *Canada and Collective Security; Odd Man Out.* (The Washington Papers/121.) New York: Praeger, with the Center for Strategic and International Studies, Georgetown Univ., 1986. 118 pp.

Johnson, Leonard V. *A General for Peace.* Toronto: J. Lorimer, 1987. 158 pp.

Johnson, Robbie. *Canadian War Service Badges, 1914-1954.* Surrey, B.C.: Johnson Books, 1995. 216 pp.

Jones, David R., Fred W. Crickard and Todd R. Yates, eds. *Ethics and Canadian Defence Policy; Proceedings of a Conference Held 22-23 March, 1990 at Acadia University, Wolfville, N.S.* Halifax: Centre for Foreign Policy Studies, Dalhousie Univ., 1992. 158 pp.

Joubert, Marie-Claude. *Par dévouement; le Cadre des Instructeurs de Cadets.* Sainte-Blandine (Qué.): Les Editions Neigette, 1994. 246 pp.

Kardash, William. *Hitler's Agents in Canada; a Revealing Story of Potentially Dangerous Fifth Column Activities in Canada among Ukrainian Canadians.* Toronto: privately printed, 1942. 33 pp.

Kardash, William. *1942; Year of Victory; Defeat the Enemy on a Second Land Front in Western Europe.* Toronto: privately printed, [1942?]. 29 pp.

Kasoff, Mark J., and Christine Gesell, eds. *Peacekeeping as an Expression of Canadian Values; Proceedings from the 8th Annual Reddin Symposium.* Bowling Green, Ohio: Canadian Studies Center at Bowling Green State Univ., 1995. 24 pp.

Kaye, V.J. *Ukranian Canadians in Canada's Wars.* J.B. Gregorovich, ed. (Materials for Ukranian Canadian History, Volume I.) Toronto: Ukranian Canadian Research Foundation, 1983. 125 pp.

Keating, Tom, and Larry Pratt. *Canada, NATO and the Bomb; the Western Alliance in Crisis.* Edmonton: Hurtig Publishers, 1988. 246 pp.

Kelsey Club, Winnipeg, Man. *Canadian Defence; What We have to Defend; Various Defence Policies.* Toronto: T. Nelson, 1937. 98 pp.

Kemp, A.E., *see* Canada. War Purchasing Commission.

Kennedy, J. de N. *History of the Department of Munitions and Supply; Canada in the Second World War.* [Ottawa]: King's Printer, 1950. 2 vols.

Keshen, Jeffrey A. *Propaganda and Censorship during Canada's Great War.* Edmonton: Univ. of Alberta Press, 1996. 333 pp.

Kimble, George H.T. *Canadian Military Geography.* Ottawa: Queen's Printer, 1949. 196 pp.

King, W.L. Mackenzie. *Agression in Hitler's Mind has no Limits; My Duty, as I See It, is to Seek above All to Preserve National Unity.* Winnipeg: privately printed, n.d. 23 pp.

*_____. *British Commonwealth Air Training Plan; Broadcast by Right Hon. W.L. Mackenzie King, M.P. Prime Minister of Canada, Sunday, December 17, 1939.* Ottawa: King's Printer, 1939. 17 pp.

_____. *Canada and the Fight for Freedom.* Toronto: Macmillan, 1944. 326 pp.

_____. *Canada and the War; Canada's Contribution to Freedom, Speech by Right Hon. W.L. Mackenzie King, M.P., Prime Minister of Canada, at a Dinner Tendered in his Honour by the Associated Canadian Organizations of New York City, New York, June 17, 1941.* Ottawa: King's Printer, 1941. 18 pp.

*_____. *Canada and the War; Canada's Fighting Men; an Address on the Opening of the Fourth Victory Loan Campaign, by Right Hon. W.L. Mackenzie King, M.P., Prime Minister of Canada, Toronto, April 19, 1943.* Ottawa: King's Printer, 1943. 15 pp.

*King, W.L. Mackenzie. *Canada and the War; Canada's Support of the Army Overseas; Broadcast by Right Hon. W.L. Mackenzie King, M.P., Prime Minister of Canada, Ottawa, November 8, 1944.* Ottawa: King's Printer, 1944. 11 pp.

_____. *Canada and the War; Mackenzie King to the People of Canada, 1940; a Series of Radio Broadcasts by Prime Minister Mackenzie King from Ottawa, February-March 1940.* Ottawa: National Liberal Federation, n.d. 104 pp.

*_____. *Canada and the War; Manpower and a Total War Effort; National Selective Service, Broadcast by Right Hon. W.L. Mackenzie King, M.P., Prime Minister of Canada, August 19, 1942.* Ottawa: King's Printer, 1942. 12 pp.

*_____. *Canada and the War; New Situations and Responsibilities. I. Canada's War Effort Viewed in Relation to the War Effort of the Allied Powers. II. Italy's Entry into the War, Broadcasts by Right Hon. W.L. Mackenzie King, M.P., Prime Minister of Canada, Friday, June 7, and Monday, June 10, 1940.* Ottawa: King's Printer, 1940. 18 pp.

*_____. *Canada and the War; the Defence of Common Liberties; an Address to the Pilgrims of the United States by Right Hon. W.L. Mackenzie King, M.P., Prime Minister of Canada, New York, December 2, 1942.* Ottawa: King's Printer, 1942. 11 pp.

_____. *Canada and the War; the Training of British Pilots and the Joint Air Training Plan; Mackenzie King Replies to Dr. Manion; a Radio Address by Right Honourable W.L. Mackenzie King, Ottawa, 8th March, 1940.* Ottawa: National Liberal Federation, n.d. 13 pp.

_____. *Canada and the War; the Unconditional Surrender of Italy (September 3, 1943); Four Years of War, 1939-1943, Broadcasts by Right Honourable W.L. Mackenzie King, M.P., Prime Minister of Canada, Ottawa, September 8 and 10, 1943.* Ottawa: King's Printer, 1943. 10 pp.

_____. *Canada and the War; Three Years of War; the Real Issue in the Struggle; Broadcast by Right Hon. W.L. Mackenzie King, M.P., Prime Minister of Canada, September 10, 1942.* Ottawa: King's Printer, 1942. 12 pp.

_____. *Canada and the War; Victory, Reconstruction and Peace.* n.p.: 1945. 142 pp.

_____. *Canada and the War; War Record of the Mackenzie King Administration; a Radio Address by Right Honourable W.L. Mackenzie King, Ottawa, 21st February, 1940.* Ottawa: National Liberal Federation, n.d. 20 pp.

*King, W.L. Mackenzie. *Canada at Britain's Side.* Toronto: Macmillan, 1941. 332 pp.

*_____. *Le Canada et la guerre.* Montréal: Editions B. Valiquette, n.d. 341 pp.

*_____. *Le Canada et la guerre; appui du Canada à son armée d'outre-mer, causerie radiophonique du très honorable W.L. Mackenzie King, M.P., Premier ministre du Canada, Ottawa, 8 novembre 1944.* Ottawa: Imprimeur du Roi, 1944. 12 pp.

_____. *Le Canada et la guerre; effort total contre guerre total; un appel en faveur de l'épargne de guerre, radiodiffusé par le très hon. Mackenzie King, M.P., Premier ministre du Canada, dimanche, le 2 février 1941.* Ottawa: Imprimeur du Roi, 1941. 12 pp.

*_____. *Le Canada et la guerre; la défense de nos communes libertés, discours prononcé lors du dîner des "Pilgrims of the United States" par le très hon. W.L. Mackenzie King, M.P., Premier ministre du Canada, New-York, le 2 décembre 1942.* Ottawa: Imprimeur du Roi, 1942. 12 pp.

*_____. *Le Canada et la guerre; les forces combattantes du Canada, discours prononcé à l'ouverture de la campagne du quatrième emprunt de la victoire, par le très honorable W.L. Mackenzie King, Premier ministre du Canada, Toronto, le 19 avril 1943.* Ottawa: Imprimeur du Roi, 1943. 15 pp.

*_____. *Le Canada et la guerre; nouvelles situations et nouvelles responsabilités. I. L'effort de guerre du Canada en regard de l'effort de guerre des puissances alliées. II. L'entrée de l'Italie dans la guerre, discours à la radio du très hon. W.L. Mackenzie King, M.P., Premier ministre du Canada, le vendredi 7 juin et le lundi 10 juin 1940.* Ottawa: Imprimeur du Roi, 1940. 20 pp.

*_____. *Le Canada et la guerre; ressources humaines et effort de guerre total; service sélectif national, discours prononcé à la T.S.F. par le très honorable W.L. Mackenzie King, M.P. Premier ministre du Canada, le 19 août, 1942.* Ottawa: Imprimeur du Roi, 1942. 13 pp.

_____. *National Security — the Issue in the Plebiscite; an Appeal to the Canadian Electorate for an Affirmative Vote on April 27th; an Address Broadcast by the Right Honourable W.L. Mackenzie King, M.P., Prime Minister of Canada, over the Canadian Broadcasting Network, April 7th, 1942.* Ottawa: King's Printer, 1942. 11 pp.

_____. *National Unity and National Survival; Responsibility to our Own and Future Generations; a Second Appeal to the Canadian Electorate for an Affirmative Vote on April 27th; an Address Broadcast by the Right Hon. W.L. Mackenzie King, M.P., Prime Minister of Canada, over the Canadian Broadcasting Corporation Network, April 24th, 1942.* Ottawa: King's Printer, 1942. 11 pp.

41

*King, W.L. Mackenzie. *L'organisation de l'effort de guerre du Canada; le Parlement et le Gouvernement; discours à la radio par le très honorable W.L. Mackenzie King, M.P., Premier ministre du Canada, mardi, le 31 octobre 1939.* Ottawa: Imprimeur du Roi, 1939. 16 pp.

*_____. *The Organization of Canada's War Effort; Parliament and the Government; Broadcast by Right Hon. W.L. Mackenzie King, M.P., Prime Minister of Canada, Tuesday, October 31, 1939.* Ottawa: King's Printer, 1939. 16 pp.

*_____. *Plan d'entraînement des aviateurs du Commonwealth britannique; discours à la radio par le très honorable W.L. Mackenzie King, M.P., Premier ministre du Canada, le dimanche 17 décembre 1939.* Ottawa: Imprimeur du Roi, 1939. 15 pp.

King, W.L. Mackenzie, et P.J.A. Cardin. *Une mesure de sécurité nationale; la question du plébiscite; les chefs disent pourquoi et comment voter; discours prononcés par le très honorable W.L. Mackenzie King, Premier ministre du Canada, et l'honorable P.-J.-A. Cardin, ministre des Transports, irradiés par le réseau français de Radio-Canada, les 7 et 9 avril 1942.* Ottawa: Imprimeur du Roi, 1942. 16 pp.

Kirkconnell, Watson. *Canada, Europe and Hitler.* Toronto: Oxford Univ. Press, 1939. 213 pp.

_____. *Our Ukranian Loyalists.* Winnipeg: privately printed, 1943. 28 pp.

_____. *Twilight of Liberty.* London: Oxford Univ. Press, 1941. 193 pp.

_____. *The Ukranian Canadians and the War.* (Oxford Pamphlets on World Affairs, no. C.3.) Toronto: Oxford Univ. Press, 1940. 30 pp.

*Knight, Eric. *C'est votre terre qu'ils veulent.* Ottawa: [Imprimeur du Roi, 1942]. 11 pp.

*_____. *They Don't Want Swamps and Jungles.* Ottawa: [King's Printer, 1942]. 11 pp.

Krawchuk, Peter. *Interned without Cause.* Pat Prokop, tr. Toronto: Kobzar Pub. Co., 1985. 124 pp.

_____. *Our Contribution to Victory.* Mary Skrypnyk, tr. Toronto: Kobzar Pub. Co., 1985. 157 pp.
Ukranian Canadians in World War II.

Kronenberg, Vernon J. *All Together Now; the Organization of the Department of National Defence in Canada, 1964-1972.* (Wellesley Paper, 3/1973.) Toronto: Canadian Institute of International Affairs, 1973. 124 pp.

Laflamme, Jean. *Les camps de détention au Québec durant la Première Guerre mondiale.* Montréal: s.i., 1973. 49 pp.

Lake, (Sir) P.H.N. *Report upon the Best Method of Giving Effect to the Recommendations of General Sir John French, Regarding the Canadian Militia.* (Sessional Paper, no. 35b.) Ottawa: King's Printer, 1910. 16 pp.

Lamb, Ken. *Milton Remembers World War II.* Milton, Ont.: Milton Historical Society, 1995. 140 pp.

Lanctot, Gustave. *Trois ans de guerre, 1939-1942.* Montréal: G. Ducharme, 1943. 32 pp.

Landells, E.A., ed. *The Military Nurses of Canada; Recollections of Canadian Military Nurses.* White Rock, B.C.: Co-Publishing, 1995. 628 pp.

Langille, Howard Peter. *Changing the Guard: Canada's Defence in a World of Transition.* Toronto: Univ. of Toronto Press, 1990. 267 pp.

Lanks, Herbert R. *Highway to Alaska.* New York: D. Appleton, 1944. 200 pp.

Lapointe, Ernest. *Causerie prononcée à la radio par l'hon. Ernest Lapointe, lundi, le 9 octobre.* Arthabaska, P.Q.: Imprimerie d'Arthabaska, [1941]. 13 pp.

Lash, Z.A. *Defence and Foreign Affairs; a Suggestion for the Empire.* Toronto: Macmillan, 1917. 86 pp.

Laurendeau, André. *La crise de la conscription, 1942.* Montréal: Editions du Jour, 1962. 157 pp.

Lauterpacht, E., ed. *The United Nations Emergency Force; Basic Documents.* London: Stevens, 1960. 49 pp.

Law, Clive M. *Canadian Military Handguns, 1855-1985.* Alexandria Bay, N.Y.: Museum Restoration Service, 1994. 123 pp.

Lawrence, W.H.C. *The Storm of '92; a Grandfather's Tale Told in 1932.* Toronto: Sheppard Pub. Co., 1889. 71 pp.
Mythical war in Canada.

Leacock, Stephen. *National Organization for War.* Ottawa: King's Printer, 1917. 11 pp.

Lee, William M. *Background to the White Paper on Defence.* Ottawa: n.p., 1964. 27 pp.

Lefebvre, Florent. *The French-Canadian Press and the War.* Translated and edited by J.H. Biggar and J.R. Baldwin. (Contemporary Affairs.) Toronto: Ryerson Press, 1940. 40 pp.

Leshchenko, L.O. *SRSR i Kanada v antyhitlerivis' kii koalitsii.* n.p.: 1973. 210 pp.

Lest We Forget; the Price of Victory. Hodgson, Man.: Hodgson Legion History Book Committee, [1991]. 288 pp.

*Letellier, Armand. *DND Language Reform: Staffing the Bilingualism Programs, 1967-1977.* (Socio-Military Series, no. 3.) Ottawa: Directorate of History, NDHQ, 1987. 260 pp.

*_____. *Réforme linguistique à la Défense nationale: la mise en marche des programmes de bilinguisme, 1967-1977.* (Collection d'histoire socio-militaire, no 3.) Ottawa: Service historique, Ministère de la Défense nationale, 1987. 258 pp.

Létourneau, Paul, éd. *Le Canada et l'OTAN après 40 ans, 1949-1989.* Québec (Qué.): Centre québécois de relations internationales, Université Laval, 1992. 216 pp.

Letter from Home see Gillis, Clarence.

*Levant, Victor. *Quiet Complicity; Canadian Involvement in the Vietnam War.* Toronto: Between the Lines, 1986. 322 pp.

*_____. *Secrète alliance; le Canada dans la guerre du Viêt-Nam.* Adapté de l'anglais par Jean-Pierre Fournier. Ville LaSalle (Qué.): Hurtubise HMH, 1990. 351 pp.

La Ligue pour la défense du Canada; ce qu'elle a fait, son attitude présente, ce qu'elle fera. Montréal: La Ligue pour la défense du Canada, 1942. 28 pp.

Longair, A.K. *Early Defence Atomic Research in Canada; with an Introduction on the Genesis of Nuclear Energy.* (Research and Development Branch CRAD Report 4/79.) Ottawa: Dept. of National Defence, 1979. 21 pp.

Loomis, Dan G. *Not Much Glory; Quelling the F.L.Q.* Toronto: Deneau, 1984. 199 pp.

Lord Dundonald; les motifs de sa révocation. s.l.: s.i., [1904?]. 16 pp.

Lord Dundonald; Orders in Council and Correspondence Showing Why He was Removed from Office; Attacked Canada's Government in Defiance of Military Regulations. (Political Pointers, no. 5.) n.p.: [1904]. 72 pp.

Lotz, Jim. *Canadians at War.* London: Bison Group, 1990. 192 pp.

Lower, A.R.M., and F.J. Parkinson, eds. *War and Reconstruction, Some Canadian Issues; Addresses Given at the Canadian Institute of Public Affairs, August 15 to 23, 1942.* Toronto: Ryerson Press, 1942. 106 pp.

Luciuk, Lubomyr Y. *Internment Operations; the Role of Old Fort Henry in World War I.* Bryan Rollason, ed. (A Delta Minibook.) Kingston, Ont.: Delta Educational Consultants, 1980. 38 pp.

MacCormac, John. *Canada; America's Problem.* New York: Viking Press, 1940. 287 pp.

Macdonald, Angus L. *Speeches of Angus L. Macdonald.* Toronto: Longmans, Green, 1960. 227 pp.

MacDonald, Brian, ed. *Airwar 2000.* Toronto: Canadian Institute of Strategic Studies, 1989. 109 pp.
Proceedings of the Canadian Institute of Strategic Studies Spring Seminar held in Toronto on 13 May 1988.

_____. *Guns and Butter: Defence and the Canadian Economy.* Toronto: Canadian Institute of Strategic Studies, 1984. 182 pp.

_____. *Parliament and Defence Policy: Preparedness or Procrastination.* ([Canadian Institute of Strategic Studies] Proceedings, Spring 1982.) Toronto: Canadian Institute of Strategic Studies, 1982. 156 pp.

McDougall, Barbara, and others. *Canada and NATO: the Forgotten Ally?* (Special Report, 1992.) Cambridge, Mass.: Institute for Foreign Policy Analysis, 1992. 81 pp.

*McInnis, Edgar. *La menace contre le Canada.* (Actualités; revue destinée aux Forces canadiennes, vol I, no 1.) Ottawa: Imprimeur du Roi, 1951. 23 pp.

* _____. *The Threat to Canada.* (Current Affairs for the Canadian Forces, vol. I, no. 1.) Ottawa: King's Printer, 1951. 23 pp.

McKercher, B.J.C., and Lawrence Aronsen, eds. *The North Atlantic Triangle in a Changing World: Anglo-American-Canadian Relations, 1902-1956.* Toronto: Univ. of Toronto Press, 1996. 298 pp.

McKinsey, Lauren, and Kim Richard Nossal, eds. *America's Alliances and Canadian-American Relations.* Toronto: Summerhill Press, 1988. 223 pp.

MacLeod, Malcolm. *Peace of the Continent.* St. John's, Nfld.: H. Cuff Publications, 1986. 86 pp.
The impact of Second World War Canadian and American bases in Newfoundland.

McLin, Jon B. *Canada's Changing Defence Policy, 1957-1963; the Problem of a Middle Power in Alliance.* Baltimore: Johns Hopkins, 1967. 251 pp.

MacMillan, Margaret O., and David S. Sorenson, eds. *Canada and NATO; Uneasy Past, Uncertain Future.* Waterloo, Ont.: Univ. of Waterloo Press, 1990. 162 pp.

The McNaughton Papers. Vol. I- . Toronto: Canadian Institute of Strategic Studies, 1991- .
Two times per year. Address issues in Canadian security.

McNeil, Bill. *Voices of a War Remembered; an Oral History of Canadians in World War Two.* Toronto: Doubleday Canada, 1991. 376 pp.

Machum, George C., comp. *Canada's V.C.'s; the Story of Canadians who have been Awarded the Victoria Cross.* Toronto: McClelland & Stewart, 1956. 208 pp.

Malone, Dick. *The Muddle in Defence; Suggestions for a Sound Defence Policy.* (Winnipeg Free Press Pamphlet, no. 92.) Winnipeg: Winnipeg Free Press, 1969. 20 pp.

_____. *A Portrait of War.* Toronto: Collins, 1983-84. 2 vols.

Maritime Defence Strategy and Resource Development in Canada's Arctic. (The Niobe Papers, Volume 1.) n.p.: Naval Officers' Association of Canada, 1990. 107 pp.

Martin, Paul. *Canada and the Quest for Peace.* New York: Columbia Univ. Press, 1967. 93 pp.

Massey, Hector J., ed. *The Canadian Military; a Profile.* n.p.: Copp Clark, 1972. 290 pp.

Massey, Vincent. *The Sword of Lionheart and Other Wartime Speeches.* Toronto: Ryerson Press, 1942. 117 pp.

Menzies, J.H. *Canada and the War; the Promise of the West.* Toronto: Copp, Clark, 1916. 117 pp.

Meredith, D.L., and J.M. Treddenick. *The Economics of Defence: a Neglected Area of Research in Canada.* (Report no. 1.) Kingston, Ont.: Centre for Studies in Defence Resources Management, Royal Military College of Canada, 1992. 31, 6 pp.

Merritt, Wm. Hamilton. *Canada and National Service.* Toronto: Macmillan, 1917. 247 pp.

Michalos, Alex C. *Militarism and the Quality of Life.* (Canadian Papers in Peace Studies, 1989, no. 1.) Toronto: Science for Peace/S. Stevens, 1989. 55 pp.

Michel, Jacques, [*pseud.*] *voir* Poisson, Camille.

Middlemiss, Danford William, and Joel Sokolsky. *Canadian Defence; Decisions and Determinants.* Toronto: Harcourt Brace Jovanovich, 1989. 249 pp.

*The Military Service Council. *For the Defence of Canada.* n.p.: 1917. 31 pp.

_____. *Military Service Act, 1917; Instructions to Registrars and Deputy Registrars; Circular no. 28.* Ottawa: n.p., 1917. 35 pp.

_____. *The Military Service Act, 1917; Manual for the Information and Guidance of Tribunals in the Consideration and Review of Claims for Exemption.* Ottawa: King's Printer, 1918. 117 pp.

The Military Service Council. *The Military Service Act, 1917; Together with the Regulations of the Governor-in-Council of 19th October, 1917, Governing Procedure and the Proclamation of the 13th October, 1917, Prefaced by Some Instructions for the Guidance of Local Tribunals.* Ottawa: n.p., 1917. 90 pp.

_____. *The Military Service Act, 1917; Together with the Regulations of the Governor-in-Council of 19th October, 1917, Governing Procedure, with Amendments Made on the 6th and 8th of November, 1917 (Unindexed), the Proclamation of the 13th October, 1917, and the Order-in-Council of the 8th Day of November, 1917, (P.C. 3168) Relating to Absentees without Leave and Evidence (Unindexed), Prefaced by Some Instructions for the Guidance of Local Tribunals.* Ottawa: King's Printer, 1917. 99 pp.

_____. *Report of the Military Service Council on the Administration of the Military Service Act, 1917.* Ottawa: King's Printer, 1918. v.p.

Miller, Carman. *Canada and the Boer War./Le Canada et la guerre des Boers.* Ottawa: National Film Board of Canada/Office national du film du Canada, [1970]. 18 pp.
Bilingual text./Texte bilingue.

Milner, Marc, ed. *Canadian Military History: Selected Readings.* (New Canadian Readings.) Toronto: Copp Clark Pitman, 1993. [400] pp.

La Minerve, Montréal, P.Q. *Sir Adolphe Caron, G.C.M.G., ministre de la Milice et ses détracteurs; ou huit années d'administration militaire.* Montréal: Cie. d'imprimerie et lithographie Gelhardt-Berthiaume, 1888. 34 pp.

Minifie, James M. *Peacemaker or Powder-Monkey; Canada's Role in a Revolutionary World.* Toronto: McClelland and Stewart, 1960. 180 pp.

The Moccasin Prints. No. 1-6. Montreal: privately printed, 1912-13.

Monk, F.D. *Address by F.D. Monk, Esq., M.P., Lachine, August 18th, 1911.* n.p.: [1911]. 13 pp.

Montreal Daily Herald. *The Story of French Canada's War Effort; Full Industrial Strength and All Economic Resources Support Democracy.* Montreal: Daily Herald, 1941. 62 pp.

Morenus, Richard. *DEW Line; Distant Early Warning; the Miracle of America's First Line of Defense.* New York: Rand McNally, 1957. 184 pp.

*Morin, René. *DND Dependents' Schools, 1921-1983.* Ottawa: Directorate of History, National Defence Headquarters, 1986. 197 pp.

*_____. *Les écoles pour les enfants des militaires canadiens, 1921-1983.* Ottawa: Service historique, Quartier général de la Défense nationale, 1986. 172 pp.

Morris, Leslie. *Whose War? A Reply to the Liberal Party's Winnipeg Free Press.* Winnipeg: privately printed, [1943?]. 45 pp.

_____. *You are Wrong Mr. Pearson! Remilitarizing the Nazis Puts Canada in Danger.* Toronto: privately printed, 1955. 16 pp.

Morrison, W. Alexander. *The Voice of Defence; the History of the Conference of Defence Associations: the First Fifty Years 1932-1982./La voix de la défense; historique de la Conférence des Associations de défense: les cinquante premières années: 1932 à 1982.* n.p./s.l.: s.i., 1982. 262/268 pp. *Bilingual text./Texte bilingue.*

Morrison, W. Alexander, ed. *The Changing Face of Peacekeeping.* Toronto: Canadian Institute of Strategic Studies, 1993. 243 pp. *Proceedings of Peacekeeping '93: an exhibition and seminar held in Ottawa March 16-17, 1993.*

_____. *A Continuing Commitment; Canada and North Atlantic Security.* Toronto: Canadian Institute of Strategic Studies, 1992. 202 pp. *Canadian Institute of Strategic Studies spring seminar.*

Morrison, William R., and Kenneth A. Coates. *Working the North; Labor and the Northwest Defense Projects 1942-1946.* n.p.: Univ. of Alaska Press, 1994. [271] pp.

Morton, Desmond. *Canada and War; a Military and Political History.* (Political Issues in their Historical Perspectives.) Toronto: Butterworths, 1981. 228 pp.

* _____. *Une histoire militaire du Canada 1608-1991.* Version française dirigée par Serge Bernier. Sillery (Qué.): Septentrion, 1992. 414 pp.

* _____. *A Military History of Canada.* Edmonton: Hurtig Publishers, 1985. 305 pp.

* _____. *1945; lorsque le Canada a gagné la guerre.* (La Société historique du Canada brochure historique no 54.) Ottawa: Société historique du Canada, 1995. 41 pp.

_____. *Ministers and Generals; Politics and the Canadian Militia, 1868-1904.* Toronto: Univ. of Toronto Press, 1970. 257 pp.

* _____. *1945; When Canada Won the War.* (The Canadian Historical Association Historical Booklet no. 54.) Ottawa: Canadian Historical Association, 1995. 35 pp.

_____. *A Peculiar Kind of Politics: Canada's Overseas Ministry in the First World War.* Toronto: Univ. of Toronto Press, 1982. 267 pp.

Morton, Desmond, and Glenn Wright. *Winning the Second Battle: Canadian Veterans and the Return to Civilian Life, 1915-1931.* Toronto: Univ. of Toronto Press, 1987. 328 pp.

48

Morton, Desmond, and J.L. Granatstein. *Marching to Armageddon; Canadians and the Great War 1914-1919.* Toronto: Lester & Orpen Dennys, 1989. 288 pp.

_____. *Victory 1945; Canadians from War to Peace.* (A Phyllis Bruce Book.) Toronto: HarperCollins Publishers, 1995. 256 pp.

Munro, Iain R. *Canada and the World Wars.* (Canada: Origins and Options.) Toronto: Wiley, 1979. 96 pp.

Murray, Howard. *The Munitionment of the Canadian Forces for Purposes of Defence; an Aide-Memoire; being a Study of Canada's Effort in the Supply of Propellants and Explosives during the War and Conclusions to be Drawn as Applying to Future Munitionment of the Military Forces of Canada.* [Ottawa: n.p., 1921.] 222 pp.
Projected in four volumes, but only the first may have been published.

Myers, C.V. *Oil to Alaska; Canol Unveiled.* Edmonton: Doublas Print. Co., [1944?]. 40 pp.

Nasmith, George Gallie. *On the Fringe of the Great Fight.* New York: Doran, n.d. 263 pp.

National Liberal Federation of Canada. *The Wartime Effort of a United Canada.* (National Liberal Federation of Canada Leaflets, [2nd Series] no. 10.) Ottawa: n.p., [1940]. 20 pp.

*New Democratic Party of Canada. International Affairs Committee. *Canada's Stake in Common Security.* n.p.: 1988. 39 pp.

Newman, Peter C. *True North: not Strong and Free; Defending the Peaceable Kingdom in the Nuclear Age.* Toronto: McClelland and Stewart, 1983. 184 pp.

Nolan, Brian. *King's War; Mackenzie King and the Politics of War, 1939-1945.* Toronto: Random House, 1988. 188 pp.

Norman, Jim, and Rita Crow, comps. *A History of the Defence Research Establishment Ottawa, 1941-1991.* (DREO Special Edition, March 1992.) Ottawa: Defence Research Establishment Ottawa, 1992. 142, 22, 2 pp.

Notre marine de guerre; que fera-t-on de la marine Laurier-Brodeur? Est-il vrai qu'elle ne servira qu'à la défense du Canada? [par] "Du Guesclin" [*pseud.*] Montréal: Imprimerie Le Devoir, 1911. 130 pp.

*Nouveau Parti démocratique du Canada. Comité des Affaires internationales. *Les enjeux du Canada dans la sécurité commune.* s.l.: s.i., 1988. 40 pp.

O'Gorman, John J. *Canadians to Arms!* Toronto: Extension Print, 1916. 14 pp.

Ollivant, Simon. *Canada: How Powerful an Ally?* (Conflict Studies, number 159.) London: Institute for the Study of Conflict, 1984. 20 pp.

Olson, Theodore, ed. *Canadian Defence and the Pursuit of Peace.* n.p.: York Centre for International and Strategic Studies, n.d. 82 pp.

On Our Naval Policy see Ross, Hendrie Drury.

Ontario Liberal Association. *Our Militia and Navy.* n.p.: [1911]. 36 pp.

Organization of Military Museums of Canada. *Bulletin.* Vol. I- . Ottawa: Queen's Printer, 1972- .

Ørvik, Nils. *Canadian Defence Policy: Choices and Directions.* (National Security Series, no. 2/80.) Kingston, Ont.: Queen's Univ. Centre for International Relations, 1980. 35 1.

Ørvik, Nils, ed. *Canada and NATO.* (National Security Series, no. 3/82.) Kingston, Ont.: Queen's Univ. Centre for International Relations, 1982. 142 pp.

Osbaldeston, Gordon F. *All the Ships that Sail; a Study of Canada's Fleets.* n.p.: n.d. 125 pp.
Report to the Treasury Board of the Study on the Utilization of the Federal Government's Marine Fleets.

Ottawa Air Training Conference, 1942. *Report of the Conference.* Ottawa: King's Printer, 1942. 25 pp.

Ozorak, Paul. *Abandoned Military Installations of Canada.* Volume I: *Ontario.* n.p.: privately printed, 1991. [293] pp.

*Page, Robert. *The Boer War and Canadian Imperialism.* (Canadian Historical Association Historical Booklet no. 44.) Ottawa: Canadian Historical Association, 1987. 27 pp.

*_____. *La guerre des Boers et l'impérialisme canadien.* Yvon de Repentigny, tr. (La Société historique du Canada brochure historique no 44.) Ottawa: La Société historique du Canada, 1987. 31 pp.

Panchuk, Bohdan. *Heroes of their Day: the Reminiscences of Bohdan Panchuk.* Lubomyr Y. Luciuk, ed. n.p.: Multicultural History Society, Ontario Heritage Foundation, 1983. 168 pp.
Ukranian Canadians in World War II.

Papineau, [Talbot Mercer]. *Captain Papineau's Letter to M. Henri Bourassa (Editor of "Le Devoir").* n.p.: n.d. 11 pp.

*Pariseau, Jean, and Serge Bernier. *French Canadians and Bilingualism in the Canadian Armed Forces.* Volume I: *1763-1969: the Fear of a Parallel Army.* (Socio-Military Series, no. 2.) Ottawa: Directorate of History, Dept. of National Defence, 1988. 447 pp.

*Pariseau, Jean, et Serge Bernier. *Les Canadiens français et le bilinguisme dans les Forces armées canadiennes.* Tome I: *1763-1969: le spectre d'une armée bicéphale.* (Collection d'histoire socio-militaire, no 2.) Ottawa: Service historique de la Défense nationale, 1987. 468 pp.

Peat, Louisa W. *Canada; New World Power.* Toronto: G.J. McLeod, 1945. 293 pp.

Peden, Murray. *Fall of an Arrow.* Stittsville, Ont.: Canada's Wings, 1978. 182 pp.

Penlington, Norman. *Canada and Imperialism, 1896-1899.* Toronto: Univ. of Toronto Press, 1965. 288 pp.

The Permanent Joint Board on Defence; Canada-United States, 1940-1975./La Commission permanente mixte de Défense; Canada-Etats-Unis, 1940-1975. n.p.: n.d./s.l.: s.i., s.d. 1 vol., unpaged./1 tome, non paginé. *Bilingual text./Texte bilingue.*

The Permanent Joint Board on Defence; Canada-United States, 1940-1965. Ottawa: Queen's Printer, 1965. 1 vol., unpaged.

Phillips-Wolley, Clive. *An Address Delivered by Clive Phillips-Wolley on Behalf of the Victoria-Esquimalt Branch, British Columbia, of the Navy League to an Audience in the City Hall, Victoria, B.C., Tuesday, May 14, 1907.* Victoria, B.C.: privately printed, n.d. 10 pp.

————. *The Canadian Naval Question; Addresses Delivered by Clive Phillips-Wolley, F.R.C.S., Vice-President, Navy League.* Toronto: W. Briggs, 1910. 70 pp.

*Pierson, Ruth Roach. *Canadian Women and the Second World War.* (Canadian Historical Association Historical Booklet no. 37.) Ottawa: Canadian Historical Association, 1983. 31 pp.

*————. *Les Canadiennes et la Seconde Guerre mondiale.* Hélène Hamel, tr. (La Société historique du Canada brochure historique no 37.) Ottawa: La Société historique du Canada, 1983. 35 pp.

————. *"They're Still Women after All": the Second World War and Canadian Womanhood.* (The Canadian Social History Series.) Toronto: McClelland and Stewart, 1986. 301 pp.

Plumptre, A.F.W. *Mobilizing Canada's Resources for War.* Toronto: Macmillan, 1941. 306 pp.

Poisson, Camille. *La participation des Canadiens français à la Grande Guerre; réponse à un livre récent de M. André Siegfried: "Le Canada, puissance internationale",* par Jacques Michel [*pseud.*] Montréal: Editions de l'A.C.-F., [1938]. 188 pp.

"Politicus" [*pseud.*] *see* Golden, L.L.L.

Pope, Maurice A. *Soldiers and Politicians; the Memoirs of Lt.-Gen. Maurice A. Pope, C.B., M.C.* Toronto: Univ. of Toronto Press, 1962. 462 pp.

Pope, R.H. *An Address Delivered by Mr. R.H. Pope at Sherbrooke, Que., on Feb 28th, 1910.* Cookshire, P.Q.: Chronicle Print, 1910. [14] pp.

Porter, Gerald. *In Retreat; the Canadian Forces in the Trudeau Years.* n.p.: Deneau & Greenberg, n.d. 232 pp.

[Power, Charles Gavan.] *A Party Politician; the Memoirs of Chubby Power.* Norman Ward, ed. Toronto: Macmillan, 1966. 419 pp.

1er Colloque d'études stratégiques et militaires ... 1981. *Les politiques de défense du Canada dans les années 1980.* (Collection études stratégiques et militaires.) Québec, P.Q.: Centre québécois de relations internationales, 1981. 127 pp.

Preston, Richard A. *Canada and "Imperial Defense", a Study of the Origins of the British Commonwealth's Defense Organization, 1867-1919.* (Duke University Commonwealth-Studies Center; Publication Number 29.) Durham, N.C.: Duke Univ. Press, 1967. 576 pp.

_____. *Canadian Defence Policy and the Development of the Canadian Nation, 1867-1917.* (Canadian Historical Association Booklets, no. 25.) Ottawa: Canadian Historical Association, 1970. 22 pp.

_____. *The Defence of the Undefended Border; Planning For War in North America, 1867-1939.* Montreal: McGill-Queen's Univ. Press, 1977. 300 pp.

Provencher, Jean. *Québec sous la loi des mesures de guerre, 1918.* Montréal: Les Editions du Boreal Express, 1971. 147 pp.

Prymak, Thomas M. *Maple Leaf and Trident; the Ukranian Canadians during the Second World War.* (Studies in Ethnic and Immigration History.) Toronto: Multicultural History Society of Ontario, 1988. 192 pp.

Purver, Ronald G. *Arms Control Options in the Arctic.* (Issue Brief no. 7.) Ottawa: Canadian Centre for Arms Control and Disarmament, 1987. 27 pp.

Ralston, J.L. *A Call for Men for the Army; an Address by Honourable J.L. Ralston, Minister of National Defence, Delivered over a National Network of Canadian Radio Stations 11th May, 1941.* Ottawa: King's Printer, 1941. 10 pp.

Ranger, Robin. *The Canadian Contribution to the Control of Chemical and Biological Warfare.* (Wellesley Paper 5/1976.) Toronto: Canadian Institute of International Affairs, 1976. 66 pp.

Reader's Digest. *The Canadians at War, 1939/45.* Montreal: Reader's Digest, 1969. 2 vols.

Reford, Robert. *Making Defence Policy in Canada.* (Behind the Headlines, vol. XXII, no. 2.) Toronto: Canadian Institute of International Affairs, 1963. 23 pp.

_____. *Merchant of Death?* (Behind the Headlines, vol. XXVII, no. 4.) Toronto: Canadian Institute of International Affairs, 1968. 28 pp.

Regehr, Ernie. *Arms Canada; the Deadly Business of Military Exports.* Toronto: J. Lorimer, 1987. 273 pp.

_____. *Making a Killing; Canada's Arms Industry.* Toronto: McClelland and Stewart, 1975. 135 pp.

Regehr, Ernie, and Simon Rosenblum, eds. *Canada and the Nuclear Arms Race.* Toronto: J. Lorimer, 1983. 268 pp.

***Règlements concernant la défense du Canada.* Ottawa: Imprimeur du Roi, 1939. 58 pp.
Réimprimé et développé 1940, 1941, 1942.

Renison, Robert John. *Impressions, September 16 to October 28, 1941; to Britain and Return.* [Toronto: privately printed, 1941?]. 31 pp.

Resolved for Victory; Resolutions of the National Workers' Total War Conference; Toronto, May 30-31, 1942. Toronto: Dominion Communist-Labour Total War Committee, [1942]. 31 pp.

Robertson, William Scot. *Canada's Commitment to NATO's Northern Flank: the Northern Base Option.* (Operational Research and Analysis Establishment ORAE Extra-Mural Paper no. 27.) Ottawa: Dept. of National Defence, 1983. 108 pp.

Robinson, C.W. *Canada and Canadian Defence; the Defensive Policy of the Dominion in Relation to the Character of her Frontier, the Events of the War of 1812-14, and her Position Today.* Toronto: Musson Book Co., 1910. 186 pp.

Robinson, David A., and Fred W. Crickard, eds. *The Canadian Army in the 21st Century; Proceedings of a Conference Held in Halifax, N.S., March 1989.* Halifax: Centre for Foreign Policy Studies, Dalhousie Univ., 1990. 80 pp.

*Rogers, Norman McL. *Canada's War Effort; Broadcast by Hon. Norman McL. Rogers, Minister of National Defence, December 20, 1939.* Ottawa: King's Printer, 1939. 17 pp.

* _____. *La part du Canada dans la guerre; discours radiodiffusé par l'honorable Norman McL. Rogers, ministre de la Défense nationale, le 20 décembre 1939.* Ottawa: Imprimeur du Roi, 1940. 18 pp.

Rosner, Gabriella. *The U.N. Emergency Force.* New York: Columbia Univ. Press, 1963. 294 pp.

Ross, Douglas Alan. *American Nuclear Revisionism, Canadian Strategic Interests, and the Renewal of NORAD.* (Behind the Headlines, vol. XXXIX.) Toronto: Canadian Institute of International Affairs, 1982. 36 pp.

[Ross, Hendrie Drury.] *On our Naval Policy.* Ottawa: n.p., [1908]. 14 pp.

Roux, E. [*pseud.*] *M. Henri Bourassa au service de l'Allemagne.* Montréal: Imprimerie Perrault, [1917]. 58 pp.

*Roy, Ferdinand. *L'appel aux armes et la réponse canadienne-française; étude sur le conflit de races.* Québec, P.Q.: J.P. Garneau, 1917. 44 pp.

*_____. *The Call to Arms and the French Canadian Reply; a Study of the Conflict of Races.* J. Squair and J.S. Will, tr. Quebec, P.Q.: J.P. Garneau, 1918. 40 pp.

Roy, Patricia E., and others. *Mutual Hostages; Canadians and Japanese during the Second World War.* Toronto: Univ. of Toronto Press, 1990. 281 pp.

Roy, R.H. *For Most Conspicuous Bravery; a Biography of Major-General George R. Pearkes, V.C., through Two World Wars.* Vancouver: Univ. of British Columbia Press, 1977. 388 pp.

Royal Canadian Legion. Baldur Branch, no. 108. *We will Remember Them.* n.p.: 1973. 1 vol., unpaged.

Royal Canadian Military Institute, Toronto, Ont. *Transactions.* Vol. I- . Toronto: privately printed, 1890- .
Title varies. Selected Papers no.1 was published in 1889. Superseded by Yearbook in 1947.

Rudmin,. Floyd W. *Bordering on Aggression; Evidence of US Military Preparations against Canada.* Hull, Que.: Voyageur Pub., 1993. 192 pp.

Rumilly, R. *La conscription.* (Histoire de la Province de Québec, XXII.) Montréal: Montréal-Editions, s.d. 256 pp.

_____. *Courcelette.* (Histoire de la Province de Québec, XXI.) Montréal: Montréal-Editions, s.d. 269 pp.

_____. *La guerre de 1939-1945.* (Histoire de la Province de Québec, XXXVIII-XLI.) Montréal: Fides, 1968-69. 4 vols.

_____. *"1914".* (Histoire de la Province de Québec, XIX.) Montréal: Montréal-Editions, s.d. 192 pp.

*Russell, E.C. *Coutumes et traditions des Forces armées canadiennes.* Jacques Gouin, tr. Québec, P.Q.: Editions du Pélican, 1980. 340 pp.

*_____. *Customs and Traditions of the Canadian Armed Forces.* n.p.: Deneau & Greenberg, 1980. 265 pp.

St. Denis, Thomas, ed. *Canada's New Field Army.* Ottawa: Conference of Defence Associations Institute, 1989. 67 pp.

St. Denis, Thomas, and Emily Atkins, eds. *The Future of Canada's Air Force.* Ottawa: Conference of Defence Associations Institute, 1990. 77 pp.

Sanders, Wilfrid. *Jack et Jacques; l'opinion publique au Canada pendant la Deuxième Guerre mondiale.* Préface de Claude Beauregard, Edwidge Munn et Béatrice Richard. Montréal: Comeau & Nadeau, 1996. 97 pp. *Rapport confidentiel, Canadian Institute of Public Opinion, 1942.*

Sandwell, B.K. *Canada and the United States Neutrality.* (Oxford Pamphlets on World Affairs, no. C.2.) Toronto: Oxford Univ. Press, 1939. 34 pp.

Santor, Donald M. *Canadians at War, 1914-1918.* (Canadiana Scrapbook.) Scarborough, Ont.: Prentice-Hall, 1978. 48 pp.

Scoble, T.C. *The Utilization of Colonial Forces in Imperial Defence (Read before the Toronto (Canada) Militia Institute, on Saturday 25th October, 1879).* London: H.M. Stationery Office, n.d. 11 pp.

Selin, Shannon. *Canada as a Nuclear Weapon-Free Zone: a Critical Analysis.* (Issue Brief no. 10.) Ottawa: Canadian Centre for Arms Control and Disarmament, 1988. 42 pp.

Shadwick, Martin W. *Who's Watching the Oceans? A Study of Canadian Maritime Air Surveillance Requirements*, prepared for the Summerside Waterfront Development Corporation. Toronto: York Univ. Centre for International and Strategic Studies, 1989. 33 pp.

Shaw, E.K. *There never was an Arrow.* Toronto: Steel Rail Educational Pub., 1979. 261 pp.

Shields, Thomas Todhunter. *Premier King's Plebiscite Speech in Commons Analyzed; an Address, Delivered in Jarvis Street Baptist Church, Toronto, Monday Evening, February 2nd, 1942.* n.p.: n.d. 32 pp.

Sherman, Michael E. *A Single Service for Canada?* (Adelphi Papers, no. 39.) London: Institute for Strategic Studies, 1967. 14 pp.

Shragge, Eric, Ronald Babin and Jean-Guy Vaillancourt, eds. *Roots of Peace; the Movement Against Militarism in Canada.* Toronto: Between the Lines, 1986. 203 pp.

Sigler, John H., ed. *International Peacekeeping in the Eighties: Global Outlook and Canadian Priorities.* (Carleton International Proceedings.) Ottawa: Norman Paterson School of International Affairs, Carleton Univ., 1982. 58 pp.

Sir Georges [sic] Cartier sur la défense du Canada. s.l.: s.i., [1909]. 13 pp.

*Smith, Goldwin. *Devant le tribunal de l'histoire; un plaidoyer en faveur des Canadiens qui ont condamné la guerre sud-africaine*. Henri Bourassa, tr. Montréal: Librairie Beauchemin, 1903. 61 pp.

*_____. *In the Court of History; an Apology for Canadians who were Opposed to the South African War*. Toronto: W. Tyrrell, 1902. 71 pp.

Smith, R. Guy C., ed. *As You Were! Ex-Cadets Remember*. [Kingston, Ont.: R.M.C. Club of Canada, 1984.] 2 vols.

Smith, Sidney E. *Report on Disarmament Discussions, 1957*. Ottawa: Queen's Printer, 1958. 40 pp.

Smye, Fred. *Canadian Aviation and the Avro Arrow*. Oakville, Ont.: privately printed, 1989. 137 pp.

Smylie, Eric. *Buttons of the Canadian Militia, Army, Naval and Air Forces, 1900-1990; Including the Canadian Expeditionary Force and the Newfoundland Forces*. St. Catharines, Ont.: Vanwell Pub., 1995. 108 pp.

Snowy Owl; Journal of the Canadian Land Forces Command and Staff College. Kingston, Ont.: privately printed, 1952-73. 18 vols.
Title varies.

Socknat, Thomas Paul. *Witness against War; Pacifism in Canada, 1900-1945*. Toronto: Univ. of Toronto Press, 1987. 370 pp.

Sokolsky, Joel J. *Defending Canada; U.S.-Canadian Defense Policies*. (A Twentieth Century Fund Paper.) New York: Priority Press Publications, 1989. 69 pp.

_____. *The Future of Canadian-American Defence Relations: Trends in U.S. Strategy and the Canadian Defence Posture*. (Centre for International Relations Occasional Paper no. 10.) Kingston, Ont.: Centre for International Relations, Queen's Univ., 1986. 55 pp.

_____. *Ogdensburg Plus Fifty and Still Counting: Canada-U.S. Defense Relations in the Post-Cold War Era*. (Canadian-American Public Policy, Number 8, December 1991.) Orono, Me.: Canadian-American Center, Univ. of Maine, 1991. 45 pp.

Sokolsky, Joel J., and Joseph T. Jockel, eds. *Fifty Years of Canada-United States Defense Cooperation; the Road from Ogdensburg*. Lewiston, N.Y.: E. Mellen Press, 1992. 417 pp.

*Stacey, C.P. *Armes, hommes et gouvernements; les politiques de guerre du Canada, 1939-1945*. Ottawa: Imprimeur de la Reine, 1970. 747 pp.

*_____. *Arms, Men and Governments; the War Policies of Canada, 1939-1945*. Ottawa: Queen's Printer, 1970. 681 pp.

Stacey, C.P. *Canada and the British Army, 1846-1871; a Study in the Practice of Responsible Government.* (Royal Empire Society Imperial Studies Series, no. 11.) London: Longmans, Green, 1936. 287 pp.

_____. *Canada and the Second World War.* (Oxford Pamphlets on World Affairs, no. C.5.) Toronto: Oxford Univ. Press, 1940. 32 pp.

_____. *The Military Problems of Canada; a Survey of Defence Policies and Strategic Conditions Past and Present.* Toronto: Ryerson Press, 1940. 184 pp.

_____. *The Undefended Border; the Myth and the Reality.* (Canadian Historical Association Booklets, no. 1.) Ottawa: Canadian Historical Association, 1953. 19 pp.

Stacey, C.P., ed. *The Arts of War and Peace, 1914-1945.* (Historical Documents of Canada, Volume V.) Toronto: Macmillan, 1972. 656 pp.

Stafford, David. *Camp X.* Toronto: Lester & Orpen Dennys, 1986. 327 pp. *British Security Co-ordination school for secret agents at Whitby, Ont.*

Stairs, Denis. *The Diplomacy of Constraint; Canada, the Korean War, and the United States.* Toronto: Univ. of Toronto Press, 1974. 373 pp.

Stevens, G.R. *The Sun is Setting on the Paleface Brave or Down the Drain a Billion a Year Goes.* Montreal: privately printed, [1968]. 16 pp.

*Stevenson, William. *A Man Called Intrepid; the Secret War.* New York: Harcourt Brace Jovanovich, 1976. 468 pp.

*_____. *Nom de code: Intrepid.* Jean Paré, tr. s.l.: Opuscule, 1979. 601 pp.

Stewart, Greig. *Shutting Down the National Dream; A.V. Roe and the Tragedy of the Avro Arrow.* Toronto: McGraw-Hill Ryerson, 1988. 320 pp.

Stewart, Larry R. *Canada's European Force 1971-1980: a Defence Policy in Transition.* (National Security Series, no. 5/80.) Kingston, Ont.: Queen's Univ. Centre for International Relations, 1980. 167 pp.

Stewart, Larry R., ed. *Canadian Defence Policy; Selected Speeches and Documents, 1964-1981.* (National Security Series, no. 1/82.) Kingston, Ont.: Queen's Univ. Centre for International Relations, 1982. 336 pp.

Strange, Thomas Bland. *The Military Aspect of Canada; a Lecture Delivered at the Royal United Service Institution.* London: Harrison, [1879]. 66 pp.

Strange, William. *Canada, the Pacific and the War.* Toronto: T. Nelson, 1937. 220 pp.

Summary of Memorandum of Agreement between the Governments of the United Kingdom, Canada, Australia and New Zealand Relating to Training of Pilots and Aircraft Crews in Canada and their Subsequent Service. n.p.: [1942]. 12 pp.

Swettenham, John. *Allied Intervention in Russia, 1918-1919; and the Part Played by Canada.* Toronto: Ryerson Press, 1967. 315 pp.

————. *Canada and the First World War.* Toronto: Ryerson Press, 1969. 160 pp.

————. *McNaughton.* Toronto: Ryerson Press, 1968-69. 3 vols.

Swettenham, John, ed. *Valiant Men; Canada's Victoria Cross and George Cross Winners.* (Canadian War Museum Historical Publication Number 7.) Toronto: Hakkert, 1973. 234 pp.

Tackaberry, R.B. *Keeping the Peace; a Canadian Military Viewpoint on Peace-Keeping Operations.* (Behind the Headlines, vol. XXVI.) Toronto: Canadian Institute of International Affairs, 1966. 26 pp.

Talmadge, Marion, and Iris Gilmore. *NORAD; the North American Air Defense Command.* New York: Dodd, Mead, 1967. 29 pp.

Tardif, H.P. *Recollections of CARDE/DREV, 1945-1995.* Courcelette, Que.: Defence Research Establishment Valcartier, 1995. 271 pp.

Taylor, Alastair. *For Canada — Both Swords and Ploughshares; a Plea for an Integrated Defence and Foreign Policy for Canada.* (Contemporary Affairs, no. 30.) Toronto: Canadian Institute of International Affairs, 1963. 67 pp.

Taylor, Alastair, David Cox and J.L. Granatstein. *Peacekeeping; International Challenge and Canadian Response.* (Contemporary Affairs, no. 39.) [Toronto]: Canadian Institute of International Affairs, 1968. 211 pp.

Taylor, Charles. *Snow Job: Canada, the United States and Vietnam (1954 to 1973).* Toronto: Anansi, n.d. 209 pp.

Texte complet des discours sur la mobilisation générale prononcés à la radio, le dimanche 23 juin 1940 par le très honorable P.-J.-A. Cardin, ministre des Travaux publics, ainsi que le message aux Canadiens-français du très honorable W.L. Mackenzie King, Premier ministre à l'occasion de la Saint-Jean-Baptiste, le 24 juin 1940. Ottawa: Imprimeur du Roi, s.d. 16 pp.

Thakur, Ramesh. *Peacekeeping in Vietnam; Canada, India, Poland, and the International Commission.* Edmonton: Univ. of Alberta Press, 1984. 375 pp.

Thibault, Jean. *Drummondville à l'heure de la guerre: 1939-1945.* Drummondville (Qué.): La Société d'histoire de Drummondville, 1994. 191 pp.

Thistle, Mel, ed. *The Mackenzie-McNaughton Wartime Letters*, with introduction and epilogue by C.J. Mackenzie. Toronto: Univ. of Toronto Press, 1975. 178 pp.

Thomas, Robert H. *The Canadian Navy: Options for the Future.* (Working Paper 41.) Ottawa: Canadian Institute for Internaional Peace and Security, 1992. 84 pp.

Thompson, John Herd. *Ethnic Miniorities during Two World Wars.* (Canada's Ethnic Groups; Booklet no. 19.) Ottawa: Canadian Historical Association, 1991. 20 pp.

_____. *The Harvests of War; the Prairie West, 1914-1918.* Toronto: McClelland and Stewart, 1978. 207 pp.

Thoughts on Defence see Coffin, W.F.

"Till the Hour of Victory"; Addresses by Right Honourable W.L. Mackenzie King, Prime Minister of Canada, Right Honourable Winston Churchill, Prime Minister of Great Britain, Right Honourable Ernest Lapointe, Minister of Justice, Delivered over the National Network of the Canadian Broadcasting Corporation, 1st June, 1941. Ottawa: King's Printer, 1941. 11 pp.

Tippett, Maria. *Lest We Forget./Souvenons-nous.* London, Ont.: London Regional Art and Historical Museums, [1989]. 71 pp.
Programme of exhibition of war art, September 9 — October 29, 1989. Bilingual text./Programme de l'exposition d'art de la guerre, 9 septembre — 29 octobre, 1989. Texte bilingue.

Toews, J.A. *Alternative Service in Canada during World War II.* Winnipeg: privately printed, [1959]. 127 pp.

Tracy, Nicholas. *Canada's Foreign Policy Objectives and Canadian Security Arrangements in the North.* (Operational Research and Analysis Establishment ORAE Extra-Mural Paper no. 8.) Ottawa: Dept. of National Defence, 1980. 98 pp.

_____. *Canada's Naval Strategy: Rooted in Experience.* (Maritime Security Occasional Paper no. 1.) Halifax: Centre for Foreign Policy Studies, Dalhousie Univ., 1995. 82 pp.

_____. *The Diplomatic Utility of Canada's Naval Forces.* (Operational Research and Analysis Establishment ORAE Report R60.) Ottawa: Dept. of National Defence, 1976. 132 pp.

Tremblay, Jeanne-D'Arc. *La défense du Québec et la famille Tremblay.* Montréal: Fides, 1988. 478 pp.

Trotter, Reginald G. *North America and the War; a Canadian View.* (Oxford Pamphlets on World Affairs, no. C.7.) Toronto: Oxford Univ. Press, 1940. 40 pp.

The True North Strong & Free? Proceedings of a Public Inquiry into Canadian Defence Policy and Nuclear Arms, sponsored by The True North Strong and Free Inquiry Society. West Vancouver, B.C.: G. Soules Book Publishers, 1987. 229 pp.

Tucker, A.B. *Canada and the War.* (Oxford Pamphlets, 1914-1915.) London: Oxford Univ. Press, [1915]. 18 pp.

Tugwell, Maurice, Brian S. MacDonald and John Marteinson. *Military Options.* (Defence of Freedom Series, 3.) Toronto: Mackenzie Institute for the Study of Terrorism, Revolution and Propaganda, 1988. 46 pp.

Turner, Arthur C. *Bulwark of the West; Implications and Problems of NATO.* (Contemporary Affairs, no. 24.) Toronto: Ryerson Press, 1953. 106 pp.

Tweedsmuir, John Buchan, baron. *Lord Minto; a Memoir*, by John Buchan. London: T. Nelson, 1924. 352 pp.

Tweedsmuir, Susan Charlotte (Grosvenor) Buchan, baroness. *Canada and the War*, by Lady Tweedsmuir. (March of Time Series, 7.) London: Pilot Press, 1942. 48 pp.

Twichell, Heath. *Northwest Epic; the Building of the Alaska Highway.* New York: St. Martin's Press, 1992. 368 pp.

Univ. of California. Committee on International Relations. *Problems of Hemispheric Defense.* Berkeley, Calif.: Univ. of California Press, 1942. 139 pp.

Vachon, Stanislas. *Le Canada et la deuxième grande guerre; la puissance occulte, tome premier.* [Montréal: Le Devoir, 1949.] 324 pp.
Les autres tomes ne furent jamais publiés.

Vaillancourt, Emile. *Le Canada et les Nations unies.* Montréal: Beauchemin, 1942. 143 pp.

Vance, Jonathan F. *Objects of Concern; Canadian Prisoners of War through the Twentieth Century.* Vancouver: UBC Press, 1994. 324 pp.

Vanguard. Vol. I-   . Ottawa: Conference of Defence Associations Institute, 1995- .
Quarterly.

Vano, Gerard S. *Canada: the Strategic and Military Pawn.* New York: Praeger, 1988. 163 pp.

Vaughan, H.H. *The Manufacture of Munitions in Canada; Presidential Address, Annual Meeting, Ottawa, Feb. 10th, 1919.* n.p.: n.d. 91 pp. *Address to the Engineering Institute of Canada.*

La vérité sur la question de la défense navale. s.l.: s.i., s.d. 38 pp.

Waiser, Bill. *Park Prisoners; the Untold Story of Western Canada's National Parks, 1915-1946.* Saskatoon, Sask.: Fifth House Publishers, 1995. 294 pp.

Warnock, John W. *Partner to Behemoth; the Military Policy of a Satellite Canada.* Toronto: New Press, 1970. 340 pp.

Warren, Falkland. *The Defence of our Empire, with Special Reference to Canada.* n.p.: [1902]. 19 pp.

West, Christopher. *Canada and Sea Power.* Toronto: McClelland & Goodchild, 1913. 172 pp.

_____. *The Defence of Canada; in the Light of Canadian History.* London: Dent, 1914. 16 pp.

Why Three Dreadnoughts? Ottawa: Modern Press, 1914. 54 pp.

Wickham, H.J. *Naval Defence of Canada.* Toronto: Murray, 1896. 11 pp.

*Wilkinson, (Sir) George Henry, W.L. Mackenzie King and Winston S. Churchill. *Canada and the War; the Lord Mayor's Luncheon in Honour of the Prime Minister of Canada, Addresses by Right Hon. Sir George Henry Wilkinson, Lord Mayor of London, Right Hon. W.L. Mackenzie King, M.P., Prime Minister of Canada and Right Hon. Winston S. Churchill, C.H., M.P., Prime Minister of Great Britain, the Mansion House, London, England, September 4, 1941.* Ottawa: King's Printer, 1941. 16 pp.

*Wilkinson, (Sir) George-Henry, W.-L. Mackenzie King et Winston Churchill. *Le Canada et la guerre; dîner offert par le Lord-maire en l'honneur du Premier ministre du Canada, discours des très honorable Sir George-Henry Wilkinson, Lord-maire de Londres, très honorable W.-L. Mackenzie King, M.P., Premier ministre du Canada, et du très honorable Winston Churchill, C.H., M.P., Premier ministre de Grande-Bretagne, à Mansion House, Londres, Angleterre, le 4 septembre 1941.* Ottawa: Imprimeur du Roi, 1941. 16 pp.

Wilkinson, J.W. *Canada's Attitude Both before and since the War with Regard to Naval Defence.* Toronto: n.p., 1918. 35 pp.

Williams-Taylor, (Sir) Frederick. *Sea Power in Relation to Canada ... Address at Annual Banquet of the Navy League of Canada.* n.p.: [1929]. 11 pp.

Willson, (Sir) John. *Canada's Relation to the Great War; an Address by Sir John Willson before the University Club of Rochester, New York, February 19, 1916.* Toronto: News Pub. Co., 1916. 1 vol., unpaged.

Wilson, Barbara M., ed. *Ontario and the First World War, 1914-1918; a Collection of Documents.* (The Publications of the Champlain Society; Ontario Series, X.) Toronto: Champlain Society, 1977. 201 pp.

*Wood, Herbert Fairlie. *Singulier champ de bataille; les opérations en Corée et leurs effets sur la politique de défense du Canada.* (Histoire officielle de l'Armée canadienne.) Ottawa: Imprimeur de la Reine, 1966. 354 pp.

*_____. *Strange Battleground; the Operations in Korea and their Effects on the Defence Policy of Canada.* (Official History of the Canadian Army.) Ottawa: Queen's Printer, 1966. 317 pp.

*Wood, Herbert Fairlie, and John Swettenham. *Silent Witnesses.* (Canadian War Museum Historical Publication Number 10; Department of Veterans Affairs Publication Number 6.) Toronto: Hakkert, 1974. 243 pp.

*Wood, Herbert Fairlie, et John Swettenham. *Témoins silencieux.* Jacques Gouin, tr. (Musée de guerre du Canada publication historique no 10; Ministère des Affaires des anciens combattants publication no 6.) Toronto: Hakkert, 1974. 249 pp.

Wood, William. *The British Command of the Sea and What It Means to Canada.* Toronto: Hunter, Rose, [1900]. 48 pp.

*Worthington, F.F. *Civil Defence and Armed Defence.* (Current Affairs for the Canadian Forces, vol. VII, no. 8.) Ottawa: Queen's Printer, 1954. 31 pp.

*_____. *La défense civile et la défense militaire.* (Actualités; revue destinée aux forces canadiennes, vol VII, no 8.) Ottawa: Imprimeur de la Reine, 1954. 31 pp.

Yost, William J. *Industrial Mobilization in Canada.* Ottawa: Conference of Defence Associations, 1983. 106 pp.

Yost, William J., ed. *In Defence of Canada's Oceans.* Ottawa: Conference of Defence Associations Institute, 1988. 58 pp.

Yost, William J., and Thomas St. Denis, eds. *Peacekeeping: Canada's Role.* Ottawa: Conference of Defence Associations Institute, 1991. 121 pp. *Conference of Defence Associations annual general meeting, Ottawa, January 1991.*

Young, George. *Who Killed Surcouf?* Queensland, N.S.: privately printed, 1986. 103 pp.

Ypres, John Pinkstone French, 1st earl *see* French, John Pinkstone French, 1st earl.

Zink, Lubor J. *Under the Mushroom Cloud.* Brandon, Man.: The Brandon Sun, 1962. 252 pp.

C. NAVAL FORCES — LES FORCES MARITIMES

1867-1914

*Appleton, Thomas E. *Usque ad Mare; a History of the Canadian Coast Guard and Marine Services.* Ottawa: Queen's Printer, 1968. 318 pp.

*_____. *Usque ad mare; historique de la Garde côtière canadienne et des Services de la Marine.* Ottawa: Ministère des Transports, 1968. 349 pp.

Arbuckle, Graeme. *Badges of the Canadian Navy.* Halifax: Nimbus Pub., 1987. 203 pp.

_____. *Customs and Traditions of the Canadian Navy.* Halifax: Nimbus Pub., 1984. 179 pp.

Bishop, William Arthur. *Courage at Sea.* (Canada's Military Heritage, Volume III.) Toronto: McGraw-Hill Ryerson, 1995. 191 pp.

Blatherwick, F.J. *Royal Canadian Navy Honours — Decorations — Medals, 1910-1968.* New Westminster, B.C. : FJB AIR Publications, 1992. 86 pp.

Bourassa, Henri, *Le projet de loi navale; sa nature, ses conséquences; discours prononcé au monument national, le 20 janvier 1910.* Montréal: le Devoir, [1910]. 37 pp.

Boutilier, James A., ed. *The RCN in Retrospect, 1910-1968.* Vancouver: Univ. of British Columbia Press, 1982. 373 pp.

Canada. Dept. of the Naval Service. *Instructions Relative to Recruiting for the Naval Service of Canada, 1910.* Ottawa: King's Printer, 1910. 35 pp.

_____. *Monthly Orders.* Ottawa: n.p., 1912-18.
Title varies. Naval Orders (1918). Continued in mimeograph form until 1936.

_____. *Naval Orders.* Ottawa: King's Printer, 1918-21. 6 vols.
Consolidation of Monthly Orders, 1912-20. Title varies.

_____. *Preliminary Training of Naval Cadets and Midshipmen, 1911.* n.p.: n.d. 29 pp.

*_____. *Report.* (Sessional Papers, no. 38 (1911-18), no. 39 (1919-21), no. 17a (1922).) Ottawa: King's Printer, 1911-22.

*Canada. Ministère du Service naval. *Rapport.* (Documents parlementaires, no 38 (1911-18), no 39 (1919-21), no 17a (1922).) Ottawa: Imprimeur du Roi, 1911-22.

[Canada. Navy.] *Canadian Naval Force and Royal Canadian Navy, 1910-1914.* Ottawa: Queen's Printer, 1955. 38 pp.

*Canada. Parlement. *Réponse à une adresse de la Chambre des Communes, en date du 29 novembre 1911, demandant copie de toute la correspondance échangée à la suite de la Conférence impériale entre le gouvernement du Canada et le gouvernement de Sa Majesté au sujet du Service naval du Canada ou d'une manière quelconque y afférant.* (Document parlementaire, no 40d.) Ottawa: Imprimeur du Roi, 1912. 19 pp.

*Canada. Parliament. *Return to an Address of the House of Commons, Dated November 29, 1911, for a Copy of all Correspondence between the Government of Canada and His Majesty's Government Subsequent to the Last Imperial Conference, Concerning the Naval Service of Canada, and in Any Way Connected with It.* (Sessional Paper, no. 40d.) Ottawa: King's Printer, 1912. 18 pp.

Canada's Navy Annual; a Special Edition of Wings Magazine. Calgary: Corvus Pub. Group, 1985- .
Title varies slightly.

Douglas, Archibald C. *Life of Admiral Sir Archibald Lucius Douglas, G.C.B., G.C.V.O., Commander of the Legion of Honour, Order of the Rising Sun of Japan, Spanish Naval Order of Merit.* Totnes, Eng.: Mortimer, 1938. 192 pp.

Douglas, W.A.B., ed. *The RCN in Transition, 1910-1985.* Vancouver: Univ. of British Columbia Press, 1988. 411 pp.

"Du Guesclin" [*pseud.*] *voir Notre marine de guerre.*

Foster, J.A. *Heart of Oak: a Pictorial History of the Royal Canadian Navy.* Toronto: Methuen, 1985. [143 pp.]

German, Tony. *The Sea is at our Gates; the History of the Canadian Navy.* Toronto: McClelland & Stewart, 1990. 360 pp.

Gough, Barry M. *Gunboat Frontier; British Maritime Authority and Northwest Coast Indians, 1846-90.* (Pacific Maritime Studies, 4.) Vancouver: Univ. of British Columbia Press, 1984. 287 pp.

*_____. *The Royal Navy and the North-West Coast of North America, 1810-1914; a Study of British Maritime Ascendency.* Vancouver: Univ. of British Columbia Press, 1971. 294 pp.

Gt. Brit. Admiralty. *Regulations for the Royal Naval Reserve Newfoundland.* London: H.M. Stationery Office, 1910. 41 pp.

[Gt. Brit. Colonial Defence Committee Canada.] *Halifax Defence Scheme.* London: H.M. Stationery Office, 1904?-12? *Amended annually.*

Hadley, Michael L., and Roger Sarty. *Tin-Pots and Pirate Ships: Candian Naval Forces & German Sea Raiders, 1880-1918.* Montreal: McGill-Queen's Univ. Press, 1991. 391 pp.

Little, C.H. *Naval Paintings/Tableaux navals/of the Second World War/de la Seconde Geurre mondiale/Naval Reserves in Canada/Les réserves navales au Canada.* Ottawa: National Museums of Canada/Musées nationaux du Canada, 1973. 30 pp. *Bilingual text./Texte bilingue.*

Longstaff, F.V. *Esquimalt Naval Base; a History of its Work and its Defences.* Vancouver: Clarke & Stuart, 1941. 189 pp.

Macdonald, William Balfour. *At Sea and by Land; the Reminiscences of William Balfour Macdonald, R.N.* S.W. Jackman, ed. Victoria, B.C.: Sono Nis Press, 1983. 136 pp.

McKee, Fraser M. *Volunteers for Sea Service; a Brief History of the Royal Canadian Naval Volunteer Reserve, its Predecessors and Successors, on its 50th Anniversary, 1973.* Toronto: privately printed, 1973. 69 pp.

Macpherson, K.R. *Canada's Fighting Ships.* (Canadian War Museum Historical Publication Number 12.) Toronto: Hakkert, 1975. 116 pp.

Macpherson, K.R., and John Burgess. *The Ships of Canada's Naval Forces, 1910-1981; a Complete Pictorial History of Canadian Warships.* Toronto: Collins, 1981. 240 pp. *Rev. eds. Toronto: Collins, 1985, and St. Catharines, Ont.: Vanwell Pub., 1993.*

[Maritime Museum of Canada.] *Souvenir of the Maritime Museum of Canada, Halifax, Nova Scotia.* [Halifax: n.p., 195-?] 44 pp.

Notre marine de guerre; que fera-t-on de la marine Laurier-Brodeur? Est-il vrai qu'elle ne servira qu'a la défense du Canada? [par] "Du Guesclin" [*pseud.*] Montréal: Imprimerie Le Devoir, 1911. 130 pp.

Preston, Richard A. *Canada and "Imperial Defense"; a Study of the Origins of the British Commonwealth's Defense Organization, 1867-1919.* (Duke University Commonwealth-Studies Center; Publication Number 29.) Durham, N.C.: Duke Univ. Press, 1967. 576 pp.

Richards, S.T. *Operation Sick Bay.* West Vancouver, B.C.: Centaur Pub., 1994. 267 pp. *The story of the Sick Berth & Medical Assistant Branch of the Royal Canadian Navy, 1910-1965.*

Royal Canadian Navy, 1910-1960; the First Fifty Years. n.p.: 1960. v.p.

Smith, Marilyn Gurney. *The King's Yard; an Illustrated History of the Halifax Dockyard.* Halifax: Nimbus Pub., 1985. 56 pp.

Smith, Waldo E.L. *The Navy Chaplain and his Parish.* Ottawa: Queen's Printer, 1967. 264 pp.

Stanley, George F.G., and Richard A. Preston. *A Short History of Kingston as a Military and Naval Centre.* Kingston, Ont.: Queen's Printer, [195-?]. 33 pp.

Swain, Hector, *History of the Naval Reserves in Newfoundland.* [St. John's, Nfld.: Provincial Archives, 1975.] 56 pp.

Tucker, Gilbert Norman. *A History of the Royal Canadian Navy.* Ottawa: King's Printer, 1951. 16 pp.

_____. *The Naval Service of Canada; its Official History.* Ottawa: King's Printer, 1952. 2 vols.

La vérité sur la question de la défense navale. s.l.: s.i., s.d. 38 pp.

Wickham, H.J. *Naval Defence of Canada.* Toronto: Murray, 1896. 11 pp.

Winters, B.A. *A Brief History of the Dockyard Terrace.* n.p.: 1989. 42 pp.

Witt, Eugene, and Jim Thomas. *Ship Repair Adventure; HMC Dockyard Esquimalt.* Victoria, B.C.: printed by Hillside Print. Co., 1985. 164 pp.

1914-1918

*Appleton, Thomas E. *Usque ad Mare; a History of the Canadian Coast Guard and Marine Services.* Ottawa: Queen's Printer, 1968. 318 pp.

*_____. *Usque ad mare; historique de la Garde côtière canadienne et des Services de la Marine.* Ottawa: Ministère de Transports, 1968. 349 pp.

Arbuckle, Graeme. *Badges of the Candadian Navy.* Halifax: Nimbus Pub., 1987. 203 pp.

_____. *Customs and Traditions of the Canadian Navy.* Halifax: Nimbus Pub., 1984. 179 pp.

Art Gallery of Toronto. *Catalogue of an Exhibition of the Canadian War Memorials, October 1926.* Toronto: privately printed, [1926]. 21 pp.

Ashbury College, Ottawa. *List of Masters and Old Boys who Served with the Colours, 1914-1919.* Ottawa: Simmons Print Co., [1919]. 33 pp.

Bank of Montreal. *Memorial of the Great War, 1914-1918; a Record of Service.* Montreal: privately printed, 1921. 261 pp.

Bidwell, R.E.S. *Random Memories.* Ottawa: privately printed, [1962. 21 pp.]

Bindon, Kathryn M. *More than Patriotism.* (A Personal Library Publication.) Don Mills, Ont.: Nelson, 1979. 192 pp.

Bird, Michael J. *The Town that Died; the True Story of the Greatest Manmade Explosion before Hiroshima.* New York: Putnam, 1962. 192 pp.

Bishop, William Arthur. *Courage at Sea.* (Canada's Military Heritage, Volume III.) Toronto: McGraw-Hill Ryerson, 1995. 191 pp.

Blatherwick, F.J. *Royal Canadian Navy Honours — Decorations — Medals, 1910-1968.* New Westminster, B.C.: FJB AIR Publications, 1992. 86 pp.

Boutilier, James A., ed. *The RCN in Retrospect, 1910-1968.* Vancouver: Univ. of British Columbia Press, 1982. 373 pp.

Canada. Dept. of the Naval Service. *The Canadian Navy List.* Ottawa: King's Printer, 1914-65.
Issued by the Dept. of National Defence from 1923.

_____. *Confidential Weekly Orders.* Ottawa: n.p., 1916-22.
Title varies. <u>Confidential Naval Orders</u> (December 1917- June 1921), <u>Naval Staff Orders</u> from June 1921.

_____. *Correspondence Relating to the Purchase of Two Submarines by the Canadian Government.* (Sessional Paper, no. 158.) Ottawa: King's Printer, 1915. 35 pp.

Canada. Dept. of the Naval Service. *Monthly Orders.* Ottawa: n.p., 1912-18.
Title varies. Naval Orders (1918). Continued in mimeograph form until 1936.

_____. *Naval Orders.* Ottawa: King's Printer, 1918-21. 6 vols.
Consolidation of Monthly Orders, 1912-20. Title varies.

_____. *Pay and Allowances for Officers and Men of the Royal Canadian Navy.* Ottawa: King's Printer, 1918. 17 pp.

_____. *Regulations for Supply and Accounting of Provisions, Clothing and Mens Traps Issued to Vessels of HMC Patrol Service; Instructions to Stewards.* Ottawa: King's Printer, 1917. v.p.

*_____. *Report.* (Sessional Papers, no. 38 (1911-18), no. 39 (1919-21), no. 17a (1922).) Ottawa: King's Printer, 1911-22.

_____. *Uniform and Clothing Regulations for Petty Officers, Men and Boys, H.M. Canadian Naval Service.* Ottawa: King's Printer, 1918. 111 pp.

Canada. Dept. of the Naval Service. Intelligence Branch. *Naval Intelligence Reports.* No. I-C. Ottawa: n.p., 1917-18.

*Canada. Directeur de l'Information publique. *L'effort du Canada pour la Guerre, 1914-1918.* Ottawa: Imprimeur du Roi, 1918. 31 pp.

Canada. Director of Public Information. *Canada's Part in the Great War.* Ottawa: n.p., 1919. 64 pp.
Also issued by Information Branch, Dept. of External Affairs.

*_____. *Canada's War Effort, 1914-1918.* Ottawa: King's Printer, 1918. 31 pp.

*Canada. Ministère du Service naval. *Rapport.* (Documents parlementaires, no 38 (1911-18), no 39 (1919-21), no 17a (1922).) Ottawa: Imprimeur du Roi, 1911-22.

[Canada. Navy.] *Canadian Naval Force and Royal Canadian Navy, 1910-1914.* Ottawa: Queen's Printer, 1955. 38 pp.

Canada's Navy Annual; a Special Edition of Wings Magazine. Calgary: Corvus Pub. Group, 1985- .
Title varies slightly.

Canadian Bank of Commerce. *Letters from the Front; being a Record of the Part Played by Officers of the Bank in the Great War, 1914-1919.* Toronto: privately printed, n.d. 2 vols.

Canadian War Records Office. *Art and War; Canadian War Memorials; a Selection of the Works Executed for the Canadian War Memorials Fund to Form a Record of Canada's Part in the Great War and a Memorial to those Canadians who have Made the Great Sacrifice.* London: n.p., 1919. 1 vol., unpaged.

Canadian War Records Office. *Canadian War Memorials Exhibition, [New York] 1919.* n.p.: n.d. 48 pp.

_____. *Thirty Canadian V.C.'s; 23rd April 1915 to 20th March 1918.* London: Skeffington, n.d. 96 pp.

Carr, William Guy. *Out of the Mists.* London: Hutchinson, n.d. 176 pp.

La Chapelle du Souvenir, Chambres du Parlement, Ottawa, Canada, [par A.F. Duguid.] Ottawa: Photogelatine Engraving Co., s.d. 1 tome, non-paginé.

Chapman, Harry. *Dartmouth's Day of Anguish; ... the Explosion, December 6, 1917 ....* Dartmouth, N.S.: Dartmouth Museum Society, 1992. 45 pp.

Corporation of British Columbia Land Surveyors. *Roll of Honour; British Columbia Land Surveyors; 1914 the Great War 1918.* n.p.: privately printed, n.d. 1 vol., unpaged.

Cranston, Bobby. *75th Anniversary, Naval Service of Canada; a Pictorial History.* Halifax: 75th Anniversary Pub. Co., [1985]. 1 vol., chiefly illus.

Creed, Catherine. *'Whose Debtors We Are'.* (Niagara Historical Society, 34.) Niagara, Ont.: Niagara Historical Society, 1922. 116 pp.

Dominion of Canada Roll of Honor; a Directory of Casualties (Deaths Only) of the World's Greatest War, 1914-1918, of the City of Toronto; Dedicated to Perpetuate Those who Made the Supreme Sacrifice, "They Shall Not be Forgotten". n.p.: C. McAlpine, 1919. 28 1.

Douglas, W.A.B., ed. *The RCN in Transition, 1910-1985.* Vancouver: Univ. of British Columbia Press, 1988. 411 pp.

Drolet, "Gil". *Loyola, the Wars: in Remembrance of "Men for Others".* Waterloo, Ont.: Laurier Centre for Military Strategic and Disarmament Studies, 1996. 44 pp.
Memorial to the war dead of Loyola High School and College.

Duguid, Archer Fortescue. *The Canadian Forces in the Great War, 1914-1919; the Record of Five Years of Active Service.* Ottawa: King's Printer, 1947. 14 pp.

Duguid, Archer Fortescue, *see also/voir aussi* *The Memorial Chamber in the Peace Tower ...; La Chapelle du Souvenir.*

Duncan-Clark, S.J., and W.R. Plewman. *Pictorial History of the Great War; [including] Canada in the Great War,* by W.S. Wallace. Toronto: J.L. Nichols, 1919. 2 vols. in 1.

Ferguson, Julie H. *Through a Canadian Periscope; the Story of the Canadian Submarine Service.* Toronto: Dundurn Press, 1995. 364 pp.

Fetherstonhaugh, R.C. *McGill University at War, 1914-1918; 1939-1945.* Montreal: McGill Univ., 1947. 437 pp.

Fighters for Freedom; Honor Roll of Halifax; the Great War, 1914-1919. Halifax: Service Pub. Co., [1919]. 191 pp.

Foster, J.A. *Heart of Oak; a Pictorial History of the Royal Canadian Navy.* Toronto: Methuen, 1985. [143 pp.]

Gardam, John. *Seventy Years After, 1914-1984.* Stittsville, Ont.: Canada's Wings, 1983. 99 pp.

[Garvin, Amelia Beers (Warnock).] *Canada's Peace Tower and Memorial Chamber, Designed by John A. Pearson, D. Arch., F.R.A.I.C., F.R.I.B.A., A.R.C.A., G.D.I.A., a Record and Interpretation by Katherine Hale [pseud.] Dedicated by the Architect to the Veterans of the Great War.* Toronto: Mundy-Goodfellow Print. Co., 1935. 29 pp.

German, Tony. *The Sea is at our Gates; the History of the Canadian Navy.* Toronto: McClelland & Stewart, 1990. 360 pp.

Godenrath, Percy F. *Lest We Forget; a Record in Art of the Dominion's Part in the War (1914-1918) and a Memorial to those Canadians who Made the Great Sacrifice, being the Gift of the Over-Seas Military Forces to the Nation; a Brief History of the Collection of War Paintings, Etchings and Sculpture, Made Possible by the Work of the Canadian War Memorials Fund and the Canadian War Record Office.* Ottawa: n.p., 1934. 46 pp.

Gt. Brit. Imperial War Graves Commission. *Beaumont-Hamel (Newfoundland) Memorial; Bearing the Names of Those Sailors, Soldiers and Merchant Seamen from Newfoundland who Fell in the Great War and have no Known Graves.* London: H.M. Stationery Office, 1929. 45 pp.

_____. *Memorials Erected at Halifax, Nova Scotia, and Victoria, British Columbia, Canada, Bearing the Names of Those Sailors, Soldiers and Merchant Seamen of Canada who Fell in the Great War and have no Known Graves.* London: H.M. Stationery Office, 1930. 24 pp.

_____. *The War Graves of the British Empire; the Register of the Names of Those who Fell in the Great War and are Buried in Cemeteries and Churchyards in Nova Scotia, Prince Edward Island and New Brunwsick, Canada.* London: H.M. Stationery Office, 1931. 92 pp.

_____. *The War Graves of the British Empire; the Register of the Names of Those who Fell in the Great War and are Buried in Cemeteries in Newfoundland.* London: H.M. Stationery Office, 1930. 19 pp.

Gt. Brit. Imperial War Graves Commission. *The War Graves of the British Empire; the Register of the Names of Those who Fell in the Great War and are Buried in Cemeteries in the Province of British Columbia, Canada.* London: H.M. Stationery Office, 1931. 48 pp.

_____. *The War Graves of the British Empire; the Register of the Names of Those who Fell in the Great War and are Buried in Cemeteries in the Province of Manitoba, Canada.* London: H.M. Stationery Office, 1931. 48 pp.

_____. *The War Graves of the British Empire; the Register of the Names of Those who Fell in the Great War and are Buried in Cemeteries in the Province of Ontario, Canada.* London: H.M. Stationery Office, 1931. 2 vols.

_____. *The War Graves of the British Empire; the Register of the Names of Those who Fell in the Great War and are Buried in Cemeteries in the Province of Quebec, Canada.* London: H.M. Stationery Office, 1931. 64 pp.

_____. *The War Graves of the British Empire; the Register of the Names of Those who Fell in the Great War and are Buried in Cemeteries in the Provinces of Saskatchewan and Alberta, Canada.* London: H.M. Stationery Office, 1931. 63 pp.

Hadley, Michael L., and Roger Sarty. *Tin-Pots and Pirate Ships: Canadian Naval Forces & German Sea Raiders, 1880-1918.* Montreal: McGill-Queen's Univ. Press, 1991. 391 pp.

Hale, Katherine, [*pseud.*] *see* Garvin, Amelia Beers (Warnock).

[Hallam, T. Douglas.] *The Spider Web; the Romance of a Flying-Boat Flight*, by P.I.X. [*pseud.*] Edinburgh: W. Blackwood, 1919. 278 pp.

Herrington, Walter S., and A.J. Wilson. *The War Work of the County of Lennox and Addington.* Napanee, Ont.: Beaver Press, 1922. 278 pp.

Hezzelwood, Oliver, *see* Trinity Methodist Church, Toronto, Ont.

*Kealy, J.D.F., and E.C. Russell. *A History of Canadian Naval Aviation, 1918-1962.* Ottawa: Queen's Printer, 1965. 164 pp.

*Kealy, J.D.F., et E.C. Russell. *Histoire de l'aéronavale canadienne, 1918-1962.* Ottawa: Imprimeur de la Reine, 1965. 185 pp.

Longstaff, F.V. *Esquimalt Naval Base; a History of its Work and its Defences.* Vancouver: Clarke & Stuart, 1941. 189 pp.

Macdonald, William Balfour. *At Sea and by Land; the Reminiscences of William Balfour Macdonald, R.N.* S.W. Jackman, ed. Victoria, B.C.: Sono Nis Press, 1983. 136 pp.

McGill Univ., Montreal, P.Q. *McGill Honour Roll, 1914-1918.* Montreal: McGill Univ., 1926. 228 pp.

McGill Univ., Montreal, P.Q. *A Memorial Service for the McGill Men and Women who Gave their Lives during the First and Second World Wars.* n.p.: [1946]. 1 vol., unpaged .

McKee, Fraser M. *The Armed Yachts of Canada.* Erin, Ont.: Boston Mills Press, 1983. 172 pp.

————. *Volunteers for Sea Service; a Brief History of the Royal Canadian Naval Volunteer Reserve, its Predecessors and Successors, on its 50th Anniversary, 1973.* Toronto: privately printed, 1973. 69 pp.

Macpherson, K.R. *Canada's Fighting Ships.* (Canadian War Museum Historical Publication Number 12.) Toronto: Hakkert, 1975. 116 pp.

Macpherson, K.R., and John Burgess. *The Ships of Canada's Naval Forces, 1910-1981; a Complete Pictorial History of Canadian Warships.* Toronto: Collins, 1981. 240 pp.
Rev. eds. Toronto: Collins, 1985, and St. Catharines, Ont.: Vanwell Pub., 1993.

[Maritime Museum of Canada.] *Souvenir of the Maritime Museum of Canada, Halifax, Nova Scotia.* [Halifax: n.p., 195-?] 44 pp.

*The Memorial Chamber in the Peace Tower, Houses of Parliament, Ottawa, Canada, [by A. F. Duguid]. Ottawa: Photogelatine Engraving Co., n.d. [34] pp.

Metson, Graham, comp. *The Halifax Explosion, December 6, 1917.* Toronto: McGraw-Hill Ryerson, n.d. 173 pp.

Miller, James Martin, and H.S. Canfield. *The People's War Book; History, Encyclopedia and Chronology of the Great World War; and Canada's Part in the War,* by W.R. Plewman. Toronto: Imperial Pub. Co., 1919. 520 pp.

Monnon, Mary Ann. *Miracles and Mysteries; the Halifax Explosion December 6, 1917.* Windsor, N.S.: Lancelot Press, 1977. 144 pp.

Ontario. Dept. of Education. *The Roll of Honour of the Ontario Teachers who Served in the Great War, 1914-1918.* Toronto: Ryerson Press, 1922. 72 pp.

Ontario Agricultural College, Guelph, Ont. *Ontario Agricultural College Honour and Service Rolls.* n.p.: n.d. 1 vol., unpaged.

Ontario Bar Association. *Roll of Honour.* n.p.: [1918.] 22 pp.

P.I.X. [*pseud.*] *see* Hallam, T. Douglas.

Parkdale Collegiate Institute, Toronto. *Roll of Service in the Great War, 1914-1919.* n.p.: n.d. 22 pp.

Parkdale Collegiate Institute, Toronto. *Their Name Liveth; a Memoir of the Boys of Parkdale Collegiate Institute who Gave their Lives in the Great War.* Toronto: privately printed, n.d. 177 pp.

Peace Souvenir; Activities of Waterloo County in the Great War, 1914-1918. Kitchener, Ont.: Kitchener Daily Telegraph, 1919. 70 pp.

Perkins, Dave. *Canada's Submariners, 1914-1923.* Erin, Ont.: Boston Mills Press, 1989. 226 pp.

Plewman, W.R., *see* Miller, James Martin.

Preston, Richard A. *Canada and "Imperial Defense"; a Study of the Origins of the British Commonwealth's Defense Organization, 1867-1919.* (Duke University Commonwealth-Studies Center; Publication Number 29.) Durham, N.C.: Duke Univ. Press, 1967. 576 pp.

Queen's Univ., Kingston, Ont. *Overseas Record; Record of Graduates, Alumni, Members of Staff, and Students of Queen's University on Active Military (Overseas) Service (to June 1st, 1917) 1914-1917.* n.p.: [1917?]. 44 pp.

Richards, S.T. *Operation Sick Bay.* West Vancouver, B.C.: Centaur Pub., 1994. 267 pp.
The story of the Sick Berth & Medical Assistant Branch of the Royal Canadian Navy, 1910-1965.

Royal Canadian Navy, 1910-1960; the First Fifty Years. n.p.: 1960. v.p.

Santor, Donald M. *Canadians at War, 1914-1918.* (Canadiana Scrapbook.) Scarborough, Ont.: Prentice-Hall, 1978. 48 pp.

Sea Breezes. Vol. I-III. Halifax: privately printed, 1914-22.
Journal of the Royal Naval College of Canada.

Smith, G. Oswald, *see University of Toronto ....*

Smith, Gaddis, *Britain's Clandestine Submarines, 1914-1915.* New Haven, Conn.: Yale Univ. Press, 1964. 155 pp.

Smith, Marilyn Gurney. *The King's Yard; an Illustrated History of the Halifax Dockyard.* Halifax: Nimbus Pub., 1985. 56 pp.

Smith, Waldo E.L. *The Navy Chaplain and his Parish.* Ottawa: Queen's Printer, 1967. 264 pp.

Stanley, George F.G., and Richard A. Preston. *A Short History of Kingston as a Military and Naval Centre.* Kingston, Ont.: Queen's Printer, [195-?]. 33 pp.

Suthren, Victor, ed. *The Oxford Book of Canadian Military Anecdotes.* Toronto: Oxford Univ. Press, 1989. 202 pp.

Swain, Hector. *History of the Naval Reserves in Newfoundland.* [St. John's, Nfld.: Provincial Archives, 1975.] 56 pp.

Swettenham, John. *Canada and the First World War.* Toronto: Ryerson Press, 1969. 160 pp.

_____. *Canada and the First World War./La participation du Canada à la Première Guerre mondiale.* Ottawa: Canadian War Museum/Musée de guerre, n.d./s.d. 56/63 pp.
Bilingual text./Texte bilingue.

Thompson, Roy J.C. *Wings of the Canadian Armed Forces, 1913-1972.* [Dartmouth], N.S.: n.p., 1973. 106 pp.

Thorburn, Ella M., and Charlotte Whitton. *Canada's Chapel of Remembrance.* Toronto: British Book Service (Canada), 1961. 68 pp.

Trinity Methodist Church, Toronto. *Trinity War Book; a Recital of Service and Sacrifice in the Great War.* Oliver Hezzelwood, comp. Toronto: privately printed, 1921. 368 pp.

Tucker, Gilbert Norman. *A History of the Royal Canadian Navy.* Ottawa: King's Printer, 1951. 16 pp.

_____. *The Naval Service of Canada; its Official History.* Ottawa: King's Printer, 1952. 2 vols.

Univ. of British Columbia. *Record of Service, 1914-1918; University of British Columbia, McGill British Columbia, Vancouver College.* Vancouver: privately printed, 1924. 142 pp.

Univ. of Manitoba. *Roll of Honour, 1914-1918.* Winnipeg: privately printed, 1923. 150 pp.

Univ. of Toronto. Univ. Schools. *The Annals, 1916-1918.* Toronto: Univ. of Toronto Press, n.d. 1 vol., unpaged.

Univ. of Toronto. Victoria College. *Acta Victoriana; War Supplement.* [Toronto]: n.p., 1919. 128 pp.

University of Toronto Roll of Service. First Edition, August 1914-August 1917. [Toronto]: Univ. of Toronto Press, n.d. 212 pp.
Also Supplement, *August 1917-October 1918.*

University of Toronto; Roll of Service, 1914-1918. G. Oswald Smith, ed. Toronto: Univ. of Toronto Press, 1921. 603 pp.

X., P.I., [*pseud.*] *see* Hallam, T. Douglas.

War Record of McGill Chapter of Delta Upsilon. Montreal: n.p., 1919. 47 pp.

Wellington Legion War Veterans Club, eds. *They Served for Freedom./A la défense de la liberté.* [Wellington, P.E.I.: Royal Canadian Legion, Wellington Branch 17/Wellington, I.P.E.: Légion royale canadienne, la filiale de Wellington no 17, 1986.] 319 pp.
Bilingual text./Texte bilingue.

Winters, B.A. *A Brief History of the Dockyard Terrace.* n.p.: 1989. 42 pp.

_____. *H.M.C.S. Discovery; a History of the Naval Reserve in Vancouver.* n.p.: [1995]. 1 vol., unpaged.

Witt, Eugene, and Jim Thomas. *Ship Repair Adventure; HMC Dockyard Esquimalt.* Victoria, B.C.: printed by Hillside Print. Co., 1985. 164 pp.

Wodehouse, R.F. *A Check List of the War Collections of World War I, 1914-1918, and World War II, 1939-1945.* Ottawa: Queen's Printer, 1968. 239 pp.

Young, A.H., and W.A. Kirkwood, eds. *The War Memorial Volume of Trinity College, Toronto.* [Toronto]: Printers Guild, 1922. 165 pp.

1919-1945

Active Service Canteen, Toronto, 1939-1945. Toronto: n.p., 1945. 1 vol., unpaged.

* Appleton, Thomas E. *Usque ad Mare; a History of the Canadian Coast Guard and Marine Services.* Ottawa: Queen's Printer, 1968. 318 pp.

* _____. *Usque ad mare; historique de la Garde côtière canadienne et des Services de la Marine.* Ottawa: Ministère des Transports, 1968. 349 pp.

Arbuckle, Graeme. *Badges of the Canadian Navy.* Halifax: Nimbus Pub., 1987. 203 pp.

_____. *Customs and Traditions of the Canadian Navy.* Halifax: Nimbus Pub., 1984. 179 pp.

Bank of Montreal. *Field of Honour; the Second World War, 1939-1945.* Montreal: n.p., 1950. 1 vol., unpaged.

Barris, Ted, and Alex Barris. *Days of Victory; Canadians Remember: 1939-1945.* Toronto: Macmillan Canada, 1995. 304 pp.

Bartlett, E.H. *The Royal Canadian Navy.* (Macmillan War Pamphlets, Canadian Series.) Toronto: Macmillan, 1942. 30 pp.

Beckles, Gordon, [*pseud.*] *see* Willson, Gordon Beckles.

Bercuson, David J. *Maple Leaf against the Axis; Canada's Second World War.* Toronto: Stoddart, 1995. 316 pp.

Bidwell, R.E.S. *Random Memories.* Ottawa: privately printed, [1962. 21 pp.]

Birney, Earle, ed. *Record of Service in the Second World War; the University of British Columbia; a Supplement to the University of British Columbia War Memorial Manuscript Record.* Vancouver: privately printed, 1955. 46 pp.

Bishop, William Arthur. *Courage at Sea.* (Canada's Military Heritage, Volume III.) Toronto: McGraw-Hill Ryerson, 1995. 191 pp.

Blakely, Tom. *Corvette Cobourg; the Role of a Canadian Warship in the Longest Sea Battle in History.* Cobourg, Ont.: Cobourg Branch, Royal Canadian Legion, n.d. 93 pp.

Blatherwick, F.J. *Royal Canadian Navy Honours — Decorations — Medals, 1910-1968.* New Westminster, B.C.: FJB AIR Publications, 1992. 86 pp.

Borthwick, J.B. *History of the 29th Canadian Motor Torpedo Boat Flotilla.* [Winnipeg: Naval Museum, H.M.C.S. Chippawa, 1991?] 66 pp.

Bourassa, Henri. *La mission Jellicoe; nouvelle poussée d'impérialisme.* [Montréal]: Editions du Devoir, 1920. 37 pp.

Boutilier, James A., ed. *The RCN in Retrospect, 1910-1968.* Vancouver: Univ. of British Columbia Press, 1982. 373 pp.

Bowering, Clifford H. *Service; the Story of the Canadian Legion, 1925-1960.* Ottawa: privately printed, 1960. 240 pp.

Bowman, Phylis. *Second World War Memories.* Port Edward, B.C.: privately printed, 1987. 84 pp.
Prince Rupert, B.C., in the Second World War.

Brantford Kinsmen Club, comp. *Album of Honour for Brant County World War II, 1939-1945.* Helen Sanders, ed. [Brantford, Ont.]: Brantford Kinsmen Club, 1946. 224 pp.

Broadfoot, Barry. *Six War Years, 1939-1945; Memories of Canadians at Home and Abroad.* Toronto: Doubleday Canada, 1974. 417 pp.

Brock, Jeffry V. *With Many Voices.* Toronto: McClelland and Stewart, 1981-83. 2 vols.

Brock, Thomas Leith. *Fight the Good Fight; Looking in on the Recruit Class at the Royal Military College of Canada during a Week in February, 1931.* Montreal: privately printed, 1964. 30 pp.

————. *The R.M.C. Vintage Class of 1934.* Victoria, B.C.: privately printed, 1985. 3 vols.

Brockington, Leonard W. *"D" Day on a Canadian Destroyer; a Talk Broadcast on the CBC Trans-Canada Network, Sunday, June 18th, 1944.* n.p.: n.d. 14 pp.

Brown, Elizabeth, Robert Brown and Quentin Brown. *The Army's Mister Brown; a Family Trilogy, 1941-1952.* Harcourt Brown, ed. Parry Sound, Ont.: privately printed, 1982. 234 pp.
Robert Brown served with the U.S. Army Air Forces in the Pacific, Quentin Brown in RCN in Atlantic and Europe. Elizabeth Brown was in UNRRA.

Bruce, Jean. *Back the Attack! Canadian Women during the Second World War — at Home and Abroad.* Toronto: Macmillan, 1985. 182 pp.

Bryden, John. *Best-Kept Secret; Canadian Secret Intelligence in the Second World War.* Toronto: Lester Pub., 1993. 390 pp.

Burrow, Len, and Emile Beaudoin. *Unlucky Lady; the Life & Death of HMCS Athabaskan, 1940-1944.* Stittsville, Ont.: Canada's Wings, 1982. 198 pp.

Burton, E.F. *Canadian Naval Radar Officers; the Story of University Graduates for whom Preliminary Training was Given in the Department of Physics, University of Toronto.* Toronto: Univ. of Toronto Press, 1946. 63 pp.

Butcher, Alan D. *I Remember Haida.* Hantsport, N.S.: Lancelot Press, 1985. 163 pp.

Cameron, James M. *Murray; the Martyred Admiral.* Hantsport, N.S.: Lancelot Press, 1980. 343 pp.

Canada. Armed Forces. H.M.C.S. Unicorn. *History of Unicorn, 1923-1973.* n.p.: n.d. v.p.

Canada. Dept. of National Defence. *Canadian Prisoners of War and Missing Personnel in the Far East.* Ottawa: King's Printer, 1945. 59 1.

_____. *Defence Forces List, Canada (Naval, Military and Air Forces).* Ottawa: King's Printer, 1930-39.
Title varies somewhat. Superseded The Militia List. *Superseded by* The Canadian Navy List, The Canadian Army List *and* The Royal Canadian Air Force List.

_____. *Digest of Opinions and Rulings; Ottawa; March 31, 1944; Compiled from the Records of the Office of the Judge Advocate-General, at National Defence Headquarters.* n.p.: [1944]. 353 pp., looseleaf.

_____. *Instructions for Engineer Services, Canada, 1936.* Ottawa: King's Printer, 1936. 152 pp.

_____. *The King's Regulations for the Government of His Majesty's Canadian Naval Service, 1945.* (B.R.C.N. 101-103.) Ottawa: King's Printer, 1945. 3 vols., looseleaf.

*_____. *Report.* Ottawa: King's Printer, 1923-59.
Title varies. Annual most years.

_____. *Royal Canadian Naval Reserve Regulations.* Ottawa: n.p., [1926]. v.p.

Canada. Dept. of National Defence (Naval Service). *Consolidated Naval Orders.* n.p.: 1927. 407 pp.
Addenda also issued.

_____. *Naval Orders.* Ottawa: n.p., 1938-45.
Title varies: Naval Monthly Orders *until September 1939. Continues mimeographed orders.*

_____. *Regulations and Instructions for the Royal Canadian Fleet Reserve, 1939.* Ottawa: King's Printer, 1939. 32 pp.

_____. *Regulations and Instructions for the Royal Canadian Naval Reserve, 1940.* Ottawa: King's Printer, 1940. 103 pp.

_____. *Regulations and Instructions for the Royal Canadian Naval Reserve, 1932.* Ottawa: King's Printer, 1932. 102 pp.

Canada. Dept. of National Defence (Naval Service). *Regulations and Instructions for the Royal Canadian Navy, 1937.* Ottawa: King's Printer, 1937. 269 pp. *Addendum published 1940.*

_____. *Regulations for Royal Canadian Naval Volunteer Reserve, 1938.* Ottawa: King's Printer, 1938. 124 pp.

_____. *The Regulations for the Organization and Administration of the Women's Royal Canadian Naval Service.* Ottawa: King's Printer, 1942. 33 pp.

_____. *Royal Canadian Naval Reserve Regulations. Vol. II: Fishermen's Reserve (West Coast).* Ottawa: King's Printer, 1939. 24 pp.

_____. *Royal Canadian Naval Volunteer Reserve Regulations, 1930, and Regulations for Entry and Service of Instructional Staff for the Royal Canadian Naval Volunteer Reserve.* Ottawa: King's Printer, 1930. v.p. *Addendum issued 1933.*

Canada. Dept. of National War Services. *Annual Report.* Ottawa: King's Printer, 1945. 3 vols.

Canada. Dept. of the Naval Service. *The Canadian Navy List.* Ottawa: King's Printer, 1914-65.
Issued by the Dept. of National Defence from 1923.

_____. *Confidential Weekly Orders.* Ottawa: n.p., 1916-22.
Title varies: Confidential Naval Orders (December 1917 — June 1921), Naval Staff Orders from June 1921.

_____. *Naval Orders.* Ottawa: King's Printer, 1918-21. 6 vols.
Consolidation of Monthly Orders, 1912-20. Title varies.

_____. *Pay and Allowances, 1920, for Officers and Men of the Royal Canadian Navy.* Ottawa: King's Printer, 1920. 28 pp.

*_____. *Report.* (Sessional Papers, no. 38 (1911-18), no. 39 (1919-21), no. 17a (1922).) Ottawa: King's Printer, 1911-22.

Canada. Dept. of Veterans Affairs. *D-Day; 1944 — June 6 — 1984./Jour J; 1944 — le 6 juin — 1984.* Ottawa: Veterans Affairs Cananda/Affaires des Anciens combattants, 1984. 22 pp.
Bilingual text./Texte bilingue.

_____. *30th Anniversary of the D-Day Landings in Normandy, 1944 — June 6 — 1974./30e anniversaire des débarquements en Normandie au jour J, 1944 — le 6 juin — 1974.* n.p./s.l.: s.i., 1974. 22 pp.
Bilingual text./Texte bilingue.

Canada. Director of Public Information. *Canada and the People's War.* n.p.: [1942]. 1 vol., unpaged.

*Canada. Director of Public Information. *Canada at War.* No. 1-45. Ottawa: King's Printer, 1941-45.

*Canada. Ministère de la Défense nationale. *Rapport.* Ottawa: Imprimeur du Roi, 1923-59.
Divergence du titre. Annuel la plupart des années.

*Canada. Ministère du Service naval. *Rapport.* (Documents parlementaires, no 38 (1911-18), no 39 (1919-21), no 17a (1922).) Ottawa: Imprimeur du Roi, 1911-22.

Canada. National Gallery. *Exhibition of Canadian War Art.* Ottawa: King's Printer, 1945. 22 pp.

Canada. National Research Council. *History of the Associate Committee on Naval Medical Research.* Ottawa: n.p., 1948. 121 pp.

Canada. Naval Service Headquarters. *Particulars of Canadian War Vessels; Half-Yearly Return.* Ottawa: King's Printer, 1940-45. 8 vols.
No issue for July 1944. Title varies somewhat.

Canada. Naval Service Headquarters. Naval Historian. *The University Naval Training Divisions*, [by Philip Chaplin]. Ottawa: Queen's Printer, 1963. 24 pp.

Canada. Navy. *Entry of Officers in the Royal Canadian Navy, Conditions of Service, etc.* Ottawa: King's Printer, 1937. [24 pp?]

_____. *Regulations and Instructions for the Royal Canadian Navy.* Ottawa: King's Printer, 1927. 407 pp.
Short title: Canadian Naval Regulations or CNRs. Originally issued under title: Consolidated Naval Orders, 1927. Title amended by Naval Order 62 of 1928.

Canada. Navy. Pacific Command. *In Commemoration of the Presentation of the King's Colour to the Royal Canadian Navy by His Late Majesty King George VI, Which Took Place at Beacon Hill Park, Victoria, British Columbia, on 30 May, 1939, at 2:30 p.m.* n.p.: [1956.] 1 vol., unpaged.

Canada. Navy. Western Command. *Presentation of the King's Colour to the Royal Canadian Navy, Western Command, by His Majesty King George VI at Beacon Hill Park, Victoria, British Columbia, on 30th May, 1939, at 2:30 P.M.* Victoria, B.C.: J.P. Buckle Print. Co., [1939]. 12 pp.

*Canada. Parlement. Chambre des Communes. Comité spécial d'enquête sur les distinctions honorifiques et les décorations. *Procès-verbaux et témoignages.* No 1-6. Ottawa: Imprimeur du Roi, 1942.

Canada. Parliament. House of Commons. Special Committee on Canteen Funds. *Minutes of Proceedings and Evidence.* No. 1-11. Ottawa: King's Printer, 1942.

*Canada. Parliament. House of Commons. Special Committee on Honours and Decorations. *Minutes of Proceedings and Evidence.* No. 1-6. Ottawa: King's Printer, 1942.

Canada. Royal Commission to Conduct an Inquiry into Certain Disorders Occurring May 7-8, 1945, in the City of Halifax. *Report on the Halifax Disorders, May 7th-8th, 1945.* Hon. Mr. Justice R.L. Kellock, Royal Commissioner. Ottawa: King's Printer, 1945. 61 pp.

*Canada. Service de l'Information. *Le Canada en guerre.* No 1-45. Ottawa: Imprimeur du Roi, 1941-45.

*_Le Canada dans la bataille de l'Atlantique._ [Ottawa; Imprimeur du Roi, 1942.] 1 tome, non paginé.

*_Canada's Battle of the Atlantic._ [Ottawa: King's Printer, 1942.] 1 vol., unpaged.

Canadian Bank of Commerce. *War Service Records, 1939-1945; an Account of the War Service of Members of the Staff during the Second World War.* D.P. Wagner and C.G. Siddall, eds. Toronto: Rous & Mann, 1947. 331 pp.

Canadian Broadcasting Corporation. Publications Branch. *We have been There; Authoritative Reports by Qualified Observers who have Returned from the War Zones, as Presented over the CBC National Network.* Toronto: Canadian Broadcasting Corporation, 1941-42. 2 vols.

Canadian Jewish Congress. *Canadian Jews in World War II.* Montreal: privately printed, 1947-48. 2 vols.

Canadian Legion War Services, Inc. *A Year of Service; a Summary of Activities on Behalf of His Majesty's Canadian Forces Rendered during Nineteen-Forty.* n.p.: n.d. 1 vol., unpaged.

Cardoulis, John N. *A Friendly Invasion; the American Military in Newfoundland, 1940-1990.* St. John's, Nfld.: Breakwater, 1990. 224 pp.

_____. *A Friendly Invasion II: a Personal Touch.* St. John's, Nfld.: Creative Publishers, 1993. 221 pp.

Carr, William Guy. *Checkmate in the North; the Axis Planned to Invade America.* Toronto: Macmillan, 1944. 304 pp.

Catley, Harry. *Gate and Gaiters; a Book of Naval Humour and Anecdotes; Including a Glossary of Naval Language for the Uninformed.* Toronto: Thorn Press, 1949. 322 pp.

Chambers, Robert W. *Halifax in Wartime; a Collection of Drawings.* Halifax: The Halifax Herald and the Halifax Mail, 1943. 1 vol., unpaged.

Charlton, Peter, and Michael Whitby, eds. *"Certified Serviceable"; Swordfish to Sea King; the Technical Story of Canadian Naval Aviation, by Those Who Made It So.* n.p.: CNATH Book Project, 1995. 496 pp.

Chrétien, Guy. *"Juno Beach", les Canadiens dans la bataille.* Caen, France: Imprimerie Lafond, s.d./n.d. 256 pp., en majeure partie ill./chiefly illus. *Texte bilingue./Bilingual text.*

Coale, Griffith. *North Atlantic Patrol, the Log of a Seagoing Artist.* New York: Farrar & Rinehart, 1942. 51 pp.

Commonwealth War Graves Commission. *The War Dead of the Commonwealth; the Register of the Names of Those who Fell in the 1939-1945 War and are Buried; Cemeteries in Canada; Cemeteries in Ontario.* London: H.M. Stationery Office, 1961. 2 vols.

_____. *The War Dead of the Commonwealth; the Register of the Names of Those who Fell in the 1939-1945 War and are Buried in Cemeteries in Canada; Cemeteries in British Columbia, Yukon Territory and Alberta.* Maidenhead, Eng.: [H.M. Stationery Office], 1972. 82 pp.

_____. *The War Dead of the Commonwealth; the Register of the Names of Those who Fell in the 1939-1945 War and are Buried in Cemeteries in Canada; Cemeteries in New Brunswick, Nova Scotia, Newfoundland and Prince Edward Island.* London: H.M. Stationery Office, 1962. 81 pp.

_____. *The War Dead of the Commonwealth; the Register of the Names of Those who Fell in the 1939-1945 War and are Buried in Cemeteries in Canada; Cemeteries in Quebec.* London: H.M. Stationery Office, 1962. 63 pp.

_____. *The War Dead of the Commonwealth; the Register of the Names of Those who Fell in the 1939-1945 War and are Buried in Cemeteries in Canada; Cemeteries in Saskatchewan and Manitoba.* London: [H.M. Stationery Office], 1963. 79 pp.

_____. *The War Dead of the Commonwealth; the Register of the Names of Those who Fell in the 1939-1945 War and have No Known Grave; the Halifax Memorial.* London: [H.M. Stationery Office], 1968. 2 vols.

Copp, Terry, and Richard Nielson. *No Price Too High; Canadians and the Second World War.* Toronto: McGraw-Hill Ryerson, 1996. 255 pp.

Corbet, E. *Calgary's Stone Frigate; HMCS Tecumseh, 1923-1973.* Calgary: Century Calgary Publications, 1975. 64 pp.

Cowling, Bill. *1413 Days: in the Wake of a Canadian DEMS Gunner.* Calgary: privately printed, 1994. [124] pp.

Cranston, Bobby. *75th Anniversary, Naval Service of Canada; a Pictorial History.* Halifax: 75th Anniversary Pub. Co., [1985]. 1 vol., chiefly illus.

Creighton, (Sir) Kenelm. *Convoy Commodore.* London: W. Kimber, 1956. 205 pp.

The Crow's Nest; a Short Account of the Seagoing Officers Club and the Newfoundland Officers Club, Issued on the Occasion of the Tenth Anniversary, 1942-1952. n.p.: printed by Guardian Press, [1952. 24 pp.]

The Crow's Nest; Fortieth Anniversary, 1942-1982. n.p.: privately printed, [1982]. 107 pp.
Officer's Club, St. John's, Nfld.

Curry, Frank. *War at Sea; a Canadian Seaman on the North Atlantic.* Toronto: Lugus, 1990. 147 pp.

Dancocks, Daniel G. *In Enemy Hands; Canadian Prisoners of War, 1939-45.* Edmonton: Hurtig, 1983. 303 pp.

Davison, Stan. *Canada's Greatest Navy! A Cartoon Seaman's Eye-View of our Sailors in World War Two.* Victoria, B.C.: privately printed, 1967. 132 pp.

————. *When Canada's Navy was Royal.* Victoria, B.C: Winged Isle Yacht Ent., [1985]. 192 pp.
Cartoons.

Desquesnes, Rémy. *Les Canadiens au secours de l'Europe./The Canadians to Europe's Rescue.* Caen, France: Mémorial musée pour la paix, 1992. 194 pp.
Texte bilingue./Bilingual text.

Douglas, W.A.B., ed. *The RCN in Transition, 1910-1985.* Vancouver: Univ. of British Columbia Press, 1988. 411 pp.

Douglas, W.A.B., and Brereton Greenhous. *Out of the Shadows; Canada in the Second World War.* Toronto: Oxford Univ. Press, 1977. 288 pp.
Rev. ed. Toronto: Dundurn Press, 1995. 304 pp.

Drolet, "Gil". *Loyola, the Wars: in Remembrance of "Men for Others".* Waterloo, Ont.: Laurier Centre for Military Strategic and Disarmament Studies, 1996. 44 pp.
Memorial to the war dead of Loyola High School and College.

Dugas, Jean-Guy. *Opération Kiebitz; un rendez-vous à Pointe Maisonette.* Caraquet, N.B.: Les Editions Franc-Jeu, 1992. 85 pp.

Duley, Margaret. *The Caribou Hut; the Story of a Newfoundland Hostel.* Toronto: Ryerson Press, 1949. 82 pp.

Dunnett, Peter J.S. *Royal Roads Military College, 1940-1990; a Pictorial Retrospect.* W. Kim Rempel, photo researcher. Victoria, B.C.: Royal Roads Military College, 1990. 159 pp.

Easton, Allan. *50 North; an Atlantic Battleground.* Toronto: Ryerson Press, 1963. 287 pp.

Elliott-Haynes Limited. *An Enquiry into the Attitude of the Canadian Civilian Public towards the Women's Armed Forces; Conducted on Behalf of the Advertising Agencies of Canada and the Joint Committee on Combined Recruiting Promotion, Women's Services of the Three Armed Forces.* Montreal: privately printed, [194-?]. 33 pp.

Essex, James W. *Victory in the St. Lawrence; Canada's Unknown War.* Erin, Ont.: Boston Mills Press, 1984. 159 pp.

Ettenger, G.H. *History of the Associate Committee on Medical Research, Ottawa, 1938-1946.* Ottawa: n.p., n.d. 46 pp.

Evans, George H. *Through the Corridors of Hell.* Antigonish, N.S.: Formac Pub. Co., 1980. 99 pp.
A Newfoundlander in the Merchant Marine.

Ferguson, Julie H. *Through a Canadian Periscope; the Story of the Canadian Submarine Service.* Toronto: Dundurn Press, 1995. 364 pp.

Fetherstonhaugh, R.C. *McGill University at War, 1914-1918; 1939-1945.* Montreal: McGill Univ., 1947. 437 pp.

For King and Country; Alberta in the Second World War. Edmonton: Provincial Museum of Alberta; Reidmore Books, 1995. 364 pp.

Foster, J.A. *Heart of Oak; a Pictorial History of the Royal Canadian Navy.* Toronto: Methuen, 1985. [143 pp.]

Fowler, T. Robert. *Valour on Juno Beach; the Canadian Awards for Gallantry, D-Day, June 6, 1944.* Burnstown, Ont.: General Store Pub. House, 1994. [104] pp.

Gaffen, Fred. *Cross-Border Warriors; Canadians in American Forces, Americans in Canadian Forces; from the Civil War to the Gulf.* Toronto: Dundurn Press, 1995. 241 pp.

_____. *Forgotten Soldiers.* Penticton, B.C.: Theytus Books, 1985. 152 pp.
Canada's native peoples in two World Wars.

Gaffen, Fred, ed./rédacteur. *The Road to Victory: a History of Canada in the Second World War./La route de la victoire: la participation du Canada à la Deuxième Guerre mondiale.* French translation/Traduction en français: Jean Pariseau. n.p./s.l.: Canadian War Museum/Musée canadien de la guerre; Esprit de corps, 1995. 84 pp.
Bilingual text./Texte bilingue.

Gardam, John. *Fifty Years After.* Burnstown, Ont.: General Store Pub. House, 1990. 141 pp.

_____. *Ordinary Heroes.* Burnstown, Ont.: General Store Pub. House, 1992. 205 pp.

Geneja, Stephen Conrad. *The Cruiser Uganda; One War — Many Conflicts; the First Documented and Eyewitness Account of Canada's Only Cruiser in World War Two and Her Part in the Pacific War.* Corbyville, Ont.: Tyendinaga Publishers, 1994. 282 pp.

[General Motors of Canada, Limited.] *Achievement.* n.p.: [1943]. 74 pp.

German, Tony. *The Sea is at our Gates; the History of the Canadian Navy.* Toronto: McClelland & Stewart, 1990. 360 pp.

Giesler, Patricia. *Valour Remembered; Canada and the Second World War, 1939-1945./Souvenirs de vaillance; la participation du Canada à la Seconde Guerre mondiale, 1939-1945.* Ottawa: Veterans Affairs Canada/Affaires des Anciens combattants Canada, 1981. 45/47 pp.
Bilingual text./Texte bilingue.

Glashan, Keith. *Montreal's Navy; Stories of HMCS Donnacona and its Predeccessors.* [Montreal]: Montreal Branch, Naval Officers' Association of Canada, [1985]. 96 pp.

Goossen, G., and others. *HMCS Naden, 1922-1965.* n.p.: n.d. 1 vol., unpaged.

Gossage, Carolyn. *Greatcoats and Glamour Boots; Canadian Women at War (1939-1945).* Toronto: Dundurn Press, 1991. 215 pp.

Granatstein, J.L., and Desmond Morton. *A Nation Forged in Fire; Canadians and the Second World War 1939-1945.* Toronto: Lester & Orpen Dennys, 1989. 287 pp.

Gt. Brit. Imperial War Graves Commission. *The War Dead of the British Commonwealth and Empire; the Register of the Names of Those who Fell in the 1939-1945 War and are Buried in Cemeteries and Churchyards in Surrey; Brookwood Military Cemetery, Woking.* London: [H.M. Stationery Office], 1958. 3 vols.

Greer, Rosamond "Fiddy". *The Girls of the King's Navy.* Victoria, B.C.: Sono Nis Press, 1983. 160 pp.

Gregory, Walter, and Michael Ticehurst. *Memories of H.M.C.S. Trentonian; Alias K368; Trenton's Own Ship.* n.p.: [1979]. 72 pp.

Gutta Percha and Rubber, Limited. *A Selection of Badge Designs of the Canadian Forces.* Toronto: n.p., n.d. 16 pp., chiefly illus.

HMCS Cornwallis. Cornwallis, N.S.: n.p., n.d. 1 vol., unpaged.

H.M.C.S. Nene; Reunion, Belleville, Ontario, 1985. Shannonville, Ont.: privately printed, [1985]. 1 vol., unpaged.

Hacking, N.R. *Naval Officers Association of British Columbia; a Record of Achievement, 1919-1959.* n.p.: n.d. 32 pp.

Hadley, Michael L. *U-Boats Against Canada; German Submarines in Canadian Waters.* Kingston, Ont.: McGill-Queen's Univ. Press, 1985. 360 pp.

Halford, Robert G. *The Unknown Navy; Canada's World War II Merchant Navy.* St. Catharines, Ont.: Vanwell Pub., 1995. 272 pp.

Harbron, John D. *The Longest Battle; the Royal Canadian Navy in the Atlantic, 1939-1945.* St. Catharines, Ont.: Vanwell Pub., 1993. 132 pp.

Hawkins, Ronald F. *We will Remember Them.* Woodstock, N.B.: privately printed, 1995. [239] pp.
Memoirs of New Brunswick Second World War veterans.

Heal, S.C. *Conceived in War, Born in Peace: Canada's Deep Sea Merchant Marine.* Vancouver: Cordillera Pub. Co., 1992. 234 pp.

Henderson, Peter A. *Guarding the Gates: a History of Canadian Forces Station St. Johns.* St. John's, Nfld.: CFS St. John's, 1992. 115 pp.

Hermann, J. Douglas. *Report to the Minister of Veterans Affairs of a Study on Canadians who were Prisoners of War in Europe during World War II./Rapport présenté au Ministre des Affaires des anciens combattants au sujet d'une enquête portant sur les Canadiens prisonniers de guerre en Europe au cours de la Seconde Guerre mondiale.* Ottawa: Queen's Printer/Imprimeur de la Reine, 1973. 56/60 pp.
Bilingual text./Texte bilingue.

Hibbert, Joyce. *Fragments of War; Stories from Survivors of World War II.* Toronto: Dundurn Press, 1985. 267 pp.

Hill, J. Kirkbride, comp. *The Price of Freedom.* Toronto: Ryerson Press, 1942-44. 2 vols.

Hitsman, J. Mackay. *Canadian Naval Policy.* Kingston, Ont.: Queen's Univ., 1940. 208 pp.

Hoare, John. *Tumult in the Clouds; a Story of the Fleet Air Arm.* London: Joseph, 1976. 208 pp.

Hodgins, J. Herbert, and others, comps. *Women at War.* Montreal: MacLean Pub., 1943. 190 pp.

Holloway, Ian. *Self-Reliance through Service; the Story of Her Majesty's Canadian Ship Scotian.* Hantsport, N.S.: Lancelot Press, 1988. 116 pp.

Hopkins, Anthony. *Songs from the Front & Rear; Canadian Servicemen's Songs of the Second World War.* Edmonton: Hurtig Publishers, 1979. 192 pp.

Horrocks, William. *In their own Words.* Ottawa: Rideau Veterans Home Residents Council, 1993. 247 pp.

Houghton, F.L., comp. *H.M.C.S. Skeena, 1931-1932; Commemorating her First Year in Commission.* Victoria, B.C.: privately printed, n.d. 80 pp.

How, Douglas. *Night of the Caribou.* Hantsport, N.S.: Lancelot Press, 1988. 153 pp.

*Jellicoe, John Rushworth Jellicoe, 1st earl. *Report of Admiral of the Fleet, Viscount Jellicoe of Scapa, G.C.B., O.M., G.C.V.O., on Mission to the Dominion of Canada, November-December, 1919.* Ottawa: n.p., n.d. 3 vols. *Vol. I also printed as Sessional Paper no. 61, 1920. Vol. II-III originally Secret .*

*Jellicoe, John Rushworth Jellicoe, 1er earl. *Rapport de l'Amiral de la Flotte le Vicomte Jellicoe de Scapa, G.C.B., O.M., G.C.V.O., sur la mission navale au Canada en novembre et décembre 1919.* (Document de la session, no 61.) Ottawa: Imprimeur du Roi, 1920. 59 pp.

Johnson, Bill. *The Prince Robert.* Sidney, B.C.: ViP Graphic Studio, 1988. 22 pp.

Johnston, Mac. *Corvettes Canada; Convoy Veterans of WW II Tell their True Stories.* Toronto: McGraw-Hill Ryerson, 1994. 310 pp.

Journal of the Edmonton Military Institute. Vol. I-IV? Edmonton: Edmonton Military Institute, 1937-46?

*Kealy, J.D.F., and E.C. Russell. *A History of Canadian Naval Aviation, 1918-1962.* Ottawa: Queen's Printer, 1965. 164 pp.

*Kealy, J.D.F., et E.C. Russell. *Histoire de l'aéronavale canadienne, 1918-1962.* Ottawa: Imprimeur de la Reine, 1965. 185 pp.

Kellock, R.L., *see* Canada. Royal Commission to Conduct an Inquiry into Certain Disorders Occurring May 7-8, 1945, in the City of Halifax.

Kelsey Club, Winnipeg, Man. *Canadian Defence; What We have to Defend; Various Defence Policies.* Toronto: T. Nelson, 1937. 98 pp.

Laing, Gertrude. *A Community Organized for War; the Story of the Greater Winnipeg Co-ordinating Board for War Services and Affiliated Organizations, 1939-1946.* Winnipeg: n.p., 1948. 103 pp.

Lamb, James B. *The Corvette Navy; True Stories from Canada's Atlantic War.* Toronto: Macmillan, 1977. 179 pp.

_____. *On the Triangle Run.* Toronto: Macmillan, 1986. 237 pp.

Lamb, Ken. *Milton Remembers World War II.* Milton, Ont.: Milton Historical Society, 1995. 140 pp.

Law, C. Anthony. *White Plumes Astern; the Short, Daring Life of Canada's MTB Flotilla.* Halifax: Nimbus Pub., 1989. 170 pp.

Lawrence, Hal. *A Bloody War; One Man's Memories of the Canadian Navy, 1939-1945.* Toronto: Macmillan, 1979. 193 pp.

_____. *Tales of the North Atlantic.* Toronto: McClelland and Stewart, 1985. 256 pp.

_____. *Victory at Sea; Tales of His Majesty's Coastal Forces.* Toronto: McClelland & Stewart, 1989. 322 pp.

Lay, H. Nelson. *Memoirs of a Mariner.* Stittsville, Ont.: Canada's Wings, 1982. 326 pp.

Leacock, Stephen, and Leslie Roberts. *Canada's War at Sea.* Montreal: A.M. Beatty, 1944. 2 vols. in 1.

Leggett, Harry Furniss. *Spindrift; Yarns of a West Coast Seaman as Told to his Grandchildren.* Victoria, B.C.: privately printed, n.d. 88 pp.

Lévesque, Thérèse. *Laisse-moi te dire ...; la guerre 1939/45 après 50 ans.* Saint-Quentin, N.-B.: Imprimerie Lévesque, 1990. 171 pp.

Little, C.H. *Naval Paintings/Tableaux navals/of the Second World War/de la Seconde Guerre mondiale/Naval Reserves in Canada/ Les réserves navales au Canada.* Ottawa: National Museums of Canada/Musées nationaux du Canada, 1973. 30 pp.
Bilingual text./Texte bilingue.

Littler, John Caldecott. *Sea Fever.* Victoria, B.C.: Kiwi Publications, 1995. [334] pp.
Memoirs of service with Royal Canadian Navy, 1940-1962.

The Log; Royal Roads Military College. Vol. V- . Victoria, B.C.: privately printed, 1942- .

Longard, John R. *Knots, Volts and Decibels; an Informal History of the Naval Research Establishment, 1940-1967.* Dartmouth, N.S.: Defence Research Establishment Atlantic, 1993. [115] pp.

Longstaff, F.V. *Esquimalt Naval Base; a History of its Work and its Defences.* Vancouver: Clarke & Stuart, 1941. 189 pp.

Lynch, Mack. *Orion Mighty Warrior.* Toronto: Lugus, 1992. 313 pp.
Memoirs of a Canadian radar officer in HMS Orion.

Lynch, Thomas G., *Canada's Flowers; History of the Corvettes of Canada, 1939-1945.* (Military Journal Special 5.) Bennington, Vt.: International Graphics, 1981. 100 pp.

Lynch, Thomas G., and James B. Lamb. *Gunshield Graffiti; Unofficial Badges of Canada's Wartime Navy.* Illus. by L.B. Jenson. Halifax: Nimbus Pub., 1984. 144 pp., chiefly illus.

*McAndrew, William J., Bill Rawling and Michael Whitby. *Liberation; the Canadians in Europe.* Montreal: Art Global, 1995. 170 pp.

*McAndrew, William J., Bill Rawling et Michael Whitby. *La Libération; les Canadiens en Europe.* Montréal: Art Global, 1995. 170 pp.

*McAndrew, William J., Donald E. Graves and Michael Whitby. *Normandy 1944; the Canadian Summer.* Montreal: Art Global, 1994. 162 pp.

*McAndrew, William J., Donald E. Graves et Michael Whitby. *Normandie 1944; l'été canadien.* Montréal: Art Global, 1994. 162 pp.

Macbeth, Jack. *Ready, Aye, Ready; an Illustrated History of the Royal Canadian Navy.* Toronto: Key Porter Books, n.d. 176 pp.

Macdonald, Angus L. *Speeches of Angus L. Macdonald.* Toronto: Longmans, Green, 1960. 227 pp.

Macdonald, Grant. *Our Canadian Armed Services,* sketches by Grant Macdonald. Montreal: Gazette, 1943. 1 vol., chiefly illus.

_____. *Sailors.* Toronto: Macmillan, 1945. 153 pp.

McElheran, Brock. *V-Bombs and Weathermaps; Reminiscences of World War II.* Montreal: McGill-Queen's Univ. Press, 1995. 199 pp.

MacFarlane, John, and Robbie Hughes. *Canada's Naval Aviators.* Victoria, B.C.: Maritime Museum of British Columbia, 1994. 182 pp.

McGill Univ., Montreal, P.Q. *A Memorial Service for the McGill Men and Women who Gave their Lives during the First and Second World Wars.* n.p.: [1946]. 1 vol., unpaged.

McGrane, J.E. *The Exeter and the North Saskatchewan.* Lac La Biche, Alta.: privately printed, 1950. 107 pp.

McKay, John, and John Harland. *The Flower Class Corvette Agassiz.* (Anatomy of the Ship.) St. Catharines, Ont.: Vanwell Pub., 1993. 160 pp.

McKee, Fraser M. *The Armed Yachts of Canada.* Erin, Ont.: Boston Mills Press, 1983. 172 pp.

_____. *HMCS Swansea; the Life and Times of a Frigate.* St. Catharines, Ont.: Vanwell Pub., 1994. 190 pp.

_____. *Volunteers for Sea Service; a Brief History of the Royal Canadian Naval Volunteer Reserve, its Predecessors and Successors, on its 50th Anniversary, 1973.* Toronto: privately printed, 1973. 69 pp.

McNeil, Bill. *Voices of a War Remembered; an Oral History of Canadians in World War Two.* Toronto: Doubleday Canada, 1991. 376 pp.

Macpherson, K.R. *Canada's Fighting Ships.* (Canadian War Museum Historical Publication Number 12.) Toronto: Hakkert, 1975. 116 pp.

_____. *Frigates of the Royal Canadian Navy, 1943-1974.* St. Catharines, Ont.: Vanwell Pub., 1989. 109 pp.

_____. *Minesweepers of the Royal Canadian Navy 1938-1945.* St. Catharines, Ont.: Vanwell Pub., 1990. 110 pp.

_____. *The River Class Destroyers of the Royal Canadian Navy.* Toronto: Musson, 1985. 103 pp.

Macpherson, K.R., and John Burgess. *The Ships of Canada's Naval Forces, 1910-1981; a Complete Pictorial History of Canadian Warships.* Toronto: Collins, 1981. 240 pp.
Rev. eds. Toronto: Collins 1985 and St. Catharines, Ont.: Vanwell Pub., 1993.

Macpherson, K.R., and Marc Milner. *Corvettes of the Royal Canadian Navy, 1939-1945.* St. Catharines, Ont.: Vanwell Pub., 1993. 174 pp.

Mansikka, Eric, comp. *Pack Up Your Troubles; Canadian War Humour.* Cartoons by Paul Gomiratto. Toronto: Methuen, 1987. 112 pp.
Second World War humour accompanied by original cartoons.

[Maritime Museum of Canada.] *Souvenir of the Maritime Museum of Canada, Halifax, Nova Scotia.* [Halifax: n.p., 195-?] 44 pp.

Mayne, J.W. *Operational Research in the Canadian Armed Forces during the Second World War.* (Operational Research and Analysis Establishment ORAE Report, no. R68.) Ottawa: Dept. of National Defence, 1978. 2 vols.

Metson, Graham, and Cheryl Lean, comps. *An East Coast Port ... Halifax at War 1939-1945.* Toronto: McGraw-Hill Ryerson, 1981. 157 pp.

Middleton, W.E. Knowles. *Radar Development in Canada: the Radio Branch of the National Research Council of Canada, 1939-1946.* Waterloo, Ont.: Wilfrid Laurier Univ. Press, 1981. 147 pp.

Milne, Gilbert A. *H.M.C.S.; One Photographer's Impressions of the Royal Canadian Navy in World War II.* Toronto: T. Allen, 1960. 141 pp.

Milner, Marc. *Canadian Naval Force Requirements in the Second World War.* (Operational Research and Analysis Establishment ORAE Extra-Mural Paper no. 20.) Ottawa: Dept. of National Defence, 1981. 113 pp.

_____. *North Atlantic Run; the Royal Canadian Navy and the Battle for the Conovys.* Toronto: Univ. of Toronto Press, 1985. 326 pp.

_____. *The U-Boat Hunters; the Royal Canadian Navy and the Offensive against Germany's Submarines.* Toronto: Univ. of Toronto Press, 1994. 326 pp.

Mirtle, Jack. *The Naden Band: a History.* Victoria, B.C.: Jackstays Pub., 1990. 167 pp.

Mowat, Farley. *The Grey Seas Under.* Toronto: McClelland and Stewart, 1958. 341 pp.

Murphy, Tony, and Paul Kenney. *The War at our Doorstep; St. John's during World War Two, an Album.* St. John's, Nfld.: H. Cuff Publications, 1989. 120 pp.

Murray, Joan. *Canadian Artists of the Second World War.* Oshawa, Ont.: Robert McLaughlin Gallery, 1981. 124 pp.

Naval Officers' Association of Canada. London Branch. *H.M.C.S. Prevost, London, Canada.* [London, Ont.: London Branch, Naval Officers' Association of Canada, 196-?] 67 pp.

Nene Lives; the Story of H.M.C.S. Nene & her Crew. n.p.: [1992]. 122 pp.

Nicholson, G.W.L. *More Fighting Newfoundlanders; a History of Newfoundland's Fighting Forces in the Second World War.* [St. John's, Nfld.]: Govt. of Nfld., 1969. 621 pp.

Nolan, Brian, and Brian Jeffrey Street. *Champagne Navy; Canada's Small Boat Raiders of the Second World War.* Toronto: Random House, 1991. 260 pp.

Nova Scotia. *Nova Scotia Helps the Fighting Man.* n.p.: [1942]. 32 pp.

O'Connor, Edward. *The Corvette Years; the Lower Deck Story.* Vancouver: Cordillera Pub. Co., 1995. 191 pp.

O'Neill, E.C., ed. *The Canadian Raleighites; Ordinary Seamen and Officers at War, 1940-1945.* Waterloo, Ont.: privately printed. 1988. 267 pp.

Outerbridge. L.M., ed. *H.M.S. Puncher, D-Day — 1944 to V.E. and V.J. — 1945.* Vancouver: privately printed, n.d. 128 pp.

Paquette, Edward R., and Charles G. Bainbridge, eds. *Honours and Awards, Canadian Naval Forces, World War II.* Victoria, B.C.: Project Gallantry, [1986]. v.p.

Parker, Mike. *Running the Gauntlet; an Oral History of Canadian Merchant Seamen in World War II.* Halifax: Nimbus Pub., 1994. 344 pp.

Popp, Carol. *The Gumboot Navy; Memories of the Men who Served in the Fisherman's Reserve — a Special Naval Unit Formed to Patrol the Coast of British Columbia during World War II.* Lantzville, B.C.: Oolichan Books, 1988. 159 pp.

Preston, Richard A. *Canada's RMC; a History of the Royal Military College.* Toronto: Univ. of Toronto Press, 1969. 415 pp.

Proulx, Benjamin A. *Underground from Hongkong.* New York: Dutton, 1943. 214 pp.

Puddester, J., ed. *The Crow's Nest (Officers Club); 30th Anniversary Souvenir, 1942-1972.* St. John's, Nfld.: privately printed, 1972. 51 pp.

Pugsley, William H. *Sailor Remember.* Toronto: Collins, 1948. 185 pp.

_____. *Saints, Devils and Ordinary Seamen; Life on the Royal Canadian Navy's Lower Deck.* Toronto: Collins, 1945. 241 pp.

The Rally Magazine. Vol. 1-? Wrecclesham, Eng.: n.p., 1939?-?
A monthly magazine for Canadian Active Service Forces.

Reader's Digest. *The Canadians at War, 1939/45.* Montreal: Reader's Digest, 1969. 2 vols.

_____. *The Tools of War, 1939/45, and a Chronology of Important Events.* Montreal: Reader's Digest, 1969. 96 pp.

Redman, Stanley R. *Open Gangway; the (Real) Story of the Halifax Navy Riot.* Hantsport, N.S.: Lancelot Press, 1981. 167 pp.

Reed, R.H. "Hank", ed. *East Camp No. 1 NAGS Yarmouth, N.S.; Memories.* Yarmouth, N.S.: R.H. Davis, 1984. 140 pp.

Reid, Max. *D.E.M.S. and the Battle of the Atlantic 1939-1945.* Ottawa: Commoners' Pub-Society, 1990. 100 pp.
Cover title: DEMS at War! Defensively Equipped Merchant Ships and the Battle of the Atlantic 1939-1945.

Revely, Henry. *The Convoy that Nearly Died; the Story of ONS 154.* London: W. Kimber, 1979. 222 pp.

Richards, S.T. *Operation Sick Bay.* West Vancouver, B.C.: Centaur Pub., 1994. 267 pp.
The story of the Sick Berth & Medical Assistant Branch of the Royal Canadian Navy, 1910-1965.

Robertson, Heather, [comp.] *A Terrible Beauty; the Art of Canada at War.* Toronto: J. Lorimer, 1977. 239 pp.

Robertson, Peter. *Irréductible vérité/Relentless Verity/les photographes militaires canadiens depuis 1885/Canadian Military Photographers since 1885.* (Les Archives publiques du Canada/Public Archives of Canada Series.) Québec, P.Q.: Les Presses de l'Université Laval, 1973. 233 pp.
Texte bilingue./Bilingual text.

Royal Canadian Navy Monthly Review (R.C.N.M.R.). Ottawa: King's Printer, 1942-45, 1947-48.

Royal Canadian Navy, 1910-1960; the First Fifty Years. n.p.: 1960. v.p.

Royal Military College of Canada, Kingston, Ont. *Regulations and Calendar of the Royal Military College of Canada, 1922.* Ottawa: King's Printer, 1923. 68 pp.

————. *Standing Orders, Amended to January, 1924.* Ottawa: King's Printer, 1924. 120 pp.

————. *Standing Orders, Amended to January, 1926.* Ottawa: King's Printer, 1926. 105 pp.

————. *Standing Orders; the Royal Military College of Canada, 1938.* Ottawa: King's Printer, 1938. 67 pp.

The Royal Military College of Canada Review. Vol. I- . Kingston, Ont.: privately printed, 1920- .

Russell, E.C. *H.M.C.S. Haida; a Brief History.* n.p.: n.d. 56 pp.

Sallans, G.H. *With Canada's Fighting Men.* Ottawa: King's Printer, 1941. 46 pp.

Salty Dips. Ottawa: Ottawa Branch, Naval Officers' Association of Canada, 1983-93. 4 vols.

*Savard, Adjutor. *The Defence of our Land.* n.p.: 1943. 12 pp.

* ————. *La défense du territoire.* s.l.: s.i., 1943. 11 pp.

*Schull, Joseph. *The Far Distant Ships; an Official Account of Canadian Naval Operations in the Second World War.* Ottawa: King's Printer, 1950. 515 pp.

* ————. *Lointains navires; compte rendu officiel des opérations de la Marine canadienne au cours de la Seconde grande Guerre.* Ottawa: Imprimeur de la Reine, 1953. 605 pp.

————. *Ships of the Great Days; Canada's Navy in World War II.* (Great Stories of Canada.) Toronto: Macmillan, 1962. 156 pp.

Sclater, William. *Haida.* Toronto: Oxford Univ. Press, 1947. 221 pp.

Sea Breezes. Vol. I-III. Halifax: privately printed, 1914-22.
Journal of the Royal Naval College of Canada.

Shea, A.A., and E. Estoriak. *Canada and the Short-Wave War.* (Behind the Headlines, vol. III.) Toronto: Canadian Institute of International Affairs, 1942. 36 pp.

Sheffield, E.F. *Portraits of the Officers in Charge of the 21st Officers' Disciplinary Course in H.M.C.S. "Cornwallis" and of the Twenty-Three Members of the Class.* Grant Macdonald, illus. [n.p.: privately printed, 1943. 32 pp.]

Six Years and a Day; the Story of the Beaver Club, 1940-1946. London: n.p., n.d. 34 pp.

Smith, Marilyn Gurney. *The King's Yard; an Illustrated History of the Halifax Dockyard.* Halifax: Nimbus Pub., 1985. 56 pp.

Smith, Waldo E.L. *The Navy Chaplain and his Parish.* Ottawa: Queen's Printer, 1967. 264 pp.

*Stacey, C.P. *Armes, hommes et gouvernements; les politiques de guerre du Canada, 1939-1945.* Ottawa: Imprimeur de la Reine, 1970. 747 pp.

*_____. *Arms, Men and Governments; the War Policies of Canada, 1939-1945.* Ottawa: Queen's Printer, 1970. 681 pp.

Stacey, C.P., and Barbara M. Wilson. *The Half-Million; the Canadians in Britian, 1939-1946.* Toronto: Univ. of Toronto Press, 1987. 198 pp.

Stanley, George F. G., and Richard A. Preston. *A Short History of Kingston as a Military and Naval Centre.* Kingston, Ont.: Queen's Printer, [195-?]. 33 pp.

Stead, Gordon W. *A Leaf upon the Sea; a Small Ship in the Mediterranean, 1941-1943.* Vancouver: Univ. of British Columbia Press, 1988. 185 pp.

Stephens, W. Ray. *The Canadian Entertainers of World War II.* Oakville, Ont.: Mosaic Press, 1993. 116 pp.

Strachan, Tony, ed. *In the Clutch of Circumstance; Reminiscences of Members of the Canadian National Prisoners of War Association.* Victoria, B.C.: Cappis Press, 1985. 285 pp.

Strange, William. *Into the Blitz; a British Journey.* Toronto: Macmillan, 1941. 318 pp.

_____. *Ships Mean Freedom.* Ottawa: King's Printer, [1942]. 63 pp.

_____. *Ships Mean Life.* [Toronto: privately printed, 1944.] 64 pp.

_____. *Ships Mean Security.* Ottawa: King's Printer, [1946]. 54 pp.

_____. *Ships Mean Victory.* [Toronto: privately printed, 1942.] 63 pp.

*Summerby, Janice. *Native Soldiers; Foreign Battlefields.* Ottawa: Communications Division, Veterans Affairs Canada, 1993. 47 pp.

*_____. *Soldats autochtones; terres étrangères.* Ottawa: Direction générale des communications, Anciens combattants Canada, 1993. 51 pp.

Suthren, Victor, ed. *The Oxford Book of Canadian Military Anecdotes.* Toronto: Oxford Univ. Press, 1989. 202 pp.

Swain, Hector. *History of the Naval Reserves in Newfoundland.* [St. John's, Nfld.: Provincial Archives, 1975.] 56 pp.

Swettenham, John. *D-Day./Jour-J.* Jacques Gouin, tr. Ottawa: National Museum of Man/Musée national de l'homme, [1970]. 27/30 pp.
Bilingual text./Texte bilingue.

Swettenham, John, and Fred Gaffen. *Canada's Atlantic War.* Toronto: Samuel-Stevens, 1979. 154 pp.

Thibault, Jean. *Drummondville à l'heure de la guerre: 1939-1945.* Drummondville (Qué): La Société d'histoire de Drummondville, 1994. 191 pp.

Thompson, Brad. *H.M.C.S. Griffon; a Naval History.* Thunder Bay, Ont.: Thunder Bay Naval Association, 1985. 98 pp.

Thompson, Roy J.C. *Wings of the Canadian Armed Forces, 1913-1972.* [Dartmouth], N.S.: n.p., 1973. 106 pp.

Thornton, J.M. *The Big 'U'; a History of HMCS Uganda/Quebec.* [Vancouver]: privately printed, 1983. 68 pp.

_____. *H.M.C.S. Discovery and Deadman's Island; a Brief History ....* n.p.: [197-?]. 52 pp.

The Tiddley Times; the W.R.C.N.S. Magazine. Ottawa: King's Printer, ?-1945.

A Tribute to Valour. St. Thomas, Ont.: printed by Sutherland Press, 1945. 169 pp.
Memorial book of Dunwich Township and village of Dutton, Ont.

Trinity College School Old Boys at War, 1899-1902, 1914-1918, 1939-1945. Port Hope, Ont.: privately printed, 1948. 245 pp.

True Canadian War Stories, selected by Jane Dewar from the pages of Legion Magazine. Toronto: Lester & Orpen Dennys, 1986. 310 pp

Tucker, Gilbert Norman. *A History of the Royal Canadian Navy.* Ottawa: King's Printer, 1951. 16 pp.

_____. *The Naval Service of Canada; its Official History.* Ottawa: King's Printer, 1952. 2 vols.

The University of Alberta in the War of 1939-45. Edmonton: n.p., 1948. 70 pp.

Univ. of Toronto. *Memorial Book, Second World War, 1939-1945.* H.E. Brown, comp. Toronto: Soldiers' Tower Committee, Univ. of Toronto, 1994. 84 pp.

Veterans' Review; a Collection of War Stories. Toronto: privately printed, 1983. 255 pp.

War Record; the McGill Chapter of Delta Upsilon, 1939-1945. Montreal: n.p., 1946. 83 pp.

Warrilow, Betty. *"Nabob"; the First Canadian-Manned Aircraft Carrier.* Owen Sound, Ont.: Escort Carriers Association, 1989. 210 pp.

Waters, John M. *Bloody Winter.* Princeton, N.J.: Van Nostrand, 1967. 279 pp.

Watt, Frederick B. *In All Respects Ready; the Merchant Navy and the Battle of the Atlantic, 1940-1945.* Scarborough, Ont.: Prentice-Hall Canada, 1985. 222 pp.

Wellington Legion War Veterans Club, eds. *They served for Freedom./A la défense de la liberté.* [Wellington, P.E.I.: Royal Canadian Legion, Wellington Branch 17/Wellington, I.P.E.: Légion royale canadienne, la filiale de Wellington no 17,] 1986. 319 pp.
Bilingual text./Texte bilingue.

Wells, George Anderson. *The Fighting Bishop; as Recounted in the Eighty-Seventh Year of his Life to his Daughter Jeanne Carden Wells.* Toronto: Cardwell House, 1971. 628 pp.

Wells, Herb. *Comrades in Arms.* St. John's, Nfld.: printed by Robinson-Blackmore Print. & Pub., 1986-88. 2 vols.
Newfoundlanders in action, Second World War.

_____. *Under the White Ensign.* Volume I. St. John's, Nfld.: printed by Robinson Blackmore Print. & Pub., 1981. 308 pp.
Cover title: A History of Newfoundland Naval Seamen, Second World War.

Whitby, Michael J. *Relentless in Chase; a History of HMCS Iroquois I and II; Comrades in Arms, Relentless in Chase.* n.p.: [1992]. 60 pp.

Whitehead, William. *Dieppe, 1942; Echoes of Disaster.* Terence Macartney-Filgate, ed. (A Personal Library Publication.) Don Mills, Ont.: Nelson, 1979. 187 pp., chiefly illus.

Whitton, Charlotte. *Canadian Women in the War Effort.* Toronto: Macmillan, 1942. 56 pp.

Wilkinson, William Arthur, and Geoff Nightingale. *Making a Difference; the Memoirs of William Arthur Wilkinson.* Windsor, Ont.: Herald Press, 1995. 163 pp.

[Willson, Gordon Beckles.] *Canada Comes to England*, by Gordon Beckles [*pseud.*] London: Hodder and Stoughton, 1941. 166 pp.

Winters, B.A. *H.M.C.S. Discovery; a History of the Naval Reserve in Vancouver.* n.p.: [1995]. 1 vol., unpaged.

Witt, Eugene, and Jim Thomas. *Ship Repair Adventure; HMC Dockyard Esquimalt.* Victoria, B.C.: printed by Hillside Print. Co., 1985. 164 pp.

Wodehouse, R.F. *A Check List of the War Collections of World War I, 1914-1918, and World War II, 1939-1945.* Ottawa: Queen's Printer, 1968. 239 pp.

Wong, Marjorie. *The Dragon and the Maple Leaf; Chinese Canadians in World War II.* London, Ont.: Pirie Pub., 1994. 274 pp.

Wright, Bruce S. *The Frogmen of Burma; the Story of the Sea Reconnaissance Unit.* Toronto: Clarke, Irwin, 1968. 152 pp.

Wright, Harold E., and Byron E. O'Leary. *Fortress Saint John; an Illustrated Military History, 1640-1985.* Saint John, N.B.: Partridge Island Research Project, 1985. 131 pp.

Wright, J., comp. *Music Ashore and Afloat; Famous Bands of the R.C.N.* Wallaceburg, Ont.: Standard Press, 1945. 1 vol., unpaged.

Young, Albert Charles. *24 Good Men and True; Members of Branch #142 of the Royal Canadian Legion.* New York: Vantage Press, 1992. 219 pp.

Young, George. *The Short Triangle; a Story of the Sea and Men who Go Down to It in Ships; the Place, the Coasts of New England and Nova Scotia; the Time, Summer — 1942.* Lunenburg, N.S.: privately printed, 1975. 79 pp.

_____. *Who Killed Surcouf?* Queensland, N.S.: privately printed, 1986. 103 pp.

Young Men's Christian Associations, Canada. *The 1st Year; a War Service Record of the Canadian Y.M.C.A. from the Outbreak of the War.* n.p.: [1940]. 23 pp.

Young Men's Christian Associations, Canada. National Council. War Services Executive. *With Arthur Jones through 5 Years of War; a Report of Canadian Y.M.C.A. War Services.* n.p.: n.d. 1 vol., unpaged.

Young, Scott. *Red Shield in Action; a Record of Canadian Salvation Army War Services in the Second Great War.* Toronto: F.F. Clarke, 1949. 149 pp.

Zarn, George. *Prairie Boys Afloat.* n.p.: privately printed, 1979. 260 pp.

Zimmerman, David. *The Great Naval Battle of Ottawa.* Toronto: Univ. of Toronto Press, 1989. 209 pp.

1946-1967

Air Force College Journal. Toronto: privately printed, 1956-64. 9 vols. *Title varies.*

*Appleton, Thomas E. *Usque ad Mare; a History of the Canadian Coast Guard and Marine Services.* Ottawa: Queen's Printer, 1968. 318 pp.

*_____. *Usque ad mare; historique de la Garde côtière canadienne et des Services de la Marine.* Ottawa: Ministère des Transports, 1968. 349 pp.

Arbuckle, Graeme. *Badges of the Canadian Navy.* Halifax: Nimbus Pub., 1987. 203 pp.

_____. *Customs and Traditions of the Canadian Navy.* Halifax: Nimbus Pub., 1984. 179 pp.

*Barton, William H. *Science and the Armed Services.* (Current Affairs for the Canadian Forces, vol. II, no. 1.) Ottawa: King's Printer, 1952. 22 pp.

*_____. *La science et les Services armés.* (Actualités; revue destinée aux Forces canadiennes, vol II, no 1.) Ottawa: Imprimeur du Roi, 1952. 22 pp

Bidwell, R.E.S. *Random Memories.* Ottawa: privately printed, [1962. 21 pp.]

Bishop, William Arthur. *Courage at Sea.* (Canada's Military Heritage, Volume III.) Toronto: McGraw-Hill Ryerson, 1995. 191 pp.

Blatherwick, F.J. *Royal Canadian Navy Honours — Decorations — Medals, 1910-1968.* New Westminster, B.C.: FJB AIR Publications, 1992. 86 pp.

Boutilier, James A., ed. *The RCN in Retrospect, 1910-1968.* Vancouver: Univ. of British Columbia Press, 1982. 373 pp.

Bowering, Clifford H. *Service; the Story of the Canadian Legion, 1925-1960.* Ottawa: privately printed, 1960. 240 pp.

Brock, Jeffry V. *With Many Voices.* Toronto: McClelland and Stewart, 1981-83. 2 vols.

Brock, Jeffry V. *see also* Canada. Naval Service Headquarters. Ad Hoc Committee on Naval Objectives.

Butcher, Alan D. *I Remember Haida.* Hantsport, N.S.: Lancelot Press, 1985. 163 pp.

CNAV Endeavour AGOR 171 Oceanographic Research Vessel. Ottawa: Queen's Printer, 1965. 1 vol., unpaged.

Canada. Armed Forces. H.M.C.S. Qu'appelle. *HMCS Qu'appelle; Commissioned September 14 1963, Paid Off April 4 1992.* Winnipeg: [printed by] Herff Jones, [1992]. 73 pp.

Canada. Armed Forces. H.M.C.S. Unicorn. *History of Unicorn, 1923-1973*. n.p.: n.d. v.p.

Canada. Canadian Forces Headquarters. *Canadian Forces Administrative Orders*. Ottawa: n.p., 1965-71.
Issued as a non-chronological sequence in which orders were discarded when obsolete. Superseded by a bilingual format in 1972.

Canada. Court Martial Appeal Board. *Court Martial Appeal Reports*. Ottawa: Queen's Printer, 1957-73. 3 vols.

*Canada. Dept. of National Defence. *The Defence Research Board, Canada*. n.p.: n.d. 1 vol, unpaged.

_____. *Defence Research Board; the First Twenty-Five Years./Conseil de recherches pour la défense; les 25 premières années*. Ottawa: Queen's Printer/Imprimeur de la Reine, 1972. 46 pp.
Bilingual text./ Texte bilingue.

_____. *The King's Regulations and Orders for the Royal Canadian Navy*. (BRCN 101-103.) Ottawa: King's Printer, 1951. 3 vols., looseleaf.

_____. *Manual of the Canadian Forces Medical Service in the Field, 1959*. Ottawa: Queen's Printer, 1959. 324 pp., looseleaf.

_____. *The Naval Officer*. Ottawa: Queen's Printer, 1956. 14 pp.

_____. *The Queen's Regulations and Orders for the Canadian Forces*. Ottawa: Queen's Printer, 1965. 3 vols., looseleaf.

_____. *The Queen's Regulations and Orders for the Royal Canadian Navy*. (BRCN 101-103.) Ottawa: Queen's Printer, 1952. 3 vols., looseleaf.

*_____. *Queens Regulations for the Canadian Services Colleges*. Ottawa: Queens Printer, 1958. 1 vol., unpaged.

*_____. *Report*. Ottawa: King's Printer, 1923-59.
Title varies. Annual most years.

*_____. *White Paper on Defence*. Ottawa: Queen's Printer, 1964. 30 pp.

Canada. Dept. of National Defence. Defence Research Board. *Review./Revue*, [par le] Conseil de recherches pour la Défense du Canada. Ottawa: Dept. of National Defence/Ministère de la Défense nationale, 1966-73.
Bilingual text. Title varies: Annual Report (1966)./Texte bilingue. Divergence du titre: Rapport annuel (1966).

*Canada. Dept. of National Defence (Naval Service). *Report on Certain "Incidents" which Occurred on Board H.M.C. Ships Athabaskan, Crescent and Magnificent, and on Other Matters Concerning the Royal Canadian Navy Made to the Minister of National Defence by a Commission Duly Appointed for the Above Purpose ... Ottawa, October, 1949*. Ottawa: King's Printer, 1949. 57 pp.

Canada. Dept. of the Naval Service. *The Canadian Navy List*. Ottawa: King's Printer, 1914-65.
Issued by the Dept. of National Defence from 1923.

Canada. Dept. of Veterans Affairs. *Commemoration; Canadians in Korea, 1978./Souvenir; Canadiens en Corée, 1978.* n.p./s.l.: s.i., [1978. 14 pp.] *Bilingual text./Texte bilingue.*

*Canada. Marine. *Carrières de la Marine pour les diplômés et les étudiants d'université.* Ottawa: Imprimeur de la Reine, 1962. 28 pp.

_____. *Carrières et formation.* Ottawa: Imprimeur de la Reine, 1964. 32 pp.

*_____. *Formation et carrières dans la Marine à l'intention des élèves des écoles secondaires.* Ottawa: Imprimeur de la Reine, 1960. 64 pp.

*Canada. Marine. Commandement maritime de l'Atlantique. *Visite du comité spécial de la défense au Commandement maritime canadien de l'Atlantique, juillet 1964; programme et renseignements.* s.l.: s.i., 1964. 1 tome, non paginé.

*Canada. Ministère de la Défense nationale. *Le conseil de recherches pour la défense, Canada.* s.l.: s.i., s.d. 1 tome, non paginé.

*_____. *Livre blanc sur la défense.* Ottawa: Imprimeur de la Reine, 1964. 34 pp.

*_____. *Ordonnances et règlements royaux applicables aux Forces canadiennes.* Ottawa: Imprimeur de la Reine, 1965. 3 tomes, feuilles mobiles.

*_____. *Rapport.* Ottawa: Imprimeur du Roi, 1923-59.
Divergence du titre. Annuel, la plupart des années.

*_____. *Règlements royaux applicables aux Collèges des services armés du Canada.* Ottawa: Imprimeur de la Reine, 1958. 1 tome, non-paginé.

*Canada. Ministère de la Défense nationale (Service naval). *Rapport sur certains incidents survenus à bord de l'Athabaskan, du Crescent et du Magnificent et sur d'autres questions relatives à la Marine royale canadienne, rapport présenté au ministre de la Défense nationale par une commission régulièrement nommée à ces fins.* Ottawa: Imprimeur du Roi, 1949. 62 pp.

Canada. National Defence Headquarters. *Supplement to Naval General Orders.* Ottawa: n.p., 1965. 1 vol., looseleaf.

Canada. Naval Service Headquarters. *General Orders.* [new series.] Ottawa: n.p., 1951-65. 3 vols., looseleaf.

_____. *General Orders.* [old series.] Ottawa: n.p., 1946-57.

_____. *Royal Canadian Navy Badges, Battle Honours, Mottoes.* Ottawa: Queen's Printer, 1964. 4 vols., looseleaf.

Canada. Naval Service Headquarters. *Uniform Instructions for the Royal Canadian Navy.* (BRCN 108.) Ottawa: Queen's Printer, 1951. 1 vol., looseleaf.

Canada. Naval Service Headquarters. Ad Hoc Committee on Naval Objectives. *Report.* Rear-Admiral Jeffry V. Brock, Chairman. Ottawa: Queen's Printer, 1961. 128 pp.
Originally classified Secret.

Canada. Naval Service Headquarters. Ad Hoc Committee on RCN Personnel Structure. *Report.* Ottawa: n.p., [1958]. v.p.

Canada. Naval Service Headquarters. Directorate of Naval Information. *The Sea, Ships and Men.* Toronto: Navy League of Canada, n.d. 48 pp.

Canada. Naval Service Headquarters. Naval Historian. *The University Naval Training Divisions*, [by Philip Chaplin]. Ottawa: Queen's Printer, 1963. 24 pp.

*Canada. Navy. *Education and Careers in the Navy for Canadian High School Students.* Ottawa: Queen's Printer, 1960. 64 pp.

_____. *General Information about the Pacific Command of the RCN.* Ottawa: Queen's Printer, 1961. 24 pp.

_____. *Handbook for Wren Officers.* Ottawa: Queen's Printer, 1962. 17 pp.

_____. *Listing of Officers on the General and Special Lists; Containing a Listing of RCN and RCN(R) Officers on Continuous Naval Duty Serving on 1 December, 1959.* Ottawa: Queen's Printer, 1960. v.p.

*_____. *R.C.N. Careers for University Graduates and Undergraduates.* Ottawa: Queen's Printer, 1962. 28 pp.

_____. *Regulations and Orders for the Royal Canadian Sea Cadets.* (BRCN 105(64).) n.p.: 1964. 1 vol., looseleaf.

_____. *The Regulations for the Government of Royal Canadian Sea Cadet Corps, 1949.* n.p.: [1949]. 51 pp.

_____. *The Royal Canadian Navy; a Career for Canadians.* Ottawa: King's Printer, 1946. 36 pp.

_____. *Royal Canadian Navy Divisional Officer's Handbook.* (BRCN 3059.) Ottawa: Queen's Printer, 1963. 241 pp.

_____. *Royal Canadian Navy Financial Manual.* (BRCN 625.) Ottawa: Queen's Printer, 1963. 2 vols.

_____. *Seaman's Handbook.* (BRCN 3029.) n.p.: [1960]. 366 pp.

_____. *Technical Apprenticeship Training, Royal Canadian Navy.* Ottawa: Queen's Printer, 1958. 14 pp.

Canada. Navy. *University Naval Training Divisions; for Cadets (R.C.N. Reserve), Royal Canadian Navy.* n.p.: [1953? 14 pp.]

_____. *Venture Plan.* Ottawa: Queen's Printer, 1955. 23 pp.

*Canada. Navy. Maritime Command, Atlantic. *Visit of the Special Committee on Defence to the Canadian Maritime Command Atlantic, July 1964; Programme and Information.* n.p.: 1964. 1 vol., unpaged.

Canada. Navy. Pacific Command. *In Commemoration of the Presentation of the King's Colour to the Royal Canadian Navy by His Late Majesty King George VI, which Took Place at Beacon Hill Park, Victoria, British Columbia, on 30 May, 1939, at 2:30 p.m.* n.p.: [1956]. 1 vol., unpaged.

Canada. Parliament. House of Commons. Special Committee on Canteen Funds. *Minutes of Proceedings and Evidence.* No. 1-10. Ottawa: King's Printer, 1947.

Canada's Navy Annual; a Special Edition of Wings Magazine. Calgary: Corvus Pub. Group, 1985- .
Title varies slightly.

Canadian Defence Quarterly. /Revue canadienne de défense. Vol. I- . Toronto: Baxter Pub., 1971- .

Canadian Services Colleges; Royal Military College of Canada, Kingston, Ontario; Royal Roads, Victoria, B.C.; Collège militaire royal de Saint-Jean, Saint-Jean, P.Q. n.p. : [195-?]. 16 pp.

Cardoulis, John N. *A Friendly Invasion; the American Military in Newfoundland, 1940-1990.* St. John's, Nfld.: Breakwater, 1990. 224 pp.

Casey, Douglas E., ed. *R.C.S.C.C. Rainbow.* n.p.: n.d. 64 pp.

Castonguay, Jacques. *Le Collège militaire royal de Saint-Jean.* Montréal: Méridien, 1989. 288 pp.
Réédition rév. et augm.: Le Collège militaire royal de Saint-Jean; une université à caractère différent. Sillery (Qué): Septentrion, 1992. 272 pp.

_____. *Collège militaire royal de Saint-Jean./ Les premiers vingt ans./ The First Twenty Years.* Adaptation anglaise: Donald A.L. Lefroy. s.l.: s.i./n.p., [1972?]. 44 pp.
Texte bilingue./ Bilingual text.

Charlton, Peter, and Michael Whitby, eds. *"Certified Serviceable"; Swordfish to Sea King; the Technical Story of Canadian Naval Aviation, by Those Who Made It So.* n.p.: CNATH Book Project, 1995. 496 pp.

Collège militaire royal de Saint-Jean. *Ouverture officielle./Official Opening.* s.l.: s.i., s.d./n.p.: n.d. 27 pp.
Texte bilingue./Bilingual text.

The Commissioning Book of H.M.C.S. Warrior, January 24th 1946. Belfast: n.p., 1946. 32 pp.

The Commissioning of HMCS Annapolis, 19 December 1964, at Halifax Shipyards Limited, Halifax, N.S./Mise en service de l'Annapolis, 19 décembre 1964, à Halifax Shipyards Limited, Halifax (N.-E.). n.p.: n.d./s.l.: s.i., s.d. 1 vol., unpaged./1 tome, non paginé.
Bilingual text./Texte bilingue.

The Commissioning of HMCS Assiniboine at Marine Industries Ltd., Sorel, P.Q., August 16, 1956. n.p.: n.d. 1 vol., unpaged.

The Commissioning of HMCS Chaudière at Halifax Shipyards, Halifax, N.S., November 14, 1959. Ottawa: Queen's Printer, 1959. 1 vol., unpaged.

The Commissioning of HMCS Columbia at Burrard Dry Dock Co., Ltd., North Vancouver, B.C., November 7, 1959. Ottawa: Queen's Printer, 1959. 1 vol., unpaged.

The Commissioning of HMCS Fraser at Yarrows Limited, Esquimalt B.C., June 28, 1957. n.p.: n.d. 1 vol., unpaged.

The Commissioning of HMCS Gatineau at HMC Dockyard, Halifax, N.S., February 17, 1959. Ottawa: Queen's Printer, 1959. 1 vol., unpaged.

The Commissioning of HMCS Grilse at the United States Naval Submarine Base, New London, Groton, Connecticut, 11th May, 1961. Ottawa: Queen's Printer, 1961. 1 vol., unpaged.

The Commissioning of HMCS Kootenay at Burrard Dry Dock Co., Ltd., North Vancouver B.C., March 7, 1959. Ottawa: Queen's Printer, 1959. 1 vol., unpaged.

The Commissioning of HMCS Mackenzie at Canadian Vickers Ltd., Montreal, P.Q., October 6, 1962. Ottawa: Queen's Printer, 1962. 1 vol., unpaged.

The Commissioning of HMCS Margaree at Halifax Shipyards, Halifax, N.S., October 5, 1957. Ottawa: Queen's Printer, 1957. 1 vol., unpaged.

The Commissioning of HMCS Ojibwa, 23 September 1965, in Her Majesty's Dockyard, Chatham, Kent, England. Ottawa: Queen's Printer, 1965. 1 vol., unpaged.

The Commissioning of HMCS Onondaga, 22 June 1967, in Her Majesty's Dockyard, Chatham, Kent, England. Ottawa: Queen's Printer, 1967. 1 vol., unpaged.

The Commissioning of HMCS Ottawa, at Canadian Vickers Ltd., Montreal, P.Q., November 10, 1956. Ottawa: Queen's Printer, 1956. 1 vol., unpaged.

The Commissioning of HMCS Provider, 28 September, 1963, at Davie Shipbuilding Limited, Lauzon, Quebec./Mise en service du Provider, 28 septembre 1963, à l'Arsenal de la Davie Shipbuilding Limited, Lauzon, Québec. n.p.: n.d./s.l.: s.i., s.d. 1 vol., unpaged./1 tome, non paginé. *Bilingual text./ Texte bilingue.*

The Commissioning of HMCS Qu'Appelle, 14 September 1963, at Davie Shipbuilding Limited, Lauzon, Quebec./Mise en service du Qu'Appelle, 14 septembre 1963, à l'Arsenal de la Davie Shipbuilding Limited, Lauzon, Québec. n.p.: n.d./s.l.: s.i., s.d. 1 vol., unpaged./1 tome, nonpaginé. *Bilingual text./ Texte bilingue.*

The Commissioning of HMCS Restigouche at Canadian Vickers Ltd., Montreal, P.Q., June 7, 1958. Ottawa: Queen's Printer, 1957. 1 vol., unpaged. *Some copies exist giving November 30, 1957 as commissioning date.*

The Commissioning of HMCS Saguenay at Halifax Shipyards Ltd., Halifax, N.S., December 15, 1956. n.p.: n.d. 1 vol., unpaged.

The Commissioning of HMCS St. Croix at Marine Industries Ltd., Sorel, P.Q., October 4, 1958. Ottawa: Queen's Printer, 1958. 1 vol., unpaged.

The Commissioning of HMCS St. Laurent at Canadian Vickers Limited, Montreal, Quebec, Saturday, October 29, 1955. n.p.: n.d. 1 vol., unpaged.

The Commissioning of HMCS Saskatchewan, February 16, 1963, at Yarrows Limited, Esquimalt, B.C. Ottawa: Queen's Printer, 1963. 1 vol., unpaged.

The Commissioning of HMCS Skeena at Burrard Dry Dock Co., Ltd., North Vancouver, B.C., March 30, 1957. n.p.: n.d. 1 vol., unpaged.

The Commissioning of HMCS Terra Nova at Victoria Machinery Depot Co. Ltd., Victoria, B.C., June 6, 1959. Ottawa: Queen's Printer, 1959. 1 vol., unpaged.

The Commissioning of HMCS Yukon, May 25, 1963, at Burrard Dry Dock Co. Ltd., North Vancouver. Ottawa: Queen's Printer, 1963. 1 vol., unpaged.

Corbet, E. *Calgary's Stone Frigate; HMCS Tecumseh, 1923-1973.* Calgary: Century Calgary Publications, 1975. 64 pp.

Coup d'oeil sur le Collège militaire royal de Saint-Jean. Ottawa: Imprimeur de la Reine, 1959. 20 pp.

Cranston, Bobby. *75th Anniversary, Naval Service of Canada; a Pictorial History.* Halifax: 75th Anniversary Pub. Co., [1985]. 1 vol., chiefly illus.

Crichton, Robert. *The Great Imposter.* New York: Random House, 1959. 218 pp.

The Crow's Nest; a Short Account of the Seagoing Officers Club and the Newfoundland Officers Club, Issued on the Occasion of the Tenth Anniversary, 1942-1952. n.p.: printed by Guardian Press, [1952. 24 pp.]

The Crowsnest; the Royal Canadian Navy's Magazine. Vol. I-XVII. Ottawa: Queen's Printer, 1948-65.

Davison, Stan. *When Canada's Navy was Royal.* Victoria, B.C.: Winged Isle Yacht Ent., [1985]. 192 pp.
Cartoons.

Le Défilé; la revue du Collège militaire royal de Saint-Jean. St-Jean, P.Q.: imprimé privé, 1952- .
Divergence du titre.

Dillon, G.M. *Canadian Naval Forces since World War II; a Decision-Making Analysis*, with comments by Dr. G.R. Lindsey and Professor Jonathan Wouk, with a reply from the author. (Dalhousie Univ. Center for Foreign Policy Studies Occasional Paper.) Halifax: Dalhousie Univ., 1972. 79 pp.

Douglas, W.A.B., ed. *The RCN in Transition, 1910-1985.* Vancouver: Univ. of British Columbia Press, 1988. 411 pp.

Dunnett, Peter J.S. *Royal Roads Military College, 1940-1990; a Pictorial Retrospect.* W. Kim Rempel, photo researcher. Victoria, B.C.: Royal Roads Military College, 1990. 159 pp.

[Elliott, Ron.] *Eight Bells and Green Ones; Memories of a Chief Boatswain [sic] Mate*, by The Buffer. n.p.: [1985]. 56 pp.
HMCS Cornwallis.

Ferguson, Julie H. *Through a Canadian Periscope; the Story of the Canadian Submarine Service.* Toronto: Dundurn Press, 1995. 364 pp.

First Canadian Minesweeping Squadron, 1962; Royal Canadian Navy. Ottawa: Queen's Printer, 1962. 1 vol., unpaged.

Fort Churchill. Ottawa: Queen's Printer, 1959. 20 pp.

Foster, J.A. *Heart of Oak; a Pictorial History of the Royal Canadian Navy.* Toronto: Methuen, 1985. [143 pp.]

_____. *Sea Wings; a Pictorial History of Canada's Waterborne Defence Aircraft.* Toronto: Methuen, 1986. 143 pp.

Gaffen, Fred. *Cross-Border Warriors; Canadians in American Forces, Americans in Canadian Forces; from the Civil War to the Gulf.* Toronto: Dundurn Press, 1995. 241 pp.

Gardam, John. *Korea Volunteer; an Oral History from Those who were There.* Burnstown, Ont.: General Store Pub. House, 1994. 262 pp.

German, Tony. *The Sea is at our Gates; the History of the Canadian Navy.* Toronto: McClelland & Stewart, 1990. 360 pp.

Glashan, Keith. *Montreal's Navy; Stories of HMCS Donnacona and its Predeccessors.* [Montreal]: Montreal Branch, Naval Officers' Association of Canada, [1985]. 96 pp.

Goodspeed, D.J. *A History of the Defence Research Board of Canada.* Ottawa: Queen's Printer, 1958. 259 pp.

Goossen, G., and others. *HMCS Naden, 1922-1965.* n.p.: n.d. 1 vol., unpaged.

Granatstein, J.L., and David J. Bercuson. *War and Peacekeeping; from South Africa to the Gulf — Canada's Limited Wars.* Toronto: Key Porter Books, 1991. 266 pp.

HMCS Cornwallis. n.p.: n.d. 1 vol., chiefly illus.

*HMCS Labrador. (Current Affairs for the Canadian Forces, vol. IX, no. 2.) Ottawa: Queen's Printer, 1955. 31 pp.

H.M.C.S. Quebec; Flagship of Rear Admiral R.E.S. Bidwell, CBE, CD, RCN, Flag Officer, Canadian Coronation Squadron, 1953. n.p..: [1953]. 16 pp.

Hacking, N.R. *Naval Officers Association of British Columbia; a Record of Achievement, 1919-1959.* n.p.: n.d. 32 pp.

Haydon, Peter T. *The 1962 Cuban Missile Crisis: Canadian Involvement Reconsidered.* Toronto: Canadian Institute of Strategic Studies, 1993. 297 pp.

Henderson, Peter A. *Guarding the Gates; a History of Canadian Forces Station St. Johns.* St. John's, Nfld.: CFS St. John's, 1992. 115 pp.

Hobson, Sharon. *The Composition of Canada's Naval Fleet, 1946-85.* Halifax: Centre for Foreign Policy Studies, Dalhousie Univ., 1986. 127 pp.

Holloway, Ian. *Self-Reliance through Service; the Story of Her Majesty's Canadian Ship Scotian.* Hantsport, N.S.: Lancelot Press, 1988. 116 pp.

Irvine, T.A. *The Ice was All Between.* Toronto: Longmans, Green, 1959. 216 pp.

*Kealy, J.D.F., and E.C. Russell. *A History of Canadian Naval Aviation, 1918-1962.* Ottawa: Queen's Printer, 1965. 164 pp.

*Kealy, J.D.F., et E.C. Russell. *Histoire de l'aéronavale canadienne, 1918-1962.* Ottawa: Imprimeur de la Reine, 1965. 185 pp.

Kilgour, Robert W. *A History of the Canadian Naval Auxiliary Vessels, [1945-1967.* Halifax: privately printed, 1967.] 44 pp.

Le "Labrador". (Actualités; revue destinée aux Forces canadiennes, vol IX, no 2.) Ottawa: Imprimeur de la Reine, 1955. 35 pp.

Lay, H. Nelson. *Memoirs of a Mariner.* Stittsville, Ont.: Canada's Wings, 1982. 326 pp.

Leggett, Harry Furniss. *Spindrift; Yarns of a West Coast Seaman as Told to his Grandchildren.* Victoria, B.C.: privately printed, n.d. 88 pp.

Littler, John Caldecott. *Sea Fever.* Victoria, B.C.: Kiwi Publications, 1995. [334] pp.
Memoirs of service with Royal Canadian Navy, 1940-1962.

The Log; Royal Roads Military College. Vol. V- . Victoria, B.C.: privately printed, 1942- .

Longard, John R. *Knots, Volts and Decibels; an Informal History of the Naval Research Establishment, 1940-1967.* Dartmouth, N.S.: Defence Research Establishment Atlantic, 1993. [115] pp.

Lynch, Thomas G. *The Flying 400; Canada's Hydrofoil Project.* Halifax: Nimbus Pub., 1983. 128 pp.

Macbeth, Jack. *Ready, Aye, Ready; an Illustrated History of the Royal Canadian Navy.* Toronto: Key Porter Books, n.d. 176 pp.

*McCracken, George W. *Votre Marine.* (Actualités; revue destinée aux Forces canadiennes, vol IV, no 8.) Ottawa: Imprimeur de la Reine, 1953. 31 pp.

*_____. *Your Navy.* (Current Affairs for the Canadian Forces, vol. IV, no. 8.) Ottawa: Queen's Printer, 1953. 31 pp.

MacFarlane, John, and Robbie Hughes. *Canada's Naval Aviators.* Victoria, B.C.: Maritime Museum of British Columbia, 1994. 182 pp.

McGrane, J.E. *The Exeter and the North Saskatchewan.* Lac La Biche, Alta.: privately printed, 1950. 107 pp.

McKee, Fraser M. *Volunteers for Sea Service; a Brief History of the Royal Canadian Naval Volunteer Reserve, its Predecessors and Successors, on its 50th Anniversary, 1973.* Toronto: privately printed, 1973. 69 pp.

Macpherson, K.R. *Canada's Fighting Ships.* (Canadian War Museum Historical Publication Number 12.) Toronto: Hakkert, 1975. 116 pp.

_____. *Frigates of the Royal Canadian Navy, 1943-1974.* St. Catharines, Ont.: Vanwell Pub., 1989. 109 pp.

Macpherson, K.R., and John Burgess. *The Ships of Canada's Naval Forces, 1910-1981; a Complete Pictorial History of Canadian Warships.* Toronto: Collins, 1981. 240 pp.
Rev. eds. Toronto: Collins, 1985 and St. Catharines, Ont.: Vanwell Pub., 1993.

Marcoux, Jules, éd. *CMR, 1952-1977; album du 25e anniversaire/25th anniversary album.* St-Jean, P.Q.: s.i./n.p., 1977. 62 pp.
Texte bilingue./Bilingual text.

[Maritime Museum of Canada.] *Souvenir of the Maritime Museum of Canada, Halifax, Nova Scotia.* [Halifax: n.p., 195-?] 44 pp.

*The Medical and Dental Services of the Canadian Forces. (Current Affairs for the Canadian Forces, vol. VI, no. 1.) Ottawa: Queen's Printer, 1954. 31 pp.

Melady, John. *Korea: Canada's Forgotten War.* Toronto: Macmillan, 1983. 215 pp.

Meyers, Edward C. *Thunder in the Morning Calm: the Royal Canadian Navy in Korea, 1950-1955.* St. Catharines, Ont.: Vanwell Pub., 1992. 248 pp.

Mills, Carl. *Banshees in the Royal Canadian Navy.* Willowdale, Ont.: Banshee Publication, 1991. [320] pp.

Mirtle, Jack. *The Naden Band: a History.* Victoria, B.C.: Jackstays Pub., 1990. 167 pp.

The Naming and Commissioning of HMCS Nipigon, 30 May, 1964, at Marine Industries Limited, Sorel, Quebec./Baptême et mise en service du Nipigon, 30 mai 1964, à Marine Industries Limited, Sorel, Québec. n.p.: n.d./s.l.: s.i., s.d. 1 vol., unpaged/1 tome, non paginé.
Bilingual text./ Texte bilingue.

Naval Officers' Association of Canada. London Branch. *H.M.C.S. Prevost, London, Canada.* [London, Ont.: London Branch, Naval Officers' Association of Canada, 196-?] 67 pp.

Paré, Lorenzo. *Les canadiens français et l'organisation militaire.* (Oeuvre des tracts, 382.) Montréal: imprime privé, [1951]. 16 pp.

Pettipas, Leo. *Aircraft of the RCN.* Winnipeg: n.p., 1988. 104 pp.

_____. *Canadian Naval Aviation, 1945-1968.* Winnipeg: n.p., 1986. 101 pp.

_____. *The Fairey Firefly in the Royal Canadian Navy.* Winnipeg: n.p., 1987. 109 pp.

_____. *The Grumman Avenger in the Royal Canadian Navy.* n.p.: 1988. 154 pp.

_____. *The Hawker Sea Fury in the Royal Canadian Navy.* n.p.: 1989. 188 pp.

_____. *The Supermarine Seafire in the Royal Canadian Navy.* Winnipeg: n.p., 1987. 86 pp.

*"Pourquoi je sers ma patrie". (Actualités; revue destinée aux Forces canadiennes, vol X, no 15.) Ottawa: Imprimeur de la Reine, 1956. 26 pp.

Presentation of the Queen's Colour to the Royal Canadian Navy by Her Majesty the Queen, Halifax, Nova Scotia, Saturday, 1st August, 1959. n.p.: n.d. 1 vol., unpaged.

*Preston, Richard A. *Au service du Canada; histoire du Royal Military College depuis la Deuxième Guerre mondiale.* s.l.: Presses de l'Université d'Ottawa, 1992. 268 pp.

_____. *Canada's RMC; a History of the Royal Military College.* Toronto: Univ. of Toronto Press, 1969. 415 pp.

*_____. *To Serve Canada; History of the Royal Military College since the Second World War.* Ottawa: Univ. of Ottawa Press, 1991. 248 pp.

Puddester, J., ed. *The Crow's Nest (Officers Club); 30th Anniversary Souvenir, 1942-1972.* St. John's, Nfld.: privately printed, 1972. 51 pp.

Pugsley, William H. *Return to Sea; the Lower Deck of the Royal Canadian Navy Revisited Eleven Years after the 1945 Demobilization.* Toronto: Collins, 1960. 249 pp.

Richards, S.T. *Operation Sick Bay.* West Vancouver, B.C.: Centaur Pub., 1994. 276 pp.
The story of the Sick Berth & Medical Assistant Branch of the Royal Candian Navy, 1910-1965.

Robertson, Peter. *Irréductible vérité/Relentless Verity/les photographes militaires canadiens depuis 1885/Canadian Military Photographers since 1885.* (Les Archives publiques du Canada/Public Archives of Canada Series.) Québec, P.Q.: Les Presses de l'Université Laval, 1973. 233 pp.
Texte bilingue./Bilingual text.

Royal Canadian Navy Monthly Review (R.C.N.M.R.). Ottawa: King's Printer, 1942-45, 1947-48.

Royal Canadian Navy, 1910-1960; the First Fifty Years. n.p.: 1960. v.p.

Royal Military College of Canada, Kingston, Ont. *The Cadet Handbook.* Kingston, Ont.: n.p., [1957?]. 59 pp., looseleaf.

The Royal Military College of Canada Review. Vol. I- . Kingston, Ont.: privately printed, 1920- .

Les services medicaux et dentaires pour les Forces armées. (Actualités; revue destinée aux Forces canadiennes, vol Vl, no 1.) Ottawa: Imprimeur de la Reine, 1954. 31 pp.

Smith, Marilyn Gurney. *The King's Yard; an Illustrated History of the Halifax Dockyard.* Halifax: Nimbus Pub., 1985. 56 pp.

Smith, Waldo E.L. *The Navy Chaplain and his Parish.* Ottawa: Queen's Printer, 1967. 264 pp.

Snowie, J. Allen. *The Bonnie; HMCS Bonaventure.* Erin, Ont.: Boston Mills Press, 1987. 336 pp.

Snowy Owl; Journal of the Canadian Land Forces Command and Staff College. Kingston, Ont.: privately printed, 1952-73. 18 vols.
Title varies.

Soward, Stuart E. *Hands to Flying Stations; a Recollective History of Canadian Naval Aviation.* Victoria, B.C.: Neptune Developments (1984), 1993-95. 2 vols.

*Stacey, C.P., H.E.W. Strange and F.H. Hitchins. *Canada's Armed Forces Today.* (Current Affairs for the Canadian Forces, vol. II, no. 9.) Ottawa: Queen's Printer, 1952. 22 pp.

*Stacey, C.P., H.E.W. Strange et F.H. Hitchins. *Les Forces armées du Canada.* (Actualités; revue destinée aux Forces canadiennes, vol II, no 9.) Ottawa: Imprimeur de la Reine, 1952. 22 pp.

*Summerby, Janice. *Native Soldiers; Foreign Battlefields.* Ottawa: Communications Division, Veterans Affairs Canada, 1993. 47 pp.

*_____. *Soldats autochtones; terres étrangères.* Ottawa: Direction générale des communications, Anciens combattants Canada, 1993. 51 pp.

Supply Mercury; for the Supply Branch of the Royal Canadian Navy. Vol. I-X. Ottawa: Queen's Printer, 1950-59.

Swain, Hector. *History of the Naval Reserves in Newfoundland.* [St. John's, Nfld.: Provincial Archives, 1975.] 56 pp.

The Telescope; a Magazine of Current Information on the Royal Canadian Navy for Officers of the R.C.N.(R) and Members of the Naval Officers' Association. Vol. I-II. Ottawa: King's Printer, 1947-48.

**The Third Canadian Escort Squadron.* n.p.: [1958? 13 pp.]

Thompson, Brad. *H.M.C.S. Griffon; a Naval History.* Thunder Bay, Ont.: Thunder Bay Naval Association, 1985. 98 pp.

Thompson, Roy J.C. *Cap Badges and Insignia of the RCN — RCAF — CAF, 1953-1978.* Colorado Springs, Col.: n.p., 1978. 75 pp.

_____. *Wings of the Canadian Armed Forces, 1913-1972.* [Dartmouth], N.S.: n.p., 1973. 106 pp.

*Thorgrimsson, Thor, and E.C. Russell. *Canadian Naval Operations in Korean Waters, 1950-1955.* Ottawa: Queen's Printer, 1965. 167 pp.

*Thorgrimsson, Thor, et E.C. Russell. *Les opérations navales du Canada dans les eaux coréennes, 1950-1955.* Ottawa: Imprimeur de la Reine, 1965. 178 pp.

Thornton, J.M. *The Big 'U'; a History of HMCS Uganda/Quebec.* [Vancouver]: privately printed, 1983. 68 pp.

_____. *H.M.C.S. Discovery and Deadman's Island; a Brief History ....* n.p.: [197-?]. 52 pp.

**La Troisième Escadre d'escorte du Canada.* s.l.: s.i., [1958? 15 pp.]

Venturian; HMCS Venture, Esquimalt, B.C. Esquimalt, B.C.: privately printed, 1955-63.
Annual.

Vondette, H.W. *Athabaskan's Rescue.* Ottawa: Queen's Printer, 1964. 19 pp.

Wave Off. Vol. I-XIV? Ottawa: n.p., 1950-64?
Magazine of Inspectorate of Naval Flight Safety, RCN.

Wellington Legion War Veterans Club, eds. *They Served for Freedom./A la défense de la liberté.* [Wellington, P.E.I.: Royal Canadian Legion, Wellington Branch 17/Wellington, I.P.E.: Légion royale canadienne, la filiale de Wellington no 17], 1986. 319 pp.
Bilingual text./Texte bilingue.

Whitby, Michael J. *Relentless in Chase; a History of HMCS Iroquois I and II; Comrades in Arms, Relentless in Chase.* n.p.: [1992]. 60 pp.

White Twist. n.p.: 1949-63?
Yearbook of the University Naval Training Divisions.

* *"Why I Serve"*, by the Serviceman. (Current Affairs for the Canadian Forces, vol. X, no. 15.) Ottawa: Queen's Printer, 1956. 26 pp.

Wilkinson, William Arthur, and Geoff Nightingale. *Making a Difference; the Memoirs of William Arthur Wilkinson.* Windsor, Ont.: Herald Press, 1995. 163 pp.

Winters, B.A. *H.M.C.S. Discovery; a History of the Naval Reserve in Vancouver.* n.p.: [1995]. 1 vol., unpaged.

Witt, Eugene, and Jim Thomas. *Ship Repair Adventure; HMC Dockyard Esquimalt.* Victoria, B.C.: printed by Hillside Print. Co., 1985. 164 pp.

D. LAND FORCES — LES FORCES TERRESTRES

1867-1914

Adam, G. Mercer. *The Canadian North-West; its History and its Troubles from the Early Days of the Fur Trade to the Era of the Railway and the Settler; with Incidents of Travel in the Region, and the Narrative of Three Insurrections.* Toronto: Rose Pub. Co., 1885. 390 pp.

Anderson, Frank. *"1885"; the Riel Rebellion.* (Frontier Book, no. 3.) n.p.: n.d. 80 pp.

————. *Riel's Manitoba Uprising.* (Frontier Book, no. 31.) Calgary: Frontier Pub., 1974. 64 pp.

Armit, W.B. *Army Museum; Halifax Citadel, Halifax, Nova Scotia.* Kentville, N.S.: n.p., [1957?]. 34 pp.

*L'Arsenal de Québec, 1880-1945. Québec, P.Q.: s.i., 1947. 166 pp.

Aston, Wm. H., comp. *History of the 21st Regiment, Essex Fusiliers of Windsor, Ontario, Canadian Militia, with a Brief History of the Essex Frontier, the War of 1812, Canadian Rebellion of 1837, Fenian Raids, War in South Africa, etc., Including an Account of the Different Actions in which the Militia of Essex have been Engaged.* Windsor, Ont.: Record Print. Co., 1902. 176 pp.

[Attwood, Peter Hinds.] *A Few Practical Hints to the Officers, N.C. Officers & Men of the 26th Battalion Relative to their Duties in Camp.* London, Ont.: Free Press Print. and Pub. Co., 1875. 15 pp.

Barnard, W.T. *The Queen's Own Rifles of Canada, 1860-1960; One Hundred Years of Canada.* Don Mills, Ont.: Ontario Pub. Co., 1960. 398 pp.

————. *A Short History of the Queen's Own Rifles of Canada.* Toronto: MacKinnon & Atkins, n.d. 22 pp.

Barnes, C.H. *Colonel Colin Clarke Harbottle, C.M.G., D.S.O., V.D.* n.p.: [1958]. 20 pp.

**Barnes, Leslie W.C.S. *Canada's Guns; an Illustrated History of Artillery.* (Canadian War Museum Historical Publication no. 15.) [Ottawa]: National Museum of Man, 1979. 112 pp.

*Barnes, Leslie W.C.S. *Histoire illustrée de l'artillerie canadienne.* (Musée canadien de la guerre publication d'histoire militaire no 15.) [Ottawa]: Musée national de l'Homme, 1979. 112 pp.

Barnett, Donald C. *Poundmaker.* (The Canadians.) Don Mills, Ont.: Fitzhenry and Whiteside, 1976. 61 pp.

Bassett, John. *John McCrae.* Markham, Ont.: Fitzhenry & Whiteside, 1984. 63 pp.

Battleford Beleaguered: 1885; the Story of the Riel Uprising from the Columns of the Saskatchewan Herald. William L. Clink, ed. Willowdale, Ont.: privately printed, 1984. v.p.

Baxter, John Babington Macauley. *Historical Records of the New Brunswick Regiment Canadian Artillery.* St. John, N.B.: Sun Print., 1896. 259 pp.

[Baylay, George Taylor, ed.] *The Regimental History of the Governor General's Foot Guards.* Ottawa: privately printed, 1948. 268 pp.

[Beach, Thomas Miller.] *Twenty-Five Years in the Secret Service; the Recollections of a Spy,* by Major Henri Le Caron [*pseud.*] London: Heinemann, 1892. 311 pp.

Beal, Bob, and Rod Macleod. *Prairie Fire; the 1885 North-West Rebellion.* Edmonton: Hurtig, 1984. 384 pp.

Beattie, Kim. *48th Highlanders of Canada, 1891-1928.* Toronto: privately printed, 1932. 434 pp.

Beauregard, George. *Le 9me bataillon au Nord-Ouest (Journal d'un militaire).* Québec, P.Q.: J.G. Gingras, 1886. 100 pp.

Beck, Norman Edward, comp. *Souvenir Number of the Reveille, the Duke of Connaught's Own, the 158th (Overseas) Battalion.* Vancouver: privately printed, 1916. 20 pp.

Begg, Alexander. *Alexander Begg's Red River Journal and Other Papers Relative to the Red River Resistance of 1869-1870.* W.L. Morton, ed. (The Publications of the Champlain Society, XXXIV.) Toronto: Champlain Society, 1956. 636 pp.

_____. *The Creation of Manitoba; or, a History of the Red River Troubles.* Toronto: A.H. Hovey, 1871. 408 pp.

Bell, K., and C.P. Stacey. *100 Years; the Royal Canadian Regiment 1883-1983.* Don Mills, Ont.: Collier Macmillan, 1983. 184 pp., chiefly illus.

Bellefeuille, E. Lef. de. *Le Canada et les Zouaves pontificaux; mémoires sur l'origine, l'enrôlement et l'expédition du contingent canadien à Rome, pendant l'année 1868.* Montréal: imprimé privé, [1868]. 263 pp.

Biggar, E.B. *The Boer War; its Causes and its Interest to Canadians with a Glossary of Cape Dutch and Kafir Terms.* Toronto: Bigger, Samuel, 1899. 38 pp.

Biggar, J. Lyons, *see* Canada. Dept. of Militia and Defence. *Manual for Use by the Canadian Army Service Corps ....*

Bindon, Kathryn M. *Queen's Men, Canada's Men; the Military History of Queen's University, Kingston.* [Kingston, Ont.]: privately printed, 1978. 180 pp.

Bird, Will R. *North Shore (New Brunswick) Regiment.* Fredericton, N.B.: Brunswick Press, 1963. 629 pp.

Bishop, William Arthur. *Courage on the Battlefield.* (Canada's Military Heritage, Volume II.) Toronto: McGraw-Hill Ryerson, 1993. 341 pp.

"Bluenose" [*pseud.*] *see "How Not to Do It".*

Boissonnault, Charles-Marie. *Histoire politico-militaire des Canadiens français (1763-1967).* Trois-Rivières, P.Q.: Editions du Bien public, 1967. 310 pp.

Boss, W. *The Stormont, Dundas and Glengarry Highlanders, 1783-1951.* Ottawa: Runge Press, 1952. 449 pp.
Revised and updated as: Boss, W., and W.J. Patterson, Up the Glens; Stormont, Dundas and Glengarry Highlanders, 1783-1994. Cornwall, Ont.: Old Book Store, 1995. 298 pp.

Boulton, [Charles Arkoll]. *Reminiscences of the North-West Rebellions; with a Record of the Raising of Her Majesty's 100th Regiment in Canada and a Chapter on Canadian Social and Political Life.* Toronto: Grip, 1886. 531 pp.
Reprinted, in part, as I Fought Riel; a Military Memoir. Heather Robertson, ed. Toronto: J. Lorimer, 1985.

A Brief Account of the Fenian Raids on the Missisquoi Frontier, in 1866 and 1870. Montreal: "Witness" Steam Print. House, 1871. 32 pp.

A Brief Historical Sketch of the Lorne Scots (Peel, Dufferin and Halton Regiment). Brampton, Ont.: Charters Pub. Co., 1943. 24 pp.

A Brief Historical Sketch of the Queen's York Rangers, 1st American Regiment. Toronto: privately printed, 1942. 30 pp.

A Brief History of the Royal Regiment of Canada, [Allied with the King's Regiment (Liverpool). Toronto: n.p., 1940.] 77 pp.

A Brief History of the Royal Regiment of Canada; Allied with the King's Regiment (Liverpool). [Toronto: n.p., 1948.] 135 pp.

Brough, H. Bruce. *Illustrated Historical Album of the Second Battalion the Queen's Own Rifles of Canada, 1856-1894.* Toronto: Toronto News Co., 1894. 80 pp.

Brown, Brian A. *Foresters; the Canadian Quest for Peace.* Erin, Ont.: Boston Mills Press, 1991. 176 pp.
The Grey & Simcoe Foresters.

Brown, Kingsley, *see* Greenhous, Brereton.

Brown, Stanley McKeown. *With the Royal Canadians.* Toronto: Publishers' Syndicate, 1900. 291 pp.

*Brown, W.J. *Les Cadets royaux de l'Armée canadienne; cent ans d'exploits, 1879-1979.* s.l.: La Ligue des Cadets de l'Armée du Canada, [1979. 12 pp.]

*_____. *The Royal Canadian Army Cadets; a Century of Achievement, 1879-1979.* n.p.: The Army Cadet League of Canada, [1979. 12 pp.]

Bruce, Walter H., and others, comps. *Historical Records of the Argyll and Sutherland Highlanders of Canada (Princess Louise's), Formerly 91st Regiment Canadian Highlanders, Canadian Militia, 1903-1928.* Hamilton, Ont.: R. Duncan, 1928. 99 pp.

Buchan, John, *see* Tweedsmuir, John Buchan, baron.

Buchan, Lawrence. *With the Infantry in South Africa; a Lecture Delivered at the Canadian Military Institute, 3rd February, 1902.* n.p.: n.d. 17 pp.

Bull, Stewart H. *The Queen's York Rangers; an Historic Regiment.* Erin, Ont.: Boston Mills Press, 1984. 248 pp.

Bull, Wm. Perkins. *From Brock to Currie; the Military Development and Exploits of Canadians in General and of the Men of Peel in Particular, 1791-1930.* Toronto: G.J. McLeod, 1935. 772 pp.

Burnham, John Hampden. *Canadians in the Imperial Naval and Military Service Abroad.* Toronto: Williamson, 1891. 238 pp.

Butler, (Sir) W.F. *Sir William Butler; an Autobiography.* London: Constable, 1911. 476 pp.

The Cameron Highlanders of Ottawa; Standing Orders and Constitution and Rules of the Officers Mess. n.p.: [1934]. 88 pp.

Cameron, James M. *Pictonians in Arms; a Military History of Pictou County, Nova Scotia.* Fredericton, N.B.: privately printed, 1969. 301 pp.

Cameron, William Bleasdell. *The War Trail of Big Bear; being the Story of the Connection of Big Bear and Other Cree Indian Chiefs and their Followers with the Canadian North-West Rebellion of 1885, the Frog Lake Massacre and Events Leading up to and Following It and of Two Month's Imprisonment in the Camp of the Hostiles.* London: Duckworth, 1926. 256 pp.

Camp, A.D., comp. *7th Toronto Regiment, Royal Regiment of Canadian Artillery, 1866-1966.* n.p.: n.d. 33 pp.

Camp Stories; Hatley Squadron, 26th Stanstead Dragoons; Headquarters and Armoury, East Hatley, Que. n.p.: n.d. 16 pp.

Camp Valcartier, P.Q., 1647 à 1957 en quelques lignes./Camp Valcartier P.Q.; a Short History, 1647-1957. s.l.: s.i./n.p.: 1957. 24 pp.
Texte bilingue./Bilingual text.

Campbell, Francis Wayland. *The Fenian Invasions of Canada of 1866 and 1870 and the Operations of the Montreal Militia Brigade in Connection Therewith; a Lecture Delivered before the Montreal Military Institute, April 23rd, 1898.* Montreal: J. Lovell, 1904. 55 pp.

[Canada. Armed Forces. 48th Highlanders of Canada.] *This is Your Regiment.* n.p.: [194-?]. 38 pp.

Canada. Armed Forces. Lake Superior Scottish Regiment. *Regimental Catechism.* Winnipeg: CFTMPC, 1977. 15 pp.

*Canada. Armée. Quartier général de l'Armée. Section historique. *Introduction à l'étude de l'histoire militaire à l'intention des étudiants canadiens,* [par C.P. Stacey]. Ottawa: [Imprimeur du Roi], 1951. 45 pp.
Editions subséquentes et révisées.

Canada. Armée. Régiment de la Chaudière. *Le Régiment de la Chaudière; notes historiques.* Québec, P.Q.: imprimé privé, 1955. 16 pp.

Canada. Army. Queen's Own Rifles of Canada. *Regimental Catechism.* n.p.: n.d. 19 pp.

Canada. Army. Royal Canadian Army Service Corps. *RCASC Diamond Jubilee Year Book 1910-1961.* Ottawa: Queen's Printer, [1962]. 95 pp.

Canada. Army. Royal Winnipeg Rifles. *Seventy-Fifth Anniversary, Royal Winnipeg Rifles, 1883-1958.* [Winnipeg: privately printed, 1958.] v.p.

*Canada. Army Headquarters. Historical Section. *Introduction to the Study of Military History for Canadian Students,* [by C. P. Stacey]. Ottawa: [King's Printer], 1951. 39 pp.
Many subsequent revised editions.

_____. *The Regiments and Corps of the Canadian Army.* (The Canadian Army List, vol. 1.) Ottawa: Queen's Printer, 1964. 253 pp.

Canada. Commission to Inquire into the Martineau Defalcation. *Report.* (Sessional Paper, no. 296.) Ottawa: King's Printer, 1903. 13 pp.

*Canada. Département [sic] du Secrétaire d'Etat. *Documents relatifs aux incursions des rebelles sudistes sur la frontière des Etats-Unis et à l'invasion du Canada par les Féniens.* Ottawa: Imprimeur de la Reine, 1869. 176 pp.

*Canada. Dept. of Militia and Defence. *Annual Report.* Ottawa: Queen's Printer, 1867-1922. *Title varies. Until 1883 was* State of the Militia of the Dominion of Canada, *with further variation in some years.*

_____. *Canadian Militia; Mobilization Regulations (Provisional), 1913.* Ottawa: King's Printer, 1912. 32 pp.

_____. *Cavalry Standing Orders.* Ottawa: Queen's Printer, 1884. v.p.

_____. *Cavalry Training, Canada, 1904.* Ottawa: King's Printer, 1904. 231 pp.

*_____. *Continuation of Appendix no. 4 of the Report of 18th May 1886, on Matters in Connection with the Suppression of the Rebellion in the North-West Territories, in 1885; Final Report of War Claims Commission.* (Sessional Paper, no. 9.) Ottawa: Queen's Printer, 1887. 80 pp.

_____. *The Department of Militia and Defence under the Honourable Sir Adolphe P. Caron, K.C.M.G.; and the Military Force of Canada.* Ottawa: Queen's Printer, 1887. 20 pp.

_____. *Dress Regulations for the Officers of the Canadian Militia.* Ottawa: King's Printer, 1907. 78 pp.

*_____. *Further Supplementary Report; Organization, Equipment, Despatch and Service of Canadian Contingents during the War in South Africa, 1899-1902.* (Sessional Paper, no. 35a.) Ottawa: King's Printer, 1903. 99 pp.

_____. *Guide for Paymasters of the Canadian Militia Consisting of the Financial Regulations (with the Exception of Those of the Permanent Force) which Have to Do with the Canadian Militia, and a Few General Remarks on the Position of Paymaster and the Duties Pertaining Thereto,* by Edwyn R. Tooley. Ottawa: n.p., 1902. 31 pp.

_____. *Infantry Training, Canada, 1904.* Ottawa: King's Printer, 1904. 206 pp.

_____. *The King's Regulations and Orders for the Canadian Militia, 1910.* Ottawa: King's Printer, 1910. 378 pp.

_____. *The King's Regulations and Orders for the Militia of Canada, 1904.* Ottawa: King's Printer, 1904. 255 pp.

_____. *Manual for the Militia Artillery of Canada.* Quebec, P.Q.: Gunnery School Press, 1875-78. v.p.

Canada. Dept. of Militia and Defence. ***Manual for Use by the Canadian Army Service Corps and Quartermasters of the Canadian Militia.*** J. Lyons Biggar, comp. Ottawa: King's Printer, 1904. 98 pp.

———. ***Memorandum for Camps of Instruction.*** Part 1: ***Instructions for Training.*** Ottawa: King's Printer, 1909?-28.
Title varies somewhat. Annual.

———. ***Memorandum Relating to Administration, Command and Staff for Camps of Training for the Canadian Militia, 1912.*** Ottawa: King's Printer, 1912. 47 pp.

———. ***The Militia List.*** Ottawa: Queen's Printer, 1867-1929.
Title and frequency vary, eg. — The Annual Volunteer and Service Militia List of Canada (1867); The Quarterly Militia List of the Dominion of Canada (1900).

———. ***Minutes of the Militia Council.*** Ottawa: King's Printer, 1905-21. 23 vols.

———. ***Musketry Regulations for the Canadian Militia (Provisional).*** Ottawa: King's Printer, 1904. 120 pp.

———. ***Pay and Allowance Regulations, 1912.*** Ottawa: King's Printer, 1912. 107 pp.

———. ***Pay and Allowances and Financial Instructions for the Militia of Canada, 1907.*** Ottawa: King's Printer, 1907. 182 pp.

———. ***Procedure in Regard to the Conduct of Business.*** Ottawa: King's Printer, 1909. 14 pp.

———. ***Regimental Standing Orders of the Canadian Permanent Army Veterinary Corps and C.A.V.C.*** Ottawa: King's Printer, 1912. 29 pp.

———. ***Regulations and Orders for the Active Militia, the Schools of Military Instruction, and the Reserve Militia (in the Cases Therein Mentioned), of the Dominion of Canada./Règlements et ordres pour la Milice active, les écoles d'instruction militaire et la Milice de réserve (dans les cas y mentionnés) de la Puissance du Canada.*** Ottawa: Queen's Printer/Imprimeur de la Reine, 1870. 171 pp.
Bilingual text./Texte bilingue.

———. ***Regulations and Orders for the Militia of Canada, 1898.*** Ottawa: Queen's Printer, 1898. 443 pp.

———. ***Regulations and Orders for the Militia of the Dominion of Canada.*** Ottawa: Queen's Printer, 1879. 348 pp.

*Canada. Dept. of Militia and Defence. *Regulations and Orders for the Militia of the Dominion of Canada, 1st September, 1887.* Ottawa: Queen's Printer, 1887. 378 pp.
At head of title: <u>Statutory Provisions.</u>

_____. *Regulations and Orders for the Militia of the Dominion of Canada, 1883.* Ottawa: Queen's Printer, 1884. 318 pp.
At head of title: <u>Statutory Provisions.</u>

_____. *Regulations for Cadet Corps.* Ottawa: King's Printer, 1910. 19 pp.

_____. *Regulations for Canadian Ordnance Services (Part I).* Ottawa: King's Printer, 1908. 164 pp.

_____. *Regulations for Engineer Services, Canada, 1909.* Ottawa: King's Printer, 1908. 233 pp.

_____. *Regulations for Supply, Transport and Barrack Services for the Canadian Militia, 1909.* Ottawa: King's Printer, 1909. 75 pp.

_____. *Regulations for the Canadian Army Veterinary Service, 1912.* Ottawa: King's Printer, 1912. 49 pp.

_____. *Regulations for the Canadian Medical Service, 1910 (Approved by the Militia Council).* Ottawa: King's Printer, 1910. 66 pp.

_____. *Regulations for the Clothing of the Canadian Militia, 1909.* [Ottawa: King's Printer], 1909. 2 vols.

_____. *Regulations for the Corps of Guides, 1913.* Ottawa: King's Printer, 1913. 13 pp.

_____. *Regulations for the Equipment of the Canadian Militia. Part 2, Section III: Engineers Field Company; Permanent and Non-Permanent Units.* Ottawa: King's Printer, 1913. 19 pp.

_____. *Regulations for the Permanent Corps Active Militia.* Ottawa: Queen's Printer, 1889. 73 pp.

_____. *Regulations for the Permanent Corps, Active Militia, Canada, September 1886.* [Ottawa: Queen's Printer, 1886.] 37 pp.

_____. *Regulations for the Royal Military College of Canada, Kingston, Ontario (Amended to 1st March, 1907).* Ottawa: King's Printer, 1907. 39 pp.

*_____. *Report of Lieutenant-Colonel W.H. Jackson, Deputy-Adjutant-General, Principal Supply, Pay and Transport Officer to the North-West Forces, and Chairman of War Claims Commission, on Matters in Connection with the Suppression of the Rebellion in the North-West Territories, in 1885.* (Sessional Paper, no. 9c.) Ottawa: Queen's Printer, 1887. 44 pp.

*Canada. Dept. of Militia and Defence. *Report of Major General Laurie, Commanding Bases and Lines of Communication, upon Matters in Connection with the Suppression of the Rebellion in the North-West Territories in 1885.* (Sessional Paper, no. 9d.) Ottawa: Queen's Printer, 1887. 39 pp.

_____. *Report of the Halifax Military Lands Board, 1915.* Ottawa: King's Printer, 1916. 171 pp.

*_____. *Report upon the Suppression of the Rebellion in the North-West Territories, and Matters in Connection Therewith, in 1885.* Ottawa: Queen's Printer, 1886. 384 pp.

_____. *Standing Orders of the Canadian Army Service Corps, 1910 (Published under the Authority of the Militia Council).* Ottawa: King's Printer, 1910. 44 pp.

_____. *Standing Orders of the Canadian Ordnance Corps, 1908.* Ottawa: King's Printer, 1908. 70 pp.

_____. *Standing Orders of the Canadian Permanent Army Service Corps (Approved by Militia Council) Published under, and Subject to the Conditions Laid Down in the K.R.&O. for the Militia, 1912.* Ottawa: King's Printer, 1912. 71 pp.

_____. *Standing Orders of the Royal Canadian Dragoons.* (Militia Book no. 2 (New Series).) Ottawa: King's Printer, 1907. 66 pp.

*_____. *Supplementary Report; Organization, Equipment, Despatch and Service of the Canadian Contingents during the War in South Africa, 1899-1900.* (Sessional Paper, no. 35a.) Ottawa: Queen's Printer, 1901. 192 pp.

*Canada. Dept. of Northern Affairs and National Resources. National Historic Sites Division. *Batoche National Historic Site.* Ottawa: Queen's Printer, 1960. 23 pp.

*Canada. Dept. of the Secretary of State. *Correspondence Relating to the Fenian Invasion, and the Rebellion of the Southern States.* Ottawa: Queen's Printer, 1869. 176 pp.

Canada. Governor-General. *Fortifications and Defence, Arms &C; Laid before Parliament by Command of His Excellency the Governor-General.* Ottawa: Queen's Printer, [1869?]. 15 pp.

Canada. Militia. Canadian Grenadier Guards. *Answers to Questions of the Day.* Montreal: Mortimer Press, [1916]. 15 pp.

Canada. Militia. Canadian Medical Service. *Manual of Establishments and Equipment.* Part I: *Peace.* Part II: *War; 1911 (Provisional).* n.p.: [1911?]. 151 pp.

Canada. Militia. Queen's Own Rifles of Canada. *Officers.* n.p.: 1893. 1 vol., chiefly ports.

Canada. Militia Headquarters. *General Orders.* Ottawa: Queen's Printer, 1899-1946.
Superseded Militia General Orders. Frequency varies.

_____. *Militia General Orders.* Ottawa: Queen's Printer, 1867-99.
Frequency varies. Superseded by Militia Orders and General Orders.

_____. *Militia Orders.* Ottawa: Queen's Printer, 1899-1940.
Superseded Militia General Orders. Frequency varies.

*Canada. Ministère de la Milice et de la Défense. *Autre rapport supplémentaire; organisation, équipement, envoi et service de Contingents canadiens pendant la guerre sud-africaine, 1899-1902.* (Document de la session, no 35a.) Ottawa: Imprimeur du Roi, 1903. 102 pp.

*_____. *Continuation de l'annexe no 4 du rapport du 19 mai 1886 sur des matières relatives à la suppression de l'insurrection du Nord-Ouest en 1885; rapport final de la Commission des comptes de la guerre.* (Document de la session, no 9b.) Ottawa: Imprimeur de la Reine, 1887. 80 pp.

*_____. *Rapport annuel.* Ottawa: Imprimeur de la Reine, 1867-1922.
Divergence du titre. Jusqu'à 1883 le titre était Rapport annuel sur l'état de la Milice de la Puissance du Canada; divers titres suivirent pendant quelques années.

*_____. *Rapport du Lieutenant-Colonel W.H. Jackson, aide adjudant-général, payeur et préposé-chef à l'approvisionnement et au transport des troupes expédiées au Nord-Ouest, et président de la commission des comptes de la guerre, sur les questions se rapportant à la répression de l'insurrection des territoires au Nord-Ouest en 1885.* (Document de la session, no 9c.) Ottawa: Imprimeur de la Reine, 1887. 45 pp.

*_____. *Rapport du Major Général Laurie, commandant la base et les lignes de communication, sur des affaires relatives à la répression de l'insurrection soulevée dans les Territoires du Nord-Ouest.* (Document de la session, no 9d.) Ottawa: Imprimeur de la Reine, 1887. 45 pp.

*_____. *Rapport supplémentaire; organisation, équipement, envoi et service des Contingents canadiens durant la guerre dans l'Afrique australe, 1899-1900.* (Document de la session, no 35a.) Ottawa: Imprimeur de la Reine, 1901. 204 pp.

*_____. *Rapport sur la répression de l'insurrection dans les Territoires du Nord-Ouest, et autres choses s'y rattachant — 1885.* Ottawa: Imprimeur de la Reine, 1886. 126 pp.

*Canada. Ministère de la Milice et de la Défense. *Règlements et ordonnances à l'usage de la Milice du Canada; 1er septembre 1887.* Ottawa: Imprimeur de la Reine, 1887. 387 pp.
En tête du titre: Dispositions statutaires.

_____. *Règles et règlements pour les écoles d'instruction militaire de la Puissance du Canada.* Ottawa: Imprimeur de la Reine, 1868. 15 pp.

*Canada. Ministère du nord canadien et des ressources nationales. Division des lieux historiques nationaux. *Lieu historique national de Batoche.* Ottawa: Imprimeur de la Reine, 1961. 24 pp.

*Canada. Parlement. *Collège militaire royal.* (Document de la session, no 48, 48a.) Ottawa: Imprimeur de la Reine, 1900. 14 pp.

*_____. *Copies d'ordres en conseil, ordres généraux, nominations et ordres de la milice relatifs aux contingents et se rapportant à l'envoi de la force militaire coloniale dans le Sud-africain.* (Document de la session, no 49.) Ottawa: Imprimeur de la Reine, 1900. 112 pp.

*_____. *Copies du décret en conseil nommant le major général comte de Dundonald commandant de la milice canadienne, 20 mai 1902, et du décret en conseil relevant le comte de Dundonald du commandement de la milice canadienne, 14 juin 1904, ainsi que de la correspondance et des autres documents s'y rattachant.* (Document de la session, no 113, 113a.) Ottawa: Imprimeur du Roi, 1904. 42 pp.

*_____. *[Correspondance relative aux pensions et gratifications, rébellion Territoires du Nord-Ouest.]* (Document de la session, no 80-80m.) Ottawa: Imprimeur de la Reine, 1886. 34 pp.

*_____. *Correspondance relative à l'envoi de contingents militaires coloniaux dans le Sud africain.* (Document de la session, no 20, 20a.) Ottawa: Imprimeur de la Reine, 1900. 54 pp.

*_____. *Correspondance relative aux troubles qui ont lieu sur la ligne du Grand-Tronk sur 1er janvier 1877.* Ottawa: Imprimeur de la Reine, 1877. 53 pp.

*_____. *Déboursés faits sur le crédit de $2,300,000 ouvert pour couvrir dépenses et pertes occasionnées par les troubles du Nord-Ouest, du 1er juillet 1885 au 15 mars 1886; aussi, relevé supplémentaire pour les approvisionnements fournis par la Cie de la Baie d'Hudson, etc.* (Document de la session, no 50.) Ottawa: Imprimeur de la Reine, 1886. 58 pp.

*_____. *Mémoire des Membres militaires du Conseil de la Milice au ministre de la Milice et de la Défense; et aussi mémoire du Membre financier du dit Conseil concernant le budget de milice pour l'exercice 1905-1906.* (Document de la session, no 130.) Ottawa: Imprimeur du Roi, 1905. 25 pp.

*Canada. Parlement. *Nominations au ministère de la Milice.* (Documents parlementaires, no 94.) Ottawa: Imprimeur du Roi, 1908. 51 pp.

*_____. *Rapport sur l'expédition de la Rivière rouge en 1870,* par S.J. Dawson. (Document de la session, no 47.) Ottawa: Imprimeur de la Reine, 1871. 31 pp.

*_____. *Réponse à un ordre de la Chambre des Communes en date du 26 février 1900; copie de tous documents, de toute correspondance, etc., concernant le choix d'officiers de la Milice canadienne pour le cours d'instruction qui se donne actuellement à Kingston sur les devoirs d'état-major.* (Document de la session, no 91.) Ottawa: Imprimeur de la Reine, 1900. 10 pp.

*_____. *Réponses à des adresses du Sénat et de la Chambre des Communes au sujet du retrait des troupes du Canada et de la défense du pays et rapport de l'honorable M. Campbell.* (Document de la session, no 46.) Ottawa: Imprimeur de la Reine, 1871. 127 pp.

*Canada Parliament. *Appointments to Militia Department.* (Sessional Paper, no. 94.) Ottawa: King's Printer, 1908. 51 pp.

*_____. *Copies of Orders in Council, General Orders, Appointments to Office and Militia Orders Affecting the Contingents, in Connection with the Despatch of the Colonial Military Force to South Africa.* (Sessional Paper, no. 49.) Ottawa: Queen's Printer, 1900. 107 pp.

*_____. *Copies of the Order in Council Appointing Major General, the Earl of Dundonald, to the Command of the Canadian Militia, 20th May, 1902, and the Order in Council Relieving from the Command of the Canadian Militia, 14th June, 1904, and also, Correspondence and Other Papers Connected Therewith.* (Sessional Paper, no. 113, 113a.) Ottawa: King's Printer, 1904. 41 pp.

*_____. *[Correspondence Concerning Militia Pensions and Medals in the Northwest Campaign.]* (Sessional Paper, no. 80-80m.) Ottawa: Queen's Printer, 1886. 34 pp.

*_____. *Correspondence Relating to the Despatch of Colonial Military Contingents to South Africa.* (Sessional Paper, no. 20, 20a.) Ottawa: Queen's Printer, 1900. 51 pp.

*_____. *Correspondence Respecting Disturbance on the Line of the Grand Trunk Railway, January 1st, 1877.* Ottawa: Queen's Printer, 1877. 53 pp.

*_____. *Expenditure under Appropriation of $2,300,000 to Defray Expenses and Losses Arising Out of Troubles in the North-West Territories, from 1st July, 1885, to 15th March, 1886; also Subsidiary Statement of Expenditure under Same Appropriation, &c., Hudson Bay Supplies, &c.* (Sessional Paper, no. 50.) Ottawa: Queen's Printer, 1886. 60 pp.

*Canada Parliament. *Memorandum from the Military Members of the Militia Council to the Minister of Militia and Defence; and also Memorandum of the Finance Member of the Militia Council Relating to the Militia Estimates for 1905-1906.* (Sessional Paper, no. 130.) Ottawa: King's Printer, 1905. 24 pp.

*_____. *Report on the Red River Expedition of 1870*, by S.J. Dawson. (Sessional Paper, no. 47.) Ottawa: Queen's Printer, 1871. 31 pp.

_____. *Return to an Order of the House of Commons Dated February 19, 1900, for Copies of all Correspondence, Telegrams, and Cablegrams that may have Passed between Major General Hutton and Lieutenant Colonel Samuel Hughes, M.P., or between these Officers and any Member of the Government of Canada or Others, Touching the Conduct of Lieutenant Colonel Hughes, M.P., in Connection with his Volunteering for Active Service in South Africa; these Papers to Include all Letters, Cablegrams and Telegrams Sent to South Africa, England or Elsewhere and Replies Received; also Any Report or Reports made by Major General Hutton on the Conduct of Lieut. Col. Hughes, M.P., in Connection with such Offer or Offers for Active Service.* (Sessional Paper, no. 77, 77a.) Ottawa: Queen's Printer, 1900. 32 pp.

*_____ . *Return to an Order of the House of Commons, Dated February 26, 1900, for a Return of All Papers and Correspondence etc., in Connection with the Selection of Officers of the Canadian Militia for the Course of Instruction in the Duties of General Staff Now Being Carried Out at Kingston.* (Sessional Paper, no. 91.) Ottawa: Queen's Printer, 1900. 10 pp.

*_____. *Returns to the Addresses of the Senate and House of Commons Relative to the Withdrawal of the Troops from the Dominion and on the Defence of the Country and Hon. Mr. Campbell's Report.* (Sessional Paper, no. 46.) Ottawa: Queen's Printer, 1871. 127 pp.

*_____. *Royal Military College.* (Sessional Paper, no. 48, 48a.) Ottawa: Queen's Printer, 1894. 14 pp.

Canada. Parliament. House of Commons. Select Committee Appointed to Inquire into the Purchase of Emergency Rations for the Use of the Canadian Troops in South Africa. *Reports.* Ottawa: Queen's Printer, 1900. 287 pp.

Canada in the Great World War; an Authentic Account of the Military History of Canada from the Earliest Days to the Close of the War of the Nations, by Various Authorities. Toronto: United Publishers, 1917-21. 6 vols.

The Canadian Artillerist; Journal of the Canadian Artillery Association. Vol. I. Kingston, Ont.: privately printed, 1905-06.

Canadian Artillery Association. *Annual Report.* n.p.: privately printed, 1876- . *Not published 1940-46.*

The Canadian Artillery Team at Shoeburyness, 1896; Extracts from the British Press. n.p.: n.d. 1 vol., unpaged.

Canadian Cavalry Association. *Proceedings.* n.p.: privately printed, 1913- .
In 1943 became Canadian Armoured Association and in 1946 Royal Canadian Armoured Corps (Cavalry) Association. Title varies, also: Annual Report and Information Digest and Annual Report.

The Canadian Fusiliers; City of London Regiment. n.p.: 1942. 12 pp.

Canadian Infantry Association. *Proceedings.* n.p.: privately printed, 1913- .
Incorporated the Proceedings of the Canadian Machine Gun Corps Association in 1936. Was the Infantry and Machine Gun Association of Canada, 1937-39. Not published 1940-45.

Canadian Military Review./Revue militaire canadienne. Vol. I-II. Québec P.Q.: privately printed/imprimé privé, 1880-81?

The Canadian Scottish Regiment. n.p.: n.d. 91 pp.

The Canadian United Service Magazine. Vol. I-IV? n.p.: privately printed 1894-98?
Title varies. Vols. I-II were titled: The V.R.I. Magazine.

Canadians in Khaki; South Africa, 1899-1900; Nominal Rolls of the Officers, Non-Commissioned Officers & Men of the Canadian Contingent and Strathcona's Horse with Casualties to Date and also R.M.C. Graduates with the Army in South Africa. Montreal: Herald Pub. Co., 1900. 127 pp.

Capon, Alan R. *His Faults Lie Gently; the Incredible Sam Hughes.* Lindsay, Ont.: F.W. Hall, 1969. 159 pp.

Castonguay, Jacques. *Les Voltigeurs de Québec; premier régiment canadien-français.* Québec, Qué: Les Voltigeurs de Québec, 1987. 523 pp.

Castonguay, Jacques, *et al. History of Canadian Forces Base Montreal and its Garrisons./Historique de la Base des Forces canadiennes Montréal et de ses garnisons.* n.p./s.l.: s.i., 1980. 181/153 pp.
Bilingual text./ Texte bilingue.

Castonguay, Jacques, [et] Armand Ross. *Le Régiment de la Chaudière.* Levis, P.Q.: imprimé privé, 1983. 644 pp.

Cavalry Standing Orders. Ottawa: printed by MacLean, Roger, 1887. 87 pp.

Cent ans d'histoire d'un régiment canadien-français; les Fusiliers Mont-Royal, 1869-1969. Montréal: Editions du Jour, 1971. 418 pp.

Centennial, 1863-1963; Presentation of Colours to the Princess of Wales' Own Regiment CA(M) by the Honourable W. Earle Rowe, P.C., Lieutenant-Governor of Ontario, Kingston, Ontario, Saturday 1st June 1963. [Kingston, Ont.: privately printed, 1963.] 15 pp.

Centennial Year, 1866-1966; 11th Field Artillery Regiment (M); 11th Field Artillery Regiment, Royal Regiment of Canadian Artillery, Canada's Oldest Artillery Regiment, Saturday, October 1, 1966. n.p.: n.d. 1 vol., unpaged.

Ceremony of Unveiling a Bronze Statue Erected on Major's Hill Park to the Memory of Ptes. Osgood and Rogers, of the Guards' Company Sharpshooters, who were Killed in the North West Rebellion in 1885. Ottawa: privately printed, 1889. 38 pp.

Chambers, Ernest J. *The Canadian Militia; a History of the Origin and Development of the Force.* Montreal: L.M. Fresco, 1907. 115 pp.

_____. *The Canadian Militia; and the Public Works Department; a History of the Origin and Development of the Force and Something about the Assistance Rendered by the Public Works Department.* Montreal: L.M. Fresco, 1907. 126 pp.

_____. *"The Duke of Cornwall's Own Rifles"; a Regimental History of the Forty-Third Regiment, Active Militia of Canada.* Ottawa: E.L. Ruddy, 1903. 82 pp.

_____. *The 5th Regiment Royal Scots of Canada Highlanders; a Regimental History.* Montreal: Guertin Print. Co., 1904. 90 pp.

_____. *The Governor-General's Body Guard; a History of the Origin, Development and Services of the Senior Cavalry Regiment in the Militia Service of the Dominion of Canada; with Some Information about the Martial Ancestry and Military Spirit of the Loyal Founders of Canada's Defensive Force.* Toronto: E.L. Ruddy, 1902. 168 pp.

_____. *Histoire du 65ème Régiment Carabiniers Mont-Royal.* Montréal: La Cie. d'Imprimerie Guertin, 1906. 151 pp.

_____. *The Montreal Highland Cadets; being a Record of the Organization and Development of a Useful and Interesting Corps.* Montreal: privately printed, 1901. 98 pp.

_____. *The 90th Regiment; Regimental History of the 90th Regiment Winnipeg Rifles.* n.p.: 1906. 99 pp.

_____. *The Origin and Services of The 3rd (Montreal) Field Battery of Artillery; with Some Notes on the Artillery of By-Gone Days and a Brief History of the Development of Field Artillery.* Montreal: E.L. Ruddy, 1898. 84 pp.

_____. *The Origin and Services of the Prince of Wales Regiment; Including a Brief History of the Militia of French Canada and of the Canadian Militia since Canada Became a British Colony; with an Account of the Different Actions in which They have Engaged, Including the North-West Rebellion of 1885.* Montreal: E.L. Ruddy, 1897. 99 pp.

Chambers, Ernest J. *The Queen's Own Rifles of Canada; a History of a Splendid Regiment's Origin, Development and Services, Including a Story of Patriotic Duties Well Performed in Three Campaigns.* Toronto: E.L. Ruddy, 1901. 156 pp.

_____. *The Royal Grenadiers; a Regimental History of the 10th Infantry Regiment of the Active Militia of Canada.* Toronto: E.L. Ruddy, 1904. 128 pp.

Champion, Thomas Edward. *History of the 10th Royals and of the Royal Grenadiers.* Toronto: Hunter, Rose, 1896. 279 pp.

[Chandler, C.M.] *The Militia in Durham County, 1812-1936; an Outline History of the Durham Regiment.* n.p.: privately printed, 1936. v.p.

Chappell, Mike. *The Canadian Army at War.* (Men-at-Arms Series, [164].) London: Osprey Pub., 1985. 48 pp.
Canadian Army uniforms.

*Chartrand, René. *Canadian Military Heritage.* Volume II: *1755-1871.* Montreal: Art Global, 1995. 238 pp.

*_____. *Le patrimoine militaire canadien; d'hier à aujourd'hui.* Tome II: *1775-1871.* Montréal: Art Global, 1995. 238 pp.

50 ans d'activités avec le 6e Régiment d'artillerie (Québec & Lévis), 1899-1949. Québec, P.Q.: Imprimerie Laflamme, 1949. 1 tome, non-paginé.

Clark, Lovell C. *The Guibord Affair.* (Canadian History through the Press.) Toronto: Holt, Rinehart & Winston, 1971. 126 pp.

Clint, H.C., comp. *A Short History of Artillery and of 57th Battery, R.C.A., 1855-1955; Formal Celebration and Reunion, Oct. 15th, 16th, 1955, Grande Allée Armouries, Quebec City.* Quebec, P.Q.: n.p., 1955. 48 pp.

Cochin, Louis. *Reminiscence of Louis Cochin, O.M.I.; a Veteran Missionary of the Cree Indians and a Prisoner in Poundmaker's Camp in 1885.* (Canadian North-West Historical Society Publications, vol. I, no. 2.) Battleford, Sask.: Star Pub. Co., 1927. 75 pp.

[Coffin, W.F.] *Thoughts on Defence; from a Canadian Point of View,* by a Canadian. Montreal: J. Lovell, 1870. 55 pp.

Cole, J.A. *Prince of Spies; Henri Le Caron.* London: Faber and Faber, 1984. 221 pp.

Corfield, William E. *Citizen Soldiers; the Canadian Fusiliers of London; the Oxford Rifles; the Perth Regiment.* London, Ont.: Royal Canadian Regiment, 1983. 86 pp.

Le Corps de Santé royal canadien. Ottawa: Imprimeur de la Reine, 1954. 11 pp.

*_The Corps of Royal Canadian Engineers._ Ottawa: Queen's Printer, 1953. 21 pp.

The Corps of Royal Canadian Engineers; a Brief History. Ottawa: King's Printer, 1948. 56 pp.

Crook, E.D., and J.K. Marteinson, eds. _A Pictorial History of the 8th Canadian Hussars (Princess Louise's)._ n.p.: privately printed, 1973. 343 pp.

Cross, Michael, and Robert Bothwell, eds. _Policy by Other Means; Essays in Honour of C.P. Stacey._ Toronto: Clarke, Irwin, 1972. 258 pp.

Cruikshank, E.A. _Camp Niagara; with a Historical Sketch of Niagara-on-the-Lake and Niagara Camp._ Niagara Falls, Ont.: F.H. Leslie, 1906. 1 vol., chiefly illus.

————. _The Origin and Official History of the Thirteenth Battalion of Infantry; and a Description of the Work of the Early Militia of the Niagara Peninsula in the War of 1812 and the Rebellion of 1837._ Hamilton, Ont.: E.L. Ruddy, 1899. 88 pp.

Cunniffe, Dick. _Scarlet, Riflegreen and Khaki; the Military in Calgary._ Calgary: Century Calgary Publications, 1975. 40 pp.

————. _The Story of a Regiment; Lord Strathcona's Horse (Royal Canadians)._ [Volume I.] n.p.: Lord Strathcona's Horse (Royal Canadians) Regimental Society, 1995. 192 pp.

Cunningham-Dunlop, C.J.A. _Mobility of the Modern Army; the Practical Use of Gig Infantry._ n.p.: n.d. 11 pp.

Curchin, Leonard A., and Brian D. Sim. _The Elgins; the Story of the Elgin Regt. (RCAC) and its Predecessors._ St. Thomas, Ont.: privately printed, 1977. 150 pp.

Cuthbertson-Muir, R. Major. _The Early Political and Military History of Burford._ Quebec, P.Q.: La Cie. d'imprimerie commerciale, 1913. 371 pp.

*Daoust, Charles R. _Cent-vingt jours de service actif; récit historique très complet de la campagne du 65ème au Nord-Ouest._ Montréal: E. Sénécal, 1886. 242 pp.

* ————. _One Hundred and Twenty Days of Active Service; a Complete Historical Narrative of the Campaign of the 65th in the North West._ Wetaskiwin, Alta.: privately printed, 1982. 176 pp.

Davidson, William McCartney. _The Life and Times of Louis Riel._ Calgary: Albertan Printers, [1952]. 114 pp.

————. _Louis Riel, 1844-1885; a Biography._ Calgary: Albertan Pub. Co., 1955. 214 pp.

Davin, Nicholas Flood. *Strathcona Horse; Speech at Lansdowne Park, March 7th, A.D. 1900, on the Occasion of the First Parade of the Strathcona Horse when a Flag from the Town of Sudbury was Presented by Her Excellency the Countess of Minto.* Ottawa: J. Hope, 1900. 20 pp.

Davis, [Robert H.] *The Canadian Militia! Its Organization and Present Condition.* Caledonia, Ont.: T. Sawle, 1873. 16 pp.

Dawson, S.J., *see/voir* Canada. Parliament. *Report on the Red River Expedition ...;* Canada. Parlement. *Rapport sur l'expédition de la Rivière rouge ....*

De Malijay, Paul. *Le Colonel d'Orsonnens; considérations sur l'organisation militaire de la Confédération canadienne; observations critiques.* Montréal: Les Presses à Vapeur du Franc-Parleur, 1874. 58 pp.

Denison, Frederick C. *Historical Record of the Governor-General's Body Guard and its Standing Orders.* Toronto: Hunter, Rose, 1876. 87 pp.

Denison, George T. *Soldiering in Canada; Recollections and Experiences.* Toronto: G.N. Morang, 1900. 364 pp.

[Denison, George T., comp.] *Reminiscences of the Red River Rebellion of 1869.* n.p.: n.d. 45 pp.

Denison, S.A. *Memoirs.* Toronto: T.H. Best Print. Co., 1927. 174 pp.

Desjardins, L.G. *Précis historique du 17ième bataillon d'infanterie de Lévis, depuis sa formation en 1862 jusqu'à 1872, suivi des ordres permanents du même corps.* Lévis, P.Q.: Les Presses à Vapeur de "L'Echo de Lévis", 1872. 89 pp.

De Trémaudan, Auguste-Henri. *Histoire de la nation métisse dans l'ouest canadien.* Montréal: Editions A. Levesque, 1935. 448 pp.

A Distinguished Military Corps; the Oldest Mounted Calvary in Canada; History of Quebec Cavalry, Now the Queen's Own Canadian Hussars; Officers who Served their Country Faithfully and Well. Quebec, P.Q.: The Chronicle, 1902. 19 pp.

Dixon, F.E., comp. *The Volunteers' Active Service Manual; or, Internal Economy and Standing Orders for Volunteers when on Active Service with Bugle Calls and Forms of all Reports, Returns &c Necessary for the Government of a Volunteer Battalion and Shewing the Everyday Duties of the Various Grades of Rank and Command.* Toronto: G.M. Adam, 1867. 131 pp.

*The Dominion Arsenal at Quebec, 1880-1945. Quebec, P.Q.: n.p., 1947. 131 pp.

Dornbusch, C.E., comp. *The Canadian Army, 1855-1958; Regimental Histories and a Guide to the Regiments.* Cornwallville, N.Y.: Hope Farm Press, 1959. 216 pp.

Dornbusch, C.E., comp. *The Canadian Army, 1855-1955; Regimental Histories and a Guide to the Regiments.* Cornwallville, N.Y.: n.p., 1957. 162 1.

_____. *The Canadian Army, 1855-1965; Lineages; Regimental Histories.* Cornwallville, N.Y.: Hope Farm Press, 1966. 179 pp.

_____. *Lineages of the Canadian Army, 1855-1961; Armour, Cavalry, Infantry.* Cornwallville, N.Y.: Hope Farm Press, 1961. 1 vol., unpaged.

Dornier, François, et Marie-Claude Joubert. *Soldats de la côte ...; Les Fusiliers du St-Laurent d'hier à aujourd'hui.* Rimouski (Qué.): La Régie, Les Fusiliers du St-Laurent, 1992. 183 pp.

D'Orsonnens, L.G. d'Odet. *Considérations sur l'organisation militaire de la Confédération canadienne.* Montréal: Typographie Duvernay, 1874. 70 pp.

Doward, Norman R. *The Queen's Own Rifles of Canada Buglers; Historical, Patriotic, Illustrated; Patriotic Souvenir.* Toronto: privately printed, 1915. 52 pp.

Drolet, Gustave A. *Zouaviana; étape de vingt-cinq ans, 1868-1893; lettres de Rome, souvenirs de voyage, études, etc.* Montréal: E. Sénécal, 1893. 460 pp.

Duguid, Archer Fortescue. *History of the Canadian Grenadier Guards, 1760-1964.* Montreal: Gazette Print. Co., 1965. 520 pp.

Dumont, Gabriel. *Gabriel Dumont Speaks.* Translated by Michael Barnholden. Vancouver: Talon Books, 1993. 79 pp.

Dundonald, Douglas Mackinnon Baillie Hamilton Cochrane, 12th earl. *My Army Life.* London: E. Arnold, 1926. 342 pp.

Dunlevie, Horace G., comp. *Our Volunteers in the North-West; a Ready Reference Handbook.* Ottawa: Daily Free Press, 1885. 52 pp.

Dunn, Jack. *The Alberta Field Force of 1885.* Calgary: privately printed, 1994. 293 pp.

Dyer, Gwynne, and Tina Viljoen. *The Defence of Canada; in the Arms of the Empire.* Toronto: McClelland & Stewart, 1990. 375 pp.

Egan, Thomas J. *History of the Halifax Volunteer Battalion and Volunteer Companies, 1859-1887.* Halifax: A. & W. Mackinlay, 1888. 182 pp.

Elliot, S.R. *Scarlet to Green; a History of Intelligence in the Canadian Army, 1903-1963.* Toronto: privately printed, 1981. 769 pp.

Evans, W. Sanford. *The Canadian Contingents and Canadian Imperialism; a Story and a Study.* Toronto: Publishers' Syndicate, 1901. 352 pp.

Extracts from General Orders for the Guidance of Troops in Affording Aid to the Civil Power. Quebec, P.Q.: Daily Evening Mercury Office, 1868. 23 pp.

The Fenian Raid of 1870, by Reporters Present at the Scenes. Montreal: Witness Print. House, 1870. 73 pp.

Fetherstonhaugh, R.C. *A Short History of the Royal Canadian Dragoons.* Toronto: Southam Press, 1932. 52 pp.

Fetherstonhaugh, R.C., and G.R. Stevens. *The Royal Canadian Regiment.* Vol. I: Montreal: Gazette Print. Co., 1936. Vol. II: London, Ont.: privately printed, 1967. 2 vols.

A Few Practical Hints to the Officers ... see Attwood, Peter Hinds.

A Few Words on Canada, by a Canadian. Ottawa: Hunter, Rose, 1871. 72 pp.

Fifth Military Tournament; to be Held in Conjunction with the Ninth Canadian Horse Show, Armouries, Toronto, Wednesday, Thursday, Friday, Saturday, April 29 and 30, May 1 and 2, 1903. n.p.: [1903]. 20 pp.

Fletcher, [Henry Charles]. *A Lecture Delivered at the Literary and Scientific Institute, Ottawa, by Col. Fletcher, Scots Fusilier Guards, Military Secretary, February, 1875.* Ottawa: n.p., n.d. 19 pp.

_____. *Memorandum on the Militia System of Canada.* Ottawa: Citizen Print. Co., 1873. 20 pp.

Flick, C.L. *A Short History of the 31st British Columbia Horse.* Victoria, B.C.: J.P. Buckle, 1922. 40 pp.

Foster, J.A. *Muskets to Missiles; a Pictorial History of Canada's Ground Forces.* Toronto: Methuen, 1987. 251 pp.

Fox, Brent. *Camp Aldershot; Serving since 1904.* (The King's Historical Society Series, number 1.) [Kentville, N.S.]: King's Historical Society, 1983. 24 pp.

Fraser, Alexander. *The 48th Highlanders of Toronto; Canadian Militia; the Origin and History of this Regiment, and a Short History of the Highland Regiments from Time to Time Stationed in Canada.* Toronto: E.L. Ruddy, 1900. 128 pp.

Fraser, W.B. *Always a Strathcona.* Calgary: Comprint Pub. Co., 1976. 252 pp.

French, John Denton Pinkstone French, 1st earl. *Report by General Sir John French, G.C.B., G.C.V.O., K.C.M.G., Inspector General of the Imperial Forces, upon his Inspection of the Canadian Military Forces.* (Sessional Paper, no. 35a.) Ottawa: King's Printer, 1910. 38 pp.

Frog Lake Massacre. Surrey, B.C.: Frontier Books, 1984. 96 pp.

From Toronto to Fort Garry see Griffin, Justin A.

Fryer, Mary Beacock. *Battlefields of Canada.* Toronto: Dundurn Press, 1986. 273 pp.

Fryer, Mary Beacock. *More Battlefields of Canada.* Toronto: Dundurn Press, 1993. 184 pp.

Gagan, David. *The Denison Family of Toronto, 1792-1925.* (Canadian Biographical Studies.) Toronto: Univ. of Toronto Press, 1973. 113 pp.

Gallant, A.M. *Pride; the History of 1390 RCACC.* Red Deer, Alta.: printed by Fletcher, [1992?]. 244 pp.

General Middleton's Defence see Middleton, (Sir) Fred.

*Le Génie royal canadien. Ottawa: Imprimeur de la Reine, 1954. 23 pp.

Goodspeed, D.J. *Battle Royal; a History of the Royal Regiment of Canada, 1862-1962.* Toronto: privately printed, 1962. 703 pp.

*Gouin, Jacques, and Lucien Brault. *Legacy of Honour; the Panets, Canada's Foremost Military Family.* Toronto: Methuen, 1985. 240 pp.

Gouin, Jacques, *et al. Bon coeur et bon bras; histoire du Régiment de Maisonneuve, 1880-1980.* Montréal: imprimé privé, 1980. 298 pp.

*Gouin, Jacques et Lucien Brault. *Les Panet de Québec; histoire d'une lignée militaire.* Montréal: Bergeron, 1984. 238 pp.

Governor General's Foot Guards, Ottawa; Seventy-Fifth Anniversary, June 8, 1872-1947. Ottawa: privately printed, 1947. 43 pp.

[Gowanlock, Theresa.] *Two Months in the Camp of Big Bear; the Life and Adventures of Theresa Gowanlock and Theresa Delaney.* Parkdale, Ont.: Times Office, 1885. 141 pp.

Granatstein, J.L., and David J. Bercuson. *War and Peacekeeping; from South Africa to the Gulf — Canada's Limited Wars.* Toronto: Key Porter Books, 1991. 266 pp.

Granatstein, J.L., and R.D Cuff, eds. *War and Society in North America.* Toronto: T. Nelson, 1971. 199 pp.

Gravel, Jean-Yves. *L'armée du Québec; un portrait social, 1868-1900.* Montréal: Les Éditions du Boréal Express, 1974. 157 pp.

_____. *Les soldats-citoyens; histoire du Régiment de Trois-Rivières, 1871-1978.* Trois-Rivières, P.Q.: Éditions du Bien Public, 1981. 153 pp.

[Gt. Brit. Colonial Defence Committee Canada.] *Halifax Defence Scheme.* London: H.M. Stationery Office, 1904?-12? *Amended annually.*

Gt. Brit. Parliament. *Correspondence Relative to the Recent Expedition to the Red River Settlement; with Journal of Operations.* (Command Paper, C298.) London: H.M. Stationery Office, 1871. 93 pp.

Gt. Brit. War Office. *Canadian Militia War Establishments (Provisional), 1912.* London: H.M. Stationery Office, 1911. 87 pp.

_____. *Regulations for the Clothing of the Canadian Militia (Permanent Units), Part I, 1909.* London: H.M. Stationery Office, 1909. 102 pp.

_____. *Regulations for the Equipment of the Canadian Militia.* London: H.M. Stationery Office, 1909. 38 pp.

Gt. Brit. War Office. General Staff. *Handbook of the Land Forces of British Dominions, Colonies and Protectorates (Other than India).* Part I: *The Dominion of Canada.* London: H.M. Stationery Office, 1908. 264 pp.

Greenhous, Brereton. *Dragoon; the Centennial History of the Royal Canadian Dragoons, 1883-1983.* Ottawa: Guild of the Royal Canadian Dragoons, 1983. 557 pp.

_____. *Guarding the Goldfields; the Story of the Yukon Field Force.* (Canadian War Museum Historical Publication no. 24.) Toronto: Dundurn Press, 1987. 222 pp.

_____. *Semper Paratus; the History of the Royal Hamilton Light Infantry (Wentworth Regiment), 1862-1977,* by Kingsley Brown, Senior, Kingsley Brown, Junior, and Brereton Greenhous. Revised and edited by Brereton Greenhous. Hamilton, Ont.: privately printed, 1977. 446 pp.

Griesbach, W.A. *I Remember.* Toronto: Ryerson Press, 1946. 353 pp.

Griffin, Frederick. *Major-General Sir Henry Mill Pellatt, CVO, DCL, VD; a Gentleman of Toronto, 1859-1939.* Toronto: Ontario Pub. Co., 1939. 30 pp.

[Griffin, Justin A.] *From Toronto to Fort Garry; an Account of the Second Expedition to Red River; Diary of a Private Soldier.* Hamilton, Ont.: Evening Times, n.d. 64 pp.

Hamilton, Fred J. *The New Declaration; a Record of the Reception of the Sixth Fusiliers of Montreal, by the Citizens of St. Albans, Vt, July 4th, 1878; being the First Occasion on which British Armed Troops have Participated in the Declaration of American Independence.* Montreal: Dawson Bros., 1878. 53 pp.

Hamilton, (Sir) Ian. *Report on the Military Institutions of Canada.* Ottawa: King's Printer, 1913. 43 pp.

Hardy, René. *Les Zouaves; une stratégie du clergé québecois au XIXe siècle.* Montréal: Boréal Express, 1980. 312 pp.

Hardy, René, *voir aussi Les Zouaves pontificaux canadiens.*

Harker, Douglas E. *The Dukes; the Story of the Men who have Served in Peace and War with the British Columbia Regiment (D.C.O.), 1883-1973.* n.p.: privately printed, 1974. 438 pp.

Harman, S. Bruce. *'Twas 26 Years Ago; Narrative of the Red River Expedition, 1870.* Toronto: Toronto Mail and Empire, 1896. 31 pp.

Harris, Stephen. *Canadian Brass: the Making of a Professional Army, 1860-1939.* Toronto: Univ. of Toronto Press, 1988. 271 pp.

Hart-McHarg, William. *From Quebec to Pretoria with the Royal Canadian Regiment.* Toronto: W. Briggs, 1902. 276 pp.

Haycock, Ronald G. *Sam Hughes; the Public Career of a Controversial Canadian, 1885-1916.* (Canadian War Museum Historical Publication no. 21.) n.p.: Wilfrid Laurier Univ. Press in collaboration with Canadian War Museum, 1986. 355 pp.

*Hildebrandt, Walter. *La bataille de Batoche; une petite guerre britannique contre des Métis retranchés.* (Etudes en archéologie, architecture et histoire.) Ottawa: Direction des lieux et des parcs historiques nationaux, Parcs Canada, 1985. 122 pp.

*_____. *The Battle of Batoche; British Small Warfare and the Entrenched Métis.* (Studies in Archaeology, Architecture and History.) Ottawa: National Historic Parks and Sites Branch, Parks Canada, 1985. 120 pp.

History of the Second Battalion, the "Queen's Own Rifles" of Toronto. n.p.: [189-?]. 1 vol., chiefly ports.

Hitsman, J. MacKay. *Safeguarding Canada, 1763-1871.* Toronto: Univ. of Toronto Press, 1968. 240 pp.

Holmes, J.G. *Dominion Artillery Association Prize Essay; on the Proportions of Artillery (Field, Siege and Garrison) Required for the Present Force of Active Militia of the Dominion, with Suggestions as to their Organization, Equipment and Localization.* Quebec, P.Q.: privately printed, 1878. 47 pp.

Houghton, C.F. *Houghton to Middleton; the Colonel with Vigor Replies to the General; Long but Interesting; Interesting Incidents of the Campaign of '85; Grave Charge Explained; Sir Fred. Middleton's Conduct towards his Second in Command as Seen by the Latter.* n.p.: 1894. 14 pp.

How, Douglas. *The 8th Hussars; a History of the Regiment.* Sussex, N.B.: Maritime Pub., 1964. 446 pp.

"How Not to Do It"; a Short Sermon on the Canadian Militia, by "Bluenose" [*pseud.*]. Quebec, P.Q.: Morning Chronicle, 1881. 29 pp.

*Howard, Joseph Kinsey. *L'empire des bois-brûlés.* Ghislain Pouliot, tr. Saint-Boniface, Man.: Editions des Plaines, 1989. 515 pp.

*_____. *Strange Empire; a Narrative of the Northwest.* New York: Morrow, 1952. 601 pp.

Hubbell, E.L. *The Winnipeg Grenadiers.* n.p.: n.d. 16 pp.

135

Hubly, Russell C. *"G" Company, or Every-Day Life of the R.C.R.; being a Descriptive Account of Typical Events in the Life of the First Canadian Contingent in South Africa.* St. John, N.B.: J. & A. McMillan, 1901. 109 pp.

Hughes, G.W., comp. *A Marchpast of the Corps and Regiments of the Canadian Army, Past and Present.* Calgary: n.p., n.d. 3 vols.

Hughes, Stuart, ed. *The Frog Lake "Massacre"; Personal Perspectives on Ethnic Conflict.* (The Carleton Library, no. 97.) Toronto: McClelland and Stewart, 1976. 364 pp.

Hunter, A.T. *History of the 12th Regiment, York Rangers; with Some Account of the Different Raisings of Militia in the County of York, Ontario.* Toronto: Murray Print. Co., 1912. 90 pp.

Hutchison, Paul P. *A Short History of the Royal Highland Regiment the Black Watch, 1725-1948.* n.p.: 1948. 39 pp.

_____. *Canada's Black Watch; the First Hundred Years, 1862-1962.* Montreal: privately printed, [1962]. 340 pp.

Huyshe, G.L. *The Red River Expedition.* London: Macmillan, 1871. 276 pp.

Illustrated Historical Album of the 2nd Battalion, the Queen's Own Rifles of Canada, 1856-1894. Toronto: Toronto News Co., 1894. 80 pp.

The Illustrated War News; Nos. 1 to 18 Inclusive; Containing All the Illustrations Referring to the North-West Rebellion of 1885, from its Outbreak to the Return and Disbanding of the Troops. Toronto: Grip, 1885. 152 pp.

An Incident in the Command of the Militia of Canada; Inspection of the 27th Battalion, at London, Ontario, June 1881, and Subsequent Correspondence. n.p.: [188-?]. 39 pp.

L'Insurrection du Nord-Ouest, 1885. [Montréal]: Le Monde, s.d. 39 pp.

*L'Intendance royale canadienne. Ottawa: Imprimeur de la Reine, 1954. 12 pp.

Irvine, [M. Bell]. *Report on the Red River Expedition of 1870.* (Command Paper, C391.) London: H.M. Stationery Office, 1871. 16 pp.

Jackson, H.M. *Canadian Prime Ministers and the Canadian Militia.* n.p.: 1958. 11 pp.

_____. *The Princess Louise Dragoon Guards; a History.* n.p.: 1952. 306 pp.

_____. *The Roll of the Regiments (the Active Militia).* Ottawa: n.p., 1959. 176 pp.

_____. *The Roll of the Regiments (the Sedentary Militia).* n.p.: 1960. 100 pp.

Jackson, H.M. *The Royal Regiment of Artillery, Ottawa, 1855-1952; a History.* Montreal: privately printed, 1952. 418 pp.

_____. *The Sherbrooke Regiment (12th Armoured Regiment).* n.p.: 1958. 229 pp.

Jackson, Louis. *Our Caughnawagas in Egypt; a Narrative of What was Seen and Accomplished by the Contingent of North American Indian Voyageurs who Led the British Boat Expedition for the Relief of Khartoum up the Cataracts of the Nile.* Montreal: W.M. Drysdale, 1885. 35 pp.

Jamieson, F.C., ed. *The Alberta Field Force of 1885.* (Canadian North-West Historical Society Publications, vol. I, no. 7.) Battleford, Sask.: n.p., 1931. 53 pp.

Johnston, Stafford. *The Fighting Perths; the Story of the First Century in the Life of a Canadian County Regiment.* Stratford, Ont.: privately printed, 1964. 133 pp.

Karpan, Arlene, and Robin Karpan. *Saskatchewan Guide to Historic Sites of the North West Rebellion.* [Regina: Tourism Saskatchewan], 1985. 76 pp.

Kennedy, H.G., ed. *History of the 101st Regiment Edmonton Fusiliers; Allied with the Royal Munster Fusiliers, 1908-1913.* n.p.: Pierce & Kennedy, [1913]. 1 vol., unpaged.

Kennedy, Howard Angus. *The North-West Rebellion.* (The Ryerson Canadian History Readers.) Toronto: Ryerson Press, 1929. 32 pp.

Kerry, A.J., and W.A. McDill. *The History of the Corps of Royal Canadian Engineers.* Ottawa: privately printed, 1962. 2 vols.

King, Horatio C. *An Account of the Visit of the Thirteenth Regiment N.G.S.N.Y. to Montreal, Canada, May, 1879.* Brooklyn, N.Y.: privately printed, 1879. 68 pp.

King, W.D., comp. *A Brief History of Militia Units Established at Various Periods at Yarmouth, Nova Scotia, 1812-1947.* Yarmouth, N.S.: privately printed, 1947. 32 pp.

Kreutzweiser, Erwin E. *The Red River Insurrection; its Causes and Events.* Gardenvale, P.Q.: Garden City Press, [1936]. 166 pp.

Labat Gaston P. *Le Livre d'or (The Golden Book) of the Canadian Contingents in South Africa; with an Appendix on Canadian Loyalty, Containing Letters, Documents, Photographs.* Montreal: n.p., 1901. v.p.

_____. *Les voyageurs canadiens à l'expédition du Soudan; ou, quatre-vingt-dix jours avec les crocodiles.* Québec, P.Q.: L.J. Demers, 1886. 214 pp.

Lachance, François. *Prise de Rome; odysée des Zouaves canadiens de Rome à Québec.* Québec, P.Q.: Léger Brousseau, 1870. 47 pp.

Laidlaw, Alexr. *From the St. Lawrence to the North Saskatchewan; being Some Incidents Connected with the Detachment of "A" Battery, Regt. Canadian Artillery, who Composed Part of the North West Field Force in the Rebellion of 1885.* Halifax: n.p., 1885. 43 pp.

Lake, (Sir) P.H.N. *Memorandum by Major General P.H.N. Lake, C.B., C.M.G., Inspector General, upon that Portion of the Report of the Civil Service Commissioners, 1908, which Deals with the Administration of the Militia.* Ottawa: King's Printer, 1908. 23 pp.

————. *Report upon the Best Method of Giving Effect to the Recommendations of General Sir John French, Regarding the Canadian Militia.* (Sessional Paper, no. 35b.) Ottawa: King's Printer, 1910. 16 pp.

Lamb, James B. *Jingo.* Toronto: Macmillan Canada, 1992. 284 pp.
Biography of Major General Thomas Bland Strange.

Lamontagne, Léopold. *Les archives régimentaires des Fusiliers du S.-Laurent.* Rimouski, P.Q.: s.i., 1943. 247 pp.

Laurie, R.C. *Reminiscences of Early Days in Battleford and with Middleton's Column.* Battleford, Sask.: privately printed, 1935. 140 pp.

Lavoie, Joseph A. *Le Régiment de Montmagny de 1869 à 1931.* s.l.: s.i., [1932]. 117 pp.

Le Caron, Henri, *see* Beach, Thomas Miller.

Leonard, R.W. *Gig Infantry.* St. Catharines, Ont.: n.p., 1908. 16 pp.

Little Black Devils see Tascona, Bruce, and Eric Wells.

Lodolini, Ello, *voir Les Zouaves pontificaux canadiens.*

The Log; Containing an Account of the 7th Fusiliers' Trip from London, Ont., to Clark's Crossing, N.W.T.; also, the Official Reports of the Officers in Charge of Boats. London, Ont.: Free Press Print. Co., 1888. 47 pp.

Lord Dundonald; les motifs de sa révocation. s.l.: s.i., [1904?]. 16 pp.

Lord Dundonald; Orders in Council and Correspondence Showing Why He was Removed from Office; Attacked Canada's Government in Defiance of Military Regulations. (Political Pointers, no. 5.) n.p.: [1904]. 72 pp.

The Lorne Scots (Peel, Dufferin and Halton Regiment). Brampton, Ont.: privately printed, 1962. 47 pp.

Lyons, Herbert H. *6th Regiment, the Duke of Connaught's Own Rifles; Souvenir Edition.* Vancouver: privately printed, 1907. 1 vol., unpaged.

McCormick, A.S. *The "Royal Canadians" in South Africa, 1899-1902.* n.p.: n.d. 13 pp.

McCourt, Edward. *Buckskin Brigadier; the Story of the Alberta Field Force.* Toronto: Macmillan, 1955. 150 pp.

_____. *Revolt in the West; the Story of the Riel Rebellion.* (Great Stories of Canada.) Toronto: Macmillan, 1958. 159 pp.

MacDermot, H.E. *Sir Thomas Roddick; his Work in Medicine and Public Life.* Toronto: Macmillan, 1938. 160 pp.

Macdonald, John A. *Troublous Times in Canada; a History of the Fenian Raids of 1866 and 1870.* Toronto: W.S. Johnston, 1910. 255 pp.

McGee, Robert. *The Fenian Raids on the Huntingdon Frontier 1866 and 1870; Centennial Issue.* n.p.: [1967]. 66 pp.

McGregor, F., ed. *LdSH (RC) '85-70'.* Winnipeg: privately printed, 1970. 62 pp.

McKee, Sandra Lynn, ed. *Gabriel Dumont; Indian Fighter.* (Frontier Books, no. 14.) [Calgary: Frontiers Unlimited, n.d.] 51 pp.

McKenzie, Thomas. *My Life as a Soldier.* St. John, N.B.: J. & A. McMillan, 1898. 202 pp.

Mackenzie-Naughton, J.D. *The Princess of Wales' Own Regiment (M.G.).* Kingston, Ont.: privately printed, 1946. 74 pp.

MacKinnon, Hedley V. *War Sketches; Reminiscences of the Boer War in South Africa, 1899-1900.* Charlottetown, P.E.I.: Examiner, 1900. 73 pp.

MacLaren, Roy. *Canadians on the Nile, 1882-1898; being the Adventures of the Voyageurs on the Khartoum Relief Expedition and Other Exploits.* Vancouver: Univ. of British Columbia Press, 1978. 184 pp.

MacLeod, [Elizabeth]. *For the Flag; or, Lays and Incidents of the South African War.* Charlottetown, P.E.I.: A. Irwin, 1901. 185 pp.

Macleod, R.C., ed. *Reminiscences of a Bungle, by One of the Bunglers; and Two Other Northwest Rebellion Diaries.* (Western Canada Reprint Series, 3.) Edmonton: Univ. of Alberta Press, 1983. 323 pp.
Diaries of Louis Redman Ord, Richard Scougall Cassels and Harold Penryn Rusden.

McMicken, Gilbert. *The Abortive Fenian Raid on Manitoba; Account by One who Knew its Secret History; a Paper Read before the Society May 11, 1888.* (Historical and Scientific Society of Manitoba Transactions, no. 32.) Winnipeg: Manitoba Free Press, 1888. 11 pp.

MacNachtan, Neil F., comp. *Guide for Duties of the Canadian Field Artillery.* Coburg, Ont.: n.p., 1904. 60 pp.

MacPherson, Pennington. *A Catechism on Military Law as Applicable to the Militia of Canada, Consisting of Questions and Answers on the Militia Act, 1883; Rules and Regulations for the Militia, 1883; the Army Act, 1881; Rules of Procedure, 1881; Queen's Regulations, 1883; Together with a Compilation of the Principal Points of the Law of Evidence.* Montreal: J. Lovell, 1886. 191 pp.

MacShane, J.R. *The Dominion Militia; Past and Present.* Halifax: J. Bowes, 1896. 40 pp.

Magnacca, Stephen A. *1871-1971; One Hundredth Anniversary of the 13 Field Battery Based at Portage La Prairie, Manitoba.* n.p.: n.d. 12 pp.

Major, J.C. *The Red River Expedition.* Winnipeg: privately printed, 1870. 28 pp.

Manarey, R. Barrie. *The Canadian Bayonet.* Edmonton: Century Press, 1971. 51 pp.

Marquis, G.E. *Le Régiment de Lévis; historique et album.* Lévis, P.Q.: s.i., 1952. 292 pp.

Marquis T.G. *Canada's Sons on Kopje and Veldt; a Historical Account of the Canadian Contingents Based on the Official Despatches of Lieutenant-Colonel W.D. Otter and the Other Commanding Officers at the Front; on the Letters and Despatches of Such War Correspondents as C. Frederick Hamilton, S.C. Simonski, Stanley McKeown Brown, John Evans and W. Richmond Smith.* Toronto: The Canada's Sons Pub. Co., 1900. 490 pp.

Marraro, Howard R. *Canadian and American Zouaves in the Papal Army, 1868-1870.* n.p.: 1945. 22 pp.

Marteinson, John, and others. *We Stand on Guard; an Illustrated History of the Canadian Army.* Montreal: Ovale, 1992. 511 pp.

Mazéas, Daniel. *Insignes armée canadienne, 1900-1914; Canadian Badges; supplément, 1920-1950.* Guingamp, France: privately printed, 1972. 116 pp.

Mellish, Annie Elizabeth. *Our Boys under Fire; or Maritime Volunteers in South Africa.* Charlottetown, P.E.I.: privately printed, 1900. 120 pp.

Melrose, Wm. *The Stanstead Cavalry; History, Opportunities and Possibilities; Dedicated to the Young Men of Stanstead County and Those who Serve in the 26th Stanstead Dragoons.* [Hartford, Conn.: Plimpton Press], 1914. 52 pp.

Merritt, Wm. Hamilton. *Regimental Standing Orders of the Governor-General's Body Guard; with Prefatory Historical Summary and Lists of Officers and Sergeant-Majors.* Toronto: Hunter, Rose, 1910. 170 pp.

Middleton, (Sir) Fred. *General Middleton's Defence; as Contained in his Parting Address to the People of Canada.* Toronto: Evening Telegram, 1890. 14 pp.

_____. *Suppression of the Rebellion in the North West Territories of Canada, 1885.* G.H. Needler, ed. (University of Toronto Studies; History and Economics Series, vol. XI.) Toronto: Univ. of Toronto Press, 1948. 80 pp.

Mika, Nick, and Helma Mika, comps. *The Riel Rebellion, 1885.* Belleville, Ont.: Mika Silk Screening, [1972]. 354 pp.

The Militia in Durham County ... see Chandler, C.M.

The Militia of Canada; from Letters to the Saturday's Special Military Column of the Empire upon Military Organization, by "The Odd File". Toronto: Hunter, Rose, 1892. 24 pp.

Miller, Carman. *Canada and the Boer War./Le Canada et la guerre des Boers.* Ottawa: National Film Board of Canada/Office national du film du Canada, [1970]. 18 pp.
Bilingual text./ Texte bilingue.

_____. *No Surrender; the Battle of Harts River, 1902.* (Canadian Battle Series no. 9.) Toronto: Canadian War Museum; Balmuir Book Pub., 1993. 31 pp.

_____. *Painting the Map Red; Canada and the South African War, 1899-1902.* (Canadian War Musem Historical Publication no. 28.) Montreal: Canadian War Museum and McGill-Queen's Univ. Press, 1993. 541 pp.

Milnes, Herbert. *A Story of the Oxford Rifles, 1798-1954.* (Oxford Museum Bulletin, no. 5.) Woodstock, Ont.: printed by Woodstock Print & Litho, 1974. 28 pp.

La Minerve, Montréal, P.Q. *Sir Adolphe Caron, G.C.M.G., ministre de la Milice et ses détracteurs; ou huit années d'administration militaire.* Montréal: Cie. d'imprimerie et lithographie Gelhardt-Berthiaume, 1888. 34 pp.

Missisquoi County Historical Society. *The Fenian Raids 1866-1870; Missisquoi County.* Stanbridge East, P.Q.: privately printed, 1967. 88 pp.

Mitchell, G.D., with B.A. Reid and W. Simcock. *RCHA — Right of the Line; an Anecdotal History of the Royal Canadian Horse Artillery from 1871.* Ottawa: RCHA History Committee, 1986. 303 pp.

Mitchell, Michael, comp. *Ducimus; the Regiments of the Canadian Infantry.* St. Hubert, Que.: Director of Infantry, Mobile Command Headquarters, 1992. 248 pp.

Moir, J.S., ed. *History of the Royal Canadian Corps of Signals, 1903-1961.* Ottawa: privately printed, 1962. 336 pp.

Montizambert, C.E. *Dominion Artillery Association Prize Essay; on the Supply, Care and Repair of Artillery Materiel, Including Small Arms and Ammunition for Canadian Militia.* Quebec, P.Q.: Gunnery School Press, 1877. 38 pp.

Moogk, Peter N., and R.V. Stevenson. *Vancouver Defended; a History of the Men and Guns of the Lower Mainland Defences, 1859-1949.* Surrey, B.C.: Antonson Pub., 1978. 128 pp.

Moore, Alexander Huggins, comp. *Sketch of the XIII Battalion A.M. with a Statistical Record of the Officers.* Hamilton, Ont.: R. Raw, 1875. 60 pp.

Morice, A.G. *A Critical History of the Red River Insurrection, after Official Documents and Non-Catholic Sources.* Winnipeg: Canadian Publishers, 1935. 375 pp.

Morris, David A. *The Canadian Militia; from 1855; an Historical Summary.* Erin, Ont.: Boston Mills Press, 1983. 328 pp.

Morrison, E.W.B. *With the Guns in South Africa.* Hamilton, Ont.: Spectator Print. Co., 1901. 307 pp.

Morton, Desmond. *Canada at Paardeberg.* (Canadian Battle Series no. 2) Ottawa: Balmuir Book Pub.; Canadian War Museum, National Museums of Canada, 1986. 27 pp.

_____. *The Canadian General, Sir William Otter.* (Canadian War Museum Historical Publication Number 9.) Toronto: Hakkert, 1974. 423 pp.

_____. *The Last War Drum; the North West Campaign of 1885.* (Canadian War Museum Historical Publication Number 5.) Toronto: Hakkert, 1972. 193 pp.

_____. *Ministers and Generals; Politics and the Canadian Militia, 1868-1904.* Toronto: Univ. of Toronto Press, 1970. 257 pp.

Morton, Desmond, and Reginald H. Roy, eds. *Telegrams of the North-West Campaign.* (Publications of the Champlain Society, XLVII.) Toronto: Champlain Society, 1972. 431 pp.

Mulvaney, Charles Pelham. *The History of the North-West Rebellion of 1885; Comprising a Full and Impartial Account of the Origin and Progress of the War, of the Various Engagements with the Indians and Half-Breeds, of the Heroic Deeds Performed by Officers and Men, and of Touching Scenes in the Field, the Camp and the Cabin; Including a History of the Indian Tribes of North-Western Canada, their Numbers, Modes of Living, Habits, Customs, Religious Rites and Ceremonies, with Thrilling Narratives of Captures, Imprisonments, Massacres and Hair-Breadth Escapes of White Settlers, etc.* Toronto: A.H. Hovey, 1885. 424 pp.

My Campaign at Niagara; being a very Veracious Account of Camp-Life and its Vicissitudes; and the Experiences, Triumphs, Trials and Sorrows of a Canadian Volunteer, by T.W. Toronto: "Pure Gold" Print. Establishment, [1871]. 95 pp.

Neale, Graham H., and Ross W. Irwin. *The Medal Roll of the Red River Campaign of 1870 in Canada.* Toronto: Charlton Press, 1982. 70 pp.

Needler, G.H. *Louis Riel; the Rebellion of 1885.* Toronto: Burns & MacEachern, 1957. 81 pp.

Nelson, H.S. *Four Months under Arms; a Reminiscence of Events Prior to, and during, the Second Riel Rebellion.* Nelson, B.C.: Nelson Daily News, n.d. 20 pp.

Nicholson, G.W.L. *Canada's Nursing Sisters.* (Canadian War Museum Historical Publication Number 13.) Toronto: S. Stevens, Hakkert, 1975. 272 pp.

_____. *The Fighting Newfoundlanders; a History of the Royal Newfoundland Regiment.* St. John's, Nfld.: Govt. of Nfld., 1964. 614 pp.

_____. *The Gunners of Canada; the History of the Royal Regiment of Canadian Artillery.* Toronto: McClelland and Stewart, 1967-72. 2 vols.

_____. *Seventy Years of Service; a History of the Royal Canadian Army Medical Corps.* Ottawa: Borealis Press, 1977. 388 pp.

Nos Croisés; ou, histoire anecdotique de l'expédition des volontaires canadiens à Rome pour la défense de l'Eglise. Montréal: Fabre et Gravel, 1871. 338 pp.

Observations on the Armed Strength of Canada. n.p.: n.d. 12 pp.

"The Odd File" *see The Militia of Canada.*

The Officers Association of the Militia of Canada. [*Semi-Annual Meeting.* No. 1-2. Ottawa: n.p., 1898-99.]

Official Souvenir Programme; Queen's Own Rifles Semi-Centennial Reunion, Toronto, June 18th to 25th, 1910. Toronto: n.p., [1910]. 39 pp.

Once in the Queen's Own, Always in the Queen's Own. n.p.: privately printed, 1932. 70 pp.

[O'Neill, John.] *Official Report of Gen. John O'Neill, President of the Fenian Brotherhood; on the Attempt to Invade Canada, May 25th, 1870; the Preparations Therefore, and the Cause of its Failure with a Sketch of his Connection with the Organization and the Motives which Led Him to Join It; also a Report of the Battle of Ridgeway, Canada West, Fought June 2nd, 1866, by Colonel Booker, Commanding the Queen's Own, and other Canadian Troops, and Colonel John O'Neill, Commanding the Fenians.* New York: J.J. Foster, 1870. 62 pp.

Ontario. Legislative Assembly. *Documents and Correspondence Regarding Petawawa Camp and Proceedings in the Legislature.* Toronto: King's Printer, 1907. 14 pp.

Oppen, William A., comp. *The Riel Rebellions; a Cartographic History./Le récit cartographique des affaires Riel.* [Toronto]: Univ. of Toronto Press in association with the Public Archives of Canada and the Canadian Government Publishing Centre/Univ. of Toronto Press avec la collaboration des Archives publiques du Canada et du Centre d'édition du gouvernement du Canada, 1979. 109 pp.
Bilingual text./ Texte bilingue.

[Ord, Lewis Redman.] *Reminiscences of a Bungle, by One of the Bunglers.* Toronto: Grip, 1887. 66 pp.

Oswald, W.R. *The Canadian Militia; an Historical Sketch; a Lecture Delivered to the Young Men's Association of St. Paul's Church, Montreal, on 8th March, 1886.* n.p.: n.d. 14 pp.

Ottawa's Heroes; Portraits and Biographies of the Ottawa Volunteers Killed in South Africa. Ottawa: Reynolds, 1900. 49 pp.

Otter, W.D., comp. *The Guide; a Manual for the Canadian Militia (Infantry); Embracing the Interior Economy, Duties, Discipline, Dress, Books and Correspondence of a Regiment in Barracks, Camp or at Home, with Bugle Calls and Instructions for Transport, Pitching Tents, etc.* Toronto: Willing & Williamson, 1880. 246 pp.
Many subsequent editions.

Ouimet, Adolphe, et B.A.T. de Montigny. *La vérité sur la question métisse au Nord-Ouest,* par Adolphe Ouimet. *Biographie et récit de Gabriel Dumont sur les événements de 1885,* par B.A.T. de Montigny. Montréal: s.i., 1889. 400 pp.

Pallas, S.M., comp. *Canadian Recipients of the Colonial Auxiliary Forces Officers' Decoration and the Colonial Auxiliary Forces Long Service Medal.* Ottawa: printed by Tri-Graphic Print., 1990. 183 pp.

Pelletier, Oscar C. *Mémoires, souvenirs de famille et récits.* Québec, P.Q.: s.i., 1940. 396 pp.

Pennefather, John P. *Thirteen Years on the Prairies; from Winnipeg to Cold Lake; Fifteen Hundred Miles.* London: K. Paul, Trench, Trubner, 1892. 127 pp.

Penny, Arthur G. *Royal Rifles of Canada, "Able and Willing" since 1862; a Short History.* n.p.: 1962. 62 pp.

Phillips, Roger, and Jerome J. Knap. *Sir Charles Ross and his Rifle.* (Historical Arms Series, no. 11.) Ottawa: Museum Restoration Service, 1969. 32 pp.

144

Phillips, Roger, F. Dupuis and J. Chadwick. *The Ross Rifle Story.* Antigonish, N.S.: privately printed, 1984. 475 pp.

Prescott, John F. *In Flanders Fields; the Story of John McCrae.* Erin, Ont.: Boston Mills Press, 1985. 144 pp.

Preston, Richard A. *Canada and "Imperial Defense"; a Study of the Origins of the British Commonwealth's Defense Organization, 1867-1919.* (Duke University Commonwealth-Studies Center; Publication Number 29.) Durham, N.C.: Duke Univ. Press, 1967. 576 pp.

_____. *Canada's RMC; a History of the Royal Military College.* Toronto: Univ. of Toronto Press, 1969. 415 pp.

Prince Edward Island. Adjutant General's Office. *Militia List of the Local Forces of Prince Edward Island; Commissioned Officers of the Reserve Militia and Volunteer Corps.* Charlottetown, P.E.I.: Queen's Printer, 1869. 43 pp.

The Queen's Birth-Day in Montreal, 24th May, 1879; Orders for the Military Review and Sham-Fight, with a Field Sketch, Showing the Position of the Troops at Different Periods of the Day. Montreal: Dawson, 1879. 12 pp.

Queen's Own Rifles of Canada Association. [*Queen's Own Rifles of Canada; Book of Remembrance, 1866-1918.* n.p.: 1932.] 1 vol., unpaged.

Quigley, John Gordon. *A Century of Rifles, 1860-1960; the Halifax Rifles (RCAC)(M); "cede nullis".* Halifax: privately printed, 1960. 230 pp.

Racette, Calvin. *Flags of the Métis.* Sherry Farrell Racette and Charles Belhameur, illus. Regina: Gabriel Dumont Institute of Native Studies and Applied Research, [1987]. 34 pp.

Rannie, William F., ed. *To the Thunderer his Arms; The Royal Canadian Ordnance Corps.* Lincoln, Ont.: privately printed, 1984. 360 pp.

The Regimental History of the Governor General's Foot Guards see Baylay, George Taylor.

Reid, Brian A. *Our Little Army in the Field; the Canadians in South Africa, 1899-1902.* St. Catharines, Ont.: Vanwell Pub., 1996. 206 pp.

Reminiscences of a Bungle see Ord, Lewis Redman.

Reminiscences of the Red River Rebellion ... see Denison, George T.

Reville, F. Douglas. *A Rebellion; a Story of the Red River Uprising.* Brantford, Ont.: Hurley Print. Co., 1912. 198 pp.

Riel, Louis. *L'amnistie aux métis de Manitoba; mémoire sur les causes des troubles du Nord-Ouest et sur les négociations qui ont amené leur règlement amiable.* Ottawa: s.i., 1874. 43 pp.

The Riel Rebellion, 1885. Montreal: Witness Print. House, n.d. 44 pp.

The Riel Rebellion — 1885. Surrey, B.C.: Frontier Books, 1984. 96 pp.

Rioux, Denise. *Les Fusiliers de Sherbrooke (1910-1980).* Sherbrooke, P.Q.: s.i., 1980. 68 pp.

Ritchie, Mary Christine. *Major-General Sir Geoffrey Twining; a Biographical Sketch and the Story of his East African Diaries.* Toronto: Macmillan, 1972. 102 pp.

Robertson, F.A. *5th (B.C.) Regiment, Canadian Garrison Artillery, and Early Defences of B.C. Coast; Historical Record.* Victoria, B.C.: privately printed, 1925. 2 vols.

Robertson, Peter. *Irréductible vérité/Relentless Verity/les photographes militaires canadiens depuis 1885/Canadian Military Photographers since 1885.* (Les Archives publiques du Canada/Public Archives of Canada Series.) Québec, P.Q.: Les Presses de l'Université Laval, 1973. 233 pp. *Texte bilingue./Bilingual text.*

Rocky Mountain Rangers; First Battalion C.A.-A.F., 1885-1941. New Westminster, B.C.: Columbian Co., 1941. 60 pp., chiefly illus.

Rogers, R.L. *History of the Lincoln and Welland Regiment.* n.p.: privately printed, 1954. 465 pp.

Roncetti, Gary A., and Edward E. Denby. *"The Canadians"; Those who Served in South Africa, 1899-1902.* n.p.: E.E. Denby, [1979]. 248 pp.

Ross, David. *The Journal of Moise Cormier, Zouaves Pontificaux, 1868-1870.* Winnipeg: Manitoba Museum of Man and Nature, 1975. 39 pp.

————. *Military Uniforms from the Collection of the New Brunswick Museum./Uniformes militaires tirés des collections du Musée du Nouveau-Brunswick.* Léandre Goguen, tr. Saint John, N.B.: New Brunswick Museum/Saint-Jean, N.-B.: Musée du Nouveau-Brunswick, 1980. 87 pp. *Bilingual text./Texte bilingue.*

Ross, David, and Grant Tyler. *Canadian Campaigns, 1860-70.* Rick Scollins, illus. (Men-at-Arms Series, 249.) London: Osprey Pub., 1992. 47 pp.

Rouleau, C.-E. *La papauté et les Zouaves pontificaux.* Québec, P.Q.: Le Soleil, 1905. 245 pp.

————. *Souvenirs de voyage d'un soldat de Pie IX.* Québec, P.Q.: L.J. Demers, 1905. 245 pp.

————. *Les Zouaves canadiens à Rome et au Canada.* Québec, P.Q.: Le Soleil, 1924. 83 pp.

————. *Les Zouaves pontificaux; précis historique.* Québec, P.Q.: Le Soleil, 1924. 50 pp.

Rowe, Kenneth. *The Postal History of the Canadian Contingents in the Anglo-Boer War, 1899-1902*. (Handbook #1 1981.) Toronto: Vincent G. Greene Philatelic Research Foundation, 1981. 104 pp.

Roy, Pierre-Georges. *La Famille Panet*. Lévis, P.Q.: J.A.K. Laflamme, 1906. 212 pp.

Roy, R.H. *Sinews of Steel; the History of the British Columbia Dragoons*. Brampton, Ont.: privately printed, 1965. 468 pp.

*The Royal Canadian Army Medical Corps. Ottawa: Queen's Printer, 1953. 10 pp.

*Royal Canadian Army Pay Corps. Ottawa: Queen's Printer, 1953. 11 pp.

*The Royal Canadian Army Service Corps. Ottawa: Queen's Printer, 1953. 11 pp.

The Royal Canadian Artillery. Ottawa: Queen's Printer, 1953. 10 pp.

Royal Canadian Horse Artillery; First Regiment, 1871-1971. Lahr, Germany: privately printed, [1971]. 32 pp.

The Royal Canadian Ordnance Corps Diamond Jubilee Yearbook. n.p.: 1963. 106 pp.

The Royal Highlanders of Canada, Allied with the Black Watch (Royal Highlanders), Montreal, Canada. London: H. Rees, 1918. 30 pp.

Royal Military College Club of Canada. *Proceedings*. No. 1-30. Quebec, P.Q.: Chronicle Print. Co., 1891-1913.

_____. *Reference Book Containing Information Respecting the Graduates, Ex-Cadets and Gentlemen Cadets, of the Royal Military College of Canada*. Ernest F. Würtele, comp. n.p.: privately printed, 1892. 64 pp.

The Royal Military College of Canada, 1876-1919. Kingston, Ont.: n.p., 1919. 16 pp.

Royal Military College of Canada, Kingston, Ont. *General Regulations*. Ottawa: Queen's Printer, 1882. 24 pp.

_____. *General Regulations*. Ottawa: Queen's Printer, 1886. 33 pp.

The Royal Rifles of Canada, Allied with the King's Royal Rifle Corps, 1862-1937; Ypres 1915, Festubert, Mont Sorrel, Somme 1916, Arras 1917, Hill 70, Ypres 1917, Amiens; South Africa 1899-1900; Great War 1914-1918. n.p.: [1937]. 21 pp.

The Royal Westminster Regiment, 1863-1988. New Westminster, B.C.: n.p., 1988. 72 pp.

Rudbach, N.E. *The Halifax Rifles (23 Armoured Regiment) R.C.A.C.R.F.; "90th" Anniversary, 14th May 1860 — 14th May 1950*. Halifax: n.p., 1950. 20 pp.

Rundle, Edwin G. *A Soldier's Life; being the Personal Reminiscences of Edwin G. Rundle.* Toronto: W. Briggs, 1909. 127 pp.

Rutherford, Tom. *An Unofficial History of the Grey and Simcoe Foresters Regiment, 1866-1973.* n.p.: n.d. 88 pp.

Ryerson, George Sterling. *Looking Backward.* Toronto: Ryerson Press, 1924. 264 pp.

Schragg, Lex. *History of the Ontario Regiment, 1866-1951.* Oshawa, Ont.: privately printed, 1951. 286 pp.

Scoble, T.C. *The Utilization of Colonial Forces in Imperial Defence (Read before the Toronto (Canada) Militia Institute, on Saturday 25th October, 1879).* London: H.M. Stationery Office, n.d. 11 pp.

Scoble, T.C., comp. *The Canadian Volunteer's Hand Book for Field Service.* Toronto: H. Rowsell, 1868. 108 pp.

Senior, Hereward. *The Last Invasion of Canada; the Fenian Raids, 1866-1870.* (Canadian War Museum Historical Publication No. 27.) Toronto: Dundurn Press in collaboration with the Canadian War Museum, Canadian Museum of Civilization, 1991. 226 pp.

Senior, Elinor Kyte. *Roots of the Canadian Army: Montreal District, 1846-1870.* Montreal: Montreal Military & Maritime Museum, 1981. 125 pp.

Sentiments of Celebration Commemorating the Jubilee of the South African War, 1899-1902, and the "Peace of Vereeniging", May 31st, 1902. Toronto: 50th Anniversary South African War Committee, 1951. 85 pp.

Service, G.T., and J.K. Marteinson. *The Gate; a History of the Fort Garry Horse.* Calgary: privately printed, 1971. 228 pp.

76th Anniversary, Her Majesty's Birthday, May 24th, 1895; Grand Military Review at London, Ontario; No. 1 Co'y R.R.C.I., 1st Hussars, London Field Battery, 7th Fusiliers, 13th Battalion, Hamilton, and Dufferin Rifles, Brantford. London, Ont.: London Print. and Lithographing Co., [1895]. 26 pp.

Sherlock, Robert A. *Experiences of the Halifax Battalion in the North-West.* Halifax: printed by J.W. Doley, 1885. 23 pp.

A Short History of the British Columbia Regiment; the "Dukes". n.p.: n.d. [11] pp.

Silver, A.I., and Marie-France Valleur. *The North-West Rebellion.* (Problems in Canadian History.) Toronto: Copp Clark, 1967. 68 pp.

Sinclair, J.D., comp. *The Queen's Own Cameron Highlanders of Canada; Twenty-Fifth Anniversary Souvenir.* Winnipeg: privately printed, 1935. 99 pp.

148

Sir Georges [*sic*] *Cartier sur la défense du Canada.* s.l.: s.i., [1909]. 13 pp.

[Slater, James.] *Three Years under the Canadian Flag as a Cavalry Soldier; a Peep behind the Scenes of Political, Municipal, Military, and Social Life in Canada.* n.p.: [1893]. 240 pp.

Souvenir de l'oeuvre des Zouaves pontificaux en Canada, Amérique du Nord. Montréal: Typ. du Nouveau Monde, [1868]. 26 pp.

Souvenir of the Visit of the "Queen's Own Rifles of Canada" to the Aldershot Command, August-September, 1910. Aldershot, Eng.: Gale & Polden, [1910]. 48 pp., chiefly illus.

Souvenir; Toronto Contingent of Volunteers for Service in Anglo-Boer War. [Toronto]: Toronto Print. Co., 1899. 1 vol., unpaged.

Stacey, C.P. *Canada and the British Army, 1846-1871; a Study in the Practice of Responsible Government.* (Royal Empire Society Imperial Studies Series, no. 11.) London: Longmans, Green, 1936. 287 pp.

Stacey, C.P., ed. *Records of the Nile Voyageurs, 1884-1885; the Canadian Contingent in the Gordon Relief Expedition.* (Publications of the Champlain Society, XXXVII.) Toronto: Champlain Society, 1959. 285 pp.

Standing Orders for the Regiment of Canadian Artillery. Ottawa: Queen's Printer, 1883. 42 pp.

Standing Orders [of the Fifth Regt. Royal Highlanders of Canada]. n.p.: 1912. 23 pp.

Standing Orders of the 1st or Prince of Wales Regt., Volunteer Rifles of Canadian Militia. Montreal: privately printed, 1878. 42 pp.

Standing Orders of the 43rd Battalion of Active Militia, the Ottawa and Carleton Rifles of Canada. Ottawa: privately printed, 1900. 35 pp.

Standing Orders of the Infantry School Corps, 1887. Ottawa: n.p., 1887. 79 pp.

Standing Orders of the Regiment of Canadian Artillery, March, 1887. Ottawa: printed by MacLean, Roger, 1887. 61 pp.

Standing Orders of the Royal Canadian Regiment. Ottawa: King's Printer, 1910. 46 pp.

Standing Orders of the Royal Regiment of Canadian Infantry. Ottawa: Queen's Printer, 1896. 42 pp.

Standing Orders of the 2nd Battalion Active Militia, the Queen's Own Rifles, of Canada. Toronto: Copp Clarke, 1883. 47 pp.

Standing Orders of the 2nd Battalion, Active Militia, the Queen's Own Rifles of Canada. Toronto: Brown, 1894. 32 pp.

Standing Orders of the 7th Regiment "Fusiliers". London, Ont.: n.p., 1906. 44 pp.

Standing Orders of the XIII Battalion A.M. of Canada; as Approved by His Excellency the Governor General, 23rd December, 1873. n.p.: [1873]. 12 pp.

Standing Orders of the 38th Battalion, the Dufferin Rifles. Brantford, Ont.: Watt & Shenston, 1886. 56 pp.

Standing Orders; Twenty-Third Battery, Canadian Field Artillery. n.p.: n.d. 16 pp.

Stanley, George F.G. *The Birth of Western Canada; a History of the Riel Rebellions.* London: Longmans, Green, 1936. 475 pp.

_____. Canada's Soldiers, 1604-1954; the Military History of an Unmilitary People. Toronto: Macmillan, 1954. 400 pp.
Subsequent revised and enlarged editions.

_____. *In the Face of Danger; the History of the Lake Superior Regiment.* Port Arthur, Ont.: privately printed, 1960. 357 pp.

_____. Nos soldats; l'histoire militaire du Canada de 1604 à nos jours. Traduction et adaptation sous la direction de Serge Bernier. Montréal: Les Editions de l'homme, 1980. 620 pp.

_____. *Toil & Trouble; Military Expeditions to Red River.* (Canadian War Museum Publication no. 25.) Toronto: Dundurn Press, 1989. 303 pp.

Stanley, George F.G., and Richard A. Preston. *A Short History of Kingston as a Military and Naval Centre.* Kingston, Ont.: Queen's Printer, [195-?]. 33 pp.

Steele, Harwood. *The Long Ride; a Short History of the 17th Duke of York's Royal Canadian Hussars.* Montreal: Gazette Print. Co., 1934. 48 pp.

Steele, (Sir) Samuel Benfield. *Forty Years in Canada; Reminiscences of the Creat Northwest with Some Account of his Service in South Africa.* Mollie Glen Niblett, ed. Toronto: McClelland, Goodchild & Stewart, 1915. 428 pp.

Stewart, Charles Herbert. *The Service of British Regiments in Canada and North America; a Resume, with a Chronological List of Uniforms Portrayed in Sources Consulted; Based on Regimental Histories Held in Department of National Defence Library.* (Department of National Defence Library Publication no. 1.) Ottawa: Queen's Printer, 1962. v.p.

Stewart, Charles Henry, comp. *The Concise Lineages of the Canadian Army, 1855 to Date.* Toronto: n.p., n.d. 161 pp.

Stirling, John. *The Colonials in South Africa, 1899-1902; their Record Based on the Despatches.* Edinburgh: Blackwood, 1907. 497 pp.

Stobie, Margaret R. *The Other Side of Rebellion; the Remarkable Story of Charles Bremner and his Furs.* Edmonton: NeWest Press, 1986. 202 pp.

Strange, Thomas Bland. *Gunner Jingo's Jubilee.* London: Remington, 1893. 546 pp.

_____. *The Military Aspect of Canada; a Lecture Delivered at the Royal United Service Institution.* London: Harrison, [1879]. 66 pp.

Stuart, (Sir) Campbell. *Opportunity Knocks Once.* London: Collins, 1952. 248 pp.

Stubbs, Roy St. George. *Men in Khaki; Four Regiments of Manitoba.* Toronto: Ryerson Press, 1941. 72 pp.

Sturdee, E.T. *Historical Records of the 62nd St. John Fusiliers (Canadian Militia).* St. John, N.B.: J. & A. McMillan, 1888. 139 pp.

Sulte, Benjamin. *L'expédition militaire de Manitoba, 1870.* Montréal: E. Sénécal, 1871. 50 pp.

_____. *Histoire de la milice canadienne-française, 1760-1897.* Montréal: Desbarats, 1897. 147 pp.

Summers, Jack L. *Tangled Web; Canadian Infantry Accoutrements, 1855-1985.* (Canadian War Museum Historical Publication no. 26.) Alexandria Bay, N.Y.: Museum Restoration Service, 1992. 146 pp.

*Summers, Jack L., and René Chartrand. *Military Uniforms in Canada, 1665-1970.* Illustrated by R.J. Marrion. (Canadian War Museum Historical Publication no. 16.) Ottawa: National Museums of Canada, 1981. 192 pp.

*Summers, Jack L., et René Chartrand. *L'uniforme militaire au Canada, 1665-1970.* Illustré par R. J. Marrion. Traduit par Jean Pariseau. (Musée canadien de la guerre publication d'histoire militaire no 16.) Ottawa: Musées nationaux du Canada, 1981. 192 pp.

Suthren, Victor, ed. *The Oxford Book of Canadian Military Anecdotes.* Toronto: Oxford Univ. Press, 1989. 202 pp.

Taché, Alexandre Antonin. *Fenian Raid; an Open Letter from Archbishop Taché to the Hon. Gilbert McMicken.* St. Boniface, Man.: n.p., 1888. 31 pp.

Tascona, Bruce. *The Militia of Manitoba; a Study of Infantry and Cavalry Regiments since 1883; a Look at Regimental Badges and Uniforms, List of Commanding Officers, Battle Honours.* n.p.: 1979. 48 pp.

_____. *XII Manitoba Dragoons: a Tribute.* Winnipeg: Manitoba Dragoons History Book Committee, 1991. 185 pp.

[Tascona, Bruce, and Eric Wells.] *Little Black Devils; a History of the Royal Winnipeg Rifles.* Winnipeg: Frye Pub., 1983. 241 pp.

Tassie, W.T. *The Rights of the Militia; Address of Major W.T. Tassie, Delivered at Association Hall, at 8 p.m. February 14th, 1902.* n.p.: n.d. 42 pp.

Telford, Murray M. *Scarlet to Green; the Colours, Uniforms and Insignia of the Grey and Simcoe Foresters.* Erin, Ont.: Boston Mills Press, 1987. 64 pp.

Tennant, Joseph F. *Rough Times, 1870-1920; a Souvenir of the 50th Anniversary of the Red River Expedition and the Formation of the Province of Manitoba.* n.p.: n.d. 271 pp.

Thompson, Roy J.C. *Cap Badges of the Canadian Officer Training Corps.* Dartmouth, N.S.: n.p., 1972. 68 pp.

Thoughts on Defence see Coffin, W.F.

Three Years under the Canadian Flag see Slater, James.

Tolton, Gordon E. *The Rocky Mountain Rangers; Southern Alberta's Cowboy Cavalry in the North West Rebellion 1885.* L. Gregory Ellis, ed. (Occasional Paper No. 28.) Lethbridge, Alta.: Lethbridge Historical Society, 1994. 93 pp.

Tooley, Edwyn R., *see* Canada. Dept. of Militia and Defence. *Guide for Paymasters ....*

*La Trésorerie militaire royale canadienne. Ottawa: Imprimeur de la Reine, 1954. 12 pp.

[Tricoche, George Nestler.] *La vie militaire à l'étranger; les milices françaises et anglaises au Canada, 1627-1900.* Paris: H. Charles-Lavauzelle, [1902]. 317 pp.

Tweedsmuir, John Buchan, baron. *Lord Minto; a Memoir,* by John Buchan. London: T. Nelson, 1924. 352 pp.

Two Months in the Camp of Big Bear ... see Gowanlock, Theresa.

Tyler, G.C.A. *The Lion Rampant; a Pictorial History of the Queen's Own Cameron Highlanders of Canada, 1910-1985.* Winnipeg: The Queen's Own Cameron Highlanders of Canada, 1985. 134 pp.

Upper Canada Historical Arms Society. *The Military Arms of Canada.* (Historical Arms Series, 1.) West Hill, Ont.: Museum Restoration Service, 1963. 47 pp.

Upton, Terence B. *The Rocky Mountain Rangers, 1898-1944; a Short History.* n.p.: n.d. 13 pp.

Urquhart, Hugh M. *Arthur Currie; the Biography of a Great Canadian.* Toronto: Dent, 1950. 363 pp.

Van Der Schee, W. *A Short History of Lord Strathcona's Horse (Royal Canadians).* n.p.: 1973. 19 1.

Victoria Rifles of Canada, 1861-1951; Historical Notes. n.p.: n.d. 14 pp.

Victoria Rifles of Canada; Youth Trained in Mind and Body in a Great Regiment. n.p.: [ca. 1936]. 16 pp.

La vie militaire à l'étranger voir Tricoche, George Nestler.

Les Voltigeurs de Québec, 1862-1952; notes historiques. s.l.: s.i., 1952. 16 pp.

Les Voltigeurs de Québec, 1862-1962; album du centenaire, mai 1962. St-François, P.Q.: imprimé privé, 1962. 31 pp.

W.,T., *see My Campaign at Niagara.*

Wallace, N. Willoughby. *The Rebellion in the Red River Settlement, 1869-70; its Cause and Suppression; a Lecture Delivered at Clifton, October 25th, 1871.* Barnstaple, Eng.: H.T. Cook, 1872. 40 pp.

Ware, Francis B. *The Story of the Seventh Regiment Fusiliers of London, Canada, 1899 to 1914; with an Epilogue, "A Few Days with the Fusiliers at War".* London, Ont.: Hunter Print. Co., 1945. 190 pp.

Warren, Arnold. *Wait for the Waggon; the Story of the Royal Canadian Army Service Corps.* Toronto: McClelland and Stewart, 1961. 413 pp.

Warriors of the Ojibway Country; 97th Regiment Algonquin Rifles of Canada. n.p.: 1908. 40 pp.

Watson, Robert. *Lower Fort Garry; a History of the Stone Fort.* Winnipeg: Hudson's Bay Company, 1928. 69 pp.

Watson, W.S., and others, eds. *The Brockville Rifles, Royal Canadian Infantry Corps (Allied with the King's Royal Rifle Corps); Semper Paratus; an Unofficial History.* Brockville, Ont.: Recorder Print. Co., 1966. 138 pp.

Wells, George Anderson. *The Fighting Bishop; as Recounted in the Eighty-Seventh Year of his Life to his Daughter Jeanne Carden Wells.* Toronto: Cardwell House, 1971. 628 pp.

Wicksteed, R.J. *The Canadian Militia.* Ottawa: MacLean, Roger, 1875. 139 pp.

Wiebe, Rudy, and Bob Beal, comps. *War in the West; Voices of the 1885 Rebellion.* Toronto: McClelland and Stewart, 1985. 192 pp.

Willcocks, K.D.H. *The Hastings and Prince Edward Regiment, Canada; a Short History.* Belleville, Ont.: n.p., 1967. 1 vol., unpaged.

Williams, Jeffery. *First in the Field; Gault of the Patricias.* St. Catharines, Ont.: Vanwell Pub., 1995. 278 pp.

Wilson, Barbara M., comp. *Military General Service, 1793-1814 (Canadian Recipients), Egypt Medal, 1882-1889 (Canadian Recipients), North West Canada, 1885; Index to the Medal Rolls.* London: Spink, 1975. 191 pp.

Wilson, Keith. *Charles Arkoll Boulton*. (Canadian Biographical Series.) Winnipeg: Faculty of Education, Univ. of Manitoba, 1984. 50 pp.

The Winnipeg Rifles, 8th Battalion, C.E.F., Allied with the Rifle Brigade (Prince Consort's Own); Fiftieth Anniversary, 1883-1933. Winnipeg: privately printed, 1933. 59 pp.

Winter, Charles F. *Lieutenant-General the Hon. Sir Sam Hughes K.C.B., M.P.; Canada's War Minister, 1911-1916; Recollections of Service as Military Secretary at Headquarters, Canadian Militia, prior to and during the Early Stages of the Great War.* Toronto: Macmillan, 1931. 182 pp.

Winton, Maurice V. *Saskatchewan's Prairie Soldiers, 1885-1980.* n.p.: n.d. 174 pp.
Cover title: *A Pictorial History of Saskatchewan's Military Badges and Medals.*

Wood, Herbert Fairlie. *Forgotten Canadians.* (Canadian Pageant.) Toronto: Longmans Canada, 1963. 134 pp.

*Woodcock, George. *Gabriel Dumont; le chef des Métis et sa patrie perdue.* Traduit par Pierre Desruisseaux et François Lanctôt. Montréal: VLB, 1986. 357 pp.

*_____. *Gabriel Dumont; the Metis Chief and his Lost World.* Edmonton: Hurtig, 1975. 256 pp.

Worthington, Larry. *The Spur and the Sprocket; the Story of the Royal Canadian Dragoons.* Kitchener, Ont.: Reeve Press, 1968. 170 pp.

Wright, Harold E., [and] Byron E. O'Leary. *Fortress Saint John; an Illustrated Military History, 1640-1985.* Saint John, N.B.: Partridge Island Research Project, 1985. 131 pp.

Würtele, A.G.G. *The Non-Professional Notes of the Cadets' Tour of Instruction to Montreal, Quebec, Halifax and Minor Places and Forming an Interesting Supplement to the Published Official Reports.* Quebec, P.Q.: Morning Chronicle Office, 1881. 87 pp.

Würtele, Ernest F., *see* Royal Military College Club of Canada.

Les Zouaves pontificaux canadiens; comprenant l'origine des Zouaves pontificaux canadiens, par René Hardy et *Les volontaires du Canada dans l'armée pontificale (1868-1870)*, par Ello Lodolini. Traduit de l'Italien par le Bureau des traductions, Secretariat d'état du Canada. (Musée national de l'homme; collection mercure; division de l'histoire dossier no 19.) Ottawa: Imprimeur de la Reine, 1976. 161 pp.

Les Zouaves pontificaux de Québec, le 20 septembre 1895. Québec, P.Q.: Imprimerie Proulx & Proulx, 1895. 19 pp.

1914-1918

Abbey, Edwin Austin. *An American Soldier; Letters of Edwin Austin Abbey, 2d.* Boston: Houghton Mifflin, 1918. 173 pp.
2nd Canadian Pioneer Battalion and 4th Canadian Mounted Rifles.

Abbink, Harry, and Cindy Abbink. *The Military Medal; Canadian Recipients, 1916-1922.* Calgary: Alison Pub. Co., 1987. v.p.

Adami, George. *War Story of the Canadian Army Medical Corps.* London: Rolls House, 1918. 286 pp.

Aitken, William Maxwell, *see* Beaverbrook, William Maxwell Aitken, baron.

Album-souvenir publié par l'amicale du 22e, au profit des oeuvres de guerre du Royal 22e, des Fusiliers Mont-Royal et du Régiment de Maisonneuve, en service outre-mer à l'occasion du 25e anniversaire de la Bataille de Courcelette (15 septembre 1916) et du 26e anniversaire de l'arrivée du 22e bataillon canadien-français à Boulogne, France (15 septembre 1915). Montréal: imprimé privé, 1941. 1 tome, non-paginé.

[Allen, E.P.S.] *The 116th Battalion in France,* by the Adjutant. Toronto: privately printed, 1921. 111 pp.

Anderson, P. *I That's Me: Escape from German Prison Camp and Other Adventures.* Edmonton: Bradburn Printers, n.d. 174 pp.

Another Garland from the Front. Mark 1-4. London: G. Pulman, 1915-19.
Title varies. Annual.

Un aperçu historique et un registre photographique du Bataillon "Acadien" d'outremer 165ième, F.E.C.; Lieut. Colonel L.C. D'Aigle, Officier Commandant. Ottawa: Mortimer, [1917]. 43 pp.

Argo, J.A. *The 2nd Can. Heavy Battery in the World War, 1914 to 1919; Record of the Battery from Mobilization in 1914 to Demobilization in 1919 Including Battle Engagements and Battery Positions; Chronology of World War, 1914 to 1919 and Miscellaneous Information; 2nd C.H.B. Old Boys Association: Constitution and Nominal Roll; also Maps of Western Front and Peace Proclamation Dated Mons, Nov 11, 1918.* [Montreal: n.p., 1932.] 117 pp., looseleaf.

Armit, W.B. *Army Museum; Halifax Citadel, Halifax, Nova Scotia.* Kentville, N.S.: n.p., [1957?]. 34 pp.

*L'Arsenal de Québec, 1880-1945. Québec, P.Q.: s.i., 1947. 166 pp.

Art Gallery of Toronto. *Catalogue of an Exhibition of the Canadian War Memorials, October 1926.* Toronto: privately printed, [1926]. 21 pp.

Ashbury College, Ottawa. *List of Masters and Old Boys who Served with the Colours, 1914-1919.* Ottawa: Simmons Print Co., [1919]. 33 pp.

At Duty's Call; Captain William Henry Victor van der Smissen; Queen's Own Rifles of Canada and 3rd Battalion (Toronto Regiment) Canadian Expeditionary Force; Born at Toronto the 6th of May, 1893, Killed on Mount Sorrel in Flanders the 13th of June, 1916. London: privately printed, n.d. 54 pp.

Babin, Lenard L., comp. *Cap Badges of the Canadian Expeditionary Forces 1914-1919, Illustrated.* John E. Snitzel, illus. Rochester, N.Y.: n.p., n.d. v.p.

Bagley, Fred, and Harvey Daniel Duncan. *A Legacy of Courage; "Calgary's Own" 137th Overseas Battalion, C.E.F.* Calgary: Plug Street Books, 1993. 260 pp.

Bagnall, F.W. *Not Mentioned in Despatches,* by Ex-Quaker. North Vancouver, B.C.: North Shore Press, 1933. 116 pp.

Bagshaw, M.E. *Maple Leaves in England*, by "The Little Mother". Manchester, Eng.: printed by Saunders, n.d. 139 pp.

[Bailey, John Beswick.] *Cinquante-quatre; being a Short History of the 54th Canadian Infantry Battalion*, by One of Them. n.p.: [1919]. 108 pp.

Baldwin, Harold. *"Holding the Line".* Chicago: A.C. McClurg, 1918. 305 pp.

Bank of Montreal. *Memorial of the Great War, 1914-1918; a Record of Service.* Montreal: privately printed, 1921. 261 pp.

_____. *Victory; a Monument in Memory of the Men in the Service of the Bank of Montreal who Fell in the Great War.* n.p.: [1924]. 19 pp.

*Barnard, Leslie G. *La Guerre des nations; le meilleur souvenir illustré de la Grande Guerre; décrivant spécialement le rôle du Canada et des Canadiens.* Montréal: Dodd-Simpson, 1914-15. 2 tomes.

*_____. *The War Pictorial; the Leading Pictorial Souvenir of the Great War; Depicting Especially the Part Played by Canada and Canadians.* Montreal: Dodd-Simpson, 1914-15. 2 vols.

Barnard, W.T. *The Queen's Own Rifles of Canada, 1860-1960; One Hundred Years of Canada.* Don Mills, Ont.: Ontario Pub. Co., 1960. 398 pp.

_____. *A Short History of the Queen's Own Rifles of Canada.* Toronto: MacKinnon & Atkins, n.d. 22 pp.

Barnes, C.H. *Colonel Colin Clarke Harbottle, C.M.G., D.S.O., V.D.* n.p.: [1958]. 20 pp.

Barnes, Leslie W.C.S. *Canada and the Science of Ballistics, 1914-1945.* (Organization of Military Museums of Canada Special Edition.) Ottawa: National Museums of Canada, 1985. 87 pp.

*Barnes, Leslie W.C.S. *Canada's Guns; an Illustrated History of Artillery.* (Canadian War Museum Historical Publication no. 15.) [Ottawa]: National Museum of Man, 1979. 112 pp.

*_____. *Histoire illustrée de l'artillerie canadienne.* (Musée canadien de la guerre publication d'histoire militaire no 15.) [Ottawa]: Musée national de l'Homme, 1979. 112 pp.

The Barrage. Vol. I-? n.p.: privately printed, 1917-? *Journal of the Canadian Reserve Artillery.*

Barry, A.L. *Batman to Brigadier.* n.p.: n.d. 90 pp.

Bassett, John. *John McCrae.* Markham, Ont.: Fitzhenry & Whiteside, 1984. 63 pp.

[Baylay, George Taylor], ed. *The Regimental History of the Governor General's Foot Guards.* Ottawa: privately printed, 1948. 268 pp.

Beattie, Kim. *48th Highlanders of Canada, 1891-1928.* Toronto: privately printed, 1932. 434 pp.

Beatty, David Pierce. *Memories of the Forgotten War; the World War I Diary of Pte. V.E. Goodwin.* Port Elgin, N.B.: Baie Verte Editions, 1988. 290 pp.

*Beaverbrook, William Maxwell Aitken, baron. *Les Canadiens en Flandre.* (Relation officielle des opérations du Corps expéditionnaire canadien.) Montréal: Beauchemin, 1916. 248 pp.

Beaverbrook, William Maxwell Aitken, baron, and Charles G.D. Roberts. *Canada in Flanders.* (The Official Story of the Canadian Expeditionary Force.) London: Hodder and Stoughton, 1916-18. 3 vols.

Beck, Norman Edward, comp. *Souvenir Number of the Reveille, the Duke of Connaught's Own, the 158th (Overseas) Battalion.* Vancouver: privately printed, 1916. 20 pp.

Bell, F. McKelvey. *The First Canadians in France; the Chronicle of a Military Hospital in the War Zone.* Toronto: McClelland, Goodchild & Stewart, 1917. 308 pp.

Bell, K., and C.P. Stacey. *100 Years; The Royal Canadian Regiment 1883-1983.* Don Mills, Ont.: Collier Macmillan, 1983. 184 pp., chiefly illus.

Bell, Ralph W. *Canada in War-Paint.* London: Dent, 1917. 208 pp.

Belton, James and E.G. Odell. *Hunting the Hun.* New York: D. Appleton, 1918. 269 pp.

Bennett, S.G. *The 4th Canadian Mounted Rifles, 1914-1919.* Toronto: privately printed, 1926. 336 pp.

Bercuson, David J. *True Patriot; the Life of Brooke Claxton, 1898-1960.* Toronto: Univ. of Toronto Press, 1993. 363 pp.

Berton, Pierre. *Vimy.* Toronto: McClelland and Stewart, 1986. 336 pp.

Biggs, E.R.J., comp. *Historical Record of the 76th Overseas Battalion of the Canadian Expeditionary Force, 1915-1916.* Toronto: Hunter, Rose, n.d. 73 pp.

Bindon, Kathryn M. *More than Patriotism.* (A Personal Library Publication.) Don Mills, Ont.: Nelson, 1979. 192 pp.

_____. *Queen's Men, Canada's Men; the Military History of Queen's University, Kingston.* [Kingston, Ont.]: privately printed, 1978. 180 pp.

Bird, C.W. *The Canadian Forestry Corps; its Inception, Development and Achievements.* London: H.M. Stationery Office, 1919. 51 pp.

Bird, Will R. *And We Go On.* Toronto: Hunter, Rose, 1930. 343 pp.

_____. *The Communication Trench.* Amherst, N.S.: privately printed, 1933. 336 pp.

_____. *Ghosts have Warm Hands.* Toronto: Clarke, Irwin, 1968. 254 pp.

_____. *North Shore (New Brunswick) Regiment.* Fredericton, N.B.: Brunswick Press, 1963. 629 pp.

_____. *Private Timothy Fergus Clancy.* Ottawa: Graphic Publishers, 1930. 325 pp.

_____. *The Story of Vimy-Ridge./La Crête de Vimy*, version française de Paul de Saint-Jullien. Arras, France: I.N.S.A.P., 1932. 24 pp.

_____. *Thirteen Years After; the Story of the Old Front Revisited, Reprinted from MacLean's Magazine with Additions.* Toronto: MacLean Pub. Co., 1932. 180 pp.

Bishop, Charles W. *The Canadian Y.M.C.A. in the Great War.* n.p.: National Council of Young Men's Christian Associations of Canada, 1924. 446 pp.

Bishop, William Arthur. *Courage on the Battlefield.* (Canada's Military Heritage, Volume II.) Toronto: McGraw-Hill Ryerson, 1993. 341 pp.

Black, Ernest G. *I Want One Volunteer.* Toronto: Ryerson Press, 1965. 183 pp.

Blay, Cecil E. *Portraits and Sketches of Hartney District Veterans; Great War 1914-1918.* Brandon, Man.: printed by Sun Pub. Co., [1921]. 82 pp.

Boissonnault, Charles-Marie. *Histoire politico-militaire des Canadiens français (1763-1967).* Trois-Rivières, P.Q.: Editions du Bien public, 1967. 310 pp.

Boss, W. *The Stormont, Dundas and Glengarry Highlanders, 1783-1951.* Ottawa: Runge Press, 1952. 449 pp.
Revised and updated as: Boss, W., and W.J. Patterson. Up the Glens; Stormont, Dundas and Glengarry Highlanders, 1783-1994. Cornwall, Ont.: Old Book Store, 1995. 298 pp.

Boyd, William. *With a Field Ambulance at Ypres.* Toronto: Musson Book Co., 1916. 110 pp.

The Brazier; a Trench Journal Printed and Published at the Front by the Canadian Scottish for the Brigade. No. 1-9? Various places: n.p., 1916-17? *Subtitle varies. A later publication of the same title was published by the 16th Battalion Association at Moose Jaw, Sask., 1926-28.*

The Brazier; Marking the 50th Anniversary of the Canadian Scottish (Princess Mary's), June 6, 1964. Victoria, B.C.: privately printed, 1964. 19 pp.

Breckon, Fred. *In the Hands of the Hun; being an Account of the Experiences of Private Fred Breckon, 8th Battalion, Canadian Expeditionary Force, during Three Years and Eight Months in German Prison Camps.* Fort Francis, Ont.: privately printed, 1919. 92 pp.

A Brief Historical Sketch of the Lorne Scots (Peel, Dufferin and Halton Regiment). Brampton, Ont.: Charters Pub. Co., 1943. 24 pp.

A Brief Historical Sketch of the Queen's York Rangers, 1st American Regiment. Toronto: privately printed, 1942. 30 pp.

A Brief History of the Active Service Battalion of the Victoria Rifles; 24th Battalion, 5th Brigade, 2nd Division, Canadian Expeditionary Force, 1914-15. Montreal: privately printed, n.d. 1 vol., chiefly illus.

Brief History of the 52nd, by W.D. Brandon, Man.: privately printed, n.d. 15 pp.

A Brief History of the Royal Regiment of Canada, [Allied with the King's Regiment (Liverpool). Toronto: n.p., 1940.] 77 pp.

A Brief History of the Royal Regiment of Canada; Allied with the King's Regiment (Liverpool). [Toronto: n.p., 1948.] 135 pp.

A Brief History of the 3rd Battalion C.E.F. (Toronto Regiment), Now the Toronto Regiment; (Allied with the King's Regiment (Liverpool)). n.p.: 1934. 47 pp.

A Brief History of the 3rd Canadian Battalion, Toronto Regiment. Toronto: Rous & Mann, [1919?] 30 pp.

A Brief Outline of the Story of the Canadian Grenadier Guards and the First Months of the Royal Montreal Regiment in the Great War, Told in an Anthology of Verse and Prose, compiled by an Officer of the Guards. Montreal: privately printed, 1926. 75 pp.

Brindle, W. *France & Flanders; Four Years Experience Told in Poem & Story.* St. John, N.B.: S. K. Smith, 1919. 84 pp.

Brown, Brian A. *Foresters; the Canadian Quest for Peace.* Erin, Ont.: Boston Mills Press, 1991. 176 pp.
The Grey & Simcoe Foresters.

Brown, Kingsley, *see* Greenhous, Brereton.

*Brown, W.J. *Les Cadets royaux de l'Armée canadienne; cent ans d'exploits, 1879-1979.* s.l.: La Ligue des Cadets de l'Armée du Canada, [1979. 12 pp.]

* _____. *The Royal Canadian Army Cadets; a Century of Achievement, 1879-1979.* n.p.: The Army Cadet League of Canada, [1979. 12 pp.]

Brown, Walter. *To the Memory of Lieutenant-Colonel James Alexander Turner, D.S.O., M.C., a Gallant Soldier who Served his Country in the Great War 1914-1918 and Fell in the Battle of Buzancy on July Twenty-six, Nineteen Eighteen.* New York: privately printed, n.d. 55 pp.

Bruce, Constance. *Humour in Tragedy; Hospital Life Behind 3 Fronts, by a Canadian Nursing Sister.* London: Skeffington, n.d. 66 pp.

Bruce, Herbert A. *Politics and the Canadian Army Medical Corps; a History of Intrigue, Containing Many Facts Omitted from the Official Records, Showing how Efforts at Rehabilitation were Baulked.* Toronto: W. Briggs, 1919. 321 pp.

_____. *Report on the Canadian Army Medical Service.* London: [H.M. Stationery Office], 1916. 168 pp.

Bruce, Walter H., and others, comps. *Historical Records of the Argyll and Sutherland Highlanders of Canada (Princess Louise's), Formerly 91st Regiment Canadian Highlanders, Canadian Militia, 1903-1928.* Hamilton, Ont.: R. Duncan, 1928. 99 pp.

Bull, Stewart H. *The Queen's York Rangers; an Historic Regiment.* Erin, Ont.: Boston Mills Press, 1984. 284 pp.

Bull, Wm. Perkins. *From Brock to Currie; the Military Development and Exploits of Canadians in General and of the Men of Peel in Particular, 1791 to 1930.* Toronto: G.J. McLeod, 1935. 772 pp.

The Bulletin of the Army Medical Corps. Vol. I-II? Toronto: n.p., 1917-19? *Title varies. Official organ of Training Depot No. 2, Canadian Army Medical Corps.*

Burns, E.L.M. *General Mud; Memoirs of Two World Wars.* Toronto: Clarke, Irwin, 1970. 254 pp.

Burns, Max, and Ken Messenger. *The Winged Wheel Patch; a History of the Canadian Military Motorcycle and Rider.* St. Catharines, Ont.: Vanwell Pub., 1993. 159 pp.

Buswell, Leslie. *Ambulance No. 10; Personal Letters from the Front.* Toronto: T. Allen, 1916. 155 pp.

Butson, A.R.C. *A History of the Military Medical Units of Hamilton, Ontario, in Peace and War, 1900-1990.* n.p.: 1990. 43 pp.

[Cadenhead, J.F.] *The Canadian Scottish; Stray Papers by a Private.* Aberdeen: Rosemount Press, 1915. 34 pp.

Calder, Donald George Scott. *The History of the 28th (Northwest) Battalion C.E.F. (October 1914 — June 1919); from the Memoirs of Brigadier General Alexander Ross.* Regina: privately printed, 1961. 277 pp.

The Call to Arms; Montreal's Roll of Honour, European War, 1914. B.K. Sandwell, ed. Montreal: Southam Press, 1914. 209 pp.

Callan, John J. *With Guns and Wagons; a Day in the Life of an Artillery Chaplain.* Charles Lyons Foster and William Smith Duthie, eds. London: Society for Promoting Christian Knowledge, 1918. 24 pp.

The Cameron Highlanders of Ottawa; Standing Orders and Constitution and Rules of the Officers Mess. n.p.: [1934]. 88 pp.

Cameron, James M. *Pictonians in Arms; A Military History of Pictou County, Nova Scotia.* Fredericton, N.B.: privately printed, 1969. 301 pp.

Cameron, Kenneth. *History of No. 1 General Hospital, Canadian Expeditionary Force.* Sackville, N.B.: privately printed, 1938. 667 pp.

Camp, A.D., comp. *7th Toronto Regiment, Royal Regiment of Canadian Artillery, 1866-1966.* n.p.: n.d. 33 pp.

Camp Valcartier, P.Q.; 1647 à 1957 en quelques lignes./Camp Valcartier P.Q.; a Short History, 1647-1957. s.l.: s.i./n.p., 1957. 24 pp.
Texte bilingue./Bilingual text.

Campbell, Len. *1st Canadian Contingent on Salisbury Plain, October 1914 — March 1915.* Amesbury, Eng.: printed by Durrington Press, [1994?]. 47 pp.

[Canada. Armed Forces. 48th Highlanders of Canada.] *This is Your Regiment.* n.p.: [194-?]. 38 pp.

Canada. Armed Forces. 4 Field Ambulance. *A History of 4 Field Ambulance.* Lahr, Germany: E. Demmer, 1992. [122] pp.

Canada. Armed Forces. Lake Superior Scottish Regiment. *Regimental Catechism.* Winnipeg: CFTMPC, 1977. 15 pp.

*Canada. Armée. Quartier général de l'Armée. Section historique. *Introduction à l'étude de l'histoire militaire à l'intention des étudiants canadiens*, [par C.P. Stacey]. Ottawa: [Imprimeur du Roi], 1951. 45 pp.
Editions subséquentes et révisées.

*_____. *La 1ère Brigade d'infanterie canadienne, 1914-1954.* (Actualités; revue destinée aux Forces canadiennes, vol VII, no 3.) Ottawa: Imprimeur de la Reine, 1954. 31 pp.

*_____. *La 1re Division d'infanterie canadienne, 1915-1955.* (Actualités; revue destinée aux Forces canadiennes, vol IX, no 1.) Ottawa: Imprimeur de la Reine, 1955. 31 pp.

Canada. Armée. Régiment de la Chaudière. *Le Régiment de la Chaudière; notes historiques.* Québec, P.Q.: imprimé privé, 1955. 16 pp.

Canada. Army. Queen's Own Rifles of Canada. *Regimental Catechism.* n.p.: n.d. 19 pp.

Canada. Army. Royal Canadian Army Service Corps. *RCASC Diamond Jubilee Year Book, 1910-1961.* Ottawa: Queen's Printer, [1962]. 95 pp.

Canada. Army. Royal Winnipeg Rifles. *Seventy-Fifth Anniversary, Royal Winnipeg Rifles, 1883-1958.* [Winnipeg: privately printed, 1958.] v.p.

[Canada. Army. Toronto Scottish Regiment.] *The Toronto Scottish Regiment.* n.p.: 1961. 24 pp.

*Canada. Army Headquarters. Historical Section. *The 1st Canadian Infantry Brigade, 1914-1954.* (Current Affairs for the Canadian Forces, vol. VII, no. 3.) Ottawa: Queen's Printer, 1954. 31 pp.

*_____. *Introduction to the Study of Military History for Canadian Students,* [by C.P. Stacey]. Ottawa: [King's Printer], 1951. 39 pp.
Many subsequent revised editions.

*_____. *The Old Red Patch; the 1st Canadian Infantry Division, 1915-1955.* (Current Affairs for the Canadian Forces, vol. IX, no. 1.) Ottawa: Queen's Printer, 1955. 31 pp.

_____. *The Regiments and Corps of the Canadian Army.* (The Canadian Army List, vol. 1.) Ottawa: Queen's Printer, 1964. 253 pp.

Canada. Dept. of Justice. Military Service Branch. *Report of the Director of the Military Service Branch to the Honourable the Minister of Justice on the Operation of the Military Service Act, 1917.* Ottawa: King's Printer, 1919. 162 pp.

Canada. Dept. of Justice. Military Sub-Committee. *Military Service Act, 1917; Pamphlet of Information and Instructions for Local Military Representatives.* n.p.: n.d. 18 pp.

*Canada. Dept. of Militia and Defence. *Annual Report*. Ottawa: Queen's Printer, 1867-1922.
Title varies. Until 1883 was State of the Militia of the Dominion of Canada, *with further variation in some years.*

_____. *Canadian Expeditionary Force Units; Instructions Governing Organization and Administration.* Ottawa: King's Printer, 1916. 109 pp.

_____. *Canadian Militia; Financial Instructions, 1914, and Standing Orders, Canadian Army Pay Corps.* Ottawa: King's Printer, 1915. 97 pp.

_____. *Canadian Militia; Pay and Allowance Regulations, 1914.* Ottawa: King's Printer, 1915. 115 pp.

_____. *Canadian Militia War Establishments (Provisional), 1914.* n.p.: n.d. 104 pp.

_____. *European War; Memorandum no. 5 Respecting Work of the Department of Militia and Defence from January 1, 1918, to October 31, 1918.* [Ottawa: King's Printer, 1919.] 103 pp.

_____. *European War; Memorandum no. 4 Respecting Work of the Department of Militia and Defence from January 1, 1917, to December 31, 1917.* [Ottawa: King's Printer, 1918.] 31 pp.

_____. *European War; Memorandum no. 6 Respecting Work of the Department of Militia and Defence from November 1, 1918, to October 31, 1919.* [Ottawa: King's Printer, 1920.] 102 pp.

_____. *European War; Memorandum no. 3 Respecting Work of the Department of Militia and Defence, from February 1, 1916, to December 31, 1916.* Ottawa: King's Printer, 1917. 83 pp.

_____. *Financial Instructions and Allowances for the Canadian Expeditionary Force, 1916.* Ottawa: King's Printer, 1916. 141 pp.

_____. *Financial Instructions for the Canadian Expeditionary Force, 1914.* Ottawa: King's Printer, 1914. 38 pp.

_____. *Historical Summary; Canadian Expeditionary Force.* [Ottawa: King's Printer, 1918.] v.p.

_____. *How to Qualify; a Short Guide for Officers and Non-Commissioned Officers of the Cavalry and Infantry, Canadian Militia.* Ottawa: King's Printer, 1915. 15 pp.

_____. *The King's Regulations and Orders for the Canadian Militia, 1917.* Ottawa: King's Printer, 1917. 422 pp.

_____. *Memoranda Respecting Work of the Department of Militia and Defence; European War, 1914-15.* Ottawa: King's Printer, 1915. 72 pp.

Canada. Dept. of Militia and Defence. *Memorandum for Camps of Instruction.* **Part 1:** *Instructions for Training.* Ottawa: King's Printer, 1909?-28. *Title varies somewhat. Annual.*

_____. *Memorandum Showing Rates of Pay and Allowances Authorized for the Canadian Expeditionary Force, the Active Militia on Home Guard Duty, and the Active Militia Called Out for Active Service, Together with Rates of Pensions Applicable in the Case of Death or Disability Incurred on Service.* n.p.: 1916. 20 pp.

_____. *The Militia List.* Ottawa: Queen's Printer, 1867-1929. *Title and frequency vary, eg — The Annual Volunteer and Service Militia List of Canada (1867), The Quarterly Militia List of the Dominion of Canada (1900).*

_____. *Minutes of the Militia Council.* Ottawa: King's Printer, 1905-21. 23 vols.

_____. *Regulations for the Cadet Services of Canada, 1915.* Ottawa: King's Printer, 1915. 14 pp.

_____. *Regulations for the Canadian Army Veterinary Service, 1916.* Ottawa: King's Printer, 1916. 51 pp.

_____. *Regulations for the Canadian Medical Service, 1914 (Approved by the Militia Council).* Ottawa: King's Printer, 1915. 62 pp.

_____. *Regulations for the Canadian Officers Training Corps, 1916.* n.p.: 1916. 26 pp.

_____. *Report of the Halifax Military Lands Board, 1915.* Ottawa: King's Printer, 1916. 171 pp.

_____. *The Return of the Troops; a Plain Account of the Demobilization of the Canadian Expeditionary Force.* Ottawa: King's Printer, 1920. 180 pp.

_____. *Returned Soldiers' Handbook; Containing Instructions and Information Dealing with Returned Warrant Officers, Non-Commissioned Officers and Men of the Canadian Expeditionary Force.* [Ottawa: King's Printer,] 1918. 84 pp.

_____. *Revised Instructions for Dealing with Deserters and Absentees without Leave.* Ottawa: King's Printer, 1918. 60 pp.

_____. *Standing Orders for the Permanent Army Medical Corps (and for the Army Medical Corps on Mobilization), 1918.* Ottawa: King's Printer, 1918. 83 pp.

Canada. Dept. of Veterans Affairs. *60th Anniversary; Vimy Ridge, 1917 — April 9 — 1977./Soixantième anniversaire; la Crête de Vimy, 1917 — le 9 avril — 1977.* n.p./s.l.: s.i., [1977]. 14 pp.
Bilingual text./Texte bilingue.

Canada. Dept. of Veterans Affairs. Directorate of Public Affairs. *The New-foundland Beaumont Hamel Memorial./Le Mémorial terre-neuvien de Beaumont-Hamel,* réalisé par la Direction des affaires publiques, Affaires des anciens combattants Canada. Ottawa: Veterans Affairs Canada/Affaires des anciens combattants Canada, 1983. 15 pp.
Bilingual text./Texte bilingue.

*Canada. Directeur de l'Information publique. *L'effort du Canada pour la Guerre, 1914-1918.* Ottawa: Imprimeur du Roi, 1918. 31 pp.

Canada. Director of Public Information. *Canada's Part in the Great War.* Ottawa: n.p., 1919. 64 pp.
Also issued by Information Branch, Dept. of External Affairs.

* _____. *Canada's War Effort, 1914-1918.* Ottawa: King's Printer, 1918. 31 pp.

Canada. Militia. Canadian Expeditionary Force. *Routine Orders.* Ottawa: n.p., ?-1920.
Supplements also issued.

Canada. Militia. Canadian Expeditionary Force. 11th Canadian Field Ambulance. *Diary of the Eleventh; being a Record of the XIth Canadian Field Ambulance (Western Universities) Feb. 1916 — May 1919.* n.p.: n.d. 128 pp.

Canada. Militia. Canadian Expeditionary Force. 1st Canadian Contingent. *Gradation List & List of Appointments, Staff & Units.* n.p.: n.d. 118 pp.

Canada. Militia. Canadian Expeditionary Force. 1st Canadian Contingent. Pay and Record Office, comp. *List of Officers and Men Serving in the First Canadian Contingent of the British Expeditionary Force, 1914.* London: H.M. Stationery Office, [1915]. 353 pp.

Canada. Militia. Canadian Expeditionary Force. Fort Garry Horse. *Standing Orders.* n.p.: n.d. 80 pp.

Canada. Militia. Canadian Grenadier Guards. *Answers to Questions of the Day.* Montreal: Mortimer Press, [1916]. 15 pp.

Canada. Militia. Military District No. 2. *Manual for Chaplains of the Canadian Expeditionary Force.* Toronto: n.p., 1916. 134 pp.

Canada. Militia Headquarters. *Canadian Expeditionary Force Nominal Rolls.* Ottawa: King's Printer, 1915-18. 13 vols.
Issued with <u>Militia Orders</u>. Number of volumes may vary.

Canada. Militia Headquarters. *General Orders.* Ottawa: Queen's Printer, 1899-1946.
Superseded Militia General Orders. Frequency varies.

_____. *Militia Orders.* Ottawa: Queen's Printer, 1899-1940.
Superseded Militia General Orders. Frequency varies.

_____. *Official List of Casualties to Members of the Canadian Expeditionary Force ....* Ottawa: King's Printer, 1914-19. 5 vols.
Issued with Militia Orders. Number of volumes may vary.

Canada. Militia Headquarters. Historical Section. *Canadian War Records.* Vol. I: *A Narrative of the Formation and Operations of the First Canadian Division, to the End of the Second Battle of Ypres, May 4, 1915.* Ottawa: King's Printer, 1920. 386 pp.
Not widely circulated because of numerous errors.

Canada. Ministère de la Milice et de la Défense. *Avantages qu'il y a dans la force permanente; conditions sous lesquelles les jeunes gens sont invités à entrer dans les troupes permanentes du Canada.* s.l.: s.i., 1914. 18 pp.

*_____. *Rapport annuel.* Ottawa: Imprimeur de la Reine, 1867-1922.
Divergence du titre. Jusqu'à 1883 le titre était Rapport annuel sur l'état de la Milice de la Puissance du Canada; divers titres suivirent pendant quelques années.

Canada. Ministry of Overseas Military Forces of Canada. *Memorandum from the Department of the Ministry of Overseas Military Forces of Canada on the Subject of Overseas Forces of Canada.* n.p.: 1918. 53 pp.

_____. *Report of the Ministry; Overseas Military Forces of Canada, 1918.* London: H.M. Stationery Office, 1919. 533 pp.

_____. *Routine Orders.* London: Canadian Print. and Stationery Services, H.M. Stationery Office, 1917-20.

Canada. Ministry of Overseas Military Forces of Canada. Accountant General's Dept. *Financial Regulations and Allowances for the Overseas Military Forces of Canada, 1918.* London: Page & Thomas, 1919. 239 pp.

*Canada. Parlement. *Correspondance concernant la discontinuation de l'usage de la carabine Ross dans l'armée canadienne.* (Document parlementaire, no 44.) Ottawa: Imprimeur du Roi, 1917. 12 pp.

*_____. *Correspondance entre l'Auditeur général et le ministère de la Milice relative aux dépenses en vertu de la Loi des credits de la guerre.* (Document parlementaire, no 122.) Ottawa: Imprimeur du Roi, 1915. 47 pp.

*Canada. Parlement. *Liste des décorations et des médailles décernées aux membres du Corps expéditionnaire canadien et aux officiers de la Milice canadienne jusqu'au 17 mars 1916.* (Document parlementaire, no 259.) Ottawa: Imprimeur du Roi, 1916. 18 pp.

*_____. *Pensions et allocations accordées aux membres des troupes expéditionnaires canadiennes depuis le commencement de la guerre jusqu'au 16 février 1916.* (Document parlementaire, no 185.) Ottawa: Imprimeur du Roi, 1916. 84 pp.

*_____. *Réponse à une adresse de la Chambre des Communes en date du 3 février 1916, donnant une copie de tous les décrets du conseil édictés depuis le 4 août 1914, relatifs aux soldats des Corps expéditionnaires canadiens, quant aux sujets suivants: pensions décrétées pour soldats en partie ou totalement invalidés, ou pour ceux dont ils étaient les soutiens; gratifications en argent ou autres aides déterminées pour le support ou le soin des soldats revenus du front en partie ou totalement invalidés; et solde, allocations ou autres gratifications accordées aux personnes dépendant des soldats durant leur service actif, et après leur retour du service, pas suite d'invalidité, quelle qu'en soit la cause.* (Document parlementaire, no 150.) Ottawa: Imprimeur du Roi, 1916. 11 pp.

*Canada. Parliament. *Correspondence between Auditor General and Militia Department Referring to Expenditure under War Appropriation Act.* (Sessional Paper, no. 122.) Ottawa: King's Printer, 1915. 44 pp.

*_____. *Correspondence Relating to the Withdrawal of the Ross Rifle from the Canadian Army Corps.* (Sessional Paper, no. 44.) Ottawa: King's Printer, 1917. 12 pp.

*_____. *List of Decorations and Medals Awarded to Members of the Canadian Expeditionary Force and Officers of the Canadian Militia to 17th March, 1916.* (Sessional Paper, no. 259.) Ottawa: King's Printer, 1916. 17 pp.

_____. *Parliamentary Memoir of George Harold Baker, Lieut.-Colonel, Fifth Canadian Mounted Rifles, Killed in Action, June 2, 1916.* Ottawa: King's Printer, 1924. 22 pp.

*_____. *Pensions Granted and Money Allowances Made to Members of Canadian Expeditionary Forces since Beginning of War to February 16, 1916.* (Sessional Paper, no. 185.) Ottawa: King's Printer, 1916. 83 pp.

*Canada. Parliament. *Return to an Address of the House of Commons, Dated the 3rd February, 1916, Showing a Copy of All Orders in Council Passed since August 4, 1914, Dealing with Members of the Canadian Expeditionary Forces in the Following Particulars; Pensions to Partially or Totally Disabled Soldiers or their Dependents; Money Allowances or Other Provisions Made for the Support or Care of Partially or Totally Disabled Returned Soldiers; and Pay Allowances or Other Consideration to Dependents of Soldiers while on Active Service, and after their Return from Active Service Because of Disablement from any Cause.* (Sessional Paper, no. 150.) Ottawa: King's Printer, 1916. 10 pp.

Canada. Parliament. House of Commons. Special Committee on Battlefield Memorials. *Battlefields Memorials; Report of the Special Committee Appointed to Consider and Report upon the Question of What Memorials, if Any, Should be Erected in the Battlefields of the Late War to Commemorate the Gallantry of the Canadian Troops; with Statements and Evidence Attached Thereto.* Ottawa: King's Printer, 1920. 18 pp.

Canada. Parliament. House of Commons. Special Committee on Boot Inquiry. *Proceedings and Evidence.* Ottawa: King's Printer, 1915.

Canada. Royal Commission Concerning Purchase of War Supplies and Sale of Small Arms Ammunition. *Evidence.* The Honourable Sir Charles Davidson, Commissioner. Ottawa: King's Printer, 1917. 3 vols.

Canada. Royal Commission on Purchase of Surgical Field Dressings and Other Surgical Supplies. *Report of the Commissioner.* The Honourable Sir Charles Davidson, Commissioner. Ottawa: King's Printer, 1917. 28 pp.

[Canada. Royal Commission to Inquire into the Purchase by and on Behalf of the Government of the Dominion of Canada, of Arms, Munitions, Implements, Materials, Horses, Supplies, and Other Things for the Purpose of the Present War.] *Report of the Commissioner Concerning Sale of Small Arms Ammunition.* Sir Charles Davidson, Commissioner. Ottawa: King's Printer, 1917. 56 pp.

Canada and her Soldiers. London: St. Clements Press, 1919. 48 pp.

Le Canada français et les conflits contemporains; actes du colloque tenu à l'Université du Québec à Montréal, le 27 août 1995, sous la direction de Claude Beauregard, Robert Comeau et Jean-Pierre Gagnon. (Cahiers d'histoire politique, no 2, hiver 1996.) s.l.: Société historique du Canada; Association québécoise d'histoire politique; Service historique, Défense nationale, 1996. 288 pp.

Canada in Action; a Souvenir of the Canadian War Memorials Exhibition; Containing Reproductions of Some of the Principal Mural Decorations, Battle Pictures, Portraits, etc, which are to Constitute Canada's Permanent War Memorial. n.p.: Canadian War Memorials Fund, 1919. 1 vol., chiefly illus.

Canada in Khaki. No. 1-3. London: Pictorial Newspaper Co. (1910), 1917-19.

Canada in the Great World War; an Authentic Account of the Military History of Canada from the Earliest Days to the Close of the War of the Nations, by Various Authorities. Toronto: United Publishers, 1917-21. 6 vols.

Canada in the Great War; an Illustrated Record of the Canadian Army in France and Flanders during the Years 1915-1918. Ottawa: Heliotype Co., 1919. 1 vol., chiefly illus.

Canada Victory Souvenir. London: Canada Newspaper Co., 1919. 72 pp.

Canada's Effort in the Great War to March, 1917. Moose Jaw, Sask.: privately printed, [1917]. 79 pp.

Canada's Heroes in the Great War; Cornwall, Alexandria, Vankleek Hill, Hawkesbury, and Intermediate Points. Vol. I. Noah J. Gareau, ed. With an historical narrative by Lt-Col. F. McKelvey Bell. Ottawa: War Publications, 1921. v.p.

Canadian Artillery Association. *Annual Report.* n.p.: privately printed, 1876- . *Not published 1940-46. Title varies.*

_____. *Officers who Served Overseas in the Great War with the Canadian Artillery, 1914-1919.* Ottawa: n.p., 1922. 258 pp.

Canadian Bank of Commerce. *Letters from the Front; being a Record of the Part Played by Officers of the Bank in the Great War, 1914-1919.* Toronto: privately printed, n.d. 2 vols.

Canadian Battlefields Memorials Commission. *Canadian Battlefield Memorials.* Ottawa: King's Printer. 1929. 84 pp.

_____. *Conditions of Competition in Design for Eight Memorial Monuments to be Erected in France and Belgium.* Ottawa: King's Printer, 1920. 53 pp.

Canadian Broadcasting Corporation. *Flanders' Fields.* n.p.: [1964]. 1 vol., unpaged.

Canadian Cavalry Association. *Proceedings.* n.p.: privately printed, 1913- . *In 1943 became Canadian Armoured Association and in 1946 Royal Canadian Armoured Corps (Cavalry) Association. Title varies, also* Annual Report *and* Information Digest and Annual Report.

The Canadian Convalescent Hospital, Bear Wood, Wokingham, Berkshire, 1915-18. London: printed by Times Pub. Co., n.d. 36 pp.

Canadian Corps Championships; France, Dominion Day, 1918. London: privately printed, [1918]. 31 pp.

Canadian Corps Trench Standing Orders. n.p. [1918]. 24 pp.

Canadian Field Comforts Commission. *With the First Canadian Contingent.* Toronto: Hodder & Stoughton, 1915. 119 pp.

The Canadian Fusiliers; City of London Regiment. n.p.: 1942. 12 pp.

Canadian Infantry Association. *Canadian Official War Photographs, with the Compliments of the Canadian Infantry Association.* Ottawa: Canadian Infantry Association, 1928. 144 pp.
Catalogue arranged by negative number.

_____. *Proceedings.* n.p.: privately printed, 1913- .
Incorporated the <u>Proceedings</u> of the Canadian Machine Gun Corps Association in 1936. Was the Infantry and Machine Gun Association of Canada, 1937-39. Not published 1940-45.

The Canadian Machine Gunner. Vol. I-II. [Seaford, Eng.]: privately printed, 1917-19.

Canadian Officers Training Corps, University of Toronto Contingent. [Toronto?]: n.p., 1937. 32 pp.

Canadian Pacific Railway Co. *Their Glory Cannot Fade.* n.p.: 1918. [15] pp.

The Canadian Scottish Regiment. n.p.: n.d. 91 pp.

A Canadian Subaltern; Billy's Letters to his Mother. London: Constable, 1917. 128 pp.
Toronto ed. titled: <u>A Sunny Subaltern; Billy's Letters from Flanders.</u>

Canadian Veteran Associates. *The Story of the Canadian Corps, 1914-1954; a Record of the Canadian Corps Re-Union, August 4, 5, 6, 1954, Toronto, Canada; the Story of Canada in the Great War of 1914-1918, as Recorded on the Walls of the Memorial Chamber in the Peace Tower at Ottawa.* Toronto: privately printed, 1954. 87 pp.

Canadian War Contingent Association. *Field Comforts for Fighting Canadians.* No. 1. Toronto: privately printed, 1917.

Canadian War Memorials Painting Exhibition, 1920; New Series; the Last Phase. n.p.: n.d. 25 pp.

[Canadian War Museum.] *La coopération canada-polonaise au cours des deux guerres mondiales./Polish-Canadian Co-operation in the Two World Wars.* Ottawa: n.p., 1973. 36 pp.
Texte bilingue./Bilingual text.

The Canadian War Pictorial. No. 1-4. London: Canadian War Records Office, [1916-18.]

Canadian War Records Office. *Art and War; Canadian War Memorials; a Selection of the Works Executed for the Canadian War Memorials Fund to Form a Record of Canada's Part in the Great War and a Memorial to those Canadians who have Made the Great Sacrifice.* London: n.p., 1919. 1 vol., unpaged.

————. *Canadian War Memorials Exhibition.* [New York]: n.p., 1919. 48 pp.

————. *Canadian War Memorials Exhibition, Royal Academy, Piccadilly, W., 1918.* n.p.: n.d. 42 pp.

————. *Souvenir; New Exhibition of Canadian Official War Photographs in Colour.* London: n.p., 1919. 16 pp., chiefly illus.

————. *Thirty Canadian V.C.'s; 23rd April 1915 to 20th March 1918.* London: Skeffington, n.d. 96 pp.

Le capitaine Jean Brillant, C.V., C.M., par ses amis. Rimouski, P.Q.: Imprimerie générale S. Vachon, 1920. 49 pp.

Capon, Alan R. *His Faults Lie Gently; the Incredible Sam Hughes.* Lindsay, Ont.: F.W. Hall, 1969. 159 pp.

Carrel, Frank. *Impressions of War.* Quebec, P.Q.: Telegraph Print. Co., 1919. 248 pp.

Carter, David J. *Behind Canadian Barbed Wire; Alien, Refugee and Prisoner of War Camps in Canada, 1914-1946.* Calgary: Tumbleweed Press, 1980. 334 pp.

Cassar, George. *Beyond Courage; the Canadians at the Second Battle of Ypres.* n.p.: Oberon Press, 1985. 218 pp.

Castonguay, Jacques. *Les Voltigeurs de Québec; premier régiment canadien-français.* Québec (Qué.): Les Voltigeurs de Québec, 1987. 523 pp.

Catalogue of the Canadian Official War Photographs Exhibition; for the Benefit of the Canadian War Memorials Fund. Toronto: privately printed, [1916?]. 14 pp.

Catalogue of Canadian War Trophies; Including Field Guns, Surrendered and Captured Planes, Flags, Uniforms, Helmets, Swords, Posters, Proclamations, Prints, etc., National Exhibition, Toronto, August 23 to September 6, 1919. n.p.: [1919]. 64 pp.

Catalogue of Canadian War Trophies; Including Field Guns, Surrendered and Captured Planes, Flags, Uniforms, Helmets, Swords, Posters, Proclamations, Prints, etc., The Armouries, Hamilton, November 3 to November 15, 1919. n.p.: [1919]. 64 pp.

Cave, Joy B. *Two Newfoundland V.C.s.* St. John's, Nfld.: Creative Printers & Publishers, 1984. 95 pp.
John B. Croak and Thomas R. Ricketts.

_____. *What Became of Corporal Pittman?* Portugal Cove, Nfld.: Breakwater Books, 1976. v.p.

Cent ans d'histoire d'un régiment canadien-français; les Fusiliers Mont-Royal, 1869-1969. Montréal: Editions du Jour, 1971. 418 pp.

Centennial, 1863-1963; Presentation of Colours to the Princess of Wales' Own Regiment CA(M) by the Honourable W. Earle Rowe, P.C., Lieutenant-Governor of Ontario, Kingston, Ontario, Saturday 1st June 1963. [Kingston, Ont.: privately printed, 1963.] 15 pp.

Centennial Year, 1866-1966; 11th Field Artillery Regiment (M); 11th Field Artillery Regiment, Royal Regiment of Canadian Artillery, Canada's Oldest Artillery Regiment, Saturday, October 1, 1966. n.p.: n.d. 1 vol., unpaged.

Chaballe, Joseph. *Histoire du 22e Bataillon canadien-français.* Tome I: *1914-1919.* Montréal: Les Editions Chantecler, 1952. 412 pp.

Chajkowsky, William E. *The History of Camp Borden, 1916-1918; Land of Sand, Sin and Sorrow.* Jordan Station, Ont.: Station Press, 1983. 106 pp.

[Chandler, C.M.] *The Militia in Durham County; 1812-1936; an Outline History of the Durham Regiment.* n.p.: privately printed, 1936. v.p.

La Chapelle du Souvenir, Chambres du Parlement, Ottawa, Canada, [par A.F. Duguid.] Ottawa: Photogelatine Engraving Co., s.d. 1 tome, non-paginé.

Chappell, Mike. *The Canadian Army at War.* (Men-at-Arms Series, [164].) London: Osprey Pub., 1985. 48 pp.
Canadian Army uniforms.

Charles, Jennifer. *John McCrae.* Ottawa: Veterans Affairs/Anciens combattants, 1988. 12 pp.
Bilingual text./Texte bilingue.

Chassé, Henri. *Souvenirs de guerre.* Québec (Qué.): Imp. de l'Evénement, 1920. 16 pp.
Royal 22e Régiment.

Chassé, Noël. *Avant la poussée finale.* Québec, P.Q.: Imprimerie "L'Événement", 1918. 98 pp.

[Chattan Club, Toronto, Ont.] *War Record of Chattan Men.* n.p.: n.d. [34] pp.

Christie, N.M. *Officers of the Canadian Expeditionary Force who Died Overseas, 1914-1919.* Ottawa: E.G. Ursual, 1989. 116 pp.

Chute, Arthur Hunt. *The Real Front.* New York: Harper, 1918. 309 pp.

50 ans d'activités avec le 6e Régiment d'artillerie (Québec & Lévis), 1899-1949.
Québec, P.Q.: Imprimerie Laflamme, 1949. 1 tome, non paginé.

Cinquante-quatre see Bailey, John Beswick.

Clark, Gregory. *War Stories.* Toronto: Ryerson Press, 1964. 171 pp.

Clark, H.D., comp. *Extracts from the War Diary and Official Records of the Second Canadian Divisional Ammunition Column.* St. John, N.B.: privately printed, 1921. 166 pp.

Claxton, Brooke. *War Diary, 10th Canadian Siege Battery, 1917-1919.* n.p.: n.d. 32 pp.

Climo, Percy L. *Cobourg 1914-1919; a Magnificent Sacrifice.* Cobourg, Ont.: privately printed, 1986. 110 pp.

Clint, H.C., comp. *A Short History of Artillery and of 57th Battery, R.C.A., 1855-1955; Formal Celebration and Reunion, Oct. 15th, 16th, 1955, Grande Allée Armouries, Quebec City.* Quebec, P.Q.: n.p., 1955. 48 pp.

Clint, M.B. *Our Bit; Memories of War Service by a Canadian Nursing Sister.* Montreal: Barwick, 1934. 177 pp.

Clyne, Henry Randolph Notman. *Vancouver's 29th; a Chronicle of the 29th in Flanders Field.* Vancouver: privately printed, 1964. 166 pp.

Coleman, Frederick. *From Mons to Ypres with the French; a Personal Narrative; Attached to Sir John French's Headquarters during the Retreat from Mons, and the 2nd Cavalry Brigade Headquarters during the Advance across the Marne and Aisne, to the 1st Cavalry Division Headquarters during the Fighting on the Lys, at Ploegsteert, Messines, and Ypres and at the Front in France and Flanders until June, 1915.* London: Sampson, Low, Marston, 1916. 324 pp.

Commemorative Number of the Western Scot; Yukon, Cariboo, Vancouver Island, 67th Pioneer Battalion, 4th Canadian Division. n.p.: n.d. 72 pp.

Commonwealth War Graves Commission. *The War Dead of the Commonwealth; the Register of the Names of Those who Fell in the Great War of 1914-1918 and are Buried in Cemeteries in France; Canadian Cemetery No. 2 Neuville-St. Vaast.* London: H.M. Stationery Office, 1967. 38 pp.

Cooper, J.A., comp. *Fourth Canadian Infantry Brigade; History of Operations, April 1915 to Demobilization.* London: Charles, n.d. 54 pp.

Corfield, William E. *Citizen Soldiers; the Canadian Fusiliers of London; the Oxford Rifles; the Perth Regiment.* London, Ont.: Royal Canadian Regiment, 1983. 86 pp.

Corneloup, Claudius. *L'épopée du vingt-deuxième.* Montréal: La Presse, 1919. 150 pp.

Corporation of British Columbia Land Surveyors. *Roll of Honour; British Columbia Land Surveyors; 1914 the Great War 1918.* n.p.: privately printed, n.d. 1 vol., unpaged.

* *Le Corps blindé royal canadien.* Ottawa: Imprimeur de la Reine, 1954. 11 pp.

* *Le Corps de Santé royal canadien.* Ottawa: Imprimeur de la Reine, 1954. 11 pp.

* *The Corps of Royal Canadian Engineers.* Ottawa: Queen's Printer, 1953. 21 pp.

The Corps of Royal Canadian Engineers; a Brief History. Ottawa: King's Printer, 1948. 56 pp.

Corrigall, D.J. *The History of the Twentieth Battalion (Central Ontario Regiment), Canadian Expeditionary Force in the Great War, 1914-18.* Toronto: privately printed, 1935. 268 pp.

Corriveau, Paul. *Le Royal 22e Régiment; 75 ans d'histoire, 1914-1989.* Québec (Qué.): La Régie du Royal 22e Régiment, 1989. 132 pp.

Cosgrave, L. Moore. *Afterthoughts of Armageddon; the Gamut of Emotions Produced by the War, Pointing a Moral that is not too Obvious.* Toronto: S.B. Gundy, 1919. 35 pp.

Coyne, F.W., comp. *Illustrated Souvenir; Dominion Orthopaedic Hospital, Christie Street, Toronto; Containing Photo Groups of Officers, Nursing Sisters, Patients, Hospital Celebrities, Distinguished Visitors and Others; Alphabetical List of Over 3000 Names of All Patients, Past and Present, Together with Present Addresses; also Names and Addresses of Officers, Nursing Sisters and Others.* Toronto: privately printed, n.d. 104 pp.

Cramm, Richard. *The First Five Hundred; being a Historical Sketch of the Military Operations of the Royal Newfoundland Regiment in Gallipoli and on the Western Front during the Great War (1914-1918).* New York: Williams, n.d. 315 pp.

Creed, Catherine. *"Whose Debtors We Are."* (Niagara Historical Society, 34.) Niagara, Ont.: Niagara Historical Society, 1922. 116 pp.

Crerar, Duff. *Padres in No Man's Land; Canadian Chaplains and the Great War.* (McGill-Queen's Studies in the History of Religion, 16.) Montreal: McGill-Queen's Univ. Press, 1995. 424 pp.

Cresswell, [C.E.] *Memorial Album Dedicated to Our Beloved Dead by Their Bereaved and Sorrowing Friends.* London, Ont.: privately printed, n.d. 279 pp.
Commemorates dead from London-Stratford-Windsor-Sarnia area.

Critchley, A. *Critch! The Memoirs of Brigadier-General A.C. Critchley.* London: Hutchinson, 1961. 256 pp.

Crook, E.D., and J.K. Marteinson, eds. *A Pictorial History of the 8th Canadian Hussars (Princess Louise's)*. n.p.: privately printed, 1973. 343 pp.

Cross, Michael, and Robert Bothwell, eds. *Policy by Other Means; Essays in Honour of C.P. Stacey*. Toronto: Clarke, Irwin, 1972. 258 pp.

Cross, W.K. *The Charlton Price Guide to First World War Canadian Infantry Badges*. Toronto: Charlton Press, 1991. 374 pp.
Subsequent eds. titled: <u>The Charlton Standard Catalogue to First World War Canadian Infantry Badges</u>.

_____. *The Charlton Standard Catalogue of First World War Canadian Corps Badges*. Toronto: Charlton Press, 1995. 254 pp.

Cunliffe, J.W. *A Canadian Soldier; George Harold Baker, M.P., Lieutenant-Colonel 5th C.M.R., Killed in Action at Ypres, June 2nd, 1916*. New York: privately printed, [1917]. 83 pp.

Cunniffe, Dick. *Scarlet, Riflegreen and Khaki; the Military in Calgary*. Calgary: Century Calgary Publications, 1975. 40 pp.

_____. *The Story of a Regiment; Lord Strathcona's Horse (Royal Canadians)*. [Volume I.] n.p.: Lord Strathcona's Horse (Royal Canadians) Regimental Society, 1995. 192 pp.

Curchin, Leonard A., and Brian D. Sim. *The Elgins; the Story of the Elgin Regt. (RCAC) and its Predecessors*. St. Thomas, Ont.: privately printed, 1977. 150 pp.

Currie, (Sir) Arthur W. *The Canadian Corps and its Part in the War* [and] *Uncle Sam and John Bull*, by Frederic William Wile. n.p.: [1920?]. 24 pp.

_____. *Canadian Corps Operations during the Year 1918; Interim Report*. Ottawa: King's Printer, 1919. 94 pp.

Currie, J.A. *"The Red Watch"; with the First Canadian Division in Flanders*. Toronto: McClelland, Goodchild & Stewart, 1916. 308 pp.

Curry, Frederic C. *From the St. Lawrence to the Yser with the 1st Canadian Brigade*. Toronto: McClelland, Goodchild & Stewart, 1916. 167 pp.

D., W., *see Brief History of the 52nd.*

Dafoe, John W. *Over the Canadian Battlefields; Notes of a Little Journey in France in March, 1919*. Toronto: T. Allen, 1919. 89 pp.

Daly-Gingras, L.J. *Standing Orders of 2nd Depot Battalion, 2nd Quebec Regiment*. Montreal: printed by Model Printing, 1918. 84 pp.

Dancocks, Daniel G. *Gallant Canadians; the Story of the Tenth Canadian Infantry Battalion, 1914-1919*. Calgary: Calgary Highlanders Regimental Funds Foundation, 1990. 251 pp.

Dancocks, Daniel G. *Legacy of Valour; the Canadians at Passchendaele.* Edmonton: Hurtig Publishers, 1986. 289 pp.

_____. *Sir Arthur Currie; a Biography.* Toronto: Methuen, 1985. 332 pp.

_____. *Spearhead to Victory; Canada and the Great War.* Edmonton: Hurtig, 1987. 294 pp.

_____. *Welcome to Flanders Fields; the First Canadian Battle of the Great War: Ypres, 1915.* (A Douglas Gibson Book.) Toronto: McClelland and Stewart, 1988. 292 pp.

Daniel, I.J.E., and D.A. Casey. *A History of the Canadian Knights of Columbus, Catholic Army Huts.* n.p.: 1922. 214 pp.

Davidson, (Sir) Charles *see* Canada. Royal Commission ....

Dawson, Coningsby. *Carry On; Letters in Wartime.* New York: J. Lane, 1917. 133 pp.
London ed. titled: Khaki Courage, Letters in Wartime.

_____. *The Glory of the Trenches; an Interpretation.* Toronto: S.B. Gundy, 1918. 141 pp.

_____. *Living Bayonets; a Record of the Last Push.* New York: J. Lane, 1919. 221 pp.

De Saint-Jullien, Paul, *see* Bird, Will R.

Desquesnes, Rémy. *Les Canadiens au secours de l'Europe./The Canadians to Europe's Rescue.* Caen, France: Mémorial musée pour la paix, 1992. 194 pp. *Texte bilingue./Bilingual text.*

De Verneuil, Marcel. *Croquis de guerre, 1915-1917.* Montréal: Editions de la Revue moderne, 1921. 84 pp.

De Wolfe, J.H., comp. *Our Heroes in the Great World War; Giving Facts and Details on Canada's Part in the Greatest War in History.* Ottawa: Patriotic Pub. Co., 1919. 415 pp.

The Diary of the 61st Battery, Canadian Field Artillery. London: Canada Newspaper Co., n.d. 99 pp.

Dinesen, Thomas. *Merry Hell! A Dane with the Canadians.* London: Jarrolds, 1929. 254 pp.

*The Dominion Arsenal at Quebec, 1880-1945. Quebec, P.Q.: n.p., 1947. 131 pp.

Dominion of Canada Roll of Honor; a Directory of Casualties (Deaths Only) of the World's Greatest War, 1914-1918, of the City of Toronto; Dedicated to Perpetuate Those who Made the Supreme Sacrifice, "They shall not be Forgotten". n.p.: C. McAlpine, 1919. 28 1.

Dornbusch, C.E., comp. *The Canadian Army, 1855-1958; Regimental Histories and a Guide to the Regiments.* Cornwallville, N.Y.: Hope Farm Press, 1959. 216 pp.

_____. *The Canadian Army, 1855-1955; Regimental Histories and a Guide to the Regiments.* Cornwallville, N.Y.: n.p., 1957. 162 l.

_____. *The Canadian Army, 1855-1965; Lineages; Regimental Histories.* Cornwallville, N.Y.: Hope Farm Press, 1966. 179 pp.

_____. *Lineages of the Canadian Army, 1855-1961; Armour, Cavalry, Infantry.* Cornwallville, N.Y.: Hope Farm Press, 1961. 1 vol., unpaged.

Dornier, François, et Mari-Claude Joubert. *Soldats de la côte ...; Les Fusiliers du St-Laurent d'hier à aujourd'hui.* Rimouski (Qué.): La Régie, Les Fusiliers du St-Laurent, 1992. 183 pp.

Douglas, J. Harvey. *Captured; Sixteen Months as a Prisoner of War.* Toronto: McClelland, Goodchild & Stewart, 1918. 195 pp.

Dow, Gene, ed. *World War One Reminiscences of a New Brunswick Veteran.* Hartland, N.B.: printed by Centennial Print., 1990. 56 pp.
Memoirs of Stephen Pike, 140th Battalion.

Doward, Norman R. *The Queen's Own Rifles of Canada Buglers; Historical, Patriotic, Illustrated; Patriotic Souvenir.* Toronto: privately printed, 1915. 52 pp.

Drage, Charles. *The Life and Times of General Two-Gun Cohen.* New York: Funk & Wagnalls, 1954. 312 pp.
London ed. titled: Two-Gun Cohen.

Drolet, "Gil". *Loyola, the Wars: in Remembrance of "Men for Others".* Waterloo, Ont.: Laurier Centre for Military Strategic and Disarmament Studies, 1996. 44 pp.
Memorial to the war dead of Loyola High School and College.

Drysdale, A.M. *Canada to Ireland; the Visit of the "Duchess of Connaught's Own".* London: T.F. Unwin, 1917. 20 pp.

Duguid, Archer Fortescue. *The Canadian Forces in the Great War, 1914-1919; the Record of Five Years of Active Service.* Ottawa: King's Printer, 1947. 14 pp.

*_____. *Histoire officielle de l'armée canadienne dans la Grande Guerre, 1914-1919.* Vol I. Ottawa: Imprimeur du Roi, 1947. 1 tome en 2 vol.

_____. *History of the Canadian Grenadier Guards, 1760-1964.* Montreal: Gazette Print. Co., 1965. 520 pp.

*_____. *Official History of the Canadian Forces in the Great War, 1914-1919.* Vol. I. Ottawa: King's Printer, 1938. 1 vol. in 2.

Duguid, Archer Fortescue, *see also/voir aussi* **The Memorial Chamber in the Peace Tower ...; La Chapelle du Souvenir.**

Duncan-Clark, S.J., and W.R. Plewman. **Pictorial History of the Great War, [including] Canada in the Great War**, by W.S. Wallace. Toronto: J.L. Nichols, 1919. 2 vols. in 1.

Dunwoody, James M. **The Colonel; Some Reminiscences.** n.p.: [1972?]. 36 pp.

Dyer, Gwynne, and Tina Viljoen. **The Defence of Canada; in the Arms of the Empire.** Toronto: McClelland & Stewart, 1990. 375 pp.

Eaton, T., Co. **Souvenir of the Camp.** n.p.: [191-? 12 pp., all illus.]

Edwards, E.W. **The Last Hundred Days of the War.** n.p.: privately printed, [1931]. 1 vol., unpaged.

Elliot, S.R. **Scarlet to Green; a History of Intelligence in the Canadian Army, 1903-1963.** Toronto: privately printed, 1981. 769 pp.

Ellis, W.D., ed. **Saga of the Cyclists in the Great War, 1914-1918.** Toronto: privately printed, 1965. 93 pp.

Engineer's Annual. Vol. I-? North Vancouver, B.C.: privately printed, 1914-? *Published by the non-commissioned officers of the 6th Field Company, Canadian Engineers.*

England, Robert. **Recollections of a Nonagenarian of Service in The Royal Canadian Regiment, 1916-1919.** n.p.: privately printed, 1983. 1 vol., unpaged.

Fallis, George O. **A Padre's Pilgrimmage.** Toronto: Ryerson Press, 1953. 166 pp.

Ferguson, Frank Byron. **Gunner Ferguson's Diary; the Diary of Gunner Frank Byron Ferguson, 1st Canadian Siege Battery, Canadian Expeditionary Force 1915-1918.** Peter G. Rogers, ed. Hantsport, N.S.: Lancelot Press, 1985. 156 pp.

Fetherstonhaugh, R.C. **McGill University at War, 1914-1918; 1939-1945.** Montreal: McGill Univ., 1947. 437 pp.

_____. **The Royal Montreal Regiment, 14th Battalion, C.E.F., 1914-1925.** Montreal: privately printed, 1927. 334 pp.

_____. **A Short History of the Royal Canadian Dragoons.** Toronto: Southam Press, 1932. 52 pp.

_____. **The 13th Battalion Royal Highlanders of Canada, 1914-1919.** Montreal: privately printed, 1925. 344 pp.

Fetherstonhaugh, R.C., comp. **No. 3 Canadian General Hospital (McGill), 1914-1919.** Montreal: Gazette Print. Co., 1928. 274 pp.

Fetherstonhaugh, R.C., comp. *The 24th Battalion, C.E.F., Victoria Rifles of Canada, 1914-1919.* Montreal: Gazette Print. Co., 1930. 318 pp.

Fetherstonhaugh, R.C., and G.R. Stevens. *The Royal Canadian Regiment.* Vol. I: Montreal: Gazette Print. Co., 1936. Vol. II: London, Ont.: privately printed, 1967. 2 vols.

The 58th Regiment Westmount Rifles; Canada Militia 1914. [Montreal?: privately printed, 1970?] 12 pp.

Fighters for Freedom; Honor Roll of Halifax; the Great War, 1914-1919. Halifax: Service Pub. Co., [1919]. 191 pp.

Filteau, Gérard. *Le Québec, le Canada et la guerre, 1914-1918.* Montréal: Editions de l'Aurore, 1977. 231 pp.

The 1st Canadian Division in the Battles of 1918. London: Barr, 1919. 55 pp.

Firth, L.M. *6th Battery, 2nd Brigade, C.F.A.* Bonn, Germany: privately printed, 1919. 53 pp.

Flahaut, Jean. *Par mon hublot; reflet du temps héroïque, 1914-1918.* Montréal: Beauchemin, 1931. 185 pp.

Flick, C.L. *"Just What Happened"; a Diary of the Mobilization of the Canadian Militia, 1914.* London, privately printed, 1917. 99 pp.

_____. *A Short History of the 31st British Columbia Horse.* Victoria, B.C.: J.P. Buckle, 1922. 40 pp.

41st Battalion French Canadians. Bramshott, Eng.: privately printed, 1915. [52] pp.

47th Battalion Yearbook, 1917. London: Jordan-Gashell, 1918. 63 pp.

The Fortyniner. Vol. I. In the field: n.p., 1915-18?
Magazine of the 49th Canadian Battalion, CEF. A magazine of the same title was published by the Forty-Ninth Battalion, the Loyal Edmonton Regiment Association beginning about 1929.

Foster, J.A. *Muskets to Missiles; a Pictorial History of Canada's Ground Forces.* Toronto:Methuen, 1987. 251 pp.

Fourth Anniversary of the Eleventh Battery, C.F.A., in France, February 1919. n.p.: 1919. 27 pp.

4th Canadian Division Standing Orders (War), 1916. London: Page & Thomas, 1916. 25 pp.

Fox, Henry L., ed. *What the "Boys" Did over There, by "Themselves".* New York: Allied Overseas Veterans Stories Co., 1918. 165 pp.

[Fraser, Donald.] *The Journal of Private Fraser, 1914-1918; Canadian Expeditionary Force.* Edited and with an introduction by Reginald H. Roy. Victoria, B.C.: Sono Nis Press, 1985. 334 pp.

Fraser, W.B. *Always a Strathcona.* Calgary: Comprint Pub. Co., 1976. 252 pp.

Frise, Jimmy. *The First Great War as Seen by Jimmy Frise.* Georgetown, Ont.: Forty-Third Battery Association, 1972. 1 vol., chiefly illus.
Cartoons.

Frost, Leslie M. *Fighting Men.* Toronto: Clarke, Irwin, 1967. 262 pp.

Gaffen, Fred. *Cross-Border Warriors; Canadians in American Forces, Americans in Canadian Forces; from the Civil War to the Gulf.* Toronto: Dundurn Press, 1995. 241 pp.

_____. *Forgotten Soldiers.* Penticton, B.C.: Theytus Books, 1985. 152 pp.
Canada's native peoples in two World Wars.

Gagnon, Jean-Pierre. *Le 22e bataillon (canadien-français), 1914-1919; étude socio-militaire.* Ottawa: Les Presses de l'Université Laval en collaboration avec le ministère de la Défense nationale et le Centre d'édition du gouvernement du Canada, 1986. [460] pp.

Gallant, A.M. *Pride; the History of 1390 RCACC.* Red Deer, Alta.: printed by Fletcher, [1992?]. 244 pp.

Gallishaw, John. *Trenching at Gallipoli; the Personal Narrative of a Newfoundlander with the Ill-Fated Dardanelles Expedition.* Toronto: S.B. Gundy, 1916. 241 pp.

Gardam, John. *Seventy Years After, 1914-1984.* Stittsville, Ont.: Canada's Wings, 1983. 99 pp.

[Garvin, Amelia Beers (Warnock).] *Canada's Peace Tower and Memorial Chamber, Designed by John A. Pearson, D. Arch., F.R.A.I.C., F.R.I.B.A., A.R.C.A., G.D.I.A., a Record and Interpretation by Katherine Hale [pseud.] Dedicated by the Architect to the Veterans of the Great War.* Toronto: Mundy-Goodfellow Print. Co., 1935. 29 pp.

* *Le Génie royal canadien.* Ottawa: Imprimeur de la Reine, 1954. 23 pp.

Gibbons, Arthur. *A Guest of the Kaiser; the Plain Story of a Lucky Soldier.* Toronto: Dent, 1919. 198 pp.

[Gibson, George Herbert Rae.] *Maple Leaves in Flanders Fields,* by Herbert Rae [*pseud.*] London: Smith, Elder, 1916. 268 pp.

Gibson, W.L., comp. *Records of the Fourth Canadian Infantry Battalion in the Great War, 1914-1918.* Toronto: MacLean Pub. Co., 1924. 274 pp.

Giesler, Patricia. *Valour Remembered; Canada and the First World War; 1918 — November 11 — 1978./Souvenirs de vaillance; la participation du Canada à la Première Guerre mondiale; 1918 — le 11 novembre — 1978.* Ottawa: Supply and Services Canada/Approvisionnements et Services Canada, 1978. 29/31 pp.
Bilingual text./Texte bilingue.

[Giles, L.C.] *Liphook, Bramshott and the Canadians.* n.p.: Bramshott and Liphook Preservation Society, 1986. 36 pp.

Godenrath, Percy F. *Lest We Forget; a Record in Art of the Dominion's Part in the War (1914-1918) and a Memorial to Those Canadians who Made the Great Sacrifice, being the Gift of the Over-Seas Military Forces to the Nation; a Brief History of the Collection of War Paintings, Etchings and Sculpture, Made Possible by the Work of the Canadian War Memorials Fund and the Canadian War Record Office.* Ottawa: n.p., 1934. 46 pp.

The Gold Stripe; a Tribute to the British Columbia Men who have been Killed, Crippled and Wounded in the Great War. No. 1-3. Vancouver: n.p., 1918-19.
Title varies. No. 3: The Gold Stripe; a Tribute to Those who were Killed, Maimed and Wounded in the Great War; a Book, One of Many Efforts to Re-Establish Some Back in Civil Life.

Goodspeed, D.J. *Battle Royal; a History of the Royal Regiment of Canada, 1862-1962.* Toronto: privately printed, 1962. 703 pp.

_____. *The Road Past Vimy; the Canadian Corps, 1914-1918.* Toronto: Macmillan, 1969. 185 pp.

Gouin, Jacques, *et al. Bon coeur et bon bras; histoire du Régiment de Maisonneuve, 1880-1980.* Montréal: imprimé privé, 1980. 298 pp.

Gould, L. McLeod. *From B.C. to Baisieux; being the Narrative History of the 102nd Canadian Infantry Battalion.* Victoria, B.C.: privately printed, 1919. 134 pp.

Gould, R.W., and S.K. Smith. *The Glorious Story of the Fighting 26th; New Brunswick's One Infantry Unit in the Greatest War of All the Ages.* n.p.: n.d. 48 pp.

Governor General's Foot Guards, Ottawa; Seventy-Fifth Anniversary, June 8, 1872-1947. Ottawa: privately printed, 1947. 43 pp.

Grafton, C.S. *The Canadian "Emma Gees"; a History of the Canadian Machine Gun Corps.* London, Ont.: privately printed, 1938. 218 pp.

Graham, Howard. *Citizen and Soldier; the Memoirs of Lieutenant-General Howard Graham.* Toronto: McClelland and Stewart, 1987. 304 pp.

Granatstein, J.L., and R.D. Cuff, eds. *War and Society in North America.* Toronto: T. Nelson, 1971. 199 pp.

Grant, Reginald. *S.O.S. Stand To!* New York: D. Appleton, 1918. 296 pp.

Gravel, Jean-Yves. *Les soldats-citoyens; histoire du Régiment de Trois-Rivières, 1871-1978.* Trois-Rivières, P.Q.: Editions du Bien Public, 1981. 153 pp.

The Great Adventure with the 4th Battery, C.F.A., B.E.F. n.p.: n.d. 70 pp.

Gt. Brit. Imperial War Graves Commission. *Beaumont-Hamel (Newfoundland) Memorial; Bearing the Names of Those Sailors, Soldiers and Merchant Seamen from Newfoundland who Fell in the Great War and have no Known Graves.* London: H.M. Stationery Office, 1929. 45 pp.

_____. *Introduction to the Register of the Vimy Memorial.* London: H.M. Stationery Office, 1931. 14 pp.

_____. *Memorials Erected at Halifax, Nova Scotia and Victoria, British Columbia, Canada, Bearing the Name of Those Sailors, Soldiers and Merchant Seamen of Canada who Fell in the Great War and have no Known Graves.* London: H.M. Stationery Office, 1930. 24 pp.

_____. *The Register of the Names of Soldiers of the Overseas Military Forces of Canada who Fell in France in the Great War, whose Graves are not Known, and who are Commemorated on the Vimy Memorial, France.* London: H.M. Stationery Office, 1930. 8 vols.

_____. *The War Graves of the British Empire; the Register of the Names of Those who Fell in the Great War and are Buried in Adanac Military Cemetery, Miraumont and Pys, France.* London: H.M. Stationery Office, 1925. 67 pp.

_____. *The War Graves of the British Empire; the Register of the Names of Those who Fell in the Great War and are Buried in Aix-Noulette Communal Cemetery and Extension, France.* London: H.M. Stationery Office, 1928. 38 pp.

_____. *The War Graves of the British Empire; the Register of the Names of Those who Fell in the Great War and are Buried in Barlin Communal Cemetery Extension, Barlin, France.* London: H.M. Stationery Office, 1922. 54 pp.

_____. *The War Graves of the British Empire; the Register of the Names of Those who Fell in the Great War and are Buried in Bois-Carré British Cemetery, Lichfield Crater and Zivy Crater, Thélus, Givenchy Road Canadian Cemetery, Neuville-St. Vaast, and Vimy Communal Cemetery, Farbus, France.* London: H.M. Stationery Office, 1930. 44 pp.

Gt. Brit. Imperial War Graves Commission. *The War Graves of the British Empire; the Register of the Names of Those who Fell in the Great War and are Buried in Canada Cemetery, Tilloy-lès-Cambrai, Ramillies and Proville British Cemeteries, Crest Cemetery, Fontaine-Notre Dame and Neuville-St. Remy Churchyard, France.* London: H.M. Stationery Office, 1925. 39 pp.

_____. *The War Graves of the British Empire; the Register of the Names of Those who Fell in the Great War and are Buried in Cemeteries and Churchyards in Nova Scotia, Prince Edward Island and New Brunswick, Canada.* London: H.M. Stationery Office, 1931. 92 pp.

_____. *The War Graves of the British Empire; the Register of the Names of Those who Fell in the Great War and are Buried in Cemeteries in Newfoundland.* London: H.M. Stationery Office, 1930. 19 pp.

_____. *The War Graves of the British Empire; the Register of the Names of Those who Fell in the Great War and are Buried in Cemeteries in the Province of British Columbia, Canada.* London: H.M. Stationery Office, 1931. 48 pp.

_____. *The War Graves of the British Empire; the Register of the Names of Those who Fell in the Great War and are Buried in Cemeteries in the Province of Manitoba, Canada.* London: H.M. Stationery Office, 1931. 48 pp.

_____. *The War Graves of the British Empire; the Register of the Names of Those who Fell in the Great War and are Buried in Cemeteries in the Province of Ontario, Canada.* London: H.M. Stationery Office, 1931. 2 vols.

_____. *The War Graves of the British Empire; the Register of the Names of Those who Fell in the Great War and are Buried in Cemeteries in the Province of Quebec, Canada.* London: H.M. Stationery Office, 1931. 64 pp.

_____. *The War Graves of the British Empire; the Register of the Names of Those who Fell in the Great War and are Buried in Cemeteries in the Provinces of Saskatchewan and Alberta, Canada.* London: H.M. Stationery Office, 1931. 63 pp.

_____. *The War Graves of the British Empire; the Register of the Names of Those who Fell in the Great War and are Buried in Courcelette British Cemetery, France.* London: H.M. Stationery Office, 1926. 42 pp.

_____. *The War Graves of the British Empire; the Register of the Names of Those who Fell in the Great War and are Buried in Ecoivres Military Cemetery, Mont-St. Eloy, France.* London: H.M. Stationery Office, 1922. 82 pp.

Gt. Brit. Imperial War Graves Commission. *The War Graves of the British Empire; the Register of the Names of Those who Fell in the Great War and are Buried in Fosse No. 10 Communal Cemetery and Extension, Sains-en-Gohelle, Beuvry Communal Cemetery and Extension, Quatre-Vents Military Cemetery, Estrée-Cauchy, Verquignel Communal Cemetery and Gouy-Servins Communal Cemetery, France.* London: H.M. Stationery Office, 1928. 51 pp.

_____. *The War Graves of the British Empire; the Register of the Names of Those who Fell in the Great War and are Buried in Hawthorn Ridge Cemeteries No. 1 and No. 2, Auchonvillers, Hunter's Cemetery, Beaumont-Hamel, Mesnil Ridge Cemetery, Miraumont Communal Cemetery, and Sunken Road and 2nd Canadian Cemeteries, Contalmaison.* London: H.M. Stationery Office, 1930. 45 pp.

_____. *The War Graves of the British Empire; the Register of the Names of Those who Fell in the Great War and are Buried in Haynecourt British Cemetery and Cantimpré Canadian Cemetery, Sailly (Nord), France.* London: H.M. Stationery Office, 1924. 31 pp.

_____. *The War Graves of the British Empire; the Register of the Names of Those who Fell in the Great War and are Buried in Iwuy Communal Cemetery, Niagara Cemetery, Iwuy, and the Communal Cemeteries at Noyelles-sur-Selle, Hordain and Thun-l'Eveque, France.* London: H.M. Stationery Office, 1929. 25 pp.

_____. *The War Graves of the British Empire; the Register of the Names of Those who Fell in the Great War and are Buried in La Chaudière Military Cemetery, Vimy, France.* London: H.M. Stationery Office, 1923. 33 pp.

_____. *The War Graves of the British Empire; the Register of the Names of Those who Fell in the Great War and are Buried in La Targette British Cemetery (Aux-Rietz) and Petit-Vimy British Cemetery, France.* London: H.M. Stationery Office, 1926. 36 pp.

_____. *The War Graves of the British Empire; the Register of the Names of Those who Fell in the Great War and are Buried in Ligny-St. Flochel British Cemetery, Averdoingt, France.* London: H.M. Stationery Office, 1922. 35 pp.

_____. *The War Graves of the British Empire; the Register of the Names of Those who Fell in the Great War and are Buried in Ontario Cemetery, Inchy-lès-Marquion, Triangle Cemetery, Inchy-en-Artois, Sucerie British Cemetery, Graincourt-lès-Havrincourt, and Moeuvres British Cemetery, France.* London: H.M. Stationery Office; 1928. 35 pp.

Gt. Brit. Imperial War Graves Commission. *The War Graves of the British Empire; the Register of the Names of Those who Fell in the Great War and are Buried in Passchendaele New British Cemetery, Belgium.* London: H.M. Stationery Office, 1928. 28 pp.

_____. *The War Graves of the British Empire; the Register of the Names of Those who Fell in the Great War and are Buried in Quarry Cemetery, Marquion Chapel Corner Cemetery, Sauchy-Lestrée and Sains-lès-Marquion British Cemetery, France.* London: H.M. Stationery Office, 1926. 30 pp.

_____. *The War Graves of the British Empire; the Register of the Names of Those who Fell in the Great War and are Buried in Quéant Communal Cemetery British Extension, Dominion and Upton Wood Cemeteries, Hendecourt-lès-Cagnicourt, Croisilles Railway Cemetery, and Ecoust Military Cemetery, Ecoust-St. Mein, France.* London: H.M. Stationery Office, 1928. 56 pp.

_____. *The War Graves of the British Empire; the Register of the Names of Those who Fell in the Great War and are Buried in Ribécourt British Cemetery, Ribécourt Road Cemetery, Trescault, Trescault Communal Cemetery, Quarry Wood Cemetery, Sains-lès-Marquion, and Bourlon Wood Cemetery, France.* London: H.M. Stationery Office, 1928. 58 pp.

_____. *The War Graves of the British Empire; the Register of the Names of Those who Fell in the Great War and are Buried in Rosières Communal Cemetery, Communal Cemetery Extension and British Cemetery, Caix Communal and British Cemeteries, Lihons French National Cemetery, Farmerville Communal Cemetery, Herleville Churchyard and Proyart Communal Cemetery, France.* London: H.M. Stationery Office, 1928. 46 pp.

_____. *The War Graves of the British Empire; the Register of the Names of Those who Fell in the Great War and are Buried in Sancourt British Cemetery, Porte-de-Paris Cemetery, Cambrai, Mill Switch British Cemetery, Tilloy-lès-Cambrai, St. Olle British and Communal Cemeteries, Raillencourt, Cantaing British Cemetery and Fontaine-Notre Dame Communal Cemetery, France.* London: H.M. Stationery Office, 1928. 39 pp.

_____. *The War Graves of the British Empire; the Register of the Names of Those who Fell in the Great War and are Buried in Sucerie Cemetery, Ablain-St. Nazaire, and Givenchy-en-Gohelle Canadian Cemetery and Zouave Valley Cemetery, Souchez, France.* London: H.M. Stationery Office, 1928. 39 pp.

Gt. Brit. Imperial War Graves Commission. *The War Graves of the British Empire; the Register of the Names of Those who Fell in the Great War and are Buried in Sun Quarry and Quebec Cemeteries, Cherisy, Quebec Cemetery, Orange Trench Cemetery, Monchy-le-Preux, Happy Valley British Cemetery, Fampoux, and Valley Cemetery, Vis-en-Artois, France.* London: H.M. Stationery Office, 1927. 38 pp.

_____. *The War Graves of the British Empire; the Register of the Names of Those who Fell in the Great War and are Buried in the Domart-sur-la-Luce Group of Cemeteries, France.* London: H.M. Stationery Office, 1928. 39 pp.

_____. *The War Graves of the British Empire; the Register of the Names of Those who Fell in the Great War and are Buried in the Fouquescourt Group of Cemeteries, France.* London: H.M. Stationery Office, 1928. 32 pp.

_____. *The War Graves of the British Empire; the Register of the Names of Those who Fell in the Great War and are Buried in Thelus Military Cemetery and Nine Elms Military Cemetery, Thelus, France.* London: H.M. Stationery Office, 1928. 44 pp.

_____. *The War Graves of the British Empire; the Register of the Names of Those who Fell in the Great War and are Buried in Villers Station Cemetery, Villers-au-Bois, France.* London: H.M. Stationery Office, 1924. 62 pp.

_____. *The War Graves of the British Empire; the Register of the Names of Those who Fell in the Great War and are Buried in Wailly Orchard Cemetery and Le Fremont Military Cemetery, Rivière, France.* London: H.M. Stationery Office, 1925. 29 pp.

Gt. Brit. War Office. *War Establishments.* Part XVI. *Canadian Forces (France), 1919.* London: H.M. Stationery Office, 1919. 328 pp.

The Great War and Canadian Society; an Oral History. Daphne Read, ed. Toronto: New Hogtown Press, 1978. 223 pp.

Green, F.G. *A History of the 6th Canadian Siege Battery; France, Belgium and Germany, 1916-1919.* n.p.: privately printed, n.d. 70 pp.

Greenhous, Brereton. *The Battle of Amiens, 8-11 August 1918.* (Canadian Battle Series, no. 15.) Toronto: Canadian War Museum; Balmuir Books, 1995. 37 pp.

_____. *Dragoon; the Centennial History of the Royal Canadian Dragoons, 1883-1983.* Ottawa: Guild of the Royal Canadian Dragoons, 1983. 557 pp.

_____. *Semper Paratus; the History of the Royal Hamilton Light Infantry (Wentworth Regiment), 1862-1977,* by Kingsley Brown, Senior, Kingsley Brown, Junior, and Brereton Greenhous. Revised and edited by Brereton Greenhous. Hamilton, Ont.: privately printed, 1977. 446 pp.

*Greenhous, Brereton, and Stephen J. Harris. *Canada and the Battle of Vimy Ridge, 9-12 April, 1917*. Ottawa: Supply and Services Canada, 1992. 149 pp.

*Greenhous, Brereton, et Stephen J. Harris. *Le Canada et la bataille de Vimy, 9-12 avril, 1917*. Fabien Saint-Jacques, tr. Ottawa: Approvisionnements et Services Canada, 1992. 151 pp.

Gregory, William T. *From Camp to Hammock with the Canadian Scottish Borderers*. [Leamington, Ont.]: n.p., 1917. 35 pp.

Griesbach W.A. *I Remember*. Toronto: Ryerson Press, 1946. 353 pp.

_____. *Observations on Cavalry Duties; Hints for Western Canadian Cavalry Men*. Edmonton: Edmonton Law Stationers, 1914. 38 1.

Griffin, Frederick. *Major-General Sir Henry Mill Pellatt, CVO, DCL, VD; a Gentleman of Toronto, 1859-1939*. Toronto: Ontario Pub. Co., 1939. 30 pp.

Grodzinski, J.R. *The Battle of Moreuil Wood*. Vancouver: Broadway Printers, [1993]. 32 pp.
Canadian Cavalry Brigade, 1918.

Groves, Hubert, comp. *Toronto Does Her "Bit"*. Toronto: Municipal Intelligence Bureau, 1918. 72 pp.

Guiou, Norman Miles. *Transfusion; a Canadian Surgeon's Story in War and in Peace*. Yarmouth, N.S.: Stoneycroft Pub., 1985. 145 pp.

Gunn, J.N. and E.E. Dutton. *Historical Records of No. 8 Canadian Field Ambulance; Canada, England, France, Belgium, 1915-1919*. Toronto: Ryerson Press, 1920. 169 pp.

Gwyn, Sandra. *Tapestry of War; a Private View of Canadians in the Great War*. Toronto: HarperCollins Publishers, 1992. 552 pp.

H., J.A., *voir Les poilus canadiens*.

Hahn, E. *The Intelligence Service within the Canadian Corps, 1914-1918*. Toronto: Macmillan, 1930. 263 pp.

Hale, Katherine, [*pseud.*] *see* Garvin, Amelia Beers (Warnock).

Halliday, H.A. *Tragic Victory./Une victoire tragique*. Ottawa: National Museum of Man, National Museums of Canada/Musée national de l'Homme, Musées nationaux du Canada, 1978. 61 pp.
Exhibition of First World War art./Exposition de l'art militaire de la Première Guerre mondiale.

Hamilton, J.H., comp. *Vancouver's Contribution to the Empire; a Souvenir of the First Overseas Contingent who Volunteered for Foreign Service from the Regiments of Vancouver and District*. Vancouver: privately printed, 1914. 32 pp.

Harker, Douglas E. *The Dukes; the Story of the Men who have Served in Peace and War with the British Columbia Regiment (D.C.O.), 1883-1973.* n.p.: privately printed, 1974. 438 pp.

Harley, Geo. E. *The Big War; a Study in Initiative and Resource.* n.p.: 1952. 41 pp.
Account of a Canadian officer in British and Canadian hospitals in England at the end of the war.

Harris, Stephen. *Canadian Brass: the Making of a Professional Army, 1860-1939.* Toronto: Univ. of Toronto Press, 1988. 271 pp.

Haycock, Ronald G. *Sam Hughes; the Public Career of a Controversial Canadian, 1885-1916.* (Canadian War Museum Historical Publication no. 21.) n.p.: Wilfrid Laurier Univ. Press in collaboration with Canadian War Museum, 1986. 355 pp.

Hayes, Joseph. *The Eighty-Fifth in France and Flanders.* Halifax: privately printed, 1920. 362 pp.
85th Battalion, C.E.F.

Herrington, Walter S., and A.J. Wilson. *The War Work of the County of Lennox and Addington.* Napanee, Ont.: Beaver Press, 1922. 278 pp.

Hewitt, G.E. *The Story of the Twenty-Eighth (North-West) Battalion, 1914-1917.* London: Charles, n.d. 24 pp.

Hezzelwood, Oliver, *see* Trinity Methodist Church, Toronto, Ont.

Historical Calendar; 21st Canadian Infantry Battalion (Eastern Ontario Regiment); Belgium — France — Germany, 1915-1919. Aldershot, Eng.: privately printed, 1919. 72 pp.

Historical Record of the No. 54 District Canadian Forestry Corps, 1916-1919. London: Bassano, 1919. 35 pp.

An Historical Sketch of the Seventy-Seventh Battalion, Canadian Expeditionary Force; Having Particular Reference to the Military Record of the Members of This Battalion, with Three Pictorial Sections, i.e., Personal Portraits, Battalion Portraits, War Views. Ottawa: War Publications, 1926. v.p.

A History of No. 7 (Queen's) Canadian General Hospital, March 26th, 1915 — Nov. 15th, 1917. London: privately printed, [1917]. 66 pp.

Hodder-Williams, Ralph, G.R. Stevens, and R.B. Mainprize. *Princess Patricia's Canadian Light Infantry.* London: Hodder and Stoughton, 1923-[57?]. 4 vols.

Holland, J.A. *The Story of the Tenth Canadian Battalion, 1914-1917.* London: Charles, n.d. 35 pp.

Holyoak, F.G. *The History of the 39th Battery, Canadian Field Artillery.* n.p.: 1919. 1 vol., unpaged.

Hopkins, J. Castell. *Canada at War; a Record of Heroism and Achievement, 1914-1918, Containing also a Story of Five Cities,* by Rev. Robert Renison. Toronto: Canadian Annual Review, 1919. 448 pp.

Horrocks, William. *In their own Words.* Ottawa: Rideau Veterans Home Residents Council, 1993. 247 pp.

How, Douglas. *The 8th Hussars; a History of the Regiment.* Sussex, N.B.: Maritime Pub., 1964. 446 pp.

Howard, Fred. *On Three Battle Fronts.* New York: V. Waring, 1918. 177 pp.

Howard, Gordon L. *The Memories of a Citizen Soldier, 1914-1945.* n.p.: n.d. 114 pp.

_____. *Sixty Years of Centennial in Saskatchewan, 1906-1968.* n.p.: n.d. 140 pp.

Howland, Harry. *The Dauntless Fannigans.* New York: Vantage Press, 1970. 377 pp.
7th Battalion, C.E.F., soldier's experiences as a prisoner of war.

Hubbell, E.L. *The Winnipeg Grenadiers.* n.p.: n.d. 16 pp.

Hughes, G.W., comp. *A Marchpast of the Corps and Regiments of the Canadian Army, Past and Present.* Calgary: n.p., n.d. 3 vols.

Humphrey, James McGivern. *The Golden Bridge of Memoirs.* Don Mills, Ont.: Nelson, 1979. 182 pp.

Hundevad, John, ed. *Guide Book of the Pilgrimmage to Vimy and the Battlefields, July-August, 1936.* Ottawa: privately printed, [1936]. 136 pp.

Hunt, M.S., comp. *Nova Scotia's Part in the Great War.* Halifax: Veteran Pub., 1920. 466 pp.

Hutchison, Paul P. *Canada's Black Watch; the First Hundred Years, 1862-1962.* Montreal: privately printed, [1962]. 340 pp.

_____. *Five Strenuous Years; the McGill Chapter of Alpha Delta Phi during the Great War.* Toronto: privately printed, n.d. 292 pp.

_____. *A Short History of the Royal Highland Regiment the Black Watch, 1725-1948.* n.p.: 1948. 39 pp.

Hyatt, A.M.J. *General Sir Authur Currie: a Military Biography.* (Canadian War Museum Historical Publication no. 22.) Toronto: Univ. of Toronto Press in collaboration with Canadian War Museum, 1987. 178 pp.

Inches, C.F. *The 1st Canadian Heavy Battery in France; Farewell Message to the N.C.O.'s and Men.* Liverpool, Eng.: C. Tinling, 1919. 31 pp.

*L'Intendance royale canadienne. Ottawa: Imprimeur de la Reine, 1954. 12 pp.

The Irish-Canadian Rangers. Montreal: privately printed, 1916. 57 pp.

Ito, Roy. *Stories of My People; a Japanese Canadian Journal.* Hamilton, Ont.: S-20 and Nisei Veterans Association, 1994. 497 pp.

————. *We Went to War; the Story of the Japanese Canadians who Served during the First and Second World Wars.* Stittsville, Ont.: Canada's Wings, 1984. 330 pp.

Jackson, H.M. *Canadian Prime Ministers and the Canadian Militia.* n.p.: 1958. 11 pp.

————. *The 127th Battalion, C.E.F.; 2nd Battalion, Canadian Railway Troops.* Montreal: privately printed, n.d. 186 pp.

————. *The Princess Louise Dragoon Guards; a History.* n.p.: 1952. 306 pp.

————. *The Roll of the Regiments (the Active Militia).* Ottawa: n.p., 1959. 176 pp.

————. *The Royal Regiment of Artillery, Ottawa, 1855-1952; a History.* Montreal: privately printed, 1952. 418 pp.

————. *The Sherbrooke Regiment (12th Armoured Regiment).* n.p.: 1958. 229 pp.

————. *The Story of the Royal Canadian Dental Corps.* Ottawa: privately printed, 1956. 475 pp.

James, F. Treve, and Thos. Johnston, eds. *Bruce in Khaki; Containing a History of the 160th Overseas Bruce Battalion and Complete Nominal Roll of All Men who were at any Time on the Strength of the Battalion.* Chesley, Ont.: privately printed, 1934. 1 vol., unpaged.

James, Fred. *Canada's Triumph; Amiens — Arras — Cambrai; August — September — October, 1918.* London: Charles, n.d. 63 pp.

Jeffery, R.A. *Catholic Army Huts; Progress Report to June 1st, 1918, and Recommendations for This Year's Campaign; Presented at the Ontario State Convention of the Knights of Columbus Held in Windsor, Ontario, on June 4th and 5th, 1918.* Windsor, Ont.: n.p., 1918. 11 pp.

Jennings, Cedric. *Canada in the First World War and the Road to Vimy Ridge./Le Canada pendant la Première Guerre mondiale et la route vers la crête de Vimy.* Ottawa: Communications Division, Veterans Affairs Canada/ Direction générale des communications, Anciens combattants Canada, 1992. 21/23 pp.
Bilingual text./Texte bilingue.

190

Johnston, G. Chalmers. *The 2nd Canadian Mounted Rifles (British Columbia Horse) in France and Flanders.* From the records of Lieutenant-Colonel G. Chalmers Johnston. M.V. McGuire and others, eds. Vernon, B.C.: privately printed, n.d. 174 pp.

Johnston, Stafford. *The Fighting Perths; the Story of the First Century in the Life of a Canadian County Regiment.* Stratford, Ont.: privately printed, 1964. 133 pp.

Jones, G.C. *Interim Report of Surgeon-General G.C. Jones, Director Medical Services, Canadians, in Reply to the Report on the Canadian Army Medical Service, by Colonel Herbert A. Bruce, Special Inspector-General, Medical Services, Canadian Expeditionary Force.* London: n.p., 1916. 163 pp.

Jones, William R. *Fighting the Hun from Saddle and Trench, by Sgt Major William R. Jones, Known among his Comrades as "Lucky Bill", no. 59 of the Royal Canadian Dragoons.* Albany, N.Y.: Aiken Book Co., 1918. 281 pp.

Kay, Hugh R. *The History of the Forty-Third Battery, C.F.A.* Niagara Falls, Ont.: privately printed, [1955?]. 23 pp.

_____. *The History of the Forty-Third Battery, C.F.A.* Vol. I. Edinburgh: privately printed, 1918. 47 pp.

Kay, Hugh R., George Magee, and F.A. MacLennan. *Battery Action; the Story of the 43rd Battery, C.F.A.* Toronto: Warrick & Rutter, n.d. 304 pp.

Kaye, V.J. *Ukranian Canadians in Canada's Wars.* J.B. Gregorovich, ed. (Materials for Ukranian Canadian History, Volume 1.) Toronto: Ukranian Canadian Research Foundation, 1983. 125 pp.

Keene, Louis. *"Crumps"; the Plain Story of a Canadian who Went.* Boston: Houghton Mifflin, 1917. 156 pp.

Kerr, Wilfred Brenton. *Arms and the Maple Leaf; Memories of Canada's Corps, 1918.* Seaforth, Ont.: Huron Expositor, 1943. 90 pp.

_____. *"Shrieks and Crashes"; being Memories of Canada's Corps, 1917.* Toronto: Hunter, Rose, 1929. 218 pp.

Kerry, A.J., and W.A. McDill. *The History of the Corps of Royal Canadian Engineers.* Ottawa: privately printed, 1962. 2 vols.

Keshen, Jeffrey A. *Propaganda and Censorship during Canada's Great War.* Edmonton: Univ. of Alberta Press, 1996. 333 pp.

Kimball, Harold G. *The 104th New Brunswick Battalion in the First World War, 1915-1918.* Fredericton, N.B.: privately printed, 1962. 20 pp.

King, W.D., comp. *A Brief History of Militia Units Established at Various Periods at Yarmouth, Nova Scotia, 1812-1947.* Yarmouth, N.S.: privately printed, 1947. 32 pp.

Kordan, Bohdan S., and Peter Melnycky. *In the Shadow of the Rockies; Diary of the Castle Mountain Internment Camp.* Edmonton: Canadian Institute of Ukrainian Studies Press, Univ. of Alberta, 1991. 143 pp.

L., R.A., *see Letters of a Canadian Stretcher Bearer.*

Laflamme, Jean. *Les camps de détention au Québec durant la Première Guerre mondiale.* Montréal: s.i., 1973. 49 pp.

_____. *Spirit Lake; un camp de concentration en Abitibi durant la Grande Guerre.* Montréal: Maxime, 1989. 59 pp.

Laird, Donald Harry. *Prisoner Five-One-Eleven.* Toronto: Ontario Press, [191-?]. 115 pp.

Lamontagne, Léopold. *Les archives régimentaires des Fusiliers du S.-Laurent.* Rimouski, P.Q.: s.i., 1943. 247 pp.

*Lapointe, Arthur J. *Souvenirs et impressions de ma vie de soldat (1916-1919); Vingt-deuxième Bataillon (1917-1918).* St-Ulric, P.Q.: s.i., 1919. 109 pp.

*_____. *Soldier of Quebec (1916-1919).* R.C. Fetherstonhaugh, tr. Montreal: Garand, 1931. 116 pp.

*La Presse, Montréal, P.Q. *Nos volontaires sous les armes; des chiffres et la vérité; 42,000 recrues natives pour Ontario; 25,000 la proportion logique pour les Canadiens-français.* Montréal: La Presse, [1916]. 39 pp.

*_____. *Our Volunteer Army; Facts and Figures.* Montreal: La Presse, 1916. 38 pp.

Lavoie, Joseph A. *Le Régiment de Montmagny de 1869 à 1931.* s.l.: s.i., [1932]. 117 pp.

_____. *Une unité canadienne; "coq-à-l'âne" sériocomique*, par E.I. Oval [*pseud.*] et E. Rastus [*pseud.* Québec, P.Q.: M.E. Martin], 1920. 162 pp.

Leash, Homer E. *131st Westminster Overseas Battalion, 1916; Headquarters, New Westminster, British Columbia.* Vancouver: n.p., 1916. 1 vol., unpaged.

LeMaistre, Susan, ed./éd. *Memorials to Canada's War Dead./Mémoriaux aux Canadiens morts à la guerre.* Ottawa: Veterans Affairs Canada/Anciens combattants Canada, [198-?]. 135 pp.
Bilingual text./Texte bilingue.

Letters of a Canadian Stretcher Bearer, by R.A.L. Anna Chapin Ray, ed. Boston: Little, Brown, 1918. 288 pp.

Lewis, R. *Over the Top with the 25th; Chronicle of Events at Vimy Ridge and Courcelette.* Halifax: H.H. Marshall, 1918. 59 pp.

Lind, [Francis Thomas]. *The Letters of Mayo Lind.* Introd. by J. Alex. Robinson. St. John's, Nfld.: Robinson, 1919. 175 pp.

Lindsey, C.B., comp. *The Story of the Fourth Canadian Division, 1916-1919.* Aldershot, Eng.: Gale & Polden, n.d. 51 pp.

The Listening Post. No. 1-32. [Bailleul, Belgium]: n.p., 1915-18. *Journal of the 7th Battalion, C.E.F. A veteran's journal of the same title was published in Montreal beginning in 1923.*

Little Black Devils see Tascona, Bruce, and Eric Wells.

"The Little Mother" *see* Bagshaw, M.E.

Livesay, J.F.B. *Canada's Hundred Days; with the Canadian Corps from Amiens to Mons, Aug 8 — Nov 11, 1918.* Toronto: Allen, 1919. 421 pp.

Logan, H.T. *History of the Canadian Machine Gun Corps, C.E.F.* n.p.: 1919. 3 vols.

Logan, J.D. *Canada's Champion Regimental Band; a Critical Study of the Musicianship of the Band of the 85th Overseas Battalion, C.E.F., Nova Scotia Highlanders; an Essay in the Appreciation of Martial and of Concert Music.* Pictou, N.S.: Advocate Print. & Pub. Co., 1916. 23 pp.

The Lorne Scots (Peel, Dufferin and Halton Regiment). Brampton, Ont.: privately printed, 1962. 47 pp.

Luciuk, Lubomyr Y. *Internment Operations; the Role of Old Fort Henry in World War I.* Bryan Rollason, ed. (A Delta Minibook.) Kingston, Ont.: Delta Educational Consultants, 1980. 38 pp.

————. *A Time for Atonement; Canada's First National Internment Operations and the Ukranian Canadians, 1914-1920.* Kingston, Ont.: The Limestone Press, 1988. 31 pp.

Luciuk, Lubomyr Y., and Ron Sorobey. *Konowal.* Kingston, Ont.: Published for the Royal Canadian Legion Branch 360 by the Kashtan Press, 1996. 18 pp. *Corporal/Caporal Filip Konowal, V.C. Trilingual text./Texte trilingue.*

Lynch, Alex. *Dad, the Motors and the Fifth Army Show.* Westport, Ont.: privately printed, 1978. 1 vol., unpaged. *1st Canadian Motor Machine Gun Brigade.*

Lynch, John William. *Princess Patricia's Canadian Light Infantry, 1917-1919.* Hicksville, N.Y.: Exposition Press, 1976. 208 pp.

MacArthur, D.C. *The History of the Fifty-Fifth Battery, C.F.A.* Hamilton, Ont.: H.S. Longhurst, 1919. 94 pp.

McBride, Herbert W. *The Emma Gees.* Indianapolis, In.: Bobbs-Merrill, 1918. 219 pp.

_____. *A Rifleman Went to War; being a Narrative of the Author's Experiences and Observations while with the Canadian Corps in France and Belgium, September 1915 — April 1917, with Particular Emphasis upon the Use of the Military Rifle in Sniping, its Place in Modern Armament, and the Work of the Individual Soldier.* Marines, N.C.: Small Arms Technical Pub. Co., 1935. 398 pp.

McClintock, Alexander. *Best o'Luck; How a Fighting Canadian Won the Thanks of Britain's King.* Toronto: McClelland, Goodchild & Stewart, 1917. 171 pp.

McClung, Nellie L., *see* Simmons, Mervin C.

Macdermot, T.W.L. *The Seventh.* Montreal: privately printed, n.d. 144 pp. *7th Canadian Siege Battery.*

MacDonald, F.B., & John J. Gardiner. *The Twenty-Fifth Battalion, Canadian Expeditionary Force; Nova Scotia's Famous Regiment in World War One.* n.p.: privately printed, 1983. 211 pp.

MacDonald. Frank. *The Kaiser's Guest.* Garden City, N.Y.: privately printed, 1918. 250 pp.

MacDonald, J.A. *Gun-Fire; an Historical Narrative of the 4th Bde C.F.A. in the Great War (1914-18).* Toronto: privately printed, 1929. 264 pp.

McEvoy, Bernard, and A.H. Finlay, comps. *History of the 72nd Canadian Infantry Battalion, Seaforth Highlanders of Canada.* Vancouver: Cowan and Brookhouse, 1920. 311 pp.

Macfie, John, [ed.] *Letters Home.* Meaford, Ont.: privately printed, 1990. 219 pp. *Letters written by Roy, John and Arthur Macfie during the First World War. Largely the 1st Battalion, C.E.F.*

McGill Univ., Montreal, P.Q. *McGill Honour Roll, 1914-1918.* Montreal: McGill Univ., 1926. 228 pp.

_____. *A Memorial Service for the McGill Men and Women who Gave Their Lives during the First and Second World Wars.* n.p.: [1946]. 1 vol., unpaged.

MacGowan, S. Douglas, Harry M. (Mac) Heckbert and Byron E. O'Leary. *New Brunswick's "Fighting 26th"; a Draft History of the 26th New Brunswick Battalion, C.E.F., 1914-1919.* n.p.: 1991. 2 vols. in 1.

McGregor, F., ed. *LdSH (RC) '85-70'.* Winnipeg: privately printed, 1970. 62 pp.

Macintyre, D.E. *Canada at Vimy.* Toronto: P. Martin, 1967. 229 pp.

McKean, G.B. *Scouting Thrills.* New York: Macmillan, 1919. 235 pp.

McKee, A. *Vimy Ridge.* London: Souvenir Press, 1966. 242 pp.
New York ed. titled: The Battle of Vimy Ridge.

McKenzie, F.A. *Canada's Day of Glory.* Toronto: W. Briggs, 1918. 342 pp.

_____. *Through the Hindenburg Line; Crowning Days on the Western Front.* London: Hodder and Stoughton, 1918. 429 pp.

Mackenzie, J.J. *Number 4 Canadian Hospital; the Letters of Professor J.J. Mackenzie from the Salonika Front; with a Memoir by his Wife Kathleen Cuffe Mackenzie.* Toronto: Macmillan, 1933. 247 pp.

Mackenzie-Naughton, J.D. *The Princess of Wales' Own Regiment (M.G.).* Kingston, Ont.: privately printed, 1946. 74 pp.

McKeown, J.D. *From Otterpool to the Rhine with the 23rd Battery, Canadian Field Artillery, via Caestre, St. Eloi, Ypres, The Somme, Vimy, Hill 70, Cinnibar Trench, Passchendaele, Arras, Amiens, Cambria* [*sic*]*, Valenciennes, Mons.* London: Charles, n.d. 48 pp.

McKillican, D.R. *A Short History of the Toronto Scottish Regiment.* n.p.: 1972. 40 pp.

Macksey, Kenneth. *The Shadow of Vimy Ridge.* Toronto: Ryerson Press, 1965. 264 pp.

_____. *Vimy Ridge.* (Pan/Ballantine Illustrated History of the First World War, no. 6.) New York: Pan/Ballantine, 1972. 160 pp.

MacLaren, Roy. *Canadians in Russia, 1918-1919.* Toronto: Macmillan, 1976. 301 pp.

MacLeod, John N. *A Pictorial Record and Original Muster Roll, 29th Battalion.* Vancouver: privately printed, 1919. 64 pp.

McMullen, Fred, and Jack Evans. *Out of the Jaws of Hunland; the Stories of Corporal Fred McMullen, Sniper, Private Jack Evans, Bomber, Canadian Soldiers, Three Times Captured and Finally Escaped from German Prison Camps.* Toronto: W. Briggs, 1918. 248 pp.

MacPhail, (Sir) Andrew. *The Medical Services.* (Official History of the Canadian Forces in the Great War, 1914-19.) Ottawa: King's Printer, 1925. 428 pp.

McWilliams, James L., and R. James Steele. *Gas! The Battle for Ypres, 1915.* St. Catharines, Ont.: Vanwell Pub., 1985. 247 pp.

_____. *The Suicide Battalion.* Edmonton: Hurtig Publishers, 1978. 226 pp.
46th Battalion (South Saskatchewan), C.E.F.

Machum, George C. *The Story of the 64th Battalion, c.e.f., 1915-16.* Montreal: privately printed, 1956. 94 pp.

Magnacca, Stephen A. *1871-1971; One Hundredth Anniversary of the 13 Field Battery Based at Portage la Prairie, Manitoba.* n.p.: n.d. 12 pp.

Major J.M. Langstaff, F.I.A., F.A.S., C.A., Barrister-at-Law; a Memorial. Toronto: Press of Miln-Bingham Co., n.d. 77 pp.

Manarey, R. Barrie. *The Canadian Bayonet.* Edmonton: Century Press, 1971. 51 pp.

Manion, R.J. *A Surgeon in Arms.* New York: D. Appleton, 1918. 310 pp.

The Maple Leaf. Vol. I-? London: Pay and Record Office, Canadian Expeditionary Force, 1915-?
Subtitle varies: The Magazine of the Canadian Expeditionary Force Pay and Record Office, The Magazine of the Overseas Military Forces of Canada, etc.

Marquis, G.E. *Le Regiment de Lévis; historique et album.* Lévis, P.Q.: s.i., 1952. 292 pp.

Marteinson, John, and others. *We Stand on Guard; an Illustrated History of the Canadian Army.* Montreal: Ovale, 1992. 511 pp.

Martin, Stuart. *The Story of the Thirteenth Battalion, 1914-1917.* London: Charles, [1918]. 19 pp.

Massey, Raymond. *When I was Young.* Toronto: McClelland and Stewart, 1976. 269 pp.
Canadian Field Artillery in France and Siberia.

Mathieson, William D. *My Grandfather's War; Canadians Remember the First World War, 1914-1918.* Toronto: Macmillan, 1981. 338 pp.

Maxwell, George A. *Swan Song of a Rustic Moralist; Memoirs.* Hicksville, N.Y.: Exposition Press, 1975. 162 pp.
Memoirs of service with 49th Battalion, C.E.F.

Mazéas, Daniel. *Insignes armée canadienne, 1900-1914; Canadian Badges; supplément, 1920-1950.* Guingamp, France: privately printed, 1972. 116 pp.

Meek, John F. *Over the Top; the Canadian Infantry in the First World War.* Orangeville, Ont.: privately printed, 1971. 188 pp.

Meighen, F.S., ed. *Photographic Record and Souvenir of the Canadian Grenadier Guards Overseas Battalion, "Eighty Seventh".* Montreal: privately printed, 1916. 55 pp.

* *The Memorial Chamber in the Peace Tower, Houses of Parliament, Ottawa, Canada,* [by A.F. Duguid]. Ottawa: Photogelatine Engraving Co., n.d. [34] pp.

Memorial of the 27th Battery, Canadian Field Artillery. London: McCorquodale, 1919. 27 pp.

Menzies, J.H. *Canada and the War; the Promise of the West.* Toronto: Copp Clark, 1916. 117 pp.

Merritt, Wm. Hamilton. *Canada and National Service.* Toronto: Macmillan, 1917. 247 pp.

The Message from Mars; being a Christmas Greeting from the Officers, Non-Commissioned Officers and Men of the 4th Canadian Division, B.E.F., to Friends the World Over. London: Carlton Studio, 1918. 60 pp.

Metson, Graham, comp. *The Halifax Explosion, December 6, 1917.* Toronto: McGraw-Hill Ryerson, n.d. 173 pp.

Military Munnings: the Canadian War Art of an Equestrian Painter from the Art Collection of the Canadian War Museum/1917-1918/Munnings, artiste militaire: les oeuvres canadiennes d'un peintre équestre provenant de la Collection d'art du Musée canadien de la guerre. n.p.: Canadian War Museum, Canadian Museum of Civilization/s.l.: Musée canadien de la guerre, Musée canadien des civilisations, 1993. 56 pp.
Bilingual text./Texte bilingue.

The Military Service Council. *Military Service Act, 1917; Instructions to Registrars and Deputy Registrars; Circular no. 28.* Ottawa: n.p., 1917. 35 pp.

_____. *The Military Service Act, 1917; Manual for the Information and Guidance of Tribunals in the Consideration and Review of Claims for Exemption.* Ottawa: King's Printer, 1918. 117 pp.

_____. *The Military Service Act, 1917; Together with the Regulations of the Governor-in-Council of 19th October, 1917, Governing Procedure and the Proclamation of the 13th October, 1917, Prefaced by Some Instructions for the Guidance of Local Tribunals.* Ottawa: n.p., 1917. 90 pp.

_____. *The Military Service Act, 1917; Together with the Regulations of the Governor-in-Council of 19th October, 1917, Governing Procedure, with Amendments Made on the 6th and 8th of November, 1917 (Unindexed), the Proclamation of the 13th October, 1917, and the Order-in-Council of the 8th Day of November, 1917, (P.C. 3168) Relating to Absentees without Leave and Evidence (Unindexed), Prefaced by Some Instructions for the Guidance of Local Tribunals.* Ottawa: King's Printer, 1917. 99 pp.

_____. *Report of the Military Service Council on the Administration of the Military Service Act, 1917.* Ottawa: King's Printer, 1918. v.p.

Military Vaudeville by 144th Overseas Battalion, C.E.F.; 3rd Battalion 90th Winnipeg Rifles, under the Patronage of His Honor the Lieutenant-Governor, Sir Douglas Cameron and the District Officer Commanding M.D. No. 10, Col. H.N. Ruttan, Winnipeg Theatre, Winnipeg, March 9th, 10th, 11th, 1916. Winnipeg: privately printed, 1916. 95 pp.

The Militia in Durham County ... see Chandler, C.M.

Millar, W.C. *From Thunder Bay through Ypres with the Fighting Fifty-Second.* n.p.: [ca. 1918]. 101 pp.

Miller, James Martin, and H.S. Canfield. *The People's War Book; History, Encyclopedia and Chronology of the Great World War; and Canada's Part in the War*, by W.R. Plewman. Toronto: Imperial Pub. Co., 1919. 520 pp.

Milnes, Herbert. *A Story of the Oxford Rifles, 1798-1954.* (Oxford Museum Bulletin, no. 5.) Woodstock, Ont.: printed by Woodstock Print & Litho, 1974. 28 pp.

Milsom, H.G. *Sunset, Night and Dawn.* [Camden, N.J.: Magrath Print. House, 1918?]. 60 pp.

Mitchell, G.D., with B.A. Reid and W. Simcock. *RCHA — Right of the Line; an Anecdotal History of the Royal Canadian Horse Artillery from 1871.* Ottawa: RCHA History Committee, 1986. 303 pp.

Mitchell, Michael, comp. *Ducimus; the Regiments of the Canadian Infantry.* St. Hubert, Que.: Director of Infantry, Mobile Command Headquarters, 1992. 248 pp.

Moir, J.S., ed. *History of the Royal Canadian Corps of Signals, 1903-1961.* Ottawa: privately printed, 1962. 336 pp.

Monaghan, Hugh B. *The Big Bombers of World War I; a Canadian's Journal.* Burlington, Ont.: R. Gentle Communications, n.d. 101 pp.

Montagu-Marsden, M. *A Short History of Captured Guns, the Great European War, 1914-1918; the British Columbia Regiment (7th Bn., (C.E.F.), the Seaforth Highlanders of Canada (72nd Bn., C.E.F.).* Vancouver: privately printed, n.d. 1 vol., unpaged.

The Montreal Standard. *Canada's Aid to the Allies, and Peace Memorial.* Frederic Yorston, ed. Montreal: Standard Pub. Co., 1918, 1 vol., unpaged, chiefly illus.

Moogk, Peter N., and R.V. Stevenson. *Vancouver Defended; a History of the Men and Guns of the Lower Mainland Defences, 1859-1949.* Surrey, B.C.: Antonson Pub., 1978. 128 pp.

Moore, Mary Macleod. *The Maple Leaf's Red Cross; the War Story of the Canadian Red Cross Overseas.* London: Skeffington, n.d. 223 pp.

More Letters From Billy; by the Author of "A Sunny Subaltern; Billy's Letters from Flanders". Toronto: McClelland, Goodchild & Stewart, 1917. 121 pp.

Morley, A.W. *Standing Orders, 144th Overseas Battalion, C.E.F., Winnipeg Rifles.* n.p.: 1916. 45 pp.

Morris, David A. *The Canadian Militia; from 1855; an Historical Summary.* Erin, Ont.: Boston Mills Press, 1983. 328 pp.

Morrison, J. Clinton. *Hell upon Earth; a Personal Account of Prince Edward Island Soldiers in the Great War, 1914-1918.* Summerside, P.E.I.: privately printed, 1995. 359 pp.

Morton, Desmond. *The Canadian General, Sir William Otter.* (Canadian War Museum Historical Publication Number 9.) Toronto: Hakkert, 1974. 423 pp.

_____. *A Peculiar Kind of Politics: Canada's Overseas Ministry in the First World War.* Toronto: Univ. of Toronto Press, 1982. 267 pp.

_____. *Silent Battle; Canadian Prisoners of War in Germany, 1914-1919.* Toronto: Lester Pub., 1992. 218 pp.

_____. *When Your Number's Up; the Canadian Soldier in the First World War.* Toronto: Random House, 1993. 354 pp.

Morton, Desmond, and J.L. Granatstein. *Marching to Armageddon; Canadians and the Great War 1914-1919.* Toronto: Lester & Orpen Dennys, 1989. 288 pp.

Mottistone, John Edward Bernard Seely, 1st baron. *Adventure.* London: W. Heinemann, 1930. 326 pp.
Commanded Canadian Cavalry Brigade 1915-1918.

Munroe, Jack. *A Dog Story of the Princess "Pats"; Mopping Up! Through the Eyes of Bobbie Burns, Regimental Mascot.* New York: H.K. Fly, [1918]. 319 pp.

Murdie, R. *Standing Orders of the 161st Canadian Infantry Battalion.* Aldershot, Eng.: Gale & Polden, 1917. 92 pp.

Murdoch. B.J. *The Red Vineyard.* Cedar Rapids, Iowa: Torch Press, 1923. 313 pp.
Memoirs of a CEF chaplain.

Murray, W.W. *Five Nines and Whiz Bangs*, by "the Orderly Sergeant". Ottawa: The Legionary, 1937. 224 pp.

_____. *The History of the 2nd Canadian Battalion (East. Ontario Regiment) Canadian Expeditionary Force in the Great War, 1914-1918.* Ottawa: n.p., 1947. 408 pp.

Murray. W.W., ed. *The Epic of Vimy.* Ottawa: The Legionary, [1936]. 223 pp.

N.R.E.F., 16th Brigade C.F.A., 67th and 68th Batteries in North Russia, September 1918 to June 1919. n.p.: n.d. 55 pp.

Nasmith, George Gallie. *Canada's Sons and Great Britain in the World War; a Complete and Authentic History of the Commanding Part Played by Canada and the British Empire in the World's Greatest War.* Toronto: J.C. Winston, 1919. 607 pp.

_____. *Canada's Sons in the World War; a Complete and Authentic Story of the Commanding Part Played by Canada and the British Empire in the World's Greatest War.* Toronto: J.C. Winston, 1919. 2 vols.

Nicholson, G.W.L. *Canada's Nursing Sisters.* (Canadian War Museum Historical Publication Number 13.) Toronto: S. Stevens, Hakkert, 1975. 272 pp.

*_____. *Canadian Expeditionary Force, 1914-1919.* (Official History of the Canadian Army in the First World War.) Ottawa: Queen's Printer, 1962. 621 pp.

*_____. *Corps expéditionnaire canadien, 1914-1919.* (Histoire officielle de la participation de l'Armée canadienne à la Première Guerre mondiale.) Ottawa: Imprimeur de la Reine, 1963. 671 pp.

_____. *The Fighting Newfoundlanders; a History of the Royal Newfoundland Regiment.* St. John's, Nfld.: Govt. of Nfld., 1964. 614 pp.

_____. *The Gunners of Canada; the History of the Royal Regiment of Canadian Artillery.* Toronto: McClelland and Stewart, 1967-72. 2 vols.

*_____. *"Nous nous souviendrons ..."; mémoriaux outremer aux morts de guerre du Canada.* Ottawa: Imprimeur de la Reine, 1973. 118 pp.

_____. *Seventy Years of Service; a History of the Royal Canadian Army Medical Corps.* Ottawa: Borealis Press, 1977. 388 pp.

*_____. *"We will Remember ..."; Overseas Memorials to Canada's War Dead.* Ottawa: Queen's Printer, 1973. 110 pp.

The 9th Mississauga Horse; and its Contribution to the Canadian Expeditionary Force. [Toronto]: n.p., n.d. 36 pp.

No Man's Land; the Battlefield Paintings/Tableaux des champs de bataille/of Mary Riter Hamilton/de Mary Riter Hamilton, 1919-1922; Organized by Angela E. Davis and Sarah M. McKinnon/Organisatrices: Angela E. Davis et Sarah M. McKinnon/University of Winnipeg Gallery November 5 — December 8, 1989/Galerie de l'Université de Winnipeg du 5 novembre au 8 décembre 1989. Winnipeg: Univ. of Winnipeg, 1989. 39 pp. *Bilingual text./Texte bilingue.*

Nominal Roll of All Officers of 120th City of Hamilton Battalion C.E.F. and Also of Other Ranks of the Battalion who Arrived in England, Showing Units with which They were Serving, or to which They were Attached on February 1st, 1917. Aldershot, Eng.: printed by Gale & Polden, 1917. 22 pp.

Norris, Armine. *"Mainly for Mother."* Toronto: Ryerson Press, n.d. 219 pp.

Noyes, Frederick W. *Stretcher Bearers ... at the Double!* Toronto: Hunter, Rose, 1937. 315 pp.

No. 3 Canadian General Hospital ... see Pirie, Alexander Howard.

O'Brien, Jack. *Into the Jaws of Death.* New York: Dodd, Mead, 1919. 295 pp.

Odds and Ends from a Regimental Diary. n.p.: n.d. 30 pp.

Officers' Gradation List; Canadian Expeditionary Force (Revised to 1st November 1915). n.p.: n.d. 234 pp.

Ogilvie, William G. *Umty-Iddy-Umty; the Story of a Canadian Signaller in the First World War.* Erin, Ont.: Boston Mills Press, 1982. 59 pp.

Ogle, Robert J. *The Faculties of Canadian Military Chaplains; a Commentary on the Faculty Sheet of December, 1955, and the Directives for Holy Week Promulgated March 14, 1956.* Ottawa: n.p., 1956. 267 pp.

O'Gorman, J.R. *Soldiers of Christ; Canadian Catholic Chaplains, 1914-1918.* Toronto: privately printed, 1936. 72 pp.

O'Gorman, J.R., comp. *The War and the 7th Bn. C.R.T.* n.p.: [1920]. 67 pp.

Oh, Canada; a Medley of Stories, Verse, Pictures and Music, Contributed by Members of the Canadian Expeditionary Force. London: Simpkin, Marshall, Hamilton, Kent, 1916. 95 pp.

On the Roll of Honour, G.L.B. Mackenzie, Lieutenant in the Third Battalion, Toronto Regiment, 1st Division, Canadian Expeditionary Force, 4th January, 1892 — 7th June, 1916. n.p.: privately printed, [1916]. 64 pp.

Once in the Queen's Own, Always in the Queen's Own. n.p.: privately printed, 1932. 70 pp.

101st Overseas Battalion, W.L.I., C.E.F.; Souvenir Programme. Winnipeg: privately printed, 1916. 88 pp.

The 116th Battalion in France see Allen, E.P.S.

Ontario. Dept. of Education. *Annals of Valour; Empire Day, Friday, May 23rd, 1919.* Toronto: King's Printer, 1919. 165 pp.

_____. *Canada's Part in the Present War; Empire Day, Thursday, May 23rd, 1918.* Toronto: King's Printer, 1918. 95 pp.

_____. *The Roll of Honour of the Ontario Teachers who Served in the Great War, 1914-1918.* Toronto: Ryerson Press, 1922. 72 pp.

Ontario Agricultural College, Guelph, Ont. *Ontario Agricultural College Honor and Service Rolls.* n.p.: n.d. 1 vol., unpaged.

Ontario Bar Association. *Roll of Honour.* n.p.: [1918]. 22 pp.

Oval, E.I., [*pseud.*] *voir* Lavoie, Joseph A.

Overseas Service of the 18th Battery, Canadian Field Artillery. n.p.: [1919]. 26 pp.

Pallas, S.M., comp. *Canadian Recipients of the Colonial Auxiliary Forces Officers' Decoration and the Colonial Auxiliary Forces Long Service Medal.* Ottawa: printed by Tri-Graphic Print., 1990. 183 pp.

Parkdale Collegiate Institute, Toronto, Ont. *Roll of Service in the Great War, 1914-1919.* n.p.: n.d. 22 pp.

_____. *Their Name Liveth; a Memoir of the Boys of Parkdale Collegiate Institute who Gave their Lives in the Great War.* Toronto: privately printed, n.d. 177 pp.

Parsons, W. David. *Pilgrimmage; a Guide to the Royal Newfoundland Regiment in World War One.* St. John's, Nfld.: Creative Publishers, 1994. 205 pp.

Peace Souvenir; Activities of Waterloo County in the Great War, 1914-1918. Kitchener, Ont.: Kitchener Daily Telegraph, 1919. 70 pp.

Pearson, George. *The Escape of a Princess Pat; Being the Full Account of the Capture and Fifteen Months' Imprisonment of Corporal Edwards, of the Princess Patricia's Canadian Light Infantry, and his Final Escape from Germany into Holland.* Toronto: McClelland, Goodchild & Stewart, 1918. 227 pp.

Peat, Harold R. *Private Peat.* Indianapolis, In.: Bobbs-Merrill, 1917. 235 pp.

Pedley, James H. *Only this; a War Retrospect.* Ottawa: Graphic Publishers, 1927. 371 pp.

Penny, Arthur G. *Royal Rifles of Canada, "Able and Willing" since 1862; a Short History.* n.p.: 1962. 62 pp.

Peterson, W.G. *Silhouettes of Mars.* London: J. Lane, 1920. 266 pp.

Peterson, (Sir) William. *"A Canadian Hospital in France."* n.p.: 1915. 12 pp. *At head of title: McGill University, Montreal, Annual University Lecture.*

Phillips, Roger, F. Dupuis and J. Chadwick. *The Ross Rifle Story.* Antigonish, N.S.: privately printed, 1984. 475 pp.

Phillips, Roger, and Jerome J. Knap. *Sir Charles Ross and his Rifle.* (Historical Arms Series, no. 11.) Ottawa: Museum Restoration Service, 1969. 32 pp.

Photographic Record of the 207th Ottawa-Carleton Battalion, C.E.F. n.p.: [1916]. 1 vol., chiefly illus.

[Pirie, Alexander Howard, comp.] *No. 3 Canadian General Hospital (McGill) in France (1915, 1916, 1917); Views Illustrating Life and Scenes in the Hospital, with a Short Description of its Origin, Organisation and Progress.* Middlesbrough, Eng.: Hood, 1918. 1 vol., unpaged.

Plewman, W.R. *see* Miller, James Martin.

Plummer, Mary. *With the First Canadian Contingent.* London: Hodder & Stoughton, 1916. 118 pp.

Les poilus canadiens; le roman du vingt-deuxième bataillon canadien-français, par J.A.H. s.l.: s.i., s.d. 47 pp.

Pontifex, Bryan, comp. *Canadian Army Service Corps, 2nd Divisional Train; Record of Service of Officers, 1914-1919.* Toronto: Carswell, 1920. 42 pp.

Pook, Ronald. *Memories of the First World War.* Allentown, Pa.: privately printed, 1986. 56 pp.

Pope, Maurice A. *Soldiers and Politicians; the Memoirs of Lt.-Gen. Maurice A. Pope, C.B., M.C.* Toronto: Univ. of Toronto Press, 1962. 462 pp.

Prescott, John F. *In Flanders Fields; the Story of John McCrae.* Erin, Ont.: Boston Mills Press, 1985. 144 pp.

Preston, Richard A. *Canada and "Imperial Defense"; a Study of the Origins of the British Commonwealth's Defense Organization, 1867-1919.* (Duke University Commonwealth-Studies Center; Publication Number 29.) Durham, N.C.: Duke Univ. Press, 1967. 576 pp.

_____. *Canada's RMC; a History of the Royal Military College.* Toronto: Univ. of Toronto Press, 1969. 415 pp.

Princess Patricia's Canadian Light Infantry Recruit's Book. [Winnipeg: n.p., 1946.] 24 pp.

Programme souvenir; publié à l'occasion du retour d'outre-mer du 22ème Bataillon (Canadien-français), mai, 1919. Québec, P.Q.: s.i., [1919]. 32 pp.

Putkowski, Julian. *The Kinmel Park Camp Riots.* Hawarden, Wales: Flintshire Historical Society, 1989. 55 pp.
Reprinted from the Flintshire Historical Society Journal, XXXII(1989).

Quebec Chronicle. *War, Victory and Peace Edition.* Quebec, P.Q.: Chronicle Print. Co., 1920. 56 pp.
Cover title: Canada's Share in War, Victory, and Peace.

Queen's Own Rifles of Canada Association. *A Brief Resumé of the Activities of the Queen's Own Rifles of Canada Association, 1914-1932.* Toronto: privately printed, 1932. 70 pp.

_____. *[Queen's Own Rifles of Canada; Book of Remembrance, 1866-1918.* n.p.: 1932.] 1 vol., unpaged.

Queen's Univ., Kingston, Ont. *Overseas Record; Record of Graduates, Alumni, Members of Staff, and Students of Queen's University on Active Military (Overseas) Service (to June 1st, 1917), 1914-1917.* n.p.: [1917?]. 44 pp.

Quigley, John Gordon. *A Century of Rifles, 1860-1960; the Halifax Rifles (RCAC)(M); "cede nullis".* Halifax: privately printed, 1960. 230 pp.

Rabjohn, R.H. *A Diary; a Story of My Experience: in France, and Belgium, during the World War, 1914-1918.* Burlington, Ont.: CDM Business Services, 1977. 1 vol., chiefly illus.

Rae, Herbert, [*pseud.*] *see* Gibson, George Herbert Rae.

Ralphson, George H. *Over There, with the Canadians at Vimy Ridge.* Chicago: M.A. Donohue, 1919. 221 pp.

Rannie, William F., ed. *To the Thunderer his Arms; The Royal Canadian Ordnance Corps.* Lincoln, Ont.: privately printed, 1984. 360 pp.

Rawling, Bill. *Surviving Trench Warfare; Technology and the Canadian Corps, 1914-1918.* Toronto: Univ. of Toronto Press, 1992. 325 pp.

Rawlinson, James H. *Through St. Dunstan's to Light.* Toronto: T. Allen, 1919. 86 pp.

Ready for Active Service; Camp Hughes, Manitoba. Winnipeg: Western News Agency, [1916]. 1 vol., chiefly illus.

The Regimental History of the Governor General's Foot Guards see Baylay, George Taylor.

Reid, Gordon. *Poor Bloody Murder; Personal Memoirs of the First World War.* Oakville, Ont.: Mosaic Press, 1980. 260 pp.

A Remembrance from the Survivors, All Ranks, of the 16th Battalion (the Canadian Scottish) C.E.F., 1914-1919, to All Ranks Now Serving in the Canadian Scottish Regiment, which Regiment Perpetuates the 16th. n.p.: n.d. 91 pp.

Renison, Robert, *see* Hopkins, J. Castell.

A Report Addressed to the Canadian Hierarchy on the Organization and Work of the Canadian Catholic Chaplains Overseas, for the Year 1917. London: privately printed, 1918. 16 pp.

Richards, R. *The Story of the Princess Patricia's Canadian Light Infantry, 1914-1917.* London: Charles, 1918. 23 pp.

Riddle, David K., and Donald G. Mitchell, comps. *The Distinguished Conduct Medal to the Canadian Expeditionary Force, 1914-1920.* Winnipeg: Kirkby-Marlton Press, 1991. 304 pp.

Riddle, David K., and Donald G. Mitchell, comps. *The Distinguished Service Order to the Canadian Expeditionary Force and Canadians in the Royal Naval Air Service, Royal Flying Corps and Royal Air Force, 1915-1920.* Winnipeg: Kirkby-Marlton Press, 1991. 130 pp.

_____. *The Military Cross to the Canadian Expeditionary Force, 1915-1921.* Winnipeg: Kirkby-Marlton Press, 1991. 390 pp.

Rioux, Denise. *Les Fusiliers de Sherbrooke (1910-1980).* Sherbrooke, P.Q.: s.i., 1980. 68 pp.

Robertson, F.A. *5th (B.C.) Regiment, Canadian Garrison Artillery, and Early Defences of B.C. Coast; Historical Record.* Victoria, B.C.: privately printed, 1925. 2 vols.

Robertson, Heather, [comp.] *A Terrible Beauty; the Art of Canada at War.* Toronto: J. Lorimer, 1977. 239 pp.

Robertson, Peter. *Irréductible vérité/Relentless Verity/les photographes militaires canadiens depuis 1885/Canadian Military Photographers since 1885.* (Les Archives publiques du Canada/Public Archives of Canada Series.) Québec, P.Q.: Les Presses de l'Université Laval, 1973. 233 pp. *Texte bilingue./Bilingual text.*

Rocky Mountain Rangers; First Battalion, C.A. — A.F., 1885-1941. New Westminster, B.C.: Columbian Co., 1941. 60 pp., chiefly illus.

Rodney, William. *Joe Boyle; King of the Klondike.* Toronto: McGraw-Hill Ryerson, 1974. 368 pp.

Rogers, R.L. *History of the Lincoln and Welland Regiment.* n.p.: privately printed, 1954. 465 pp.

Roll Call of Canadian Irish. Toronto: n.p., 1916. 32 pp.

Rosen, Albert, & Peter Martin. *Canadian Expeditionary Force Military Cap Badges of World War I.* Toronto: Alternative Graphics, 1985. 124 pp.

Rossiter, Ivan. *In Kultured Kaptivity; Life and Death in Germany's Prison Camps and Hospitals.* Indianapolis, In.: Bobbs-Merrill, 1918. 244 pp.

Roy, R.H. *For Most Conspicuous Bravery; a Biography of Major-General George R. Pearkes, V.C., through Two World Wars.* Vancouver: Univ. of British Columbia Press, 1977. 388 pp.

_____. *Sherwood Lett; his Life and Times.* Vancouver: UBC Alumni Association, Univ. of British Columbia, 1991. 180 pp.

_____. *Sinews of Steel; the History of the British Columbia Dragoons.* Brampton, Ont.: privately printed, 1965. 468 pp.

*The Royal Canadian Armoured Corps. Ottawa: Queen's Printer, 1953. 11 pp.

The Royal Canadian Army Medical Corps. Ottawa: Queen's Printer, 1953. 10 pp.

Royal Canadian Army Pay Corps. Ottawa: Queen's Printer, 1953. 11 pp.

The Royal Canadian Army Service Corps. Ottawa: Queen's Printer, 1953. 11 pp.

The Royal Canadian Artillery. Ottawa: Queen's Printer, 1953. 10 pp.

Royal Canadian Horse Artillery; First Regiment, 1871-1971. Lahr, Germany: privately printed, [1971]. 32 pp.

Royal Canadian Military Institute, Toronto, Ont. *The Golden Book.* Toronto: privately printed, 1927. 1 vol., unpaged.

The Royal Canadian Ordnance Corps Diamond Jubilee Yearbook. n.p.: 1963. 106 pp.

The Royal Highlanders of Canada, Allied with the Black Watch (Royal Highlanders), Montreal, Canada. London: H. Rees, 1918. 30 pp.

The Royal Military College of Canada, 1876-1919. Kingston, Ont.: n.p., 1919. 16 pp.

Royal Military College of Canada, Kingston, Ont. *Regulations for the Royal Military College of Canada Kingston, Ont.; Amended to May 1917.* Ottawa: King's Printer, 1917. 25 pp.

_____. *The Stone Frigate.* Kingston, Ont.: privately printed, 1914. 301 pp.

The Royal Rifles of Canada, Allied with the King's Royal Rifle Corps, 1862-1937; Ypres 1915, Festubert, Mont Sorrel, Somme 1916, Arras 1917, Hill 70, Ypres 1917, Amiens; South Africa 1899-1900; Great War 1914-1918. n.p.: [1937]. 21 pp.

The Royal Westminster Regiment, 1863-1988. New Westminster, B.C.: n.p., 1988. 72 pp.

Ruck, Calvin W. *Canada's Black Battalion; No. 2 Construction, 1916-1920.* Halifax: Society for the Protection and Preservation of Black Culture in Nova Scotia, 1986. 143 pp.

Rudbach, N.E. *The Halifax Rifles (23 Armoured Regiment) R.C.A.C.R.F.; "90th" Anniversary, 14th May 1860 — 14th May 1950.* Halifax: n.p., 1950. 20 pp.

Russenholt, E.S., comp. *Six Thousand Canadian Men; being the History of the 44th Battalion Canadian Infantry, 1914-1919.* Winnipeg: privately printed, 1932. 364 pp.

Rutherford, Tom. *An Unofficial History of the Grey and Simcoe Foresters Regiment, 1866-1973.* n.p.: n.d. 88 pp.

Rutledge, Stanley A. *Pen Pictures from the Trenches.* Toronto: W. Briggs, 1918. 159 pp.

Ryerson, George Sterling. *Looking Backward.* Toronto: Ryerson Press, 1924. 264 pp.

Santor, Donald M. *Canadians at War, 1914-1918.* (Canadiana Scrapbook.) Scarborough, Ont.: Prentice-Hall, 1978. 48 pp.

Schragg, Lex. *History of the Ontario Regiment, 1866-1951.* Oshawa, Ont.: privately printed, 1951. 286 pp.

Scott, Frederic George. *The Great War as I Saw It.* Toronto: Goodehill, 1922. 327 pp.

Scudamore, T.V. *Lighter Episodes in the Life of a Prisoner of War.* Aldershot, Eng.: Gale & Polden, 1933. 92 pp.

_____. *A Short History of the 7th Battalion, C.E.F.* Vancouver: privately printed, 1930. 1 vol., unpaged.

Second Contingent, Military District No. 10, 1915; in Commemoration of the Second Contingent Going to the Front from Military District No. 10, Canada, 1915. [Winnipeg: n.p., 1915.] 1 vol., chiefly illus.

Seely, J.E.B. *see* Mottistone, John Edward Bernard Seely, 1st baron.

Service, G.T., and J.K. Marteinson. *The Gate; a History of the Fort Garry Horse.* Calgary: privately printed, 1971. 228 pp.

78th Overseas Battalion (Winnipeg Grenadiers). Winnipeg: Advance Photo Co., 1916. 35 pp., chiefly illus.

75th Battalion; Book of the Battalion. Toronto: privately printed, [1916]. 36 pp.

77th Overseas Battalion, Canadian Expeditionary Force, Ottawa. Ottawa: privately printed, [1916]. 1 vol., chiefly illus.

Sharpe, Robert J. *The Last Day, the Last Hour; the Currie Libel Trial.* Agincourt, Ont.: Published for The Osgoode Society by the Carswell Co. of Canada, 1988. 270 pp.

Sheldon-Williams, Ralf Frederic Lardy. *The Canadian Front in France and Flanders.* Inglis Sheldon-Williams, illus. London: A. and C. Black, 1920. 208 pp.

A Short History and Photographic Record of 106th Overseas Battalion, C.E.F., Nova Scotia Rifles, Lieut. Col. Robert Innes, Commanding Officer. [Ottawa]: Mortimer, 1916. 47 pp.

A Short History & Photographic Record of the Nova Scotia Overseas Highland Brigade, C.E.F., Composed of the 85th Nova Scotia Highlanders, 193rd Nova Scotia Highlanders, 219th Overseas Highland Battalion, Lieut. Col. A.H. Borden, Brigadier. Halifax: Mortimer, 1916. v.p.

A Short History and Photographic Record of the 73rd Battalion, Canadian Expeditionary Force, Royal Highlanders of Canada; Allied with the Black Watch. Ottawa: privately printed, n.d. 47 pp.

A Short History of the British Columbia Regiment; the "Dukes". n.p.: n.d. [11] pp.

Short Memoirs of the Third Canadian Divisional Mechanical Transport Company; Organized April 14th, 1918, Demobilized May 1st, 1919. London: privately printed, [1919]. 34 pp.

Sifton, C., comp. *The Diary of the 13th Battery, Canadian Field Artillery, 1914-1919.* London: privately printed, 1919. 47 pp.

Sime, J.G. *Canada Chaps.* Toronto: S.B. Gundy, 1917. 270 pp.

Simmons, [Mervin C.] *Three Times Out,* told by Private Simmons, written by Nellie L. McClung. Toronto: T. Allen, 1918. 247 pp.

Sinclair, J.D., comp. *The Queen's Own Cameron Highlanders of Canada; Twenty-Fifth Anniversary Souvenir.* Winnipeg: privately printed, 1935. 99 pp.

Singer, H.C., and A.A. Peebles. *History of Thirty-First Battalion C.E.F. from its Organization, November, 1914, to its Demobilization, June, 1919.* Calgary: privately printed, [1939]. 515 pp.

Six Bits. Vol. I, no. 1-7. Toronto: privately printed, 1919-20.
Published by the 75th Battalion Overseas Association.

The 60th C.F.A. Battery Book, 1916-1919. London: Canada Newspaper Co., [1919]. 190 pp.

60th Canadian Battalion B.E.F. (Victoria Rifles of Canada). n.p.: [1917. 10 pp.]

Skuce, J.E. *CSEF; Canada's Soldiers in Siberia, 1918-1919.* Ottawa: Access to History Publications, 1990. 148 pp.

Smith, G. Oswald, *see University of Toronto ....*

Smith, Joseph S. *Over There and Back in Three Uniforms; being the Experiences of an American Boy in the Canadian, British and American Armies at the Front and through No Man's Land.* New York: Dutton, 1917. 244 pp.

Snell, A.E. *The C.A.M.C. with the Canadian Corps during the Last Hundred Days of the Great War.* Ottawa: King's Printer, 1924. 292 pp.

Social Service Council of Canada. *Moral Conditions among our Soldiers Overseas; Official and Other Reliable Evidence.* Toronto: privately printed, [191-?]. 12 pp.

Société des Vétérans français de la Grande Guerre. *Livre d'or des réservistes français du Canada.* Montréal: imprimé privé, 1921. 34 pp.

Souvenir Album of Officers, N.C.Os. and Men of the 50th Overseas Battalion C.E.F., European War. Calgary: Stafford & Kent, n.d. 1 vol., chiefly illus.

Souvenir Book of the 79th Cameron Highlanders of Canada. Winnipeg: n.p., 1916. 32 pp.

Souvenir of Sewell Camp; a Canadian Military Training Ground, 1915. Winnipeg: Western News Agency, [1915]. 1 vol., chiefly illus.

Souvenir of Valcartier Camp. Montreal: G. Clark, n.d. 1 vol., unpaged. *Bound vol. of postcards with captions.*

Souvenir, 231st Overseas Battalion, C.E.F., 3rd Battn., 72nd Seaforth Highlanders of Canada. Vancouver: n.p., 1917. 41 pp.

Souvenir Valcartier Camp, Canada, 16 Scenes from Camp Life. Montreal: T.H. Davies, n.d. [16 pp., chiefly illus.].

*Speaight, Robert. *Georges P. Vanier; soldat, diplomate et gouverneur général.* (Vies canadiennes.) Montréal: Fides, 1972. 530 pp.

*_____. *Vanier; Soldier, Diplomat and Governor General.* Toronto: Collins, 1970. 488 pp.

Standing Orders of the 163rd Battalion Canadian Expeditionary Force. London: H. Rees, 1917. 119 pp.

*Stanley, George F.G. *Canada's Soldiers, 1604-1954; the Military History of an Unmilitary People.* Toronto: Macmillan, 1954. 400 pp. *Subsequent revised and enlarged editions.*

_____. *In the Face of Danger; the History of the Lake Superior Regiment.* Port Arthur, Ont.: privately printed, 1960. 357 pp.

*_____. *Nos soldats; l'histoire militaire du Canada de 1604 à nos jours.* Traduction et adaptation sous la direction de Serge Bernier. Montréal: Les Editions de l'homme, 1980. 620 pp.

Stanley, George F.G., and Richard A. Preston. *A Short History of Kingston as a Military and Naval Centre.* Kingston, Ont.: Queen's Printer, [195-?]. 33 pp.

Steele, Harwood. *The Canadians in France, 1915-1918.* Toronto: Copp Clark, 1920. 364 pp.

_____. *The Long Ride; a Short History of the 17th Duke of York's Royal Canadian Hussars.* Montreal: Gazette Print. Co., 1934. 48 pp.

Steven, Walter T. *In This Sign.* Toronto: Ryerson Press, 1948. 182 pp.

Stevens, G.R. *A City Goes to War.* Brampton, Ont.: Charters Pub., 1964. 431 pp.
Loyal Edmonton Regiment.

Stewart, Charles Henry, comp. *The Concise Lineages of the Canadian Army, 1855 to Date.* Toronto: n.p., n.d. 163 pp.

_____. *"Overseas"; the Lineages and Insignia of the Canadian Expeditionary Force, 1914-1919.* Toronto: Little and Stewart, 1970. 167 pp.

The Story of the Sixty-Sixth C.F.A. Edinburgh: Turnbull & Spears, 1919. 148 pp.

Strachan, Tony, ed. *In the Clutch of Cirmcumstance; Reminiscences of Members of the Canadian National Prisoners of War Association.* Victoria, B.C.: Cappis Press, 1985. 285 pp.

The Strathconian. Calgary: n.p., 1914-?, 1927-38, 1947- .
Regimental journal of the Lord Strathcona's Horse (Royal Canadians). Re-numbered from no. 1 after each gap in publication.

Stuart, (Sir) Campbell. *Opportunity Knocks Once.* London: Collins, 1952. 248 pp.

Stubbs, Roy St. George. *Men in Khaki; Four Regiments of Manitoba.* Toronto: Ryerson Press, 1941. 72 pp.

*Summerby, Janice. *Native Soldiers; Foreign Battlefields.* Ottawa: Communications Division, Veterans Affairs Canada, 1993. 47 pp.

*_____. *Soldats autochtones; terres étrangères.* Ottawa: Direction générale des communications, Anciens combattants Canada, 1993. 51 pp.

Summers, Jack L. *Tangled Web: Canadian Infantry Accoutrements, 1885-1985.* (Canadian War Museum Historical Publication no. 26.) Alexandria Bay, N.Y.: Museum Restoration Service, 1992. 146 pp.

*Summers, Jack L., and René Chartrand. *Military Uniforms in Canada, 1665-1970.* Illustrated by R.J. Marrion. (Canadian War Museum Historical Publication no. 16.) Ottawa: National Museums of Canada, 1981. 192 pp.

*Summers, Jack L., et René Chartrand. *L'uniforme militaire du Canada, 1665-1970.* Illustré par R.J. Marrion. Traduit par Jean Pariseau. (Musée canadien de la guerre publication d'histoire militaire no 16.) Ottawa: Musées nationaux du Canada, 1981. 192 pp.

A Sunny Subaltern; Billy's Letters from Flanders. Toronto: McClelland, Goodchild & Stewart, 1916. 175 pp.
London ed. titled: <u>A Canadian Subaltern, Billy's Letters to his Mother</u>.

Suthren, Victor, ed. *The Oxford Book of Canadian Militiary Anecdotes.* Toronto: Oxford Univ. Press, 1989. 202 pp.

210

Swalm, E.J. *Nonresistance under Test; the Experiences of a Conscientious Objector, as Encountered in the Late World War.* Kitchener, Ont.: Cober Print. Service, 1938. 55 pp.

Swanston, Victor N. *Who Said War is Hell! No. 12895, Private Victor N. Swanston, Fifth Battalion, Canadian Expeditionary Force, World War I.* Saskatoon, Sask.: n.p., 1983. 62 pp.

Swettenham, John. *Allied Intervention in Russia, 1918-1919; and the Part Played by Canada.* Toronto: Ryerson Press, 1967. 315 pp.

_____. *Breaking the Hindenburg Line.* (Canadian Battle Series no. 3.) Ottawa: Balmuir Book Pub.; Canadian War Museum, National Museums of Canada, 1986. 22 pp.

_____. *Canada and the First World War.* Toronto: Ryerson Press, 1969. 160 pp.

_____. *Canada and the First World War./La participation du Canada à la Première Guerre mondiale.* Ottawa: Canadian War Museum/Musée de guerre, n.d./s.d. 56/63 pp.
Bilingual text./Texte bilingue.

_____. *McNaughton.* Toronto: Ryerson Press, 1968-69. 3 vols.

_____. *To Seize the Victory; the Canadian Corps in World War I.* Toronto: Ryerson Press, 1965. 265 pp.

T., R.H., *see* Tupper, Reginald H.

Tamblyn, D.S. *The Horse in War, and Famous Canadian War Horses.* Kingston, Ont.: Jackson Press, n.d. 120 pp.

The Tank Tatler. Vol. I. n.p.: 1918-19.
Official publication of the First Battalion Canadian Tank Corps.

Tascona, Bruce. *From the Forks to Flanders Fields; the Story of the 27th City of Winnipeg Battalion 1914-1919.* Winnipeg: privately printed, 1995. 128 pp.

_____. *The Militia of Manitoba; a Study of Infantry and Cavalry Regiments since 1883; a Look at Regimental Badges and Uniforms, List of Commanding Officers, Battle Honours.* n.p.: 1979. 48 pp.

_____. *XII Manitoba Dragoons: a Tribute.* Winnipeg: Manitoba Dragoons History Book Committee, 1991. 185 pp.

[Tascona, Bruce, and Eric Wells.] *Little Black Devils; a History of the Royal Winnipeg Rifles.* Winnipeg: Frye Pub., 1983. 241 pp.

Taylor, Leonard W. *The Sourdough and the Queen; the Many Lives of Klondike Joe Boyle.* Toronto: Methuen, 1983. 394 pp.

Telford, Murray M. *Scarlet to Green; the Colours, Uniforms and Insignia of the Grey and Simcoe Foresters.* Erin, Ont.: Boston Mills Press, 1987. 64 pp.

3rd Contingent from 1st & 2nd Divisions, Ontario; in Commemoration of the 3rd Contingent Going to the Front from the 1st and 2nd Divisions, Ontario ... 1915. n.p.: G. R. Gibbons, n.d. 1 vol., chiefly illus.

Thomas, Hartley Munro. *UWO Contingent COTC; the History of the Canadian Officers' Training Corps at the University of Western Ontario.* London, Ont.: Univ. of Western Ontario, 1956. 422 pp.

Thompson, Roy J.C. *Cap Badges of the Canadian Officer Training Corps.* Dartmouth, N.S.: n.p., 1972. 68 pp.

_____. *Wings of the Canadian Armed Forces, 1913-1972.* [Dartmouth], N.S.: n.p., 1973. 106 pp.

Thorburn, Ella M., and Charlotte Whitton. *Canada's Chapel of Remembrance.* Toronto: British Book Service (Canada), 1961. 68 pp.

Thorn, J.C. *Three Years a Prisoner in Germany; the Story of Major J.C. Thorn, a First Canadian Contingent Officer, who was Captured by the Germans at Ypres on April 24th, 1915; Relating his Many Attempts to Escape (Once Disguised as a Widow) and Life in the Various Camps and Fortresses.* n.p.: 1919. 152 pp.

Thurston, Arthur. *A Monument Speaks; ... and Tells the Story of its Dead.* Yarmouth, N.S.: A. Thurston Publications, [1989]. 397 pp.
Biographies of those on Yarmouth's First World War memorial.

Tippett, Maria. *Art at the Service of War; Canada, Art, and the Great War.* Toronto: Univ. of Toronto Press, 1984. 136 pp.

Tompkins, Stuart Ramsay. *A Canadian's Road to Russia; Letters from the Great War Decade.* Doris H. Pieroth, ed. Edmonton: Univ. of Alberta Press, 1989. 466 pp.
Service with the Canadian Expeditionary Force in Europe 1916-1918 and Siberia 1919.

Topp, C. Beresford. *The 42nd Battalion, C.E.F., Royal Highlanders of Canada in the Great War.* Montreal: privately printed, 1931. 412 pp.

Toronto's Roll of Honour Fighting the Empire's Battles; an Alphabetical Directory of the Toronto Members of the First and Second Contingents. Toronto: Stevenson & Hevey, 1915. 120 pp.

*La Trésorerie militaire royale canadienne. Ottawa: Imprimeur de la Reine, 1954. 12 pp.

Tributes to the Memory of Corp. G. Gordon Galloway, B.A., 26th Battery, C.F.A., Killed in Action in Flanders, Feb. 10, 1916; Aged 21 yrs. 8 mos. n.p.: n.d. 27 pp.

Trinity Methodist Church, Toronto, Ont. *Trinity War Book; a Recital of Service and Sacrifice in the Great War.* Oliver Hezzelwood, comp. Toronto: privately printed, 1921. 368 pp.

True Canadian War Stories, selected by Jane Dewar from the pages of Legion Magazine. Toronto: Lester & Orpen Dennys, 1986. 310 pp.

Tucker, A.B. *The Battle Glory of Canada; being the Story of the Canadians at the Front, Including the Battle of Ypres.* London: Cassell, [1915]. 168 pp.

[Tupper, Reginald H.] *Victor Gordon Tupper; a Brother's Tribute*, by R.H.T. London: privately printed, 1921. 66 pp.

Turner, H.S. *With the Tenth Field Company, Canadian Engineers, C.E.F.* [Goderich, Ont.: n.p., 1936-41.] 3 vols.

Twenty-Third Battery, Field Artillery; Active Service, 1915. London: Roberts & Leete, [1915. 31 pp.]

226th Overseas Battalion, C.E.F., North-Western Manitoba. Winnipeg: privately printed, n.d. 60 pp.

Two Thousand Officers and Men of the 64th Battalion, C.E.F.; Sussex, New Brunswick, October, 1915. n.p.: n.d. 15 pp.
Nominal roll.

Tyler, G.C.A. *The Lion Rampant; a Pictorial History of the Queen's Own Cameron Highlanders of Canada, 1910-1985.* Winnipeg: The Queen's Own Cameron Highlanders of Canada, 1985. 134 pp.

Univ. of British Columbia. *Record of Service, 1914-1918; University of British Columbia, McGill British Columbia, Vancouver College.* Vancouver: privately printed, 1924. 142 pp.

Univ. of Manitoba. *Roll of Honour, 1914-1918.* Winnipeg: privately printed, 1923. 150 pp.

Univ. of Toronto. Univ. Schools. *The Annals, 1916-1918.* Toronto: Univ. of Toronto Press, n.d. 1 vol., unpaged.

Univ. of Toronto. Victoria College. *Acta Victoriana; War Supplement.* [Toronto]: n.p., 1919. 128 pp.

University of Toronto Roll of Service. First edition, August, 1914 — August, 1917. [Toronto]: Univ. of Toronto Press, n.d. 212 pp.
Also Supplement, August 1917 — October, 1918.

University of Toronto; Roll of Service, 1914-1918. G. Oswald Smith, ed. Toronto: Univ. of Toronto Press, 1921. 603 pp.

Unknown Soldiers, by One of Them. New York: Vantage Press, 1959. 170 pp.

Upper Canada Historical Arms Society. *The Military Arms of Canada.* (Historical Arms Series, 1.) West Hill, Ont.: Museum Restoration Service, 1963. 47 pp.

Upton, Terence B. *The Rocky Mountain Rangers, 1898-1944; a Short History.* n.p.: n.d. 13 pp.

Urquhart, Hugh M. *Arthur Currie; the Biography of a Great Canadian.* Toronto: Dent, 1950. 363 pp.

_____. *The History of the 16th Battalion (the Canadian Scottish) Canadian Expeditionary Force in the Great War, 1914-1919.* Toronto: Macmillan, 1932. 853 pp.

The Vancouver Battalion. Vol. I, no. 1. Vancouver: privately printed, 1915. 34 pp.
Journal of the 29th (Vancouver) Battalion, CEF. Apparently no further numbers were published.

Van Der Schee, W. *A Short History of Lord Strathcona's Horse (Royal Canadians).* n.p.: 1973. 19 1.

Veterans' Review; a Collection of War Stories. Toronto: privately printed, 1983. 255 pp.

Victoria Rifles of Canada, 1861-1951; Historical Notes. n.p.: n.d. 14 pp.

Victoria Rifles of Canada; Youth Trained in Mind and Body in a Great Regiment. n.p.: [ca. 1936]. 16 pp.

Les Voltigeurs de Québec, 1862-1952; notes historiques. s.l.: s.i., 1952. 16 pp.

Les Voltigeurs de Québec, 1862-1962; album du centenaire, mai 1962. St-François, P.Q.: imprimé privé, 1962. 31 pp.

WUB; Western Universities Battalion — 196th. Vol. I-? Camp Hughes, Man.: n.p., 1916-?

Waiser, Bill. *Park Prisoners; the Untold Story of Western Canada's National Parks, 1915-1946.* Saskatoon, Sask.: Fifth House Publishers, 1995. 294 pp.

Walker, William K. *Canadian Motor Machine Gun Brigade with British Fifth Army, March-April 1918.* n.p.: 1957. [15 pp.]

Wallace, John F. *Dragons of Steel; Canadian Armour in Two World Wars.* Burnstown, Ont.: General Store Pub. House, 1995. 283 pp.

The War Diaries. Volume One: *Canadian Railway Troops during World War I; First Battalion, Canadian Overseas Railway Construction Corps, November 1917 — April 1918.* Peter Wilson, ed. Campbellford, Ont.: Wilson's Pub. Co., 1995. 1 vol., unpaged.

War Record of Chattan Men see Chattan Club, Toronto, Ont.

War Record of McGill Chapter of Delta Upsilon. Montreal: n.p., 1919. 47 pp.

Ware, Francis B. *The Story of the Seventh Regiment Fusiliers of London, Canada, 1899 to 1914; with an Epilogue, "A Few Days with the Fusiliers at War".* London. Ont.: Hunter Print. Co., 1945. 190 pp.

Warren, Arnold. *Wait for the Waggon; the Story of the Royal Canadian Army Service Corps.* Toronto: McClelland and Stewart, 1961. 413 pp.

Watson, W.S., and others, eds. *The Brockville Rifles, Royal Canadian Infantry Corps (Allied with the King's Royal Rifle Corps); Semper Paratus; an Unofficial History.* Brockville, Ont.: Recorder Print. Co., 1966. 138 pp.

Weatherbe, K., comp. *From the Rideau to the Rhine; the 6th Field Co. and Battalion Canadian Engineers in the Great War; a Narrative.* Toronto: Hunter-Rose Co., 1928. 519 pp.

Wellington Legion War Veterans Club, eds. *They Served for Freedom./A la défense de la liberté.* [Wellington, P.E.I.: Royal Canadian Legion, Wellington Branch 17/Wellington, I.P.E.: Légion royale canadienne, la filiale de Wellington no 17], 1986. 319 pp.
Bilingual text./Texte bilingue.

Wells, Clifford Almon. *From Montreal to Vimy Ridge and Beyond; the Correspondence of Lieut. Clifford Almon Wells, B.A., of 8th Battalion Canadians, B.E.F., November, 1915 — April, 1917.* O.C.S. Wallace, ed. Toronto: McClelland, Goodchild & Stewart, 1917. 321 pp.

Wells, George Anderson. *The Fighting Bishop; as Recounted in the Eighty-Seventh Year of his Life to his Daughter Jeanne Carden Wells.* Toronto: Cardwell House, 1971. 628 pp.

Wheeler, Victor W. *The 50th Battalion in No Man's Land.* Calgary: Comprint Pub. Co., 1980. 447 pp.

Willcocks, K.D.H. *The Hastings and Prince Edward Regiment, Canada; a Short History.* Belleville, Ont.: n.p., 1967. 1 vol., unpaged.

Williams, Jeffery. *First in the Field; Gault of the Patricias.* St. Catharines, Ont.: Vanwell Pub., 1995. 278 pp.

_____. *Princess Patricia's Canadian Light Infantry.* (Famous Regiments.) London: L. Cooper, 1972. 110 pp.

Williams, S.H. *Stand to Your Horses; through the First World War, 1914-1918, with the Lord Strathcona's Horse (Royal Canadians).* Winnipeg: privately printed, 1961. 308 pp.

Willson, Gordon Beckles. *From Quebec to Picadilly and Other Places; Some Anglo-Canadian Memories.* London: J. Cape, 1929. 366 pp.

————. *In the Ypres Salient; the Story of a Fortnight's Canadian Fighting, June 2-16, 1916.* London: W. Cloes, n.d. 79 pp.

Wilson, Barbara M., ed. *Ontario and the First World War, 1914-1918; a Collection of Documents.* (The Publications of the Champlain Society; Ontario Series, X.) Toronto: Champlain Society, 1977. 201 pp.

Wilson-Simmie, Katherine M. *Lights Out; a Canadian Nursing Sister's Tale.* Belleville, Ont.: Mika Pub., 1981. 168 pp.

Winnington-Ingram, Arthur F. *'Life for Ever and Ever'; Preached by the Right Hon. and Right Rev. Arthur F. Winnington-Ingram, D.D., Lord Bishop of London, at the Canadian Memorial Service, St. Paul's Cathedral, May 10th, 1915.* London: Wells Gardner, Darton, n.d. 19 pp.

Winnipeg Grain Exchange Honor Roll; Resident Members and Employees who Enlisted and Fought in the Great War, August 4th, 1914 — November 11th, 1918. n.p.: n.d. 1 vol., unpaged.

The Winnipeg Rifles, 8th Battalion, C.E.F., Allied with the Rifle Brigade (Prince Consort's Own); Fiftieth Anniversary, 1883-1933. Winnipeg: privately printed, 1933. 59 pp.

Winter, Charles F. *Lieutenant-General the Hon. Sir Sam Hughes K.C.B., M.P.: Canada's War Minister, 1911-1916; Recollections of Service as Military Secretary at Headquarters, Canadian Militia, Prior to and during the Early Stages of the Great War.* Toronto: Macmillan, 1931. 182 pp.

Winton, Maurice V. *Saskatchewan's Prairie Soldiers, 1885-1980.* n.p.: n.d. 174 pp.
Cover title: A Pictorial History of Saskatchewan's Military Badges and Medals.

With the 4th Canadian Div'l Signal Coy C.E. on Active Service. n.p.: n.d. 111 pp.

Wodehouse, R.F. *A Check List of the War Collections of World War I, 1914-1918, and World War II, 1939-1945.* Ottawa: Queen's Printer, 1968. 239 pp.

Wood, Herbert Fairlie. *Vimy!* Toronto: Macmillan, 1967. 186 pp.

Worthington, Larry. *Amid the Guns Below; the Story of the Canadian Corps, 1914-1919.* Toronto: McClelland and Stewart, 1965. 171 pp.

Worthington, Larry. *The Spur and the Sprocket; the Story of the Royal Canadian Dragoons.* Kitchener, Ont.: Reeve Press, 1968. 170 pp.

_____. *"Worthy"; a Biography of Major-General F.F. Worthington, C.B., M.C., M.M.* Toronto: Macmillan, 1961. 236 pp.

Wright, Harold E., and Byron E. O'Leary. *Fortress Saint John; an Illustrated Military History, 1640-1985.* Saint John, N.B.: Partridge Island Research Project, 1985. 131 pp.

Young, A.H., ed. *The War Book of Upper Canada College, Toronto.* Toronto: privately printed, 1923. 322 pp.

Young, A.H., and W.A. Kirkwood, eds. *The War Memorial Volume of Trinity College, Toronto.* [Toronto]: Printers Guild, 1922. 165 pp.

Young, Albert Charles. *24 Good Men and True; Members of Branch #142 of the Royal Canadian Legion.* New York: Vantage Press, 1992. 219 pp.

Young Men's Christian Associations, Canada. *The Camera with the Canadian Forestry Corps in Great Britain.* London: n.p., n.d. 24 pp., chiefly illus.

Young Men's Christian Associations, Canada. National Council. *The Achievements of the Young Men's Christian Associations in the Great War.* Toronto: privately printed, [1935]. 20 pp.

_____. *On Leave; How the Red Triangle Club, Toronto, Provides for the Soldier while Off Duty.* Toronto: privately printed, 1917. 1 vol., unpaged.

1919-1945

A15 Link. Vol. I-II. Shilo Camp, Man.: n.p., 1943-45.
Monthly journal of A15 Canadian Infantry Training Centre.

Abautret, René. *Dieppe, le sacrifice des Canadiens, 19 août 1942.* Paris: R. Laffont, 1969. 250 pp.

Active Service Canteen, Toronto, 1939-1945. Toronto: n.p., 1945. 1 vol., unpaged.

Adleman, Robert H., and George Walton. *The Devil's Brigade.* Philadelphia: Chilton Books, 1966. 259 pp.

Aernoudts, Karel. *Waar de rode klaproos bloeit; een episode uit de Tweede Wereldoorlog; strijd om de vrijmaking van de linker Scheldemonding, september, oktober, november 1944.* Oostburg, Neth.: W.J. Pieters, 1972. 201 pp.

The Alaska Highway Today; a Brief History and Guide to Those Seeking New Scenic Thrills in North America's Last Frontier ... that Rugged, Vast Hinterland Now Traversed by the Famous Alaska Highway ... Linking Bustling Cities of Canada and the United States of America to the Awe-Inspiring Land of the Midnight Sun. Edmonton: printed by Douglas Print. Co., [1951]. 1 vol., unpaged.

Aldershot News. Vol. I-III? Aldershot, N.S.: n.p., 1943-46?
Monthly 1943-44; bimonthly 1945-46. Journal of A14 Canadian Infantry Training Centre.

Alexander, G.M., ed. *4th Canadian Armoured Brigade.* [Mitcham, Eng.: privately printed, n.d.] 47 pp.

*Allard, Jean V. *Mémoires du Général Jean V. Allard.* Collaboration spéciale de Serge Bernier. s.l.: Editions de Mortagne, 1985. 533 pp.

*_____. *The Memoirs of General Jean V. Allard,* written in cooperation with Serge Bernier. Vancouver: Univ. of British Columbia Press, 1988. 366 pp.

Allister, William. *A Handful of Rice.* London: Secker and Warburg, 1961. 288 pp.
Hong Kong and prisoners of war.

_____. *Where Life and Death Hold Hands.* Toronto: Stoddart, 1989. 245 pp.

Amey, Ada. *Here Come the Khaki Skirts ... the Women Volunteers; a Pictorial Review of the Canadian Women's Army Corps during the Second World War.* Cobalt, Ont.: Highway Book Shop, 1988. 169 pp.

Armit, W.B. *Army Museum; Halifax Citadel Halifax, Nova Scotia.* Kentville, N.S.: n.p., [1957?]. 34 pp.

218

*L'Arsenal de Québec, 1880-1945. Québec, P.Q.: s.i., 1947. 166 pp.

Atkin, Ronald. *Dieppe 1942; the Jubilee Disaster.* London: Macmillan, 1980. 306 pp.

Austin, A.B. *We Landed at Dawn; the Story of the Dieppe Raid.* New York: Harcourt, Brace, 1943. 217 pp.

B.M.A. Blitz. Vol. I-IV. Brockville, Ont.: privately printed, 1942-45. *Journal of the Officers' Training Centre, Brockville.*

Bank of Montreal. *Field of Honour; the Second World War, 1939-1945.* Montreal: n.p., 1950. 1 vol., unpaged.

Barnard, W.T. *The Queen's Own Rifles of Canada, 1860-1960; One Hundred Years of Canada.* Don Mills, Ont.: Ontario Pub. Co., 1960. 398 pp.

_____. *A Short History of the Queen's Own Rifles of Canada.* Toronto: Mackinnon & Atkins, n.d. 22 pp.

Barnes, C.H. *Colonel Colin Clarke Harbottle, C.M.G., D.S.O., V.D.* n.p.: [1958]. 20 pp.

Barnes, Leslie W.C.S. *Canada and the Science of Ballistics, 1914-1945.* (Organization of Military Museums of Canada Special Edition.) Ottawa: National Museums of Canada, 1985. 87 pp.

*_____. *Canada's Guns; an Illustrated History of Artillery.* (Canadian War Museum Historical Publication no. 15.) [Ottawa]: National Museum of Man, 1979. 112 pp.

*_____. *Histoire illustrée de l'artillerie canadienne.* (Musée canadien de la guerre publication d'histoire militaire no 15.) [Ottawa]: Musée national de l'Homme, 1979. 112 pp.

Barrass, R., and T.J.H. Sloan. *The Story of 657 Air O.P. Squadron R.A.F., January 31st, 1943, to May 8th, 1945.* London: Whitefriars Press, n.d. 96 pp.

Barrett, W.W. *The History of 13 Canadian Field Regiment, Royal Canadian Artillery, 1940-1945.* n.p.: n.d. 188 pp.

Barris, Ted, and Alex Barris. *Days of Victory; Canadians Remember: 1939-1945.* Toronto: Macmillan Canada, 1995. 304 pp.

Bartlett, Jack Fortune. *1st Battalion, the Highland Light Infantry of Canada, 1940-1945.* Galt, Ont.: privately printed, n.d. 126 pp.

Bates, Maxwell. *A Wilderness of Days; an Artist's Experiences as a Prisoner of War in Germany.* Victoria, B.C.: Sono Nis Press, 1978. 133 pp.

Batten, Jack. *The Spirit of the Regiment; an Account of the 48th Highlanders from 1956 to 1991.* n.p.: n.d. 171 pp.

[Baylay, George Taylor], ed. *The Regimental History of the Governor General's Foot Guards.* Ottawa: privately printed, 1948. 268 pp.

Beattie, Kim. *Dileas; History of the 48th Highlanders of Canada, 1929-1956.* Toronto: privately printed, 1957. 847 pp.

_____. *48th Highlanders of Canada, 1891-1928.* Toronto: privately printed, 1932. 434 pp.

Beckles, Gordon, [*pseud.*] *see* Willson, Gordon Beckles.

Beeching, William C. *Canadian Volunteers, Spain, 1936-1939.* Regina: Canadian Plains Research Center, Univ. of Regina, 1989. 212 pp.

Bell, J. Mackintosh. *Sidelights on the Siberian Campaign.* Toronto: Ryerson Press, 1923. 132 pp.

Bell, K. *Curtain Call.* Toronto: Intaglio Gravure, 1953. 136 pp.

_____. *The Way We Were.* Toronto: Univ. of Toronto Press, 1988. 255 pp. *Pictorial history of 1st Canadian Army operations.*

Bell, K., and C.P. Stacey. *Not in Vain.* Toronto: Univ. of Toronto Press, 1973. 143 pp.

_____. *100 Years; the Royal Canadian Regiment 1883-1983.* Don Mills, Ont.: Collier Macmillan, 1983. 184 pp., chiefly illus.

Bell, T.J. *Into Action with the 12th Field.* T.E. Jarvis, ed. n.p.: n.d. 159 pp.

Bercuson, David J. *Battalion of Heroes; the Calgary Highlanders in World War II.* Calgary: Calgary Highlanders Regimental Funds Foundation, 1994. 297 pp.

_____. *Maple Leaf against the Axis; Canada's Second World War.* Toronto: Stoddart, 1995. 316 pp.

Bercuson, David J., and S.F. Wise, eds. *The Valour and the Horror Revisited.* Montreal: McGill-Queen's Univ. Press, 1994. 185 pp. *Discussion of television series by Brian McKenna and Terence McKenna.*

Bernage, Georges. *Les Canadiens face à la Hitlerjugend, Normandie, 7 au 9 juin 44.* s.l.: Editions Heimdal, 1991. [80] pp.

Bernard, Yves, et Caroline Bergeron. *Trop loin de Berlin; des prisonniers allemands au Canada (1939-1946).* Sillery (Qué.): Septentrion, 1995. [359] pp.

Bezeau, M.V. *University of Ottawa Contingent, Canadian Officers Training Corps.* n.p.: 1968. 15 pp.

Bindon, Kathryn M. *Queen's Men, Canada's Men; the Military History of Queen's University, Kingston.* [Kingston, Ont.]: privately printed, 1978. 180 pp.

Bird, Will R. *No Retreating Footsteps; the Story of the North Nova Scotia Highlanders.* Kentville, N.S.: privately printed, n.d. 399 pp.

_____. *North Shore (New Brunswick) Regiment.* Fredericton, N.B.: Brunswick Press, 1963. 629 pp.

_____. *The Two Jacks; the Amazing Adventures of Major Jack M. Veness and Major Jack L. Fairweather.* Toronto: Ryerson Press, 1954. 209 pp.

Birney, Earle, ed. *Record of Service in the Second World War; the University of British Columbia; a Supplement to the University of British Columbia War Memorial Manuscript Record.* Vancouver: privately printed, 1955. 46 pp.

Bishop, William Arthur. *Courage on the Battlefield.* (Canada's Military Heritage, Volume II.) Toronto: McGraw-Hill Ryerson, 1993. 341 pp.

Blackburn, George G. *The Guns of Normandy; a Soldier's Eye View, France 1944.* Toronto: McClelland & Stewart, 1995. 511 pp.

Blue & Gold. Vol. I- . Winnipeg: n.p., 1934- .
Frequency varies, but chiefly annual. Regimental journal of the Fort Garry Horse.

Bobak, Molly Lamb. *Double Duty; Sketches and Diaries of Molly Lamb Bobak, Canadian War Artist.* Carolyn Gossage, ed. Toronto: Dundurn Press, 1992. 156 pp.

Boissonnault, Charles-Marie. *Histoire du Royal 22e Régiment.* Québec, P.Q.: Editions du Pélican, 1964. 414 pp.

_____. *Histoire politico-militaire des Canadiens français (1763-1967).* Trois-Rivières, P.Q.: Editions du Bien public, 1967. 310 pp.

Boss, W. *The Stormont, Dundas and Glengarry Highlanders, 1783-1951.* Ottawa: Runge Press, 1952. 449 pp.
Revised and updated as: Boss, W., and W.J. Patterson, Up the Glens; Stormont, Dundas and Glengarry Highlanders, 1783-1994. Cornwall, Ont.: Old Book Store, 1995. 298 pp.

Bowering, Clifford H. *Service; the Story of the Canadian Legion, 1925-1960.* Ottawa: privately printed, 1960. 240 pp.

Bowman, Bob. *Dieppe.* Ottawa: Wartime Information Board, [1942?]. 11 pp.

Bowman, Phylis. *Second World War Memories.* Port Edward, B.C.: privately printed, 1987. 84 pp.
Prince Rupert, B.C., in the Second World War.

Bowman, Phylis. *We Skirted the War!* Prince Rupert, B.C.: privately printed, 1975. 133 pp.

Bradford, R.C., ed. *Decorations and Awards Received during World War II, 1939-1945, by The Hastings and Prince Edward Regiment.* Belleville, Ont.: privately printed, 1986. 115 pp.

Brantford Kinsmen Club, comp. *Album of Honor for Brant County; World War II, 1939-1945.* Helen Sanders, ed. [Brantford, Ont.]: Brantford Kinsmen Club, 1946. 224 pp.

The Brazier; Marking the 50th Anniversary of the Canadian Scottish (Princess Mary's), June 6, 1964. Victoria, B.C.: privately printed, 1964. 19 pp.

Brebner, Phyllis Lee. *The Alaska Highway; a Personal & Historical Account of the Building of the Alaska Highway.* Erin, Ont.: Boston Mills Press, 1985. 80 pp.

A Brief Historical Sketch of the Lorne Scots (Peel, Dufferin and Halton Regiment). Brampton, Ont.: Charters Pub. Co., 1943. 24 pp.

A Brief Historical Sketch of the Queen's York Rangers, 1st American Regiment. Toronto: privately printed, 1942. 30 pp.

A Brief History of the Royal Regiment of Canada, [Allied with the King's Regiment (Liverpool). Toronto: n.p., 1940.] 77 pp.

A Brief History of the Royal Regiment of Canada; Allied with the King's Regiment (Liverpool). [Toronto: n.p., 1948.] 135 pp.

A Brief History of the 3rd Battalion C.E.F. (Toronto Regiment), Now the Toronto Regiment; (Allied with the King's Regiment (Liverpool)). n.p.: 1934. 47 pp.

The Brigade. Vol. I-III? Winnipeg: privately printed, 1942-46?
Journal of the 38th Reserve Brigade.

British Great War Veterans of America, Inc. *Official Souvenir Book in Commemoration of the Visit to New York of the Fifth Royal Highlanders of Canada, the "Black Watch" of Montreal on Memorial Day, 1925.* New York: n.p., 1925. 1 vol., unpaged.

Broadfoot, Barry. *Six War Years, 1939-1945; Memories of Canadians at Home and Abroad.* Toronto: Doubleday Canada, 1974. 417 pp.

Brock, Thomas Leith. *Fight the Good Fight; Looking in on the Recruit Class at the Royal Military College of Canada during a Week in February, 1931.* Montreal: privately printed, 1964. 30 pp.

_____. *The R.M.C. Vintage Class of 1934.* Victoria, B.C.: privately printed, 1985. 3 vols.

Brodsky, G.W. Stephen. *God's Dodger; the Story of a Front Line Chaplain 1905-1945; Lieutenant Colonel (The Reverend) R.O. "Rusty" Wilkes, M.C., C.D.* Sidney, B.C.: Elysium Pub. Co., 1993. 264 pp.
Chaplain to the Royal Canadian Regiment in England, Sicily and Italy.

Brooker, Chris. *The Standard Catalogue of Canadian Cap Badges of World War II.* London, Ont.: privately printed, 1984. 30 pp.

Brown, Brian A. *Foresters; the Canadian Quest for Peace.* Erin, Ont.: Boston Mills Press, 1991. 176 pp.
The Grey & Simcoe Foresters.

Brown, Kingsley, *see* Greenhous, Brereton.

*Brown, W.J. *Les Cadets royaux de l'Armée canadienne; cent ans d'exploits, 1879-1979.* s.l: La ligue des Cadets de l'Armée du Canada, [1979. 12 pp.]

*_____. *The Royal Canadian Army Cadets; a Century of Achievement, 1879-1979.* n.p.: The Army Cadet League of Canada, [1979. 12 pp.]

Bruce, Jean. *Back the Attack! Canadian Women during the Second World War — at Home and Abroad.* Toronto: Macmillan, 1985. 182 pp.

Bruce, Walter H., and others, comps. *Historical Records of the Argyll and Sutherland Highlanders of Canada (Princess Louise's), Formerly 91st Regiment Canadian Highlanders, Canadian Militia, 1903-1928.* Hamilton, Ont.: R. Duncan, 1928. 99 pp.

Bryden, John. *Best-Kept Secret; Canadian Secret Intelligence in the Second World War.* Toronto: Lester Pub., 1993. 390 pp.

_____. *Deadly Allies; Canada's Secret War, 1937-1947.* Toronto: McClelland & Stewart, 1989. 314 pp.

Buchanan, G.B. *The March of the Prairie Men; a Story of the South Saskatchewan Regiment.* Weyburn, Sask.: privately printed, [1957?]. 75 pp.

Buckingham, N.A. *A Brief History of the 4th Canadian Armoured Brigade in Action July 1944 — May 1945.* n.p.: privately printed, 1945. 47 pp.

Bull, Stewart H. *The Queen's York Rangers; an Historic Regiment.* Erin, Ont.: Boston Mills Press, 1984. 248 pp.

Bull, Wm. Perkins. *From Brock to Currie; the Military Development and Exploits of Canadians in General and of the Men of Peel in Particular, 1791 to 1930.* Toronto: G.J. McLeod, 1935. 772 pp.

Burch, E.T. *"So I Said to the Colonel."* Toronto: Ryerson Press, 1941. 72 pp.

Burhans, R.D. *The First Special Service Force; a War History of the North Americans, 1942-1944.* Washington: Infantry Journal Press, 1947. 376 pp.

Burns, E.L.M. *General Mud; Memoirs of Two World Wars.* Toronto: Clarke, Irwin, 1970. 254 pp.

_____. *Manpower in the Canadian Army, 1939-1945.* Toronto: Clarke, Irwin, 1956. 184 pp.

Burns, Max, and Ken Messenger. *The Winged Wheel Patch; a History of the Canadian Military Motorcycle and Rider.* St. Catharines, Ont.: Vanwell Pub., 1993. 159 pp.

Butson, A.R.C. *A History of the Military Medical Units of Hamilton, Ontario, in Peace and War, 1900-1990.* n.p.: 1990. 43 pp.

CAM. Vol. I-II. Ottawa: King's Printer, 1943-45.
Journal of the Directorate of Mechanical Maintenance, National Defence Headquarters.

The Calgary Regiment. n.p.: n.d. 17 pp.

Callan, Les. *From "D" Day to Victory, Normandy and on with the Fighting Canadians.* Toronto: Longmans, Green, 1945. 126 pp.

Cambon, Ken. *Guest of Hirohito.* Vancouver: PW Press, 1990. 184 pp.
Royal Rifles of Canada at Hong Kong.

The Cameron Highlanders of Ottawa: Standing Orders and Constitution and Rules of the Officers Mess. n.p.: [1934]. 88 pp.

Cameron, James M. *Pictonians in Arms; a Military History of Pictou County, Nova Scotia.* Fredericton, N.B.: privately printed, 1969. 301 pp.

Camp, A.D., comp. *7th Toronto Regiment, Royal Regiment of Canadian Artillery, 1866-1966.* n.p.: n.d. 33 pp.

Camp Valcartier, P.Q.; 1647 à 1957 en quelques lignes./Camp Valcartier P.Q.; a Short History, 1647-1957. s.l.: s.i./n.p.: 1957. 24 pp.
Texte bilingue./Bilingual text.

Campbell, Ian J., and/et Robert L. Bennett. *Abbaye d'Ardenne, June 1944; Twenty Canadian Prisoners of War./Abbaye d'Ardenne, juin 1944; 20 prisonniers de guerre canadiens.* Buron, France: L'Association des Amis du Canada, 1984. 19 pp.
Bilingual text./Texte bilingue.

Campbell, John P. *Dieppe Revisited; a Documentary Investigation.* London: F. Cass, 1993. 247 pp.

[Canada. Armed Forces. 48th Highlanders of Canada.] *This is Your Regiment.* n.p.: [194-?]. 38 pp.

Canada. Armed Forces. 4 Field Ambulance. *A History of 4 Field Ambulance.* Lahr, Germany: E. Demmer, 1992. [122] pp.

Canada. Armed Forces. Lake Superior Scottish Regiment. *Regimental Catechism.* Winnipeg: CFTMPC, 1977. 15 pp.

*Canada. Armée. Quartier général de l'Armée. Section historique. *Introduction à l'étude de l'histoire militaire à l'intention des étudiants canadiens,* [par C.P. Stacey]. Ottawa: [Imprimeur du Roi], 1951. 45 pp.
Editions subséquentes et revisées.

*_____. *La 1ère Brigade d'infanterie canadienne, 1914-1954.* (Actualités; revue destinée aux Forces canadiennes, vol VII, no 3.) Ottawa: Imprimeur de la Reine, 1954. 31 pp.

*_____. *La 1re Division d'infanterie canadienne, 1915-1955.* (Actualités; revue destinée aux Forces canadiennes, vol IX, no 1.) Ottawa: Imprimeur de la Reine, 1955. 31 pp.

Canada. Armée. Régiment de la Chaudière. *Le Régiment de la Chaudière; notes historiques.* Québec, P.Q.: imprimé privé, 1955. 16 pp.

*Canada. Armée. Service feminin de l'Armée canadienne. *CWAC — compact; vue d'ensemble sur le CWAC.* s.l.: s.i., s.d. 32 pp.

[Canada. Army.] *The Man in Battledress.* n.p.: [1941]. 41 pp.

Canada. Army. Canadian Military Headquarters. *Canadian Army (Overseas) Routine Orders.* London: n.p., 1940-47.
Title varies. Issued as Canadian Active Service Force (Overseas) Routine Orders *until December 1940. Supplements also issued.*

Canada. Army. Canadian Military Headquarters. Quartermaster-General's Branch. *Vehicle Data Book; Canadian Army Overseas; Armoured Tracked Vehicles, Armoured Wheeled Vehicles, Tractors, Transporters, "B" Vehicles, Trailers.* n.p.: 1944. 210 pp.

Canada. Army. Canadian Scottish Regiment (Princess Mary's). *History of the Regiment from Mobilization to Present Day.* Utrecht, Neth.: privately printed, [1945]. 31 pp.

*Canada. Army. Canadian Women's Army Corps. *CWAC Digest; Facts about the C.W.A.C.* n.p.: n.d. 32 pp.

Canada. Army. 1st Canadian Armoured Carrier Regiment. *The History of the Kangaroos.* n.p.: Imit Hergelo, 1945. 11 pp.

Canada. Army. 1st Canadian Army Headquarters. Supplies and Transport Branch. *An Account of Operations of Supplies and Transport Service, First Canadian Army, France and Belgium, 23 July 44 — 31 Oct 44.* Printed in the field, 1944. 254 pp.

Canada. Army. First Canadian Army Headquarters and Gt. Brit. Air Force. 35 Reconnaissance Wing. *Air Recce.* London: n.p., n.d. 66 pp.

Canada. Army. 1 Canadian Special Wireless Group. *1 Canadian Special Wireless Group; Royal Canadian Corps of Signals; Souvenir Booklet, 1944-45.* n.p.: privately printed, [1945]. 32 pp.

Canada. Army. 19 Canadian Army Field Regiment. *Regimental History, September 1941 — July 1945.* Deventer, Neth.: privately printed, 1945. 131 pp.

Canada. Army. No. 3 Canadian Public Relations Group. *The Maple Leaf Scrapbook.* Belgium: n.p., [194-?]. 40 pp.

Canada. Army. Queen's Own Rifles of Canada. *Regimental Catechism.* n.p.: n.d. 19 pp.

Canada. Army. Royal Canadian Army Service Corps. *RCASC Diamond Jubilee Year Book, 1910-1961.* Ottawa: Queen's Printer, [1962]. 95 pp.

Canada. Army. Royal Canadian Engineers. 1 Canadian Field (Air) Survey Company. *433; 1 Cdn Fd (Air) Svy Coy RCE, Sep 44 — May 45; 4 Cdn Fd Svy Coy RCE, Jun 43 — Sep 44.* n.p.: [1945?]. 75 pp. *Cover title: Air Survey Review, June 1943 — May 1945.*

Canada. Army. Royal Canadian Engineers. 2nd Battalion. *The Story of 2 Bn R.C.E.* Zwolle, Neth.: privately printed, 1945. 1 vol., unpaged.

Canada. Army. Royal Canadian Engineers. 3rd Field (Reproduction) Survey Company. *432; 3rd Field (Reproduction) Survey Company, Royal Canadian Engineers, 1939-1945 (on Active Service).* [n.p.: 1945?]. 1 vol., unpaged.

Canada. Army. Royal Canadian Engineers. 23 Field Company. *The Twenty-Third Story.* [London, Ont.: n.p., 1947.] 86 pp.

Canada. Army. Royal Winnipeg Rifles. *Seventy-Fifth Anniversary, Royal Winnipeg Rifles, 1883-1958.* [Winnipeg: privately printed, 1958.] v.p.

[Canada. Army. Toronto Scottish Regiment.] *The Toronto Scottish Regiment.* n.p.: 1961. 24 pp.

Canada. Army. Victoria Rifles of Canada. *The Victorian, 1st Battalion 1940-1941.* n.p.: [1941]. 36 pp.

Canada. Army Headquarters. Director of Artillery. *Standing Orders for the Royal Regiment of Canadian Artillery.* Don Mills, Ont.: T.H. Best, 1963. 62 pp.

*Canada. Army Headquarters. Historical Section. *The 1st Canadian Infantry Brigade, 1914-1954.* (Current Affairs for the Canadian Forces, vol. VII, no. 3.) Ottawa: Queen's Printer, 1954. 31 pp.

*_____. *Introduction to the Study of Military History for Canadian Students,* [by C.P. Stacey]. Ottawa: [King's Printer], 1951. 39 pp. *Many subsequent revised editions.*

*Canada. Army Headquarters. Historical Section. **The Old Red Patch; the 1st Canadian Infantry Division, 1915-1955.** (Current Affairs for the Canadian Forces, vol. IX, no. 1.) Ottawa: Queen's Printer, 1955. 31 pp.

_____ . **The Regiments and Corps of the Canadian Army.** (The Canadian Army List, vol. 1.) Ottawa: Queen's Printer, 1964. 253 pp.

*Canada. Commission royale sur le Corps expéditionnaire canadien envoyé dans la Colonie de la Couronne de Hong-Kong. **Rapport**, par Sir Lyman P. Duff, commissaire royal. Ottawa: Imprimeur du Roi, 1942. 64 pp.

*Canada. Dept. of Militia and Defence. **Annual Report.** Ottawa: Queen's Printer, 1867-1922.
Title varies.

_____ . **Memorandum for Camps of Instruction.** Part 1: **Instructions for Training.** Ottawa: King's Printer, 1909?-28.
Title varies somewhat. Annual.

_____ . **The Militia List.** Ottawa: Queen's Printer, 1867-1929.
Title and frequency vary. Superseded by <u>Defence Forces List, Canada.</u>

_____ . **Minutes of the Militia Council.** Ottawa: King's Printer, 1905-21. 23 vols.

_____ . **Pay and Allowance Regulations for the Permanent Force and Non-Permanent Active Militia, 1920.** Ottawa: King's Printer, 1920. 170 pp. *Reprinted with amendments 1924, 1927, 1937.*

_____ . **The Return of the Troops; a Plain Account of the Demobilization of the Canadian Expeditionary Force.** Ottawa: King's Printer, 1920. 180 pp.

Canada. Dept. of Munitions and Supply. Army Engineering Design Branch. **Design Record; Canadian Developed Military Vehicles, World War II.** Ottawa: n.p., 1945. 8 vols.
Reprinted by Directorate of Vehicle Development, Dept. of National Defence. 8 vols. in 2.

Canada. Dept. of National Defence. **The Canadian Army List.** Ottawa: King's Printer, 1940-66.
Title varies, eg. — <u>Gradation List, Canadian Army Active</u> *(1940-45);* <u>Canadian Army (Regular) List</u> *(1959-66).*

_____ . **Canadian Prisoners of War and Missing Personnel in the Far East.** Ottawa: King's Printer, 1945. 59 1.

*_____ . **The Canadians in Britain, 1939-1944.** (The Canadian Army at War, no. 1.) Ottawa: King's Printer, [1945]. 172 pp.

227

Canada. Dept. of National Defence. ***Defence Forces List, Canada (Naval, Military and Air Forces)***. Ottawa: King's Printer, 1930-39.
Title varies somewhat. Superseded <u>The Militia List</u>. Superseded by <u>The Canadian Navy List</u>, <u>The Canadian Army List</u> and <u>The Royal Canadian Air Force List</u>.

_____. ***Digest of Opinions and Rulings; Ottawa; March 31, 1944; Compiled from the Records of the Office of the Judge Advocate-General, at National Defence Headquarters***. n.p.: [1944]. 353 pp., looseleaf.

_____. ***Dress Regulations for the Officers of the Canadian Militia***. Ottawa: King's Printer, 1932. [50] pp.

*_____. ***50 Questions and Answers about CWAC***. Ottawa: King's Printer, 1944. 13 pp.

_____. ***Financial Regulations and Instructions for the Canadian Active Service Force (Canada)***. Ottawa: King's Printer, 1939. 87 pp.

_____. ***Financial Regulations and Instructions for the Canadian Active Service Force (Overseas)***. Ottawa: King's Printer, 1939. 123 pp.

*_____. ***From Pachino to Ortona; the Canadian Campaign in Sicily and Italy, 1943***. (The Canadian Army at War, no. 2.) Ottawa: King's Printer, [1945]. 160 pp.

_____. ***Instructions for Engineer Services, Canada, 1936***. Ottawa: King's Printer, 1936. 152 pp.

_____. ***Instructions for the Canadian Chaplain Service, Canadian Active Service Force***. Ottawa: King's Printer, 1939. 13 pp.

_____. ***Instructions for the Canadian Officers' Training Corps, 1936***. Ottawa: King's Printer, 1936. 78 pp.

_____. ***Instructions for the Canadian Officers' Training Corps, 1929***. Ottawa: King's Printer, 1929. 68 pp.

_____. ***Instructions for the Royal Canadian Army Medical Corps and the Canadian Army Dental Corps, 1937***. Ottawa: King's Printer, 1937. 162 pp.

_____. ***Instructions for the Royal Canadian Army Pay Corps, 1938***. Ottawa: King's Printer, 1938. 68 pp.

_____. ***The King's Regulations and Orders for the Canadian Militia***. Ottawa: King's Printer, 1939. 409 pp.

_____. ***The King's Regulations and Orders for the Canadian Militia, 1926***. Ottawa: King's Printer, 1926. 477 pp.

_____. ***Memorandum on Training of the Canadian Militia***. Ottawa: King's Printer, 1934. 200 pp.

Canada. Dept. of National Defence. *Regulations and Instructions for the Clothing of the Non-Permanent Active Militia, 1928.* Ottawa: King's Printer, 1928. 40 pp.

_____. *Regulations and Instructions for the Clothing of the Non-Permanent Active Militia, 1926.* Ottawa: King's Printer, 1927. 32 pp.

_____. *Regulations and Instructions for the Equipment of the Canadian Militia.* Ottawa: King's Printer, 1930. 227 pp.

*_____. *Regulations for the Cadet Services of Canada, 1942.* Ottawa: King's Printer, 1942. 56 pp.

*_____. *Regulations for the Cadet Services of Canada, 1928.* Ottawa: King's Printer, 1928. 53 pp.

_____. *Regulations for the Canadian Medical Service, 1923 (Approved by the Defence Council).* Ottawa: King's Printer, 1923. 118 pp.

_____. *Regulations for the Clothing of the Canadian Militia. Part I: Permanent Active Militia.* Ottawa: King's Printer, 1935. 83 pp.

_____. *Regulations for the Clothing of the Canadian Militia. Part I: Permanent Active Militia.* Ottawa: King's Printer, 1924. 77 pp.

*_____. *Report.* Ottawa: King's Printer, 1923-59.
Title varies. Annual most years.

_____. *War Dress Regulations for the Officers and Other Ranks of the Canadian Army (1943).* Ottawa: King's Printer, 1943. 85 pp.

_____. *Where Do We Go from Here? Facts for the Guidance of Canadian Army Personnel.* n.p.: [1945]. 28 pp.

Canada. Dept. of National War Services. *Annual Report.* Ottawa: King's Printer, 1945. 3 vols.

Canada. Dept. of Veterans Affairs. *Canadians in Asia, 1945-1985./Les Canadiens en Asie, 1945-1985.* Ottawa: Veterans Affairs Canada/Anciens combattants Canada, 1985. 28 pp.
Bilingual text./Texte bilingue.

_____. *D-Day; 1944 — June 6 — 1984./Jour J; 1944 — le 6 juin — 1984.* Ottawa: Veterans Affairs Canada/Affaires des anciens combattants, 1984. 22 pp.
Bilingual text./Texte bilingue.

_____. *30th Anniversary of the D-Day Landings in Normandy, 1944 — June 6 — 1974./30e anniversaire des débarquements en Normandie au jour J, 1944 — le 6 juin — 1974.* n.p./s.l.: s.i., 1974. 22 pp.
Bilingual text./Texte bilingue.

Canada. Dept. of Veterans Affairs. *30th Anniversary of the Dieppe Raid, 19 August 1942./Le trentième anniversaire du Raid de Dieppe (19 août 1942).* n.p./s.l.: s.i., 1972. [16] pp.
Bilingual text./Texte bilingue.

_____. *35th Anniversary; the Raid on Dieppe, 1942 August 19 1977./35ième anniversaire; le coup de main de Dieppe, 1942 le 19 août 1977.* n.p./s.l.: s.i., [1977]. 14 pp.
Bilingual text./Texte bilingue.

Canada. Dept. Of Veterans Affairs. Directorate of Public Relations. *Commemoration; Canadians in Hong Kong, 1980./Souvenir; Canadiens à Hong Kong, 1980,* [par la] Direction des relations publiques, Ministère des Affaires des anciens combattants. Ottawa: Supply and Services Canada/ Approvisionnements et Services Canada, 1980. 15/16 pp.
Bilingual text./Texte bilingue.

_____. *Netherlands/Canada/Pays-Bas/Nederland, 1945-1980; Commemoration/Souvenir/Ter Herinnering.* n.p.: n.d./s.l.: s.i., s.d. 47 pp.
Trilingual text./Texte trilingue.

Canada. Dept. of Veterans Affairs. Public Affairs Division. *Uncommon Courage; Canadian Secret Agents in the Second World War./Un courage peu ordinaire; les agents secrets canadiens au cours de la Seconde Guerre mondiale.* Ottawa: Veterans Affairs Canada/Anciens combattants Canada, 1985. 27 pp.
Bilingual text./Texte bilingue.

Canada. Director of Public Information. *Canada and the People's War.* n.p.: [1942]. 1 vol., unpaged.

*_____. *Canada at War.* No. 1-45. Ottawa: King's Printer, 1941-45.

_____. *Canada's Modern Army./L'Armée moderne du Canada,* [par le] Service de l'Information. Ottawa: n.p./s.i., 1941. 15 pp., chiefly illus./en majeure partie ill.
Bilingual text./Texte bilingue.

Canada. Militia. Canadian Expeditionary Force. *Routine Orders.* Ottawa: n.p., ?-1920.
Supplements also issued

Canada. Militia. Canadian Machine Gun Corps. *Canadian Machine Gun Corps; Organization, Administration and Duties.* London: Page and Thomas, 1919. 129 pp.

Canada. Militia Headquarters. *General Orders.* Ottawa: Queen's Printer, 1899-1946.
Superseded <u>Militia General Orders</u>. Frequency varies.

Canada. Militia Headquarters. *Militia Orders.* Ottawa: Queen's Printer, 1899-1940.
Superseded Militia General Orders. Frequency varies.

*Canada. Ministère de la Défense nationale. *Les Canadiens en Grande-Bretagne, 1939-1944.* (L'Armée canadienne à la Guerre, no 1.) Ottawa: Imprimeur du Roi, 1946. 188 pp.

*_____. *50 questions et réponses au sujet du CWAC.* Ottawa: Imprimeur du Roi, 1944. 13 pp.

*_____. *De Pachino à Ortona; la campagne des Canadiens en Sicile et en Italie, 1943.* (L'Armée canadienne à la Guerre, no 2.) Ottawa: Imprimeur du Roi, 1946. 168 pp.

*_____. *Rapport.* Ottawa: Imprimeur du Roi, 1923-59.
Divergence du titre. Annuel la plupart des années.

_____. *Réglement applicable au service des Corps de Cadets du Canada, 1942./Regulations for the Cadet Services of Canada,* [by Dept. of National Defence.] Ottawa: Imprimeur du Roi/King's Printer, 1942. 103 pp.
Texte bilingue./Bilingual text.

_____. *Réglement et instructions d'ordre financier applicables à l'Armée active (Canada).* Ottawa: Imprimeur du Roi, 1942. 114 pp.

*_____. *Réglements concernant les services des cadets du Canada, 1928.* Ottawa: Imprimeur du Roi, 1928. 53 pp.

*Canada. Ministère de la Milice et de la Défense. *Rapport annuel.* Ottawa: Imprimeur de la Reine, 1867-1922.
Divergence du titre.

Canada. Ministry of Overseas Military Forces of Canada. *Routine Orders.* London: Canadian Print. and Stationery Services, H.M. Stationery Office, 1917-20.

*Canada. National Defence Headquarters. *Canadian Army Orders.* [Ottawa: King's Printer], 1941-64.
From 1947 issued as a non-chronological series with orders being discarded when obsolete. Supplements also issued from 1947.

_____. *Canadian Army Routine Orders.* Ottawa: n.p., 1939-46.
Title varies. Issued as Canadian Active Service Force Routine Orders until December 1940. Supplements also issued.

[Canada. National Defence Headquarters. General Staff.] *Canadian Army and Air Force Winter Warfare Research Programme, 1944-1945; Exercise Eskimo "Dry Cold".* [Ottawa]: Dept. of National Defence, [1945]. 3 vols.
Originally classified Restricted.

Canada. National Gallery. *Exhibition of Canadian War Art.* Ottawa: King's Printer, 1945. 22 pp.

Canada. National Research Council. *Medical Research and Development in the Canadian Army during World War II, 1942-1946.* n.p.: n.d. v.p.

*Canada. Parlement. Chambre des Communes, Comité spécial d'enquête sur les distinctions honorifiques et les décorations. *Procès-verbaux et témoignages.* No 1-6. Ottawa: Imprimeur du Roi, 1942.

Canada. Parliament. House of Commons. Special Committee on Canteen Funds. *Minutes of Proceedings and Evidence.* No. 1-11. Ottawa: King's Printer, 1942.

*Canada. Parliament. House of Commons. Special Committee on Honours and Decorations. *Minutes of Proceedings and Evidence.* No. 1-6. Ottawa: King's Printer, 1942.

*Canada. Quartier général de la Défense nationale. *Ordres de l'Armée canadienne.* [Ottawa: Imprimeur du Roi], 1941-64.
Publiés en série de façon non chronologique à partir de 1947; les ordres périmés sont remplacés. Des suppléments sont également publiés à partir de 1947.

Canada. Royal Commission on the Bren Machine Gun Contract. *Report.* Henry Hague Davis, Commissioner. Ottawa: King's Printer, 1939. 52 pp.

*Canada. Royal Commission on the Canadian Expeditionary Force to the Crown Colony of Hong Kong. *Report*, by Sir Lyman P. Duff, Royal Commissioner. Ottawa: King's Printer, 1942. 61 pp.

Canada. Royal Commission to Conduct an Inquiry into Certain Disorders Occurring May 7-8, 1945, in the City of Halifax. *Report on the Halifax Disorders, May 7th-8th, 1945.* Hon. Mr. Justice R.L. Kellock, Royal Commissioner. Ottawa: King's Printer, 1945. 61 pp.

*Canada. Service de l'Information. *Le Canada en guerre.* No 1-45. Ottawa: Imprimeur du Roi, 1941-45.

Canadian Armoured Association *see* Canadian Cavalry Association.

Canadian Army Handbook on District Courts-Martial, 1941 (December)./Armée canadienne, aide-mémoire pour la conduite des cours martiales de district, 1941. Ottawa: King's Printer/Imprimeur du Roi, 1942. 79 pp.
Bilingual text./Texte bilingue.

Canadian Army Training Memorandum. No. 1-72. Ottawa: King's Printer, 1941-47.

Canadian Artillery Association. *Annual Report.* n.p.: privately printed, 1876- .
Not published 1940-46. Title varies.

Canadian Artillery Association. *Artillery Summary.* Vol. I-XIII. n.p.: privately printed, 1921-42.

Canadian Bank of Commerce. *War Service Records, 1939-1945; an Account of the War Service of Members of the Staff during the Second World War.* D.P. Wagner and C.G. Siddall, eds. Toronto: Rous & Mann, 1947. 331 pp.

Canadian Broadcasting Corporation. Publications Branch. *We have been There; Authoritative Reports by Qualified Observers who have Returned from the War Zones, as Presented over the CBC National Network.* Toronto: Canadian Broadcasting Corporation, 1941-42. 2 vols.

Canadian Cavalry Association. *Proceedings.* n.p.: privately printed, 1913- .
In 1943 became Canadian Armoured Association and in 1946 Royal Canadian Armoured Corps (Cavalry) Association. Title varies: also Annual Report and Information Digest and Annual Report.

Canadian Defence Quarterly. Vol. I-XVI. Ottawa: privately printed, 1923-39.

The Canadian Fusiliers; City of London Regiment. n.p.: 1942. 12 pp.

Canadian Infantry Association. *Proceedings.* n.p.: privately printed, 1913- .
Incorporated the Proceedings of the Canadian Machine Gun Corps Association in 1936. Was the Infantry and Machine Gun Association of Canada, 1937-39. Not published 1940-45.

Canadian Jewish Congress. *Canadian Jews in World War II.* Montreal: privately printed, 1947-48. 2 vols.

Canadian Legion War Services, Inc. *A Year of Service; a Summary of Activities on Behalf of His Majesty's Canadian Forces Rendered during Nineteen-Forty.* n.p.: n.d. 1 vol., unpaged.

Canadian Machine Gun Corps Association. *Proceedings.* n.p.: privately printed, 1928-35.
Superseded by Infantry and Machine Gun Association of Canada Proceedings.

Canadian Officers Training Corps, University of Toronto Contingent. [Toronto?]: n.p., 1937. 32 pp.

Canadian Press. *Maple Leaf in Italy; a Sequel to Red Patch in Sicily; the Canadian Campaign on the Mainland*, frontline dispatches by CP war correspondents. n.p.: Canadian Press, 1944. 13 pp.

The Canadian Provost Corps; Silver Jubilee, 1940-1965. Ottawa: privately printed, 1965. 96 pp.

The Canadian Scottish Regiment. n.p.: n.d. 91 pp.

Canadian Signals Training Centre, Vimy Barracks, Barriefield, Ont. Kingston, Ont.: printed by Salsbury Press, 1945. 28 pp.

[Canadian War Museum.] *La coopération canada-polonaise au cours des deux guerres mondiales./Polish-Canadian Co-operation in the Two World Wars.* Ottawa: n.p., 1973. 36 pp.
Texte bilingue./Bilingual text.

Capon, Alan R. *Mascots of the Hastings and Prince Edward Regiment.* Picton, Ont.: Picton Gazette, 1977. 31 pp.

Cardoulis, John N. *A Friendly Invasion; the American Military in Newfoundland, 1940-1990.* St. John's, Nfld.: Breakwater, 1990. 224 pp.

_____. *A Friendly Invasion II: a Personal Touch.* St. John's, Nfld.: Creative Publishers, 1993. 221 pp.

Carter, David J. *Behind Canadian Barbed Wire; Alien, Refugee and Prisoner of War Camps in Canada, 1914-1946.* Calgary: Tumbleweed Press, 1980. 334 pp.

Cash, Gwen. *A Million Miles from Ottawa.* Toronto: Macmillan, 1942. 152 pp.

Cassidy, G.L. *Warpath; the Story of the Algonquin Regiment, 1939-1945.* Toronto: Ryerson Press, 1948. 372 pp.

Castonguay, Jacques. *Les Voltigeurs de Québec; premier régiment canadien-français.* Québec (Qué.): Les Voltigeurs de Québec, 1987. 523 pp.

Castonguay, Jacques, *et al. History of Canadian Forces Base Montreal and its Garrisons./Historique de la Base des Forces canadiennes Montréal et de ses garnisons.* n.p./s.l.: s.i., 1980. 181/153 pp.
Bilingual text./Texte bilingue.

Castonguay, Jacques, et Armand Ross. *Le Régiment de la Chaudière.* Lévis, P.Q.: imprimé privé, 1983. 644 pp.

Cederberg, Fred. *The Long Road Home; the Autobiography of a Canadian Soldier in Italy in World War II.* Toronto: General Pub., 1984. 257 pp.

Cent ans d'histoire d'un régiment canadien-français; les Fusiliers Mont-Royal, 1869-1969. Montréal: Editions du Jour, 1971. 418 pp.

Centennial, 1863-1963; Presentation of Colours to the Princess of Wales' Own Regiment CA(M) by the Honourable W. Earle Rowe, P.C., Lieutenant-Governor of Ontario, Kingston, Ontario, Saturday 1st June 1963. [Kingston, Ont.: privately printed, 1963.] 15 pp.

Centennial Year, 1866-1966; 11th Field Artillery Regiment (M); 11th Field Artillery Regiment, Royal Regiment of Canadian Artillery, Canada's Oldest Artillery Regiment, Saturday, October 1, 1966. n.p.: n.d. 1 vol., unpaged.

The Centurion (Nulli Secundus); Official Journal of 100th Canadian Army Basic (R) Training Centre. No. 1-? Portage la Prairie, Man.: n.p., 1941-?

Chafe, Edward W. *Gunners; World War II: 166th (Newfoundland) Field Regiment Royal Artillery.* St. John's, Nfld.: Creative Publishers, 1987. 162 pp.

Chambers, Robert W. *Halifax in Wartime; a Collection of Drawings.* Halifax: The Halifax Herald and the Halifax Mail, 1943. 1 vol., unpaged.

[Chandler, C.M.] *The Militia in Durham County, 1812-1936; an Outline History of the Durham Regiment.* n.p.: privately printed, 1936. v.p.

Chappell, Mike. *The Canadian Army at War.* (Men-at-Arms Series, [164].) London: Osprey Pub., 1985. 48 pp.
Canadian Army uniforms.

Châtillon, Claude. *Carnets de guerre; Ottawa — Casa Berardi, 1941-1944.* (Collection «Visages», no 1.) Ottawa: Editions du Vermillon, 1987. 163 pp.
Royal 22e Régiment.

Chevaliers de Colomb. Services de guerre des Chevaliers de Colomb canadiens, 1939-1947; l'oeuvre des huttes militaires des Chevaliers de Colomb. Montréal: s.i., 1948. 280 pp.

Chrétien, Guy. *"Juno Beach" les Canadiens dans la bataille.* Caen, France: Imprimerie Lafond, s.d./n.d. 256 pp., en majeure partie ill./chiefly illus.
Texte bilingue./Bilingual text.

————. *Juno Beach: les Canadiens débarquent.* s.l.: Editions Heimdal, 1979. 96 pp.

50 ans d'activités avec le 6e Régiment d'artillerie (Québec & Lévis), 1899-1949. Québec, P.Q.: Imprimerie Laflamme, 1949. 1 tome, non paginé.

Clark, Gregory. *War Stories.* Toronto: Ryerson Press, 1964. 171 pp.

Clark, Thomas, and Harry Pugh. *Canadian Airborne Insignia, 1942 — Present.* (Elite Insignia Guide, 4.) Arlington, Va.: C & D Enterprise, 1994. 158 pp.

Claude-Laboissière, Alphonse. *Journal d'un aumônier militaire canadien, 1939-1945.* Montréal: Editions françaises, 1948. 330 pp.

Claxton, Brooke. *Notes on Military Law and Discipline for Canadian Soldiers.* n.p.: [1939]. 37 pp.

Clegg, Howard. *A Canuck in England; Journal of a Canadian Soldier.* Toronto: Harrap, 1942. 160 pp.

Clint, H.C., comp. *A Short History of Artillery and of 57th Battery, R.C.A., 1855-1955; Formal Celebration and Reunion, Oct. 15th, 16th, 1955, Grande Allée Armouries, Quebec City.* Quebec, P.Q.: n.p., 1955. 48 pp.

Coates, Kenneth. *North to Alaska.* Toronto: McClelland & Stewart, 1992. 304 pp.
Alaska Highway.

Coates, Kenneth, ed. *The Alaska Highway; Papers of 40th Anniversary Symposium.* Vancouver: Univ. of British Columbia Press, 1985. 208 pp.

Coates, Kenneth, and W.R. Morrison. *The Alaska Highway in World War II; the U.S. Army of Occupation in Canada's Northwest.* Toronto: Univ. of Toronto Press, 1992. 309 pp.

Cohen, Stan. *The Forgotten War; a Pictorial History of World War II in Alaska and Northwestern Canada.* Missoula, Mont.: Pictorial Histories Pub. Co., 1981. 260 pp.

_____. *The Trail of 42; a Pictorial History of the Alaska Highway.* Missoula, Mont.: Pictorial Histories Pub. Co., 1979. 101 pp.

Colton, E. Bert, comp. *History of the 42nd. Infantry Reserve Company, Veterans Guard of Canada, Attached to the Black Watch (RHR) of Canada during the Period of World War II.* Montreal: privately printed, 1947. 28 pp.

Comfort, Charles Fraser. *Artist at War.* Toronto: Ryerson Press, 1956. 187 pp.

Commonwealth War Graves Commission. *The War Dead of the Commonwealth; the Register of the Names of Those who Fell in the 1939-1945 War and are Buried; Cemeteries in Canada; Cemeteries in Ontario.* London: H.M. Stationery Office, 1961. 2 vols.

_____. *The War Dead of the Commonwealth; the Register of the Names of Those who Fell in the 1939-1945 War and are Buried in Cemeteries in Canada; Cemeteries in British Columbia, Yukon Territory and Alberta.* Maidenhead, Eng.: [H.M. Stationery Office], 1972. 82 pp.

_____. *The War Dead of the Commonwealth; the Register of the Names of Those who Fell in the 1939-1945 War and are Buried in Cemeteries in Canada; Cemeteries in New Brunswick, Nova Scotia, Newfoundland and Prince Edward Island.* London: H.M. Stationery Office, 1962. 81 pp.

_____. *The War Dead of the Commonwealth; the Register of the Names of Those who Fell in the 1939-1945 War and are Buried in Cemeteries in Canada; Cemeteries in Quebec.* London: H.M. Stationery Office, 1962. 63 pp.

_____. *The War Dead of the Commonwealth; the Register of the Names of Those who Fell in 1939-1945 War and are Buried in Cemeteries in Canada; Cemeteries in Saskatchewan and Manitoba.* London: [H.M. Stationery Office], 1963. 79 pp.

_____. *The War Dead of the Commonwealth; the Register of the Names of Those who Fell in the 1939-1945 War and have No Known Grave; the Halifax Memorial.* London: [H.M. Stationery Office], 1968. 2 vols.

The Connecting File. Vol. I- . London. Ont.: privately printed, 1921- . *Journal of The Royal Canadian Regiment.*

Conrod, W. Hugh. *Athene, Goddess of War; the Canadian Women's Army Corps; their Story.* Dartmouth, N.S.: Writing and Editorial Services, 1983. 397 pp.

Copp, Terry. *The Brigade; the Fifth Canadian Infantry Brigade, 1939-1945.* Stoney Creek, Ont.: Fortress Publications, 1992. 208 pp.

_____. *A Canadian's Guide to the Battlefields of Normandy.* Waterloo, Ont.: Canadian Battle of Normandy Foundation/LCMSDS, Wilfrid Laurier Univ., 1994. 174 pp.

_____. *A Canadian's Guide to the Battlefields of Northwest Europe.* Waterloo, Ont.: Wilfrid Laurier Univ.; Canadian Battle of Normandy Foundation, 1995. 236 pp.

Copp, Terry, and Bill McAndrew. *Battle Exhausion; Soldiers and Psychiatrists in the Canadian Army, 1939-1945.* Montreal: McGill-Queen's Univ. Press, 1990. 249 pp.

Copp, Terry and Richard Nielsen. *No Price Too High; Canadians and the Second World War.* Toronto: McGraw-Hill Ryerson, 1996. 255 pp.

Copp, Terry, and Robert Vogel. *Maple Leaf Route: Antwerp.* Alma, Ont.: Maple Leaf Route, 1984. 143 pp.

_____. *Maple Leaf Route: Caen.* Alma, Ont.: Maple Leaf Route, 1983. 119 pp.

_____. *Maple Leaf Route: Falaise.* Alma, Ont.: Maple Leaf Route, 1983. 143 pp.

_____. *Maple Leaf Route: Scheldt.* Alma, Ont.: Maple Leaf Route, 1985. 143 pp.

_____. *Maple Leaf Route: Victory.* Alma, Ont.: Maple Leaf Route, 1988. 144 pp.

Corfield, William E. *Citizen Soldiers; the Canadian Fusiliers of London; the Oxford Rifles; the Perth Regiment.* London, Ont.: Royal Canadian Regiment, 1983. 86 pp.

*Cormier, Ronald. *The Forgotten Soldiers; Stories from Acadian Veterans of the Second World War.* Fredericton, N.B.: New Ireland Press, 1992. 174 pp.

* _____. *«J'ai vécu la guerre.» Témoignages de soldats acadiens, 1939-1945.* Moncton, N.-B.: Editions d'Acadie, 1988. [254] pp.

Cornelius, J.R. *Cadet Training as a National Wealth.* Ottawa: King's Printer, 1923. 12 pp.

**Le Corps blindé royal canadien.* Ottawa: Imprimeur de la Reine, 1954. 11 pp.

**Le Corps de Santé royal canadien.* Ottawa: Imprimeur de la Reine, 1954. 11 pp.

The Corps of Royal Canadian Engineers. Ottawa: Queen's Printer, 1953. 21 pp.

The Corps of Royal Canadian Engineers; a Brief History. Ottawa: King's Printer, 1948. 56 pp.

[Corrigan, Cecil Edwin.] *Tales of a Forgotten Theatre,* by "Pooch" [*pseud.*] Winnipeg: Day Publishers, 1969. 223 pp.

Corriveau, Paul. *Le Royal 22e Régiment; 75 ans d'histoire, 1914-1989.* Québec (Qué): La Régie du Royal 22e Régiment, 1989. 132 pp.

Couffon, Claude. *A Caen avec les Canadiens.* (Collections "Patrie".) Paris: Rouff, 1949. 24 pp.

Coughlin, Bing. *Herbie.* n.p.: T. Nelson, 1946. 190 pp.

_____. *This Army; a Portfolio of Cartoons Drawn on the Italian Battle Front for the Maple Leaf, Canadian Army Newspaper.* Rome: No. 2 Canadian Public Relations Group, 1944-45. 2 vols., chiefly illus.

Coursaget, A.C., comp. *Histoire d'une petite plage normande devenue grande dans le souvenir des français par l'héroïsme du "Royal Regiment of Canada".* Paris: R. Girard, 1946. 1 tome, en majeure partie ill.

Couture, Claude-Paul. *Opération "Jubilee", Dieppe, 19 août 1942.* Paris: Editions France-Empire, 1969. 662 pp.

*[Cras, Hervé.] *Dieppe; the Dawn of Decision,* by Jacques Mordal [*pseud.*] Mervyn Savill, tr. Toronto: Ryerson Press, 1963. 285 pp.

*_____. *Les Canadiens à Dieppe,* par Jacques Mordal [*pseud.*] Paris: Presses de la Cité, 1962. 343 pp.

Crook, E.D., and J.K. Marteinson, eds. *A Pictorial History of the 8th Canadian Hussars (Princess Louise's).* n.p.: privately printed, 1973. 343 pp.

The Crow's Nest; Fortieth Anniversary, 1942-1982. n.p.: privately printed, [1982]. 107 pp.
Officers' Club, St. John's, Nfld.

Cunniffe, Dick. *Scarlet, Riflegreen and Khaki; the Military in Calgary.* Calgary: Century Calgary Publications, 1975. 40 pp.

_____. *The Story of a Regiment; Lord Strathcona's Horse (Royal Canadians).* [Volume I.] n.p.: Lord Strathcona's Horse (Royal Canadians) Regimental Society, 1995. 192 pp.

Curchin, Leonard A., and Brian D. Sim. *The Elgins; the Story of the Elgin Regt. (RCAC) and its Predecessors.* St. Thomas, Ont.: privately printed, 1977. 150 pp.

Dancocks, Daniel G. *The D-Day Dodgers; the Canadians in Italy, 1943-1945.* Toronto: McClelland & Stewart, 1991. 508 pp.

238

Dancocks, Daniel G. *In Enemy Hands; Canadian Prisoners of War, 1939-45.* Edmonton: Hurtig, 1983. 303 pp.

Darby, H., and M. Cunliffe. *A Short Story of 21 Army Group; the British and Canadian Armies in the Campaigns in North West Europe, 1944-45.* Aldershot, Eng.: Gale and Polden, 1949. 147 pp.

Davis, Eldon S. *An Awesome Silence; a Gunner Padre's Journey through the Valley of the Shadow.* Carp, Ont.: Creative Bound, [1991]. 142 pp.
1st Canadian Division in Italy.

Davis, Henry Hague, *see* Canada. Royal Commission on the Bren Machine Gun Contract.

Desjardins, Maurice. *Momo s'en va-t-en guerre.* Montréal: Ferron Editeur, 1973. 159 pp.

Desquesnes, Rémy. *Les Canadiens au secours de l'Europe./The Canadians to Europe's Rescue.* Caen, France: Mémorial musée pour la paix, 1992. 194 pp.
Texte bilingue./Bilingual text.

Diary of 65 Canadian Tank Transporter Company, Royal Canadian Army Service Corps. Editorial research and composition: Norman Lafrance. Coldwater, Ont.: privately printed, [1983]. 199 pp.

* *The Dominion Arsenal at Quebec, 1880-1945.* Quebec, P.Q.: n.p., 1947. 131 pp.

Donoghue, Jack. *The Edge of War.* Calgary: Detselig Enterprises, 1988. 149 pp.
Memoirs of a public relations officer with 1st Canadian Army.

_____. *PR; Fifty Years in the Field.* Toronto: Dundurn Press, 1993. 188 pp.

Dornbusch, C.E., comp. *The Canadian Army, 1855-1958; Regimental Histories and a Guide to the Regiments.* Cornwallville, N.Y.: Hope Farm Press, 1959. 216 pp.

_____. *The Canadian Army, 1855-1955; Regimental Histories and a Guide to the Regiments.* Cornwallville, N.Y.: n.p., 1957. 162 1.

_____. *The Canadian Army, 1855-1965; Lineages; Regimental Histories.* Cornwallville, N.Y.: Hope Farm Press, 1966. 179 pp.

_____. *Lineages of the Canadian Army, 1855-1961; Armour, Cavalry, Infantry.* Cornwallville, N.Y.: Hope Farm Press, 1961. 1 vol., unpaged.

Dornier, François, et Marie-Claude Joubert. *Soldats de la côte ...; Les Fusiliers du St-Laurent d'hier à aujourd'hui.* Rimouski (Qué.): La Régie, Les Fusiliers du St-Laurent, 1992. 183 pp.

Dorosh, Michael A. *Canuck.* Volume I: *Clothing and Equipping the Canadian Soldier, 1939-1945; Battle Dress, Weapons and Equipment.* Missoula, Mont.: Pictorial Histories Pub. Co., 1995. 156 pp.

Dorward, David M. *The Gold Cross; One Man's Window on the War.* Toronto: Canadian Stage and Arts Publications, 1978. 92 pp.
Reminiscences of the Sicilian campaign.

Douglas, W.A.B., and Brereton Greenhous. *Out of the Shadows; Canada in the Second World War.* Toronto: Oxford Univ. Press, 1977. 288 pp.
Rev. ed. Toronto: Dundurn Press, 1995. 304 pp.

Drage, Charles. *The Life and Times of General Two-Gun Cohen.* New York: Funk & Wagnalls, 1954. 312 pp.
London ed. titled: Two-Gun Cohen.

Drive to the Rhine; the First Canadian Army in Action; Dispatches by CP Correspondents. [Toronto: Canadian Press, 1945.] 21 pp.

Drolet, "Gil". *Loyola, the Wars: in Remembrance of "Men for Others".* Waterloo, Ont.: Laurier Centre for Military Strategic and Disarmament Studies, 1996. 44 pp.
Memorial to the war dead of Loyola High School and College.

Duff, (Sir) Lyman P., *see/voir* Canada. Royal Commission on the Canadian Expeditionary Force to the Crown Colony of Hong Kong; Canada. Commission royale sur le Corps expéditionnaire canadien envoyé dans la Colonie de la Couronne de Hong-Kong.

Duguid, Archer Fortescue. *History of the Canadian Grenadier Guards, 1760-1964.* Montreal: Gazette Print. Co., 1965. 520 pp.

Duley, Margaret. *The Caribou Hut; the Story of a Newfoundland Hostel.* Toronto: Ryerson Press, 1949. 82 pp.

Dumais, Lucien A. *Un Canadien français à Dieppe.* Paris: Editions France-Empire, 1968. 283 pp.

_____. *Un Canadien français face à la Gestapo.* Montréal: Editions du Jour, 1969. 280 pp.

Dumais, Lucien A., and Hugh Popham. *The Man who Went Back.* London: L. Cooper, 1975. 213 pp.

Duncan, Donald Albert. *Some Letters and other Writings.* Halifax: Imperial Pub. Co., 1945. 199 pp.

Dunkelman, Ben. *Dual Allegiance; an Autobiography.* Toronto: Macmillan, 1976. 336 pp.

Dunwoody, James M. *The Colonel; Some Reminiscences.* n.p.: [1972?]. 36 pp.

Dyer, Gwynne, and Tina Viljoen. *The Defence of Canada; in the Arms of the Empire.* Toronto: McClelland & Stewart, 1990. 375 pp.

Edelstein, H. *All Quiet in Canada — and Why; "Cpl. Ray's" Pen and Camera Pictures of the War (1939-1944) with Verse Comment and Later Poems.* Ottawa: privately printed, 1944. 41 pp.

Edwards, Charles A. *Canadian Army Formation Signs, 1939-1985; a Collector's and Historian's Comprehensive Guide to the Cloth Formation Signs Worn by the Canadian Army in 1939-1985.* Michael J. Langenfeld, illus. Grayslake, Ill.: Pass in Review Publications, 1987. 50 pp.

Einer kam durch see/voir Werra, Franz von.

Elliot, S.R. *Scarlet to Green; a History of Intelligence in the Canadian Army, 1903-1963.* Toronto: privately printed, 1981. 769 pp.

Elliott-Haynes Limited. *An Enquiry into the Attitude of the Canadian Civilian Public towards the Women's Armed Forces; Conducted on Behalf of the Advertising Agencies of Canada and the Joint Committee on Combined Recruiting Promotion, Women's Services of the Three Armed Forces.* Montreal: privately printed, [194-?]. 33 pp.

Ellis, Chris, and Peter Chamberlain. *Ram and Sexton.* (AFV, no. 13.) Windsor, Eng.: Profile Publications, n.d. 20 pp.

Ellis, Jean M., and Isabel Dingman. *Face Powder and Gunpowder.* Toronto: S.J.R. Saunders, 1947. 229 pp.

English, John A. *The Canadian Army and the Normandy Campaign; a Study of Failure in High Command.* New York: Praeger, 1991. 347 pp.
    Reprinted as: Failure in High Command; the Canadian Army and the Normandy Campaign. *Ottawa: Golden Dog Press, 1995.*

Ettenger, G.H. *History of the Associate Committee on Medical Research Ottawa, 1938-1946.* Ottawa: n.p., n.d. 46 pp.

Europe WW2. (Canadian Military Vehicle Series, vol. 1.) Rockwood, Ont.: Canadian Military Historical Society, [1978]. 210 pp.
    Reprint of Vehicle Data Book; Canadian Army Overseas *with additions. 2d. ed. titled:* Canada's Fighting Vehicles: Europe 1943-45.

Falardeau, Victor, et Jean Parent. *La musique du Royal 22e Régiment; 50 ans d'histoire, 1922-1972.* Québec, P.Q.: Editions Garneau, 1976. 243 pp.

Falconer, D.W. *Battery Flashes of W.W.II; a Thumb-Nail Sketch of Canadian Artillery Batteries during the 1939-1945 Conflict.* [Victoria, B.C.: n.p., 1985.] 514 pp.

Fallis, George O. *A Padre's Pilgrimage.* Toronto: Ryerson Press, 1953. 166 pp.

Farran, Roy. *The History of the Calgary Highlanders, 1921-54.* n.p.: Bryant Press, [1954]. 222 pp.

Farrel, J.C., and others. *Memoirs of 4 Canadian Armoured Troops Workshop, Royal Canadian Electrical and Mechanical Engineers.* Enschede, Neth.: n.p., 1945. 74 pp.

Feasby, W.R. *Official History of the Canadian Medical Services, 1939-1945.* Ottawa: Queen's Printer, 1956. 2 vols.

Ferguson, Ted. *Desperate Siege; the Battle of Hong Kong.* Toronto: Doubleday, 1980. 252 pp.

Fetherstonhaugh, R.C. *McGill University at War, 1914-1918; 1939-1945.* Montreal: McGill Univ., 1947. 437 pp.

_____. *The Royal Montreal Regiment, 14th Battalion, C.E.F., 1914-1925.* Montreal: privately printed, 1927. 334 pp.

_____. *The Royal Montreal Regiment, 1925-1945.* Westmount, P.Q.: privately printed, 1949. 298 pp.

_____. *A Short History of the Royal Canadian Dragoons.* Toronto: Southam Press, 1932. 52 pp.

Fetherstonhaugh, R.C., and G.R. Stevens. *The Royal Canadian Regiment.* Vol. I: Montreal: Gazette Print. Co., 1936. Vol. II: London, Ont.: privately printed, 1967. 2 vols.

Fifty Years of Armour/Cinquante ans de blindé/Royal Canadian Armoured Corps/Le Corps blindé royal canadien/1940-1990. Ottawa: Esprit de corps, [1990]. 43 pp.
Bilingual text./Texte bilingue.

50 Years of Canadian Electrical and Mechanical Engineering./50 ans de Génie électrique et mécanique canadien. Ottawa: n.p./s.i., [1994]. 111 pp.
Bilingual text./Texte bilingue.

First Battalion, Rocky Mountain Rangers. n.p.: [1944?]. 13 pp.

First Battalion the Canadian Scottish Regiment, Victoria, B.C. ... Souvenir Programme of the Civic Welcome Extended by the Citizens of Victoria, B.C., on the Homecoming of Vancouver Island's Own Regiment, December, 1945. Victoria, B.C.: Economy Press, 1945. 32 pp.

1st Battalion, the Saskatoon Light Infantry (M.G.), Canadian Army Overseas; Honour Roll, 10th July 1943 to 8th May, 1945, Sicily, Italy, Holland. n.p.: privately printed, n.d. 15 pp.

Flatt, S.A. *History of the 6th Field Company, Royal Canadian Engineers, 1939-1945.* Vancouver: privately printed, n.d. 141 pp.

*Florentin, Eddy. *Battle of the Falaise Gap.* Mervyn Savill, tr. London: Elek Books, 1965. 336 pp.

242

*Florentin, Eddy. *Stalingrad en Normandie.* Paris: Presses de la Cité, 1964. 389 pp.

For King and Country; Alberta in the Second World War. Edmonton: Provincial Museum of Alberta; Reidmore Books, 1995. 364 pp.

Forbes, D.F. *North Nova Scotia Highlanders.* Varel, Germany: n.p., [1945]. 32 pp.

Forbes, J. Charles. *Fantassin; pour mon pays, la gloire et ... des prunes.* Sillery (Qué.): Septentrion, 1994. 451 pp.
Le Régiment de Maisonneuve dans la Deuxième Guerre mondiale, le Royal 22e Régiment en Corée.

The Fort Garry Horse, C.A.S.F. (Allied with 4th/7th Dragoon Guards). Winnipeg: n.p., 1939. 47 pp.

Foster, J.A. *Meeting of Generals,* by Tony Foster. Toronto: Methuen, 1986. 559 pp.

_____. *Muskets to Missiles; a Pictorial History of Canada's Ground Forces.* Toronto: Methuen, 1987. 251 pp.

Fowler, T. Robert. *Valour in the Victory Campaign; the 3rd Canadian Infantry Division Gallantry Decorations, 1945.* Burnstown, Ont.: General Store Pub. House, 1995. 235 pp.

_____. *Valour on Juno Beach; the Canadian Awards for Gallantry, D-Day, June 6, 1944.* Burnstown, Ont.: General Store Pub. House, 1994. [104] pp.

Fraser, W.B. *Always a Strathcona.* Calgary: Comprint Pub. Co., 1976. 252 pp.

Frost, C. Sydney. *Once a Patricia (Memoirs of a Junior Infantry Officer in World War II).* St. Catharines, Ont.: Vanwell Pub., [1988]. 564 pp.

Fryer, Mary Beacock. *More Battlefields of Canada.* Toronto: Dundurn Press, 1993. 184 pp.

Gaffen, Fred. *Cross-Border Warriors; Canadians in American Forces, Americans in Canadian Forces; from the Civil War to the Gulf.* Toronto; Dundurn Press, 1995. 241 pp.

_____. *Forgotten Soldiers.* Penticton, B.C.: Theytus Books, 1985. 152 pp.
Canada's native peoples in two World Wars.

_____. *Ortona, Christmas 1943.* (Canadian Battle Series no. 5.) Ottawa: Balmuir Book Pub.; Canadian War Museum, National Museums of Canada, 1988. 64 pp.

Gaffen, Fred, ed./rédacteur. *The Road to Victory: a History of Canada in the Second World War./La route de la victoire: la participation du Canada à la Deuxième Guerre mondiale.* French translation/Traduction en français: Jean Pariseau. n.p./s.l.: Canadian War Museum/Musée canadien de la guerre; Esprit de corps, 1995. 84 pp.
Bilingual text./Texte bilingue.

Gagnon, Jean-Paul. *Mon journal de guerre.* Sainte-Foy, P.Q.: imprimé privé, 1968. 64 pp.
4e Régiment d'artillerie moyenne.

Gallant, A.M. *Pride; the History of 1390 RCACC.* Red Deer, Alta.: printed by Fletcher, [1992?]. 244 pp.

Galloway, Strome. *"55 Axis"; with The Royal Canadian Regiment, 1939-1945.* Montreal: Provincial Pub. Co., 1946. 232 pp.
Reprinted in 1979, titled: <u>A Regiment at War, the Story of The Royal Canadian Regiment, 1939-1945</u>.

_____. *The General Who Never Was.* Belleville, Ont.: Mika Pub. Co., 1981. 296 pp.
Reprinted as <u>Bravely into Battle</u>. Toronto: Stoddart, 1988.

_____. *Some Died at Ortona; The Royal Canadian Regiment in Action in Italy 1943, a Diary by Strome Galloway.* n.p.: The Royal Canadian Regiment, [1983]. 223 pp.

*_____. *30th Anniversary; the Canadians in Italy, April 22 to May 3, 1975.* n.p.: [1975]. 28 pp.

*_____. *Trentième anniversaire; les Canadiens en Italie, du 22 avril au 3 mai 1975.* s.l.: s.i., [1975]. 31 pp.

_____. *With the Irish against Rommel; a Diary of 1943.* Langley, B.C.: Battleline Books, 1984. [182] pp.

Gardam, John. *Fifty Years After.* Burnstown, Ont.: General Store Pub. House, 1990. 141 pp.

_____. *Ordinary Heroes.* Burnstown, Ont.: General Store Pub. House, 1992. 205 pp.

[Garneau, Grant S., and others.] *The Royal Rifles of Canada in Hong Kong, 1941-1945.* Sherbrooke, P.Q.: n.p., 1980. 433 pp.

Gavin, T.M., ed. *The Story of 1 Canadian Survey Regiment, RCA, 1939-1945.* n.p.: privately printed, 1945. 99 pp.

[General Motors of Canada, Limited.] *Achievement.* n.p.: [1943]. 74 pp.

Le Génie royal canadien. Ottawa: Imprimeur de la Reine, 1954. 23 pp.

Giesler, Patricia. *Commemoration; Dieppe, August 19, 1942./Commémoration; Dieppe, le 19 août 1942.* Ottawa: Veterans Affairs Canada/Affaires des anciens combattants Canada, 1982. 1 vol., unpaged./1 tome, non-paginé.
Bilingual text./Texte bilingue.

_____. *Valour Remembered; Canada and the Second World War, 1939-1945./Souvenirs de vaillance; la participation du Canada à la Seconde Guerre mondiale, 1939-1945.* Ottawa: Veterans Affairs Canada/Affaires des anciens combattants Canada, 1981. 45/47 pp.
Bilingual text./Texte bilingue.

[Giles, L.C.] *Liphook, Bramshott and the Canadians.* n.p.: Bramshott and Liphook Preservation Society, 1986. 36 pp.

The Goat see The Springbok.

Goodspeed, D.J. *Battle Royal; a History of the Royal Regiment of Canada, 1862-1962.* Toronto: privately printed, 1962. 703 pp.

Gordon, David A. *The Stretcher Bearers.* Stroud, Ont.: Pacesetter Press, 1995. 127 pp.
Memoirs of a member of 24 Canadian Field Ambulance, attached to the Perth Regiment.

Gossage, Carolyn. *Greatcoats and Glamour Boots; Canadian Women at War (1939-1945).* Toronto: Dundurn Press, 1991. 215 pp.

Gouin, Jacques. *Lettres de guerre d'un Québecois, 1942-1945.* Montréal: Editions du Jour, 1975. 341 pp.

_____. *Par la bouche de nos canons; histoire du 4e Régiment d'artillerie moyenne/4th Cdn Medium Regt RCA/1941-1945.* [Montréal]: Gasparo, 1970. 248 pp.

*Gouin, Jacques and Lucien Brault. *Legacy of Honour; the Panets, Canada's Foremost Military Family.* Toronto: Methuen, 1985. 240 pp.

Gouin, Jacques, *et al. Bon coeur et bon bras; histoire du Régiment de Maisonneuve, 1880-1980.* Montréal: imprimé privé, 1980. 298 pp.

*Gouin, Jacques, et Lucien Brault. *Les Panet de Québec; histoire d'une lignée militaire.* Montréal: Bergeron, 1984. 238 pp.

Governor General's Foot Guards, Ottawa; Seventy-Fifth Anniversary, June 8, 1872-1947. Ottawa: privately printed, 1947. 43 pp.

The Governer General's Horse Guards Home Coming, Queen Elizabeth Building, C.N.E., May 22-23-24 1964. n.p.: [1964]. 31 pp.

The Governor General's Horse Guards, 1939-1945. Toronto: Canadian Military Journal, [1953]. 243 pp.

Grafton, C.S. *The Canadian "Emma Gees"; a History of the Canadian Machine Gun Corps*. London, Ont.: privately printed, 1938. 218 pp.

Graham, Dominick. *The Price of Command; a Biography of General Guy Simonds*. Toronto: Stoddart, 1993. 345 pp.

Graham, Howard. *Citizen and Soldier; the Memoirs of Lieutenant-General Howard Graham*. Toronto: McClelland and Stewart, 1987. 304 pp.

Granastein, J.L. *The Generals; the Canadian Army's Senior Commanders in the Second World War*. Toronto: Stoddart, 1993. 370 pp.

_____. *Normandy 1944./Normandie 1944*. Ottawa: Communications Division, Veterans Affairs Canada/Direction générale des communications, Anciens combattants Canada, 1994. 58/62 pp.
Bilingual text./Texte bilingue.

Granatstein, J.L., and Desmond Morton. *Bloody Victory; Canadians and the D-Day Campaign 1944*. Toronto: Lester & Orpen Dennys, 1984. 240 pp.

_____. *A Nation Forged in Fire; Canadians and the Second World War 1939-1945*. Toronto: Lester & Orpen Dennys, 1989. 287 pp.

Granatstein, J.L., and R.D. Cuff, eds. *War and Society in North America*. Toronto: T. Nelson, 1971. 199 pp.

Grant, D.W. *"Carry On"; the History of the Toronto Scottish Regiment (M.G.), 1939-1945*. Toronto: privately printed, 1949. 177 pp.

Gravel, Jean-Yves. *Les soldats-citoyens; histoire du Régiment de Trois-Rivières, 1871-1978*. Trois-Rivières, P.Q.: Editions du Bien Public, 1981. 153 pp.

Gt. Brit. Army. British Army of the Rhine, and Canada. Army Headquarters. Historical Section. *British Army of the Rhine; Battlefield Tour, Second Day; 2 Canadian Corps Operations Astride the Road Caen-Falaise, 7-8 August, 1944 (Operation Totalize)*. n.p.: 1947. 71 pp.

Gt. Brit. Army. 21 Army Group Headquarters. Canadian Section. *Canadian Routine Orders (21 Army Group)*. n.p.: 1944-45.
Title varies. Issued as <u>Canadian Routine Orders (British Army of the Rhine)</u> from August 1945.

Gt. Brit. Imperial War Graves Commission. *The War Dead of the British Commonwealth and Empire; the Register of the Names of Those who Fell in the 1939-1945 War and are Buried in Cemeteries and Churchyards in Surrey; Brookwood Military Cemetery, Woking*. London: [H.M. Stationery Office], 1958. 3 vols.

_____. *The War Dead of the British Commonwealth and Empire; the Register of the Names of Those who Fell in the 1939-1945 War and are Buried in Cemeteries in Belgium; Adegem Canadian War Cemetery*. London: H.M. Stationery Office, 1956. 42 pp.

Gt. Brit. Imperial War Graves Commission. *The War Dead of the British Commonwealth and Empire; the Register of the Names of Those who Fell in the 1939-1945 War and are Buried in Cemeteries in France; Beny-sur-mer Canadian War Cemetery.* London: H.M. Stationery Office, 1955. 2 vols.

_____. *The War Dead of the British Commonwealth and Empire; the Register of the Names of Those who Fell in the 1939-1945 War and are Buried in Cemeteries in France; Bretteville-sur-Laize Canadian War Cemetery.* London: H.M. Stationery Office, 1955. 3 vols.

_____. *The War Dead of the British Commonwealth and Empire; the Register of the Names of Those who Fell in the 1939-1945 War and are Buried in Cemeteries in France; Calais War Cemetery, Calais Canadian War Cemetery.* London: H.M. Stationery Office, 1956. 43 pp.

_____. *The War Dead of the British Commonwealth and Empire; the Register of the Names of Those who Fell in the 1939-1945 War and are Buried in Cemeteries in France; Dieppe Canadian War Cemetery; Janval Cemetery, Dieppe.* London: H.M. Stationery Office, 1956. 40 pp.

_____. *The War Dead of the British Commonwealth and Empire; the Register of the Names of Those who Fell in the 1939-1945 War and are Buried in Cemeteries in Hong Kong.* London: H.M. Stationery Office, 1956-58. 2 vols.

_____. *The War Dead of the British Commonwealth and Empire; the Register of the Names of Those who Fell in the 1939-1945 War and are Buried in Cemeteries in Italy; Agira Canadian War Cemetery, Sicily.* London: H.M. Stationery Office, 1953. 29 pp.

_____. *The War Dead of the British Commonwealth and Empire; the Register of the Names of Those who Fell in the 1939-1945 War and are Buried in Cemeteries in Italy; Argenta Gap War Cemetery; Bologna War Cemetery; Villanova Canadian War Cemetery.* London: H.M. Stationery Office, 1953. 70 pp.

_____. *The War Dead of the British Commonwealth and Empire; the Register of the Names of Those who Fell in the 1939-1945 War and are Buried in Cemeteries in Italy; Moro River Canadian War Cemetery, Ortona.* London: H.M. Stationery Office, 1954. 2 vols.

_____. *The War Dead of the British Commonwealth and Empire; the Register of the Names of Those who Fell in the 1939-1945 War and are Buried in Cemeteries in Italy; Ravenna War Cemetery.* London: [H.M. Stationery Office], 1956. 44 pp.

Gt. Brit. Imperial War Graves Commission. *The War Dead of the British Commonwealth and Empire; the Register of the Names of Those who Fell in the 1939-1945 War and are Buried in Cemeteries in the Netherlands; Bergen-Op-Zoom Canadian War Cemetery.* London: H.M. Stationery Office, 1957. 50 pp.

_____. *The War Dead of the British Commonwealth and Empire; the Register of the Names of Those who Fell in the 1939-1945 War and are Buried in Cemeteries in the Netherlands; Groesbeek Canadian War Cemetery, Nijmegen.* London: H.M. Stationery Office, 1956. 2 vols.

_____. *The War Dead of the British Commonwealth and Empire; the Register of the Names of Those who Fell in the 1939-1945 War and are Buried in Cemeteries in the Netherlands; Holten Canadian War Cemetery; Holten General Cemetery.* London: H.M. Stationery Office, 1956. 64 pp.

Greenhous, Brereton. *Dragoon; the Centennial History of the Royal Canadian Dragoons, 1883-1983.* Ottawa: Guild of the Royal Canadian Dragoons, 1983. 557 pp.

_____. *Dieppe, Dieppe.* Montréal: Art Global, 1992. 155 pp.

_____. *Semper Paratus; the History of the Royal Hamilton Light Infantry (Wentworth Regiment), 1862-1977,* by Kingsley Brown, Senior, Kingsley Brown, Junior, and Brereton Greenhous. Revised and edited by Brereton Greenhous. Hamilton, Ont.: privately printed, 1977. 446 pp.

Gregg, William. *Blueprint for Victory; the Story of Military Vehicle Design and Production in Canada from 1937-45.* (Canadian Military Vehicle Series, Volume III.) Rockwood, Ont.: Canadian Military Historical Society, 1981. 208 pp.

Gregg, William, ed. *Canadian Military Vehicle Profiles.* (Canadian Military Vehicle Series, Volume II.) Rockwood, Ont.: Canadian Military Historical Society, [1981-82]. 1 vol., looseleaf.

Griffin, Frederick. *Major-General Sir Henry Mill Pellatt, CVO, DCL, VD; a Gentleman of Toronto, 1859-1939.* Toronto: Ontario Pub. Co., 1939. 30 pp.

Grimshaw, Louis E. *"Ex coelis"; the Badges and Insignia of the Canadian Airborne Forces; a History of Canadian Airborne Badges and the Units and Men who Wore Them "ex coelis".* Edmonton: Lone Pine Pub., 1981. 80 pp.

Grogan, John Patrick. *Dieppe and Beyond; for a Dollar and a Half a Day.* Renfrew, Ont.: Juniper Books, 1982. 118 pp.

Gunning, C. *North Bay's Fort Chippewa, 1939-1945.* North Bay, Ont.: printed by Detail Printing & Graphics, 1991. 138 pp.

Gutta Percha and Rubber, Limited. *A Selection of Badge Designs of the Canadian Forces.* Toronto: n.p., n.d. 16 pp., chiefly illus.

Halton, Matthew. *Ten Years to Alamein.* Toronto: S.J.R. Saunders, 1944. 319 pp.

Harker, Douglas E. *The Dukes; the Story of the Men who have Served in Peace and War with the British Columbia Regiment (D.C.O.), 1883-1973.* n.p.: privately printed, 1974. 438 pp.

_____. *The Story of the British Columbia Regiment, 1939-1945.* [Vancouver: n.p., 1950.] 1 vol., unpaged.

Harris, Stephen. *Canadian Brass: the Making of a Professional Army, 1860-1939.* Toronto: Univ. of Toronto Press, 1988. 271 pp.

Hawkins, Ronald F. *We will Remember Them.* Woodstock, N.B.: privately printed, 1995. [239] pp.
Memoirs of New Brunswick Second World War veterans.

Hayes, Geoffrey. *The Lincs: a History of the Lincoln and Welland Regiment at War.* Alma, Ont.: Maple Leaf Route, 1986. 139 pp.

Heaps, Leo. *Escape from Arnhem; a Canadian among the Lost Paratroops.* Toronto: Macmillan, 1945. 159 pp.

_____. *The Evaders.* New York: W. Morrow, 1976. 245 pp.
London ed. titled: The Grey Goose of Arnhem.

Hello, Canada! Canada's Mackenzie Papineau Battalion, 1837-1937; 15th Brigade I.B.; "Fascism shall be Destroyed". n.p.: n.d. 46 pp.

Henderson, Peter A. *Guarding the Gates; a History of Canadian Forces Station St. Johns.* St. John's, Nfld.: CFS St. John's, 1992. 115 pp.

Henry, C.E. *Regimental History of the 18th Armoured Car Regiment (XII Manitoba Dragoons).* Deventer, Neth.: privately printed, n.d. 151 pp.

Henry, Hugh G. *Dieppe through the Lens of the German War Photographer.* Photos: Jean Paul Pallud. London: After the Battle, n.d. 63 pp.

Henry, Jacques. *La Normandie en flammes; journal de guerre du capitaine Gérard Leroux, officier d'intelligence au Régiment de la Chaudière.* Condé-sur-Noireau, France: Editions C. Corlet, 1984. 454 pp.

Hermann, J. Douglas. *Report to the Minister of Veterans Affairs of a Study on Canadians who were Prisoners of War in Europe during World War II./Rapport présenté au ministre des Affaires des Anciens combattants au sujet d'une enquête portant sur les Canadiens prisonniers de guerre en Europe au cours de la Seconde Guerre mondiale.* Ottawa: Queen's Printer/Imprimeur de la Reine, 1973. 56/60 pp.
Bilingual text./Texte bilingue.

Hibbert, Joyce. *Fragments of War; Stories from Survivors of World War II.* Toronto: Dundurn Press, 1985. 267 pp.

Hickey, R.M. *The Scarlet Dawn.* Campbellton, N.B.: Tribune Publishers, 1949. 277 pp.

Hill, B. Kirkbride, comp. *The Price of Freedom.* Toronto: Ryerson Press, 1942-44. 2 vols.

Hillsman, John Burwell. *Eleven Men and a Scalpel.* Winnipeg: Columbia Press, 1948. 144 pp.

History; 49th Battalion (C.E.F.), the Loyal Edmonton Regiment. Edmonton: Bradburn Printers, n.d. 16 pp.

History of 17th Field Regiment, Royal Canadian Artillery, 5th Canadian Armoured Division. Groningen, Neth.: J. Niemeijer, 1946. 107 pp.

The History of the 8th Canadian Light Anti-Aircraft Regiment, R.C.A. Amersfoort, Neth.: n.p., 1945. 124 pp.

A History of the First Hussars Regiment. London, Ont.: privately printed, 1951. 172 pp.

A History of the First Hussars Regiment, 1856-1980. n.p.: 1981. 195 pp. *An updating of 1951 ed.*

The History of the Second Field Regiment R.C.A. Sep 1939 — Jun 1945. n.p.: n.d. 79, xxiv pp.

A History of the 7th Anti-Tank Regiment, Royal Canadian Artillery. n.p.: n.d. 22 pp.

History of the 7th Canadian Medium Regiment ... see Lockwood, A.M.

History of the 6th. Canadian Anti-Tank Regiment, Royal Canadian Artillery, 1st April 1942 — 24th June 1945. n.p.: n.d. 38 pp.

The History of the 65th Canadian Anti-Tank Battery, Royal Canadian Artillery, 9 September 1941 — 20 September 1945. Lochem, Neth.: privately printed, 1945. 36 pp.

The History of the Third Canadian Light Anti-Aircraft Regiment from 17 Aug '40 to 7 May '45; World War II. Deventer, Neth.: privately printed, [1945]. 50 pp.
Reprinted in Calgary, 1955.

The History of the 23rd Field Regiment ... see Smith, Lawrence N.

History, 1 Anti-Tank Regiment, RCA, 5 Sep. '39 — 31 Jul. '45; World War II. n.p.: [1945]. v.p.

Hoar, Victor. *The Mackenzie-Papineau Battalion; Canadian Participation in the Spanish Civil War.* [Toronto]: Copp, Clark, 1969. 285 pp.
Reprinted as: Howard, Victor, with Mac Reynolds. The Mackenzie-Papineau Battalion; the Canadian Contingent in the Spanish Civil War. (Carleton Library Series, Number 137.) Ottawa: Carleton Univ. Press, 1986. 285 pp.

Hodder-Williams, Ralph, G.R. Stevens and R.B. Mainprize. *Princess Patricia's Canadian Light Infantry.* London: Hodder and Stoughton, 1923-[57?]. 4 vols.

Hodgins, J. Herbert, and others, comps. *Women at War.* Montreal: MacLean Pub., 1943. 190 pp.

Holberton, Fred. G. *39th Field Battery, Royal Canadian Artillery, World War II.* (Occasional Paper no. 23.) Lethbridge, Alta.: Lethbridge Historical Society, 1991. 14 pp.

Hopkins, Anthony. *Songs from the Front & Rear; Canadian Servicemen's Songs of the Second World War.* Edmonton: Hurtig Publishers, 1979. 192 pp.

Horrocks, William. *In their own Words.* Ottawa: Rideau Veterans Home Residents Council, 1993. 247 pp.

The Horse Guard; Souvenir Programme of the Regimental Reunion, May, 1954. n.p.: [1954]. 36 pp.

How, Douglas. *The 8th Hussars; a History of the Regiment.* Sussex, N.B.: Maritime Pub., 1964. 446 pp.

Howard, Gordon L. *The Memories of a Citizen Soldier, 1914-1945.* n.p.: n.d. 114 pp.

_____. *Sixty Years of Centennial in Saskatchewan, 1906-1968.* n.p.: n.d. 140 pp.

Hubbell, E.L. *The Winnipeg Grenadiers.* n.p.: n.d. 16 pp.

Hughes, G.W., comp. *A Marchpast of the Corps and Regiments of the Canadian Army, Past and Present.* Calgary: n.p., n.d. 3 vols.

Huizinga, M.H. *Maple Leaf Up; de Canadese opmars in Noord-Nederland, april 1945.* Groningen, Neth.: J. Niemeijer, 1980. 295 pp.

Humphrey, James McGivern. *The Golden Bridge of Memoirs.* Don Mills, Ont.: Nelson, 1979. 182 pp.

*Hunter, T. Murray. *Le Canada à Dieppe.* (Musée canadien de la guerre publication d'histoire militaire no 17.) s.l.: Balmuir Book Pub., 1982. 61 pp.

*_____. *Canada at Dieppe.* (Canadian War Museum Historical Publication no. 17.) n.p.: Balmuir Book Pub., 1982. 61 pp.

Hutchison, Paul P. *Canada's Black Watch; the First Hundred Years, 1862-1962.* Montreal: privately printed, [1962]. 340 pp.

_____. *A Short History of the Royal Highland Regiment the Black Watch, 1725-1948.* n.p.: 1948. 39 pp.

In Memoriam; the Perth Regiment, 4th September 1939 to 8th May 1945. n.p.: [1945]. 20 pp.

L'Intendance royale canadienne. Ottawa: Imprimeur de la Reine, 1954. 12 pp.

The Irish Regiment of Canada; Memorial Service to Honour our Gallant Dead, Canada, England, Italy, Holland, June 1940 — to — May 1945, Heerenveen, Holland, Sunday, July 1st, 1945. Groningen, Neth.: privately printed, 1945. 1 vol., unpaged.

Ito, Roy. *Stories of my People; a Japanese Canadian Journal.* Hamilton, Ont.: S-20 and Nisei Veterans Association, 1994. 497 pp.

_____. *We Went to War; the Story of the Japanese Canadians who Served during the First and Second World Wars.* Stittsville, Ont.: Canada's Wings, 1984. 330 pp.

Jackson, H.M. *Canadian Prime Ministers and the Canadian Militia.* n.p.: 1958. 11 pp.

_____. *The Princess Louise Dragoon Guards; a History.* n.p.: 1952. 306 pp.

_____. *The Roll of the Regiments (the Active Militia).* Ottawa: n.p., 1959. 176 pp.

_____. *The Royal Regiment of Artillery, Ottawa, 1855-1952; a History.* Montreal: privately printed, 1952. 418 pp.

_____. *The Sherbrooke Regiment (12th Armoured Regiment).* n.p.: 1958. 229 pp.

_____. *The Story of the Royal Canadian Dental Corps.* Ottawa: privately printed, 1956. 475 pp.

Jackson, H.M., ed. *The Argyll and Sutherland Highlanders of Canada (Princess Louise's), 1928-1953.* Montreal: privately printed, 1953. 497 pp.

Johnson, Charles Monroe. *Action with the Seaforths.* New York: Vantage Press, 1954. 342 pp.

Johnston, Murray. *Canada's Craftsmen; the Story of the Corps of Royal Canadian Electrical and Mechanical Engineers and of the Land Ordnance Engineering Branch.* n.p.: 1983. 291 pp.

Johnston, Stafford. *The Fighting Perths; the Story of the First Century in the Life of a Canadian County Regiment.* Stratford, Ont.: privately printed, 1964. 133 pp.

Jones, Gwilym. *To the Green Fields Beyond; a Soldier's Story.* Burnstown, Ont.: General Store Pub. House, 1993. 201 pp.
Memoir of service in the Three Rivers Regiment.

Jones, Ted. *Both Sides of the Wire; the Fredericton Internment Camp.* Fredericton, N.B.: New Ireland Press, 1988-89. 2 vols.

Jones, William. *Twelve Months with Tito's Partisans.* Bedford, Eng.: Bedford Books, 1946. 128 pp.

Journal of the Edmonton Military Institute. Vol. I-IV? Edmonton: Edmonton Military Institute, 1937-46?

Joy, Edward H. *Gentlemen from Canada.* London: Hodder & Stoughton, 1943. 92 pp.

Juteau, Maurice (Pipo). *L'envers de ma guerre.* Ste-Sabine, P.Q.: imprimé privé, 1982. 203 pp.
Mémoires du service au Royal 22e Régiment.

_____. *Ma drôle de guerre; tiré du soldat qui pense.* Ste-Sabine, P.Q.: imprimé privé, 1980. 172 pp.
Mémoires du service au Royal 22e Régiment.

Kardash, William. *I Fought for Canada in Spain ....* (Timely Topics, no. 3.) Toronto: New Era Publishers, n.d. 30 pp.

Kaufman, David, and Michiel Horn. *A Liberation Album; Canadians in the Netherlands, 1944-45.* Toronto: McGraw-Hill Ryerson, 1980. 175 pp.

Kelly, Arthur J. *"There's a Goddam Bullet for Everyone ...."* Elizabeth Kelly, ed. Paris, Ont.: Tyoweronh Arts and Pub. Co., 1979. 339 pp.

Kelsey Club, Winnipeg, Man. *Canadian Defence; What We have to Defend; Various Defence Policies.* Toronto: T. Nelson, 1937. 98 pp.

Kellock, R.L., *see* Canada. Royal Commission to Conduct an Inquiry into Certain Disorders Occurring May 7-8, 1945, in the City of Halifax.

Kembar, A.K., and W.T. Gundy. *The Six Years of 6 Canadian Field Regiment, Royal Canadian Artillery; September 1939 — September 1945.* n.p.: privately printed, 1945. 128 pp.

Kerr, Ashton L. *"The Cherry Beret"; Distant Recollections of World War II as Remembered by One of the First Canloan Officers.* Westmount, P.Q.: printed by Centrav Graphics, n.d. 117 pp.

Kerr, John. *A Souvenir War History of the 8th Canadian Field Squadron, Royal Canadian Engineers.* Zutphen, Neth.: privately printed, n.d. 1 vol., unpaged.

Kerry, A.J., and W.A. McDill. *The History of the Corps of Royal Canadian Engineers.* Ottawa: privately printed, 1962. 2 vols.

King, W.D., comp. *A Brief History of Militia Units Established at Various Periods at Yarmouth, Nova Scotia, 1812-1947.* Yarmouth, N.S.: privately printed, 1947. 32 pp.

Kitching, George. *Mud and Green Fields; the Memoirs of Major General George Kitching.* (Canadians at War Series.) Langley, B.C.: Battleline Books, 1986. 329 pp.

*Knights of Columbus. *War Services of Canadian Knights of Columbus, 1939-1947; a History of the Work of the Knights of Columbus Canadian Army Huts.* Montreal: privately printed, 1948. 260 pp.

Krawchuck, Peter. *Interned without Cause.* Pat Prokop, tr. Toronto: Kobzar Pub. Co., 1985. 124 pp.

Krepps, Rex G. *Sparks of Flame.* Oliver, B.C.: privately printed, 1990. 239 pp. *Reminiscences of No. 8 Canadian General Hospital.*

Laing, Gertrude. *A Community Organized for War; the Story of the Greater Winnipeg Co-ordinating Board for War Services and Affiliated Organizations, 1939-1946.* Winnipeg: n.p., 1948. 103 pp.

Lake, Harold. *Perhaps They Left Us Up There*. St. John's, Nfld.: H. Cuff Publications, 1995. 205 pp.
Training in England and fighting in North Africa and Italy with the 166th (Newfoundland) Field Regiment, Royal Artillery.

Lamb, Ken. *Milton Remembers World War II.* Milton, Ont.: Milton Historical Society, 1995. 140 pp.

Lamontagne, Léopold. *Les archives régimentaires des Fusiliers du S.-Laurent.* Rimouski, P.Q.: s.i., 1943. 247 pp.

Landells, E.A. ed. *The Military Nurses of Canada; Recollections of Canadian Military Nurses.* White Rock, B.C.: Co-Publishing, 1995. 628 pp.

Lannoy, Danny. *For Freedom./Voor de Vrijheid./Pour la liberté.* n.p./s.l.: Brugsch Handelsblad, 1984. 256 pp.
Trilingual text. 40th anniversary of the liberation of Belgium./Texte trilingue. 40e anniversaire de la libération de la Belgique.

Lavoie, Joseph A. *Le Régiment de Montmagny de 1869 à 1931.* s.1.: s.i., [1932]. 117 pp.

Leasor, James. *Green Beach.* London: Heinemann, 1975. 250 pp.

Legermuseum Delft. *Victory Parade; Canadian War Artists in Holland 1944/45.* Delft, Neth.: Legermuseum Delft, 1990. 64 pp.

Legge, Walter R. *The Bomber Press in England; the Story of the Visit of Twelve Canadian Editors to Canadian Forces in Great Britian, August 20th to October 3rd, 1942, as Written for the Weekly Press of Canada.* Granby, P.Q.: printed by Granby Leader-Mail, n.d. 91 pp.

LeMaistre, Susan, ed./éd. *Memorials to Canada's War Dead./Mémoriaux aux Canadiens morts à la guerre.* Ottawa: Veterans Affairs Canada/Anciens combattants Canada, [198-?]. 135 pp.
Bilingual text./Texte bilingue.

Lévesque, Thérèse. *Laisse-moi te dire ...; la guerre 1939/45 après 50 ans.* Saint-Quentin, N.-B.: Imprimerie Lévesque, 1990. 171 pp.

Lindsay, Oliver. *At the Going Down of the Sun; Hong Kong and South-East Asia, 1941-1945.* London: H. Hamilton, 1981. 258 pp.

_____. *The Lasting Honour; the Fall of Hong Kong, 1941.* London: H. Hamilton, 1978. 226 pp.

Little Black Devils see Tascona, Bruce, and Eric Wells.

[Lockwood, A.M., comp.] *History of the 7th Canadian Medium Regiment, R.C.A.; from 1st September, 1939 to 8th June, 1945.* n.p.: n.d. 111 pp.

Londerville, J.D. *The Pay Services of the Canadian Army Overseas in the War of 1939-45.* Ottawa: privately printed, 1950. 315 pp.

The Lorne Scots (Peel, Dufferin and Halton Regiment). Brampton, Ont.: privately printed, 1962. 47 pp.

The Loyal Edmonton Regiment Memorial Booklet Including the Memorial Service, a Short History of the Regiment, the Roll of Honour. Nijkerk, Neth.: privately printed, 1945. 38 pp.

Lucas, James S., and James Barker. *The Killing Ground; the Battle of the Falaise Gap, August 1944.* London: Batsford, 1978. 176 pp.

Luxton, E.C. *1st Battalion, the Regina Rifle Regiment, 1939-1946.* n.p.: n.d. 70 pp.

Lyman, Tom. *5 LAA W/S RCEME; Unit History, 1943-1945.* n.p.: 1945. 1 vol., unpaged.

*McAndrew, William J., Bill Rawling and Michael Whitby. *Liberation; the Canadians in Europe.* Montreal: Art Global, 1995. 170 pp.

*McAndrew, William J., Bill Rawling et Michael Whitby. *La Libération; les Canadiens en Europe.* Montréal: Art Global, 1995. 170 pp.

*McAndrew, William J., Donald E. Graves and Michael Whitby. *Normandy 1944; the Canadian Summer.* Montreal: Art Global, 1994. 162 pp.

*McAndrew, William J., Donald E. Graves et Michael Whitby. *Normandie 1944; l'été canadien.* Montréal: Art Global, 1994. 162 pp.

McAvity, J.M. *Lord Strathcona's Horse (Royal Canadians); a Record of Achievement.* Toronto: n.p., 1947. 280 pp.

Macbeth, John Douglas. *Somewhere in England; War Letters of a Canadian Officer on Overseas Service.* (Macmillan War Pamphlets; Canadian Series, no. 4.) Toronto: Macmillan, 1941. 32 pp.

Macdonald, B.J.S. *The Trial of Kurt Meyer.* Toronto: Clarke, Irwin, 1954. 216 pp.

Macdonald, Grant. *Our Canadian Armed Services*, sketches by Grant Macdonald. Montreal: Gazette, 1943. 1 vol., chiefly illus.

Macdougall, G.L. *A Short History of the 29 Cdn Armd Recce Regt (South Alberta Regiment).* Amsterdam: Spin's Pub. Co., [1945?]. 87 pp.

McGill Univ., Montreal, P.Q. *A Memorial Service for the McGill Men and Women who Gave their Lives during the First and Second World Wars.* n.p.: [1946]. 1 vol., unpaged.

McGregor, F., ed. *LdSH (RC) '85-70'.* Winnipeg: privately printed, 1970. 62 pp.

McKee, Alexander. *Caen, Anvil of Victory.* London: Souvenir Press, 1964. 368 pp.

Mackenzie-Naughton, J.D. *The Princess of Wales' Own Regiment (M.G.).* Kingston, Ont.: privately printed, 1946. 74 pp.

McKillican, D.R. *A Short History of the Toronto Scottish Regiment.* n.p.: 1972. 40 pp.

McMahon, J.S. *Professional Soldier; a Memoir of General Guy Simonds, CB, CBE, DSO, CD.* Winnipeg: McMahon Investments, 1985. 87 pp.

MacLaren, Roy. *Canadians behind Enemy Lines, 1939-1945.* Vancouver: Univ. of British Columbia Press, 1981. 330 pp.

_____. *Canadians in Russia, 1918-1919.* Toronto: Macmillan, 1976. 301 pp.

McNeil, Bill. *Voices of a War Remembered; an Oral History of Canadians in World War Two.* Toronto: Doubleday Canada, 1991. 376 pp.

Madsen, C.M.V., and R.J. Henderson. *German Prisoners of War in Canada and their Artifacts, 1940-1948.* Regina, Sask.: privately printed, 1993. 203 pp.

Magnacca, Stephen A. *1871-1971; One Hundredth Anniversary of the 13 Field Battery Based at Portage la Prairie, Manitoba.* n.p.: n.d. 12 pp.

Maguire, E. *Dieppe, August 19.* London: Cape, 1963. 205 pp.

Malone, Dick. *Missing from the Record.* Toronto: Collins, 1946. 227 pp.

_____. *A Portrait of War.* Toronto: Collins, 1983-84. 2 vols.

Maltby, R.G. *The Calgary Regiment.* Hilversum, Neth.: privately printed, 1945. 17 pp.

256

Manarey, R. Barrie. *The Canadian Bayonet.* Edmonton: Century Press, 1971. 51 pp.

Mandar, Allin J. *Line Clear for Up Trains; a History of No. 1 Canadian Railway Operating Group, R.C.E., 1943-1945.* Alexandria Bay, N.Y.: Museum Restoration Sevice, 1991. 110 pp.

Mansikka, Eric, comp. *Pack Up your Troubles; Canadian War Humour.* Cartoons by Paul Gomiratto. Toronto: Methuen, 1987. 112 pp.
Second World War humour accompanied by original cartoons.

Marchand, Gérard. *Le Régiment de Maisonneuve vers la victoire, 1944-1945.* Montréal: Les Presses Libres, 1980. 266 pp.

Marcotte, Jean-Marie. *Mektoub! C'était écrit; "les récits du capitaine".* Montréal: Editions Lumen, 1946. 204 pp.

Marquis, G.E. *Le Régiment de Lévis; historique et album.* Lévis, P.Q.: s.i., 1952. 292 pp.

Marteinson, John, [and others]. *We Stand on Guard; an Illustrated History of the Canadian Army.* Montreal: Ovale, 1992. 511 pp.

Martin, Charles Cromwell, and Roy Whitsed. *Battle Diary; from D-Day and Normandy to the Zuider Zee and VE.* Toronto: Dundurn Press, 1994. 191 pp.

Massey, Raymond. *When I was Young.* Toronto: McClelland and Stewart, 1976. 269 pp.
Canadian Field Artillery in France and Siberia.

Maule, Henry. *Caen; the Brutal Battle and Break-Out from Normandy.* Newton Abbot, Eng.: David & Charles, 1976. 176 pp.

Mayne, J.W. *Operational Research in the Canadian Armed Forces during the Second World War.* (Operational Research and Analysis Establishment ORAE Report, no. R68.) Ottawa: Dept. of National Defence, 1978. 2 vols.

Mazéas, Daniel. *Croquis d'insignes armée canadienne, 1920-1950; Canadian Badges.* Guingamp, France; privately printed, 1970. 64 pp.

_____. *Insignes armée canadienne, 1900-1914; Canadian Badges; supplément, 1920-1950.* Guingamp, France: privately printed, 1972. 116 pp.

Meanwell, R.W. *1 Battalion, the Essex Scottish Regiment (Allied with the Essex Regiment), 1939-1945; a Brief Narrative.* Aldershot, Eng.: Gale & Polden, 1946. 95 pp.

Melady, John. *Escape from Canada! The Untold Story of German POWs in Canada, 1939-1945.* Toronto: Macmillan, 1981. 210 pp.

257

Mellor, John. *Forgotten Heroes; the Canadians at Dieppe.* Toronto: Methuen, 1975. 163 pp.

*Memorandum sur l'instruction de l'Armée canadienne. No 1-72. Ottawa: Imprimeur du Roi, 1941-47.

Metson, Graham, and Cheryl Lean, comps. *Alex Colville; Diary of a War Artist.* Halifax: Nimbus Pub., 1981. 159 pp.

Middleton, W.E. Knowles. *Radar Development in Canada: the Radio Branch of the National Research Council of Canada, 1939-1946.* Waterloo, Ont.: Wilfrid Laurier Univ. Press, 1981. 147 pp.

The Militia in Durham County ... see Chandler, C.M.

Milnes, Herbert. *A Story of the Oxford Rifles, 1798-1954.* (Oxford Museum Bulletin, no. 5.) Woodstock, Ont.: printed by Woodstock Print & Litho, 1974. 28 pp.

Mimms, John A. *Spam Medal Heroes.* Barrie, Ont.: Video Text, 1984. 154 pp. *1st Canadian Anti-Tank Regiment.*

Mitchell, G.D., with B.A. Reid and W. Simcock. *RCHA — Right of the Line; an Anecdotal History of the Royal Canadian Horse Artillery from 1871.* Ottawa: RCHA History Committee, 1986. 303 pp.

Mitchell, Howard. *"My War"; with the Saskatoon Light Infantry (M.G.), 1939-1945.* n.p.: privately printed, n.d. 129 pp.

Mitchell, Michael, comp. *Ducimus; the Regiments of the Canadian Infantry.* St. Hubert, Que.: Director of Infantry, Mobile Command Headquarters, 1992. 248 pp.

Mitchell, Steve. *They were Invincible; Dieppe and After.* Bracebridge, Ont.: Herald-Gazette, 1976. 132 pp.

Miville-Deschênes, Charles. *Souvenirs de guerre.* Québec, P.Q.: s.i., 1946. 128 pp.

Mobilization & Creation of the 1st Canadian Overseas Corps, 1939-1942./La mobilisation & la création du Ier Corps canadien outre-mer, 1939-1942. Ottawa: National Defence Department/Ministère de la Défense nationale, 1995. 36 pp.
Bilingual text./Texte bilingue.

Moir, J.S., ed. *History of the Royal Canadian Corps of Signals, 1903-1961.* Ottawa: privately printed, 1962. 336 pp.

Moogk, Peter N., and R.V. Stevenson. *Vancouver Defended; a History of the Men and Guns of the Lower Mainland Defences, 1859-1949.* Surrey, B.C.: Antonson Pub., 1978. 128 pp.

Mordal, Jacques, [*pseud.*] *see/voir* Cras, Hervé.

Morris, David A. *The Canadian Militia; from 1855; an Historical Summary.* Erin, Ont.: Boston Mills Press, 1983. 328 pp.

Morrison, W. Alexander and Ted Slaney. *The Breed of Manly Men; the History of the Cape Breton Highlanders.* Toronto: Canadian Institute of Strategic Studies and The Cape Breton Highlanders Association, 1994. 410 pp.

Morrison, William R., and Kenneth A. Coates. *Working the North; Labor and the Northwest Defense Projects 1942-1946.* n.p.: Univ. of Alaska Press, 1994. [271] pp.

Morton, Desmond. *The Canadian General, Sir William Otter.* (Canadian War Museum Historical Publication Number 9.) Toronto: Hakkert, 1974. 423 pp.

Moulton, J.L. *Battle for Antwerp; the Liberation of the City and the Opening of the Scheldt 1944.* London: I. Allan, 1978. 208 pp.

Mowat, Farley. *And No Birds Sang.* Toronto: McClelland and Stewart, 1979. 250 pp.

_____. *My Father's Son; Memories of War and Peace.* Toronto: Key Porter Books, 1992. 340 pp.

_____. *The Regiment.* Toronto: McClelland and Stewart, 1955. 312 pp. *The Hastings and Prince Edward Regiment in the Second World War.*

Munro, Ross. *Gauntlet to Overlord; the Story of the Canadian Army.* Toronto: Macmillan, 1946. 477 pp.

_____. *Red Patch in Sicily; the Story of the 1st Canadian Division in Action; Dispatches by Ross Munro.* Toronto: Canadian Press, 1943. 13 pp.

Murphy, Tony, and Paul Kenney. *The War at our Doorstep; St. John's during World War Two, an Album.* St. John's, Nfld.: H. Cuff Publications, 1989. 120 pp.

Murray, Joan. *Canadian Artists of the Second World War.* Oshawa, Ont.: Robert McLaughlin Gallery, 1981. 124 pp.

N.R.E.F. 16th Brigade C.F.A., 67th and 68th Batteries in North Russia, September 1918 to June 1919. n.p.: n.d. 55 pp.

Nicholson, G.W.L. *Canada's Nursing Sisters.* (Canadian War Museum Historical Publication Number 13.) Toronto: S. Stevens, Hakkert, 1975. 272 pp.

*_____. *The Canadians in Italy, 1943-1945.* (Official History of the Canadian Army in the Second World War, vol. II.) Ottawa: Queen's Printer, 1956. 807 pp.

*_____. *Les Canadiens en Italie, 1943-1945.* (Histoire officielle de la participation de l'Armée canadienne dans la Seconde Guerre mondiale, vol II.) Ottawa: Imprimeur de la Reine, 1960. 851 pp.

Nicholson, G.W.L. *The Gunners of Canada; the History of the Royal Regiment of Canadian Artillery.* Toronto: McClelland and Stewart, 1967-72. 2 vols.

_____. *More Fighting Newfoundlanders; a History of Newfoundland's Fighting Forces in the Second World War.* [St. John's, Nfld.]: Govt. of Nfld., 1969. 621 pp.

*_____. *"Nous nous souviendrons ...";* mémoriaux outre-mer aux morts de guerre du Canada.* Ottawa: Imprimeur de la Reine, 1973. 118 pp.

_____. *Seventy Years of Service; a History of the Royal Canadian Army Medical Corps.* Ottawa: Borealis Press, 1977. 388 pp.

*_____. *"We Will Remember ..."; Overseas Memorials to Canada's War Dead.* Ottawa: Queen's Printer, 1973. 110 pp.

Nicholson, L.H. *Battle-Dress Patrol; No. 1 Provost Company (R.C.M.P.), 1939-1945.* Ottawa: Access to History Publications, 1992. 56 pp.
Reprinted from R.C.M.P. Quarterly, XLVII(1946-47).

Nieuwenhuys, Jan. *"Daàg"; the Canadian Army in Holland.* Amsterdam: De La Mar Publicity, 1945. 1 vol., chiefly illus.
Cartoons.

Noblston, Allen. *5 Canadian Light Anti-Aircraft Regiment; Regimental History; World War II (1 March 1941 — 8 May 1945).* Groningen, Neth.: privately printed, 1945. 64 pp.

Nolan, Brian. *Airborne; the Heroic Story of the 1st Canadian Parachute Battalion in the Second World War.* Toronto: Lester Pub., 1995. 227 pp.

*Nord, Max, comp. *Merci Canada.* Afdeling, Neth.: Stichting Wereldtentoonstelling, 1967. 192 pp.

*_____. *Thank You, Canada.* Afdeling, Neth.: Stichting Wereldtentoonstelling, 1967. 192 pp.

Nova Scotia. *Nova Scotia Helps the Fighting Man.* n.p.: [1942]. 32 pp.

Officers' Directory 1st Cdn Armd Bde., Holland, June 7, 1945. n.p.: 1945. 25 1.

Ogle, Robert J. *The Faculties of Canadian Military Chaplains; a Commentary on the Faculty Sheet of December, 1955 and the Directives for Holy Week Promulgated March 14, 1956.* Ottawa: n.p., 1956. 267 pp.

Oldfield, J.E. *The Westminsters' War Diary; an Unofficial History of the Westminster Regiment (Motor) in World War II.* New Westminster, B.C.: privately printed, 1964. 209 pp.

Once in the Queen's Own, Always in the Queen's Own. n.p.: privately printed, 1932. 70 pp.

Ortona; medaglia d'oro al valor civile, settembre 1943 — giugno 1944. Roma: Ristampa, 1960. 249 pp.

Osler, John G. *2nd Canadian Medium Regiment, R.C.A.; Regimental History, 18 January 1942 — 30 June 1945.* Deventer, Neth.: privately printed, 1945. 119 pp.

Pallas, S.M., comp. *Canadian Recipients of the Colonial Auxiliary Forces Officers' Decoration and the Colonial Auxiliary Forces Long Service Medal.* Ottawa: printed by Tri-Graphic Print., 1990. 183 pp.

Parrot, D.F. *Princess Patricia's Regiment, 1939-1941.* n.p.: privately printed, [1990]. 60 pp.
Personal memoir.

Paterson, R.A. *A History of the 10th Canadian Infantry Brigade.* n.p.: privately printed, 1945. 78 pp.

Patterson, Tom. *They Never Rationed Courage; Letters Home from the War, 1940-1945.* Stratford, Ont.: Mercury Press, 1995. 236 pp.
Memoirs of the Canadian Dental Corps in England and North West Europe.

Pavey, Walter G. *An Historical Account of the 7th Canadian Reconnaissance Regiment (17th Duke of York's Royal Canadian Hussars) in the World War, 1939-1945.* Montreal: privately printed, [1948]. 139 pp.

Pearce, Donald. *Journal of a War, North-West Europe, 1944-1945.* Toronto: Macmillan, 1965. 188 pp.

Pellatt, Reginald. *A Guide to Riflemen of the Queen's Own Rifles of Canada.* Toronto: privately printed, 1924. 40 pp.

————. *Standing Orders of the Queen's Own Rifles of Canada.* [Toronto: n.p., 1925.] 77 pp.

Penny, Arthur G. *Royal Rifles of Canada, "Able and Willing" since 1862; a Short History.* n.p.: 1962. 62 pp.

Pepin, J.C. *Mes cinq ans à la Légion; histoire véridique vécue par l'auteur lui-même.* Beauceville, P.Q.: L'Eclaireur, 1932. 150 pp.

Peppard, Herb. *The Light Hearted Soldier; a Canadian's Exploits with the Black Devils in WW II.* Halifax: Nimbus Pub., 1994. 196 pp.
1st Special Service Force.

Phillips, Norman, and J. Nikerk. *Holland and the Canadians.* Amsterdam: Contact Pub., 1945. 72 pp.

A Pictorial Review of Military District No. 10, 1939-1940. Winnipeg: Winnipeg Saturday Post, [1940?]. 100 pp., chiefly illus.

Pierson, Ruth Roach. *"They're Still Women after All": the Second World War and Canadian Womanhood.* (The Canadian Social History Series.) Toronto: McClelland and Stewart, 1986. 301 pp.

Pipet, Albert. *Mourir à Caen.* Paris: Presses de la Cité, 1974. 249 pp.

"Pooch" [*pseud.*] *see* Corrigan, Cecil Edwin.

Pope, Maurice A. *Soldiers and Politicians; the Memoirs of Lt.-Gen. Maurice A. Pope, C.B., M.C.* Toronto: Univ. of Toronto Press, 1962. 462 pp.

Poulin, J.G. *696 heures d'enfer avec le Royal 22e Régiment; récit vécu et inspiré d'un journal tenu tant bien que mal au front.* Montréal: Beauchemin, 1946. 181 pp.

Pouliot, Henri. *Légionnaire! Histoire véridique et vécue d'un Québecois simple soldat à la Légion étrangère.* Québec, P.Q.: Imprimerie le "Soleil", 1931. 300 pp.

Powley, A.E. *Broadcast from the Front; Canadian Radio Overseas in the Second World War.* (Canadian War Museum Historical Publication Number 11.) Toronto: Hakkert, 1975. 189 pp.

Presentation of Colours by His Excellency the Earl of Bessborough; the 1st (13th) and 2nd (42nd) Battalions, the Black Watch (Royal Highlanders) of Canada; at the McGill Stadium, Montreal, May 28th, 1931; Programme of Ceremonies. n.p.: n.d. 18 pp.

Presentation of Colours to 1st Battalion, the Royal Regiment of Canada and the South Saskatchewan Regiment, by His Majesty the King, at Witley, Surrey, England, 16th July, 1943. Aldershot, Eng.: privately printed, [1943]. 1 vol., chiefly illus.

Presentation of Colours to the Carleton & York Regiment and the Edmonton Regiment by His Majesty the King at Caterham, Surrey, England, Dominion Day, 1st July, 1941. Aldershot, Eng.: privately printed, [1941]. 1 vol., chiefly illus.

Presentation of Colours to the First Battalion the Saskatoon Light Infantry by Her Majesty the Queen, at Caterham, Surrey, England, 24th October, 1941. Aldershot, Eng.: privately printed, [1941]. 1 vol., unpaged.

Presentation of Colours to the Toronto Scottish Regiment (M.G.) by Her Majesty the Queen, Colonel-in-Chief; the Toronto Scottish Regiment (M.G.), Monday, May 22nd, 1939, in the Forenoon on the Grounds of the University of Toronto. [n.p.: 1939. 18 pp.]

Preston, Richard A. *Canada's RMC; a History of the Royal Military College.* Toronto: Univ. of Toronto Press, 1969. 415 pp.

Princess Patricia's Canadian Light Infantry Recruit's Book. [Winnipeg: n.p., 1946.] 24 pp.

Programme-souvenir; le Régiment de Hull, mai 1964; publication autorisée par le Lt-Col. Guy de Marlis, C.D., Commandant, le Régiment de Hull; programme-souvenir publié pour marquer le 50e anniversaire du Régiment de Hull et le 25e anniversaire du Manège de Salaberry. Hull, P.Q.: imprimé privé, [1964]. 60 pp.

Programme-souvenir; ouverture officielle du Manège de Salaberry par Son Excellence Lord Tweedsmuir, Gouverneur général, samedi, le 28 janvier, 1939./Program-Souvenir; Official Opening of the Manège de Salaberry by His Excellency Lord Tweedsmuir, Governor-General, Saturday, January 28, 1939. s.l.: s.i., s.d./n.p.: n.d. 1 tome, non paginé./1 vol., unpaged.
Texte bilingue./Bilingual text. Titre en couverture/Cover title: Le Régiment de Hull.

Proulx, Benjamin A. *Underground from Hongkong.* New York: Dutton, 1943. 214 pp.

Prouse, A. Robert. *Ticket to Hell via Dieppe; from a Prisoner's Wartime Log 1942-1945.* Toronto: Van Nostrand Reinhold, 1982. 192 pp.

Queen-Hughes, R.W. *Whatever Men Dare; a History of the Queen's Own Cameron Highlanders of Canada, 1935-1960.* Winnipeg: privately printed, 1960. 247 pp.

Queen's Own Rifles of Canada Association. *A Brief Resumé of the Activities of the Queen's Own Rifles of Canada Association, 1914-1932.* Toronto: privately printed, 1932. 70 pp.

————. *Yearbook.* [Toronto: n.p.], 1923-47. 18 vols.
Not issued 1939-44, 1946.

Quigley, John Gordon. *A Century of Rifles, 1860-1960; the Halifax Rifles (RCAC)(M); "cede nullis".* Halifax: privately printed, 1960. 230 pp.

RCCS; Second Canadian Armoured Brigade Signals. n.p.: n.d. 40 pp.

Raddall, Thomas H. *West Novas; a History of the West Nova Scotia Regiment.* Toronto: privately printed, 1947. 326 pp.

The Rally Magazine. Vol. I-? Wrecclesham, Eng.: n.p., 1939?-?
A monthly magazine for Canadian Active Service Forces.

Ralston, J.L. *A Call for Men for the Army; an Address by Honourable J.L. Ralston, Minister of National Defence, Delivered over a National Network of Canadian Radio Stations 11th May, 1941.* Ottawa: King's Printer, 1941. 10 pp.

The Ranger. Vol. I-V. Vancouver: privately printed, 1942-45.
Journal of the Pacific Coast Militia Rangers.

Rannie, William F., ed. *To the Thunderer his Arms; The Royal Canadian Ordnance Corps*. Lincoln, Ont.: privately printed, 1984. 360 pp.

Rawling, Bill. *Hell and High Water; Battles for the Rhineland, 1945*. (Canadian Battle Series, no. 14.) Toronto: Canadian War Museum; Balmuir Books, 1995. 34 pp.

Reader's Digest. *The Canadians at War, 1939/45*. Montreal: Reader's Digest, 1969. 2 vols.

_____. *The Tools of War, 1939/45, and a Chronology of Important Events*. Montreal: Reader's Digest, 1969. 96 pp.

Redman, Stanley R. *Open Gangway; the (Real) Story of the Halifax Navy Riot*. Hantsport, N.S.: Lancelot Press, 1981. 167 pp.

Regimental History, 85 Cdn Bridge Coy, June, 1941 — May, 1945. [Zwolle, Neth.: n.p., 1945.] 82 pp.

The Regimental History of the Governor General's Foot Guards see Baylay, George Taylor.

Regimental Standing Orders of the Royal Canadian Army Service Corps, 1925. Ottawa: King's Printer, 1925. 162 pp.

Regulations for the Canadian Army Veterinary Service, 1923. Ottawa: King's Printer, 1923. 60 pp.

Reyburn, Wallace. *Glorious Chapters; the Canadians at Dieppe*. Toronto: Oxford Univ. Press, 1943. 165 pp.
London ed. titled: Rehearsal for Invasion.

_____. *Some of It was Fun*. Peter Whalley, illus. Toronto: T. Nelson, 1949. 199 pp.

Reynolds, Quentin. *Dress Rehearsal; the Story of Dieppe*. New York: London House, 1943. 278 pp.

Rioux, Denise. *Les Fusiliers de Sherbrooke (1910-1980)*. Sherbrooke, P.Q.: s.i., 1980. 68 pp.

Roberts, James Alan. *The Canadian Summer; the Memoirs of James Alan Roberts*. Toronto: Univ. of Toronto Bookroom, 1981. 253 pp.
Commanded 12th Manitoba Dragoons and 8th Canadian Infantry Brigade in North West Europe, 1944-45.

Robertson, F.A. *5th (B.C.) Regiment, Canadian Garrison Artillery, and Early Defences of B.C. Coast; Historical Record*. Victoria, B.C.: privately printed, 1925. 2 vols.

Robertson, Heather, [comp.] *A Terrible Beauty; the Art of Canada at War.* Toronto: J. Lorimer, 1977. 239 pp.

Robertson, Peter. *Irréductible vérité/Relentless Verity/les photographes militaires canadiens depuis 1885/Canadian Military Photographers since 1885.* (Les Archives publiques du Canada/Public Archives of Canada Series.) Québec, P.Q.: Les Presses de l'Université Laval, 1973. 233 pp.
Texte bilingue./Bilingual text.

*Robertson, Terence. *Dieppe; journée de honte, journée de gloire.* R. Jouan, tr. Paris: Presses de la Cité, 1963. 379 pp.

*_____. *The Shame and the Glory; Dieppe.* Toronto: McClelland and Stewart, 1962. 432 pp.

Rocky Mountain Rangers; First Battalion C.A. — A.F., 1885-1941. New Westminster, B.C.: Columbian Co., 1941. 60 pp., chiefly illus.

Roe, Kathleen Robson. *War Letters from the C.W.A.C. (Canadian Women's Army Corp [sic]).* Toronto: Kakabeka Pub. Co., 1976. 169 pp.

Rogers, R.L. *History of the Lincoln and Welland Regiment.* n.p.: privately printed, 1954. 465 pp.

Rollifson, M.O. *Green Route Up; Fourth Canadian Armoured Division.* The Hague, Neth.: Mouton, 1945. 119 pp.

Roodman, H.S., and P.A. Rylaarsdom, eds. *To Honour the Memory of Those who Fell in World War II —.— Queen's Own Cameron Highlanders of Canada.* Amersfoort, Neth.: Nieuborg Print. Plant, 1945. 1 vol., unpaged.

Ross, Alexander M. *Slow March to a Regiment.* (Armchair General Series.) St. Catharines, Ont.: Vanwell Pub., 1993. 235 pp.
17th Field Regiment, Royal Canadian Artillery.

Ross, Armand et Michel Gauvin. *Le geste du Régiment de la Chaudière.* B.J. Van Der Velde, ed. Rotterdam: imprimé privé, 1945. 179 pp.

Ross, Richard M. *The History of the 1st Battalion Cameron Highlanders of Ottawa (M.G.).* Ottawa: privately printed, 1946. 96 pp.

Rowland, Barry D., [ed.] *Herbie and Friends; Cartoons in Wartime.* Toronto: Natural Heritage/Natural History, 1990. 103 pp.

Rowland, Barry D., and J. Douglas MacFarlane. *The Maple Leaf Forever; the Story of Canada's Foremost Armed Forces Newspaper.* Toronto: Natural Heritage/Natural History, 1987. 160 pp.

Rowland, David Parsons. *The Padre.* [Edited by] Barry D. Rowland. Scarborough, Ont.; Amethyst, 1982. 172 pp.
Padre to Irish Regiment of Canada.

Roy, Patricia E., and others. *Mutual Hostages; Canadians and Japanese during the Second World War.* Toronto: Univ. of Toronto Press, 1990. 281 pp.

*Roy, R.H. *Débarquement et offensive des Canadiens en Normandie.* Traduit par Roland Marquis. (Musée canadien de la guerre publication d'histoire militaire no 19.) Saint-Laurent, Qué.: Editions du Trécarré en collaboration avec le Musée canadien des civilisations, 1986. 471 pp.

_____. *For Most Conspicuous Bravery; a Biography of Major-General George R. Pearkes, V.C., through Two World Wars.* Vancouver: Univ. of British Columbia Press. 1977. 388 pp.

*_____. *1944; the Canadians in Normandy.* (Canadian War Museum Historical Publication no. 19.) n.p.: Macmillan, 1984. 359 pp.

_____. *Ready for the Fray (Deas Gu Cath); the History of the Canadian Scottish Regiment (Princess Mary's), 1920-1955.* Vancouver: privately printed, 1958. 509 pp.

_____. *The Seaforth Highlanders of Canada, 1919-1965.* Vancouver: privately printed, 1969. 559 pp.

_____. *Sherwood Lett; his Life and Times.* Vancouver: UBC Alumni Association, Univ. of British Columbia, 1991. 180 pp.

_____. *Sinews of Steel; the History of the British Columbia Dragoons.* Brampton, Ont.: privately printed, 1965. 468 pp.

**The Royal Canadian Armoured Corps.* Ottawa: Queen's Printer, 1953. 11 pp.

**The Royal Canadian Army Medical Corps.* Ottawa: Queen's Printer, 1953. 10 pp.

**Royal Canadian Army Pay Corps.* Ottawa: Queen's Printer, 1953. 11 pp.

**The Royal Canadian Army Service Corps.* Ottawa: Queen's Printer, 1953. 11 pp.

The Royal Canadian Artillery. Ottawa: Queen's Printer, 1953. 10 pp.

Royal Cdn. Artillery; History of the 4th Cdn. Anti-Tank Battery, June 1940 — July 1945. n.p.: [1945]. 60 pp.

Royal Canadian Dragoons, 1939-1945. Montreal: privately printed, 1946. 233 pp.

Royal Canadian Horse Artillery; First Regiment, 1871-1971. Lahr, Germany: privately printed, [1971]. 32 pp.

The Royal Canadian Ordnance Corps Diamond Jubilee Yearbook. n.p.: 1963. 106 pp.

Royal Military College of Canada, Kingston, Ont. *Regulations and Calendar of the Royal Military College of Canada, 1922.* Ottawa: King's Printer, 1923. 68 pp.

Royal Military College of Canada, Kingston, Ont. *Standing Orders, Amended to January, 1924*. Ottawa: King's Printer, 1924. 120 pp.

_____. *Standing Orders, Amended to January, l926*. Ottawa: King's Printer, 1926. 105 pp.

_____. *Standing Orders; the Royal Military College of Canada, 1938*. Ottawa: King's Printer, 1938. 67 pp.

The Royal Military College of Canada Review. Vol. I- . Kingston, Ont.: privately printed, 1920- .

The Royal Rifles of Canada, Allied with the King's Rifle Corps, 1862-1937; Ypres 1915, Festubert, Mont Sorrel, Somme 1916, Arras 1917, Hill 70, Ypres 1917, Amiens; South Africa 1899-1900; Great War 1914-1918. n.p.: [1937]. 21 pp.

Le Royal 22e Régiment Armée active du Canada, Londres, du 17 au 21 avril mil neuf cent quarante. Aldershot, Angleterre: imprimé privé, 1940. [20] pp.

The Royal Westminster Regiment, 1863-1988. New Westminster, B.C.: n.p., 1988. 72 pp.

Rudbach, N.E. *The Halifax Rifles (23 Armoured Regiment) R.C.A.C.R.F.; "90th" Anniversary, 14th May 1860 — 14th May 1950*. Halifax: n.p., 1950. 20 pp.

Rudler, Raymond. *Le jubilé des Canadiens*. Paris: Presses de la Cité, 1972. 309 pp.

Ruffee, G.E.M., and J.B. Dickie. *The History of the 14th Field Regiment, Royal Canadian Artillery, 1940-1945*. Amsterdam: Wereldbibliotheek N.V., 1945. 61 pp.

Rutherford, T.H., comp. *Honour Roll; Royal Canadian Armoured Corps; World War II*. Oromocto, N.B.: privately printed, 1972. 1 vol., unpaged.

Rutherford, Tom. *An Unofficial History of the Grey and Simcoe Foresters Regiment, 1866-1973*. n.p.: n.d. 88 pp.

Sabourin, J. Armand. *This was Dieppe*. n.p.: National War Finance Committee of the Province of Quebec, n.d. 1 vol., unpaged.

Saint-Pierre, Marjolaine. *Léo Gariépy; un héros récupéré; célébré en France, ignoré ici; biographie*. Varennes (Qué.): Les Editions de Varennes, 1993. 147 pp.

Sallans, G.H. *With Canada's Fighting Men*. Ottawa: King's Printer, 1941. 46 pp.

The Salute; Official Organ of the 103rd C.A.(B)T.C., Fort Garry, Manitoba. Vol. I-III. n.p.: privately printed, 1942-45.

Sanderson, Robert Miles, and Marie Sanderson. *Letters from a Soldier; the Wartime Experiences of a Candian Infantryman, 1943-1945.* Waterloo, Ont.: Escart Press, 1993. 213 pp.
Edited letters and journal of Coporal Robert Miles Sanderson, Essex Scottish Regiment.

Savage, J.M. *The History of the 5th Canadian Anti-Tank Regiment, 10 Sept. 1941 — 10 June 1945.* John P. Claxton, ed. Lochem, Neth.: privately printed, [1945]. 83 pp.

*Savard, Adjutor. *The Defence of Our Land.* n.p.: 1943. 12 pp.

*_____. *La défense du territoire.* s.l.: s.i., 1943. 11 pp.

Schmidt, John. *"This was no ⊕YXNH Picnic!" 2.4 Years of Wild and Woolly Mayhem in Dawson Creek.* Hanna, Alta.: Gorman & Gorman, 1991. 355 pp.
Building the Alaska Highway.

Schragg, Lex. *History of the Ontario Regiment, 1866-1951.* Oshawa, Ont.: privately printed, 1951. 286 pp.

Scislowski, Stanley. *Return to Italy, 1975; a Modern-Day Pilgrimage.* n.p.: [1977]. 73 pp.

Sealey, D. Bruce, and Peter Van de Vyvere. *Thomas George Prince.* (Manitobans in Profile.) Winnipeg: Peguis Publishers, 1981. 52 pp.

The Sentry. Vol. I-? Camp Sussex, N.B.: n.p., 1941-?
Published semi-monthly under sponsorship of Y.M.C.A.

The Sentry. Vol. I-? Ottawa: privately printed, 1940?-?
Journal of District Depot, Military District No. 3.

Service, G.T., and J.K. Marteinson. *The Gate; a History of the Fort Garry Horse.* Calgary: privately printed, 1971. 228 pp.

Le Service Jociste du Soldat. *Nos Canadiens en service.* Montréal: Les Editions Ouvrières, 1943-44. 3 vols.

Sévigny, Pierre. *Face à l'ennemi.* Montréal: Beauchemin, 1946. 167 pp.

Sexton, Donal J. *A Guide to Canadian Shoulder Titles, 1939-1985; a Collector's and Historian's Comprehensive Guide to the Cloth Shoulder Titles Worn by the Regiments and Corps of the Canadian Army in 1939-1985.* Hinsdale, Ill.: Pass in Review Publications, 1987. 97 pp.

Shapiro, L.S.B. *They Left the Back Door Open; a Chronicle of the Allied Campaign in Sicily and Italy.* Toronto: Ryerson Press, 1944. 191 pp.

Shea, A.A., and E. Estoriak. *Canada and the Short-Wave War.* (Behind the Headlines, vol. III.) Toronto: Canadian Institute of International Affairs, 1942. 36 pp.

A Short History of the British Columbia Regiment; the "Dukes". n.p.: n.d. [11] pp.

The Signalman. Vol. I-IV? Kingston, Ont.: King's Printer, 1942-46?

Simonds, Peter. *Maple Leaf Up Maple Leaf Down; the Story of the Canadians in the Second World War.* New York: Island Press, 1946. 356 pp.

Sinclair, J.D., comp. *The Queen's Own Cameron Highlanders of Canada; Twenty-Fifth Anniversary Souvenir.* Winnipeg: privately printed, 1935. 99 pp.

Singer, Burrell M., and R.J.S. Langford. *Handbook of Canadian Military Law.* Toronto: Copp Clark, 1941. 272 pp.

Sirois, Georges. *Centre d'instruction (élémentaire) no 71 d'Edmunston.* (Revue de la Société historique du Madawaska, vol XX, nos 1-2-3.) Edmunston, N.-B.: Société historique du Madawaska, 1993. 88 pp.

Six Years and a Day; the Story of the Beaver Club, 1940-1946. London: n.p., n.d. 34 pp.

Skuce, J.E. *CSEF; Canada's Soldiers in Siberia, 1918-1919.* Ottawa: Access to History Publications, 1990. 148 pp.

Slinger, J.E., and D. McNichol. *History of the 11th Canadian Armoured Regiment (the Ontario Regiment) in the Field, 1939-1945.* Harlingen, Neth.: Flevo Press, 1945. 44 pp.

Smith, Doug. *Bless 'em All.* Vancouver: privately printed, 1967. 152 pp.

————. *Memoirs of an Old Sweat.* Vancouver: privately printed, 1961. 154 pp.

Smith, John Owen. *All Tanked Up ...; the Canadians in Headley during World War II; Compiled from the Memories of Villagers and Veterans.* Headley Down, Eng.: privately printed, 1994. [35] pp.

Smith, Kenneth B. *"Duffy's Regiment".* Don Mills, Ont.: printed by T.H. Best Print Co., 1983. 222 pp.
Angus Duffy and the Hastings and Prince Edward Regiment.

[Smith, Lawrence N.] *The History of the 23rd Field Regiment (SP) R.C.A., World War II.* St. Catharines, Ont.: privately printed, n.d. 81 pp.

Smith, Waldo E.L. *What Time the Tempest; an Army Chaplain's Story.* Toronto: Ryerson Press, 1953. 305 pp.

Smith, Wilfred I. *Code Word CANLOAN.* Toronto: Dundurn Press, 1992. 346 pp.
Loan of Canadian officers to British Army.

Snowie, J. Allan, *Bloody Buron; the Battle of Buron, Normandy — 08 July 1944.* Erin, Ont.: The Boston Mills Press, 1984. 120 pp.
Highland Light Infantry of Canada.

South Saskatchewan Regiment; Welcome Home, Weyburn, November 1945. Estevan, Sask.: Mercury Print, n.d. 12 pp.

*Speaight, Robert. *Georges P. Vanier; soldat, diplomate et gouverneur-général.* (Vies canadiennes.) Montréal: Fides, 1972. 530 pp.

*_____. *Vanier; Soldier, Diplomat and Governor General.* Toronto: Collins, 1970. 488 pp.

Spencer, R.A. *History of the Fifteenth Canadian Field Regiment; Royal Canadian Artillery, 1941 to 1945.* Amsterdam: Elsevier, 1945. 302 pp.

Spittael, George E. *Libera me.* Eeklo, Belgium: Drukkerij Pauwels, 1988. 446 pp. *Liberation of Belgium by 1st Canadian Army in 1944./Libération de la Belgique par 1re Armée canadienne au 1944.*

The Springbok. Various places: n.p., 1923- . *Regimental journal of the Royal Canadian Dragoons. Title varies:* The Goat *(1923-36).*

*Stacey, C.P. *L'Armée canadienne, 1939-1945; résumé historique officiel.* Ottawa: Imprimeur du Roi, 1949. 364 pp.

*_____. *Armes, hommes et gouvernements; les politiques de guerre du Canada, 1939-1945.* Ottawa: Imprimeur de la Reine, 1970. 747 pp.

*_____. *Arms, Men and Governments; the War Policies of Canada, 1939-1945.* Ottawa: Queen's Printer, 1970. 681 pp.

*_____. *La campagne de la victoire; les opérations dans le Nord-Ouest de l'Europe, 1944-45.* (Histoire officielle de la participation de l'Armée canadienne à la Seconde Guerre mondiale, vol III.) Ottawa: Imprimeur de la Reine, 1960. 837 pp.

*_____. *Canada's Battle in Normandy; the Canadian Army's Share in the Operations 6 June — 1 September, 1944.* (The Canadian Army at War, no. 3.) Ottawa: King's Printer, 1946. 159 pp.

*_____. *The Canadian Army 1939-1945; an Official Historical Summary.* Ottawa: King's Printer, 1948. 312 pp.

*_____. *Les Canadiens dans la bataille de Normandie; la participation de l'Armée canadienne aux opérations du 6 juin au 1er septembre 1944.* (L'Armée canadienne à la Guerre, no 3.) Ottawa: Imprimeur du Roi, 1946. 159 pp.

_____. *A Date with History; Memoirs of a Canadian Historian.* Ottawa: Deneau, [1982]. 293 pp.

*_____. *Six années de guerre; l'Armée au Canada, en Grande-Bretagne et dans le Pacifique.* (Histoire officielle de la participation de l'Armée canadienne à la Seconde Guerre mondiale, vol I.) Ottawa: Imprimeur de la Reine, 1957. 652 pp.

*Stacey, C.P. *Six Years of War; the Army in Canada, Britain and the Pacific.* (Official History of the Canadian Army in the Second World War, vol. I.) Ottawa: Queen's Printer, 1955. 629 pp.

*_____. *The Victory Campaign; the Operations in North West Europe, 1944-45.* (Official History of the Canadian Army in the Second World War, vol. III.) Ottawa: Queen's Printer, 1960. 770 pp.

Stacey, C.P., and Barbara M. Wilson. *The Half-Million; the Canadians in Britian, 1939-1946.* Toronto: Univ. of Toronto Press, 1987. 198 pp.

Stalmann, Reinhart. *Die Ausbrecherkönige von Kanada.* [Hamburg, Germany]: Sternbücher, 1958. 191 pp.

Standing Orders of Princess Patricia's Canadian Light Infantry. Ottawa: King's Printer, 1920. 42 pp.

Standing Orders of the Royal Canadian Regiment. Ottawa: T. Mulvey, [1920?]. 78 pp.

*Stanley, George F.G. *Canada's Soldiers, 1604-1954; the Military History of an Unmilitary People.* Toronto: Macmillan, 1954. 400 pp.
Subsequent revised and enlarged editions.

_____. *In the Face of Danger; the History of the Lake Superior Regiment.* Port Arthur, Ont.: privately printed, 1960. 357 pp.

*_____. *Nos soldats; l'histoire militaire du Canada de 1604 à nos jours.* Traduction et adaptation sous la direction de Serge Bernier. Montréal: Les Editions de l'homme, 1980. 620 pp.

Stanley, George F.G., and Richard A. Preston. *A Short History of Kingston as a Military and Naval Centre.* Kingston, Ont.: Queen's Printer, [195-?]. 33 pp.

Steele, Harwood. *The Long Ride; a Short History of the 17th Duke of York's Royal Canadian Hussars.* Montreal: Gazette Print. Co., 1934. 48 pp.

Stephens, W. Ray. *The Canadian Entertainers of World War II.* Oakville, Ont.: Mosaic Press, 1993. 116 pp.

_____. *The Harps of War.* Oakville, Ont.: Frederick Harris Music Co., 1985. 271 pp.
Bandsman in Princess Patricia's Canadian Light Infantry. Somewhat fictionalized.

Steven, Walter T. *In this Sign.* Toronto: Ryerson Press, 1948. 182 pp.

Stevens, G.R. *A City Goes to War.* Brampton, Ont.: Charters Pub., 1964. 431 pp.
Loyal Edmonton Regiment.

_____. *The Sun is Setting on the Paleface Brave or Down the Drain a Billion a Year Goes.* Montreal: privately printed, [1968]. 16 pp.

Stewart, Charles Henry, comp. *The Concise Lineages of the Canadian Army, 1855 to Date.* Toronto: n.p., n.d. 163 pp.

Stormont, Dundas and Glengarry Highlanders; a Brief History, 1784-1945; Presented to Members of the First Battalion upon their Return from Overseas. Cornwall, Ont.: n.p., [1945]. 39 pp.

The Story of the 69th Light Anti-Aircraft Battery, R.C.A. Toronto: T.H. Best Print. Co., n.d. 179 pp.

Strachan, Tony ed. *In the Clutch of Circumstance; Reminiscences of Members of the Canadian National Prisoners of War Association.* Victoria, B.C.: Cappis Press, 1985. 285 pp.

The Strathconian. Calgary: n.p., 1914-?, 1927-38, 1947- .
Regimental journal of the Lord Strathcona's Horse (Royal Canadians). Re-numbered from no.1 after each gap in publication.

Street, Brian Jeffrey. *The Parachute Ward; a Canadian Surgeon's Wartime Adventures in Yugoslavia.* Toronto: Lester & Orpen Dennys, 1987. 306 pp. *Major Colin Scott Dafoe.*

Stuart, (Sir) Campbell. *Opportunity Knocks Once.* London: Collins, 1952. 248 pp.

Stubbs, Roy St. George. *Men in Khaki; Four Regiments of Manitoba.* Toronto: Ryerson Press, 1941. 72 pp.

Stursberg, Peter. *Journey into Victory; Up the Alaska Highway and to Sicily and Italy.* London: Harrap, 1944. 160 pp.

————. *The Sound of War; Memoirs of a CBC Correspondent.* Toronto: Univ. of Toronto Press, 1993. 313 pp.

*Summerby, Janice. *Native Soldiers; Foreign Battlefields.* Ottawa: Communications Division, Veterans Affairs Canada, 1993. 47 pp.

*————. *Soldats autochtones; terres étrangères.* Ottawa: Direction générale des communications, Anciens combattants Canada, 1993. 51 pp.

Summers, Jack L. *Tangled Web; Canadian Infantry Accoutrements, 1855-1985.* (Canadian War Museum Historical Publication no. 26.) Alexandria Bay, N.Y.: Museum Restoration Service, 1992. 146 pp.

*Summers, Jack L., and René Chartrand. *Military Uniforms in Canada, 1665-1970.* Illustrated by R.J. Marrion. (Canadian War Museum Historical Publication no. 16.) Ottawa: National Museums of Canada, 1981. 192 pp.

*Summers, Jack L., et René Chartrand. *L'uniforme militaire au Canada, 1665-1970.* Illustré par R.J. Marrion. Traduit par Jean Pariseau. (Musée canadien de la guerre publication d'histoire militaire no 16.) Ottawa: Musées nationaux du Canada, 1981. 192 pp.

Suthren, Victor, ed. *The Oxford Book of Canadian Military Anecdotes.* Toronto: Oxford Univ. Press, 1989. 202 pp.

Swettenham, John. *Allied Intervention in Russia, 1918-1919; and the Part Played by Canada.* Toronto: Ryerson Press, 1967. 315 pp.

_____. *D-Day./Jour-J.* Jacques Gouin, tr. Ottawa: National Museum of Man/Musée national de l'homme, [1970]. 27/30 pp.
Bilingual text./Texte bilingue.

_____. *McNaughton.* Toronto: Ryerson Press, 1968-69. 3 vols.

The Tank, Canada. Vol. I-V. Camp Borden, Ont.: n.p., 1940-45.
Official organ, Canadian Armoured Corps.

Tascona, Bruce. *The Militia of Manitoba; a Study of Infantry and Cavalry Regiments since 1883; a Look at Regimental Badges and Uniforms, List of Commanding Officers, Battle Honours.* n.p.: 1979. 48 pp.

_____. *XII Manitoba Dragoons: a Tribute.* Winnipeg: Manitoba Dragoons History Book Committee, 1991. 185 pp.

[Tascona, Bruce, and Eric Wells.] *Little Black Devils; a History of the Royal Winnipeg Rifles.* Winnipeg: Frye Pub., 1983. 241 pp.

Telford, Murray M. *Scarlet to Green; the Colours, Uniforms and Insignia of the Grey and Simcoe Foresters.* Erin, Ont.: Boston Mills Press, 1987. 64 pp.

Thibault, Jean. *Drummondville à l'heure de la guerre: 1939-1945.* Drummondville (Qué.): La Société d'histoire de Drummondville, 1994. 191 pp.

Thomas, Hartley Munro. *UWO Contingent COTC; the History of the Canadian Officers' Training Corps at the University of Western Ontario.* London, Ont.: Univ. of Western Ontario, 1956. 422 pp.

Thompson, R.W. *Dieppe at Dawn; the Story of the Dieppe Raid.* London: Hutchinson, 1956. 215 pp.
New York ed. titled: At Whatever Cost.

_____. *The Eighty-Five Days; the Story of the Battle of the Scheldt.* London: Hutchinson, 1957. 235 pp.

Thompson, Roy J.C. *Cap Badges of the Canadian Officer Training Corps.* Dartmouth, N.S.: n.p., 1972. 68 pp.

_____. *Wings of the Canadian Armed Forces, 1913-1972.* [Dartmouth], N.S.: n.p., 1973. 106 pp.

Tierney, Ruth. *Petticoat Warfare.* Belleville, Ont.: Mika Pub. Co., 1984. 82 pp.
Memoirs of service in Canada in Canadian Women's Army Corps.

Tompkins, Stuart Ramsay. *A Canadian's Road to Russia; Letters from the Great War Decade.* Doris H. Pieroth, ed. Edmonton: Univ. of Alberta Press, 1989. 466 pp.
Service with the Canadian Expeditionary Force in Europe 1916-1918 and Siberia 1919.

Tooley, Robert. *Invicta; the Carleton and York Regiment in the Second World War.* Fredericton, N.B.: New Ireland Press, 1989. 471 pp.

Toronto Garrison Military Tournament ...; Programme. Toronto: printed by Southam Press, [1926, 1927, 1929, 1934]. 4 vols.

* La Trésorerie militaire royale canadienne. Ottawa: Imprimeur de la Reine, 1954. 12 pp.

A Tribute to Valour. St. Thomas, Ont.: printed by Sutherland Press, 1945. 169 pp.
Memorial book of Dunwich Township and village of Dutton, Ont.

Trinity College School Old Boys at War, 1899-1902, 1914-1918, 1939-1945. Port Hope, Ont.: privately printed, 1948. 245 pp.

Tripp, F.R. *Canada's Army in World War II; Badges and Histories of the Corps and Regiments.* n.p.: n.d. 1 vol., chiefly illus.

Trooping the Colours, Annual Inspection and Ceremony of Hamilton Central Collegiate Institute, Royal Army [sic] Cadet Corps, no. 62; Affiliation with R.H.L.I. (Old 13th Regiment), May 5th, 1944, 8 p.m., The Armouries, Hamilton, Ont., Canada. n.p.: [1944]. 1 vol., unpaged.

True Canadian War Stories, selected by Jane Dewar from the pages of Legion Magazine. Toronto: Lester & Orpen Dennys, 1986. 310 pp.

Turner, T.H. *Mechanics to Mars; the Story of the Canadian Ordnance Corps Training Centre at Barriefield, Ontario.* Barriefield, Ont.: n.p., n.d. 16 pp.

The 23rd Canadian Field Regiment (S.P.) Royal Canadian Artillery; a Compilation of All the Photos Used to Illustrate the Featured Articles of the "S.P." Paper. n.p.: n.d. 72 pp.

Twichell, Heath. *Northwest Epic; the Building of the Alaska Highway.* New York: St. Martin's Press, 1992. 368 pp.

Tyler, G.C.A. *The Lion Rampant; a Pictorial History of the Queen's Own Cameron Highlanders of Canada, 1910-1985.* Winnipeg: The Queen's Own Cameron Highlanders of Canada, 1985. 134 pp.

Ukranian Canadian Veterans; Royal Canadian Legion; Memorial Souvenir Book 1. Montreal: Ukranian Canadian Veterans Association, 1986. 192 pp. *Chiefly reprint of the Ukranian Canadian Servicemen's Associations' newsletters, 1943-46.*

The University of Alberta in the War of 1939-45. Edmonton: n.p., 1948. 70 pp.

Univ. of Toronto. *Memorial Book, Second World War, 1939-1945.* H.E. Brown, comp. Toronto: Soldiers' Tower Committee, Univ. of Toronto, 1994. 84 pp.

Upper Canada Historical Arms Society. *The Military Arms of Canada.* (Historical Arms Series, 1.) West Hill, Ont.: Museum Restoration Service, 1963. 47 pp.

Upton, Terence B. *The Rocky Mountain Rangers, 1898-1944; a Short History.* n.p.: n.d. 13 pp.

Urquhart, Hugh M. *Arthur Currie; the Biography of a Great Canadian.* Toronto: Dent, 1950. 363 pp.

Vallée, Pierre. *Prisonnier à l'Oflag 79.* Montréal: Editions de l'homme, 1964. 123 pp.

Van Der Schee, W. *A Short History of Lord Strathcona's Horse (Royal Canadians).* n.p.: 1973. 19 1.

Vanguard; the Fort Garry Horse in the Second World War. Doetinchem, Neth.: privately printed, 1945. 196 pp.

Vanier, Georges-P. *Paroles de guerre.* Montréal: Beauchemin, 1944. 148 pp.

Veldheer, Peter A. *"Daar komen de Canadezen ...!"; de zegevierende opmars van het Eerste Canadese Legerkorps over de Veluwe naar West-Nederland in 1945.* Arnhem: Gijsbers & Van Loon, 1982. 227 pp.

Veldheer, Peter A., [en] E.v.d. Weerd. *De Slag om de Veluwe, 1945; de bevrijding van de Veluwe door Britse en Canadese troepen in april van het laatste oorlogsjarr.* Arnhem: Gysbers & Van Loon, 1981. 231 pp.

Vennat, Pierre. *Dieppe n'aurait pas dû avoir lieu.* Montréal: Méridien, 1991. [201] pp.

Verrault, Georges. *Journal d'un prisonnier de guerre au Japon, 1941-1945.* Sillery (Qué.): Septentrion, 1993. 313 pp.
Soldat à Hong-Kong, 1941.

Veterans' Review; a Collection of War Stories. Toronto: privately printed, 1983. 255 pp.

Victoria Rifles of Canada, 1861-1951; Historical Notes. n.p.: n.d. 14 pp.

Victoria Rifles of Canada; Youth Trained in Mind and Body in a Great Regiment. n.p.: [ca. 1936]. 16 pp.

Vincent, Carl. *No Reason Why; the Canadian Hong Kong Tragedy — an Examination.* Stittsville, Ont.: Canada's Wings, 1981. 281 pp.

Vokes, Chris, and John P. Maclean. *Vokes; My Story.* Ottawa: Gallery Books, 1985. 233 pp.

Les Voltigeurs de Québec, 1862-1952; notes historiques. s.l.: s.i., 1952. 16 pp.

Les Voltigeurs de Québec, 1862-1962; album du centenaire, mai 1962. St-François, P.Q.: imprimé privé, 1962. 31 pp.

Waiser, Bill. *Park Prisoners; the Untold Story of Western Canada's National Parks, 1915-1946.* Saskatoon, Sask.: Fifth House Publishers, 1995. 294 pp.

Walker, D.E., comp. *A Resume of the Story of 1st Battalion the Saskatoon Light Infantry (MG), Canadian Army, Overseas.* Saskatoon, Sask.: privately printed, n.d. 139 pp.

Wallace, John F. *Dragons of Steel; Canadian Armour in Two World Wars.* Burnstown, Ont.: General Store Pub. House, 1995. 283 pp.

Walmsley, R.Y., and B.J.P. Whalley. *The History of the First Med. Regt., 1940-1945.* Amsterdam: Spin's Pub. Co., 1945. 121 pp.

Wamper, Hans. *Dieppe; Die Fewährung des Küstenwestwalles.* Berlin: E.S. Mittler, 1943. 97 pp.

War Record; the McGill Chapter of Delta Upsilon, 1939-1945. Montreal: n.p., 1946. 83 pp.

Warren, Arnold. *Wait for the Wagon; the Story of the Royal Canadian Army Service Corps.* Toronto: McClelland and Stewart, 1961. 413 pp.

Watson, W.S., and others, eds. *The Brockville Rifles, Royal Canadian Infantry Corps (Allied with the King's Royal Rifle Corps); Semper Paratus; an Unofficial History.* Brockville, Ont.: Recorder Print. Co., 1966. 138 pp.

Watts, E.M. *Some Soldiers; the Story of 80(R) Company, Veteran's Guard of Canada.* Brampton, Ont.: privately printed, 1960. 24 pp.

Weerd, Evert van de, en Gerjan Crebolder. *Bevrijdings-kroniek; Noord-West Veluwe, Nijkerk — Patten Ermelo — Harderwijk — Nunspeet — Hoevelaken, April — November 1945.* Barneveld, Neth.: BDU, 1983. 108 pp.

————. *Bevrijdings-kroniek; West-Veluwe, September 1944 — November 1945.* Barneveld, Neth.: BDU, 1981. 108 pp.

Weerd, Evert van de, Peter A. Veldheer en Gerjan Crebolder. *Bevrijdingsatlas Veluwe.* Barneveld, Neth.: BDU, 1985. 144 pp.

Weisbord, Merrily, and Merilyn Simonds Mohr. *The Valour and the Horror.* Toronto: HarperCollins, 1991. 171 pp.
From the film series by Brian McKenna and Terence McKenna.

Welcome Home, 14th C.A.(T.)R. Calgary Regiment (Tank). [Calgary: n.p., 1945]. 14 pp.

Wellington Legion War Veterans Club, eds. *They Served for Freedom./A la défense de la liberté.* [Wellington, P.E.I.: Royal Canadian Legion, Wellington Branch 17/Wellington, I.P.E.: Légion royale canadienne, la filiale de Wellinton no 17,] 1986. 319 pp.
Bilingual text./Texte bilingue.

Wells, George Anderson. *The Fighting Bishop; as Recounted in the Eighty-Seventh Year of his Life to his Daughter Jeanne Carden Wells.* Toronto: Cardwell House, 1971. 628 pp.

Wells, Herb. *Comrades in Arms.* St. John's, Nfld.: printed by Robinson-Blackmore Print. & Pub., 1986-88. 2 vols.
Newfoundlanders in action, Second World War.

Wentzel, Fritz. *Single or Return? The Story of a German P.O.W. in British Camps, and the Escape of Lieutenant Franz Von Werra.* Edward Fitzgerald, tr. London: W. Kimber, 1954. 172 pp.

[Werra, Franz von.] *Einer kam durch; Fluchtbericht des Fliegerleutnants Franz Von Werra.* Hamburg, Germany: Verlag der Sternbücher, [1959]. 244 pp.

Whitaker, W. Denis, and Shelagh Whitaker. *Dieppe; Tragedy to Triumph.* Toronto: McGraw-Hill Ryerson, 1992. 372 pp.

_____. *Rhineland; the Battle to End the War.* Toronto: Stoddart, 1989. 422 pp.

_____. *Tug of War; the Canadian Victory that Opened Antwerp.* Toronto: Stoddart, 1984. 461 pp.

*Whitcombe, Fred, and Blair Gilmour. *The Pictorial History of Canada's Army Overseas, 1939-1945.* Montreal: Whitcombe Gilmour, 1947. 262 pp.

*Whitcombe, Fred, et Blair Gilmour. *L'histoire illustrée de l'Armée canadienne outre-mer, 1939-1945.* Placide Labelle, tr. Montréal: Whitcombe Gilmour, s.d. 280 pp.

Whitehead, William. *Dieppe, 1942; Echoes of Disaster.* Terence Macartney-Filgate, ed. (A Personal Library Publication.) Don Mills, Ont.: Nelson, 1979. 187 pp., chiefly illus.

Whitton, Charlotte. *Canadian Women in the War Effort.* Toronto: Macmillan, 1942. 56 pp.

Wilkinson, Arthur Campbell. *Ottawa to Caen; Letters.* Alta R. Wilkinson, ed. Ottawa: Tower Books, 1947. 122 pp.

Willcocks, K.D.H. *The Hastings and Prince Edward Regiment, Canada; a Short History.* Belleville, Ont.: n.p., 1967. 1 vol., unpaged.

Willes, John A. *Out of the Clouds; the History of the 1st Canadian Parachute Battalion.* Kingston, Ont.: n.p., 1981. 251 pp.

Williams, C.D., ed. *Sabretache; the Memorial Journal of the VIII Recce Association.* n.p.: VIII Recce Association, [1966]. 79 pp.
14th Canadian Hussars.

Williams, Jeffery. *First in the Field; Gault of the Patricias.* St. Catharines, Ont.: Vanwell Pub., 1995. 278 pp.

————. *The Long Left Flank; the Hard Fought Way to the Reich, 1944-1945.* Toronto: Stoddart, 1988. 348 pp.
1st Canadian Army in North West Europe.

————. *Princess Patricia's Canadian Light Infantry.* (Famous Regiments.) London: L. Cooper, 1972. 110 pp.

[Willson, Gordon Beckles.] *Canada Comes to England,* by Gordon Beckles [*pseud.*] London: Hodder and Stoughton, 1941. 166 pp.

Wilson, J.E., and others. *A History of 2 Cdn H.A.A. Regt.* Soesterberg, Neth.: privately printed, 1945. 59 pp.

Windsor, John. *Blind Date.* Sidney, B.C.: Gray's Pub., 1962. 192 pp.

————. *The Mouth of the Wolf.* Sidney, B.C.: Gray's Pub., 1967. 224 pp.

The Winnipeg Rifles, 8th Battalion, C.E.F., Allied with the Rifle Brigade (Prince Consort's Own); Fiftieth Anniversary, 1883-1933. Winnipeg: privately printed, 1933. 59 pp.

Winton, Maurice V. *Saskatchewan's Prairie Soldiers, 1885-1980.* n.p.: n.d. 174 pp.
Cover title: A Pictorial History of Saskatchewan's Military Badges and Medals.

Wodehouse, R.F. *A Check List of the War Collections of World War I, 1914-1918, and World War II, 1939-1945.* Ottawa: Queen's Printer, 1968. 239 pp.

Women in Khaki. n.p.: n.d. 32 pp.

Wonders, William C. *The 'Sawdust Fusiliers'; the Canadian Forestry Corps in the Scottish Highlands in World War Two.* Montreal: Canadian Pulp and Paper Association, [1991]. 129 pp.

Wong, Marjorie. *The Dragon and the Maple Leaf; Chinese Canadians in World War II.* London, Ont.: Pirie Pub., 1994. 274 pp.

Wood, Alan. *The Falaise Road.* Toronto: Macmillan, 1944. 64 pp.

Wood, Gordon. *The Story of the Irish Regiment of Canada, 1939-1945.* Heerenveen, Neth.: privately printed, 1945. 87 pp.

Wood, J.E.R., ed. *Detour; the Story of Oflag IV C.* J.F. Watton, illus. London: Falcon Press, 1946. 183 pp.

Worthington, Larry. *The Spur and the Sprocket; the Story of the Royal Canadian Dragoons.* Kitchener, Ont.: Reeve Press, 1968. 170 pp.

_____. *"Worthy"; a Biography of Major-General F.F. Worthington, C.B., M.C., M.M.* Toronto: Macmillan, 1961. 236 pp.

Wright, Harold E., and Byron E. O'Leary. *Fortress Saint John; an Illustrated Military History, 1640-1985.* Saint John, N.B.: Partridge Island Research Project, 1985. 131 pp.

The York Ranger. No. 1. [Toronto]: n.p., 1922.
Only one number published.

Young, Albert Charles. *24 Good Men and True; Members of Branch #142 of the Royal Canadian Legion.* New York: Vantage Press, 1992. 219 pp.

Young, C.R. *Notes on Elementary Military Law for Canadian Officers.* [Toronto]: Univ. of Toronto Press, 1939. 70 pp.

Young Men's Christian Associations, Canada. *The 1st Year; a War Service Record of the Canadian Y.M.C.A. from the Outbreak of the War.* n.p.: [1940]. 23 pp.

Young Men's Christian Associations, Canada. National Council. War Services Executive. *With Arthur Jones through 5 Years of War; a Report of Canadian Y.M.C.A. War Services.* n.p.: n.d. 1 vol., unpaged.

Young, Scott. *Red Shield in Action; a Record of Canadian Salvation Army War Services in the Second Great War.* Toronto: F.F. Clarke, 1949. 149 pp.

Zepeda Turcios, Roberto. *Caminos de Renunciĉion.* Tegucigalpa, Honduras: Talles Tipograficos de la Imprenta Caldéron, 1947. 244 pp.

1946-1967

Adams, James. *Bull's Eye; the Assassination and Life of Supergun Inventor Gerald Bull.* New York: Times Books, 1992. 317 pp.

Air Force College Journal. Toronto: privately printed, 1956-64. 9 vols. *Title varies.*

*Allard, Jean V. *Mémoires du Général Jean V. Allard.* Collaboration spéciale de Serge Bernier. s.l: Editions de Mortagne, 1985. 533 pp.

*_____. *The Memoirs of General Jean V. Allard,* written in cooperation with Serge Bernier. Vancouver: Univ. of British Columbia Press, 1988. 366 pp.

L'Amicale du 22e. Vol. I-XVIII. Québec, P.Q.: imprimé privé, 1947-64. *Remplacé par La Citadelle.*

Armour Review. Vol. I-VIII. Camp Borden, Ont.: n.p., 1965-73. *Annual. Title varies. Vol. I: RCAC Bulletin. Vol. II-V: RCAC Review. Official organ of the Royal Canadian Armoured Corps.*

Barnard, W.T. *The Queen's Own Rifles of Canada, 1860-1960; One Hundred Years of Canada.* Don Mills, Ont.: Ontario Pub. Co., 1960. 398 pp.

_____. *A Short History of the Queen's Own Rifles of Canada.* Toronto: MacKinnon & Atkins, n.d. 22 pp.

*Barnes, Leslie W.C.S. *Canada's Guns; an Illustrated History of Artillery.* (Canadian War Muscum Historical Publication no. 15.) [Ottawa]: National Museum of Man, 1979. 112 pp.

*_____. *Histoire illustrée de l'artillerie canadienne.* (Musée canadien de la guerre publication d'histoire militaire no 15.) [Ottawa]: Musée national de l'Homme, 1979. 112 pp.

*Barton, William H. *Science and the Armed Services.* (Current Affairs for the Canadian Forces, vol. II, no. 1.) Ottawa: King's Printer, 1952. 22 pp.

*_____. *La science et les Services armés.* (Actualités; revue destinée aux Forces canadiennes, vol II, no 1.) Ottawa: Imprimeur du Roi, 1952. 22 pp.

Batten, Jack. *The Spirit of the Regiment; an Account of the 48th Highlanders from 1956 to 1991.* n.p.: n.d. 171 pp.

Beattie, Kim. *Dileas; History of the 48th Highlanders of Canada, 1929-1956.* Toronto: privately printed, 1957. 847 pp.

Bell, K., and C.P. Stacey. *100 Years; the Royal Canadian Regiment 1883-1983.* Don Mills, Ont.: Collier Macmillan, 1983. 184 pp., chiefly illus.

Bezeau, M.V. *University of Ottawa Contingent, Canadian Officers Training Corps.* n.p.: 1968. 15 pp.

Bindon, Kathryn M. *Queen's Men, Canada's Men; the Military History of Queen's University, Kingston.* [Kingston, Ont.]: privately printed, 1978. 180 pp.

Bird, Will R. *North Shore (New Brunswick) Regiment.* Fredericton, N.B.: Brunswick Press, 1963. 629 pp.

Bishop, William Arthur. *Courage on the Battlefield.* (Canada's Military Heritage, Volume II.) Toronto: McGraw-Hill Ryerson, 1993. 341 pp.

Blue & Gold. Vol. I- . Winnipeg: n.p., 1934- .
Frequency varies, but chiefly annual. Regimental journal of the Fort Garry Horse.

Boissonault, Charles-Marie. *Histoire politico-militaire des Canadiens français (1763-1967).* Trois-Rivières, P.Q.: Editions du Bien public, 1967. 310 pp.

Boss, W. *The Stormont, Dundas and Glengarry Highlanders, 1783-1951.* Ottawa: Runge Press, 1952. 449 pp.
Revised and updated as: Boss, W., and W.J. Patterson, Up the Glens; Stormont, Dundas and Glengarry Highlanders, 1783-1994. Cornwall, Ont.: Old Book Store, 1995. 298 pp.

Bowering, Clifford H. *Service; the Story of the Canadian Legion, 1925-1960.* Ottawa: privately printed, 1960. 240 pp.

The Brazier; Marking the 50th Anniversary of the Canadian Scottish (Princess Mary's), June 6, 1964. Victoria, B.C.: privately printed, 1964. 19 pp.

A Brief History of the Royal Regiment of Canada; Allied with the King's Regiment (Liverpool). [Toronto: n.p., 1948.] 135 pp.

Brown, Brian A. *Foresters; the Canadian Quest for Peace.* Erin, Ont.: Boston Mills Press, 1991. 176 pp.
The Grey & Simcoe Foresters.

Brown, Kingsley, *see* Greenhous, Brereton.

*Brown, W.J. *Les Cadets royaux de l'Armée canadienne; cent ans d'exploits, 1879-1979.* s.l.: La Ligue des Cadets de l'Armée du Canada, [1979. 12 pp.]

*_____. *The Royal Canadian Army Cadets; a Century of Achievement, 1879-1979.* n.p.: The Army Cadet League of Canada, [1979. 12 pp.]

Bull, Stewart H. *The Queen's York Rangers; an Historic Regiment.* Erin, Ont.: Boston Mills Press, 1984. 248 pp.

Burns, E.L.M. *Between Arab and Israeli.* Toronto: Clarke, Irwin, 1962. 336 pp.

Burns, Max, and Ken Messenger. *The Winged Wheel Patch; a History of the Canaian Military Motorcycle and Rider.* St. Catharines, Ont.: Vanwell Pub., 1993. 159 pp.

Butson, A.R.C. *A History of the Military Medical Units of Hamilton, Ontario, in Peace and War, 1900-1990.* n.p.: 1990. 43 pp.

Cahiers des Voltigeurs. Vol I, nos 1-8. s.l.: L'Amicale des Anciens Voltigeurs de Québec, 1954-66.
Irrégulier.

Cameron, James M. *Pictonians in Arms; a Military History of Pictou County, Nova Scotia.* Fredericton, N.B.: privately printed, 1969. 301 pp.

Camp, A.D., comp. *7th Toronto Regiment, Royal Regiment of Canadian Artillery, 1866-1966.* n.p.: n.d. 33 pp.

Camp Valcartier, P.Q.; 1647 à 1957 en quelques lignes./Camp Valcartier P.Q.; a Short History 1647-1957. s.l.: s.i./n.p.: 1957. 24 pp.
Texte bilingue./Bilingual text.

[Canada. Armed Forces. 8th Canadian Hussars (Princess Louise's).] *The 8th Canadian Hussars (Princess Louise's), 1962-1987.* G.H. MacDonald, ed.-in-chief. n.p.: 1987. 162 pp.

Canada. Armed Forces. 4 Field Ambulance. *A History of 4 Field Ambulance.* Lahr, Germany: E. Demmer, 1992. [122] pp.

Canada. Armed Forces. Lake Superior Scottish Regiment. *Regimental Catechism.* Winnipeg: CFTMPC, 1977. 15 pp.

[Canada. Armed Forces. 3rd Regiment, Royal Canadian Horse Artillery.] *Third Regiment, 1953-1983.* Brandon, Man.: privately printed, n.d. 1 vol., chiefly illus.

*Canada. Armée. Quartier général de l'Armée. Section historique. *L'Armée canadienne en Corée; les opérations des Nations unies (1950-1953) et leurs répercussions; court récit officiel.* Ottawa: Imprimeur de la Reine, 1956. 118 pp.

* _____. *La 1re Division d'infanterie canadienne, 1915-1955.* (Actualités; revue destinée aux Forces canadiennes, vol IX, no 1.) Ottawa: Imprimeur de la Reine, 1955. 31 pp.

Canada. Armée. Régiment de la Chaudière. *Le Régiment de la Chaudière; notes historiques.* Québec, P.Q.: imprimé privé, 1955. 16 pp.

*Canada. Army. *Army Life.* Ottawa: Queen's Printer, [195-?]. 1 vol., unpaged.

_____. *Remember ... It's Your Army; Recruiting Information.* Ottawa: Queen's Printer, 1953. 15 pp.

_____. *Winter Exercise Musk Ox, 1946.* Ottawa: King's Printer, 1947. 168 pp.
Originally classified Confidential.

Canada. Army. The Black Watch (Royal Highland Regiment) of Canada. *The Black Watch (Royal Highland Regiment) of Canada; the Regimental Book.* Montreal: privately printed, 1965. 1 vol., unpaged, looseleaf.

Canada. Army. Canadian Guards. *The Changing of the Guard; Your Souvenir Guide Book.* n.p.: n.d. 24 pp.

Canada. Army. Canadian Guards. 2nd Battalion. *Changing the Guard, by 2nd Battalion, the Canadian Guards on Parliament Hill, Ottawa, Canada.* n.p.: n.d. 16 pp.

Canada. Army. Canadian Military Headquarters. *Canadian Army (Overseas) Routine Orders.* London: n.p., 1940-47.
Title varies. Issued as Canadian Active Service Force (Overseas) Routine Orders *until December 1940. Supplements also issued.*

Canada. Army. Canadian Officers' Training Corps. Carleton Univ. Contingent. *Unit Notes.* n.p.: 1966. 53 pp.

[Canada. Army. Lorne Scots (Peel, Dufferin and Halton Regiment).] *Dress Instructions; The Lorne Scots (P.D. & H. Regt.).* n.p.: 1966. 1 vol., chiefly illus.

Canada. Army. Princess Patricia's Canadian Light Infantry. *Regimental Dress Instructions.* n.p.: 1963. 1 vol., looseleaf.

Canada. Army. Queen's Own Rifles of Canada. *Regimental Catechism.* n.p.: n.d. 19 pp.

_____. *Regimental Standing Orders for the Queen's Own Rifles of Canada.* n.p.: 1965. 1 vol., looseleaf.

Canada. Army. Royal Canadian Army Service Corps. *RCASC Diamond Jubilee Year Book, 1910-1961.* Ottawa: Queen's Printer, [1962]. 95 pp.

[Canada. Army. Royal Canadian Ordnance Corps.] *Standing Orders for the Royal Canadian Ordnance Corps.* Cobourg, Ont.: printed by Haynes Print. Co., 1965. 118 pp., looseleaf.

Canada. Army. Royal Winnipeg Rifles. *Seventy-Fifth Anniversary, Royal Winnipeg Rifles, 1883-1958.* [Winnipeg: privately printed, 1958.] v.p.

[Canada. Army. Toronto Scottish Regiment.] *The Toronto Scottish Regiment.* n.p.: 1961. 24 pp.

Canada. Army Headquarters. Director of Artillery. *Standing Orders for the Royal Regiment of Canadian Artillery.* Don Mills, Ont.: T.H. Best, 1963. 62 pp.

Canada. Army Headquarters. Directorate of Manning. *Canadian Army Manual for the Canadian Officers Training Corps (Short Title: COTC Manual), 1962.* Ottawa: n.p., [1962]. 1 vol., looseleaf.

Canada. Army Headquarters. Directorate of Manning. *The Canadian Regular Army.* Ottawa: Queen's Printer, 1955. 49 pp.

*Canada. Army Headquarters. Historical Section. *Canada's Army in Korea; the United Nations Operations, 1950-53, and their Aftermath; a Short Official Account.* Ottawa: Queen's Printer, 1956. 108 pp.

*_____. *The Old Red Patch; the 1st Canadian Infantry Division 1915-1955.* (Current Affairs for the Canadian Forces, vol. IX, no. 1.) Ottawa: Queen's Printer, 1955. 31 pp.

_____. *The Regiments and Corps of the Canadian Army.* (The Canadian Army List, vol. I.) Ottawa: Queen's Printer, 1964. 253 pp.

Canada. Canadian Forces Headquarters. *Canadian Forces Administrative Orders.* Ottawa: n.p., 1965-71.
Issued as a non-chronological sequence in which orders were discarded when obsolete. Superseded by a bilingual format in 1972.

Canada. Court Martial Appeal Board. *Court Martial Appeal Reports.* Ottawa: Queen's Printer, 1957-73. 3 vols.

Canada. Dept. of National Defence. *The Canadian Army List.* Ottawa: King's Printer, 1940-66.
Title varies, eg. — Gradation List, Canadian Army Active (1940-45); Canadian Army (Regular) List (1959-66).

*_____. *The Defence Research Board, Canada.* n.p.: n.d. 1 vol., unpaged.

_____. *Defence Research Board; the First Twenty-Five Years./Conseil de recherches pour la défense; les 25 premières années.* Ottawa: Queen's Printer/Imprimeur de la Reine, 1972. 46 pp.
Bilingual text./Texte bilingue.

_____. *Instructions for the Royal Canadian Army Medical Corps; Effective 1 November 1948.* n.p.: n.d. v.p.

_____. *The King's Regulations and Orders for the Canadian Army.* Ottawa: King's Printer, 1951. 3 vols. in 1.

_____. *Manual of the Canadian Forces Medical Service in the Field, 1959.* Ottawa: Queen's Printer, 1959. 324 pp., looseleaf.

_____. *Pay and Allowance Regulations for the Canadian Army, 1946.* Ottawa: King's Printer, 1946. 1 vol., looseleaf.

*_____. *The Queen's Regulations and Orders for the Cadet Services of Canada and the Royal Canadian Army Cadets, 1956.* Ottawa: Queen's Printer, 1956. 1 vol., looseleaf.

_____. *The Queen's Regulations and Orders for the Canadian Army.* Ottawa: Queen's Printer, 1959. 3 vols., looseleaf.

*Canada. Dept. of National Defence. *The Queen's Regulations and Orders for the Canadian Army.* Ottawa: Queen's Printer, 1952. 3 vols., looseleaf.

*_____. *The Queen's Regulations and Orders for the Canadian Forces.* Ottawa: Queen's Printer, 1965. 3 vols., looseleaf.

*_____. *Queen's Regulations for the Canadian Services Colleges.* Ottawa: Queen's Printer, 1958. 1 vol., unpaged.

_____. *Regulations for Canadian Ordnance Services, 1948.* n.p.: n.d. 70 1.

_____. *Regulations for the Organization and Control of the Royal Canadian Army Cadets, 1948.* Ottawa: King's Printer, 1949. 41 pp.

*_____. *Report.* Ottawa: King's Printer, 1923-59.
Title varies. Annual most years.

*_____. *White Paper on Defence.* Ottawa: Queen's Printer, 1964. 30 pp.

Canada. Dept. of National Defence. Defence Research Board. *Review./Revue,* [par le] Conseil de recherches pour la Défense du Canada. Ottawa: Dept. of National Defence/Ministère de la Défense nationale, 1966-73.
Bilingual text. Title varies: Annual Report (1966)./Texte bilingue. Divergence du titre: Rapport annuel (1966).

Canada. Dept. of Veterans Affairs. *Commemoration; Canadians in Korea 1978./Souvenir; Canadiens en Corée, 1978.* n.p./s.l.: s.i., [1978. 14 pp.]
Bilingual text./Texte bilingue.

Canada. Militia Headquarters. *General Orders.* Ottawa: Queen's Printer, 1899-1946.
Superseded Militia General Orders. Frequency varies.

* Canada. Ministère de la Défense nationale. *Le Conseil de recherches pour la défense, Canada.* s.l.: s.i., s.d. 1 tome, non-paginé.

*_____. *Livre blanc sur la défense.* Ottawa: Imprimeur de la Reine, 1964. 34 pp.

*_____. *Ordonnances et règlements royaux applicables aux Forces canadiennes.* Ottawa: Imprimeur de la Reine, 1965. 3 tomes, feuilles mobiles.

*_____. *Ordonnances et règlements royaux applicables aux Services des Cadets du Canada et au Corps royal des Cadets de l'Armée canadienne, 1956.* Ottawa: Imprimeur de la Reine, 1957. 1 tome, feuilles mobiles.

*_____. *Rapport.* Ottawa: Imprimeur du Roi, 1923-59.
Divergence du titre. Annuel, la plupart des années.

*_____. *Règlements royaux applicables aux Collèges des services armés du Canada.* Ottawa: Imprimeur de la Reine, 1958. 1 tome, nonpaginé.

*Canada. Ministère de la Défense nationale (Armée). *La vie dans l'Armée.* Ottawa: Imprimeur de la Reine, 1956. 1 tome, non-paginé.

*Canada. National Defence Headquarters. *Canadian Army Orders.* [Ottawa: King's Printer], 1941-64.
From 1947 issued as a non-chronological series, with orders being discarded when obsolete. Supplements also issued from 1947.

_____. *Canadian Army Routine Orders.* Ottawa: n.p., 1939-46.
Title varies. Issued as Canadian Active Service Force Routine Orders *until December 1940. Supplements also issued.*

Canada. Parliament. House of Commons. Special Committee on Canteen Funds. *Minutes of Proceedings and Evidence.* No. 1-10. Ottawa: King's Printer, 1947.

*Canada. Quartier général de la Défense nationale. *Ordres de l'Armée canadienne.* [Ottawa: Imprimeur du Roi], 1941-64.
Publiés en série de façon non chronologique, à partir de 1947; les ordres périmés sont remplacés. Des suppléments sont également publiés à partir de 1947.

**The Canadian Army Journal.* Vol. I-XIX. Ottawa: King's Printer, 1947-65.

**Canadian Army Training Memorandum.* No. 1-72. Ottawa: King's Printer, 1941-47.

Canadian Artillery Association. *Annual Report.* n.p.: privately printed, 1876- .
Not published 1940-46. Title varies.

Canadian Cavalry Association. *Proceedings.* n.p.: privately printed, 1913- .
In 1943 became Canadian Armoured Association and in 1946 Royal Canadian Armoured Corps (Cavalry) Association. Title varies: also Annual Report *and* Information Digest and Annual Report.

Canadian Defence Quarterly./Revue canadienne de défense. Vol. I- . Toronto: Baxter Pub., 1971 - .

The Canadian Forces Dental Services Bulletin./Bulletin du Service dentaire des Forces canadiennes. Ottawa: n.p./s.i., 1960- .
Quarterly. Title varies: The Royal Canadian Dental Corps Quarterly *(1960-70) and* The Canadian Forces Dental Services Quarterly./Bulletin du Service dentaire des Forces canadiennes *(1970-79). Bilingual text./ Trimestriel. Divergence du titre:* The Royal Canadian Dental Corps Quarterly *(1960-70) et* The Canadian Forces Dental Service Quarterly./Bulletin du Service dentaire des Forces canadiennes *(1970-79). Texte bilingue.*

The Canadian Guardsman. n.p.: privately printed, 1956-69.

The Canadian Gunner. Vol. I- . n.p.: privately printed, 1965- .

Canadian Infantry Association. *Proceedings.* n.p.: privately printed, 1913- .
Incorporated the Proceedings of the Canadian Machine Gun Corps Association in 1936. Was the Infantry and Machine Gun Association of Canada, 1937-39. Not published 1940-45.

The Canadian Intelligence Quarterly; the Journal of the Canadian Intelligence Corps. Vol. I-VI. n.p.: privately printed, 1963-68.

The Canadian Provost Corps; Silver Jubilee, 1940-1965. Ottawa: privately printed, 1965. 96 pp.

The Canadian Scottish Regiment. n.p.: n.d. 91 pp.

Canadian Services Colleges; Royal Military College of Canada, Kingston, Ontario; Royal Roads, Victoria, B.C.; Collège militaire royal de Saint-Jean, Saint-Jean, P.Q. n.p.: [195-?]. 16 pp.

Capon, Alan R. *Mascots of the Hastings and Prince Edward Regiment.* Picton, Ont.: Picton Gazette, 1977. 31 pp.

Cardoulis, John N. *A Friendly Invasion; the American Military in Newfoundland, 1940-1990.* St. John's, Nfld.: Breakwater, 1990. 224 pp.

Castonguay, Jacques. *Les bataillons et le dépôt du Royal 22e Régiment; vingt ans d'histoire, 1945-1965.* Québec, P.Q.: imprimé privé, 1974. 284 pp.

_____. *Collège militaire royal de Saint-Jean./Les premiers vingt ans./The First Twenty Years.* Adaptation anglaise: Donald A.L. Lefroy. s.l.: s.i./n.p., [1972?]. 44 pp.
Texte bilingue./Bilingual text.

_____. *Le Collège militaire royal de Saint-Jean.* Montréal: Méridien, 1989. 288 pp.
Réédition rév. et augm.: Le Collège militaire royal de Saint-Jean; une université à caractère différent. Sillery (Qué.): Septentrion, 1992. 272 pp.

_____. *Les Voltigeurs de Québec; premier régiment canadien-français.* Québec (Qué.): Les Voltigeurs de Québec, 1987. 523 pp.

Castonguay, Jacques, *et al. History of Canadian Forces Base Montreal and its Garrisons./Historique de la Base des Forces canadiennes Montréal et de ses garnisons.* n.p./s.1: s.i., 1980. 181/153 pp.
Bilingual text./Texte bilingue.

Castonguay, Jacques, et Armand Ross. *Le Régiment de la Chaudière.* Lévis, P.Q.: imprimé privé, 1983. 644 pp.

Cent ans d'histoire d'un régiment canadien-français; les Fusiliers Mont-Royal, 1869-1969. Montréal: Editions du Jour, 1971. 418 pp.

Centennial, 1863-1963; Presentation of Colours to the Princess of Wales' Own Regiment CA(M) by the Honourable W. Earle Rowe, P.C., Lieutenant-Governor of Ontario, Kingston, Ontario, Saturday 1st June 1963. [Kingston, Ont.: privately printed, 1963.] 15 pp.

Centennial Year, 1866-1966; 11th Field Artillery Regiment (M); 11th Field Artillery Regiment, Royal Regiment of Canadian Artillery, Canada's Oldest Artillery Regiment, Saturday, October 1, 1966. n.p.: n.d. 1 vol., unpaged.

The Ceremony of Trooping the Colour of the Second Battalion, The Royal Canadian Regiment; Taking the Salute, General C. Foulkes, Chairman Chiefs of Staff Committee, London, Ontario, 27th October 1956. n.p.: [1956]. 1 vol., unpaged.

Chappell, Mike. *The Canadian Army at War.* (Men-at-Arms Series, [164].) London: Osprey Pub., 1985. 48 pp.
Canadian Army uniforms.

Charters, David A. *Armed Forces and Political Purpose: Airborne Forces and the Canadian Army in the 1980s.* Fredericton, N.B.: Univ. of New Brunswick Centre for Conflict Studies, 1984. 145 pp.

50 ans d'activités avec le 6e Régiment d'artillerie, (Québec & Lévis), 1899-1949. Québec, P.Q.: Imprimerie Laflamme, 1949. 1 tome, non-paginé.

La Citadelle. Vol I- . Québec, P.Q.: s.i., 1965- .
Bimestriel. La revue de l'Association du 22e, Inc. Remplace L'Amicale du 22e.

Clark, Thomas, and Harry Pugh. *Canadian Airborne Insignia, 1942 — Present.* (Elite Insignia Guide, 4.) Arlington, Va.: C & D Enterprise, 1994. 158 pp.

Clint, H.C., comp. *A Short History of Artillery and of 57th Battery, R.C.A., 1855-1955; Formal Celebration and Reunion, Oct. 15th, 16th, 1955, Grande Allée Armouries, Quebec City.* Quebec, P.Q.: n.p., 1955. 48 pp.

Coates, Kenneth. *North to Alaska.* Toronto: McClelland & Stewart, 1992. 304 pp.
Alaska Highway.

Coates, Kenneth, ed. *The Alaska Highway; Papers of 40th Anniversary Symposium.* Vancouver: Univ. of British Columbia Press, 1985. 208 pp.

Collège militaire royal de Saint-Jean. *Ouverture officielle./Official Opening.* s.l.: s.i., s.d./n.p.: n.d. 27 pp.
Texte bilingue./Bilingual text.

The Connecting File. Vol. I- . London, Ont.: privately printed, 1921- .
Journal of The Royal Canadian Regiment.

Corfield, William E. *Citizen Soldiers; the Canadian Fusiliers of London; the Oxford Rifles; the Perth Regiment.* London, Ont.: Royal Canadian Regiment, 1983. 86 pp.

*Le Corps blindé royal canadien. Ottawa: Imprimeur de la Reine, 1954. 11 pp.

*Le Corps de Santé royal canadien. Ottawa: Imprimeur de la Reine, 1954. 11 pp.

*The Corps of Royal Canadian Engineers. Ottawa: Queen's Printer, 1953. 21 pp.

Corriveau, Paul. *Le Royal 22e Régiment; 75 ans d'histoire, 1914-1989.* Québec (Qué.): La Régie du Royal 22e Régiment, 1989. 132 pp.

Coup d'oeil sur le Collège militare royal de Saint-Jean. Ottawa: Imprimeur de la Reine, 1959. 20 pp.

Crook, E.D., and J.K. Marteinson, eds. *A Pictorial History of the 8th Canadian Hussars (Princess Louise's).* n.p.: privately printed, 1973. 343 pp.

Cross, Michael, and Robert Bothwell, eds. *Policy by Other Means; Essays in Honour of C.P. Stacey.* Toronto: Clarke, Irwin, 1972. 258 pp.

Cunniffe, Dick. *Scarlet, Riflegreen and Khaki; the Military in Calgary.* Calgary: Century Calgary Publications, 1975. 40 pp.

Curchin, Leonard A., and Brian D. Sim. *The Elgins; the Story of the Elgin Regt. (RCAC) and its Predeccessors.* St. Thomas, Ont.: privately printed, 1977. 150 pp.

Le Défilé; la revue du Collège militaire royal de Saint-Jean. Saint-Jean, P.Q.: imprimé privé, 1952- .
Divergence du titre.

Donoghue, Jack. *PR; Fifty Years in the Field.* Toronto: Dundurn Press, 1993. 188 pp.

Dornbusch, C.E., comp. *The Canadian Army, 1855-1958; Regimental Histories and a Guide to the Regiments.* Cornwallville, N.Y.: Hope Farm Press, 1959. 216 pp.

_____. *The Canadian Army, 1855-1955; Regimental Histories and a Guide to the Regiments.* Cornwallville, N.Y.: n.p., 1957. 162 1.

_____. *The Canadian Army, 1855-1965; Lineages; Regimental Histories.* Cornwallville, N.Y.: Hope Farm Press, 1966. 179 pp.

_____. *Lineages of the Canadian Army, 1855-1961; Armour, Cavalry, Infantry.* Cornwallville, N.Y.: Hope Farm Press, 1961. 1 vol., unpaged.

Dornier, François, et Marie-Claude Joubert. *Soldats de la côte ...; Les Fusiliers du St-Laurent d'hier à aujourd'hui.* Rimouski (Qué.): La Régie, Les Fusiliers du St-Laurent, 1992. 183 pp.

Drolet, "Gil". *Loyola, the Wars: in Remembrance of "Men for Others".* Waterloo, Ont.: Laurier Centre for Military Strategic and Disarmament Studies, 1996. 44 pp.
Memorial to the war dead of Loyola High School and College.

Duguid, Archer Fortescue. *History of the Canadian Grenadier Guards, 1760-1964.* Montreal: Gazette Print. Co., 1965. 520 pp.

Dunkelman, Ben. *Dual Allegiance; an Autobiography.* Toronto: Macmillan, 1976. 336 pp.

Dunnett, Peter J.S. *Royal Roads Military College, 1940-1990; a Pictorial Retrospect.* W. Kim Rempel, photo researcher. Victoria, B.C.: Royal Roads Militray College, 1990. 159 pp.

Edwards, Charles A. *Canadian Army Formation Signs, 1939-1985; a Collector's and Historian's Comprehensive Guide to the Cloth Formation Signs Worn by the Canadian Army in 1939-1985.* Michael J. Langenfeld, illus. Grayslake, Ill.: Pass in Review Publications, 1987. 50 pp.

Elliot, S.R. *Scarlet to Green; a History of Intelligence in the Canadian Army, 1903-1963.* Toronto: privately printed, 1981. 769 pp.

Falardeau, Victor, et Jean Parent. *La musique du Royal 22e Régiment; 50 ans d'histoire, 1922-1972.* Québec, P.Q.: Editions Garneau, 1976. 243 pp.

Farran, Roy. *The History of the Calgary Highlanders, 1921-54.* n.p.: Bryant Press, [1954]. 222 pp.

Fetherstonhaugh, R.C., and G.R. Stevens. *The Royal Canadian Regiment.* Vol. I: Montreal: Gazette Print. Co., 1936. Vol. II: London, Ont.: privately printed, 1967. 2 vols.

Fifty Years of Armour/Cinquante ans de blindé/Royal Canadian Armoured Corps/Le Corps blindé royal canadien/1940-1990. Ottawa: Esprit de corps, [1990]. 43 pp.
Bilingual text./Texte bilingue.

50 Years of Canadian Electrical and Mechanical Engineering./50 ans de Génie électrique et mécanique canadien. Ottawa: n.p./s.i., [1994]. 111 pp.
Bilingual text./Texte bilingue.

First Battalion, Princess Patricia's Canadian Light Infantry and the King's Own Calgary Regiment; the Ceremony of Presentation of Colours by Her Majesty Queen Elizabeth II, Beacon Hill Park, Victoria, British Columbia, Friday, July 17th, 1959. Victoria, B.C.: privately printed, [1959]. 16 pp.

Forbes, J. Charles. *Fantassin; pour mon pays, la gloire et ... des prunes.* Sillery (Qué.): Septentrion, 1994. 451 pp.
Le Régiment de Maisonneuve dans la Deuxième Guerre mondiale, le Royal 22e Régiment en Corée.

Fort Churchill. Ottawa: Queen's Printer, 1959. 20 pp.

Foster, J.A. *Muskets to Missiles; a Pictorial History of Canada's Ground Forces.* Toronto: Methuen, 1987. 251 pp.

4 CMBG; Canada's NATO Brigade./ 4e GBMC; Brigade canadienne au service de l'OTAN. Lahr, Germany/Allemagne: M. Schauenburg, 1983. 1 vol., unpaged./1 tome, non paginé.
Bilingual text./Texte bilingue.

Fox, Brent. *Camp Aldershot; Serving since 1904.* (The King's Historical Society Series, number 1.) [Kentville, N.S.]: King's Historical Society, 1983. 24 pp.

Franklin, B.A.J. *The Airborne Bridge; the Canadian Special Air Service Company.* n.p.: privately printed, 1988. 170 pp.

Fraser, W.B. *Always a Strathcona.* Calgary: Comprint Pub. Co., 1976. 252 pp.

Gaffen, Fred. *Cross-Border Warriors; Canadians in American Forces, Americans in Canadian Forces; from the Civil War to the Gulf.* Toronto: Dundurn Press, 1995. 241 pp.

_____. *In the Eye of the Storm; a History of Canadian Peacekeeping.* Toronto: Deneau & Wayne, 1987. 302 pp.

_____. *Unknown Warriors; Canadians in Vietnam.* Toronto: Dundurn Press, 1990. 366 pp.

Gallant, A.M. *Pride; the History of 1390 RCACC.* Red Deer, Alta.: printed by Fletcher, [1992?]. 244 pp.

Gardam, John. *The Canadian Peacekeeper./Le gardien de la paix canadien.* Burnstown, Ont.: General Store Pub. House, 1992. 69 pp.
Bilingual text./Texte bilingue.

_____. *Korea Volunteer; an Oral History from Those who were There.* Burnstown, Ont.: General Store Pub. House, 1994. 262 pp.

The Gauntlet; RCAC School COTC. Camp Borden, Ont.: privately printed, 1953?-59?
Annual.

*Le Génie royal canadien. Ottawa: Imprimeur de la Reine, 1954. 23 pp.

Giesler, Patricia. *Commemoration; Canadians in Korea, 1983./Commemoration; Canadiens en Corée, 1983.* Ottawa: Veterans Affairs Canada/Affaires des Anciens combattants Canada, [1983]. 15/17 pp.
Bilingual text./Texte bilingue.

_____. *Valour Remembered; Canadians in Korea./Souvenirs de vaillance; les Canadiens en Corée.* Ottawa: Veterans Affairs Canada/Affaires des Anciens combattants Canada, 1982. [28/29 pp.]
Bilingual text./Texte bilingue.

Goodspeed, D.J. *Battle Royal; a History of the Royal Regiment of Canada, 1862-1962.* Toronto: privately printed, 1962. 703 pp.

Goodspeed, D.J. *A History of the Defence Research Board of Canada.* Ottawa: Queen's Printer, 1958. 259 pp.

Gouin, Jacques, *et al. Bon coeur et bon bras; histoire du Régiment de Maisonneuve, 1880-1980.* Montréal: imprimé privé, 1980. 298 pp.

The Governor General's Horse Guards Home Coming, Queen Elizabeth Building, C.N.E., May 22-23-24 1964. n.p.: [1964]. 31 pp.

Graham, Dominick. *The Price of Command; a Biography of General Guy Simonds.* Toronto: Stoddart, 1993. 345 pp.

Graham, Howard. *Citizen and Soldier; the Memoirs of Lieutenant-General Howard Graham.* Toronto: McClelland and Stewart, 1987. 304 pp.

Granatstein, J.L., and David J. Bercuson. *War and Peacekeeping; from South Africa to the Gulf — Canada's Limited Wars.* Toronto: Key Porter Books, 1991. 266 pp.

Granatstein, J.L., and Douglas Lavender. *Shadows of War, Faces of Peace; Canada's Peacekeepers.* Photographs by Boris Spremo. Toronto: Key Porter Books, 1992. 160 pp.

Granatstein, J.L., and R.D. Cuff, eds. *War and Society in North America.* Toronto: T. Nelson, 1971. 199 pp.

Gravel, Jean-Yves. *Les soldats-citoyens; histoire du Régiment de Trois-Rivières, 1871-1978.* Trois-Rivières, P.Q.: Editions du Bien public, 1981. 153 pp.

Greenhous, Brereton. *Dragoon; the Centennial History of the Royal Canadian Dragoons, 1883-1983.* Ottawa: Guild of the Royal Canadian Dragoons, 1983. 557 pp.

_____. *Semper Paratus; the History of the Royal Hamilton Light Infantry (Wentworth Regiment), 1862-1977,* by Kingsley Brown, Senior, Kingsley Brown, Junior, and Brereton Greenhous. Revised and edited by Brereton Greenhous. Hamilton, Ont.: privately printed, 1977. 446 pp.

Grimshaw, Louis E. *"Ex coelis"; the Badges and Insignia of the Canadian Airborne Forces; a History of Canadian Airborne Badges and the Units and Men who Wore Them "ex coelis".* Edmonton: Lone Pine Pub., 1981. 80 pp.

Harker, Douglas E. *The Dukes; the Story of the Men who have Served in Peace and War with the British Columbia Regiment (D.C.O.), 1883-1973.* n.p.: privately printed, 1974. 438 pp.

Hempenstall, Robert. *Find the Dragon; the Canadian Army in Korea, 1950-1953.* Edmonton: Four Winds Pub. Co., 1995. 380 pp.

Henderson, Peter A. *Guarding the Gates; a History of Canadian Forces Station St. Johns.* St. John's, Nfld.: CFS St. John's, 1992. 115 pp.

A History of the First Hussars Regiment, 1856-1980. n.p.: 1981. 195 pp. *An updating of 1951 ed.*

Hodder-Williams, Ralph, G.R. Stevens and R.B. Mainprize. *Princess Patricia's Canadian Light Infantry.* London: Hodder and Stoughton, 1923-[57?]. 4 vols.

Horrocks, William. *In their own Words.* Ottawa: Rideau Veterans Home Residents Council, 1993. 247 pp.

The Horse Guard; Souvenir Programme of the Regimental Reunion, May, 1954. n.p.: [1954]. 36 pp.

How, Douglas. *The 8th Hussars; a History of the Regiment.* Sussex, N.B.: Maritime Pub., 1964. 446 pp.

Hubbell, E.L. *The Winnipeg Grenadiers.* n.p.: n.d. 16 pp.

Hughes, G.W., comp. *A Marchpast of the Corps and Regiments of the Canadian Army, Past and Present.* Calgary: n.p., n.d. 3 vols.

Hutchison, Paul P. *Canada's Black Watch; the First Hundred Years, 1862-1962.* Montreal: privately printed, [1962]. 340 pp.

*L'Intendance royale canadienne. Ottawa: Imprimeur de la Reine, 1954. 12 pp.

Jackson, H.M. *Canadian Prime Ministers and the Canadian Militia.* n.p.: 1958. 11 pp.

_____. *The Roll of the Regiments (the Active Militia).* Ottawa: n.p., 1959. 176 pp.

_____. *The Royal Regiment of Artillery, Ottawa, 1855-1952; a History.* Montreal: privately printed, 1952. 418 pp.

_____. *The Sherbrooke Regiment (12th Armoured Regiment).* n.p.: 1958. 229 pp.

_____. *The Story of the Royal Canadian Dental Corps.* Ottawa: privately printed, 1956. 475 pp.

Jackson, H.M., ed. *The Argyll and Sutherland Highlanders of Canada (Princess Louise's), 1928-1953.* Montreal: privately printed, 1953. 497 pp.

Johnston, Murray. *Canada's Craftsmen; the Story of the Corps of Royal Canadian Electrical and Mechanical Engineers and of the Land Ordnance Engineering Branch.* n.p.: 1983. 291 pp.

Johnston, Stafford. *The Fighting Perths; the Story of the First Century in the Life of a Canadian County Regiment.* Stratford, Ont.: privately printed, 1964. 133 pp.

Journal de l'Armée canadienne. Vol. I-XIX. Ottawa: Imprimeur du Roi, 1947-65.

Juteau, Maurice (Pipo). *L'envers de ma guerre.* Ste-Sabine, P.Q.: imprimé privé, 1982. 203 pp.
Mémoires du service au Royal 22e Régiment.

_____. *Ma drôle de guerre; tiré du soldat qui pense.* Ste-Sabine, P.Q.: imprimé privé, 1980. 172 pp.
Mémoires du service au Royal 22e Régiment.

Kerry, A.J., and W.A. McDill. *The History of the Corps of Royal Canadian Engineers.* Ottawa: privately printed, 1962. 2 vols.

King, W.D., comp. *A Brief History of Militia Units Established at Various Periods at Yarmouth, Nova Scotia, 1812-1947.* Yarmouth, N.S.: privately printed, 1947. 32 pp.

Kitching, George. *Mud and Green Fields; the Memoirs of Major General George Kitching.* (Canadians at War Series.) Langley, B.C.: Battleline Books, 1986. 329 pp.

LeMaistre, Susan, ed./éd. *Memorials to Canada's War Dead./Mémoriaux aux Canadiens morts à la guerre.* Ottawa: Veterans Affairs Canada/Anciens combattants Canada, [198-?]. 135 pp.
Bilingual text./Texte bilingue.

The Link. Vol. I-IV? Rivers, Man.: privately printed, 1948-51?
Journal of Canadian Joint Air Training Centre, Rivers, Man.

Little Black Devils see Tascona, Bruce, and Eric Wells.

The Log; Royal Roads Military College. Vol. V- . Victoria, B.C.: privately printed, 1942- .

The Lorne Scots (Peel, Dufferin and Halton Regiment). Brampton, Ont.: privately printed, 1962. 47 pp.

*McCracken, George W. *Votre armée.* (Actualités; revue destinée aux Forces canadiennes, vol IV, no 10.) Ottawa: Imprimeur de la Reine, 1953. 31 pp.

* _____. *Your Army.* (Current Affairs for the Canadian Forces, vol. IV, no. 10.) Ottawa: Queen's Printer, 1953. 31 pp.

McGregor, F., ed. *LdSH (RC) '85-70'.* Winnipeg: privately printed, 1970. 62 pp.

Mackenzie, Lewis. *Peacekeeper; the Road to Sarajevo.* Vancouver: Douglas & McIntyre, 1993. 345 pp.

Mackenzie-Naughton, J.D. *The Princess of Wales' Own Regiment (M.G.).* Kingston, Ont.: privately printed, 1946. 74 pp.

McKeown, Michael G. *Kapyong Remembered; Anecdotes from Korea; Second Battalion, Princess Patricia's Canadian Light Infantry; Korea, 1950-1951.* n.p.: [1976]. 40 pp.

McKillican, D.R. *A Short History of the Toronto Scottish Regiment.* n.p.: 1972. 40 pp.

Magnacca, Stephen A. *1871-1971; One Hundredth Anniversary of the 13 Field Battery Based at Portage la Prairie, Manitoba.* n.p.: n.d. 12 pp.

Manarey, R. Barrie. *The Canadian Bayonet.* Edmonton: Century Press, 1971. 51 pp.

Maple Leaf Services Serving the Canadian Army. Ottawa: Queen's Printer, 1958. 18 pp.

Marcoux, Jules, éd. *CMR, 1952-1977; album du 25e anniversaire./25th Anniversary Album.* St-Jean, P.Q.: s.i./n.p., 1977. 62 pp. *Texte bilingue./Bilingual text.*

Marquis, G.E. *Le Régiment de Lévis; historique et album.* Lévis, P.Q.: s.i., 1952. 292 pp.

Marteinson, John, and others. *We Stand on Guard; an Illustrated History of the Canadian Army.* Montreal: Ovale, 1992. 511 pp.

Martin, Paul. *Canada and the Quest for Peace.* New York: Columbia Univ. Press, 1967. 93 pp.

Mazéas, Daniel. *Croquis d'insignes armée canadienne, 1920-1950; Canadian Badges.* Guingamp, France: privately printed, 1970. 64 pp.

————. *Insignes armée canadienne, 1900-1914; Canadian Badges: supplément, 1920-1950.* Guingamp, France: privately printed, 1972. 116 pp.

*The Medical and Dental Services of the Canadian Forces. (Current Affairs for the Canadian Forces, vol. VI, no. 1.) Ottawa: Queen's Printer, 1954. 31 pp.

Melady, John. *Korea: Canada's Forgotten War.* Toronto: Macmillan, 1983. 215 pp.

*Memorandum sur l'instruction de l'Armée canadienne. No 1-72. Ottawa: Imprimeur du Roi, 1941-47.

Milnes, Herbert. *A Story of the Oxford Rifles, 1798-1954.* (Oxford Museum Bulletin, no. 5.) Woodstock, Ont.: printed by Woodstock Print & Litho, 1974. 28 pp.

Mitchell, G.D., with B.A. Reid and W. Simcock. *RCHA — Right of the Line; an Anecdotal History of the Royal Canadian Horse Artillery from 1871.* Ottawa: RCHA History Committee, 1986. 303 pp.

Mitchell, Michael, comp. *Ducimus; the Regiments of the Canadian Infantry.* St. Hubert, Que.: Director of Infantry, Mobile Command Headquarters, 1992. 248 pp.

Moir, J.S., ed. *History of the Royal Canadian Corps of Signals, 1903-1961.* Ottawa: privately printed, 1962. 336 pp.

Moogk, Peter N., and R.V. Stevenson. *Vancouver Defended; a History of the Men and Guns of the Lower Mainland Defences, 1859-1949.* Surrey, B.C.: Antonson Pub., 1978. 128 pp.

Morris, David A. *The Canadian Militia; from 1855; an Historical Summary.* Erin, Ont.: Boston Mills Press, 1983. 328 pp.

Morrison, W. Alexander, and Stephanie A. Blair. *Canada and Peacekeeping; Dedication and Service.* Clementsport, N.S.: Lester B. Pearson Canadian International Peacekeeping Training Centre, 1995. 32 pp.

Nicholson, G.W.L. *Canada's Nursing Sisters.* (Canadian War Museum Historical Publication Number 13.) Toronto: S. Stevens, Hakkert, 1975. 272 pp.

_____. *The Gunners of Canada; the History of the Royal Regiment of Canadian Artillery.* Toronto: McClelland and Stewart, 1967-72. 2 vols.

_____. *Seventy Years of Service; a History of the Royal Canadian Army Medical Corps.* Ottawa: Borealis Press, 1977. 388 pp.

The Northwest Highway System; Canadian Army, General Information, Camp Takhini, Whitehorse, Y.T. Ottawa: Queen's Printer, 1961. 25 pp.

Notes for RCEME Officers Pending Issue of Corps Standing Orders. Ottawa: Queen's Printer, 1963. 44 pp.
Originally Restricted.

Ogle, Robert J. *The Faculties of Canadian Military Chaplains; a Commentary on the Faculty Sheet of December, 1955 and the Directives for Holy Week Promulgated March 14, 1956.* Ottawa: n.p., 1956. 267 pp.

Paré, Lorenzo. *Les canadiens français et l'organisation militaire.* (Oeuvre des tracts, 382.) Montréal: imprimé privé, [1951]. 16 pp.

The Patrician. Vol. I- . Edmonton: privately printed, 1948- .
Regimental journal of the Princess Patricia's Canadian Light Infantry.

Peacock, Robert S. *Kim-chi, Asahi and Rum; a Platoon Commander Remembers Korea 1952-1953.* n.p.: Lugus, 1994. 161 pp.

Penny, Arthur G. *Royal Rifles of Canada, "Able and Willing" since 1862; a Short History.* n.p.: 1962. 62 pp.

* *"Pourquoi je sers ma patrie".* (Actualités; revue destinée aux Forces canadiennes, vol X, no 15.) Ottawa: Imprimeur de la Reine, 1956. 26 pp.

The Powder Horn; Chronicle of the Queen's Own Rifles of Canada. Calgary, Victoria, B.C.: privately printed, 1960-70.

Presentation of Colours and Squadron Standard to The Loyal Edmonton Regiment (3 PPCLI) and 418 Squadron (City of Edmonton) RCAF by Her Royal Highness Princess Alexandra, Saturday, May 27th, 1967, Hamilton Gault Barracks, Edmonton, Alberta. [Edmonton: printed by] Edmonton Printers, [1967]. 16 pp.

Presentation of Colours by Her Majesty Queen Elizabeth II, to Canadian Grenadier Guards (6th Battalion, Canadian Guards), 48th Highlanders of Canada, the Argyll and Sutherland Highlanders of Canada (Princess Louise's.) Ottawa: n.p., 1959. 20 pp.

Presentation of Colours by His Excellency Major-General Georges P. Vanier, D.S.O., M.C., E.D., the Governor-General of Canada to the Royal Hamilton Light Infantry (Wentworth Regiment), Hamilton, Ontario, 30th June, 1962. n.p.: [1962]. 20 pp.

Presentation of Colours to the Second Battalion, The Royal Canadian Regiment, by Field-Marshal His Royal Highness the Duke of Edinburgh, Colonel-in-Chief of the Regiment, Nominated by Her Majesty the Queen to Make this Presentation, Fort York, Germany, 17th October 1955. Aldershot, Eng.: privately printed, 1955. [12] pp.

Presentation of Guidons and Colours by Her Majesty Queen Elizabeth II to 1st Battalion, the Canadian Guards, the Ontario Regiment, the Sherbrooke Hussars, 1st Hussars, the Cameron Highlanders of Ottawa, Ottawa, 5 July 1967. Ottawa: Queen's Printer, 1967. 1 vol., unpaged.

Presentation of New Colours to The Highland Light Infantry of Canada by Her Royal Highness the Princess Margaret, C.I., G.C.V.O., Colonel-in-Chief of the Regiment, Nominated by Her Majesty the Queen to Make this Presentation, Hamilton, Ontario, August 1st, 1958. Ottawa: Queen's Printer, 1958. 1 vol., unpaged.

Presentation of New Colours to The Perth Regiment by Lt.-Col. The Honourable John Keiller Mackay, DSO, BD, QC, LLD, Lieutenant-Governor of Ontario, Saturday, June 30, 1962 at Queen's Park, Stratford, Ontario, and Laying Up of Old Colours, Preacher: Major The Rev. D.C. Smith, MC, CD, Chaplain of The Perth Regiment 1940-1945, Sunday, July 1, 1962, at St. James Church, Stratford, Ontario. n.p.: [1962]. 1 vol., unpaged.

*Preston, Richard A. *Au service du Canada; histoire du Royal Military College depuis la Deuxième Guerre mondiale.* s.l.: Presses de l'Université d'Ottawa, 1992. 286 pp.

Preston, Richard A. *Canada's RMC; a History of the Royal Military College.* Toronto: Univ. of Toronto Press, 1969. 415 pp.

*_____. *To Serve Canada; a History of the Royal Military College since the Second World War.* Ottawa: Univ. of Ottawa Press, 1991. 248 pp.

Programme-souvenir; le Régiment de Hull, mai 1964; publication autorisée par le Lt-Col. Guy de Marlis, C.D., Commandant, le Régiment de Hull; programme-souvenir publié pour marquer le 50e anniversaire du Régiment de Hull et le 25e anniversaire du Manège de Salaberry. Hull, P.Q.: imprimé privé, [1964]. 60 pp.

Queen-Hughes, R.W. *Whatever Men Dare; a History of the Queen's Own Cameron Highlanders of Canada, 1935-1960.* Winnipeg: privately printed, 1960. 247 pp.

The Queen's Own Rifles of Canada Association. *Yearbook.* [Toronto: n.p.], 1923-47. 18 vols.
Not issued 1939-44, 1946.

Quigley, John Gordon. *A Century of Rifles, 1860-1960; the Halifax Rifles (RCAC)(M); "cede nullis".* Halifax: privately printed, 1960. 230 pp.

R.C.E.M.E. Quarterly. Vol. I-V. Ottawa: King's Printer, 1949-53.

The RCOC Quarterly. Vol. I-VII. Ottawa: n.p., 1947-54?

Rannie, William F., ed. *To the Thunderer his Arms; The Royal Canadian Ordnance Corps.* Lincoln, Ont.: privately printed, 1984. 360 pp.

Review of the Regiment and Presentation of New Colours to the First and Third Battalions by the Colonel-in-Chief His Royal Highness the Prince Philip, Duke of Edinburgh, London, Ontario, 2nd July 1959. n.p.: [1959]. 1 vol., unpaged.
The Royal Canadian Regiment.

La revue régimentaire; le Régiment de Maisonneuve. Vol I-VIII. Montréal: imprimé privé, 1960-72.

Rioux, Denise. *Les Fusiliers de Sherbrooke (1910-1980).* Sherbrooke, P.Q.: s.i., 1980. 68 pp.

Robertson, Peter. *Irréductible vérité/Relentless Verity/les photographes militaires canadiens depuis 1885/Canadian Military Photographers since 1885.* (Les Archives publiques du Canada/Public Archives of Canada Series.) Québec, P.Q.: Les Presses de l'Université Laval, 1973. 233 pp.
Texte bilingue./Bilingual text.

Rosner, Gabriella. *The U.N. Emergency Force.* New York: Columbia Univ. Press, 1963. 294 pp.

Roy, R.H. *Ready for the Fray (Deas Gu Cath); the History of the Canadian Scottish Regiment (Princess Mary's), 1920-1955.* Vancouver: privately printed, 1958. 509 pp.

_____. *The Seaforth Highlanders of Canada, 1919-1965.* Vancouver: privately printed, 1969. 559 pp.

_____. *Sinews of Steel; the History of the British Columbia Dragoons.* Brampton, Ont.: privately printed, 1965. 468 pp.

*The Royal Canadian Armoured Corps. Ottawa: Queen's Printer, 1953. 11 pp.

Royal Canadian Armoured Corps (Cavalry) Association *see* Canadian Cavalry Association.

*The Royal Canadian Army Medical Corps. Ottawa: Queen's Printer, 1953. 10 pp.

*Royal Canadian Army Pay Corps. Ottawa: Queen's Printer, 1953. 11 pp.

*The Royal Canadian Army Service Corps. Ottawa: Queen's Printer, 1953. 11 pp.

The Royal Canadian Artillery. Ottawa: Queen's Printer, 1953. 10 pp.

Royal Canadian Horse Artillery; First Regiment, 1871-1971. Lahr, Germany: privately printed, [1971]. 32 pp.

The Royal Canadian Ordnance Corps Diamond Jubilee Yearbook. n.p.: 1963. 106 pp.

Royal Canadian Signals Quarterly. Vol. I-II? Ottawa: King's Printer, 1951-52?

Royal Military College of Canada, Kingston, Ont. *The Cadet Handbook.* Kingston, Ont.: n.p., [1957?]. 59 pp., looseleaf.

The Royal Military College of Canada Review. Vol. I- . Kingston, Ont.: privately printed, 1920- .

Le Royal 22e Régiment; remise de nouveaux drapeaux aux 1er, 2eme et 3eme bataillons par Sa Majesté la Reine Elizabeth II; les plaines d'Abraham, le 23 juin 1959. Aldershot, Angleterre: imprimé privé, 1959. [16] pp.

The Royal Westminster Regiment, 1863-1988. New Westminster, B.C.: n.p., 1988. 72 pp.

Rudbach, N.E. *The Halifax Rifles (23 Armoured Regiment) R.C.A.C.R.F.; "90th" Anniversary, 14th May 1860 — 14th May 1950.* Halifax: n.p., 1950. 20 pp.

Rutherford, Tom. *An Unofficial History of the Grey and Simcoe Foresters Regiment, 1866-1973.* n.p.: n.d. 88 pp.

Schragg, Lex. *History of the Ontario Regiment, 1866-1951.* Oshawa, Ont.: privately printed, 1951. 286 pp.

Sealey, D. Bruce, and Peter Van de Vyvere. *Thomas George Prince.* (Manitobans in Profile.) Winnipeg: Peguis Publishers, 1981. 52 pp.

Service, G.T., and J.K. Marteinson. *The Gate; a History of the Fort Garry Horse.* Calgary: privately printed, 1971. 228 pp.

*Les services médicaux et dentaires pour les Forces armées. (Actualités; revue destinée aux Forces canadiennes, vol VI, no 1.) Ottawa: Imprimeur de la Reine, 1954. 31 pp.

Sexton, Donal J. *A Guide to Canadian Shoulder Titles, 1939-1985; a Collector's and Historian's Comprehensive Guide to the Cloth Shoulder Titles Worn by the Regiments and Corps of the Canadian Army in 1939-1985.* Hinsdale, Ill.: Pass in Review Publications, 1987. 97 pp.

A Short History of the British Columbia Regiment; the "Dukes". n.p.: n.d. [11] pp.

The Signalman. Vol. I-IV? Kingston, Ont.: King's Printer, 1942-46?

Smith, Kenneth B. *"Duffy's Regiment".* Don Mills, Ont.: printed by T.H. Best Print. Co., 1983. 222 pp.
Angus Duffy and the Hastings and Prince Edward Regiment.

Snowy Owl; Journal of the Canadian Land Forces Command and Staff College. Kingston, Ont.: privately printed, 1952-73. 18 vols.
Title varies.

South Alberta Light Horse; Calgary Highlanders; the Ceremony of the Presentation of Guidon and New Colours by Her Royal Highness Princess Alexandra, Currie Barracks, Calgary, Alberta, Thursday, May 25th, 1967. Calgary: Burnand Print. Co., [1967]. 15 pp.

The Springbok. Various places: n.p., 1923- .
Regimental journal of the Royal Canadian Dragoons. Title varies: The Goat *(1923-36).*

Stacey, C.P. *A Date with History; Memoirs of a Canadian Historian.* Ottawa: Deneau, [1982]. 293 pp.

**Stacey, C.P., H.E.W. Strange and F.H. Hitchins. *Canada's Armed Forces Today.* (Current Affairs for the Canadian Forces, vol. II, no. 9.) Ottawa: Queen's Printer, 1952. 22 pp.

**Stacey, C.P., H.E.W. Strange et F.H. Hitchins. *Les Forces armées du Canada.* (Actualités; revue destinée aux Forces canadiennes, vol II, no 9.) Ottawa: Imprimeur de la Reine, 1952. 22 pp.

**Stanley, George F.G. *Canada's Soldiers, 1604-1954; the Military History of an Unmilitary People.* Toronto: Macmillan, 1954. 400 pp.
Subsequent revised and enlarged editions.

Stanley, George F.G. *In the Face of Danger; the History of the Lake Superior Regiment.* Port Arthur, Ont.: privately printed, 1960. 357 pp.

*_____. *Nos soldats; l'histoire militaire du Canada de 1604 à nos jours.* Traduction et adaptation sous la direction de Serge Bernier. Montréal: Les Editions de l'homme, 1980. 620 pp.

Stanley, George F.G., and Richard A. Preston. *A Short History of Kingston as a Military and Naval Centre.* Kingston, Ont.: Queen's Printer, [195-?]. 33 pp.

Stefaniuk, M.E. *8th Canadian Hussars (Princess Louise's), 1957-1967.* n.p.: privately printed, 1967. 154 pp.

Steven, Walter T. *In this Sign.* Toronto: Ryerson Press, 1948. 182 pp.

Stevens, G.R. *The Sun is Setting on the Paleface Brave or Down the Drain a Billion a Year Goes.* Montreal: privately printed, [1968]. 16 pp.

Stewart, Charles Henry, comp. *The Concise Lineages of the Canadian Army, 1855 to Date.* Toronto: n.p., n.d. 163 pp.

Stone, James R., and Jacques Castonguay. *Korea 1951; Two Canadian Battles.* (Canadian Battle Series no. 6.) Ottawa: Balmuir Book Pub.; Canadian War Museum, National Museums of Canada, 1988. 51 pp.

The Strathconian. Calgary: n.p., 1914-?, 1927-38, 1947- .
Regimental journal of the Lord Strathcona's Horse (Royal Canadians). Re-numbered from no. 1 after each gap in publication.

Stuart, (Sir) Campbell. *Opportunity Knocks Once.* London: Collins, 1952. 248 pp.

*Summerby, Janice. *Native Soldiers; Foreign Battlefields.* Ottawa: Communications Division, Veterans Affairs Canada, 1993. 47 pp.

*_____. *Soldats autochtones; terres étrangères.* Ottawa: Direction générale des communications, Anciens combattants Canada, 1993. 51 pp.

Summers, Jack L. *Tangled Web: Canadian Infantry Accoutrements, 1855-1985.* (Canadian War Museum Historical Publication no. 26.) Alexandria Bay, N.Y.: Museum Restoration Service, 1992. 146 pp.

*Summers, Jack L., and René Chartrand. *Military Uniforms in Canada, 1665-1970.* Illustrated by R.J. Marrion. (Canadian War Museum Historical Publication no. 16.) Ottawa: National Museums of Canada, 1981. 192 pp.

*Summers, Jack L., et René Chartrand. *L'uniforme militaire au Canada, 1665-1970.* Illustré par R.J. Marrion. Traduit par Jean Pariseau. (Musée canadien de la guerre publication d'histoire militaire no 16.) Ottawa: Musées nationaux du Canada, 1981. 192 pp.

Suthren, Victor, ed. *The Oxford Book of Canadian Military Anecdotes.* Toronto: Oxford Univ. Press, 1989. 202 pp.

Tackaberry, R.B. *Keeping the Peace; a Canadian Military Viewpoint on Peace-Keeping Operations.* (Behind the Headlines, vol. XXVI.) Toronto: Canadian Institute of International Affairs, 1966. 26 pp.

Tascona, Bruce. *The Militia of Manitoba; a Study of Infantry and Cavalry Regiments since 1883; a Look at Regimental Badges and Uniforms, List of Commanding Officers, Battle Honours.* n.p.: 1979. 48 pp.

_____. *XII Manitoba Dragoons: a Tribute.* Winnipeg: Manitoba Dragoons History Book Committee, 1991. 185 pp.

[Tascona, Bruce, and Eric Wells.] *Little Black Devils; a History of the Royal Winnipeg Rifles.* Winnipeg: Frye Pub., 1983. 241 pp.

Taylor, Alastair, David Cox and J.L. Granatstein. *Peacekeeping; International Challenge and Canadian Response.* (Contemporary Affairs, no. 39.) [Toronto]: Canadian Institute of International Affairs, 1968. 211 pp.

Telford, Murray M. *Scarlet to Green; the Colours, Uniforms and Insignia of the Grey and Simcoe Foresters.* Erin, Ont.: Boston Mills Press, 1987. 64 pp.

Thompson, Roy J.C. *Canadian Army Cap Badges, 1953-1973.* [Dartmouth], N.S.: n.p., 1973. 215 pp.

_____. *Cap Badges of the Canadian Officer Training Corps.* Dartmouth, N.S.: n.p., 1972. 68 pp.

_____. *Wings of the Canadian Armed Forces, 1913-1972.* [Dartmouth], N.S.: n.p., 1973. 106 pp.

The Toronto Scottish Regimental Gazette. Vol. I. n.p.: privately printed, 1946-50.

*La Trésorerie militaire royale canadienne. Ottawa: Imprimeur de la Reine, 1954. 12 pp.

True Canadian War Stories, selected by Jane Dewar from the pages of Legion Magazine. Toronto: Lester & Orpen Dennys, 1986. 310 pp.

Tyler, G.C.A. *The Lion Rampant; a Pictorial History of the Queen's Own Cameron Highlanders of Canada, 1910-1985.* Winnipeg: The Queen's Own Cameron Highlanders of Canada, 1985. 134 pp.

Upper Canada Historical Arms Society. *The Military Arms of Canada.* (Historical Arms Series, 1.) West Hill, Ont.: Museum Restoration Service, 1963. 47 pp.

Van Der Schee, W. *A Short History of Lord Strathcona's Horse (Royal Canadians).* n.p.: 1973. 19 l.

Victoria Rifles of Canada, 1861-1951; Historical Notes. n.p.: n.d. 14 pp.

Les Voltigeurs de Québec, 1862-1952; notes historiques. s.l.: s.i., 1952. 16 pp.

Les Voltigeurs de Québec, 1862-1962; album du centenaire, mai 1962. St-François, P.Q.: imprimé privé, 1962. 31 pp.

Vox Pat. Vol. I-IV? n.p.: privately printed, 1954-57?
Title varies, vol. I no. 1-2 titled: 2 VP; You Name It. Journal of 2nd Battalion, Princess Patricia's Canadian Light Infantry.

Warren, Arnold. *Wait for the Wagon; the Story of the Royal Canadian Army Service Corps.* Toronto: McClelland and Stewart, 1961. 413 pp.

Watson, W.S., and others, eds. *The Brockville Rifles, Royal Canadian Infantry Corps (Allied with the King's Royal Rifle Corps); Semper Paratus; an Unofficial History.* Brockville, Ont.: Recorder Print. Co., 1966. 138 pp.

Wellington Legion War Veterans Club, eds. *They Served for Freedom./A la défense de la liberté.* [Wellington, P.E.I.: Royal Canadian Legion, Wellington Branch 17/Wellington, I.P.E.: Légion royale canadienne, la filiale de Wellington no 17], 1986. 319 pp.
Bilingual text./Texte bilingue.

* *"Why I Serve"*, by the Serviceman. (Current Affairs for the Canadian Forces, vol. X, no. 15.) Ottawa: Queen's Printer, 1956. 26 pp.

Willcocks, K.D.H. *The Hastings and Prince Edward Regiment, Canada; a Short History.* Belleville, Ont.: n.p., 1967. 1 vol., unpaged.

Williams, Jeffery. *Princess Patricia's Canadian Light Infantry.* (Famous Regiments.) London: L. Cooper, 1972. 110 pp.

The Windsor Regiment (Royal Canadian Armoured Corps); Presentation of the Guidon by The Honourable W. Earl Rowe, PC, Lieutenant-Governor of Ontario, Windsor Stadium, Windsor, Ontario, Sunday, June 16th, 1963. n.p.: [1963]. 12 pp.

Winton, Maurice V. *Saskatchewan's Prairie Soldiers, 1885-1980.* n.p.: n.d. 174 pp.
Cover title: A Pictorial History of Saskatchewan's Military Badges and Medals.

*Wood, Herbert Fairlie. *Singulier champ de bataille; les opérations en Corée et leurs effets sur la politique de défense du Canada.* (Histoire officielle de l'Armée canadienne.) Ottawa; Imprimeur de la Reine, 1966. 354 pp.

* _____. *Strange Battleground; the Operations in Korea and their Effects on the Defence Policy of Canada.* (Official History of the Canadian Army.) Ottawa: Queen's Printer, 1966. 317 pp.

Worthington, Larry. *The Spur and the Sprocket; the Story of the Royal Canadian Dragoons.* Kitchener, Ont.: Reeve Press, 1968. 170 pp.

Worthington, Larry. *"Worthy"; a Biography of Major-General F.F. Worthington, C.B., M.C., M.M.* Toronto: Macmillan, 1961. 236 pp.

E. AIR FORCES — LES FORCES AÉRIENNES

1867-1918

Air Heroes in the Making; the Imperial Royal Flying Corps. n.p.: n.d. 19 pp.

Airforce. Vol. I- . Ottawa: Air Force Productions, 1977- .
Quarterly. *Recommended by the Royal Canadian Air Force Association.*

Art Gallery of Toronto. *Catalogue of an Exhibition of the Canadian War Memorials, October 1926.* Toronto: privately printed, [1926]. 21 pp.

Ashbury College, Ottawa. *List of Masters and Old Boys who Served with the Colours, 1914-1919.* Ottawa: Simmons Print. Co., [1919]. 33 pp.

Bank of Montreal. *Memorial of the Great War, 1914-1918; a Record of Service.* Montreal: privately printed, 1921. 261 pp.

_____. *Victory; a Monument in Memory of the Men in the Service of the Bank of Montreal who Fell in the Great War.* n.p.: [1924]. 19 pp.

Bindon, Kathryn M. *More than Patriotism.* (A Personal Library Publication.) Don Mills, Ont.: Nelson, 1979. 192 pp.

Bishop, William A. *Winged Peace.* New York: Viking Press, 1944. 175 pp.

_____. *Winged Warfare.* Toronto: McClelland, Goodchild and Stewart, 1918. 272 pp.

Bishop, William Arthur. *Courage in the Air.* (Canada's Military Heritage, Volume 1.) Toronto: McGraw-Hill Ryerson, 1992. 307 pp.

_____. *The Courage of the Early Morning; a Son's Biography of a Famous Father; the Story of Billy Bishop.* Toronto: McClelland & Stewart, 1965. 211 pp.

Blay, Cecil E. *Portraits and Sketches of Hartney District Veterans; Great War 1914-1918.* Brandon, Man.: printed by Sun Pub. Co., [1921]. 82 pp.

The C.A.H.S. Journal. Vol. I- . Willowdale, Ont.: Canadian Aviation Historical Society, 1963- .

Cadet Wing Review; R.A.F. Long Branch, Ont. Vol. I. Toronto: privately printed, 1918.

Canada. Air Force. *Canada's Air Heritage.* Ottawa: King's Printer, 1941. 23 pp.

Canada. Air Force Headquarters. Air Historical Section. *RCAF Logbook; a Chronological Outline of the Origin, Growth and Achievement of the Royal Canadian Air Force.* Ottawa: King's Printer, 1949. 96 pp.

Canada. Director of Public Information. *Canada's Part in the Great War.* Ottawa: n.p., 1919. 64 pp.
Also issued by Information Branch, Dept. of External Affairs.

Canada. Ministry of Overseas Military Forces of Canada. *Report of the Ministry; Overseas Military Forces of Canada, 1918.* London: H.M. Stationery Office, 1919. 533 pp.

Canada. Parliament. Senate. Standing Committee on Social Affairs, Science and Technology. *Production and Distribution of the National Film Board Production "The Kid who Couldn't Miss."/Production et distribution du film de l'Office national de film intitulé «The Kid Who Couldn't Miss»,* rapport du Comité sénatorial des affaires sociales, des sciences et de la technologie. n.p.: Supply and Services Canada/s.l.: Approvisionnements et Services Canada, 1986. 21/22 pp.

Canada in Action; a Souvenir of the Canadian War Memorials Exhibition; Containing Reproductions of Some of the Principal Mural Decorations, Battle Pictures, Portraits, etc, which are to Constitute Canada's Permanent War Memorial. n.p.: Canadian War Memorials Fund, 1919. 1 vol., chiefly illus.

Canada in the Great World War; an Authentic Account of the Military History of Canada from the Earliest Days to the Close of the War of the Nations, by Various Authorities. Toronto: United Publishers, 1917-21. 6 vols.

Canadian Bank of Commerce. *Letters from the Front; being a Record of the Part Played by Officers of the Bank in the Great War, 1914-1919.* Toronto: privately printed, n.d. 2 vols.

Canadian Broadcasting Corporation. *Flanders' Fields.* n.p.: [1964]. 1 vol., unpaged.

Canadian Infantry Association. *Canadian Official War Photographs, with the Compliments of the Canadian Infantry Association.* Ottawa: Canadian Infantry Association, 1928. 144 pp.
Catalogue arranged by negative number.

Canadian Pacific Railway Co. *Their Glory Cannot Fade.* n.p.: 1918. [15] pp.

Canadian War Memorials Painting Exhibition, 1920; New Series; the Last Phase. n.p.: n.d. 25 pp.

The Canadian War Pictorial. No. 1-4. London: Canadian War Records Office, [1916-18.]

Canadian War Records Office. *Art and War; Canadian War Memorials; a Selection of the Works Executed for the Canadian War Memorials Fund to Form a Record of Canada's Part in the Great War and a Memorial to Those Canadians who have Made the Great Sacrifice.* London: n.p., 1919. 1 vol., unpaged.

_____. *Canadian War Memorials Exhibition, [New York] 1919.* n.p.: n.d. 48 pp.

_____. *Thirty Canadian V.C.'s; 23rd April 1915 to 20th March 1918.* London: Skeffington, n.d. 96 pp.

Carisella, P.J., and James W. Ryan. *Who Killed the Red Baron; the Final Answer.* Wakefield, Mass.: Daedalus, 1969. 254 pp.

Carr, William Guy. *Out of the Mists.* London: Hutchinson, n.d. 176 pp.

Carroll, Warren. *Wings, 1913-1945; Royal Flying Corps, Royal Naval Air Service, Canadian Aviation Corps, Royal Canadian Naval Air Service, Canadian Air Force, Royal Canadian Air Force, Fleet Air Arm, Royal Air Force, Armies of Great Britain and Canada.* Thornhill, Ont.: n.p., 1981. 127 pp.
Flying badges.

Castonguay. Jacques. *Unsung Mission; History of the Chaplaincy Service (RC) of the R.C.A.F.* Montreal: Institut de Pastorale, 1968. 173 pp.

Catalogue of Canadian War Trophies; Including Field Guns, Surrendered and Captured Planes, Flags, Uniforms, Helmets, Swords, Posters, Proclamations, Prints, etc., National Exhibition, Toronto, August 23 to September 6, 1919. n.p.: [1919]. 64 pp.

Catalogue of Canadian War Trophies; Including Field Guns, Surrendered and Captured Planes, Flags, Uniforms, Helmets, Swords, Posters, Proclamations, Prints, etc., The Armouries, Hamilton, November 3 to November 15, 1919. n.p.: [1919]. 64 pp.

Chajkowsky, William E. *The History of Camp Borden, 1916-1918; Land of Sand, Sin and Sorrow.* Jordan Station, Ont.: Station Press, 1983. 106 pp.

_____. *Royal Flying Corps; Borden to Texas to Beamsville.* Cheltenham, Ont.: Boston Mills Press, 1979. 127 pp.

La Chapelle du Souvenir, Chambres du Parlement, Ottawa, Canada, [par A.F. Duguid.] Ottawa: Photogelatine Engraving Co., s.d. 1 tome, non-paginé.

Clark, Don. *Wild Blue Yonder; an Air Epic.* Seattle, Wash.: Superior, 1972. 172 pp.

Collishaw, Raymond, and R.V. Dodds. *Air Command; a Fighter Pilot's Story.* London: W. Kimber, 1973. 256 pp.

Corporation of British Columbia Land Surveyors. *Roll of Honour; British Columbia Land Surveyors; 1914 the Great War 1918.* n.p.: privately printed, n.d. 1 vol., unpaged.

Cosgrove, Edmund. *Canada's Fighting Pilots.* (Canadian Portraits.) Toronto: Clarke, Irwin, 1965. 190 pp.

Costello, W. Brian. *A Nursery of the Air Force; the Story of the Carleton Place Great War Airmen and the Brown/Richthofen Saga.* Carleton Place, Ont.: Forest Beauty Products, 1979. 187 pp.

Creed. Catherine. *"Whose Debtors We Are".* (Niagara Historical Society, 34.) Niagara, Ont.: Niagara Historical Society, 1922. 116 pp.

Cresswell, [C.E.] *Memorial Album Dedicated to our Beloved Dead by their Bereaved and Sorrowing Friends.* London, Ont.: privately printed, n.d. 279 pp.
Commemorates dead from London-Stratford-Windsor-Sarnia area.

Critchley, A. *Critch! The Memoirs of Brigadier-General A.C. Critchley.* London: Hutchinson, 1961. 256 pp.

Cross, Michael, and Robert Bothwell, eds. *Policy by Other Means; Essays in Honour of C.P. Stacey.* Toronto: Clarke, Irwin, 1972. 258 pp.

Dodds, Ronald. *The Brave Young Wings.* Stittsville, Ont.: Canada's Wings, 1980. 293 pp.

Dominion of Canada Roll of Honor; a Directory of Casualties (Deaths Only) of the World's Greatest War, 1914-1918, of the City of Toronto; Dedicated to Perpetuate Those who Made the Supreme Sacrifice, "They shall not be Forgotten". n.p.: C. McAlpine, 1919. 28 1.

Drew, George A. *Canada's Fighting Airmen.* Toronto: MacLean Pub. Co., 1930. 305 pp.

Drolet, "Gil". *Loyola, the Wars: in Remembrance of "Men for Others".* Waterloo, Ont.: Laurier Centre for Military Strategic and Disarmament Studies, 1996. 44 pp.
Memorial to the war dead of Loyola High School and College.

Duguid, Archer Fortescue. *The Canadian Forces in the Great War, 1914-1919; the Record of Five Years of Active Service.* Ottawa: King's Printer, 1947. 14 pp.

Duguid, Archer Fortescue, *see also/voir aussi The Memorial Chamber in the Peace Tower ...; La Chapelle du Souvenir ....*

Duncan-Clark, S.J., and W.R. Plewman. *Pictorial History of the Great War,* [including] *Canada in the Great War,* by W.S. Wallace. Toronto: J.L. Nichols, 1919. 2 vols. in 1.

Ellis, Frank H. *Canada's Flying Heritage*. Toronto: Univ. of Toronto Press, 1954. 398 pp.

_____. *Fifty Years of Adventure and Progress in Canadian Skies*. Toronto: Ryerson Press, 1959. 230 pp.

Fetherstonhaugh, R.C. *McGill University at War, 1914-1918; 1939-1945*. Montreal: McGill Univ., 1947. 437 pp.

Fighters for Freedom; Honor Roll of Halifax; the Great War, 1914-1919. Halifax: Service Pub. Co., [1919]. 191 pp.

Foster, J.A. *For Love and Glory; a Pictorial History of Canada's Air Forces*. Toronto: McClelland & Stewart, 1989. 143 pp.

_____. *Sea Wings; a Pictorial History of Canada's Waterborne Defence Aircraft*. Toronto: Methuen, 1986. 143 pp.

Fuller, G.A., J.A. Griffin and K.M. Molson. *125 Years of Canadian Aeronautics; a Chronology 1840-1965*. Willowdale, Ont.: Canadian Aviation Historical Society, 1983. 328 pp.

Gardam, John. *Seventy Years After, 1914-1984*. Stittsville, Ont.: Canada's Wings, 1983. 99 pp.

[Garvin, Amelia Beers (Warnock).] *Canada's Peace Tower and Memorial Chamber, Designed by John A. Pearson, D. Arch., F.R.A.I.C., F.R.I.B.A., A.R.C.A., G.D.I.A., a Record and Interpretation by Katherine Hale [pseud.] Dedicated by the Architect to the Veterans of the Great War*. Toronto: Mundy-Goodfellow Print. Co., 1935. 29 pp.

Godenrath, Percy F. *Lest We Forget; a Record in Art of the Dominion's Part in the War (1914-1918) and a Memorial to Those Canadians who Made the Great Sacrifice, being the Gift of the Over-Seas Military Forces to the Nation; a Brief History of the Collection of War Paintings, Etchings and Sculpture, Made Possible by the Work of the Canadian War Memorials Fund and the Canadian War Record Office*. Ottawa: n.p., 1934. 46 pp.

Gordon, John. *... Of Men and Planes*. Ottawa: Love Print., 1968. 3 vols.

_____. *Winged Sentries./Sentinelles de l'air*. Claude Rousseau, illus. n.p./s.l.: s.i., 1963. 104 pp.
Bilingual text./ Texte bilingue.

Graves, Sandham. *The Lost Diary*. Victoria, B.C.: C.F. Banford, 1941. 131 pp.

Gt. Brit. Imperial War Graves Commission. *The War Graves of the British Empire; the Register of the Names of Those who Fell in the Great War and are Buried in Cemeteries and Churchyards in Nova Scotia, Prince Edward Island and New Brunswick, Canada*. London: H.M. Stationery Office, 1931. 92 pp.

Gt. Brit. Imperial War Graves Commission. *The War Graves of the British Empire; the Register of the Names of Those who Fell in the Great War and are Buried in Cemeteries in Newfoundland.* London: H.M. Stationery Office, 1930. 19 pp.

_____. *The War Graves of the British Empire; the Register of the Names of Those who Fell in the Great War and are Buried in Cemeteries in the Province of British Columbia, Canada.* London: H.M. Stationery Office, 1931. 48 pp.

_____. *The War Graves of the British Empire; the Register of the Names of Those who Fell in the Great War and are Buried in Cemeteries in the Province of Manitoba, Canada.* London: H.M. Stationery Office, 1931. 48 pp.

_____. *The War Graves of the British Empire; the Register of the Names of Those who Fell in the Great War and are Buried in Cemeteries in the Province of Ontario, Canada.* London: H.M. Stationery Office, 1931. 2 vols.

_____. *The War Graves of the British Empire; the Register of the Names of Those who Fell in the Great War and are Buried in Cemeteries in the Province of Quebec, Canada.* London: H.M. Stationery Office, 1931. 64 pp.

_____. *The War Graves of the British Empire; the Register of the Names of Those who Fell in the Great War and are Buried in Cemeteries in the Provinces of Saskatchewan and Alberta, Canada.* London: H.M. Stationery Office, 1931. 63 pp.

Greenhous, Brereton, ed./éd. *A Rattle of Pebbles: the First World War Diaries of Two Canadian Airmen./Un crépitement de galets: les journaux de deux aviateurs canadiens de la Première Guerre mondiale.* (Department of National Defence/Ministère de la Défense nationale/Directorate of History/ Service historique/Monograph no. 4./Monographie no 4.) Ottawa: Canadian Government Publishing Centre, Supply and Services Canada, 1987. 366 pp. *Diaries of John Bernard "Don" Brophy and Harold Price./Journaux de John Bernard "Don" Brophy et de Harold Price.*

Groves, Hubert, comp. *Toronto Does Her "Bit".* Toronto: Municipal Intelligence Bureau, 1918. 72 pp.

Hale, Katherine, [*pseud.*] *see* Garvin, Amelia Beers (Warnock).

[Hallam, T. Douglas.] *The Spider Web; the Romance of a Flying-Boat Flight,* by P.I.X. [*pseud.*] Edinburgh: W. Blackwood, 1919. 278 pp.

Halliday, H.A. *Chronology of Canadian Military Aviation.* (National Museum of Man Mercury Series; Canadian War Museum Paper, no. 6.) Ottawa: [Queen's Printer], 1975. 168 pp.

Halliday, H.A. *Tragic Victory./Une victoire tragique.* Ottawa: National Museum of Man, National Museums of Canada/Musée national de l'Homme, Musées nationaux du Canada, 1978. 61 pp.
Exhibition of First World War war art./Exposition de l'art militaire de la Première Guerre mondiale.

Hampson, Bill. *Canadian Flying Services Emblems & Insignia (1914-1984).* Vancouver: privately printed, 1986. 193 pp.

Harris, John Norman. *Knights of the Air; Canadian Aces of World War I.* (Great Stories of Canada, no. 18.) Toronto: Macmillan, 1958. 156 pp.

Hartney, Harold E. *Up and at 'Em.* Stanley M. Ulanoff, ed. (Air Combat Classics.) Garden City, N.Y.: Doubleday, 1971. 360 pp.

Herrington, Walter S., and A.J. Wilson. *The War Work of the County of Lennox and Addington.* Napanee, Ont.: Beaver Press, 1922. 278 pp.

Hezzelwood, Oliver, *see* Trinity Methodist Church, Toronto, Ont.

High Flight. Vol. I-III. Stittsville Ont.: Canada's Wings, [1981?-85.]

Holman, R.F. *Best in the West; the Story of Number 2 Canadian Forces Flying Training School and Flying Training in Canada.* Moose Jaw, Sask.: Big 2 Fund, 15 Wing Moose Jaw, 1995. [223] pp.

Horrocks, William. *In their own Words.* Ottawa: Rideau Veterans Home Residents Council, 1993. 247 pp.

The Illustrated Review of Aviation in Canada; Celebrating the Golden Anniversary of Powered Flight in Canada. Montreal: privately printed, [1959]. 1 vol., unpaged.

*Kealy, J.D.F., and E.C. Russell. *A History of Canadian Naval Aviation, 1918-1962.* Ottawa: Queen's Printer, 1965. 164 pp.

*Kealy, J.D.F., et E.C. Russell. *Histoire de l'aéronavale canadienne, 1918-1962.* Ottawa: Imprimeur de la Reine, 1965. 185 pp.

Langeste, Tom, comp. *Words on the Wing; Slang, Aphorisms, Catchphrases and Jargon of Canadian Military Aviation since 1914.* Toronto: Canadian Institute of Strategic Studies, 1995. 330 pp.

McCaffery, Dan. *Air Aces; the Lives and Times of Twelve Canadian Fighter Pilots.* Toronto: J. Lorimer, 1990. 234 pp.

_____. *Billy Bishop; Canadian Hero.* Toronto: J. Lorimer, 1988. 227 pp.

McGill Univ., Montreal, P.Q. *McGill Honour Roll, 1914-1918.* Montreal: McGill Univ., 1926. 228 pp.

_____. *A Memorial Service for the McGill Men and Women who Gave their Lives during the First and Second World Wars.* n.p.: [1946]. 1 vol., unpaged.

*Main, J.R.K. *Les voyageurs de l'air; historique de l'aviation civile au Canada, 1859-1967.* Ottawa: Imprimeur de la Reine, 1967. 433 pp.

*_____. *Voyageurs of the Air; a History of Civil Aviation in Canada.* Ottawa: Queen's Printer, 1967. 397 pp.

Mathieson, William D. *Billy Bishop, VC.* (The Canadians.) Markham, Ont.: Fitzhenry & Whiteside, 1989. 63 pp.

_____. *My Grandfather's War; Canadians Remember the First World War, 1914-1918.* Toronto: Macmillan, 1981. 338 pp.

Mazéas, Daniel. *Insignes armée canadienne, 1900-1914; Canadian Badges; supplément, 1920-1950.* Guingamp, France: privately printed, 1972. 116 pp.

The Memorial Chamber in the Peace Tower, Houses of Parliament, Ottawa, Canada, [by A.F. Duguid.] Ottawa: Photogelatine Engraving Co., n.d. [34] pp.

Milberry, Larry. *Aviation in Canada.* Toronto: McGraw-Hill Ryerson, 1979. 272 pp.

Milberry, Larry, ed. *Sixty Years; the RCAF and CF Air Command 1924-1984.* Toronto: CANAV Books, 1984. 480 pp.

Miller, James Martin, and H.S. Canfield. *The People's War Book; History, Encyclopedia and Chronology of the Great World War; and Canada's Part in the War,* by W.R. Plewman. Toronto: Imperial Pub. Co., 1919. 520 pp.

*Molson, K.M. *Canada's National Aviation Museum; its History and Collections.* Ottawa: National Aviation Museum, National Museum of Science and Technology, 1988. 291 pp.

*_____. *Le Musée national de l'aviation du Canada; son histoire et ses collections.* Ottawa: Musée national de l'aviation, Musée national des sciences et de la technologie, 1988. [288] pp.

Molson, K.M., and H.A. Taylor. *Canadian Aircraft since 1909.* Stittsville, Ont.: Canada's Wings, 1982. 530 pp.

Monaghan, Hugh B. *The Big Bombers of World War I; a Canadian's Journal.* Burlington, Ont.: R. Gentle Communications, n.d. 101 pp.

Musciano, Walter A. *Lt. Col. William Barker, Canada's All-Around Ace.* New York: Hobby Helpers Publishers, 1973. 56 pp.

Le Musée national de l'aviation; un survol. Ottawa: Musée national de l'aviation, 1991. 64 pp.

Myles, Eugenie Louise. *Airborne from Edmonton.* Toronto: Ryerson Press, 1959. 280 pp.

National Aeronautical Collection. Ottawa: Queen's Printer, 1967. 36 pp.

312

National Aeronautical Collection./Collection aéronautique nationale. n.p.: n.d./s.l.: s.i., s.d. 36 pp.
Bilingual text./Texte bilingue.

*The National Aviation Museum; a Flypast. Ottawa: National Aviation Museum, 1991. 64 pp.

Northern Flight; Canada's Aviation Heritage Magazine. Vol. I- . Thornhill, Ont.: Northern Flight Publications, 1992- .

O'Kiely, Elizabeth. *Gentleman Air Ace; the Duncan Bell-Irving Story.* Madeira Park, B.C.: Harbour Pub., 1992. 216 pp.

Ontario. Dept. of Education. *The Roll of Honour of the Ontario Teachers who Served in the Great War, 1914-1918.* Toronto: Ryerson Press, 1922. 72 pp.

Ontario Agricultural College, Guelph, Ont. *Ontario Agricultural College Honor and Service Rolls.* n.p.: n.d. 1 vol., unpaged.

Ontario Bar Association. *Roll of Honour.* n.p.: [1918]. 22 pp.

P.I.X. [*pseud.*] *see* Douglas, T. Hallam.

Parkdale Collegiate Institute, Toronto, Ont. *Roll of Service in the Great War, 1914-1919.* n.p.: n.d. 22 pp.

_____. *Their Name Liveth; a Memoir of the Boys of Parkdale Collegiate Institute who Gave their Lives in the Great War.* Toronto: privately printed, n.d. 177 pp.

Peace Souvenir; Activities of Waterloo County in the Great War, 1914-1918. Kitchener, Ont.: Kitchener Daily Telegraph, 1919. 70 pp.

Pigott, Peter. *Flying Canucks; Famous Canadian Aviators.* Toronto: Hounslow, 1994. 178 pp.

Plewman, W.R., *see* Miller, James Martin.

Queen's Univ., Kingston, Ont. *Overseas Record; Record of Graduates, Alumni, Members of Staff, and Students of Queen's University on Active Military (Overseas) Service (to June 1st, 1917) 1914-1917.* n.p.: [1917?]. 44 pp.

Riddle, David K., and Donald G. Mitchell, comps. *The Distinguished Service Order to the Canadian Expeditionary Force and Canadians in the Royal Naval Air Service, Royal Flying Corps and Royal Air Force, 1915-1920.* Winnipeg: Kirkby-Marlton Press, 1991. 130 pp.

_____. *The Military Cross to the Canadian Expeditionary Force, 1915-1921.* Winnipeg: Kirkby-Marlton Press, 1991. 390 pp.

Roberts, Leslie. *There shall be Wings; a History of the Royal Canadian Air Force.* Toronto: Clarke, Irwin, 1959. 250 pp.

Robertson, Heather, [comp.] *A Terrible Beauty; the Art of Canada at War.* Toronto: J. Lorimer, 1977. 239 pp.

Royal Canadian Military Institute, Toronto, Ont. *The Golden Book.* Toronto: privately printed, 1927. 1 vol., unpaged.

Sandwell, A.H. *Planes over Canada.* London: T. Nelson, 1938. 120 pp.

Santor, Donald M. *Canadians at War, 1914-1918.* (Canadiana Scrapbook.) Scarborough, Ont.: Prentice-Hall, 1978. 48 pp.

Shores, Christopher. *History of the Royal Canadian Air Force.* (A Bison Book.) Toronto: Royce Publications, 1984. 128 pp.

Shrive, Frank J. *The Diary of a P.B.O.*; *Poor Bloody Observer.* Norman Shrive, ed. Erin, Ont.: Boston Mills Press, 1981. 88 pp.
Observer in North Russia 1918-19.

Smith, G. Oswald, *see University of Toronto ....*

Stedman, Ernest W. *From Boxkite to Jet; Memoirs of Air Vice-Marshall Ernest W. Stedman.* [Toronto]: Univ. of Toronto Press, 1963. 1 vol., unpaged.
Reprints of articles from Canadian Aviation. An enlarged edition was published as From Boxkite to Jet; the Memoirs of an Aeronautical Engineer. (National Museum of Man Mercury Series; Canadian War Museum Paper, no. 1.) Ottawa: Queen's Printer, 1972.

Sullivan, Alan. *Aviation in Canada, 1917-1918; being a Brief Account of the Work of the Royal Air Force Canada, the Aviation Department of the Imperial Munitions Board and the Canadian Aeroplanes Limited.* Toronto: Rous & Mann, 1919. 318 pp.

Swettenham, John. *Canada and the First World War.* Toronto: Ryerson Press, 1969. 160 pp.

_____. *Canada and the First World War./La participation du Canada à la Première Guerre mondiale.* Ottawa: Canadian War Museum/Musée de guerre, n.d./s.d. 56/63 pp.
Bilingual text./ Texte bilingue.

Thompson, Roy J.C. *Wings of the Canadian Armed Forces, 1913-1972.* [Dartmouth], N.S.: n.p., 1973. 106 pp.

Thorburn, Ella M., and Charlotte Whitton. *Canada's Chapel of Remembrance.* Toronto: British Book Service (Canada), 1961. 68 pp.

Titler, Dale M. *The Day the Red Baron Died.* New York: Walker, 1970. 329 pp.

Trinity Methodist Church, Toronto, Ont. *Trinity War Book; a Recital of Service and Sacrifice in the Great War.* Oliver Hezzelwood, comp. Toronto: privately printed, 1921. 368 pp.

Univ. of British Columbia. *Record of Service, 1914-1918; University of British Columbia, McGill British Columbia, Vancouver College.* Vancouver: privately printed, 1924. 142 pp.

Univ. of Manitoba. *Roll of Honour, 1914-1918.* Winnipeg: privately printed, 1923. 150 pp.

Univ. of Toronto. Univ. Schools. *The Annals, 1916-1918.* Toronto: Univ. of Toronto Press, n.d. 1 vol., unpaged.

Univ. of Toronto. Victoria College. *Acta Victoriana; War Supplement.* [Toronto]: n.p., 1919. 128 pp.

University of Toronto Roll of Service. First Edition, August, 1914 — August, 1917. [Toronto]: Univ. of Toronto Press, n.d. 212 pp.
Also Supplement, August 1917 — October, 1918.

University of Toronto; Roll of Service, 1914-1918. G. Oswald Smith, ed. Toronto: Univ. of Toronto Press, 1921. 603 pp.

Wallace, W.S., *see* Duncan-Clark, S.J.

War Record of McGill Chapter of Delta Upsilon. Montreal: n.p., 1919. 47 pp.

Wheeler, William J. *Images of Flight; a Canadian Aviation Portfolio.* Willowdale, Ont.: Hounslow, 1992. 134 pp.

Williams, Jack. *Wings over Niagara; Aviation in the Niagara District, 1911-1944.* St. Catharines, Ont.: Niagara Aviation Pioneers, [1982]. 1 vol., unpaged.

Wilson, J.A. *Development of Aviation in Canada, 1879-1948.* Ottawa: Dept. of Transport Air Services Branch, n.d. 105 pp.

*Wise, S.F. *Les aviateurs canadiens dans la Première Guerre mondiale.* (Histoire officielle de l'Aviation royale du Canada, Tome premier.) s.l.: Ministère de la Défense nationale du Canada, 1982. 835 pp.

*_____. *Canadian Airmen and the First World War.* (The Official History of the Royal Canadian Air Force, Volume I.) n.p.: Univ. of Toronto Press in co-operation with the Dept. of National Defence and the Canadian Government Pub. Centre, Supply and Services Canada, 1980. 771 pp.

*Wodehouse, R.F. *Aviation Paintings from the Art Collection of the Canadian War Museum.* Ottawa: [Queen's Printer], 1972. 84 pp.

_____. *A Check List of the War Collections of World War I, 1914-1918, and World War II, 1939-1945.* Ottawa: Queen's Printer, 1968. 239 pp.

*_____. *Tableaux de l'aviation militaire; provenant de la Collection d'art du Musée de guerre canadien.* Ottawa: [Imprimeur de la Reine], 1972. 84 pp.

X., P.I., [*pseud.*] *see* Hallam, T. Douglas.

Yates, Harry A. *Memoirs of a World War I Pilot,* [edited] by Douglas Eaton Eagles [and] Elizabeth Joan (Yates) Eagles. Sarnia, Ont.: n.p., 1985. v.p.

Young, A.H., and W.A. Kirkwood, eds. *The War Memorial Volume of Trinity College, Toronto.* [Toronto]: Printers Guild, 1922. 165 pp.

Young, Albert Charles. *24 Good Men and True; Members of Branch #142 of the Royal Canadian Legion.* New York: Vantage Press, 1992. 219 pp.

1919-1945

Abbott, Kim. *Gathering of Demons; 407 Demon Squadron of the Royal Canadian Air Force, during its First Year of Operations, between May 8, 1941, and June 30, 1942, When It was Engaged on Low Level Shipping Attacks along the Coast of Occupied Europe.* Perth, Ont.: Inkerman House, 1987. 228 pp.

Active Service Canteen, Toronto, 1939-1945. Toronto: n.p., 1945. 1 vol., unpaged.

The Adastrian; being the Journal of No. 31 E.F.T.S. Royal Air Force, De Winton, Alberta, Canada. No. 1-? De Winton, Alta.: n.p., 1942-?

Adelberg, Philip, ed. *414 Squadron (1941-1975); a Short History.* n.p.: 1975. 1 vol., unpaged.

The Adventura; Magazine of the Royal Air Force Station Pennfield, New Brunswick. n.p.: ?-1944.

Advertising Club of Montreal. *Visit of His Majesty's Airship R-100, Canada — 1930.* n.p.: [1930]. 96 pp.

Aer-Log. Vol. 1-? Brandon, Man.: privately printed, 1943-?
Journal of No. 12 Service Flying Training School, RCAF.

Agreement Amending and Extending the British Commonwealth Air Training Plan Agreement of December 17, 1939, Relating to Training of Pilots and Aircraft Crews in Canada and their Subsequent Service, between the United Kingdom, Canada, Australia and New Zealand, Dated at Ottawa, June 5, 1942. Ottawa: King's Printer, 1942. 28 pp.

Agreement Relating to Training of Pilots and Aircraft Crews in Canada and their Subsequent Service between the United Kingdom, Canada, Australia and New Zealand, Signed at Ottawa, December 17, 1939. Ottawa: King's Printer, 1941. 19 pp.

The Air Force Guide, by "Group Captain". Toronto: Copp Clark, 1940. 180 pp.

Air Force Review. Vol. I-VI. Gardenvale, P.Q., Toronto: Anglo-American Pub. Co., 1940-45.
Title varies. Vol. IV-VI titled: Aviation Review.

Airforce. Vol. I- . Ottawa: Air Force Productions, 1977- .
Quarterly. Recommended by the Royal Canadian Air Force Association.

The Aircraftsman. Vol. I-V? St. Thomas, Ont.: n.p., 1940-44?
Journal of the Technical Training School, RCAF, St. Thomas, Ont.

Alcorn, Douglas, and Raymond Souster. *From Hell to Breakfast.* Toronto: Intruder Press, 1980. 339 pp.
Personal narrative of service in the RCAF chiefly with no. 418 Squadron.

317

Allison, Les. *Canadians in the Royal Air Force.* Roland, Man.: privately printed, 1978. 216 pp.
220 pp. with separately printed epilogue.

Allison, Les, and Henry Hayward. *They shall not Grow Old; a Book of Remembrance.* Brandon, Man.: Commonwealth Air Training Plan Museum, [1991?]. 892 pp.

Annis, Clare L. *Airpower 1952; Three Speeches.* n.p.: n.d. v.p.

Ashton, Martin. *The Canadian Medal Rolls — Distinguished Flying Medal (1939-1945).* Toronto: Charlton Press, 1984. 99 pp.

Bank of Montreal. *Field of Honour; the Second World War, 1939-1945.* Montreal: n.p., 1950. 1 vol., unpaged.

Barrass, R., and T.J.H. Sloan. *The Story of 657 Air O.P. Squadron R.A.F., January 31st, 1943, to May 8th, 1945.* London: Whitefriars Press, n.d. 96 pp.

Barris, Ted. *Behind the Glory.* Toronto: Macmillan Canada, 1992. 358 pp.
British Commonwealth Air Training Plan.

Barris, Ted, and Alex Barris. *Days of Victory; Canadians Remember: 1939-1945.* Toronto: Macmillan Canada, 1995. 304 pp.

A Battle for Truth; Canadian Aircrews Sue the CBC over Death by Moonlight: Bomber Command. Agincourt, Ont.: Ramsay Business Systems, 1994. 252 pp.

Bayly, G.H.U. "Terk" "Bill". *Cats; Memoirs of 413 Squadron.* n.p.: Graphic Image, 1993. 71 pp.

The Beam; No. 1 Wireless School R.C.A.F. Vol. I-? Montreal: n.p., 1942-?

Beckles, Gordon, [*pseud.*] see Willson, Gordon Beckles.

Bercuson, David J. *Maple Leaf against the Axis; Canada's Second World War.* Toronto: Stoddart, 1995. 316 pp.

Bercuson, David J., and S.F. Wise, eds. *The Valour and the Horror Revisited.* Montreal: McGill-Queen's Univ. Press, 1994. 185 pp.
Discussion of television series by Brian McKenna and Terence McKenna.

Berger, Monty, and Brian Jeffrey Street. *Invasions without Tears; the Story of Canada's Top-Scoring Spitfire Wing in Europe during the Second World War.* n.p.: Random House of Canada, 1994. 240 pp.
No. 126 Wing, RCAF.

Bernier, Robert. *Jacques Chevrier, chef d'escadrille, R.C.A.F.; tombé en service au large de Cap-Chat.* Montréal: Editions de l'A.C.J.C., 1943. 95 pp.

Beurling, George F., and Leslie Roberts. *Malta Spitfire; the Story of a Fighter Pilot.* Toronto: Oxford Univ. Press, 1943. 235 pp.

Birney, Earle, ed. *Record of Service in the Second World War; the University of British Columbia; a Supplement to the University of British Columbia War Memorial Manuscript Record.* Vancouver: privately printed, 1955. 46 pp.

Bishop, William A. *What Aviation Means to Canada.* Montreal: privately printed, 1936. 25 pp.

_____. *Winged Peace.* New York: Viking Press, 1944. 175 pp.

Bishop, William Arthur. *Courage in the Air.* (Canada's Military Heritage, Volume 1.) Toronto: McGraw-Hill Ryerson, 1992. 307 pp.

_____. *The Splendid Hundred; the True Story of Canadians who Flew in the Greatest Air Battle of World War II.* Toronto: McGraw-Hill Ryerson, 1994. 170 pp.
Battle of Britain, 1940.

Black, Don. *Skies were Filled; a Pictorial Review of Saskatchewan and the British Commonwealth Air Training Plan, 1939-1989.* Regina: privately printed, 1989. 78 pp., chiefly illus.

Blatherwick, F.J. *Royal Canadian Air Force Honours — Decorations — Medals, 1920-1968.* New Westminster, B.C.: FJB Air Publications, 1991. 176 pp.

Bottomley, Nora. *424 Squadron History.* [Belleville, Ont.]: The Hangar Bookshelf, 1985. 137 pp.

Bowering, Clifford H. *Service; the Story of the Canadian Legion, 1925-1960.* Ottawa: privately printed, 1960. 240 pp.

Bowman, Phylis. *Second World War Memories.* Port Edward, B.C.: privately printed, 1987. 84 pp.
Prince Rupert, B.C., in the Second World War.

Bracken, Robert. *Spitfire; the Canadians.* Erin, Ont.: Stoddart, Boston Mills Press, 1995. [160] pp.

Brantford Kinsmen Club, comp. *Album of Honour for Brant County; World War II, 1939-1945.* Helen Sanders, ed. [Brantford, Ont.]: Brantford Kinsmen Club, 1946. 224 pp.

Brisson, Pierre. *Défendez le Saguenay; les cinquante ans de la Base de Forces canadiennes de Bagotville, 1942-1992/the Fifty Years History of Canadian Forces Base Bagotville, 1942-1992.* Rejean Cardin et/and Marie Novak, tr. s.l.: s.i./n.p., 1992. 34/31 pp.
Texte bilingue./Bilingual text.

The British Commonwealth Air Training Plan. Ottawa: King's Printer, 1941. 10 pp.

* *The British Commonwealth Air Training Plan, 1939-1945; an Historical Sketch and Record of the Ceremony at R.C.A.F. Station Trenton.* Ottawa: King's Printer, 1949. 58 pp.

Broadfoot, Barry. *Six War Years, 1939-1945; Memories of Canadians at Home and Abroad.* Toronto: Doubleday Canada, 1974. 417 pp.

Brock, Thomas Leith. *Fight the Good Fight; Looking in on the Recruit Class at the Royal Military College of Canada during a Week in February, 1931.* Montreal: privately printed, 1964. 30 pp.

_____. *The R.M.C. Vintage Class of 1934.* Victoria, B.C.: privately printed, 1985. 3 vols.

Brown, Elizabeth, Robert Brown and Quentin Brown. *The Army's Mister Brown; a Family Trilogy, 1941-1952.* Harcourt Brown, ed. Parry Sound Ont.: privately printed, 1982. 234 pp.
Robert Brown served with U.S. Army Air Forces in the Pacific, Quentin Brown in RCN in Atlantic and Europe. Elizabeth Brown was in UNRRA.

Brown, George, and Michel Lavigne. *Canadian Wing Commanders of Fighter Command in World War II.* Langley, B.C.: Battleline Books, 1984. [346 pp.]

Brown, Kingsley. *Bonds of Wire; a Memoir.* Toronto: Collins, 1989. 267 pp.
RCAF prisoner of war in Stalag Luft 3.

Bruce, Jean. *Back the Attack! Canadian Women during the Second World War — at Home and Abroad.* Toronto: Macmillan, 1985. 182 pp.

Buckham, Robert. *Forced March to Freedom; an Illustrated Diary of Two Forced Marches and the Interval Between — January to May, 1945.* Stittsville, Ont.: Canada's Wings, 1984. 98 pp.

Butt, Bob. *Le Dakota de l'Aviation royale du Canada et les Forces canadiennes: 1943[sic]- — De la débutante à la grande dame./The Royal Candian Air Force and Canadian Forces Dakota: 1943[sic]- — From Debutante to Matriarch.* Winnipeg: Design & typeset — Media One Productions, 1989. 71 pp.
Texte bilingue./Bilingual text.

The C.A.H.S. Journal. Vol. I- . Willowdale, Ont.: Canadian Aviation Historical Society, 1963- .

Calgary Wings. No. 1-? Calgary: privately printed, 1941-?
Journal of No. 37 Service Flying Training School, RAF.

Canada. Air Board. *Air Regulations 1920; with which are Printed the Air Board Act, the Convention Relating to International Air Navigation, and Certain Directions Given and Forms Approved for Use under the Regulations.* Ottawa: King's Printer, 1920. 139 pp.

Canada. Air Board. *Regulations for the Canadian Air Force and the Air Board Act, August 31, 1920.* Ottawa: King's Printer, 1920. 196 pp.

_____. *Report.* Ottawa: King's Printer, 1920-23. 4 vols.

Canada. Air Force. *The Canadian Air Force List.* Ottawa: King's Printer, 1921?-22?

_____. *Dress Regulations for the Royal Canadian Air Force, 1925.* Ottawa: King's Printer, 1926. 41 pp.

_____. *Exhibition of Paintings and Drawings.* Ottawa: King's Printer, 1944. 28 pp.

_____. *Final Report of the Chief of the Air Staff to the Members of the Supervisory Board, British Commonwealth Air Training Plan; a Summary of the British Commonwealth Air Training Plan from its Inception on December 17, 1939, to Termination on March 31, 1945.* n.p.: 1945. 63 pp.

_____. *Information Relating to Enlistment, Terms of Service, Pay, etc., of Airmen and Boys in the Royal Canadian Air Force.* Ottawa: King's Printer, 1930. 10 pp.

_____. *Regulations and Instructions for the Clothing of the Royal Canadian Air Force, 1927.* (C.A.P. 9.) Ottawa: King's Printer, n.d. 71 pp.

_____. *The Royal Canadian Air Force List.* Ottawa: n.p., 1942-66. *Issued in mimeographed form until 1942. Frequency varies.*

_____. *Weekly Orders.* Ottawa: [King's Printer, 1920-25]. 1 vol., looseleaf.

Canada. Air Force. 409 Squadron. *1941-1945; the Nighthawks.* Hengelo, Neth.: n.p., n.d. 80 pp.

Canada. Air Force. 435 Squadron. *Chinthe.* Victoria, B.C.: privately printed, n.d. 166 pp.

Canada. Air Force. 436 Squadron. *Canucks Unlimited; the Record in Story and Picture of the History, Life and Experiences of the Men of 436 R.C.A.F. Squadron, India-Burma, 1944-1945.* Toronto: n.p., n.d. 93 pp.

[Canada. Air Force. 666 Squadron.] *Battle History 666.* Epe, Neth.: privately printed, 1945. 37 pp.

Canada. Air Force. 39 Reconnaissance Wing. *Flap; 39 Reconnaissance Wing.* J.H. Marsters, ed. Hamburg: privately printed, 1945. 1 vol., unpaged.

Canada. Air Force. No. 8 Air Observer School. *From the First to the Last Flight; a Pictorial History of the Operations and Personnel of the Royal Canadian Air Force and Quebec Airways (Observers) Ltd., 1941-1945.* n.p.: n.d. 127 pp.

Canada. Air Force. No. 5 Bombing and Gunnery School. *Dafoe Doings.* Dafoe, Sask.: n.p., n.d. 20 pp.

Canada. Air Force. No. 4 Initial Training School. *"All for One — One for All"; 1st Anniverary; No. 4 Initial Training School, Royal Canadian Air Force, Edmonton, Alberta.* Edmonton: privately printed, [1942]. 1 vol., unpaged.

_____. *Christmas and New Year's Greetings, 1942-43.* Edmonton: privately printed, n.d. 1 vol., unpaged.

[Canada. Air Force. No. 1 Technical Training School.] *St. Thomas, Ontario, Canada.* n.p.: n.d. 19 l., chiefly illus.

Canada. Air Force. No. 7 Air Observer School. *The Record; a Souvenir of No. 7 Air Observer School, R.C.A.F., Portage la Prairie, Manitoba, Operated by Portage Air Observer School Ltd., 1941-1945.* n.p.: n.d. 100 pp.

[Canada. Air Force. No. 24 Elementary Flying Training School.] *Sky; Memories of Abbotsford.* n.p.: [1944]. 23 pp.

[Canada. Air Force. No. 2 Bombing and Gunnery School.] *R.C.A.F. "Bomb Bursts".* Regina: Caxton Press, 1943. 1 vol., unpaged.

Canada. Air Force. No. 2 Initial Training School. *ITS News; Second Anniversary.* Regina: n.p., 1942. 60 pp.

Canada. Air Force. Technical Training School. Y.M.C.A. Services. Supervisors, comp. *The Royal Canadian Air Force Technical Training School, St. Thomas, Ontario.* St. Thomas, Ont.: privately printed, n.d. 21 pp.

Canada. Air Force Headquarters. *Flying Regulations for the Royal Canadian Air Force.* (C.A.P. 100.) n.p.: 1940. 1 vol., looseleaf.

_____. *General and Routine Orders.* Ottawa: n.p., 1940-65.
Title varies. Routine Orders from 1947. Supplements also issued. Issued in mimeographed form from 1933.

Canada. Air Force Headquarters. Air Historical Section. *Among the Few; a Sketch of the Part Played by Canadian Airmen in the Battle of Britain (July 10th — October 31st, 1940).* (A.F.P. 49.) n.p.: 1948. 36 pp.

_____. *RCAF Logbook; a Chronological Outline of the Origin, Growth and Achievement of the Royal Canadian Air Force.* Ottawa: King's Printer, 1949. 96 pp.

_____. *The R.C.A.F. Overseas.* Toronto: Oxford Univ. Press, 1944-49. 3 vols.

Canada. Air Force Overseas Headquarters. *Overseas Orders.* London: n.p., 1943-46.
Issued in mimeographed form from 1940.

_____. *Publication No. 1.* London: n.p., 1942. v.p.

Canada. Armed Forces. Canadian Forces Base Greenwood. *50 Years; the History of CFB Greenwood, 1942-1992.* Winnipeg: C. Kelman, [1992]. 148 pp.

[Canada. Armed Forces. Canadian Forces Base Portage la Prairie.] *Portage la Prairie; Fifty Years of Flying Training: 1940-1990.* Southport, Man.: Manitoba Airshow 1990, 1990. 181 pp.

[Canada. Armed Forces. Canadian Forces Base Shearwater.] *From White-Caps to Contrails; a History of a Modern Air Formation.* n.p.: 1981. 108 pp.
History of 880 MR, VU 32, VT 406, HS 423 and HS 443 Squadrons.

[Canada. Armed Forces. Canadian Forces Base Summerside.] *"Forty Years" 1941-1981; a History of the Base at Summerside, Prince Edward Island.* n.p.: n.d. 22 pp.

[Canada. Armed Forces. 408 Squadron.] *408 Squadron History.* n.p.: 1984. 107 pp.

[Canada. Armed Forces. 404 Squadron.] *404 Squadron History.* Winnipeg: C. Kelman, n.d. 121 pp.

[Canada. Armed Forces. 415 Squadron.] *Swordfish; the Story of 415 Squadron.* n.p.: [1982?]. 71 pp.

[Canada. Armed Forces. 409 Squadron.] *Nighthawk! A History of 409 (Night Fighter) Squadron, 1941-1977.* Courtenay, B.C.: privately printed, n.d. 93 pp.

Canada. Armed Forces. 401 Squadron. *1934-1984; Escadrille — 401 — Squadron.* n.p.: [1984]. 1 vol., unpaged.

[Canada. Armed Forces. 430 Squadron. *Escadrille 430 Squadron.*] Lac-Etchemin, P.Q.: privately printed/imprimé privé, 1981. 288 pp.
Bilingual text./Texte bilingue.

Canada. Armed Forces. 434 Squadron. *434 Squadron ... a History.* n.p.: privately printed, [1977]. 155 pp.
New ed.: [Belleville, Ont.]: Hangar Bookshelf, 1984.

[Canada. Armed Forces. 437 Squadron.] *437 Squadron History.* [Belleville, Ont.]: Hangar Bookshelf, 1985. 113 pp.

[Canada. Armed Forces. 433 Squadron.] *433 Squadron History.* [Belleville, Ont.]: Hangar Bookshelf, 1985. 112 pp.

[Canada. Armed Forces. 425 Squadron.] *425 Alouette.* n.p.: n.d./s.l.: s.i., s.d. 101 pp.
Bilingual texte./Texte bilingue.

Canada. Armed Forces. 400 Squadron. *400 Squadron; the First Half Century.* n.p.: [1982?]. 17 pp.

Canada. Army. First Canadian Army Headquarters and Gt. Brit. Air Force. 35 Reconnaissance Wing. *Air Recce.* London: n.p., n.d. 66 pp.

Canada. Dept. of National Defence. *Canadian Prisoners of War and Missing Personnel in the Far East.* Ottawa: King's Printer, 1945. 59 1.

_____. *Defence Forces List, Canada (Naval, Military and Air Forces).* Ottawa: King's Printer, 1930-39.
Title varies somewhat. Superseded The Militia List. *Superseded by* The Canadian Navy List, The *Canadian Army List and* The Royal Canadian Air Force List.

_____. *Digest of Opinions and Rulings; Ottawa; March 31, 1944; Compiled from the Records of the Office of the Judge Advocate-General, at National Defence Headquarters.* n.p.: [1944]. 353 pp., looseleaf.

_____. *Financial Regulations and Instructions for the Royal Canadian Air Force on Active Service (Canada), Effective September 1st, 1939.* Ottawa: King's Printer, 1940. 88 pp.

_____. *Financial Regulations for the Royal Canadian Air Force on Active Service, 1945.* (C.A.P. 2.) Ottawa: King's Printer, 1945. 154 pp.

_____. *Instructions for Engineer Services, Canada, 1936.* Ottawa: King's Printer, 1936. 152 pp.

_____. *King's Regulations and Orders for the Royal Canadian Air Force, 1924.* Ottawa: King's Printer, 1924. 494 pp.

_____. *King's Regulations for the Royal Canadian Air Force, 1943.* (C.A.P. 4.) Ottawa: King's Printer, 1943. 404 pp.

_____. *Pay and Allowance Regulations for the Royal Canadian Air Force, Permanent and Auxiliary, 1924.* Ottawa: King's Printer, 1924. 1 vol., looseleaf.

*_____. *Report.* Ottawa: King's Printer, 1923-59.
Title varies. Annual most years.

*_____. *Report on Civil Aviation.* Ottawa: King's Printer, 1924-32. 9 vols.

Canada. Dept. of National War Services. *Annual Report.* Ottawa: King's Printer, 1945. 3 vols.

Canada. Dept. of Veterans Affairs. *Canadians in Asia, 1945-1985./Les Canadiens en Asie, 1945-1985.* Ottawa: Veterans Affairs Canada/Anciens combattants Canada, 1984. 28 pp.
Bilingual text./Texte bilingue.

_____. *D-Day; 1944 — June 6 — 1984./Jour J; 1944 — le 6 juin — 1984.* Ottawa: Veterans Affairs Canada/Affaires des Anciens combattants, 1984. 22 pp.
Bilingual text./Text bilingue.

Canada. Dept. of Veterans Affairs. *30th Anniversary of the D-Day Landings in Normandy, 1944 — June 6 — 1974./30e anniversaire des débarquements en Normandie au jour J, 1944 — le 6 juin — 1974.* n.p./s.l.: s.i., 1974. 22 pp.
Bilingual texte./Texte bilingue.

Canada. Director of Public Information. *Canada and the People's War.* n.p.: [1942]. 1 vol., unpaged.

*_____. *Canada at War.* No. 1-45. Ottawa: King's Printer, 1941-45.

*Canada. Ministère de la Défense nationale. *Rapport.* Ottawa: Imprimeur du Roi, 1923-59.
Divergence du titre. Annuel, la plupart des années.

*_____. *Rapport sur l'aviation civile.* Ottawa: Imprimeur du Roi, 1924-32. 9 tomes.

Canada. National Gallery. *Exhibition of Canadian War Art.* Ottawa: King's Printer, 1945. 22 pp.

Canada. National Research Council. *History of the Associate Committee on Aviation Medical Research, 1939-1945.* Edgar C. Black, ed. Ottawa: King's Printer, 1946. 212 pp.

*Canada. Parlement. Chambre des Communes. Comité spécial d'enquête sur les distinctions honorifiques et les décorations. *Procès-verbaux et témoignages.* No 1-6. Ottawa: Imprimeur du Roi, 1942.

Canada. Parliament. House of Commons. Special Committee on Canteen Funds. *Minutes of Proceedings and Evidence.* No. 1-11. Ottawa: King's Printer, 1942.

*Canada. Parliament. House of Commons. Special Committee on Honours and Decorations. *Minutes of Proceedings and Evidence.* No. 1-6. Ottawa: King's Printer, 1942.

Canada. Royal Commission to Conduct an Inquiry into Certain Disorders Occurring May 7-8, 1945, in the City of Halifax. *Report on the Halifax Disorders, May 7th-8th, 1945.* Hon. Mr. Justice R.L. Kellock, Royal Commissioner. Ottawa: King's Printer, 1945. 61 pp.

*Canada. Service de l'Information. *Le Canada en guerre.* No 1-45. Ottawa: Imprimeur du Roi, 1941-45.

Canadian Air Cadet. Vol. I-VII. Toronto: Air Cadet League of Canada, 1941-48.

Canadian Bank of Commerce. *War Service Records, 1939-1945; an Account of the War Service of Members of the Staff during the Second World War.* D.P. Wagner and C.G. Siddall, eds. Toronto: Rous & Mann, 1947. 331 pp.

Canadian Broadcasting Corporation. Publications Branch. *We have been There; Authoritative Reports by Qualified Observers who have Returned from the War Zones, as Presented over the CBC National Network.* Toronto: Canadian Broadcasting Corporation, 1941-42. 2 vols.

Canadian Jewish Congress. *Canadian Jews in World War II.* Montreal: privately printed, 1947-48. 2 vols.

Canadian Legion War Services, Inc. *A Year of Service; a Summary of Activities on Behalf of His Majesty's Canadian Forces Rendered during Nineteen-Forty.* n.p.: n.d. 1 vol., unpaged.

Canadian War Museum. *La coopération canada-polonaise au cours des deux guerres mondiales./Polish-Canadian Co-operation in the Two World Wars.* Ottawa: n.p., 1973. 36 pp.
Texte bilingue./Bilingual text.

_____. *Four War Artists./Quatre artistes de guerre.* Ottawa: Canadian War Museum/Musée canadien de la guerre, 1981. 41 pp.
Bilingual text./ Texte bilingue.

Cardoulis, John N. *A Friendly Invasion; the American Military in Newfoundland, 1940-1990.* St. John's, Nfld.: Breakwater, 1990. 224 pp.

_____. *A Friendly Invasion II: a Personal Touch.* St. John's, Nfld.: Creative Publishers, 1993. 221 pp.

Carlson, Don. *R.C.A.F. Padre with Spitfire Squadrons.* Red Deer, Alta.: privately printed, n.d. 71 pp.

Carr, William Guy. *Checkmate in the North; the Axis Planned to Invade America.* Toronto: Macmillan, 1944. 304 pp.

Carroll, Warren. *Wings, 1913-1945; Royal Flying Corps, Royal Naval Air Service, Canadian Aviation Corps, Royal Canadian Naval Air Service, Canadian Air Force, Royal Canadian Air Force, Fleet Air Arm, Royal Air Force, Armies of Great Britain and Canada.* Thornhill, Ont.: n.p., 1981. 127 pp.
Flying badges.

Carter, William S. *Anglo-Canadian Wartime Relations, 1939-1945; RAF Bomber Command and No. 6 (Canadian) Group.* New York: Garland Pub., 1991. 204 pp.

Castonguay, Jacques. *La 16e Escadre Saint-Jean; ses antecédents — ses unités (1941-1994).* Saint-Roch-des-Aulnaies (Qué.): La Beaucassière, 1994. 206 pp.

_____. *Unsung Mission; History of the Chaplaincy Service (RC) of the R.C.A.F.* Montreal: Institut de Pastorale, 1968. 173 pp.

Castonguay, Jacques, *et al. History of Canadian Forces Base Montreal and its Garrisons./Historique de la Base des Forces canadiennes Montréal et de ses garnisons.* n.p./s.l.: s.i., 1980. 181/153 pp.
Bilingual text./Texte bilingue.

Chapman, J.K. *River Boy at War.* Fredericton, N.B.: Fiddlehead Poetry Books & Goose Lane Editions, 1985. 103 pp.
Memoirs of no. 415 Squadron.

Charlton, Peter, and Michael Whitby, eds. *"Certified Serviceable"; Swordfish to Sea King; the Technical Story of Canadian Naval Aviation, by Those Who Made It So.* n.p: CNATH Book Project, 1995. 496 pp.

The Chinook. Vol. I-? Lethbridge, Alta.: n.p., 1942-?
Journal of No. 8 Bombing and Gunnery School, RCAF.

Chirol, J.-M. *Héros du ciel et de la terre, 1943-1944.* [Saint-Dizier, France]: s.i., 1979. 125 pp.
Lancaster II DS689 de l'escadron 426.

Chrétien, Guy. *"Juno Beach" les Canadiens dans la bataille.* Caen, France: Imprimerie Lafond, s.d./n.d. 256 pp., en majeure partie ill./chiefly illus.
Texte bilingue./Bilingual text.

Christie, Carl A., with Fred Hatch. *Ocean Bridge: the History of RAF Ferry Command.* Toronto: Univ. of Toronto Press, 1995. 458 pp.

50e/th/anniversaire/Anniversary;/Cité de Montréal/"Wildcats", Corps d'aviation royale du Canada, Forces armées canadiennes/City of Montreal/Wildcats, Royal Canadian Air Force, Canadian Armed Forces/Escadrille/18/118/438/ Squadron. s.l.: s.i./n.p., 1984. 42 pp.

City of Winnipeg 402 Squadron, 1932-1974. n.p.: n.d. 1 vol., unpaged.

Cohen, Stan. *The Forgotten War; a Pictorial History of World War II in Alaska and Northwestern Canada.* Missoula, Mont.: Pictorial Histories Pub. Co., 1981. 260 pp.

Collins, Robert. *The Long and the Short and the Tall; an Ordinary Airman's War.* Saskatoon, Sask.: Western Producer Prairie Books, 1986. 134 pp.

Collishaw, Raymond, and R.V. Dodds. *Air Command; a Fighter Pilot's Story.* London: W. Kimber, 1973. 256 pp.

Commonwealth War Graves Commission. *The War Dead of the Commonwealth; the Register of the Names of Those who Fell in the 1939-1945 War and are Buried; Cemeteries in Canada; Cemeteries in Ontario.* London: H.M. Stationery Office, 1961. 2 vols.

Commonwealth War Graves Commission. *The War Dead of the Commonwealth; the Register of the Names of Those who Fell in the 1939-1945 War and are Buried in Cemeteries in Canada; Cemeteries in British Columbia, Yukon Territory and Alberta.* Maidenhead, Eng.: [H.M. Stationery Office], 1972. 82 pp.

_____. *The War Dead of the Commonwealth; the Register of the Names of Those who Fell in the 1939-1945 War and are Buried in Cemeteries in Canada; Cemeteries in New Brunswick, Nova Scotia, Newfoundland and Prince Edward Island.* London: H.M. Stationery Office, 1962. 81 pp.

_____. *The War Dead of the Commonwealth; the Register of the Names of Those who Fell in the 1939-1945 War and are Buried in Cemeteries in Canada; Cemeteries in Quebec.* London: H.M. Stationery Office, 1962. 63 pp.

_____. *The War Dead of the Commonwealth; the Register of the Names of Those who Fell in the 1939-1945 War and are Buried in Cemeteries in Canada; Cemeteries in Saskatchewan and Manitoba.* London: [H.M. Stationery Office], 1963. 79 pp.

Connolly, Don. *Painting Planes; the Aviation Art of Don Connolly.* Stittsville, Ont.: Canada's Wings, 1982. [75] pp.

Conrad, Peter C. *Training for Victory; the British Commonwealth Air Training Plan in the West.* Saskatoon, Sask.: Western Producer Prairie Books, 1989. 102 pp.

Contact. Vol. I- . Gardenvale, P.Q., Trenton, Ont.: n.p., 1942- .
Journal of RCAF Station Trenton, Ont. Continues to be issued as a newspaper, with occasional issues in magazine format. Frequency, numbering vary.

Contact! Vol. I-IV. Mossbank, Sask.: n.p., 1941-44.
Journal of No. 2 Bombing and Gunnery School, RCAF. Title varies. Vol. IV titled: Target.

Copp, Terry, and Richard Nielsen. *No Price Too High; Canadians and the Second World War.* Toronto: McGraw-Hill Ryerson, 1996. 255 pp.

Cosgrove, Edmund. *Canada's Fighting Pilots.* (Canadian Portraits.) Toronto: Clarke, Irwin, 1965. 190 pp.

_____. *The Evaders.* Toronto: Clarke, Irwin, 1970. 301 pp.

Coughlin, Tom. *The Dangerous Sky; Canadian Airmen in World War II.* Toronto: Ryerson Press, 1968. 214 pp.

Countryman, Barry. *R100 in Canada.* Erin, Ont.: The Boston Mills Press, 1982. 128 pp.

Crandall, Max E. *Farm Boy Goes to War.* Sicamous, B.C.: privately printed, 1984. 100 pp.
Armourer with No. 111 Squadron in the Aleutian campaign, No. 440 Squadron in North West Europe.

Critchley, A. *Critch! The Memoirs of Brigadier-General A.C. Critchley.* London: Hutchinson, 1961. 256 pp.

Critical Moments; Profiles of Members of the Greater Vancouver Branch of the Aircrew Association. n.p.: 1990. 345 pp.

The Crow's Nest; Fortieth Anniversary, 1942-1982. n.p.: privately printed, [1982]. 107 pp.
Officer's Club, St. John's, Nfld.

The Dafoe Digest. Vol. I-? Saskatoon, Sask.: privately printed, 1942-?
Journal of No. 5 Bombing and Gunnery School RCAF.

Dancocks, Daniel G. *In Enemy Hands; Canadian Prisoners of War, 1939-45.* Edmonton: Hurtig, 1983. 303 pp.

Deller, K.M. *Per Ardua ad Usquam (Through Adversity Anywhere); a History of the CMU's and 1 CEU.* n.p.: [1984?]. 136 pp.
Contruction Engineering in RCAF and Canadian Forces.

The Demon Squadron; 407 Squadron in War and Peace, May 1941 — June 1952, June 1952 — June 1975. n.p.: privately printed, [1975]. 46 pp.

Desmares, [Joseph]. *L'incident du cimetière St.-Germain[-]de-la-Lieue.* Bayeux, France: "La Renaissance du Bessin," 1946. 24 pp.
La mort de William Kennedy Ferguson, RCAF, 15 janvier 1943.

Desquesnes, Rémy. *Les Canadiens au secours de l'Europe./The Canadians to Europe's Rescue.* Caen, France: Mémorial musée pour la paix, 1992. 194 pp.
Texte bilingue./Bilingual text.

"Digby to Downsview"; a 411 Squadron History, 1941-1981. n.p.: n.d. 21 pp.

Dornier, François. *Des bombardiers au-dessus du fleuve; historique de la 9e Ecole de Bombardement et de Tir de Mont-Joli (1941-1945).* Mont-Joli, P.Q.: imprimé privé, 1989. 55 pp.

*Douglas, W.A.B. *La création d'une aviation militaire nationale.* Responsable de l'édition française: Jean Pariseau. (Histoire officialle de l'Aviation royale du Canada, tome II.) s.l.: Ministère de la Défense nationale et le Centre d'édition du gouvernement du Canada, Approvisionnements et Services Canada, 1987. 881 pp.

*_____. *The Creation of a National Air Force.* (The Official History of the Royal Canadian Air Force, Volume II.) n.p.: Univ. of Toronto Press in co-operation with the Dept. of National Defence and the Canadian Government Pub. Centre, Supply and Services Canada, 1986. 797 pp.

Douglas, W.A.B., and Brereton Greenhous. *Out of the Shadows; Canada in the Second World War.* Toronto: Oxford Univ. Press, 1977. 288 pp.
Rev. ed. Toronto: Dundurn Press, 1995. 304 pp.

The Drift Recorder. Winnipeg: n.p., ?-1945.
Journal of No. 5 Air Observer School, RCAF.

Drolet, "Gil". *Loyola, the Wars: in Rememberance of "Men for Others".* Waterloo, Ont.: Laurier Centre for Military Strategic and Disarmament Studies, 1996. 44 pp.
Memorial to the war dead of Loyola High Shcool and College.

Dudley-Mathiesen, Vi. *Sweet 'n' Sour.* Sidney, B.C.: Family Compact, 1985. 288 pp.
Memories of service in RCAF Women's Division, 1942-1957.

Duffin, W.K.G. *With the RCAF in Europe, June, 1944 to August, 1945; a Personal Memoir.* Ross Duffin, ed. n.p.: [1994]. 24 pp.

Duley, Margaret. *The Caribou Hut; the Story of a Newfoundland Hostel.* Toronto: Ryerson Press, 1949. 82 pp.

Dunmore, Spencer. *Wings for Victory; the Remarkable Story of the British Commonwealth Air Training Plan in Canada.* Toronto: McClelland & Stewart, 1994. 399 pp.

Dunmore, Spencer, and William Carter. *Reap the Whirlwind; the Untold Story of 6 Group, Canada's Bomber Force of World War II.* Toronto: McClelland & Stewart, 1991. 437 pp.

Elliott-Haynes Limited. *An Enquiry into the Attitude of the Canadian Civilian Public towards the Women's Armed Forces; Conducted on Behalf of the Advertising Agencies of Canada and the Joint Committee on Combined Recruiting Promotion, Women's Services of the Three Armed Forces.* Montreal: privately printed, [194-?]. 33 pp.

Ellis, Frank H. *Canada's Flying Heritage.* Toronto: Univ. of Toronto Press, 1954. 398 pp.

_____. *Fifty Years of Adventure and Progress in Canadian Skies.* Toronto: Ryerson Press, 1959. 230 pp.

Emmott, Norman. *One Foot on the Ground.* Toronto: Lugus, 1992. 257 pp.

English, Allan D. *The Cream of the Crop; Canadian Aircrew, 1939-1945.* Montreal: McGill-Queen's Univ. Press, 1996. 239 pp.

Ettenger, G.H. *History of the Associate Committee on Medical Research, Ottawa, 1938-1946.* Ottawa: n.p., n.d. 46 pp.

Everard, Hedley. *A Mouse in My Pocket; Memoirs of a Fighter Pilot.* Picton, Ont.: Valley Floatplane Services, 1988. 408 pp.

330

Fetherstonhaugh, R.C. *McGill University at War, 1914-1918; 1939-1945.* Montreal: McGill Univ., 1947. 437 pp.

Field, Peter J. *Canada's Wings.* London: Unwin, 1942. 126 pp.

Fletcher, David C., and Doug MacPhail. *Harvard! The North American Trainers in Canada.* San Josef, B.C.: DCF Flying Books, [1990]. 208 pp.

The Fly Paper. Vol. I-? Jarvis, Ont.: privately printed, 1943-? *Journal of No. 1 Bombing and Gunnery School, RCAF.*

The Flying Gopher; the Journal of the Royal Air Force, No. 41 Service Flying Training School, Weyburn, Saskatchewan, Canada. Vol. I-? Weyburn, Sask.: privately printed, 1942-?

Foothill Fliers. Vol. I-III? Calgary: privately printed, 1941-45? *Journal of No. 3 Service Flying Training School, RCAF.*

For King and Country; Alberta in the Second World War. Edmonton: Provincial Museum of Alberta; Reidmore Books, 1995. 364 pp.

Foster, J.A. *For Love and Glory; a Pictorial History of Canada's Air Forces.* Toronto: McClelland & Stewart, 1989. 143 pp.

_____. *Sea Wings; a Pictorial History of Canada's Waterborne Defence Aircraft.* Toronto: Methuen, 1986. 143 pp.

Foulds, Glen. *[419 Squadron History.]* Burnaby, B.C.: printed by Crosstown Printers, [1988?]. 108 pp.

440 Squadron History. Stittsville, Ont.: Canada's Wings, 1983. 103 pp.

417 Squadron History. Stittsville, Ont.: Canada's Wings, 1983. 104 pp.

416 Squadron see Hovey, H. Richard.

407 Squadron RCAF (Overseas). n.p.: 1945. 60 pp.

421 Squadron History. [Stittsville, Ont.: 421 Tactical Fighter Squadron and Canada's Wings, 1982.] 107 pp.

427 Lion Squadron, 1942-1970. Marceline, Mo.: Walsworth, n.d. 76 pp.

422 Sqn; This Arm shall do It, 1942-1970. Marceline, Mo.: Walsworth, n.d. 64 pp.

402 Squadron, Royal Canadian Air Force; We Stand on Guard, 1932-1952. n.p.: n.d. 14 pp.

Fowler, T. Robert. *Valour on Juno Beach; the Canadian Awards for Gallantry, D-Day, June 6, 1944.* Burnstown, Ont.: General Store Pub. House, 1994. [104] pp.

Fraser, Donald A. *Live to Look Again; Memoirs of a Canadian Pilot with the RAF during WWII.* Belleville, Ont.: Mika Pub. Co., 1984. 243 pp.

Frazer, W.W. *A Trepid Aviator; Bombay to Bangkok.* Burnstown, Ont.: General Store Pub. House, 1995. 265 pp.
RCAF pilot in Nos. 215 and 356 Squadrons, RAF, 1944-1945.

Fuller, G.A., J.A. Griffin and K.M. Molson. *125 Years of Canadian Aeronautics; a Chronology 1840-1965.* Willowdale, Ont.: Canadian Aviation Historical Society, 1983. 328 pp.

Gaffen, Fred. *Cross-Border Warriors; Canadians in American Forces, Americans in Canadian Forces; from the Civil War to the Gulf.* Toronto: Dundurn Press, 1995. 241 pp.

_____. *Forgotten Soldiers.* Penticton, B.C.: Theytus Books, 1985. 152 pp.
Canada's native peoples in two World Wars.

Gaffen, Fred, ed./rédacteur. *The Road to Victory: a History of Canada in the Second World War./La route de la victoire: la participation du Canada à la Deuxième Guerre mondiale.* French translation/Traduction en français: Jean Pariseau. n.p./s.l.: Canadian War Museum/Musée canadien de la guerre; Esprit de corps, 1995. 84 pp.
Bilingual text./Texte bilingue.

Gardam, John. *Fifty Years After.* Burnstown, Ont.: General Store Pub. House, 1992. 141 pp.

_____. *Ordinary Heroes.* Burnstown, Ont.: General Store Pub. House, 1992. 205 pp.

[General Motors of Canada, Limited.] *Achievement.* n.p.: [1943]. 74 pp.

Gibson, Colin. *"Air Power in Canada"; an Address by Col. the Hon. Colin Gibson, M.C., M.A., Minister of National Defence for Air, to the Empire Club of Toronto, February 28, 1946.* n.p.: n.d. 11 pp.

Giesler, Patricia. *Valour Remembered; Canada and the Second World War, 1939-1945./Souvenirs de vaillance; la participation du Canada à la Seconde Guerre mondiale, 1939-1945.* Ottawa: Veterans Affairs Canada/Affaires des anciens combattants Canada, 1981. 45/47 pp.
Bilingual text./Texte bilingue.

Gilman, William. *Our Hidden Front.* New York: Reynal & Hitchcock, 1944. 266 pp.

Giloteaux, Paulin. *Une "âme-hostie" canadienne; Jean-François Bittner, novice "père blanc" et aviateur-bombardier, 1919-1943.* Le Quesnoy, France: Oeuvres Charitable, 1952. 139 pp.

Godefroy, Hugh Constant. *Lucky Thirteen.* Stittsville, Ont.: Canada's Wings, 1983. 274 pp.
RCAF fighter pilot during the Second World War.

Godsell, Philip H. *The Romance of the Alaska Highway.* Toronto: Ryerson Press, 1944. 235 pp.

Gordon, John. ... *Of Men and Planes.* Ottawa: Love Print., 1968. 3 vols.

_____.*Winged Sentries./Sentinelles de l'air.* Claude Rousseau, illus. n.p.: 1963. 104 pp.
Bilingual text./ Texte bilingue.

Gossage, Carolyn. *Greatcoats and Glamour Boots; Canadian Women at War (1939-1945).* Toronto: Dundurn Press, 1991. 215 pp.

Grahame, Fred B. *My Radar Service Record in WWII.* Dundas, Ont.: Magra Pub., 1993. 54 pp.

Granatstein, J.L., and Desmond Morton. *A Nation Forged in Fire; Canadians and the Second World War 1939-1945.* Toronto: Lester & Orpen Dennys, 1989. 287 pp.

Gray, Edwin. *In All Thy Ways; Letters from a Canadian Flying Officer in Training in Canada and England and in Action in North Africa; F/O Edwin (Ted) Gray.* Toronto: privately printed, n.d. 47 pp.

[Gt. Brit. Air Force. No. 35 Elementary Flying Training School.] *A History of No. 35 E.F.T.S., R.A.F., Neepawa.* Neepawa, Man.: Neepawa Press, n.d. 1 vol., unpaged.

Gt. Brit. Imperial War Graves Commission. *The War Dead of the British Commonwealth and Empire; the Register of the Names of Airmen who Fell in the 1939-1945 War and have No Known Graves; the Ottawa Memorial.* London: H.M. Stationery Office, 1959. 37 pp.

_____. *The War Dead of the British Commonwealth and Empire; the Register of the Names of Those who Fell in the 1939-1945 War and are Buried in Cemeteries and Churchyards in Surrey; Brookwood Military Cemetery, Woking.* London: [H.M. Stationery Office], 1958. 3 vols.

_____. *The War Dead of the British Commonwealth and Empire; the Register of the Names of Those who Fell in the 1939-1945 War and are Buried in Cemeteries in Italy; Ravenna War Cemetery.* London: [H.M. Stationery Office], 1956. 44 pp.

Gt. Brit. Ministry of Information. *Atlantic Bridge; the Official Account of R.A.F. Transport Command's Ocean Ferry.* London: H.M. Stationery Office, 1945. 75 pp.

*Greenhous, Brereton. *Dieppe, Dieppe.* Montréal: Art Global, 1992. 155 pp.

Greenhous, Brereton, and others. *The Crucible of War, 1939-1945.* (The Official History of the Royal Canadian Air Force, Volume III.) n.p.: Univ. of Toronto Press in cooperation with the Department of National Defence and the Canadian Government Pub. Centre, Supply and Services Canada, 1994. 1096 pp.

Griffin, D.F. *First Steps to Tokyo; the Royal Canadian Air Force in the Aleutians.* Toronto: Dent, 1944. 50 pp.

Griffin, J.A. *Canadian Military Aircraft; Serials & Photographs, 1920-1968./Avions militaires canadiens; numéros de série et photographies, 1920-1968.* (Canadian War Museum Publication Number 69-2./Musée de guerre du Canada publication numéro 69-2.) Ottawa: Queen's Printer/ Imprimeur de la Reine, 1969. 691 pp.
Bilingual text./Texte bilingue.

_____. *A Tradition of Fighters./Une tradition de combat aérien.* n.p./s.l.: s.i., [198-?]. 54 pp.
Bilingual text./Texte bilingue.

"Group Captain" *see* The Air Force Guide.

Gutta Percha and Rubber, Limited. *A Selection of Badge Designs of the Canadian Forces.* Toronto: n.p., n.d. 16 pp., chiefly illus.

Hagedorn, Hermann. *Sunward I've Climbed; the Story of John Magee, Poet and Soldier, 1922-1941.* New York: Macmillan, 1943. 166 pp.

Halliday, H.A. *Chronology of Canadian Military Aviation.* (National Museum of Man Mercury Series; Canadian War Museum Paper, no. 6.) Ottawa: [Queen's Printer], 1975. 168 pp.

_____. *The Little Blitz.* (Canadian Battle Series no. 4.) Ottawa: Balmuir Book Pub.; Canadian War Museum, National Museums of Canada, 1986. 26 pp.

_____. *No. 242 Squadron; the Canadian Years; the Story of the RAF's "All-Canadian" Fighter Squadron.* Stittsville, Ont.: Canada's Wings, 1981. 177 pp.

_____. *The Tumbling Sky.* Stittsville, Ont.: Canada's Wings, 1978. 324 pp.

_____. *Typhoon and Tempest; the Canadian Story.* Toronto: CANAV Books, 1992. 207 pp.

_____. *Woody; a Fighter Pilot's Album.* Toronto: CANAV Books, 1987. 143 pp.
Wing Commander Vernon C. Woodward.

Hammond, H.R.L., and others, eds. [*401 Squadron.*] n.p.: privately printed, n.d. 1 vol., unpaged.

Hampson, Bill. *Canadian Flying Services Emblems & Insignia (1914-1984)*. Vancouver: privately printed, 1986. 193 pp.

Hansen, W.J. *"My Life in the R.C.A.F."* Edmonton: privately printed, 1943. 1 vol., chiefly illus.
Recruits book for No. 3 Manning Depot, RCAF.

The Happy Warrior; a Book in Memory of the Life and Work of G/C the Rev. R.M. Frayne, C.D., D.D., Director of Religious Administration (P), the Royal Canadian Air Force. Toronto: United Church Pub. House, 1953. 103 pp.

Harding, John. *The Dancin' Navigator.* Guelph, Ont.: privately printed, 1988. 144 pp.
Memoirs of RCAF navigator in Bomber Command and transport operations.

Harsh, George. *Lonesome Road.* New York: Norton, 1971. 222 pp.
Memoirs of an American on a Georgia chain gang and as an RCAF air gunner officer in North West Europe and as a prisoner of war.

Harvey, J. Douglas. *Boys, Bombs and Brussels Sprouts; a Knees-Up, Wheels-Up Chronicle of WWII.* Toronto: McClelland and Stewart, 1981. 210 pp.

_____. *Laughter-Silvered Wings; Remembering the Air Force II.* Toronto: McClelland and Stewart, 1984. 277 pp.

_____. *The Tumbling Mirth; Remembering the Air Force.* Toronto: McClelland and Stewart, 1983. 263 pp.

Harvie, John D. *Missing in Action; an RCAF Navigator's Story.* Montreal: McGill-Queen's Univ. Press, 1995. 243 pp.
Memoirs of No. 433 Squadron, evasion and as a prisoner of war, including Buchenwald.

*Hatch, F.J. *The Aerodrome of Democracy: Canada and the British Commonwealth Air Training Plan, 1939-1945.* (Department of National Defence Directorate of History Monograph Series no. 1.) Ottawa: Directorate of History, Dept. of National Defence, 1983. 223 pp.

* _____. *Le Canada, aérodrome de la démocratie: le plan d'entraînement aérien du Commonwealth britannique, 1939-1945.* (Service historique du Ministère de la Défense nationale monographie no 1.) Ottawa: Service historique, Ministère de la Défense nationale, 1983. 247 pp.

Hawkins, Ronald F. *We will Remember Them.* Woodstock, N.B.: privately printed, 1995. [239] pp.
Memoirs of New Brunswick Second World War veterans.

Hearn, Owen. *Bing, R.C.A.F.; a Proud and Grateful Memory of Warrant Officer Albert Joseph Michael De Cruyenaere, R.C.A.F., Killed in Action in North Burma, March 1943.* n.p.: privately printed, n.d.

Hearn, Owen. *Verne, R.C.A.F.; a Companion Book to That of Bing, R.C.A.F.; Written in Proud and Grateful Memory of his Friend, Flying Officer Vernon Bartlett Graves Butler, R.C.A.F., Killed in Action in Manipur, Assam, March 1944.* n.p.: privately printed, n.d.

Henderson, Peter A. *Guarding the Gates; a History of Canadian Forces Station St. Johns.* St. John's, Nfld.: CFS St. John's, 1992. 115 pp.

Hermann, J. Douglas. *Report to the Minister of Veterans Affairs of a Study on Canadians who were Prisoners of War in Europe during World War II./Rapport présenté au ministre des Affaires des anciens combattants au sujet d'une enquête portant sur les Canadiens prisonniers de guerre en Europe au cours de la Seconde Guerre mondiale.* Ottawa: Queen's Printer/Imprimeur de la Reine, 1973. 56/60 pp.
Bilingual text./Texte bilingue.

Hibbert, Joyce. *Fragments of War; Stories from Survivors of World War II.* Toronto: Dundurn Press, 1985. 267 pp.

High Flight. Vol. I-III. Stittsville Ont.: Canada's Wings, [1981?]-85.

Hill, B. Kirkbride, comp. *The Price of Freedom.* Toronto: Ryerson Press, 1942-44. 2 vols.

A History of No. 5 E.F.T.S. (R.C.A.F.); High River and Lethbridge, Alberta. D.C. Jones, comp. n.p.: 1945. 82 pp.

Hitchins, F.H. *Air Board, Canadian Air Force and Royal Canadian Air Force.* (National Museum of Man Mercury Series; Canadian War Museum Paper, no. 2.) Ottawa: Queen's Printer, 1972. 475 pp.

Hoare, John. *Tumult in the Clouds; a Story of the Fleet Air Arm.* London: Joseph, 1976. 208 pp.

Hobbs, Charlie. *Past Tense; Charlie's Story.* Burnstown, Ont.: General Store Pub. House, 1994. 208 pp.
Memoir of RCAF air gunner in RAF bomber squadrons and as a prisoner of war.

Hodgins, J. Herbert, and others, comps. *Women at War.* Montreal: MacLean Pub., 1943. 190 pp.

Holliday, Joe. *The Wooden Wonder Aircraft of World War II; Mosquito!* Toronto: Doubleday Canada, 1970. 236 pp.

Holman, R.F. *Best in the West; the Story of Number 2 Canadian Forces Flying Training School and Flying Training in Canada.* Moose Jaw, Sask.: Big 2 Fund, 15 Wing Moose Jaw, 1995. [223] pp.

Hopkins, Anthony. *Songs from the Front & Rear; Canadian Servicemen's Songs of the Second World War.* Edmonton: Hurtig Publishers, 1979. 192 pp.

Horrocks, William. *In their own Words*. Ottawa: Rideau Veterans Home Residents Council, 1993. 247 pp.

[Hovey, H. Richard, and others.] *416 Squadron*. n.p.: 1974. 133 pp.
   Rev. and updated ed.: 416 Squadron History. Belleville, Ont.: Hangar Bookshelf, 1984. 160 pp.

Hundeby, Irv. *Only an Erk with the Thunderbirds*. Elbow, Sask.: printed by Apex Designs Graphics, 1985. 190 pp.
   Groundcrew with No. 426 Squadron.

Hunt, Lloyd, and others. *We Happy Few*. Ottawa: Canadian Fighter Pilots' Association, 1986. 168 pp.

The Illustrated Review of Aviation in Canada; Celebrating the Golden Anniversary of Powered Flight in Canada. Montreal: privately printed, [1959]. 1 vol., unpaged.

In Transit; the Magazine of No. 31 R.A.F. Depot, Moncton, N.B. Vol. I-? Moncton, N.B.: n.p., 1942-?

Iverach, John A. *Chronicles of a Nervous Navigator*. Winnipeg: privately printed, [1992?]. 259 pp.
   Memoirs of an RCAF officer flying with RAF flying boat squadrons from Britain, on special duties and in the Far East.

Jackson, Fred, and others. *The Story of "418"; the City of Edmonton Intruder Squadron, R.C.A.F.* n.p.: n.d. 72 pp.

Jacobson, Ray. *426 Squadron History*. n.p.: [1988]. 187 pp.

Johnson, E.A. "Rick", ed. *Trenton; 50 Years of Air Force*. Trenton, Ont.: n.p., 1981. 160 pp.

Johnson, J.E. *Wing Leader*. Toronto: Clarke, Irwin, 1956. 320 pp.

Johnson, Sara E. *"To Spread their Wings"*. Spruce Grove, Alta.: Saraband Productions, 1990. [126 pp.]
   Memoir of R.C.A.F. (W.D.)

Jones, D.C., *see A History of No. 5 E.F.T.S. ....*

Journal of the Edmonton Military Institute. Vol. I-IV? Edmonton: Edmonton Military Institute, 1937-46?

Karkut, E.T., ed. *The History of 6 RD and the Aerospace Maintenance Development Unit*. Erin, Ont.: The Boston Mills Press, 1990. 120 pp.

*Kealy, J.D.F., and E.C. Russell. *A History of Canadian Naval Aviation, 1918-1962*. Ottawa: Queen's Printer, 1965. 164 pp.

*Kealy, J.D.F., et E.C. Russell. *Histoire de l'aéronavale canadienne, 1918-1962*. Ottawa: Imprimeur de la Reine, 1965. 185 pp.

Kellock, R.L., *see* Canada. Royal Commission to Conduct an Inquiry into Certain Disorders Occurring May 7-8, 1945, in the City of Halifax.

Kelsey Club, Winnipeg, Man. *Canadian Defence; What We have to Defend; Various Defence Policies.* Toronto: T. Nelson, 1937. 98 pp.

Kemp, Hugh. *28 True Adventure Stories; Canada's Aces.* Winnipeg: Contemporary Publishers, 1944. 50 pp.
Also titled: Adventure in the Skies, the Thrilling Achievements of Canada's Greatest Air Aces. n.p: n.d.

Kennedy, I.F. *Black Crosses off my Wingtip.* Burnstown, Ont.: General Store Pub. House, 1994. 183 pp.

Kent, J.A. *One of the Few.* London: W. Kimber, 1971. 255 pp.

Kernaghan, Tom. *Bomb Aimer; the World War II Memoirs of Flying Officer Tom Kernaghan*, as related to D.J. Kernaghan. Belleville, Ont.: n.p., 1994. 49 pp.
British Commonwealth Air Training Plan and No. 420 Squadron.

Kerr, W.K. *Bibliography of Canadian Reports in Aviation Medicine, 1939-1945.* n.p.: Defence Research Board, 1962. v.p.

*King, W.L. Mackenzie. *British Commonwealth Air Training Plan; Broadcast by Right Hon. W.L. Mackenzie King, M.P. Prime Minister of Canada, Sunday, December 17, 1939.* Ottawa: King's Printer, 1939. 17 pp.

————. *Canada and the War; the Training of British Pilots and the Joint Air Training Plan; Mackenzie King Replies to Dr. Manion; a Radio Address by Right Honourable W.L. Mackenzie King, Ottawa, 8th March, 1940.* Ottawa: National Liberal Federation, n.d. 13 pp.

* ————. *Plan d'entraînement des aviateurs du Commonwealth britannique; discours à la radio par le très honorable W.L. Mackenzie King, M.P., Premier ministre du Canada, le dimanche 17 décembre 1939.* Ottawa: Imprimeur du Roi, 1939. 15 pp.

Kostenuk, Samuel, and John Griffin. *RCAF Squadron Histories and Aircraft, 1924-1968.* (Canadian War Museum Historical Publication 14.) Toronto: S. Stevens, Hakkert, 1977. 255 pp.

Laing, Gertrude. *A Community Organized for War; the Story of the Greater Winnipeg Co-ordinating Board for War Services and Affiliated Organizations, 1939-1946.* Winnipeg: n.p., 1948. 103 pp.

Lamb, Ken. *Milton Remembers World War II.* Milton, Ont.: Milton Historical Society, 1995. 140 pp.

Langeste, Tom, comp. *Words on the Wing; Slang, Aphorisms, Catchphrases and Jargon of Canadian Military Aviation since 1914.* Toronto: Canadian Institute of Strategic Studies, 1995. 330 pp.

Large, W.S. *The Diary of a Canadian Fighter Pilot.* K.B. Conn, ed. Toronto: R. Saunders, 1944. 64 pp.

Lavender, Emerson, and Norman Sheffe. *The Evaders; True Stories of Downed Canadian Airmen and their Helpers in World War II.* Toronto: McGraw-Hill Ryerson, 1992. 262 pp.

Lavigne, J.P.A. Michel, and J.F. "Stocky" Edwards. *Kittyhawk Pilot; Wing Commander J.F. (Stocky) Edwards.* Battleford, Sask.: Turner-Warwick Publications, 1983. 308, xxiv pp.

Lee, A.M. *Chatham; an Airfield History.* Fredericton, N.B.: privately printed, 1989. 116 pp.

Legermuseum Delft. *Victory Parade; Canadian War Artists in Holland 1944/45.* Delft, Neth.: Legermuseum Delft, 1990. 64 pp.

Leigh, Z. Lewis. *And I shall Fly.* Toronto: CANAV Books, 1985. 211 pp.

Lévesque, Thérèse. *Laisse-moi te dire ...; la guerre 1939/45 après 50 ans.* Saint-Quentin, N.-B.: Imprimerie Lévesque, 1990. 171 pp.

London Air Observer; Published Monthly in the Interests of the Personnel of No. 4 Air Observer School, Leavens Bros. (Training) Limited. Vol. I-? London, Ont.: n.p., 1943-?

M.T.B. Vol. I-III? Rivers, Man.: privately printed, 1943-45?
Cover title: Message to Base. Journal of No. 1 Central Navigation School, RCAF.

McAlister, Alec. *Hi-Sky! The Ups and Downs of a Pinfeather Pilot.* Toronto: Ryerson Press, 1944. 124 pp.

*McAndrew, Willliam J., Bill Rawling and Michael Whitby. *Liberation; the Canadians in Europe.* Montreal: Art Global, 1995. 170 pp.

*McAndrew, William J., Bill Rawling et Michael Whitby. *La libération; les Canadiens en Europe.* Montréal: Art Global, 1995. 170 pp.

*McAndrew, William J., Donald E. Graves and Michael Whitby. *Normandy 1944; the Canadian Summer.* Montreal: Art Global, 1994. 162 pp.

*McAndrew, William J., Donald E. Graves et Michael Whitby. *Normandie 1944; l'été canadien.* Montréal: Art Global, 1994. 162 pp.

McCaffery, Dan. *Air Aces; the Lives and Times of Twelve Canadian Fighter Pilots.* Toronto: J. Lorimer, 1990. 234 pp.

_____. *Battlefields in the Air; Canadians in the Allied Bomber Command.* Toronto: J. Lorimer, 1995. 196 pp.

McClenaghan, John, and Derek Blatchford. *411 City of North York Squadron; 50 Years of History, 1941-1991.* Winnipeg: John/David Associates, 1992. 190 pp.

Macdonald, Grant. *Our Canadian Armed Services,* sketches by Grant Macdonald. Montreal: Gazette, 1943. 1 vol., chiefly illus.

MacDonald, Grant, and Terry Strocel. *442 Squadron History.* n.p.: [1987]. 144 pp.

MacFarlane, John, and Robbie Hughes. *Canada's Naval Aviators.* Victoria, B.C.: Maritime Museum of British Columbia, 1994. 182 pp.

McGill Univ., Montreal, P.Q. *A Memorial Service for the McGill Men and Women who Gave their Lives during the First and Second World Wars.* n.p.: [1946]. 1 vol., unpaged.

McIntosh, Dave. *Terror in the Starboard Seat.* Don Mills, Ont.: General Pub. Co., 1980. 184 pp.

McIntosh, Dave, ed. *High Blue Battle.* Toronto: Stoddart, 1990. 178 pp.
The war diary of No. 1 (401) Fighter Squadron, RCAF.

McKay, Russell. *One of the Many.* Burnstown, Ont.: General Store Pub. House, 1989. 167 pp.
Service with No. 420 Squadron, 1944-45.

MacLaren, Roy. *Canadians in Russia, 1918-1919.* Toronto: Macmillan, 1976. 301 pp.

McLean, N.B. *Report of the Hudson Strait Expedition, 1927-28.* Ottawa: King's Printer, 1929. 221 pp.

MacMillan, D.A. *Only the Stars Know.* Toronto: Dent, 1944. 138 pp.

McNeil, Bill. *Voices of a War Remembered; an Oral History of Canadians in World War Two.* Toronto: Doubleday Canada, 1991. 376 pp.

McQuiston, John H. *Tannoy Calling; a Story of Canadian Airmen Flying against Nazi Germany.* New York: Vantage Press, 1990. 210 pp.
No. 415 Squadron.

McVicar, Don. *Ferry Command.* Shrewsbury, Eng.: Airlife Pub., 1981. 213 pp.

_____. *North Atlantic Cat.* Shrewsbury, Eng.: Airlife Pub., 1983. 216 pp.
Ferrying aircraft to United Kingdom.

*Main, J.R.K. *Les voyageurs de l'air; historique de l'aviation civile au Canada, 1859-1967.* Ottawa: Imprimeur de la Reine, 1967. 433 pp.

* _____. *Voyageurs of the Air; a History of Civil Aviation in Canada.* Ottawa: Queen's Printer, 1967. 397 pp.

Manning the R.C.A.F.; Short History of the Directorate of Manning. n.p.: n.d. 25 pp.

Mansikka, Eric, comp. *Pack Up your Troubles; Canadian War Humour.* Cartoons by Paul Gomiratto. Toronto: Methuen, 1987. 112 pp. *Second World War humour accompanied by original cartoons.*

Mayne, J.W. *Operational Research in the Canadian Armed Forces during the Second World War.* (Operational Research and Analysis Establishment ORAE Report, no. R68.) Ottawa: Dept. of National Defence, 1978. 2 vols.

Mazéas, Daniel. *Insignes armée canadienne, 1900-1914; Canadian Badges; supplément, 1920-1950.* Guingamp, France: privately printed, 1972. 116 pp.

*Melnyk, T.W. *Canadian Flying Operations in South East Asia, 1941-1945.* (Department of National Defence Directorate of History Occasional Paper, Number One.) Ottawa: Queen's Printer, 1976. 179 pp.

*_____. *Les opérations aériennes du Canada dans le sud-est Asiatique, 1941-1945.* Jacques Gouin, tr. (Ministère de la Défense nationale Service historique Document occasionnel, numéro 1.) Ottawa: Imprimeur de la Reine, 1976. 202 pp.

Memories of Linton; Home of the Goose and Thunderbird Squadrons. n.p.: n.d. 15 pp.

Merrick, Bob. *410 Squadron; a History.* n.p.: n.d. 114 pp.

Middleton, W.E. Knowles. *Radar Development in Canada: the Radio Branch of the National Research Council of Canada, 1939-1946.* Waterloo, Ont.: Wilfrid Laurier Univ. Press, 1981. 147 pp.

Milberry, Larry. *Aviation in Canada.* Toronto: McGraw-Hill Ryerson, 1979. 272 pp.

Milberry, Larry, ed. *Sixty Years; the RCAF and CF Air Command 1924-1984.* Toronto: CANAV Books, 1984. 480 pp.

Milberry, Larry, and Hugh A. Halliday. *The Royal Canadian Air Force at War 1939-1945.* Toronto: CANAV Books, 1990. 480 pp.

Military Aviation. Vol. I-? Toronto: privately printed, 1940-?

Milne, Ramsay H. *Sailor Boy to Typhoon Pilot.* Duncan, B.C.: printed by Solitaire Press, 1988. 301 pp.

Miville-Deschênes, Charles. *Souvenirs de guerre.* Québec, P.Q.: s.i., 1946. 128 pp.

*Molson, K.M. *Canada's National Aviation Museum; its History and Collections.* Ottawa: National Aviation Museum, National Museum of Science and Technology, 1988. 291 pp.

*_____. *Le Musée national de l'aviation du Canada; son histoire et ses collections.* Ottawa: Musée national de l'aviation, Musée national des sciences et de la technologie, 1988. [288] pp.

Molson, K.M., and H.A. Taylor. *Canadian Aircraft since 1909.* Stittsville, Ont.: Canada's Wings, 1982. 530 pp.

Monnon, Ernest F., and Mary Ann Monnon. *"Right On, You Got the Elbow Out!"; Wartime Memoirs of the R.C.A.F.* Toronto: Natural Heritage/Natural History, 1990. 96 pp.
Radio telephone officer with No. 143 Wing.

The Mont Joli Target. Vol. I. Mont Joli, P.Q.: n.p., 1944-45.
Journal of No. 9 Bombing and Gunnery School, RCAF.

The Moose Squadron; 1941-45, the War Years of 419 Squadron. Winnipeg: CFTMPC, 1977. 303 pp.

Morgan, Len. *The AT-6 Harvard.* (Famous Aircraft.) New York: Arco Pub. Co., 1965. 1 vol., unpaged.

Morneault, J.C. *424 Tiger Squadron, 1935-1977.* n.p.: [1978]. 31 pp.

Morris, Jerrold. *Canadian Artists and Airmen, 1940-45.* Toronto: The Morris Gallery, n.d. 207 pp.

The Moth Monthly. Vol. I-II. Caron, Sask.: privately printed, 1942-43.
Journal of No. 33 Elementary Flying Training School, RCAF. Vol. II, no. 3-12 titled: The Tailspin.

Moule, Dick. *The Radar Mechanics' Secret War, 1940-1945.* Calgary: privately printed, 1993. 119 pp.

The Mount Hope Meteor. Vol. I-? Mount Hope, Ont.: privately printed, 1942-?
Journal of No. 33 Air Navigation School, RCAF.

Murray, Joan. *Canadian Artists of the Second World War.* Oshawa, Ont.: Robert McLaughlin Gallery, 1981. 124 pp.

Le Musée national de l'aviation; un survol. Ottawa: Musée national de l'aviation, 1991. 64 pp.

Myles, Eugenie Louise. *Airborne from Edmonton.* Toronto: Ryerson Press, 1959. 280 pp.

National Aeronautical Collection. Ottawa: Queen's Printer, 1967. 36 pp.

National Aeronautical Collection./Collection aéronautique nationale. n.p.: n.d./s.l.: s.i., s.d. 36 pp.
Bilingual text./Texte bilingue.

The National Aviation Museum; a Flypast. Ottawa: National Aviation Museum, 1991. 64 pp.

Nicholson, G.W.L. *More Fighting Newfoundlanders; a History of Newfoundland's Fighting Forces in the Second World War.* [St. John's, Nfld.]: Govt. of Nfld., 1969. 621 pp.

1939-1989/50th Anniversary Reunion, 4-6 August 1989/50ième anniversaire réunion, 4-6 août 1989 [412 Squadron/Escadrille]. n.p./s.l.: s.i., [1989]. 28 pp.
Bilingual text./Texte bilingue.

Nolan, Brian. *Hero; the Buzz Beurling Story.* Toronto: Lester & Orpen Dennys, 1981. 201 pp.

Northern Flight; Canada's Aviation Heritage Magazine. Vol. I- . Thornhill, Ont.: Northern Flight Publications, 1992- .

Norway. Air Force. Training Centre, Ontario. *"Little Norway" in Pictures; R.N.A.F. in Canada.* n.p.: n.d. 1 vol., unpaged.

Nova Scotia. *Nova Scotia Helps the Fighting Man.* n.p.: [1942]. 32 pp.

No. 8 on Parade. Vol. I-? Winnipeg: n.p., 1942-?
Journal of No. 8 Repair Depot, RCAF.

Number Four Hundred & Four Squadron, Royal Canadian Air Force. n.p.: [1972]. 62 pp.

No. 9 Flyer. Vol. I. Centralia, Ont.: n.p., 1944-45?
Journal of No. 9 Service Flying Training School, RCAF.

No. 19 Service Flying Training School, Vulcan, Alberta, Royal Canadian Air Force, Annual, 1944. n.p.: privately printed, n.d. 51 pp.

Obodiac, Stanlee. *Pennfield Ridge.* Wembley, Eng.: privately printed, 1949. 100 pp.

Olmsted, Bill. *Blue Skies; the Autobiography of a Canadian Spitfire Pilot in World War II.* Toronto: Stoddart, 1987. 261 pp.

[Ontario County Flying Training School, Limited.] *Souvenir Booklet, No. 20 Elementary Flying Training School, Limited R.C.A.F., 1941-1944.* Oshawa, Ont.: privately printed, [1945].

Ottawa Air Training Conference, 1942. *Report of the Conference.* Ottawa: King's Printer, 1942. 25 pp.

Over Seas; the Magazine of the Royal Air Force, Greenwood, Nova Scotia, Canada. Vol. I-? n.p.: 1942-?

Page, Bette, comp. *Mynarski's Lanc; the Story of Two Famous Canadian Lancaster Bombers KB726 & FM213.* Erin, Ont.: Boston Mills Press, 1989. 192 pp.

Page, Ron D., and William Cumming. *Fleet; the Flying Years*. Erin, Ont.: Boston Mills Press, 1990. 152 pp.

The Patrician. Vol. I-? Sidney, B.C.: privately printed, 1941-?
Magazine of the Royal Air Force, British Columbia.

343

The Paulson Post. Vol. I-? Paulson, Man.: privately printed, 1942-?
Journal of No. 7 Bombing and Gunnery School, RCAF.

Pearcy, Arthur. *The Dakota; a History of the Douglas Dakota in RAF and RCAF Service.* London: I. Allan, 1972. 320 pp.

Peden, Murray. *A Thousand shall Fall.* Stittsville, Ont.: Canada's Wings, 1979. 473 pp.

The Penhold Log. Vol. I-V. Penhold, Alta.: privately printed, 1941-44.
Journal of No. 36 Service Flying Training School, RCAF.

Per ardua; a Pictorial History of RCAF, Torbay. n.p.: 1944. [64] pp.

Pickett, James. *Into the Sausage Machine; the History of 22 Wing.* North Bay, Ont.: privately printed, 1994. 145 pp.

Pickler, Ron, and Larry Milberry. *Canadair; the First Fifty Years.* Toronto: CANAV Books, 1995. 392 pp.

Pigott, Peter. *Flying Canucks; Famous Canadian Aviators.* Toronto: Hounslow, 1994. 178 pp.

Pilots, Observers and Air Gunners for the Royal Canadian Air Force. n.p.: n.d. [20 pp.]

Pioneer; Official Journal, No. 31 SFTS, Canada, Royal Air Force. Vol. I-II. Kingston, Ont.: privately printed, 1941-42.

Le plan d'entraînement aérien du Commonwealth britannique. Ottawa: Imprimeur du Roi, 1941. 11 pp.

Le plan d'entraînement aérien du Commonwealth britannique, 1939-1945; résumé historique et compte rendu de la cérémonie qui s'est déroulée à la station du CARC de Trenton. Ottawa: Imprimeur du Roi, 1950. 61 pp.

Powell, Griffith. *Ferryman.* Shrewsbury, Eng.: Airlife Pub., 1982. 221 pp.
North Atlantic aircraft ferrying.

Prairie Flyer; the Magazine of No. 32 S.F.T.S. R.A.F. Vol. I-? Moose Jaw, Sask.: privately printed, 1941-?

Preston, Richard A. *Canada's RMC; a History of the Royal Military College.* Toronto: Univ. of Toronto Press, 1969. 415 pp.

Pukka Gen. Vol. I-IV. Debert, N.S.: privately printed, 1942-44.
Journal of No. 31 Operational Training Unit, RAF.

RCA Victor Co. *Symbol of Air Supremacy.* n.p.: n.d. [12] pp.

The Rally Magazine. Vol. I-? Wrecclesham, Eng.: n.p., 1939?-?
A monthly magazine for Canadian Active Service Forces.

Reader's Digest. *The Canadians at War, 1939/45.* Montreal: Reader's Digest, 1969. 2 vols.

_____. *The Tools of War, 1939/45, and a Chronology of Important Events.* Montreal: Reader's Digest, 1969. 96 pp.

Recte Volare. Vol. I-? Port Albert, Ont.: n.p., 1942-?
Journal of No. 31 Air Navigation School, RAF.

Redman, Stanley R. *Open Gangway; the (Real) Story of the Halifax Navy Riot.* Hantsport, N.S.: Lancelot Press, 1981. 167 pp.

Reed, R.H. "Hank", ed. *East Camp No. 1 NAGS Yarmouth, N.S.; Memories.* Yarmouth, N.S.: R.H. Davis, 1984. 140 pp.

The Regina Elementary Flying Training School Limited; a Company Incorporated under the Dominion Companies Act for the Sole Purpose of Operating No. 15 Elementary Flying Training School, a Unit of the British Commonwealth Air Training Plan, from November, 1940, to August, 1944. n.p.: n.d. 24 pp.

The Repair-O-Scope. Vol. I-? St. Johns, P.Q.: n.p., 1944-?
Journal of No. 9 Repair Depot, RCAF.

Rivac, Richard. *Tail Gunner Takes Over.* London: Jarrolds, n.d. 112 pp.

Roberts, Leslie. *Canada's War in the Air.* Montreal: A.M. Beatty, 1942. 157 pp.

_____. *There shall be Wings; a History of the Royal Canadian Air Force.* Toronto: Clarke, Irwin, 1959. 250 pp.

Robertson, Heather, [comp.] *A Terrible Beauty; the Art of Canada at War.* Toronto: J. Lorimer, 1977. 239 pp.

Robertson, Peter. *Irréductible vérité/Relentless Verity/les photographes militaires canadiens depuis 1885/Canadian Military Photographers since 1885.* (Les Archives publiques du Canada/Public Archives of Canada Series.) Québec, P.Q.: Les Presses de l'Université Laval, 1973. 233 pp.
Texte bilingue./Bilingual text.

Robinson, J.R., and Fred B. Grahame. *Radar Officers of the Royal Canadian Air Force, 1940-1946.* Dundas, Ont.: Magra Pub., 1995. 100 pp.

Rogers, Betty (Fillmore). *A Girl in Blue; my Days in the R.C.A.F.* Port Elgin, N.B.: printed by Mount Allison Reprographics Dept., Mount Allison Univ., 1993. 152 pp.

Royal Military College of Canada, Kingston, Ont. *Regulations and Calendar of the Royal Military College of Canada, 1922.* Ottawa: King's Printer, 1923. 68 pp.

Royal Military College of Canada, Kingston, Ont. *Standing Orders, Amended to January, 1924.* Ottawa: King's Printer, 1924. 120 pp.

_____. *Standing Orders, Amended to January, 1926.* Ottawa: King's Printer, 1926. 105 pp.

_____. *Standing Orders; the Royal Military College of Canada, 1938.* Ottawa: King's Printer, 1938. 67 pp.

The Royal Military College of Canada Review. Vol. I- . Kingston, Ont.: privately printed, 1920- .

Sallans, G.H. *With Canada's Fighting Men.* Ottawa: King's Printer, 1941. 46 pp.

Sandwell, A.H. *Planes over Canada.* London: T. Nelson, 1938. 120 pp.

Sargent, J. William. *Sgt Sargent's Trenton.* Belleville, Ont.: Hangar Books, 1985. 144 pp.

Savard, Adjutor. *Les ailes canadiennes françaises.* s.l.: s.i., 1944. 1 tome, non paginé.

*_____. *The Defence of our Land.* n.p.: 1943. 12 pp.

*_____. *La défense du territoire.* s.l.: s.i., 1943. 11 pp.

Schmidt, John. *"This Was No ⊕YXNH Picnic!" 2.4 Years of Wild and Woolly Mayhem in Dawson Creek.* Hanna, Alta.: Gorman & Gorman, 1991. 355 pp. *Building the Alaska Highway.*

Segal, Jean Brown. *Wings of the Morning.* Toronto: Macmillan, 1945. 151 pp.

The Sentinel. No. 1-11? n.p.: 1944-45? *Journal of No. 32 Radio Unit, RCAF, Port-aux-Basques, Nfld.*

Shea, A.A., and E. Estoriak. *Canada and the Short-Wave War.* (Behind the Headlines, vol. III.) Toronto: Canadian Institute of International Affairs, 1942. 36 pp.

Shores, Christopher. *History of the Royal Canadian Air Force.* (A Bison Book.) Toronto: Royce Publications, 1984. 128 pp.

Shrive, Frank J. *The Diary of a P.B.O.*; *Poor Bloody Observer.* Norman Shrive, ed. Erin, Ont.: Boston Mills Press, 1981. 88 pp. *Observer in North Russia, 1918-19.*

Silver, L. Ray. *Last of the Gladiators; a World War II Bomber Navigator's Story.* Shrewsbury, Eng.: Airlife, 1995. 192 pp. *RCAF in No. 10 Squadron, RAF, and prisoner of war.*

Simpson, Allan, and others. *We Few.* Ottawa: Canadian Fighter Pilots Association, 1983. 167 pp.

Six Years and a Day; the Story of the Beaver Club, 1940-1946. London: n.p., n.d. 34 pp.

Skelding, Wm. *419 Repair and Salvage Unit, Royal Canadian Air Force; Operation Overlord, 1944-1945.* n.p.: n.d. [42] pp.

Smith, Gladys E. *Forty Nights to Freedom; the True Prisoner of War Escape Story of Wing Commander Stewart F. Cowan (Ret.).* Winnipeg: Queenston House Pub. Co., 1984. 219 pp.

Smith, I. Norman. *The British Commonwealth Air Training Plan.* Toronto: Macmillan, 1941. 28 pp.

Sparks. Vol. I-? Guelph, Ont.: n.p., 1942-?
Journal of No. 4 Wireless School, RCAF. Began publication as a newspaper.

Squires, Clinton H. *Share my Flights.* n.p.: 1984. 56 pp.

*Stacey, C.P. *Armes, hommes et gouvernements; les politiques de guerre du Canada, 1939-1945.* Ottawa: Imprimeur de la Reine, 1970. 747 pp.

*_____. *Arms, Men and Governments; the War Policies of Canada, 1939-1945.* Ottawa: Queen's Printer, 1970. 681 pp.

Stacey, C.P., and Barbara M. Wilson. *The Half-Million; the Canadians in Britain, 1939-1946.* Toronto: Univ. of Toronto Press, 1987. 198 pp.

Stalmann, Reinhart. *Die Ausbrecherkönige von Kanada.* [Hamburg]: Sternbücher, 1958. 191 pp.

Stedman, Ernest W. *From Boxkite to Jet; Memoirs of Air Vice-Marshall Ernest W. Stedman.* [Toronto]: Univ. of Toronto Press, 1963. 1 vol., unpaged.
Reprints of articles from Canadian Aviation. An enlarged edition was published as From Boxkite to Jet; the Memoirs of an Aeronautical Engineer (National Museum of Man Mercury Series; Canadian War Museum Paper no. 1.) Ottawa: Queen's Printer, 1972.

Stephens, W. Ray. *The Canadian Entertainers of World War II.* Oakville, Ont.: Mosaic Press, 1993. 116 pp.

Stofer, Eric. *RCAF Station Ucluelet B.C. (Recollections).* Victoria, B.C.: privately printed, 1995. [221] pp.

_____. *Unsafe for Aircrew.* Victoria, B.C.: privately printed, 1989. 413 pp.

Stofer, Ken. *Dear Mum; the Story of Victor Edward "Candy" Syrett, a Canadian in the Royal Air Force during World War Two.* Victoria, B.C.: Kenlyn Pub., 1991. 29 pp.

Strachan, Tony, ed. *In the Clutch of Circumstance; Reminiscences of Members of the Canadian National Prisoners of War Association.* Victoria, B.C.: Cappis Press, 1985. 285 pp.

Summary of Memorandum of Agreement between the Governments of the United Kingdom, Canada, Australia and New Zealand Relating to Training of Pilots and Aircraft Crews in Canada and their Subsequent Service. n.p.: [1942]. 12 pp.

*Summerby, Janice. *Native Soldiers; Foreign Battlefields.* Ottawa: Communications Division, Veterans Affairs Canada, 1993. 47 pp.

*_____. *Soldats autochtones; terres étrangères.* Ottawa: Direction générale des communications, Anciens combattants Canada, 1993. 51 pp.

Sutherland, Alice Gibson. *Canada's Aviation Pioneers; 50 Years of McKee Trophy Winners.* Toronto: McGraw-Hill Ryerson, 1978. 304 pp.

Sutherland Brown, A. *Indian Days — Burmese Nights; Personal Reminiscences of Wartime Service with the RAF.* Victoria, B.C.: n.p., 1992. 33 pp.

Suthren, Victor, ed. *The Oxford Book of Canadian Militiary Anecdotes.* Toronto: Oxford Univ. Press, 1989. 202 pp.

Swan, Minto. *Props, Bars and Pulpits or Minto's Minutes.* Kingston, Ont.: privately printed, n.d. 143 pp.
Cover title: Padre Minto Remembers.

Sweanor, George. *It's All Pensionable Time.* Vol. I. n.p.: n.d. v.p.

Swettenham, John. *D-Day./Jour-J.* Jacques Gouin, tr. Ottawa: National Museum of Man/Musée national de l'Homme, [1970]. 27/30 pp.
Bilingual text./Texte bilingue.

The Swift; a Review of Current Events. No. 1-? Swift Current, Sask.: Sun Print. & Pub. Co., 1942-?
Journal of No. 39 Service Flying Training School, RAF.

[Tait, Stuart.] *408 Goose Squadron Reunion, 1987.* n.p.: [1987]. 34 pp.

Taschereau, Gabriel. *Du salpêtre dans le gruau; souvenirs d'escadrille (1939-1945).* Sillery (Qué.): Septentrion, 1993. 344 pp.
Escadrille 425.

Thibault, Jean. *Drummondville à l'heure de la guerre: 1939-1945.* Drummondville (Qué.): La Société d'histoire de Drummondville, 1994. 191 pp.

Thompson, Roy J.C. *Wings of the Canadian Armed Forces, 1913-1972.* [Dartmouth], N.S.: n.p., 1973. 106 pp.

Thompson, Walter R. *Lancaster to Berlin.* London: Goodall Publications, 1985. 242 pp.

Thumbs Up. Vol. I-? Dartmouth, N.S.: privately printed, 1941-?
   *Published by airmen of RCAF Station Dartmouth. Vol. I, no. 1-4 were
   published by airmen of No. 4 Repair Depot, RCAF.*

Thurston, Arthur. *Bluenose Spitfires.* Hantsport, N.S.: Lancelot Press, 1979. 92
   pp.

Torontow, Cy. *Up, Up and — Oy Vay.* Ottawa: privately printed, 1990. 155 pp.
   Memoires of RCAF service 1939-1968.

Tracer. Vol. I-? Winnipeg: privately printed, 1944-?
   Journal of No. 3 Bombing and Gunnery School, RCAF.

A Tribute to Valour. St. Thomas, Ont.: printed by Sutherland Press, 1945. 169
   pp.
   Memorial book of Dunwich Township and village of Dutton, Ont.

Trinity College School Old Boys at War, 1899-1902, 1914-1918, 1939-1945. Port
   Hope, Ont.: privately printed, 1948. 245 pp.

True Canadian War Stories, selected by Jane Dewar from the pages of Legion
   Magazine. Toronto: Lester & Orpen Dennys, 1986. 310 pp.

25th Anniversary Reunion; Royal Canadian Air Force (Women's Division).
   Toronto: n.p., 1966. 1 vol., unpaged.

Twichell, Heath. *Northwest Epic; the Building of the Alaska Highway.* New
   York: St. Martin's Press, 1992. 368 pp.

*Ukranian Canadian Veterans; Royal Canadian Legion; Memorial Souvenir
   Book 1.* Montreal: Ukranian Canadian Veterans Association, 1986. 192 pp.
   *Chiefly reprint of the Ukranian Canadian Servicemen's Associations
   newsletters, 1943-46.*

The University of Alberta in the War of 1939-45. Edmonton: n.p., 1948. 70 pp.

Univ. of Toronto. *Memorial Book, Second World War, 1939-1945.* H.E. Brown,
   comp. Toronto: Soldiers' Tower Committee, Univ. of Toronto, 1994. 84 pp.

Vaughan, Arnold P. *418 City of Edmonton Squadron History.* n.p.: [1984]. 117
   pp.

Velleman, Alexander. *The RCAF as Seen from the Ground (A Worm's-Eye
   View).* Stittsville, Ont.: Canada's Wings, 1986. 3 vols.

Veterans' Review; a Collection of War Stories. Toronto: privately printed, 1983.
   255 pp.

Vincent, Carl. *The Blackburn Shark.* (Canada's Wings, vol. 1.) Stittsville, Ont.:
   Canada's Wings, 1974. 98 pp.

Vincent, Carl, J.D. Oughton and E. Vincent. *Consolidated Liberator & Boeing Fortress*. (Canada's Wings, vol. 2.) Stittsville, Ont.: Canada's Wings, 1975. 246 pp.

[Virden Flying Training School, Limited.] *Virden Days; Memories of No. 19 E.F.T.S., R.C.A.F., 1941-1944.* Winnipeg: Sautes and Pollards, [1945]. 94 pp.

Wagner, Gordon. *How Papa Won the War.* Courtenay, B.C.: Flying-W-Pub. Co., 1989. 237 pp.

War Record; the McGill Chapter of Delta Upsilon, 1939-1945. Montreal: n.p., 1946. 83 pp.

Watt, Sholto. *I'll Take the High Road; a History of the Beginning of the Atlantic Air Ferry in Wartime.* Fredericton, N.B.: Brunswick Press, 1960. 169 pp.

Watts, Jack. *Nickels and Nightingales.* Burnstown, Ont.: General Store Pub. House, 1995. 285 pp.
Memoirs of an RCAF observer in Nos. 10, 462 and 109 Squadrons, RAF, in North West Europe and the Desert Air Force.

Weisbord, Merrily, and Merilyn Simonds Mohr. *The Valour and the Horror.* Toronto: HarperCollins, 1991. 171 pp.
From the television series by Brian McKenna and Terence McKenna.

Wellington Legion War Veterans Club, eds. *They Served for Freedom./A la Défense de la liberté.* [Wellington, P.E.I.: Royal Canadian Legion, Wellinton Branch 17/Wellington, I.P.E.: Légion royale canadienne, la filiale de Wellington no 17], 1986. 319 pp.
Bilingual text./Texte bilingue.

Wells, Herb. *Comrades in Arms.* St. John's, Nfld.: printed by Robinson-Blackmore Print. & Pub., 1986-88. 2 vols.
Newfoundlanders in action, Second World War.

West, Bruce. *The Man who Flew Churchill.* Toronto: McGraw-Hill Ryerson, 1975. 201 pp.

Wheeler, William J. *Images of Flight; a Canadian Aviation Portfolio.* Willowdale, Ont.: Hounslow, 1992. 134 pp.

Whitehead, William. *Dieppe, 1942; Echoes of Disaster.* Terence Macartney-Filgate, ed. (A Personal Library Publication.) Don Mills, Ont.: Nelson, 1979. 187 pp., chiefly illus.

Whitton, Charlotte. *Canadian Women in the War Effort.* Toronto: Macmillan, 1942. 56 pp.

Williams, Jack. *Wings over Niagara; Aviation in the Niagara District, 1911-1944.* St. Catharines, Ont.: Niagara Aviation Pioneers, [1982]. 1 vol., unpaged.

Williams, James N. *The Plan; [Memories of the British Commonwealth Air Training Plan].* Stittsville, Ont.: Canada's Wings, 1984. 222 pp.

[Willson, Gordon Beckles.] *Canada Comes to England,* by Gordon Beckles [*pseud.*] London: Hodder and Stoughton, 1941. 166 pp.

Wilson, J.A. *Development of Aviation in Canada, 1879-1948.* Ottawa: Dept. of Transport Air Services Branch, n.d. 105 pp.

Windy Wings. Vol. I-IV? Claresholm, Alta.: privately printed, 1941-44?
Title varies. Vol. I titled: No. 15 S.F.T.S. Review. Journal of No. 15 Service Flying Training School, RCAF.

Wings. Vol. I-? Picton, Ont.: privately printed, 1941-?
Journal of RAF Station Picton and of No. 31 Bombing and Gunnery School, RAF.

Wings. Vol. I-? Yorkton, Sask.: n.p., 1941-?
Journal of No. 11 Service Flying Training School, RCAF.

Wings; Log of the R.C.A.F. Vol. I-? Ottawa: privately printed, 1943-?
Published monthly for Air Force personnel by the Air Force Headquarters Station Fund.

Wings over Borden; the Pioneer R.C.A.F. Journal. Vol. I-? Camp Borden, Ont.: n.p., 1942-?

*Wodehouse, R.F. *Aviation Paintings from the Art Collection of the Canadian War Museum.* Ottawa: [Queen's Printer], 1972. 84 pp.

_____. *A Check List of the War Collections of World War I, 1914-1918, and World War II, 1939-1945.* Ottawa: Queen's Printer, 1968. 239 pp.

* _____. *Tableaux de l'aviation militaire; provenant de la Collection d'art du Musée de guerre canadien.* Ottawa: [Imprimeur de la Reine], 1972. 84 pp.

Wong, Marjorie. *The Dragon and the Maple Leaf; Chinese Canadians in World War II.* London, Ont.: Pirie Pub., 1994. 274 pp.

Woolley, H.W. *No Time Off for Good Behavior.* Burnstown, Ont.: General Store Pub. House, 1990. 188 pp.
Canadian prisoner of war in Germany.

Wright, Harold E., [and] Byron E. O'Leary. *Fortress Saint John; an Illustrated Military History, 1640-1985.* Saint John, N.B.: Partridge Island Research Project, 1985. 131 pp.

Wyatt, Bernie. *Maximum Effort; the Big Bombing Raids.* Erin, Ont.: Boston Mills Press, 1986. 164 pp.

_____. *Two Wings and a Prayer.* Erin, Ont.: The Boston Mills Press, 1984. 136 pp.
Reminiscences of fifty Canadian and American air force veterans of the Second World War.

Wynn, Edgar J. *Bombers Across.* New York: Dutton, 1944. 178 pp.
Atlantic Ferry Organization.

Young, Albert Charles. *24 Good Men and True; Members of Branch #142 of the Royal Canadian Legion.* New York: Vantage Press, 1992. 219 pp.

Young Men's Christian Associations, Canada. *The 1st Year; a War Service Record of the Canadian Y.M.C.A. from the Outbreak of the War.* n.p.: [1940]. 23 pp.

Young Men's Christian Associations, Canada. National Council. War Services Executive. *With Arthur Jones through 5 Years of War; a Report of Canadian Y.M.C.A. War Services.* n.p.: n.d. 1 vol., unpaged.

Young, Scott. *Red Shield in Action; a Record of Canadian Salvation Army War Services in the Second Great War.* Toronto: F.F. Clarke, 1949. 149 pp.

Ziegler, Mary. *The Story of the Women's Division, Royal Canadian Air Force.* Hamilton, Ont.: privately printed, 1973. 173 pp.

1946-1967

Adams, James. *Bull's Eye; the Assassination and Life of Supergun Inventor Gerald Bull*. New York: Times Books, 1992. 317 pp.

Adelberg, Philip, ed. *414 Squadron (1941-1975); a Short History*. n.p.: 1975. 1 vol., unpaged.

Air Cadet Annual. Ottawa: Air Cadet League of Canada, 1949-69.

Air Force College Journal. Toronto: privately printed, 1956-64. 9 vols. *Title varies*.

Airforce. Vol. I- . Ottawa: Air Force Productions, 1977- .
   Quarterly. Recommended by the Royal Canadian Air Force Association.

Annis, Clare L. *Airpower 1952; Three Speeches*. n.p.: n.d. v.p.

The Arrowhead Tribune. Vol. I-VII. Marville, France: n.p., 1961-67.
   Semi-weekly. Journal of No. 1 (Fighter) Wing.

The Arrowheads *see* Organ, Richard.

Aviation in Modern Defence; the Story of the Expanding Royal Canadian Air Force. n.p.: n.d. [12] pp.

Aylore. Vol. I-? Aylmer, Ont.: privately printed, 1954-?
   Monthly. Journal of RCAF Station Aylmer, Ont.

Baglow, Bob. *Canucks Unlimited; Royal Canadian Air Force CF-100 Squadrons and Aircraft, 1952-1963*. Ottawa: Canuck Publications, 1985. [124] pp.

*Barton, William H. *Science and the Armed Services*. (Current Affairs for the Canadian Forces, vol. II, no. 1.) Ottawa: King's Printer, 1952. 22 pp.

* _____ . *La science et les Services armés*. (Actualités; revue destinée aux Forces canadiennes, vol II, no 1.) Ottawa: Imprimeur du Roi, 1952. 22 pp.

Bashow, David L. *Starfighter: a Loving Restrospective of the CF-104 Era in Canadian Fighter Aviation, 1961-1986*. Stoney Creek, Ont.: Fortress Publications, 1991. 223 pp.

Bishop, William Arthur. *Courage in the Air*. (Canada's Military Heritage, Volume 1.) Toronto: McGraw-Hill Ryerson, 1992. 307 pp.

Blatherwick, F.J. *Royal Canadian Air Force Honours — Decorations — Medals, 1920-1968*. New Westminster, B.C.: FJB Air Publications, 1991. 176 pp.

The Boeing Company. Vertol Division. *Hand-Over Ceremony; First Canadian Army CH-113A (Voyageur) Helicopter to the Canadian Government, RCAF Station Rockcliffe, Ontario, November 10, 1964*. n.p.: n.d. 1 vol., looseleaf.

Bottomley, Nora. *424 Squadron History.* [Belleville, Ont.]: Hangar Bookshelf, 1985. 137 pp.

Bowering, Clifford H. *Service; the Story of the Canadian Legion, 1925-1960.* Ottawa: privately printed, 1960. 240 pp.

Brisson, Pierre. *Défendez le Saguenay; les cinquante ans de la Base des Forces canadiennes de Bagotville, 1942-1992/the Fifty Years History of Canadian Forces Base Bagotville, 1942-1992.* Rejean Cardin et/and Marie Novak, tr. s.l.: s.i./n.p., 1992. 34/31 pp.
Texte bilingue./Bilingual text.

Butt, Bob. *Le Dakota de l'Aviation royale du Canada et les Forces canadiennes: 1943[sic]- — De la débutante à la grande dame./The Royal Canadian Air Force and Canadian Forces Dakota: 1943[sic]- — From Debutante to Matriarch.* Winnipeg: Design & Typeset — Media One Productions, 1989. 71 pp.
Texte bilingue./Bilingual text.

The C.A.H.S. Journal. Vol. I- . Willowdale, Ont.: Canadian Aviation Historical Society, 1963- .

CF-104 Starfighter, 1961-1986. n.p./s.i., [1986]. 106 pp.
Bilingual text./Texte bilingue.

Campagna, Palmiro. *Storms of Controversy; the Secret Avro Arrow Files Revealed.* Toronto: Stoddart, 1992. 228 pp.

Canada. Air Force. *Dress Orders for the Royal Canadian Air Force.* (C.A.P. 6.) Ottawa: Queen's Printer, 1958. v.p.

_____. *A Plan for your Future.* Ottawa: King's Printer, 1948. 65 pp.

_____. *Regulations and Orders for the Royal Canadian Air Cadets.* (CAP 496.) n.p.: 1956. 1 vol., looseleaf.

_____. *The Royal Canadian Air Force List.* Ottawa: n.p., 1942-66.
Issued in mimeographed form until 1942. Frequency varies.

*Canada. Air Force. Air Defence Command Headquarters. *The Ground Observer Corps.* (Current Affairs for the Canadian Forces, vol. VIII, no. 6.) Ottawa: Queen's Printer, 1955. 31 pp.

Canada. Air Force. 1 Fighter Wing. *The First Year, 1951-52; 1 Fighter Wing, R.C.A.F.; North Luffenham, Rutland, England.* n.p.: 1953. 96 pp.

Canada. Air Force. Rescue Co-ordination Centre, Halifax, N.S. *Search & Rescue; Atlantic Area.* (RCAF Pamphlet 35.) Ottawa: Queen's Printer, 1958. 30 pp.

Canada. Air Force. Training Command. *Training in the Royal Canadian Air Force.* Scott Air Force Base, Ill.: n.p., n.d. 143 pp.

Canada. Air Force Headquarters. *Air Force Administrative Orders*. Ottawa: n.p., 1947?-65.

Issued as a non-chronological sequence in which orders were discarded when obsolete. Gradually superseded an older series of mimeographed administrative orders.

————. *General and Routine Orders*. Ottawa: n.p., 1940-65.

Title varies. <u>Routine Orders</u> from 1947. Supplements also issued. Issued in mimeographed form from 1933.

[Canada. Air Force Overseas Headquarters.] *Overseas Orders*. London: n.p., 1943-46.

Issued in mimeographed form from 1940.

Canada. Armed Forces. Canadian Forces Base Greenwood. *50 Years; the History of CFB Greenwood, 1942-1992*. Winnipeg: C. Kelman, [1992]. 148 pp.

[Canada. Armed Forces. Canadian Forces Base Portage la Prairie.] *Portage la Prairie; Fifty Years of Flying Training: 1940-1990*. Southport, Man.: Manitoba Airshow 1990, 1990. 181 pp.

[Canada. Armed Forces. Canadian Forces Base Shearwater.] *From White-Caps to Contrails; a History of a Modern Air Formation*. n.p.: 1981. 108 pp.

History of 880 MR, VU 32, VT 406, HS 423 and HS 443 Squadrons.

[Canada. Armed Forces. Canadian Forces Base Summerside.] *"Forty Years" 1941-1981; a History of the Base at Summerside, Prince Edward Island*. n.p.: n.d. 22 pp.

[Canada. Armed Forces. Canadian Forces Station Holberg.] *Canadian Forces Station Holberg, San Josef, British Columbia; the First 30 Years*. Altona, Man.: printed by Friesen Yearbooks, [1984]. 1 vol., unpaged.

[Canada. Armed Forces. 408 Squadron.] *408 Squadron History*. n.p.: 1984. 107 pp.

[Canada. Armed Forces. 415 Squadron.] *Swordfish; the Story of 415 Squadron*. n.p.: [1982?]. 71 pp.

[Canada. Armed Forces. 404 Squadron.] *404 Squadron History*. Winnipeg: C. Kelman, n.d. 121 pp.

[Canada. Armed Forces. 409 Squadron.] *Nighthawk! A History of 409 (Night Fighter) Squadron, 1941-1977*. Courtenay, B.C.: privately printed, n.d. 93 pp.

Canada. Armed Forces. 401 Squadron. *1934-1984; Escadrille — 401 — Squadron*. n.p.: [1984]. 1 vol., unpaged.

[Canada. Armed Forces. 430 Squadron. *Escadrille 430 Squadron*.] Lac-Etchemin, P.Q.: privately printed/imprimé privé, 1981. 288 pp.

Bilingual text./Texte bilingue.

Canada. Armed Forces. 434 Squadron. *434 Squadron ... a History.* n.p.: privately printed, [1977]. 155 pp.
New ed. [Belleville, Ont.]: Hangar Bookshelf, 1984. 113 pp.

[Canada. Armed Forces. 437 Squadron.] *437 Squadron History.* [Belleville, Ont.]: Hangar Bookshelf, 1985. 113 pp.

[Canada. Armed Forces. 433 Squadron.] *433 Squadron History.* [Belleville, Ont.]: Hangar Bookshelf, 1985. 112 pp.

[Canada. Armed Forces. 425 Squadron.] *425 Alouette.* n.p.: n.d./s.l.: s.i., s.d. 101 pp.
Bilingual text./Texte bilingue.

Canada. Armed Forces. 400 Squadron. *400 Squadron; the First Half Century.* n.p.: [1982?]. 17 pp.

Canada. Army. *Winter Exercise Musk Ox, 1946.* Ottawa: King's Printer, 1947. 168 pp.
Originally classified Confidential.

*Canada. Aviation. Quartier général du Commandement de l'Air. *Le Corps des observateurs terrestres.* (Actualités; revue destinée aux Forces canadiennes, vol VIII, no 6.) Ottawa: Imprimeur de la Reine, 1955. 31 pp.

Canada. Canadian Forces Headquarters. *Canadian Forces Administrative Orders.* Ottawa: n.p., 1965-71.
Issued as a non-chronological sequence in which orders were discarded when obsolete. Superseded by a bilingual format in 1972.

Canada. Court Martial Appeal Board. *Court Martial Appeal Reports.* Ottawa: Queen's Printer, 1957-73. 3 vols.

*Canada. Dept. of National Defence. *The Defence Research Board, Canada.* n.p.: n.d. 1 vol., unpaged.

_____. *Defence Research Board; the First Twenty-Five Years./Conseil de recherches pour la défense; les 25 premières années.* Ottawa: Queen's Printer/Imprimeur de la Reine, 1972. 46 pp.
Bilingual text./Texte bilingue.

_____. *The King's Regulations and Orders for the Royal Canadian Air Force.* (C.A.P. 4.) Ottawa: King's Printer, 1951. 3 vols., looseleaf.

_____. *Manual of the Canadian Forces Medical Service in the Field, 1959.* Ottawa: Queen's Printer, 1959. 324 pp., looseleaf.

*_____. *The Queen's Regulations and Orders for the Canadian Forces.* Ottawa: Queen's Printer, 1965. 3 vols., looseleaf.

*_____. *The Queen's Regulations and Orders for the Royal Canadian Air Force.* (CAP 4.) Ottawa: Queen's Printer, 1953. 3 vols., looseleaf.

Canada. Dept. of National Defence. ***The Queen's Regulations and Orders for the Royal Canadian Air Force.*** (CAP 4.) Ottawa: Queen's Printer, 1952. 3 vols., looseleaf.

*_____. ***Queen's Regulations for the Canadian Services Colleges.*** Ottawa: Queen's Printer, 1958. 1 vol., unpaged.

*_____. ***Report.*** Ottawa: King's Printer, 1923-59.
Title varies. Annual most years.

*_____. ***White Paper on Defence.*** Ottawa: Queen's Printer, 1964. 30 pp.

Canada. Dept. of National Defence. Defence Research Board. ***Review./Revue,*** [par le] Conseil de recherches pour la Défense du Canada. Ottawa: Dept. of National Defence/Ministère de la Défense nationale, 1966-73.
Bilingual text. Title varies: <u>Annual Report</u> *(1966)./Texte bilingue. Divergence du titre:* <u>Rapport annuel</u> *(1966).*

Canada. Dept. of Veterans Affairs. ***Commemoration; Canadians in Korea, 1978./Souvenir; Canadiens en Corée, 1978.*** n.p./s.l.: s.i., [1978. 14 pp.]
Bilingual text./Texte bilingue.

[Canada. Forces armées. Station des Forces canadiennes Chibougamau.] ***SFC Chibougamau; 25è anniversaire, 1962-1987.*** s.l.: s.i., s.d. 148 pp.

*Canada. Ministère de la Défense nationale. ***Le Conseil de recherches pour la défense, Canada.*** s.1.: s.i., s.d. 1 tome, non-paginé.

*_____. ***Livre blanc sur la défense.*** Ottawa: Imprimeur de la Reine, 1964. 34 pp.

*Canada. Ministère de la Défense nationale. ***Ordonnances et règlements royaux applicables au Corps d'aviation royal canadien.*** (CAP 4.) Ottawa: Imprimeur de la Reine, 1953. 3 tomes, feuilles mobiles.

*_____. ***Ordonnances et règlements royaux applicables aux Forces canadiennes.*** Ottawa: Imprimeur de la Reine, 1965. 3 tomes, feuilles mobiles.

*_____. ***Rapport.*** Ottawa: Imprimeur du Roi, 1923-59.
Divergence du titre. Annuel, la plupart des années.

*_____. ***Règlements royaux applicables aux Collèges des services armés du Canada.*** Ottawa: Imprimeur de la Reine, 1958. 1 tome, non paginé.

Canada. Parliament. House of Commons. Special Committee on Canteen Funds. ***Minutes of Proceedings and Evidence.*** No. 1-10. Ottawa: King's Printer, 1947.

Canadair Limited. ***Argus Mk. II Maritime Patrol Aircraft.*** n.p.: 1961. 31 pp.

_____. ***CL-44G Strategic Military Transport.*** n.p.: n.d. 26 pp.

Canadian Air Cadet. Vol. I-VII. Toronto: Air Cadet League of Canada, 1941-48.

Canadian Defence Quarterly./Revue canadienne de défense. Vol. I- . Toronto: Baxter Pub., 1971- .

Canadian Services Colleges; Royal Military College of Canada, Kingston, Ontario; Royal Roads, Victoria, B.C.; Collège militaire royal de Saint-Jean, Saint-Jean, P.Q. n.p.: [195-?]. 16 pp.

Cardoulis, John N. *A Friendly Invasion; the American Military in Newfoundland, 1940-1990.* St. John's, Nfld.: Breakwater, 1990. 224 pp.

Castonguay, Jacques. *Le Collège militaire royal de Saint-Jean.* Montréal: Méridien, 1989. 288 pp.
Réédition rév. et augm.: Le Collège militaire royal de Saint-Jean; une université à caractère différent. Sillery (Qué.): Septentrion, 1992. 272 pp.

_____. *Collège militaire royal de Saint-Jean./Les premiers vingt ans./The First Twenty Years.* Adaptation anglaise: Donald A.L. Lefroy. s.l.: s.i./n.p., [1972?]. 44 pp.
Texte bilingue./Bilingual text.

_____. *La 16e Escadre Saint-Jean; ses antecédents — ses unités (1941-1994).* Saint-Roch-des-Aulnaies (Qué.): La Beaucassière, 1994. 206 pp.

_____. *Unsung Mission; History of the Chaplaincy Service (RC) of the R.C.A.F.* Montreal: Institut de Pastorale, 1968. 173 pp.

Castonguay, Jacques, *et al. History of Canadian Forces Base Montreal and its Garrisons./Historique de la Base des Forces canadiennes Montréal et de ses garnisons.* n.p./s.l.: s.i., 1980. 181/153 pp.
Bilingual text./Texte bilingue.

Charlton, Peter, and Michael Whitby, eds. *"Certified Serviceable"; Swordfish to Sea King; the Technical Story of Canadian Naval Aviation, by Those Who Made It So.* n.p.: CNATH Book Project, 1995. 496 pp.

Chatair. Vol. [I]-III. Chatham, N.B.: n.p., 1957-61.
Journal of RCAF Station Chatham, N.B. Initially numbered vol. VIII.

Childerhose, Chick. *Wild Blue.* Victoria, B.C.: Hoot Publications, 1978. 346 pp.

50e/th/anniversaire/Anniversary; Cité de Montréal/"Wildcats", Corps d'aviation royale du Canada, Forces armées canadiennes/City of Montreal/Wildcats, Royal Canadian Air Force, Canadian Armed Forces/Escadrille/18/118/438/ Squadron. s.l.: s.i./n.p., 1984. 42 pp.

City of Winnipeg 402 Squadron, 1932-1974. n.p.: n.d. 1 vol., unpaged.

The Clinton Mercury. Vol. I-? Clinton, Ont.: n.p., 1953-?
Journal of RCAF Station Clinton, Ont.

Collège militaire royal de Saint-Jean. *Ouverture officielle./Official Opening*. s.l.: s.i., s.d./n.p.: n.d. 27 pp.
Texte bilingue./Bilingual text.

Connolly, Don. *Painting Planes; the Aviation Art of Don Connolly*. Stittsville, Ont.: Canada's Wings, 1982. [75] pp.

Coup d'oeil sur le Collège militaire royal de Saint-Jean. Ottawa: Imprimeur de la Reine, 1959. 20 pp.

Le Défilé: la revue du Collège militaire royal de Saint-Jean. St-Jean, P.Q.: imprimé privé, 1952- .
Divergence du titre.

Deller, K.M. *Per Ardua ad Usquam (Through Adversity Anywhere); a History of the CMUs and 1 CEU*. n.p.: [1984?]. 136 pp.
Construction engineering in the RCAF and Canadian Forces.

The Demon Squadron; 407 Squadron in War and Peace, May 1941 — June 1952, June 1952 — June 1975. n.p.: privately printed, [1975]. 46 pp.

"Digby to Downsview"; a 411 Squadron History, 1941-1981. n.p.: n.d. 21 pp.

Dow, James. *The Arrow*. Toronto: J. Lorimer, 1979. 160 pp.

Dudley-Mathiesen, Vi. *Sweet 'n' Sour*. Sidney, B.C.: Family Compact, 1985. 228 pp.
Memories of service in RCAF Women's Division, 1942-1957.

Dunnett, Peter J.S. *Royal Roads Military College, 1940-1990; a Pictorial Retrospect*. W. Kim Rempel, photo researcher. Victoria, B.C.: Royal Roads Military College, 1990. 159 pp.

Edwards, B.A., ed. *CFS Sioux Lookout, 1953-1983*. n.p.: Inter-Collegiate Press, [1984]. 1 vol., unpaged.

Ellis, Frank H. *Canada's Flying Heritage*. Toronto: Univ. of Toronto Press, 1954. 398 pp.

_____. *Fifty Years of Adventure and Progress in Canadian Skies*. Toronto: Ryerson Press, 1959. 230 pp.

Emmott, Norman. *One Foot on the Ground*. Toronto: Lugus, 1992. 257 pp.

The End of a Decade; a Pictorial Essay of 447 Surface to Air Missile Squadron from its Inception in 1962 until Closure in 1972. n.p.: n.d. 1 vol., unpaged.

Eternal Vigilance is the Price of Safety; an Active Auxiliary for Citizens of Ottawa. n.p.: n.d. 1 vol., unpaged.
No. 2416 Aircraft Control and Warning Squadron.

Fletcher, David C., and Doug MacPhail. *Harvard! The North American Trainers in Canada*. San Josef, B.C.: DCF Flying Books, [1990]. 208 pp.

Flight Comment. Ottawa: King's Printer, 1949- .
   Title until 1953: Crash Comment. Bilingual text from 1976, no 3. Frequency varies.

Fort Churchill. Ottawa: Queen's Printer, 1959. 20 pp.

440 Squadron History. Stittsville, Ont.: Canada's Wings, 1983. 103 pp.

417 Squadron History. Stittsville, Ont.: Canada's Wings, 1983. 104 pp.

416 Squadron see Hovey, H. Richard.

421 Squadron History. [Stittsville, Ont.: 421 Tactical Fighter Squadron and Canada's Wings, 1982.] 107 pp.

427 Lion Squadron, 1942-1970. Marceline, Mo.: Walsworth, n.d. 76 pp.

422 Sqn; This Arm shall do It, 1942-1970. Marceline, Mo.: Walsworth, n.d. 64 pp.

402 Squadron, Royal Canadian Air Force; We Stand on Guard, 1932-1952. n.p.: n.d. 14 pp.

4 Wing Baden-Soellingen, Sept 1953 — June 1970. J. David, ed. Marceline, Mo.: Walsworth, [1971]. 206 pp.

Foster, J.A. *For Love and Glory; a Pictorial History of Canada's Air Forces.* Toronto: McClelland & Stewart, 1989. 143 pp.

_____. *Sea Wings; a Pictorial History of Canada's Waterborne Defence Aircraft.* Toronto: Methuen, 1986. 143 pp.

Foulds, Glen. [*419 Squadron History.*] Burnaby, B.C.: printed by Crosstown Printers, [1988?]. 108 pp.

Fraser, Dan, ed. *CFS Sydney; 25 Jubilee Booklet, 1953-1978.* n.p.: [1978]. 40 pp.

Fuller, G.A., J.A. Griffin and K.M. Molson. *125 Years of Canadian Aeronautics; a Chronology 1840-1965.* Willowdale, Ont.: Canadian Aviation Historical Society, 1983. 328 pp.

Gaffen, Fred. *In the Eye of the Storm; a History of Canadian Peacekeeping.* Toronto: Deneau & Wayne, 1987. 302 pp.

Gardam, John. *The Canadian Peacekeeper./Le gardien de la paix canadien.* Burnstown, Ont.: General Store Pub. House, 1992. 69 pp.
   Bilingual text./Texte bilingue.

_____. *Korea Volunteer; an Oral History from Those who were There.* Burnstown, Ont.: General Store Pub. House, 1994. 262 pp.

Gibson, Colin. *"Air Power in Canada"; an Address by Col. the Hon. Colin Gibson, M.C., M.A., Minister of National Defence for Air, to the Empire Club of Toronto, February 28, 1946.* n.p.: n.d. 11 pp.

Goodspeed, D.J. *A History of the Defence Research Board of Canada.* Ottawa: Queen's Printer, 1958. 259 pp.

Gordon, John. ... *Of Men and Planes.* Ottawa: Love Print., 1968. 3 vols.

_____. *Winged Sentries./Sentinelles de l'air.* Claude Rousseau, illus. n.p.: 1963. 104 pp.
Bilingual text./Texte bilingue.

Granatstein, J.L., and David J. Bercuson. *War and Peacekeeping; from South Africa to the Gulf — Canada's Limited Wars.* Toronto: Key Porter Books, 1991. 266 pp.

Griffin. J.A. *Canadian Military Aircraft; Serials & Photographs, 1920-1968./Avions militaires canadiens; numéros de série et photographies, 1920-1968.* (Canadian War Museum Publication Number 69-2./Musée de guerre du Canada publication numéro 69-2.) Ottawa: Queen's Printer/ Imprimeur de la Reine, 1969. 691 pp.
Bilingual text./Texte bilingue.

_____. *A Tradition of Fighters./Une tradition de combat aérien.* n.p./s.l.: s.i., [198-?]. 54 pp.
Bilingual text./Texte bilingue.

Halliday, H.A. *Chronology of Canadian Military Aviation.* (National Museum of Man Mercury Series: Canadian War Museum Paper, no. 6.) Ottawa: [Queen's Printer], 1975. 168 pp.

Hammond, H.R.L., and others, eds. [*401 Squadron.*] n.p.: privately printed, n.d. 1 vol., unpaged.

Hampson, Bill. *Canadian Flying Services Emblems & Insignia (1914-1984).* Vancouver: privately printed, 1986. 193 pp.

The Happy Warrior; a Book in Memory of the Life and Work of G/C the Rev. R.M. Frayne, C.D., D.D., Director of Religious Administration (P), the Royal Canadian Air Force. Toronto: United Church Pub. House, 1953. 103 pp.

Harvey, J. Douglas. *426 Squadron around the World Flight; North Star 17525 — Special Flight no. 160; Trip Diary 09 June — 07 July 1956.* n.p.: 1956. 22 pp.

_____. *Laughter-Silvered Wings; Remembering the Air Force II.* Toronto: McClelland and Stewart, 1984. 277 pp.

_____. *The Tumbling Mirth; Remembering the Air Force.* Toronto: McClelland and Stewart, 1983. 263 pp.

Haydon, Peter T. *The 1962 Cuban Missile Crisis: Canadian Involvement Reconsidered.* Toronto: Canadian Institute of Strategic Studies, 1993. 297 pp.

Henderson, Peter A. *Guarding the Gates; a History of Canadian Forces Station St. Johns.* St. John's, Nfld.: CFS St. John's, 1992. 115 pp.

High Flight. Vol. I-III. Stittsville, Ont.: Canada's Wings, [1981?-85.]

Hinse, Jean-Robert, éd. *Station des Forces canadiennes/Canadian Forces Station/Senneterre, 1953-1978; album-anniversaire/Anniversary Album.* s.l.: imprimé privé/n.p.: privately printed, [1978]. 1 tome, non-paginé/1 vol., unpaged.
Texte bilingue./Bilingual text.

Holman, R.F. *Best in the West; the Story of Number 2 Canadian Forces Flying Training School and Flying Training in Canada.* Moose Jaw, Sask.: Big 2 Fund, 15 Wing Moose Jaw, 1995. [223] pp.

[Hovey, H. Richard, and others.] *416 Squadron.* n.p.: 1974. 133 pp.
Rev. and updated ed.: 416 Squadron History. Belleville, Ont.: Hangar Bookshelf, 1984. 160 pp.

Humby, P.A., ed. *CFS Sioux Lookout, 1953-1978.* Winnipeg: Inter-Collegiate Press, [1978]. 1 vol., unpaged.

The Illustrated Review of Aviation in Canada; Celebrating the Golden Anniversary of Powered Flight in Canada. Montreal: privately printed, [1959]. 1 vol., unpaged.

Jacobson, Ray. *426 Squadron History.* n.p.: [1988]. 187 pp.

Jockel, Joseph T. *No Boundaries Upstairs; Canada, the United States, and the Origins of North American Air Defence, 1945-1958.* Vancouver: Univ. of British Columbia Press, 1987. 160 pp.

Johnson, E.A. "Rick", ed. *Trenton; 50 Years of Air Force.* Trenton, Ont.: n.p., 1981. 160 pp.

Johnson, Leonard V. *A General for Peace.* Toronto: J. Lorimer, 1987. 158 pp.

Johnston, Wilf, and Andy Wilson, eds. *Gypsumville; 24 Years of Vigilance/24 ans de vigilance.* n.p./s.l.: CFS/BFC Gypsumville, [1987]. 80 pp.

Joos, Gerhard. *The Canadair Sabre.* (Profile Publications, number 186.) Leatherhead, Eng.: Profile Publications, 1967. [11 pp.]

Karkut, E.T., ed. *The History of 6 RD and the Aerospace Maintenance Development Unit.* Erin, Ont.: Boston Mills Press, 1990. 120 pp.

*Kealy, J.D.F., and E.C. Russell. *A History of Canadian Naval Aviation, 1918-1962.* Ottawa: Queen's Printer, 1965. 164 pp.

*Kealy, J.D.F., et E.C. Russell. *Histoire de l'aéronavale canadienne, 1918-1962.* Ottawa: Imprimeur de la Reine, 1965. 185 pp.

Kostenuk, Samuel, and John Griffin. *RCAF Squadron Histories and Aircraft, 1924-1968.* (Canadian War Museum Historical Publication 14.) Toronto: S. Stevens, Hakkert, 1977. 255 pp.

Kvas, Peter, with Hattie A. Perry. *Lobster, Lighthouse and Long-Range Radar; a History of Canadian Forces Station Barrington to 1987.* Stone Horse, N.S.: Canadian Forces Station Barrington, 1987. 126 pp.

Langar Log. Vol I-XI. Langar, Eng.: privately printed, 1952-63.
Journal of No. 30 Air Materiel Base, RCAF.

Langeste, Tom, comp. *Words on the Wing; Slang, Aphorisms, Catchphrases and Jargon of Canadian Military Aviation since 1914.* Toronto: Canadian Institute of Strategic Studies, 1995. 330 pp.

The Last CF-100 to Fly; Souvenir Program, Dedication Ceremonies, April 16, 1983./Le dernier CF-100 à voler; programme souvenir, cérémonie de remise, le 16 avril 1983. n.p./s.l.: s.i., [1983]. 1 vol., unpaged./1 tome, non-paginé.
Bilingual text./Texte bilingue.

Lee, A.M. *Chatham; an Airfield History.* Fredericton, N.B.: privately printed, 1989. 116 pp.

Leigh, Z. Lewis. *And I shall Fly.* Toronto: CANAV Books, 1985. 211 pp.

The Link. Vol. I-V? Calgary: privately printed, 1955-59?
Journal of RCAF Station Lincoln Park.

The Link. Vol. I-IV? Rivers, Man.: privately printed, 1948-51?
Journal of Canadian Joint Air Training Centre, Rivers, Man.

The Log; Royal Roads Military College. Vol. V- . Victoria, B.C.: privately printed, 1942- .

Lyzum, Jim. *Canadian Profile; CF-100 Canuck.* (Aircraft no. 3.) Vanier, Ont.: Sabre Model Supplies Pub., 1985. 52 pp.

Macaw, H.B., éd. *25 années de service; 1953-1978; 25 Years of Service.* n.p./s.l.: s.i., [1978]. v.p.
SFC/CFS Moisie. Texte bilingue./Bilingual text.

McCaffery, Dan. *Air Aces; the Lives and Times of Twelve Canadian Fighter Pilots.* Toronto: J. Lorimer, 1990. 234 pp.

McClenaghan, John, and Derek Blatchford. *411 City of North York Squadron; 50 Years of History, 1941-1991.* Winnipeg: John/David Associates, 1992. 190 pp.

*McCracken, George W. *Les aviateurs de l'OTAN au Canada.* (Actualités; revue destinée aux Forces canadiennes, vol IV, no 1.) Ottawa: Imprimeur de la Reine, 1953. 31 pp.

*McCracken, George W. *NATO Air Training in Canada.* (Current Affairs for the Canadian Forces, vol. IV, no. 1.) Ottawa: Queen's Printer, 1953. 31 pp.

*_____. *Votre Aviation.* (Actualités; revue destinée aux Forces canadiennes, vol V, no 3.) Ottawa: Imprimeur de la Reine, 1953. 31 pp.

*_____. *Your Air Force.* (Current Affairs for the Canadian Forces, vol. V, no. 3.) Ottawa: Queen's Printer, 1953. 31 pp.

MacDonald, Grant, and Terry Strocel. *422 Squadron History.* n.p.: [1987]. 144 pp.

MacFarlane, John, and Robbie Hughes. *Canada's Naval Aviators.* Victoria, B.C.: Maritime Museum of British Columbia, 1994. 182 pp.

McIntyre, Bob. *Canadian Profile; CF-104 Starfighter.* (Aircraft no. 1.) Vanier, Ont.: Sabre Model Supplies Pub., 1984. 52 pp.

_____. *Canadian Profile; CF-101 Voodoo.* (Aircraft no. 2.) Vanier, Ont.: Sabre Model Supplies Pub., 1984. 52 pp.

MacMillan, James. *CF 100.* Oakville, Ont.: Tarka Press, 1981. 104 pp.

McQuarrie, John. *Canadian Fighter Pilot; a Legacy of Courage and Dedication.* Whitby, Ont.: McGraw-Hill Ryerson, 1992. 223 pp.

*Main, J.R.K. *Les voyageurs de l'air; historique de l'aviation civile au Canada, 1859-1967.* Ottawa: Imprimeur de la Reine, 1967. 433 pp.

*_____. *Voyageurs of the Air; a History of Civil Aviation in Canada.* Ottawa: Queen's Printer, 1967. 397 pp.

Marcoux, Jules, éd. *CMR, 1952-1977; album du 25e anniversaire./25th Anniversary Album.* St-Jean, P.Q.: s.i./n.p., 1977. 62 pp.
Texte bilingue./Bilingual text.

Mazéas, Daniel. *Insignes armée canadienne, 1900-1914; Canadian Badges; supplément, 1920-1950.* Guingamp, France: privately printed, 1972. 116 pp.

The Medical and Dental Services of the Canadian Forces. (Current Affairs for the Canadian Forces, vol. VI, no. 1.) Ottawa: Queen's Printer, 1954. 31 pp.

Melady, John. *Korea: Canada's Forgotten War.* Toronto: Macmillan, 1983. 215 pp.

Merrick, Bob. *410 Squadron; a History.* n.p.: n.d. 114 pp.

Milberry, Larry. *AIRCOM; Canada's Air Force.* Toronto: CANAV Books, 1991. 191 pp.

_____. *Aviation in Canada.* Toronto: McGraw-Hill Ryerson, 1979. 272 pp.

_____. *The Avro CF-100.* Toronto: CANAV Books, 1981. 203 pp.

Milberry, Larry. *The Canadair Sabre.* Toronto: CANAV Books, 1986. 372 pp.

Milberry, Larry, ed. *Sixty Years; the RCAF and CF Air Command 1924-1984.* Toronto: CANAV Books, 1984. 480 pp.

Mills, Carl. *Banshees in the Royal Canadian Navy.* Willowdale, Ont.: Banshee Publication, 1991. [320] pp.

The Moisie Monitor. Vol. I-? Moisie, P.Q.: n.p., 1954-?
Quarterly journal of no. 211 Aircraft Warning Squadron and RCAF Station Moisie, P.Q.

Mokler, R.J. *Aircraft Down; a Personal Account of Search, Survival and Rescue in the Canadian North.* New York: Exposition Press, 1968. 110 pp.

*Molson, K.M. *Canada's National Aviation Museum; its History and Collections.* Ottawa: National Aviation Museum, National Museum of Science and Technology, 1988. 291 pp.

*_____. *Le Musée national de l'aviation du Canada; son histoire et ses collections.* Ottawa: Musée national de l'aviation, Musée national des sciences et de la technologie, 1988. [288] pp.

Molson, K.M., and H.A. Taylor. *Canadian Aircraft since 1909.* Stittsville, Ont.: Canada's Wings, 1982. 530 pp.

Morneault, J.C. *424 Tiger Squadron, 1935-1977.* n.p.: [1978]. 31 pp.

Morrison, W. Alexander, and Stephanie A. Blair. *Canada and Peacekeeping; Dedication and Service.* Clementsport, N.S.: Lester B. Pearson Canadian International Peacekeeping Training Centre, 1995. 32 pp.

**Le Musée national de l'aviation; un survol.* Ottawa: Musée national de l'aviation, 1991. 64 pp.

Myles, Eugenie Louise. *Airborne from Edmonton.* Toronto: Ryerson Press, 1959. 280 pp.

National Aeronautical Collection. Ottawa: Queen's Printer, 1967. 36 pp.

National Aeronautical Collection./Collection aéronautique nationale. n.p.: n.d./s.l.: s.i., s.d. 36 pp.
Bilingual text./Texte bilingue.

**The National Aviation Museum; a Flypast.* Ottawa: National Aviation Museum, 1991. 64 pp.

1939-1989/50th Anniversary Reunion, 4-6 August 1989/50ième anniversaire réunion, 4-6 août 1989 [412 Squadron/Escadrille]. n.p./s.l.: s.i., [1989]. 28 pp.
Bilingual text./Texte bilingue.

Northern Flight; Canada's Aviation Heritage Magazine. Vol. I- . Thornhill, Ont.: Northern Flight Publications, 1992- .

Number Four Hundred & Four Squadron, Royal Canadian Air Force. n.p.: [1972]. 62 pp.

[Organ, Richard, and others.] *Avro Arrow; the Story of the Avro Arrow from its Evolution to its Extinction,* [by] The Arrowheads. Cheltenham, Ont.: Boston Mills Press, 1980. 180 pp.

Page, Bette, comp. *Mynarski's Lanc; the Story of Two Famous Canadian Lancaster Bombers KB726 & FM213.* Erin, Ont.: Boston Mills Press, 1989. 192 pp.

Page, Ron D. *Avro Canuck; CF 100 All Weather Fighter.* Erin, Ont.: Boston Mills Press, [1981]. 192 pp.

Paré, Lorenzo. *Les canadiens français et l'organisation militaire.* (Oeuvre des tracts, 382.) Montréal: imprimé privé, [1951]. 16 pp.

Pearcy, Arthur. *The Dakota; a History of the Douglas Dakota in RAF and RCAF Service.* London: I. Allan, 1972. 320 pp.

Peden, Murray. *Fall of an Arrow.* Stittsville, Ont.: Canada's Wings, 1978. 182 pp.

Pettipas, Leo. *Aircraft of the RCN.* Winnipeg: n.p., 1988. 104 pp.

_____. *Canadian Naval Aviation, 1945-1968.* Winnipeg: n.p., 1986. 101 pp.

_____. *The Fairey Firefly in the Royal Canadian Navy.* Winnipeg: n.p., 1987. 109 pp.

_____. *The Grumman Avenger in the Royal Canadian Navy.* n.p.: 1988. 154 pp.

_____. *The Hawker Sea Fury in the Royal Canadian Navy.* n.p.: 1989. 188 pp.

_____. *The Supermarine Seafire in the Royal Candian Navy.* Winnipeg: n.p., 1987. 86 pp.

Philp, O.B., and Bill Johnson. *Snowbirds from the Beginning.* Sidney, B.C.: Porthole Press, 1990. 255 pp.

Phipps, Brian, ed. *Silver Jubilee Celebration, June 14-17, 1979, Canadian Forces Base Cold Lake.* n.p.: [1979]. 1 vol., unpaged.

Pickett, James. *Into the Sausage Machine; the History of 22 Wing.* North Bay, Ont.: privately printed, 1994. 145 pp.

Pickler, Ron, and Larry Milberry. *Canadair; the First Fifty Years.* Toronto: CANAV Books, 1995. 392 pp.

Polumin, Nicholas. *Arctic Unfolding; Experiences and Observations during a Canadian Airborne Expedition in Northern Ungava, the Northwest Territories, and the Arctic Archipelago.* London: Hutchinson, 1949. 348 pp.

"Pourquoi je sers ma patrie". (Actualités; revue destinée aux Forces canadiennes, vol X, no 15.) Ottawa: Imprimeur de la Reine, 1956. 26 pp.

Presentation of Colours and Squadron Standard to The Loyal Edmonton Regiment (3 PPCLI) and 418 Squadron (City of Edmonton) RCAF by Her Royal Highness Princess Alexandra, Saturday, May 27th, 1967, Hamilton Gault Barracks, Edmonton, Alberta. [Edmonton: printed by] Edmonton Printers, [1967]. 16 pp.

*Preston, Richard A. *Au service du Canada; histoire du Royal Military College depuis la Deuxième Guerre mondiale.* s.l.: Presses de l'Université d'Ottawa, 1992. 268 pp.

_____. *Canada's RMC; a History of the Royal Military College.* Toronto: Univ. of Toronto Press, 1969. 415 pp.

*_____. *To Serve Canada; a History of the Royal Military College since the Second World War.* Ottawa: Univ. of Ottawa Press, 1991. 248 pp.

Roberts, Leslie. *There shall be Wings; a History of the Royal Canadian Air Force.* Toronto: Clarke, Irwin, 1959. 250 pp.

Robertson, Peter. *Irréductible vérité/Relentless Verity/les photographes militaires canadiens depuis 1885/Canadian Military Photographers since 1885.* (Les Archives publiques du Canada/Public Archives of Canada Series.) Québec, P.Q.: Les Presses de l'Université Laval, 1973. 233 pp.
Texte bilingue./Bilingual text.

Roundel. Vol. I-XVII. Ottawa: Queen's Printer, 1948-65.
Journal of the RCAF.

Royal Military College of Canada, Kingston, Ont. *The Cadet Handbook.* Kingston, Ont.: n.p., [1957?]. 59 pp., looseleaf.

The Royal Military College of Canada Review. Vol. I- . Kingston, Ont.: privately printed, 1920- .

Schwarzwaldflieger (Black Forest Flyer). Vol. I-X. Baden-Soellingen, Germany: privately printed, 1954-63.
Journal of No. 4 (Fighter) Wing, RCAF.

Les services médicaux et dentaires pour les Forces armées. (Actualités; revue destinée aux Forces canadiennes, vol VI, no 1.) Ottawa: Imprimeur de la Reine, 1954. 31 pp.

Shaw, E.K. *There never was an Arrow.* Toronto: Steel Rail Educational Pub., 1979. 261 pp.

Shores, Christopher. *History of the Royal Canadian Air Force.* (A Bison Book.) Toronto: Royce Publications, 1984. 128 pp.

Simpson, Allan, and others. *We Few.* Ottawa: Canadian Fighter Pilots Association, 1983. 167 pp.

Smith, G.Y. *Seek and Save; the History of 103 Rescue Unit.* Erin, Ont.: Boston Mills Press, 1990. 137 pp.

Smye, Fred. *Canadian Aviation and the Avro Arrow.* Oakville, Ont.: privately printed, 1989. 137 pp.

Snowy Owl; Journal of the Canadian Land Forces Command and Staff College. Kingston, Ont.: privately printed, 1952-73. 18 vols.
Title varies.

Soward, Stuart E. *Hands to Flying Stations; a Recollective History of Canadian Naval Aviation.* Victoria, B.C.: Neptune Developments (1984), 1993-95. 2 vols.

*Stacey, C.P., H.E.W. Strange and F.H. Hitchins. *Canada's Armed Forces Today.* (Current Affairs for the Canadian Forces, vol. II, no. 9.) Ottawa: Queen's Printer, 1952. 22 pp.

*Stacey, C.P., H.E.W. Strange et F.H. Hitchins. *Les Forces armées du Canada.* (Actualités; revue destinée aux Forces canadiennes, vol II, no 9.) Ottawa: Imprimeur de la Reine, 1952. 22 pp.

Stewart, Greig. *Shutting Down the National Dream; A.V. Roe and the Tragedy of the Avro Arrow.* Toronto: McGraw-Hill Ryerson, 1988. 320 pp.

Sutherland, Alice Gibson. *Canada's Aviation Pioneers; 50 Years of McKee Trophy Winners.* Toronto: McGraw-Hill Ryerson, 1978. 304 pp.

[Tait, Stuart.] *408 Goose Squadron Reunion, 1987.* n.p.: [1987]. 34 pp.

Talepipe. Vol. I-? North Luffenham, Eng., Marville, France: privately printed, 1952-?
Title varies: Vol. I, no. 1 & 2 titled: You Name It? Journal of No. 1 Fighter Wing, RCAF.

Thompson, Roy J.C. *Cap Badges and Insignia of the RCN — RCAF — CAF, 1953-1978.* Colorado Springs, Col.: n.p., 1978. 75 pp.

_____. *Wings of the Canadian Armed Forces, 1913-1972.* [Dartmouth], N.S.: n.p., 1973. 106 pp.

Torontow, Cy. *Up, Up and — Oy Vay.* Ottawa: privately printed, 1990. 155 pp.
Memoirs of RCAF service 1939-1968.

25th Anniversary Reunion; Royal Canadian Air Force (Women's Division). Toronto: n.p., 1966. 1 vol., unpaged.

25th NORAD Region. Baton Rouge, La.: Army & Navy Pub. Co., n.d. 370 pp.

Uplands Times. Vol. I-? Ottawa: privately printed, 1954-?

Vaughan, Arnold P. *418 City of Edmonton Squadron History.* n.p.: [1984]. 117 pp.

Velleman, Alexander. *The RCAF as Seen from the Ground (A Worm's-Eye View).* Stittsville, Ont.: Canada's Wings, 1986. 3 vols.

Vincent, Carl, J.D. Oughton and E. Vincent. *Consolidated Liberator & Boeing Fortress.* (Canada's Wings, vol. 2.) Stittsville, Ont.: Canada's Wings, 1975. 246 pp.

Ward, Richard, and Gerhard W. Joos, comps. *Canadair Sabre Mk. 1-6, Commonwealth Sabre Mk. 30-32; in RCAF-RAF-RAAF-Luftwaffe & Foreign Service.* (Airco-Aircam Aviation Series, no. 24 (vol. 2).) Canterbury, Eng.: Osprey Publications, 1971. 1 vol., chiefly illus.

Wheeler, William J. *Images of Flight; a Canadian Aviation Portfolio.* Willowdale, Ont.: Hounslow, 1992. 134 pp.

* *"Why I Serve",* by the Serviceman. (Current Affairs for the Canadian Forces, vol. X, no. 15.) Ottawa: Queen's Printer, 1956. 26 pp.

Wilson, J.A. *Development of Aviation in Canada, 1879-1948.* Ottawa: Dept. of Transport Air Services Branch, n.d. 105 pp.

Ziegler, Mary. *The Story of the Women's Division, Royal Canadian Air Force.* Hamilton, Ont.: privately printed, 1973. 173 pp.

F. THE UNIFIED CANADIAN FORCES SINCE 1968 — LES FORCES CANADIENNES UNIFIÉES DEPUIS 1968

Adams, James. *Bull's Eye; the Assassination and Life of Supergun Inventor Gerald Bull.* New York: Times Books, 1992. 317 pp.

Adelberg, Philip, ed. *414 Squadron (1941-1975); a Short History.* n.p.: 1975. 1 vol., unpaged.

Air Command 10th Anniversary; Air Force Day/Commandement aérien 10ième anniversaire; Journée de Forces aériennes/Canadian Forces Base Winnipeg/Base des Forces canadiennes Winnipeg/8 Sept. 1985. n.p.: [1985]. 28 pp.

Airforce. Vol. I- . Ottawa: Air Force Productions, 1977- .
Quarterly. Recommended by the Royal Canadian Air Force Association.

Alford, R.A., ed. *Canadian Forces Base Esquimalt.* n.p.: [1979]. 78 pp.

*Allard, Jean V. *Mémoires du Général Jean V. Allard.* Collaboration spéciale de Serge Bernier. s.l.: Editions de Mortagne, 1985. 533 pp.

*_____. *The Memoirs of General Jean V. Allard*, written in cooperation with Serge Bernier. Vancouver: Univ. of British Columbia Press, 1988. 366 pp.

Arbuckle, Graeme. *Badges of the Canadian Navy.* Halifax: Nimbus Pub., 1987. 203 pp.

_____. *Customs and Traditions of the Canadian Navy.* Halifax: Nimbus Pub., 1984. 179 pp.

Armour Bulletin/Journal de l'arme blindée. Vol. I- . Oromocto, N.B.: n.p., 1973- .
Semi-annual/Semestriel. Title varies./Divergence du titre. Vol. I-II: Armoured Department Semi-Annual Bulletin. Vol. III-VII: Armour Newsletter. Vol. VIII-XXV: Armour Bulletin des Blindés. Journal of the Armour Branch./Journal de l'arme blindée. Bilingual text./Texte bilingue.

Armour Review. Vol. I-VIII. Camp Borden, Ont.: n.p., 1965-73.
Annual. Title varies. Vol. I: RCAC Bulletin. Vol. II-V: RCAC Review. Official organ of the Royal Canadian Armoured Corps.

Audet, Pierre, éd. *Le Deuxième Bataillon du Royal 22e Régiment à Chypre, 1969.* Chypre: imprimé par les Presses Zavallis, 1969. 131 pp., en majeure partie ill.

Baraton, Jean Pierre. *Snowbirds; 1971-1990, a 20 Year History.* Calgary: J.P.B. Publications, n.d. 166 pp.

*Barton, William H. *Recherche, développement et instruction; dans le domaine de la défense chimique et biologique au sein du ministère de la Défense nationale et des Forces canadiennes.* Ottawa: Ministère de la Défense nationale, 1988. 60 pp.

*_____. *Research, Development and Training; in Chemical and Biological Defence within the Department of National Defence and the Canadian Forces.* Ottawa: Dept. of National Defence, 1988. 54 pp.

Bashow, David L. *Starfighter: a Loving Restrospective of the CF-104 Era in Canadian Fighter Aviation, 1961-1986.* Stoney Creek, Ont.: Fortress Publications, 1991. 223 pp.

_____. *Sting of the Hornet; McDonell Douglas F/A-18 in Canadian Service.* Ottawa: Canuck Publications, 1987. 72 pp.

Batten, Jack. *The Spirit of the Regiment; an Account of the 48th Highlanders from 1956 to 1991.* n.p.: n.d. 171 pp.

Bennett, Chris. *Superbase 20; Baden Söllingen; the Hornet's Nest.* London: Osprey Aerospace, 1991. 128 pp.

Blais, Pierre. *Loup solitaire; un mercenaire québécois pleure le Viêt-nam.* Montréal: v/b éditeur, 1991. 388 pp.

Bland, Douglas. *Chiefs of Defence; Government and the Unified Command of the Canadian Armed Forces.* Toronto: [Canadian Institute of Strategic Studies], 1995. 314 pp.

Boss, W. *The Stormont, Dundas and Glengarry Highlanders, 1783-1951.* Ottawa: Runge Press, 1952. 449 pp.
Revised and updated as: Boss, W., and W.J. Patterson, Up the Glens; Stormont, Dundas and Glengarry Highlanders, 1783-1994. Cornwall, Ont.: Old Book Store, 1995. 298 pp.

Blue & Gold. Vol. I- . Winnipeg: n.p., 1934- .
Frequency varies, but chiefly annual. Regimental journal of the Fort Garry Horse.

Bottomley, Nora. *424 Squadron History.* [Belleville, Ont.]: The Hangar Bookshelf, 1985. 137 pp.

Le bouc en mission; 2e Bataillon, Royal 22e Régiment. No 1- . Nicosie, Chypre: s.i., 1987- .

Bricker, Calvin. *Canada's Reserves and Peacekeeping; a Workshop Report.* n.p.: York Centre for International and Strategic Studies, [1988]. 62 pp.

Brisson, Pierre. *Défendez le Saguenay; les cinquante ans de la Base des Forces canadiennes de Bagotville, 1942-1992/the Fifty Years History of Canadian Forces Base Bagotville, 1942-1992.* Rejean Cardin et/and Marie Novak, tr. s.l.: s.i./n.p., 1992. 34/31 pp.
Texte bilingue./Bilingual text.

Brown, Brian A. *Foresters; the Canadian Quest for Peace.* Erin, Ont.: Boston Mills Press, 1991. 176 pp.
The Grey & Simcoe Foresters.

*Brown, W.J. *Les Cadets royaux de l'Armée canadienne; cent ans d'exploits, 1879-1979.* s.l.: La Ligue des Cadets de l'Armée du Canada, [1979. 12 pp.]

*_____. *The Royal Canadian Army Cadets; a Century of Achievement, 1879-1979.* n.p.: The Army Cadet League of Canada, [1979. 12 pp.]

Buker, Peter Edward. *The Closure of CFB Gimli and the Post-Closure Development of the Gimli Region.* (Operational Research and Analysis Establishment Directorate of Social and Economic Analysis, ORAE Project Report no. PR 317.) Ottawa: Dept. of National Defence, 1985. 31 pp.

Bull, Stewart H. *The Queen's York Rangers; an Historic Regiment.* Erin, Ont.: Boston Mills Press, 1984. 248 pp.

Burns, Max, and Ken Messenger. *The Winged Wheel Patch; a History of the Canadian Military Motorcycle and Rider.* St. Catharines, Ont.: Vanwell Pub., 1993. 159 pp.

Butson, A.R.C. *A History of the Military Medical Units of Hamilton, Ontario, in Peace and War, 1900-1990.* n.p.: 1990. 43 pp.

Butt, Bob. *Le Dakota de l'Aviation royale du Canada et les Forces canadiennes: 1943[sic]- — De la débutante à la grande dame./The Royal Canadian Air Force and Canadian Forces Dakota: 1943[sic]- — From Debutante to Matriarch.* Winnipeg: Design & Typeset — Media One Productions, 1989. 71 pp.
Texte bilingue./Bilingual text.

CF-104 Starfighter, 1961-1986. n.p./s.l.: s.i., [1986]. 106 pp.
Bilingual text./Texte bilingue.

CRDV/DREV/Centre de recherches pour la Défense, Valcartier/Defence Research Establishment Valcartier. s.l.: s.i., s.d./n.p.: n.d. 62 pp.
Texte bilingue./Bilingual text.

Canada. Armed Forces. Aerospace Engineeering Test Establishment. *AETE Handbook.* Cold Lake Alta.: n.p., 1985. 48, 9 pp.

Canada. Armed Forces. Air Command Headquarters. *Commemorative Booklet; the Formation of Wings in Air Command./Livret commémoratif; la formation des escadres au sein du Commandement aérien*, [par le] Quartier général du Commandement aérien. Winnipeg: n.p./s.l.: s.i., 1993. 38 pp. *Bilingual text./Texte bilingue.*

[Canada. Armed Forces. Canadian Airborne Regiment.] *Regimental Standing Orders.* Calgary: n.p., 1976. 1 vol., looseleaf.

[Canada. Armed Forces. Canadian Forces Base Borden.] *Canadian Forces Base Borden; Canada's Largest Training Base.* n.p.: 1972. 1 vol., unpaged. *Subsequent revised editions.*

_____. *Welcome to Canadian Forces Base Borden./Bienvenue à la Base des Forces canadiennes Borden.* n.p.: n.d./s.l.: s.i., s.d. 56 pp. *Bilingual text./Texte bilingue.*

[Canada. Armed Forces. Canadian Forces Base Calgary.] *Canadian Forces Base Calgary; Home of the Army of the West./Base des Forces canadiennes Calgary; siège de "l'Armée de l'Ouest"/1983.* n.p.: n.d./s.l.: s.i., s.d. 48 pp. *Bilingual text./Texte bilingue.*

[Canada. Armed Forces. Canadian Forces Base Chatham.] *Welcome to Canadian Forces Base Chatham./Bienvenue à la Base des Forces canadiennes Chatham.* n.p./s.l.: National Military Publishers of Canada, 1982. 28 pp. *Bilingual text./Texte bilingue.*

[Canada. Armed Forces. Canadian Forces Base Chilliwack.] *1983-1984/Base Information Directory, Canadian Forces Base Chilliwack/Informations générales, Base des Forces canadiennes de Chilliwack.* n.p./s.l.: National Military Publishers of Canada, 1983. 44 pp. *Bilingual text./Texte bilingue.*

[Canada. Armed Forces. Canadian Forces Base Cold Lake.] *Cold Lake; Vigil Borealis.* n.p.: n.d./s.l.: s.i., s.d. 30 pp. *Bilingual text./Texte bilingue.*

_____. *Welcome to Canadian Forces Base Cold Lake./Bienvenue à la Base des Forces canadiennes de Cold Lake.* n.p.: n.d./s.l.: s.i., s.d. 32 pp. *Bilingual text./Texte bilingue.*

[Canada. Armed Forces. Canadian Forces Base Esquimalt.] *Canadian Forces Base Esquimalt./Base des Forces canadiennes Esquimalt.* n.p./s.l.: s.i., 1984. 108 pp. *Bilingual text./Texte bilingue.*

[Canada. Armed Forces. Canadian Forces Base Greenwood.] *Canadian Forces Base Greenwood Base des Forces canadiennes.* n.p./s.l.: National Military Publishers of Canada, 1983. 60 pp. *Bilingual text./Texte bilingue.*

[Canada. Armed Forces. Canadian Forces Base Greenwood.] *Welcome to C.F.B. Greenwood; Armed Forces Day 1972.* n.p.: [1972]. 36 pp.

[Canada. Armed Forces. Canadian Forces Base Kingston.] *Canadian Forces Base Kingston Base des Forces canadiennes.* n.p./s.l.: s.i., 1984. 78 pp. *Bilingual text./Texte bilingue.*

[Canada. Armed Forces. Canadian Forces Base Moose Jaw.] *Canadian Forces Base Moose Jaw; Welcome — Bienvenue.* n.p.: n.d. 76 pp.

[Canada. Armed Forces. Canadian Forces Base North Bay.] *1983/Base Information Directory; Canadian Forces Base North Bay/Informations générales; Base des Forces canadiennes de North Bay.* n.p./s.l.: National Military Publishers of Canada, 1983. 42 pp. *Bilingual text./Texte bilingue.*

_____. *Welcome; Air Defence Command; Canadian Forces Base North Bay.* [North Bay, Ont.: n.p., 197-?] 35 pp.

_____. *Welcome to Canadian Forces Base North Bay./Bienvenue; Base des Forces canadienne [sic] North Bay.* n.p.: n.d./s.l.: s.i., s.d. 13 pp. *Bilingual text./Text bilingue.*

[Canada. Armed Forces. Canadian Forces Base Ottawa.] *Welcome to CFB Ottawa./Bienvenue à la BFC Ottawa.* n.p./s.l.: s.i., 1983. 74 pp. *Bilingual text./Texte bilingue.*

[Canada. Armed Forces. Canadian Forces Base Petawawa.] *Canadian Forces Base Petawawa/Base des Forces canadiennes.* n.p./s.l.: National Military Publishers of Canada, 1983. 56 pp. *Bilingual text./Texte bilingue.*

[Canada. Armed Forces. Canadian Forces Base Portage la Prairie.] *Portage la Prairie; Fifty Years of Flying Training: 1940-1990.* Southport, Man.: Manitoba Airshow 1990, 1990. 181 pp.

_____. *Welcome to Canadian Forces Base/Bienvenue à la Base des Forces canadiennes/Portage la Prairie.* Victoria, B.C.: National Publishers, 1984. 28 pp. *Bilingual text./Texte bilingue.*

_____. *Welcome to Canadian Forces Base Portage la Prairie./Bienvenue à Base des Forces canadiennes.* n.p.: n.d./s.l.: s.i., s.d. 12 pp. *Bilingual text./Texte bilingue.*

_____. *Welcome to Canadian Forces Base Portage la Prairie./Bienvenue à la Base des Forces canadiennes de Portage la Prairie.* n.p.: n.d./s.l.: s.i., s.d. 14 pp. *Bilingual text./Texte bilingue.*

[Canada. Armed Forces. Canadian Forces Base Shearwater.] *From White-Caps to Contrails; a History of a Modern Air Formation.* n.p.: 1981. 108 pp. *History of 880 MR, VU 32, VT 406, HS 423 and HS 443 Squadrons.*

[Canada. Armed Forces. Canadian Forces Base Shilo.] *Canadian Forces Base Shilo; Home of Canadian Artillery.* n.p.: n.d. 85 pp.

[Canda. Armed Forces. Canadian Forces Base Summerside.] *Canadian Forces Base Summerside./Base des Forces canadiennes Summerside.* n.p./s.l.: National Military Publishers of Canada, 1983. 48 pp. *Bilingual text./Texte bilingue.*

_____. *"Forty Years" 1941-1981; a History of the Base at Summerside, Prince Edward Island.* n.p.: n.d. 22 pp.

[Canada. Armed Forces. Canadian Forces Base Toronto.] *Canadian Forces Base Toronto.* n.p.: 1980. 36 pp.

[Canada. Armed Forces. Canadian Forces Base Trenton.] *Canadian Forces Base Trenton./ Base des Forces canadiennes Trenton.* n.p./s.l.: National Military Publishers of Canada, 1983. 48 pp. *Bilingual text./Texte bilingue.*

[Canada. Armed Forces. Canadian Forces Base Winnipeg.] *Canadian Forces Base Winnipeg Base des Forces canadiennes.* n.p./s.l.: s.i., 1983. 88 pp. *Bilingual text./Texte bilingue.*

_____. *Welcome; Canadian Forces Base Winnipeg./Bienvenue; Base des Forces canadiennes Winnipeg.* n.p./s.l.: s.i., 1975. 37 pp. *Bilingual text./Texte bilingue.*

[Canada. Armed Forces. Canadian Forces Station Holberg.] *Canadian Forces Station Holberg, San Josef, British Columbia; the First 30 Years.* Altona, Man.: printed by Friesen Yearbooks, [1984]. 1 vol., unpaged.

[Canada. Armed Forces. 8th Canadian Hussars (Princess Louise's.)] *The 8th Canadian Hussars (Princess Louise's), 1962-1987.* G.H. MacDonald, ed.-in-chief. n.p.: 1987. 162 pp.

_____. *The 8th Hussar.* Vol. I- . Various places: 8th Canadian Hussars (Princess Louise's), 1977- . *Biweekly. Vol. II, nos. 1-9, October 1978 — March 1979 reprinted, with introduction and additional material as: <u>The 8th Hussar; Cyprus 1978-79</u>.*

_____. *Regimental Standing Orders.* n.p.: 1972. 123 l., looseleaf.

[Canada. Armed Forces. 48th Highlanders of Canada.] *48th Highlanders Tattoo.* n.p.: [1969]. 24 pp.

Canada. Armed Forces. 4 Field Ambulance. *A History of 4 Field Ambulance.* Lahr, Germany: E. Demmer, 1992. [122] pp.

[Canada. Armed Forces. 408 Squadron.] *408 Squadron History.* n.p.: 1984. 107 pp.

[Canada. Armed Forces. 415 Squadron.] *Swordfish; the Story of 415 Squadron.* n.p.: [1982?]. 71 pp.

[Canada. Armed Forces. 404 Squadron.] *404 Squadron History.* Winnipeg: C. Kelman, n.d. 121 pp.

Canada. Armed Forces. 409 Squadron. *Nighthawk! A History of 409 (Night Fighter) Squadron.* Courtenay, B.C.: privately printed, 1978. 92 pp.

Canada. Armed Forces. 401 Squadron. *1934-1984; Escadrille — 401 — Squadron.* n.p.: [1984]. 1 vol., unpaged.

Canada. Armed Forces. 434 Squadron. *434 Squadron ... a History.* n.p.: privately printed, [1977]. 155 pp.
New ed. [Belleville, Ont.]: Hangar Bookshelf, 1984.

[Canada. Armed Forces. 437 Squadron.] *437 Squadron History.* [Belleville, Ont.]: Hangar Bookshelf, 1985. 113 pp.

[Canada. Armed Forces. 433 Squadron.] *433 Squadron History.* [Belleville, Ont.]: Hangar Bookshelf, 1985. 112 pp.

[Canada. Armed Forces. 430 Squadron. *Escadrille 430 Squadron.*] Lac-Etchemin, P.Q.: privately printed/imprimé privé, 1981. 288 pp.
Bilingual text./Texte bilingue.

[Canada. Armed Forces. 425 Squadron.] *425 Alouette.* n.p.: n.d./s.l.: s.i., s.d. 101 pp.
Bilingual text./Texte bilingue.

[Canada. Armed Forces. 429 Squadron.] *Welcome to ... 429 (Composite) Squadron, C.F.B. Winnipeg.* Winnipeg: Canadian Forces Training Materiel Production Centre, 1978. 14 pp.

Canada. Armed Forces. 400 Squadron. *400 Squadron; the First Half Century.* n.p.: [1982?]. 17 pp.

Canada. Armed Forces. HMCS Qu'appelle. *HMCS Qu'appelle; Commissioned September 14 1963, Paid Off April 4 1992.* Winnipeg: [printed by] Herff Jones, [1992]. 73 pp.

Canada. Armed Forces. H.M.C.S. Unicorn. *History of Unicorn, 1923-1973.* n.p.: n.d. v.p.

Canada. Armed Forces. Lake Superior Scottish Regiment. *Regimental Catechism.* Winnipeg: CFTMPC, 1977. 15 pp.

[Canada. Armed Forces. Logistics Branch.] *Logistics Newsletter/Bulletin de la Logistique* [par le Service de la Logistique, Forces armées du Canada.] Ottawa: National Defence/Défense nationale, 1991- .
Bilingual text. Frequency varies./Texte bilingue. La périodicité varie.

Canada. Armed Forces. Mapping and Charting Establishment. *History, Organization and Technical Functions./Histoire, l'organisation et les fonctions techniques*, [par le] Service de Cartographie. n.p./s.l.: s.i., [1976?]. 14 pp.
Bilingual text./Texte bilingue.

Canada. Armed Forces. Maritime Command. *Maritime Command, Halifax, N.S.; Media Information Booklet.* n.p.: n.d. 42 pp.

Canada. Armed Forces. 1 Combat Engineer Regiment. *Change-of-Command Ceremonies, 28 July 1978; CFB Chilliwack, Vedder Crossing, B.C.* n.p.: [1978.] 16 pp.

[Canada. Armed Forces. Princess Patricia's Canadian Light Infantry.] *Manual of Customs and Traditions of Princess Patricia's Canadian Light Infantry.* n.p.: 1974. 1 vol., looseleaf.

Canada. Armed Forces. Princess Patricia's Canadian Light Infantry. 1st Battalion Group. *Op Harmony Dispatches.* Souvenir ed. Croatia: n.p., 1994. v.p.

Canada. Armed Forces. Princess Patricia's Canadian Light Infantry. 2nd Battalion Group. *The Sandbag.* Souvenir ed. Daruvar, Croatia: n.p., 1993. v.p.

[Canada. Armed Forces. Princess Patricia's Canadian Light Infantry. 3rd Battalion Group.] *Op Harmony Chronicle; 3 PPCLI Battalion Group.* No. 1-10. Daruvar, Croatia: n.p., 1992-93.
Assembled into a souvenir book with additional illus.

Canada. Armed Forces. Royal Canadian Regiment. 1st Battalion Group. *The First Royal Canadian Regiment Battalion Group; Cyprus 74-75.* n.p.: [1975]. 84 pp., chiefly illus.

Canada. Armed Forces. Royal Canadian Regiment. 2nd Battalion Group. *Operation Cavalier.* n.p.: [1993]. 129 pp.
United Nations service in Bosnia-Hercegovina.

[Canada. Armed Forces. Royal Regiment of Canadian Artillery.] *Standing Orders for The Royal Regiment of Canadian Artillery.* Brandon, Man.: privately printed, [1977]. 1 vol., looseleaf.

[Canada. Armed Forces. 3rd Regiment, Royal Canadian Horse Artillery.] *Third Regiment, 1953-1983.* Brandon, Man.: privately printed, n.d. 1 vol., chiefly illus.

Canada. Canadian Forces Headquarters. *Canadian Forces Administrative Orders.* Ottawa: n.p., 1965-71.
Issued as a non-chronological sequence in which orders were discarded when obsolete. Superseded by a bilingual format in 1972.

Canada. Court Martial Appeal Board. *Court Martial Appeal Reports.* Ottawa: Queen's Printer, 1957-73. 3 vols.

Canada. Dept. of National Defence. *CF-18 Acceptance Ceremony./Cérémonie de réception du CF-18* [par le] ministère de la Défense nationale. n.p./s.l.: s.i., [1982]. 1 vol., unpaged./1 tome, non paginé.
Bilingual text./Texte bilingue.

_____. *Canadian Patrol Frigate Project; Navy Modernization./Projet de la frégate canadienne de patrouille; modernisation de la marine.* n.p.: National Defence/s.l.: Défense nationale, [1991?]. 32 pp.
Bilingual text./Texte bilingue.

_____. *Canadian Forces Dress Manual./Manuel sur la tenue des Forces canadiennes* [par le] ministère de la Défense nationale. (CFP/PFC 265.) [Ottawa: Dept. of National Defence/Ministère de la Défense nationale, 1977.] 1 vol., looseleaf./1 tome, feuilles mobiles.
Bilingual text./Texte bilingue.

_____. *Canadian Patrol Frigate Program./Programme de la frégate canadienne de patrouille* [par le] ministère de la Défense nationale. n.p./s.l.: s.i., [1982.] 17 pp.
Bilingual text./Texte bilingue.

_____. *Defence/Défense, 1971-90* [par le] ministère de la Défense nationale. Ottawa: Dept. of National Defence/Ministère de la Défense nationale, 1972-91.
Annual. Bilingual text./Annuel. Texte bilingue.

_____. *Research and Development Branch, Department of National Defence./Bureau de recherche et de développement, ministère de la Défense nationale.* n.p.: n.d./s.l.: s.i., s.d. 33 pp.
Bilingual text./Texte bilingue.

* _____. *White Paper on Defence.* Ottawa: Information Canada, 1971. 50 pp.
Cover title: Defence in the 70s.

Canada. Dept. of National Defence. Defence Research Board. *Review./Revue* [par le] Conseil des recherches pour la Défense du Canada. Ottawa: Dept. of National Defence/Ministère de la Défense nationale, 1966-73.
Bilingual text. Title varies: Annual Report (1966)./Texte bilingue. Divergence du titre: Rapport annuel (1966).

Canada. Dept. of National Defence. Defence Research Establishment Ottawa. *Annual Report.* Ottawa: n.p., 1974- .
Continues earlier classified reports.

_____. *Defence Research Establishment Ottawa (DREO).* n.p.: 1981. 24 pp.

Canada. Dept. of National Defence. Defence Research Establishment Valcartier. *Annual Report./Rapport annuel* du Centre de recherches pour la Défense, Valcartier. Courcelette, P.Q.: Defence Research Establishment Valcartier/Centre de recherches pour la Défense, Valcartier, 1969- .
Bilingual text. Canadian Armament Research and Development Establishment was renamed Defence Research Establishment Valcartier in 1969. Most annual reports of CARDE are classified./Texte bilingue. Le Centre canadien de recherches et perfectionnement des armes fut rebaptisé Centre de recherches pour la Défense Valcartier en 1969. La plupart des rapports annuels de CCRPA sont classifiées.

Canada. Dept. of National Defence. Ministerial Committee on the Canadian Military Colleges. *Report./Rapport* du Comité ministériel sur les Collèges militaires canadiens, [Ministère de la Défense nationale]. Ottawa: National Defence/Défense nationale, 1993. 52/56 pp.
Bilingual text./Texte bilingue.

[Canada. Forces armées. Base des Forces canadiennes de Bagotville.] *Bienvenue/Welcome/BFC Bagotville.* s.l.: s.i., s.d./n.p.: n.d. 68 pp.
Texte bilingue./Bilingual text.

[Canada. Forces armées. Base des Forces canadiennes de Montréal.] *Bienvenue à la BFC Montréal./Welcome to CFB Montreal.* s.l./n.p.: National Military Publishers of Canada, s.d./n.d. 104 pp.
Texte bilingue./Bilingual text.

[Canada. Forces armées. Base des Forces canadiennes de Saint-Jean.] *Bienvenue/Welcome/à la/to/BFC Saint-Jean.* s.l./n.p.: National Military Publishers, s.d./n.d. 51 pp.
Texte bilingue./Bilingual text.

[Canada. Forces armées. Base des Forces canadiennes de Valcartier.] *Bienvenue/Welcome/à la/to/BFC Valcartier.* s.l./n.p.: National Military Publishers Canada, s.d./n.d. 64 pp.
Texte bilingue./Bilingual text.

[Canada. Forces armées. Ecole technique des Forces canadiennes.] *10e anniversaire; Ecole technique des Forces canadiennes, BFC St-Jean, 1969-1979.* s.l.: s.i., s.d. 88 pp.

[Canada. Forces armées. NCSM Montcalm.] *75e anniversaire du Service naval du Canada; journal souvenir du NCSM Montcalm.* s.l.: s.i., [1985]. 50 pp.

[Canada. Forces armées. Royal 22e Régiment.] *Manuel d'information à l'intention des membres du Royal 22e Régiment.* s.l.: imprimé privé, 1976. 1 tome, feuilles mobiles.

Canada. Forces armées. Royal 22e Régiment. 2 Groupe-bataillon. *La Citadelle en Croatie; GB 2eR22eR — BATCAN 1; album souvenir, avril-septembre 95.* [Rastevic, Croatie: s.i., 1995.] p.m.

[Canada. Forces armées. Station des Forces canadiennes Chibougamau.] *SFC Chibougamau; 25e anniversaire, 1962-1987.* s.l.: s.i., s.d. 148 pp.

*[Canada. Ministère de la Défense nationale.] *Livre blanc sur la politique de défense.* Ottawa: Information Canada, 1971. 54 pp.
Titre de la couverture: La défense dans les années 70.

[Canada. National Defence Headquarters.] *Canadian Forces Administrative Orders./Ordonnances administratives des Forces canadiennes* [par le Quartier général de la Défense nationale.] n.p./s.l.: Dept. of National Defence/Ministère de la Défense nationale, 1972- . various vols., looseleaf/tomes multiples, feuilles mobiles.
Bilingual text. Issued as a non-chronological sequence in which orders are discarded when obsolete. Supersedes unilingual format./Texte bilingue. Parues sur une base irregulière, les derniers ordres annulant les précédents. Remplace l'édition unilingue.

[Canada. National Defence Headquarters. Chief of Research and Development.] *Research and Development Branch Review./Bureau de recherche et développement revue* [par le Chef, Recherche et développement, Quartier général de la Défense nationale.] n.p.: Dept. of National Defence/s.l.: Ministère de la Défense nationale, 1981- .
Annual. Bilingual text./Annuel. Texte bilingue.

Canada. National Defence Headquarters. Director General Official Languages. *Official Languages in the Canadian Forces./Les langues officielles dans les Forces canadiennes* [par le] Directeur général des langues officielles, Quartier général de la Défense nationale. n.p./s.l.: s.i., 1982. 24/26 pp.
Bilingual text./Texte bilingue.

*Canada. National Defence Headquarters. Director General Personnel Research and Development. *Personnel Research and Development Annual Report.* [Ottawa]: Dept. of National Defence, 1981- .
Annual.

Canada. National Defence Headquarters. Director General Public Affairs. *Defence Matters./Questions de défense* [par le Directeur général — Affairs publiques, Quartier général de la Défense nationale.] Vol. I- . Ottawa: Dept. of National Defence/Ministère de la Défense nationale, 1995- .
First pilot issue was 1er December 1995. Bilingual text./La première édition-pilote était le 1 décembre 1995. Texte bilingue.

[Canada. National Defence Headquarters. Director of Ceremonial.] *Badges of the Canadian Forces./Les insignes des Forces canadiennes* [par le Directeur — Cérémonial, Quartier général de la Défense nationale.] (CFP/PFC 267.) Ottawa: Dept. of National Defence/Ministère de la Défense nationale, 1976. 1 vol., looseleaf/1 tome, feuilles mobiles.
Bilingual text./Texte bilingue.

_____. *Canadian Forces Dress Instructions./Instructions sur la tenue des Forces canadiennes* [par le Directeur — Cérémonial, Quartier général de la Défense nationale.] (A-AD-265-000/AG-001.) n.p./s.l.: Dept. of National Defence/Ministère de la Défense nationale, 1988. 1 vol., looseleaf/1 tome, feuilles mobiles.
Bilingual text. Amended and re-issued annually./Texte bilingue. Modifié et republié annuellement.

_____. *Canadian Forces Dress Manual./Manuel sur la tenue des Forces canadiennes* [par le Directeur — Cérémonial, Quartier général de la Défense nationale.] (CFP/PFC 265.) Ottawa: Dept. of National Defence/Ministère de la Défense nationale, 1979. 1 vol., looseleaf/1 tome, feuilles mobiles.
Supplement/Supplément, 1986. Bilingual text./Texte bilingue.

Canada. National Defence Headquarters. Surgeon General. *Canadian Forces Medical Services Information Booklet./Services de santé des Forces canadiennes, brochure d'information* [par le] Chef du Service de Santé, Quartier général de la Défense nationale. n.p./s.l.: s.i., 1977. 23/24 pp.
Bilingual text./Texte bilingue.

*Canada. Quartier général de la Défense nationale. Directeur général Recherche et développement (personnel). *Rapport annuel; recherche et développement (personnel).* [Ottawa]: Ministère de la Défense nationale, 1981- .
Annuel.

Le Canada français et les conflits contemporains; actes du colloque tenu à l'Université du Québec à Montréal, le 27 août 1995, sous la direction de Claude Beauregard, Robert Comeau et Jean-Pierre Gagnon. (Cahiers d'histoire politique, no 2, hiver 1996.) s.l.: Société historique du Canada; Association québécoise d'histoire politique; Service historique, Défense nationale, 1996. 288 pp.

Canada's Air Force; a Special Edition of Wings Magazine. Calgary: Corvus Pub. Group, 1984. 146 pp.

Canada's Navy Annual; a Special Edition of Wings Magazine. Calgary: Corvus Pub. Group, 1985- .
Title varies slightly.

Canadian Armed Forces and Military Procurement Review. Vol. I-IX. Ottawa: Garrex Enterprises, 1967-76.
Title varies: became Canadian Armed Forces Review; a Magazine of Military and Government Procurement (July-August 1968) and Government and Military Business (October 1973). Frequency varies.

Canadian Defence Quarterly./Revue canadienne de défense. Vol. I- . Toronto: Baxter Pub., 1971- .

Canadian Forces CP-140 Aurora. Burbank, Calif.: Lockheed-California, 1976. 32 pp.

Canadian Forces canadiennes/Communications and Electronics Newsletter/ Bulletin des communications et de l'électronique. Ottawa: n.p./s.i., [1973]- . *Bilingual text./Texte bilingue.*

Canadian Forces College Review./Revue; Collège des Forces canadiennes. Toronto: n.p./s.i., 1975- .
Bilingual text. Title varies. Annual./Texte bilingue. Divergence du titre. Annuel.

The Canadian Forces Dental Services Bulletin./Bulletin du Service dentaire des Forces canadiennes. Ottawa: n.p./s.i., 1960- .
Quarterly. Title varies: The Royal Canadian Dental Corps Quarterly (1960-70) and The Canadian Forces Dental Services Quarterly./Bulletin du Service dentaire des Forces canadiennes (1970-79). Bilingual text./ Trimestriel. Divergence du titre: The Royal Canadian Dental Corps Quarterly (1960-70) et The Canadian Forces Dental Services Quarterly./Bulletin du Service dentaire des Forces canadiennes (1970-79). Texte bilingue.

Canadian Forces Persian Gulf Deployment. n.p.: Esprit de corps/Der Kanadier, [1990]. 16 pp.

Canadian Grenadier Guards; Presentation of Colours by Her Majesty The Queen, Colonel in Chief of the Regiment, Rideau Hall, 30th June 1992. n.p.: n.d. 12 pp.

The Canadian Gunner. Vol. I- . n.p.: privately printed, 1965- .

Cardoulis, John N. *A Friendly Invasion; the American Military in Newfoundland, 1940-1990.* St. John's, Nfld.: Breakwater, 1990. 224 pp.

Castonguay, Jacques. *Le 5e Régiment d'artillerie légère du Canada et ses prédecesseurs à Québec.* Courcelette (Qué.): 5e Régiment d'artillerie légère du Canada, 1993. 237 pp.

_____. *Le Collège militaire royal de Saint-Jean.* Montréal: Meridien, 1989. 288 pp.
Réédition rév. et augm.: Le Collège militaire royal de Saint-Jean; une université à caractère différent. Sillery (Qué.): Septentrion, 1992. 272 pp.

Castonguay, Jacques. *Collège militaire royal de Saint-Jean./Les premiers vingt ans./The First Twenty Years.* Adaptation anglaise: Donald A.L. Lefroy. s.l.: s.i./n.p., [1972?]. 44 pp.
Texte bilingue./Bilingual text.

_____. *La 16e Escadre Saint-Jean; ses antecédents — ses unités (1941-1994).* Saint-Roch-des-Aulnaies (Qué.): La Beaucassière, 1994. 206 pp.

_____. *Les Voltigeurs de Québec; premier régiment canadien-français.* Québec (Qué.): Les Voltigeurs de Québec, 1987. 523 pp.

Castonguay, Jacques, *et al. History of Canadian Forces Base Montreal and its Garrisons./ Historique de la Base des Forces canadiennes Montréal et de ses garnisons.* n.p./s.l.: s.i., 1980. 181/153 pp.
Bilingual text./Texte bilingue.

Castonguay, Jacques, [et] Armand Ross. *Le Régiment de la Chaudière.* Lévis, P.Q.: imprimé privé, 1983. 644 pp.

Charlton, Peter, and Michael Whitby, eds. *"Certified Serviceable"; Swordfish to Sea King; the Technical Story of Canadian Naval Aviation, by Those Who Made It So.* n.p.: CNATH Book Project, 1995. 496 pp.

Charters, David A. *Armed Forces and Political Purpose: Airborne Forces and the Canadian Army in the 1980s.* Fredericton, N.B.: Univ. of New Brunswick Centre for Conflict Studies, 1984. 145 pp.

50e/the/annniversaire/Anniversary;/Cité de Montréal/"Wildcats", corps d'aviation royale du Canada, Forces armées canadiennes/City of Montreal/Wildcats, Royal Canadian Air Force, Canadian Armed Forces/Escadrille/18/118/438/Squadron. s.l.: s.i./n.p., 1984. 42 pp.

La Citadelle. Vol. I- . Québec, P.Q.: s.i., 1965- .
Bimestriel. La revue de l'Association du 22e, Inc. Remplace L'Amicale du 22e.

La Citadelle de Québec; résidence du/of the/Royal 22e Régiment. Québec, P.Q.: La Musée du Royal 22e Regiment, [197-?. 40 pp.]
Texte bilingue./Bilingual text.

City of Winnipeg 402 Squadron, 1932-1974. n.p.: n.d. 1 vol., unpaged.

Clark, Thomas and Harry Pugh. *Canadian Airborne Insignia, 1942 — Present.* (Elite Insignia Guide, 4.) Arlington, Va.: C & D Enterprise, 1994. 158 pp.

Code, David E., and Ian Cameron, eds. *Canadian Forces and the Modern World.* Ottawa: Conference of Defence Associations Institute, 1993. 142 pp.
Conference of Defence Associations Institute Ninth Annual Seminar, January 1993.

Collier, Dianne. *Hurry Up and Wait; an Inside Look at Life as a Canadian Military Wife.* Carp, Ont.: Creative Bound, 1994. 183 pp.

The Commissioning of HMCS Algonquin, 3 November 1973 at Davie Shipbuilding Ltd., Lauzon, Quebec./Mise en service de l'Algonquin, le 3 novembre 1973, aux chantiers de la Davie Shipbuilding Ltd., Lauzon, Québec. n.p.: n.d./s.l.: s.i., s.d. 1 vol., unpaged./1 tome, non paginé. *Bilingual text./Texte bilingue.*

The Commissioning of HMCS Athabaskan, 30 September 1972, at Davie Shipbuilding Ltd. Lauzon, Quebec./Mise en service de l'Athabaskan, le 30 septembre 1972, aux chantiers de la Davie Shipbuilding Ltd. Lauzon, Québec. n.p.: n.d./s.l.: s.i., s.d. 1 vol., unpaged./1 tome, non paginé. *Bilingual text./Texte bilingue.*

The Commissioning of HMCS Cormorant, 10 November 1978, at Davie Shipbuilding Ltd. Lauzon, Quebec./Mise en service du Cormorant, 10 novembre 1978, aux chantiers de la Davie Shipbuilding Ltd. Lauzon, Québec. n.p./s.l.: s.i., [1978]. 1 vol., unpaged./1 tome, non paginé. *Bilingual text./Texte bilingue.*

The Commissioning of HMCS Moresby & HMCS Anticosti, 7 May 1989./L'armement du NCSM Moresby et du NCSM Anticosti, le 7 mai 1989. n.p./s.l.: s.i., [1989]. 1 vol., unpaged./1 tome, non paginé. *Bilingual text./Texte bilingue.*

The Commissioning of HMCS Preserver at Saint John Shipbuilding and Dry Dock Co., Ltd., Saint John N.B./Mise en service du Preserver à la Saint John Shipbuilding and Dry Dock Co., Ltd., Saint John, N.B. n.p.: n.d./s.l.: s.i., s.d. 1 vol., unpaged./1 tome, non paginé. *Bilingual text./Texte bilingue.*

The Commissioning of HMCS Protecteur, 30 August 1969, at Saint John Shipbuilding and Dry Dock Co., Ltd., Saint John N.B./Mise en service du Protecteur, 30 août 1969, à la Saint John Shipbuilding and Dry Dock Co., Ltd., Saint John N.-B. n.p.: n.d./s.l.: s.i., s.d. 1 vol., unpaged./1 tome, non paginé. *Bilingual text./Texte bilingue.*

The Connecting File. Vol. I- . London, Ont.: privately printed, 1921- . *Journal of The Royal Canadian Regiment.*

Connolly, Don. *Painting Planes; the Aviation Art of Don Connolly.* Stittsville, Ont.: Canada's Wings, 1982. [75] pp.

Corfield, William E. *Citizen Soldiers; the Canadian Fusiliers of London; the Oxford Rifles; the Perth Regiment.* London, Ont.: Royal Canadian Regiment, 1983. 86 pp.

Corriveau, Paul. *Le Royal 22e Régiment; 75 ans d'histoire, 1914-1989.* Québec (Qué.): La Régie du Royal 22e Régiment, 1989. 132 pp.

Cotton, C.A. *Military Attitudes and Values of the Army in Canada.* (Report 79-5.) Willowdale, Ont.: Canadian Forces Personnel Applied Research Unit, 1979. v.p.

Coulon, Jocelyn, et Yvan Cliche. *La Dernière Croisade; la guerre du Golfe et le rôle caché du Canada.* Montréal: Méridien, 1992. [226] pp.

Cranston, Bobby. *75th Anniversary, Naval Service of Canada; a Pictorial History.* Halifax: 75th Anniversary Pub. Co., [1985]. 1 vol., chiefly illus.

Crickard, Fred W., and Gregory L. Witol, eds. *The Reserves, Society, and Operational Roles: Comparative Perspectives.* (The Niobe Papers, Volume 7.) Halifax: Naval Officers' Association of Canada, 1995. 163 pp.

Crook, E.D., and J.K. Marteinson, eds. *A Pictorial History of the 8th Canadian Hussars (Princess Louise's).* n.p.: privately printed, 1973. 343 pp.

Cunniffe, Dick. *Scarlet, Riflegreen and Khaki; the Military in Calgary.* Calgary: Century Calgary Publications, 1975. 40 pp.

Curchin, Leonard A., and Brian D. Sim. *The Elgins; the Story of the Elgin Regt. (RCAC) and its Predecessors.* St. Thomas, Ont.: privately printed, 1977. 150 pp.

Cushnie, J.E., ed. *Welcome to Canadian Forces Base Penhold/Bienvenue à la Base des Forces canadiennes Penhold/"the Best in the West"/"la meilleure de l'Ouest".* n.p./s.l.: National Military Publishers of Canada, 1983. 40 pp. *Bilingual text./Texte bilingue.*

Deere, David N., ed. *Desert Cats; the Canadian Fighter Squadron in the Gulf War.* Stoney Creek, Ont.: Fortress Publications, 1991. [143] pp.

Defence Research Establishment Ottawa (DREO). n.p.: 1981. 24 pp.

Defence Research Establishment Suffield, Alberta. n.p.: 1976. 1 vol., chiefly illus.

Le Défilé; la revue du Collège militaire royal de Saint-Jean. St-Jean, P.Q.: imprimé privé, 1952- . *Divergence du titre.*

Deller, K.M. *Per Ardua ad Usquam (Through Adversity Anywhere); a History of the CMUs and 1 CEU.* n.p.: [1984?]. 136 pp. *Construction engineering in the RCAF and Canadian Forces.*

The Demon Squadron; 407 Squadron in War and Peace, May 1941 — June 1952, June 1952 — June 1975. n.p.: privately printed, [1975]. 46 pp.

Dick, Wm., ed. *Welcome to Canadian Forces Base Penhold; the Best in the West.* n.p.: [1980]. 36 pp.

"Digby to Downsview"; a 411 Squadron History, 1941-1981. n.p.: n.d. 21 pp.

Dillon, G.M. *Canadian Naval Forces since World War II; a Decision-Making Analysis*, with comments by Dr. G.R. Lindsey and Professor Jonathan Wouk, with a reply from the author. (Dalhousie Univ. Center for Foreign Policy Studies Occasional Paper.) Halifax: Dalhousie Univ., 1972. 79 pp.

Dornier, François, et Marie-Claude Joubert. *Soldats de la côte ...; Les Fusiliers du St-Laurent d'hier à aujourd'hui.* Rimouski (Qué.): La Régie, Les Fusiliers du St-Laurent, 1992. 183 pp.

Dosé, Daniel C. *NORAD: a New Look.* (National Security Series, no. 1/83.) Kingston, Ont.: Queen's Univ. Centre for International Relations, 1983. 93 pp.

Douglas, W.A.B., ed. *The RCN in Transition, 1910-1985.* Vancouver: Univ. of British Columbia Press, 1988. 411 pp.

Droit de Cité de la Ville de Montréal, septembre 1982. s.l.: imprimé par Atelier M.P. Dama, [1982. 16 pp.]
Les Fusiliers Mont-Royal.

Drouin, Marc, and François Saillant. *The Mohawk Trial; Not Guilty.* Montreal: Regroupement de Solidarité avec les Autochtones, 1992. 109 pp.
Oka crisis, 1990.

Duchaîne, Jean-François. *Rapport sur les événements d'octobre 1970.* s.l.: Ministère de la Justice, Gouvernement du Québec, 1980. 256 pp.
2ᵉ éd., 1981, comprenant les passages retenus dans la 1ʳᵉ éd.

Dunnett, Peter J.S. *Royal Roads Military College, 1940-1990; a Pictorial Retrospect.* W. Kim Rempel, photo researcher. Victoria, B.C.: Royal Roads Military College, 1990. 159 pp.

EME Journal; the Magazine of the Land Electrical and Mechanical Engineers./Journal du GEM; la revue du Génie électrique et mécanique — Terre. Ottawa: n.p./s.l.: s.i., 1975- .
Bilingual text. Title varies: Land Technical Bulletin technique (1975-77), LORE Technical Bulletin technique du GM TER (1977-84)./Texte bilingue. Divergence du titre: Land Technical Bulletin technique (1975-77), LORE Technical Bulletin technique du GEM TER (1977-84).

Edwards, B.A., ed. *CFS Sioux Lookout, 1953-1983.* n.p.: Inter-Collegiate Press, [1984]. 1 vol., unpaged.

Edwards, Charles A. *Canadian Army Formation Signs, 1939-1985; a Collector's and Historian's Comprehensive Guide to the Cloth Formation Signs Worn by the Canadian Army in 1939-1985.* Michael J. Langenfeld, illus. Grayslake, Ill.: Pass in Review Publications, 1987. 50 pp.

En garde. Vol. I- . Rimouski, P.Q.: La Régie du Régiment, Les Fusiliers du St-Laurent, 1983- .
3 fois par année.

The End of a Decade; a Pictorial Essay of 447 Surface to Air Missile Squadron from its Inception in 1962 until Closure in 1972. n.p.: n.d. 1 vol., unpaged.

Esprit de corps/The Inflight Magazine of the Canadian Forces/Journal de vol des Forces canadiennes. Vol. I-IV. Ottawa: n.p./s.i., 1990-91.
Bilingual text. Frequency varies./Texte bilingue. La périodicité varie./Became: Esprit de corps; the Canadian Military Then and Now. Vol. I- . Ottawa: n.p., 1991- .

Evans, L.J., ed. *Airborne Régiment aéroporté/journal du dixième anniversaire, 1968-1978/Tenth Anniversary Journal, 1968-1978.* n.p.: n.d./s.l.: s.i., s.d. 156 pp.
Bilingual text./Texte bilingue.

Excelsior. No. 1- . n.p./s.l.: s.i., 1991- .
Air Reserve newsletter. Bilingual text. Irregular./Revue de la Réserve aérienne. Texte bilingue. Irrégulier.

Falardeau, Victor, et Jean Parent. *La musique du Royal 22e Régiment; 50 ans d'histoire, 1922-1972.* Québec, P.Q.: Editions Garneau, 1976. 243 pp.

Fast, Beverly G. *Snowbirds Flying High; Canada's Snowbirds Celebrate 25 Years.* Saskatoon, Sask.: Sandra Lynn Rempel, 1995. 58 pp.

Ferguson, Julie H. *Through a Canadian Periscope; the Story of the Canadian Submarine Service.* Toronto: Dundurn Press, 1995. 364 pp.

Fifty Years of Armour/Cinquante ans de blindé/Royal Canadian Armoured Corps/Le Corps blindé royal canadien/1940-1990. Ottawa: Esprit de corps, [1990]. 43 pp.
Bilingual text./Texte bilingue.

50 Years of Canadian Electrical and Mechanical Engineering./50 ans de Génie électrique et mécanique canadien. Ottawa: n.p./s.i., [1994]. 111 pp.
Bilingual text./Texte bilingue.

Fighter Forum. No. 1- . Westwin, Man., Hornell Heights, Ont.: n.p./s.i., 1977- .
Irregular. Bilingual text from 1983./Irrégulier. Texte bilingue depuis 1983.

1st Hussars Guidon Weekend, 11, 12, 13 June 1993. n.p.: [1993. 16 pp.]

Flight Comment. Ottawa: King's Printer, 1949- .
Title until 1953: Crash Comment. Bilingual text from 1976, no. 3. Frequency varies.

Fortin, Marc, éd. *Le troisième Bataillon du Royal 22e Régiment à Chypre, 1968-1969.* Chypre: imprimé par les Presses Zavallis, 1969. 110 pp., en majeure partie ill.

Forum; Conference of Defence Associations. Vol. II- . Ottawa: Conference of Defence Associations, 1987- .

Foster, J.A. *For Love and Glory; a Pictorial History of Canada's Air Forces.* Toronto: McClelland & Stewart, 1989. 143 pp.

_____. *Heart of Oak; a Pictorial History of the Royal Canadian Navy.* Toronto: Methuen, 1985. [143 pp.]

_____. *Muskets to Missiles; a Pictorial History of Canada's Ground Forces.* Toronto: Methuen, 1987. 251 pp.

Foulds, Glen. *[419 Squadron History.]* Burnaby, B.C.: printed by Crosstown Printers, [1988?]. 108 pp.

4 CMBG; Canada's NATO Brigade./4e GBMC; Brigade canadienne au service de l'OTAN. Lahr, Germany/Allemagne: M. Schauenburg, 1983. 1 vol., unpaged./1 tome, non paginé.
Bilingual text./Texte bilingue.

440 Squadron History. Stittsville, Ont.: Canada's Wings, 1983. 103 pp.

417 Squadron History. Stittsville, Ont.: Canada's Wings, 1983. 104 pp.

416 Squadron see Hovey, H. Richard.

421 Squadron History. [Stittsville, Ont.: 421 Tactical Fighter Squadron and Canada's Wings, 1982.] 107 pp.

427 Lion Squadron, 1942-1970. Marceline, Mo.: Walsworth, n.d. 76 pp.

422 Sqn; This Arm shall Do It, 1942-1970. Marceline, Mo.: Walsworth, n.d. 64 pp.

4 Service Battalion, 1969-1989; 20 Years of History. n.p.: [1989]. 83 pp.

4 Wing Baden-Soellingen, Sept 1953 — June 1970. J. David, ed. Marceline, Mo.: Walsworth, [1971]. 206 pp.

Fox, Brent. *Camp Aldershot; Serving since 1904.* (The King's Historical Society Series, number 1.) [Kentville, N.S.]: King's Historical Society, 1983. 24 pp.

Fragments of 1 Airborne Battery (RCA), the Canadian Airborne Regiment. Pembroke, Ont.: printed by D.F. Runge, [1977?]. 113 pp.

Fraser, Dan, ed. *CFS Sydney; 25 Jubilee Booklet, 1953-1978.* n.p.: [1978]. 40 pp.

Fraser, W.B. *Always a Strathcona.* Calgary: Comprint Pub. Co., 1976. 252 pp.

Gaffen, Fred. *Cross-Border Warriors; Canadians in American Forces, Americans in Canadian Forces; from the Civil War to the Gulf.* Toronto: Dundurn Press, 1995. 241 pp.

_____. *In the Eye of the Storm; a History of Canadian Peacekeeping.* Toronto: Deneau & Wayne, 1987. 302 pp.

_____. *Unknown Warriors; Canadians in Vietnam.* Toronto: Dundurn Press, 1990. 366 pp.

Gagnon, Réginald. *Fait d'armes à Oka.* Québec (Qué.): Arion, 1994. 189 pp.

Gallant, A.M. *Pride; the History of 1390 RCACC.* Red Deer, Alta.: printed by Fletcher, [1992?]. 244 pp.

Gardam, John. *The Canadian Peacekeeper./Le gardien de la paix canadien.* Burnstown, Ont.: General Store Pub. House, 1992. 69 pp.
Bilingual text./Texte bilingue.

Gian, M.S., and S.H. Woodend. *The Social Impact of Canadian Forces Bases upon their Host Communities — an Interim Report.* (Defence Research Analysis Establishment Directorate of Social and Economic Analysis Report no. DRAE R48.) Ottawa: Dept. of National Defence, 1974. 84 1.

Glashan, Keith. *Montreal's Navy; Stories of HMCS Donnacona and its Predeccessors.* [Montreal]: Montreal Branch, Naval Officers' Association of Canada, [1985]. 96 pp.

Gludish, M.S., ed. *CFB Trenton; RCAF 60th Anniversary.* Trenton, Ont.: n.p., 1984. 64 pp.

Goetze, Bernd A. *Military Professionalism; the Canadian Officer Corps.* (National Security Series, no. 3/76.) Kingston, Ont.: Queen's Univ. Centre for International Relations, 1976. v.p.

Goodfellow, T.H. *A Profile of the Militiaman of 1970.* (Defence Research Analysis Establishment Directorate of Social and Economic Analysis Report no. DRAE R53.) Ottawa: Dept. of National Defence, 1974. 26 pp.

_____. *Reserve Force Study.* (Operational Research and Analysis Establishment ORAE Report no. R61.) Ottawa: Dept. of National Defence, 1976. 121 pp.

Goodleaf, Donna. *Entering the War Zone; a Mohawk Perspective on Resisting Invasions.* Penticton, B.C.: Theytus Books, 1995. 189 pp.

Gouin, Jacques, *et al. Bon coeur et bon bras; histoire du Régiment de Maisonneuve, 1880-1980.* Montréal: imprimé privé, 1980. 298 pp.

Granatstein, J.L., and David J. Bercuson. *War and Peacekeeping; from South Africa to the Gulf — Canada's Limited Wars.* Toronto: Key Porter Books, 1991. 266 pp.

Granatstein, J.L., and Douglas Lavender. *Shadows of War, Faces of Peace; Canada's Peacekeepers.* Photographs by Boris Spremo. Toronto: Key Porter Books, 1992. 160 pp.

Gravel, Jean-Yves. *Les soldats-citoyens; histoire du Régiment de Trois-Rivières, 1871-1978.* Trois-Rivières, P.Q.: Editions du Bien Public, 1981. 153 pp.

Gray, Colin S. *Canada's Maritime Forces.* (Wellesley Paper 1.) Toronto: Canadian Institute of International Affairs, 1973. 79 pp.

Greenhous, Brereton. *Dragoon; the Centennial History of the Royal Canadian Dragoons, 1883-1983.* Ottawa: Guild of the Royal Canadian Dragoons, 1983. 557 pp.

_____. *Semper Paratus; the History of the Royal Hamilton Light Infantry (Wentworth Regiment), 1862-1977*, by Kingsley Brown, Senior, Kingsley Brown, Junior and Brereton Greenhous. Revised and edited by Brereton Greenhous. Hamilton, Ont.: privately printed, 1977. 446 pp.

Gregory, James W., ed. *Welcome to Canadian Forces Base Comox.* n.p.: [1980]. 48 pp.

Griffin, J.A. *A Tradition of Fighters./Une tradition de combat aérien.* n.p./s.l.: s.i., [198-?]. 54 pp.
Bilingual text./Texte bilingue.

Grimshaw, Louis E. *"Ex coelis"; the Badges and Insignia of the Canadian Airborne Forces; a History of Canadian Airborne Badges and the Units and Men who Wore Them "ex coelis".* Edmonton: Lone Pine Pub., 1981. 80 pp.

Gronbeck-Jones, D.A., et/and T. Holodwisky, comps. *Cinquième Régiment, 1968-1978.* Valcartier (Qué.): 5e Régiment d'artillerie légère du Canada, 1978. 32 pp.
Texte bilingue./Bilingual text.

Haggart, Ron, and Aubrey E. Golden. *Rumours of War.* Toronto: New Press, 1971. 311 pp.
October crisis, 1970.

Hampson, Bill. *Canadian Flying Services Emblems & Insignia (1914-1984).* Vancouver: privately printed, 1986. 193 pp.

Harker, Douglas E. *The Dukes; the Story of the Men who have Served in Peace and War with the British Columbia Regiment (D.C.O.), 1883-1973.* n.p.: privately printed, 1974. 438 pp.

Harrington, Don A., ed. *Welcome to Canadian Forces Base Comox./Bienvenue à la Base des Forces canadiennes de Comox.* n.p./s.l.: National Military Publishers of Canada, 1982. 62 pp.
Bilingual text./Texte bilingue.

Harrison, Deborah, and Lucie Laliberté. *No Life like It; Military Wives in Canada.* Toronto: J. Lorimer, 1994. 266 pp.

Heaps, Leo. *Operation Morning Light; Terror in our Skies, the True Story of Cosmos 954.* New York: Paddington Press, 1978. 208 pp.

Henderson, Peter A. *Guarding the Gates; a History of Canadian Forces Station St. Johns.* St. John's, Nfld.: CFS St. John's, 1992. 115 pp.

Henderson, Thomas. *A History of the Base Construction Engineering Branch of CFB Halifax, 1946-1991.* n.p.: 1991. 59 pp.

High Flight. Vol. I-III. Stittsville, Ont.: Canada's Wings, [1981?-85].

Hinse, Jean-Robert, éd. *Station des Forces canadiennes/Canadian Forces Station/Senneterre, 1953-1978; album-anniversaire/Anniversary Album.* s.l.: imprimé privé/n.p.: privately printed, [1978]. 1 tome, non paginé./1 vol., unpaged.
Texte bilingue./Bilingual text.

A History of the First Hussars Regiment, 1856-1980. n.p.: 1981. 195 pp.
An updating of 1951 ed.

Hobson, Sharon. *The Composition of Canada's Naval Fleet, 1946-85.* Halifax: Centre for Foreign Policy Studies, Dalhousie Univ., 1986. 127 pp.

Holland, J.A. Kent, D.G. Clarke [and/et] Renaud Préfontaine, eds. *Canadian Forces Base Edmonton./Base des Forces canadiennes Edmonton.* n.p./s.l.: National Military Publishers of Canada, 1983. 110 pp.
Bilingual text./Texte bilingue.

Holloway, Ian. *Self-Reliance through Service; the Story of Her Majesty's Canadian Ship Scotian.* Hantsport, N.S.: Lancelot Press, 1988. 116 pp.

Holman, R.F. *Best in the West; the Story of Number 2 Canadian Forces Flying Training School and Flying Training in Canada.* Moose Jaw, Sask.: Big 2 Fund, 15 Wing Moose Jaw, 1995. [223] pp.

Hornung, Rick. *One Nation under the Sun.* Toronto: Stoddart, 1991. 294 pp.
Mohawk crisis, 1990.

[Hovey, H. Richard, and others.] *416 Squadron.* n.p.: 1974. 133 pp.
Rev. and updated ed.: 416 Squadron History. Belleville, Ont.: Hangar Bookshelf, 1984. 160 pp.

Hubel, J.R.M., ed. *Guide Book: Official Marches of the Canadian Forces; a Centennial Celebration of the Royal Canadian Military Institute.* Ottawa: Royal Canadian Military Institute, 1989. 40 pp.

Hughes, G.W., comp. *A Marchpast of the Corps and Regiments of the Canadian Army, Past and Present.* Calgary: n.p., n.d. 3 vols.

Humby, P.A., ed. *CFS Sioux Lookout, 1953-1978.* Winnipeg: Inter-Collegiate Press, [1978]. 1 vol., unpaged.

Infantry Journal. Vol. I- . Oromocto, N.B.: n.p., 1973- .
Irregular. Title varies. Vol. I-V: Infantry Newsletter. Journal of the Infantry Branch.

Intelligence Branch/Journal/du service de renseignements militaires. No. 1- . Ottawa: Dept. of National Defence/Ministère de la Défense nationale, 1985- . *Bilingual text. Twice yearly./Texte bilingue. Semi-annuellement.*

Intercom. Vol. [I]- . n.p./s.l.: s.i., 1965- .
Title varies. Originally published, unnumbered, as CFCS Intercom, and Restricted. Bilingual text from 1978. Frequency varies. Journal of Canadian Forces Communication Command./Divergence du titre. Publié originalement à diffusion restreinte et sans identification de tome, sous le titre CFCS Intercom. La périodicité varie. Journal du Commandement des communications des Forces canadiennes.

International Commission of Control and Supervision, Military Component, Canadian Delegation, January-June 1973. n.p.: n.d. 101 pp.

Jacobson, Ray. *426 Squadron History.* n.p.: [1988]. 187 pp.

Jarymowycz, Roman Johann. *Mobile Command/La Force mobile/RV 83/Wainwright, Alta, mai-juin.* n.p.: Department of National Defence/s.l.: Ministère de la Défense nationale, 1983. 1 vol., chiefly illus./1 tome, en majeure partie ill.
Cartoons with bilingual captions./Caricatures avec des rubriques bilingues.

_____. *RV 81; Rendezvous 81, 01 jun/juin — 06 jul/juil, Gagetown, New Brunswick/Nouveau Brunswick.* n.p.: Department of National Defence/s.l.: Ministère de la Défense nationale, 1981. 1 vol., chiefly illus./1 tome, en majeure partie ill.
Cartoons with bilingual captions./Caricatures avec des rubriques bilingues.

Johnson, E.A. "Rick", ed. *Trenton; 50 Years of Air Force.* Trenton, Ont.: n.p., 1981. 160 pp.

Johnson, Leonard V. *A General for Peace.* Toronto: J. Lorimer, 1987. 158 pp.

Johnston, Murray. *Canada's Craftsmen; the Story of the Corps of Royal Canadian Electrical and Mechanical Engineers and of the Land Ordnance Engineering Branch.* n.p.: 1983. 291 pp.

Johnston, Wilf, and Andy Wilson, eds. *Gypsumville; 24 Years of Vigilance/24 ans de vigilance.* n.p./s.l.: CFS/BFC Gypsumville, [1987]. 80 pp.

Joubert, Marie-Claude. *Par dévouement; le Cadre des Instructeurs de Cadets.* Sainte-Blandine (Qué.): Les Editions Neigette, 1994. 246 pp.

Kanadanin/Groupe de bataille/1R22R/Battle Group. No. 1-6. Daruvar, Croatie: Groupe de bataille du 1er R22eR, mars-septembre 1992.
Recueilli comme un livre, intitulé/Collected as a book, titled: UNPROFOR/FORPRONU/Groupe de bataille/1er Bataillon Royal 22e Régiment/Battle Group/Livre souvenir/Souvenir Book/Croatie-Sarajevo 1992.

Karkut, E.T., ed. *The History of 6 RD and the Aerospace Maintenance Development Unit.* Erin, Ont.: The Boston Mills Press, 1990. 120 pp.

Kellett, N.A. *Analysis of Some of the Elements of the Social Interaction between CFBs and their Host Communities.* (Operational Research and Analysis Establishment Directorate of Social and Economic Analysis Project Report no. PR114.) Ottawa: Dept. of National Defence, 1978. [43] pp.

Kvas, Peter, with Hattie A. Perry. *Lobster, Lighthouse and Long-Range Radar; a History of Canadian Forces Station Barrington to 1987.* Stone Horse, N.S.: Canadian Forces Station Barrington, 1987. 126 pp.

Lacroix, D.J., comp. *The First Battalion of The Royal Canadian Regiment in Cyprus, 28 March to 10 October 1970.* Nicosia, Cyprus: printed by Zavallis Press, 1970. 119 pp.

Langeste, Tom, comp. *Words on the Wing; Slang, Aphorisms, Catchphrases and Jargon of Canadian Military Aviation since 1914.* Toronto: Canadian Institute of Strategic Studies, 1995. 330 pp.

The Last CF-100 to Fly; Souvenir Program, Dedication Ceremonies, April 16, 1983./Le dernier CF-100 à voler; programme souvenir, cérémonie de remise, le 16 avril 1983. n.p/s.l.: s.i., [1983]. 1 vol., unpaged./1 tome, non paginé.
Bilingual text./Texte bilingue.

LeBreton, Marcel. *The Socio-Economic Impact of CADIN/Pinetree Phase 1.* (Operational Research and Analysis Establishment Directorate of Social and Economic Anaylsis, ORAE Project Report no. PR346.) Ottawa: Dept. of National Defence, 1985. 19, 4 pp.

_____. *The Socio-Economic Impact of CFS Beausejour on its Surrounding Region.* (Operational Research and Analysis Establishment Directorate of Social and Economic Analysis, ORAE Project Report no. PR338.) Ottawa: Dept. of National Defence, 1985. 33, 4 pp.

_____. *The Socio-Economic Impact of CFS Falconbridge on its Surrounding Area.* (Operational Research and Analysis Establishment Directorate of Social and Economic Analysis, ORAE Project Report no. PR343.) Ottawa: Dept. of National Defence, 1985. 35, 4 pp.

LeBreton, Marcel. *The Socio-Economic Impact of CFS Lac St-Denis on its Surrounding Region.* (Operational Research and Analysis Establishment Directorate of Social and Economic Analysis, ORAE Project Report no. PR334.) Ottawa: Dept. of National Defence, 1985. 36, 4 pp.

————. *The Socio-Economic Impact of CFS Yorkton on its Surrounding Area.* (Operational Research and Anaylsis Establishment Directorate of Social and Economic Analysis, ORAE Project Report no. PR344.) Ottawa: Dept. of National Defence, 1985. 33, 4 pp.

LeBreton, Marcel, and M. Thiessen. *The Impact of CFB Comox on the Comox-Strathcona Regional District.* (Operational Reserach and Analysis Establishment Directorate of Social and Economic Analysis, ORAE Project Report no. PR201.) Ottawa: Dept. of National Defence, 1982. v.p.

Lee, A.M. *Chatham; an Airfield History.* Fredericton, N.B.: privately printed, 1989. 116 pp.

Lee, Robert Mason. *Death and Deliverance; the Haunting True Story of the Hercules Crash at the North Pole.* Toronto: Macfarlane Walter & Ross, 1992. 217 pp.

Little Black Devils see Tascona, Bruce, and Eric Wells.

The Log; Royal Roads Military College. Vol. V- . Victoria, B.C.: privately printed, 1942- .

Loomis, Dan G. *Not Much Glory; Quelling the F.L.Q.* Toronto: Deneau, 1984. 199 pp.

Lord Strathcona's Horse (Royal Canadians); the Presentation of the New Guidon by Field Marshal Sir Richard Hull, GCB, DSO, Fort Beausejour, Iserlohn, Germany, 26 July 1968, 1100 hrs. Iserlohn, Germany: printed by Welz, [1968. 19 pp.]

Lovell, D.W., ed. *Canadian Forces Base Calgary; Home of the Army of the West.* Calgary: National Publishers, 1979. 72 pp.

Lycan, J.A. *Ubique Quandoque; a History of 4 Service Battalion.* n.p.: Jostens Canada, [1993]. 152 pp.

Lynch, Thomas G. *The Flying 400; Canada's Hydrofoil Project.* Halifax: Nimbus Pub., 1983. 128 pp.

Lyzum, Jim. *Canadian Profile; CF-100 Canuck.* (Aircraft no. 3.) Vanier, Ont.: Sabre Model Supplies Pub., 1985. 52 pp.

Macaw, H.B., ed. *25 années de service; 1953-1978; 25 Years of Service.* n.p.: [1978]. v.p.
  SFC/CFS Moisie. Texte bilingue./Bilingual text.

McClenaghan, John, and Derek Blatchford. *411 City of North York Squadron; 50 Years of History, 1941-1991.* Winnipeg: John/David Associates, 1992. 190 pp.

MacDonald, Grant, and Terry Strocel. *442 Squadron History.* n.p.: [1987]. 144 pp.

MacDonald, J.D., ed. *The Canadian Airborne Regiment/Le Régiment Aéroporté du Canada/Cyprus/Chypre, 1974.* Nicosia, Cyprus/Chypre: printed by Zavallis Press, n.d./imprimé par Zavallis Press, s.d. 44 pp. *Bilingual text./Texte bilingue.*

MacFarlane, John, and Robbie Hughes. *Canada's Naval Aviators.* Victoria, B.C.: Maritime Museum of British Columbia, 1994. 182 pp.

McGregor, F., ed. *LdSH '85-70'.* Winnipeg: privately printed, 1970. 62 pp.

McIntyre, Bob. *Canadian Profile; CF-104 Starfighter.* (Aircraft no. 1.) Vanier, Ont.: Sabre Model Supplies Pub., 1984. 52 pp.

_____. *Canadian Profile; CF-101 Voodoo.* (Aircraft no. 2.) Vanier, Ont.: Sabre Model Supplies Pub., 1984. 52 pp.

_____. *Canadian Profile: Canadair CF-5.* (Aircraft no. 4.) Vanier, Ont.: Sabre Model Supplies Pub., 1985. 52 pp.

McKee, Fraser M. *Volunteers for Sea Service; a Brief History of the Royal Canadian Naval Volunteer Reserve, its Predecessors and Successors, on its 50th Anniversary, 1973.* Toronto: privately printed, 1973. 69 pp.

MacKenzie, Lewis. *Peacekeeper; the Road to Sarajevo.* Vancouver: Douglas & McIntyre, 1993. 345 pp.

McKillican, D.R. *A Short History of the Toronto Scottish Regiment.* n.p.: 1972. 40 pp.

MacLaine, Craig, and Michael S. Boxendale. *This Land is our Land; the Mohawk Revolt at Oka.* Photography: Robert Galbraith. Montreal: Optimum Pub. International, 1990. 121 pp.

MacMillan, James. *CF 100.* Oakville, Ont.: Tarka Press, 1981. 104 pp.

Macpherson, K.R. *Canada's Fighting Ships.* (Canadian War Museum Historical Publication Number 12.) Toronto: Hakkert, 1975. 116 pp.

_____. *Frigates of the Royal Canadian Navy, 1943-1974.* St. Catharines, Ont.: Vanwell Pub., 1989. 109 pp.

Macpherson, K.R., and John Burgess. *The Ships of Canada's Naval Forces, 1910-1981; a Complete Pictorial History of Canadian Warships.* Toronto: Collins, 1981. 240 pp. *Rev. eds. Toronto: Collins, 1985 and St. Catharines, Ont.: Vanwell Pub., 1993.*

McQuarrie, John. *Between the Lines; Canadians in the Service of Peace.* Toronto: Macmillan Canada, 1993. [184] pp.

_____. *Canadian Fighter Pilot; a Legacy of Courage and Dedication.* Whitby, Ont.: McGraw-Hill Ryerson, 1992. 223 pp.

McQuarrie, John, and David O'Malley. *Canadian Wings; the Passion and the Force.* Toronto: McGraw-Hill Ryerson, 1990. 205 pp., chiefly illus.

McRoberts, B.G. *Canadian Forces' Education as a Contributor to National Development.* (Defence Research Analysis Establishment Management and Policy Analysis Team Report no. DRAE 37.) Ottawa: Dept. of National Defence, 1973. 51 1.

*Macksey, Kenneth. *First Clash.* Winnipeg: Canadian Forces Training Materiel Production Centre, 1984. 211 pp.
4th Canadian Mechanized Brigade Group in fictional war in Europe.

*_____. *Premier choc.* Winnipeg: Centre de production du matériel d'instruction, 1987. 231 pp.
4e Groupe brigade mécanisé du Canada dans une guerre imaginaire en Europe.

Madill, D.S., rédacteur. *Le 2e Bataillon, Royal 22e Régiment et la Batterie 'Q', 5e Régiment d'Artillerie légère du Canada à Chypre, 1975.* Chypre: imprimé par les Presses Zavallis, 1975. 1 tome non paginé, en majeure partie ill.

Magnacca, Stephen A. *1871-1971; One Hundredth Anniversary of the 13 Field Battery Based at Portage la Prairie, Manitoba.* n.p.: n.d. 12 pp.

Marcoux, Jules, éd. *CMR, 1952-1977; album du 25e anniversaire/25th Anniversary Album.* St-Jean, P.Q.: s.i./n.p., 1977. 62 pp.
Texte bilingue./Bilingual text.

Marteinson, John, and others. *We Stand on Guard; an Illustrated History of the Canadian Army.* Montreal: Ovale, 1992. 511 pp.

Mayne, J.W., and G.D. Kaye. *An Introduction to Military Operational Research in Canada.* (Operational Research and Analysis Establishment ORAE Report no. R94.) Ottawa: Dept. of National Defence, 1985. [184] pp.

Medicus; the Medical Branch Journal/la revue de la Branche des services de santé. Ottawa: Dept. of National Defence/Ministère de la Défense nationale, 1989- .
Bilingual text./Texte bilingue.

Merrick, Bob. *410 Squadron; a History.* n.p.: n.d. 114 pp.

Milberry, Larry. *AIRCOM; Canada's Air Force.* Toronto: CANAV Books, 1991. 191 pp.

_____. *Aviation in Canada.* Toronto: McGraw-Hill Ryerson, 1979. 272 pp.

Milberry, Larry. *The Avro CF-100.* Toronto: CANAV Books, 1981. 203 pp.

_____. *Canada's Air Force Today.* Toronto: CANAV Books, 1987. 152 pp.

_____. *Canada's Air Force Today — 1991 Update.* Toronto: CANAV Books, 1991. 24 pp.

Milberry, Larry, ed. *Sixty Years; the RCAF and CF Air Command 1924-1984.* Toronto: CANAV Books, 1984. 480 pp.

1871-1971, centenaire, Le 12e Régiment blindé du Canada et Le 12e Régiment blindé du Canada (Milice), Trois-Rivières, Qué., 19 septembre 1971. s.l.: s.i., s.d. [16 pp.]

Miller, Duncan (Dusty) E., and Sharon Hobson. *The Persian Excursion; the Canadian Navy in the Gulf War.* Clementsport, N.S.: Canadian Peacekeeping Press and the Canadian Institute of Strategic Studies, 1995. 239 pp.

Mirtle, Jack. *The Naden Band: a History.* Victoria, B.C.: Jackstays Pub., 1990. 167 pp.

Mitchell, G.D., with B.A. Reid and W. Simcock. *RCHA — Right of the Line; an Anecdotal History of the Royal Canadian Horse Artillery from 1871.* Ottawa: RCHA History Committee, 1986. 303 pp.

Mitchell, Michael, comp. *Ducimus; the Regiments of the Canadian Infantry.* St. Hubert, Que.: Director of Infantry, Mobile Command Headquarters, 1992. 248 pp.

Molson, K.M., and H.A. Taylor. *Canadian Aircraft since 1909.* Stittsville, Ont.: Canada's Wings, 1982. 530 pp.

Morneault, J.C. *424 Tiger Squadron, 1935-1977.* n.p.: [1978]. 31 pp.

Morris, David A. *The Canadian Militia; from 1855; an Historical Summary.* Erin, Ont.: Boston Mills Press, 1983. 328 pp.

Morrison, C.A. *Voyage into the Unknown; the Search for and Recovery of Cosmos 954.* Stittsville, Ont.: Canada's Wings, 1982. 154 pp.

Morrison, W. Alexander, ed. *The Changing Face of Peacekeeping.* Toronto: Canadian Institute of Strategic Studies, 1993. 243 pp.
Proceedings of Peacekeeping '93: an exhibition and seminar held in Ottawa March 16-17, 1993.

Morrison, W. Alexander, and Stephanie A. Blair. *Canada and Peacekeeping; Dedication and Service.* Clementsport, N.S.: Lester B. Pearson Canadian International Peacekeeping Training Centre, 1995. 32 pp.

Mummery, Robert. *Snowbirds; Canada's Ambassadors of the Sky.* n.p.: Reidmore Book, n.d. 1 vol., chiefly illus.

Le Musée national de l'aviation; un survol. Ottawa: Musée national de l'aviation, 1991. 64 pp.

The Naming and Commissioning of HMCS Huron, 16 December 1972, at Marine Industries Ltd. Sorel, Quebec./Baptême et mise en service de l'Huron, le 16 décembre 1972, aux chantiers de la Marine Industrie Limitée, Sorel, Québec. n.p.: n.d./s.l.: s.i., s.d. 1 vol., unpaged./1 tome, non paginé.
Bilingual text./Texte bilingue.

The Naming and Commissioning of HMCS Iroquois, 29 July 1972, at Marine Industries Ltd. Sorel, Quebec./Baptême et mise en service de l'Iroquois, le 29 juillet 1972, aux chantiers de la Marine Industrie Limitée, Sorel, Québec. n.p.: n.d./s.l.: s.i., s.d. 1 vol., unpaged./1 tome non paginé.
Bilingual text./Texte bilingue.

The National Aviation Museum; a Flypast. Ottawa: National Aviation Museum, 1991. 64 pp.

Nicholson, G.W.L. *Canada's Nursing Sisters.* (Canadian War Museum Historical Publication Number 13.) Toronto: S. Stevens, Hakkert, 1975. 272 pp.

_____. *Seventy Years of Service; a History of the Royal Canadian Army Medical Corps.* Ottawa: Borealis Press, 1977. 388 pp.

Nicks, D.A. *Lahr — Schwarzwald 25; 1967-1992.* Ottawa: Dept. of National Defence, 1992. 127 pp.
Cover title/Titre de la couverture: Lahr — Schwarzwald; Base des Forces canadiennes Lahr/Canadian Forces Base Lahr. *Bilingual text./Texte bilingue.*

1939-1989/50th Anniversary Reunion, 4-6 August 1989/50ième anniversaire, réunion, 4-6 août 1989 [412 Squadron/Escadrille]. n.p./s.l.: s.i., [1989]. 28 pp.
Bilingual text./Texte bilingue.

Nixon, Rod, ed. *The Aurora Software Development Unit; the First Ten Years.* n.p.: 1990. 91 pp.
Cover title: The First Ten Years; ASDU Reunion Souvenir Book, August 1980 — August 1990.

Northern Flight; Canada's Aviation Heritage Magazine. Vol. I- . Thornhill, Ont.: Northern Flight Publications, 1992- .

Official Opening of the Brennan Building; by Mrs. Jean Brennan and the Honourable Henry Perrin Beatty, PC, MP, Solicitor General of Canada, Canadian Forces School of Administration and Logistics, Canadian Forces Base Borden, Borden, Ontario, Thursday, September 5, 1985./Ouverture officielle de L'Edifice Brennan; par Mme Jean Brennan et L'honorable Henry Perrin Beatty, PC, MP, Solliciteur général du Canada, Ecole d'administration et de logistique des Forces canadiennes, Base des Forces canadiennes de Borden, Borden, Ontario, le jeudi 5 septembre 1985. n.p./s.l.: s.i., [1985]. 12 pp.
Bilingual text./Texte bilingue.

*The Order of Military Merit. n.p.: n.d. 12 pp.

Order of Military Merit; Commanders, Officers, Members./Ordre du Mérite militaire; commandeurs, officiers, membres. n.p./s.l.: s.i., 1977. 23 pp.
Bilingual text./Texte bilingue.

*L'Ordre du Mérite militaire. s.l.: s.i., s.d. 12 pp.

Page, Ron D. *Avro Canuck; CF 100 All Weather Fighter.* Erin, Ont.: Boston Mills Press, [1981]. 192 pp.

Pallas, S.M., and/et N.G. Woods, eds. *Changing the Guard; Official Programme./La relève de la garde; le programme officiel.* Ottawa: Governer General's Foot Guards Foundation, 1986. 24 pp.
Bilingual text./Text bilingue.

The Patrician. Vol. I- . Edmonton: privately printed, 1948- .
Regimental journal of the Princess Patricia's Canadian Light Infantry.

The Peacekeeping Monument Competition; Creating a National Symbol./Le concours pour le monument au maintien de la paix; la création d'un symbole national. Ottawa: National Capital Commission, Cultural Programs/Commission de la Capitale nationale, Programmes culturels, 1991. 26 pp.
Bilingual text./Texte bilingue.

Periscope/the Professional Journal of the Canadian Forces Physical Education and Recreation Branch/le journal professionel de la Section de l'Education physique et des loisirs. Vol. I- . Ottawa: n.p./s.i., 1969- .
Annual. Bilingual text./Annuel. Texte bilingue.

Philp, O.B., and Bill Johnson. *Snowbirds from the Beginning.* Sidney, B.C.: Porthole Press, 1990. 255 pp.

Phipps, Brian, ed. *Silver Jubilee Celebration, June 14-17, 1979, Canadian Forces Base Cold Lake.* n.p.: [1979]. 1 vol., unpaged.

Pickett, James. *Into the Sausage Machine; the History of 22 Wing.* North Bay, Ont.: privately printed, 1994. 145 pp.

Pickler, Ron, and Larry Milberry. *Canadair; the First Fifty Years.* Toronto: CANAV Books, 1995. 392 pp.

The Powder Horn; Chronicle of the Queen's Own Rifles of Canada. Calgary, Victoria, B.C.: privately printed, 1960-70.

Presentation of Colours and Medals, Third Battalion Princess Patricia's Canadian Light Infantry, The Right Honourable Countess Mountbatten of Burma, CBE, CD, JP, DL, Colonel-in-Chief, and Major-General H.C. Pitts, MC, CD, Colonel-of-the-Regiment Presiding, United Nations Protected Area, Sector West, in the Republic of Croatia. n.p.: 1993. 14 pp.

Presentation of Colours to The North Saskatchewan Regiment (The Saskatoon Light Infantry) (MG), by His Excellency The Right Homourable Jules Léger, CC CMM CD, Governor General of Canada, 25 Oct 1975. n.p.: n.d. [16 pp].

Presentation of Colours to Third Battalion The Royal Canadian Regiment by The Colonel-in-Chief, Field Marshal, His Royal Highness, The Prince Philip, Duke of Edinburgh, KG, PC, KT, OM, GBE, CD, Parliament Hill, 2 August 1973./La remise des drapeaux au Troisième Bataillon, The Royal Canadian Regiment par Le Colonel d'Honneur, Le Field Maréchal, Son Altesse royale, Le Prince Philip, duc d'Edinbourg, KG, PC, KT, OM, GBE, CD, Colline parlementaire, 2 août 1973. Pembroke, Ont.: privately printed/imprimé privé, [1973]. 1 vol., unpaged./1 tome, non paginé. *Bilingual text./Texte bilingue.*

Presentation of Squadron Standard to 880 Maritime Reconnaissance Squadron by His Honour, The Honorable Joseph Aubin Doiron, B.A., D.D.S., L.L.D., The Lieutenant-Governor of the Province of Prince Edward Island, CFB Summerside, Slemon Park, Prince Edward Island, September 26, 1981./La remise de l'étenard d'escadrille au 880 Escardille [sic] de reconnaissance maritime, par son honneur, l'honorable Joseph Aubin Doiron, B.A., D.D.S., L.L.D., le Lieutenant-gouverneur de la province de l'Ile-du-Prince Edouard, BCF Summerside, Selmon [sic] Park, Ile-du-Prince Edouard, le 26 septembre 1981. n.p.: n.d./s.l.: s.i., s.d. [17/15 pp.] *Bilingual text./Texte bilingue.*

Presentation of Squadron Standard to 427 Heavy Bomber, Fighter, Strike/Attack, Tactical Helicopter Squadron by Her Honour, The Honourable Pauline M. McGibbon, OC, BA, LLD, DU (OTT), BAA (Theatre), The Lieutenant Governor of the Province of Ontario, CFB Petawawa, Petawawa, Ontario, May 23, 1976. Pembroke, Ont.: printed by D.F. Runge, [1976]. 1 vol., unpaged.

Presentation of Squadron Standards to 424 Transport & Rescue Squadron, 437 Transport Squadron by Her Excellency The Right Honorable Jeanne Sauvé, P.C., C.C., C.M.M., C.D., Governor General of Canada, June 23, 1985, CFB Trenton, Astra, Ontario./Remise des étendards aux 424e Escadron de Transport & Sauvetage, 437e Escadron de Transport par son Excellence la très honorable Jeanne Sauvé, C.P, C.C., C.M.M., C.D., Gouverneur général du Canada, le 23 juin 1985, BFC Trenton, Astra, Ontario. n.p., n.d./s.l., s.i., s.d. [20 pp.]
Bilingual text./Texte bilingue.

Presentation of the 450 Tactical Helicopter Squadron's Standard by His Excellency The Right Honorable Ramon John Hnatyshyn, Governor General of Canada, 7 Wing Ottawa, 18 June 1994./Présentation de l'étendard au 450ième Escadron tactique d'Helicoptères par Son Excellence Ramon John Hnatyshyn, 7e Escadre Ottawa, 18 juin, 1994. n.p.: n.d./s.l.: s.i., s.d. [20/15 pp.]
Bilingual text./Texte bilingue.

Presentation of the New Queen's Colour and Regimental Colour to the Princess Louise Fusiliers by Her Royal Highness The Princess Margaret, Countess of Snowdon, Colonel-in-Chief, Halifax, Nova Scotia, Wednesday, 6 July, 1988. n.p.: n.d. [12 pp.]

Presentation of the Queen's Colour to the Hastings and Prince Edward Regiment by His Excellency Roland Michener, C.C., C.D., the Governor General of Canada on Saturday, the 14th Day of March, 1970, Belleville, Ontario. n.p.: n.d. [12 pp.]

*Preston, Richard A. *Au service du Canada; histoire du Royal Military College depuis la Deuxième Guerre mondiale.* s.l.: Presses de l'Université d'Ottawa, 1992. 268 pp.

*_____. *To Serve Canada; a History of the Royal Military College since the Second World War.* Ottawa: Univ. of Ottawa Press, 1991. 248 pp.

Prise d'armes du NCSM Ville de Québec/Commissioning of HMCS Ville de Québec; Quai 22/Pier 22, Québec, Québec, 14 juillet/July 1994. s.l.: s.i./n.p., [1994]. 35 pp.
Texte bilingue./Bilingual text.

Prise d'armes, remise de nouveaux drapeaux et passation de commandement du 4e Bataillon Royal 22e Régiment (Châteauguay) par le Colonel du Régiment le Lieutenant-général J.J. Paradis, CMM, CD, Saint-Jérome, le 2 mai 1993. s.l.: s.i., s.d. [28 pp.]

Programme-souvenir; Le Régiment de Hull, juin 1974; publication autorisée par le Lcol. R.E. Dormer, C.D., A.D.C., Commandant, Le Régiment de Hull; programme-souvenir publié pour marquer le 60e anniversaire du Régiment de Hull et le 35e anniversaire du manège de Salaberry. Hull, P.Q.: imprimé privé, [1974]. 32 pp.

Provider. n.p.: [1985]. 1 vol., unpaged.
HMCS Provider yearbook.

Publication de l'histoire régimentaire; Lévis, le 4 juin 1983. s.l.: s.i., [1983]. 15 pp.
Le Régiment de la Chaudière.

Puddester, J., ed. *The Crow's Nest (Officers Club); 30th Anniversary Souvenir, 1942-1972.* St. John's, Nfld.: privately printed, 1972. 51 pp.

Qatar, 1er, Bataillon Cie C, Royal 22e Régiment, décembre 90 — mars 91. Directeur: Richard V. Blanchette. Ottawa: Esprit de corps, s.d. 80 pp.

Quadrant. Vol. I- . Shilo, Man.: Royal Regiment of Canadian Artillery, 1984- . *Bi-annual.*

Rankin-Lowe, Jeff, and Andrew Cline. *The Aircraft of the Canadian Armed Forces; a Checklist of Current Aircraft and Disposals.* London, Ont.: Sirius Productions, 1995. 108 pp.

Le Régiment du Saguenay; prise d'armes sous la présidence du Colonel P. Giroux, CD, Commandant District no 3, à l'occasion de la passation de commandement entre le Lieutenant-Colonel G. Vachon, CD, et le Lieutenant-Colonel C. Rhainds, CD, manège militaire Saguenay, le 10 mai 1987. s.l.: s.i., s.d. [27 pp.]

La revue régimentaire; le Régiment de Maisonneuve. Vol. I-VIII. Montréal: imprimé privé, 1960-72.

Rioux, Denise. *Les Fusiliers de Sherbrooke (1910-1980).* Sherbrooke, P.Q.: s.i., 1980. 68 pp.

Robinson, Maurice, Beverly Hall and Paul Price. *Royal Roads; a Celebration.* Victoria, B.C.: Natural Light Productions, 1995. 102 pp., chiefly illus.

Rockett, Melanie E. *Sky Hawks; There's No Life like It!* Edmonton: Proof Positive Productions, 1988. 95 pp.

The Rocky Mountain Rangers; Presentation of Colours, 10 March 1983, KXA, Kamloops, B.C. n.p.: printed by Thompson Valley Print., [1983]. 12 pp.

Ross, D.A. *An Outline of Canada's Defence Scientific Information Service.* (DSIS Technical Memorandum 3/74 (ODG).) Ottawa: Research and Development Branch, Dept. of National Defence, 1974. 16 pp.

Royal Canadian Horse Artillery; First Regiment, 1871-1971. Lahr, Germany: privately printed, [1971]. 32 pp.

The Royal Military College of Canada, 1876-1976/[Presentation of a Queen's Colour to the Royal Military College of Canada by His Excellency The Right Honourable Jules Léger, C.C., C.M.M., C.D., Governor General of Canada, 13 May 1976/La remise d'un nouveau drapeau de la Reine au Royal Military College of Canada par Son Excellence le très honorable Jules Léger, C.C., C.M.M., C.D., Gouverneur général du Canada, 13 mai 1976. n.p./s.l.: s.i., 1976.] 20 pp.
Bilingual text./Texte bilingue.

The Royal Military College of Canada Review. Vol. I- . Kingston, Ont.: privately printed, 1920- .

Le Royal 22e Régiment; remise de nouveaux drapeaux aux 1er, 2ième et 3ième Bataillons par Son Excellence le Gouverneur général du Canada, les Plaines d'Abraham, le 4 juillet 1982. s.l.: s.i., s.d. 1 tome, non paginé.

The Royal Westminster Regiment, 1863-1988. New Westminster, B.C.: n.p., 1988. 72 pp.

Rutherford, Tom. *An Unofficial History of the Grey and Simcoe Foresters Regiment, 1866-1973.* n.p.: n.d. 88 pp.

Rycquart, Barbara. *The Snowbirds Story.* London, Ont.: Third Eye, 1987. 93 pp.

St. Denis, Thomas, ed. *Canada's New Field Army.* Ottawa: Conference of Defence Associations Institute, 1989. 67 pp.

St. Denis, Thomas, and Emily Atkins, eds. *The Future of Canada's Air Force.* Ottawa: Conference of Defence Associations Institute, 1990. 77 pp.

Savard, Claude. *Journal intime d'un béret bleu canadien en ex-Yougoslavie.* Outremont (Qué.): Les Editions Quebecor, 1994. 196 pp.
Le Royal 22e Régiment.

Second Battalion, Princess Patricia's Canadian Light Infantry; Souvenir Booklet Commemorating the Presentation of Colours by General J.V. Allard CC, CBE, DSO, ED, CD, Chief of Defence Staff, Fort MacLeod, Deilinghofen, Germany, Monday 5th of May, 1969. n.p.: n.d. [16 pp.]

Service, G.T., and J.K. Marteinson. *The Gate; a History of the Fort Garry Horse.* Calgary: privately printed, 1971. 228 pp.

Sexton, Donal J. *A Guide to Canadian Shoulder Titles, 1939-1985; a Collector's and Historian's Comprehensive Guide to the Cloth Shoulder Titles Worn by the Regiments and Corps of the Canadian Army in 1939-1985.* Hinsdale, Ill.: Pass in Review Publications, 1987. 97 pp.

Shaw, Robbie. *Superbase 18; Cold Lake; Canada's Northern Guardian.* London: Osprey Aerospace, 1990. 127 pp., chiefly col. illus.

Shores, Christopher. *History of the Royal Canadian Air Force.* (A Bison Book.) Toronto: Royce Publications, 1984. 128 pp.

Smith, G.Y. *Seek and Save; the History of 103 Rescue Unit.* Erin, Ont.: Boston Mills Press, 1990. 137 pp.

Smith, Marilyn Gurney. *The King's Yard; an Illustrated History of the Halifax Dockyard.* Halifax: Nimbus Pub., 1985. 56 pp.

Snowie, J. Allen. *The Bonnie; HMCS Bonaventure.* Erin, Ont.: Boston Mills Press, 1987. 336 pp.

Snowy Owl; Journal of the Canadian Land Forces Command and Staff College. Kingston, Ont.: privately printed, 1952-73. 18 vols.
Title varies.

Soward, Stuart E. *Hands to Flying Stations; a Recollective History of Canadian Naval Aviation.* Victoria, B.C.: Neptune Developments (1984), 1993-95. 2 vols.

The Springbok. Various places: n.p., 1923- .
Regimental journal of The Royal Canadian Dragoons. Title varies: The Goat *(1923-36).*

Stailing, Libby, ed. *Canadian Forces Base Halifax.* n.p.: 1984. 76 pp.

* Stanley, George F.G. *Canada's Soldiers, 1604-1954; the Military History of an Unmilitary People.* Toronto: Macmillan, 1954. 400 pp.
Subsequent revised and enlarged editions.

* _____. *Nos soldats; l'histoire militaire du Canada de 1604 à nos jours.* Traduction et adaptation sous la direction de Serge Bernier. Montréal: Les Editions de l'homme, 1980. 620 pp.

The Strathconian. Calgary: n.p., 1914-?, 1927-38, 1947- .
Regimental journal of the Lord Strathcona's Horse (Royal Canadians). Re-numbered from no. 1 after each gap in publication.

Summers, Jack L. *Tangled Web; Canadian Infantry Accoutrements, 1855-1985.* (Canadian War Museum Historical Publication no. 26.) Alexandria Bay, N.Y.: Museum Restoration Service, 1992. 146 pp.

* Summers, Jack L., and René Chartrand. *Military Uniforms in Canada, 1665-1970.* Illustrated by R.J. Marrion. (Canadian War Museum Historical Publication no. 16.) Ottawa: National Museums of Canada, 1981. 192 pp.

* Summers, Jack L., et René Chartrand. *L'uniforme militaire au Canada, 1665-1970.* Illustré par R.J. Marrion. Traduit par Jean Pariseau. (Musée canadien de la guerre publication d'histoire militaire no 16.) Ottawa: Musées nationaux du Canada, 1981. 192 pp.

Sutherland, Alice Gibson. *Canada's Aviation Pioneers; 50 Years of McKee Trophy Winners.* Toronto: McGraw-Hill Ryerson, 1978. 304 pp.

[Tait, Stuart.] *408 Goose Squadron Reunion, 1987.* n.p.: [1987]. 34 pp.

[Tascona, Bruce, and Eric Wells.] *Little Black Devils; a History of the Royal Winnipeg Rifles.* Winnipeg: Frye Pub., 1983. 241 pp.

Telford, Murray M. *Scarlet to Green; the Colours, Uniforms and Insigna of the Grey and Simcoe Foresters.* Erin, Ont.: Boston Mills Press, 1987. 64 pp.

Thompson, Brad. *H.M.C.S. Griffon; a Naval History.* Thunder Bay, Ont.: Thunder Bay Naval Association, 1985. 98 pp.

Thompson, Roy J.C. *Canadian Army Cap Badges, 1953-1973.* [Dartmouth], N.S.: n.p., 1973. 215 pp.

_____. *Cap Badges and Insignia of the RCN — RCAF — CAF, 1953-1978.* Colorado Springs, Col.: n.p., 1978. 75 pp.

_____. *Wings of the Canadian Armed Forces, 1913-1972.* [Dartmouth], N.S.: n.p., 1973. 106 pp.

Thornton, J.M. *H.M.C.S. Discovery and Deadman's Island; a Brief History ....* n.p.: [197-?]. 52 pp.

La Tourelle. Courcelette, P.Q.: s.i., 1975- .
Bulletin annuel du 12e Régiment blindé du Canada.

Tracy, Nicholas. *The Diplomatic Utility of Canada's Naval Forces.* (Operational Research and Analysis Establishment ORAE Report R60.) Ottawa: Dept. of National Defence, 1976. 132 pp.

Trooping of the Colour, Third Battalion Princess Patricia's Canadian Light Infantry and Review of the Battalion by Major General G.R. Pearkes, VC, CC, PC, CB, DSO, MC, CD, Royal Athletic Park, Victoria, British Columbia, Monday, 1 July 1974. n.p.: printed by Colonist Printers, [1974]. 1 vol., unpaged.

Tyler, G.C.A. *The Lion Rampant: a Pictorial History of the Queen's Own Cameron Highlanders of Canada, 1910-1985.* Winnipeg: The Queen's Own Cameron Highlanders of Canada, 1985. 134 pp.

Ubique/the Magazine of the Canadian Military Engineers/la revue du Génie militaire canadien. Ottawa: Director General Military Engineering Operations, National Defence Headquarters, 1968- .
Frequency varies. Title varies. Until Vol. XIII, 1981 was: The Canadian Military Engineer. Volumes not numbered until Vol. XII, 1980. Not published 1979.

U.S. Dept. of Energy. Nevada Operations Office, Las Vegas, Nevada. *Operation Morning Light; Northwest Territories, Canada — 1978; a Non-Technical Summary of U.S. Participation.* Washington: U.S. Govt. Print. Off., 1978. 81 pp.

Van Der Schee, W. *A Short History of Lord Strathcona's Horse (Royal Canadians).* n.p.: 1973. 19 l.

Vanguard. Vol. I- . Ottawa: Conference of Defence Associations Institute, 1995- .
Quarterly.

Vaughan, Arnold P. *418 City of Edmonton Squadron History.* n.p.: [1984]. 117 pp.

West Nova; the Journal of the West Nova Scotia Regiment. Vol. I- . Kentville, N.S.: n.p., 1986- .

Wheeler, William J. *Images of Flight; a Canadian Aviation Portfolio.* Willowdale, Ont.: Hounslow, 1992. 134 pp.

Whitby, Michael J. *Relentless in Chase; a History of HMCS Iroquois I and II; Comrades in Arms, Relentless in Chase.* n.p.: [1992]. 60 pp.

Willcocks, K.D.H. *The Hastings and Prince Edward Regiment, Canada; Customs and Traditions of the Regiment.* Belleville, Ont.: n.p., 1968. 29 pp.

Willett, J.C. *A Heritage at Risk: the Canadian Militia as a Social Institution.* (IUS Special Editions on Armed Forces and Society, no. 1.) Boulder, Col.: Westview Press, 1987. 269 pp.
Also published as: Canada's Militia; a Heritage at Risk. Ottawa: Conference of Defence Associations Institute, 1990.

Williams, Jon D., ed. *Presentation of Colours to 441, 439, 421 Tactical Fighter Squadrons, 4 May 1973.* n.p.: [1973]. 1 vol., unpaged.

Winters, B.A. *H.M.C.S. Discovery; a History of the Naval Reserve in Vancouver.* n.p.: [1995]. 1 vol., unpaged.

Winton, Maurice V. *Saskatchewan's Prairie Soldiers, 1885-1980.* n.p.: n.d. 174 pp.
Cover title: A Pictorial History of Saskatchewan's Military Badges and Medals.

Witt, Eugene, and Jim Thomas. *Ship Repair Adventure; HMC Dockyard Esquimalt.* Victoria, B.C.: printed by Hillside Print. Co., 1985. 164 pp.

York, Geoffrey, and Loreen Pindera. *People of the Pines; the Warriors and the Legacy of Oka.* Boston: Little Brown, 1991. 438 pp.

Index

INDEX

SUBJECTS

Aboriginal soldiers: 84, 94, 110, 137, 180, 210, 243, 272, 291, 332, 348
Acadians: 155, 237
Admirals *see* General officers
Aid to the civil power: 44, 123, 124, 128, 131, 391, 395
Air accidents investigation: 360, 388
Air Board: 36, 320, 336
Airborne forces: 25, 235, 248, 249, 260, 278, 288, 291, 292, 374, 384, 388, 391
Aircraft
    General: 309, 333, 334, 361, 365
    Avro CF-100 Canuck: 353, 363, 364, 366, 394-396, 398, 400
    Avro CF-105 Arrow: 11, 30, 51, 55-57, 354, 359, 366-368
    Avro Lancaster: 343, 366
    Blackburn Shark: 349
    Boeing B-17 Fortress: 350, 369
    Boeing CH-113 Voyageur: 353
    Canadair CF-5: 396
    Canadair CF-104 Starfighter: 353, 364, 372, 373, 396
    Canadair CL-28 Argus: 357
    Canadair CL-44 Yukon: 357
    Canadair Sabre: 362, 365, 396
    Consolidated B-24 Liberator: 350, 369
    De Havilland Mosquito: 336
    Douglas C-47 Dakota: 320, 344, 354, 366, 373
    Fairey Firefly: 108, 366
    Ferrying *see* Ferrying of aircraft.
    Grumman TBF Avenger: 108, 366
    Hawker Sea Fury: 108, 366
    Hawker Tempest: 334
    Hawker Typhoon: 334
    Lockheed CP-140 Aurora: 383, 399
    McDonnell CF-101 Voodoo: 364, 396
    McDonnell F2H Banshee: 108, 365
    McDonnell-Douglas CF-18: 372, 379
    North American AT-6 Harvard: 331, 342, 359
    North American Sabre *see* Canadair Sabre

INDEX

SUJETS

Acadiens: 155, 237

Accord d'Ogdensburg, 1940: 56

Aéronavale: 68, 71, 74, 81, 86, 87, 89, 95, 102, 105-108, 110, 111, 310, 311, 327, 331, 336, 337, 340, 358, 360, 362, 364, 366-368, 376, 382, 384, 389, 396, 405

Aéronefs

Général: 309, 333, 334, 361, 365

Avro CF-100 Canuck: 353, 363, 364, 366, 394-396, 398, 400

Avro CF-105 Arrow: 11, 30, 51, 55-57, 354, 359, 366-368

Avro Lancaster: 343, 366

Blackburn Shark: 349

Boeing B-17 Fortress: 350, 369

Boeing CH-113 Voyageur: 353

Canadair CF-5: 396

Canadair CF-104 Starfighter: 353, 364, 372, 373, 396

Canadair CL-28 Argus: 357

Canadair CL-44 Yukon: 357

Canadair Sabre: 362, 365, 369

Consolidated B-24 Liberator: 350, 369

Convoyage *voir* Convoyage des aéronefs

De Havilland Mosquito: 336

Douglas C-47 Dakota: 320, 344, 354, 366, 373

Fairey Firefly: 108, 366

Grumman TBF Avenger: 108, 366

Hawker Sea Fury: 108, 366

Hawker Tempest: 334

Hawker Typhoon: 334

Lockheed CP-140 Aurora: 383, 399

McDonnell CF-101 Voodoo: 364, 396

McDonnell F2H Banshee: 108, 365

McDonnell-Douglas CF-18: 372, 379

North American AT-6 Harvard: 331, 342, 359

North American Sabre *voir* Canadair Sabre

Northrop CF-5 *voir* Canadair CF-5

R-100, aérostat britannique: 317, 328

Northrop CF-5 *see* Canadair CF-5

R-100, British airship: 317, 328

Supermarine Seafire: 108, 366

Supermarine Spitfire: 319

Aircrew Association of Canada: 329

Alaska Highway: 5, 26, 33, 43, 60, 218, 222, 236, 268, 272, 274, 288, 296, 333, 346, 349

Alberta: 32, 84, 243, 331

Aldershot, N.S.: 132, 218, 291, 389

Aleutian Campaign, 1942-1943: 235, 236, 334

Alexandria, Ont.: 169

Alpha Delta Phi *see* McGill University

Allied Intervention in Russia *see* Russia

Americans in Canadian Service: 84, 105, 180, 243, 291, 332, 390

Amiens, 1918: 186, 190, 193

Anecdotes, Military: 73, 94, 151, 173, 210, 273, 302, 348

Architecture, Military: 26

Arctic, Canadian: 10, 11, 27, 31, 33-35, 38, 46-48, 52, 59, 259, 367

Armoured Fighting Vehicles: 225, 241

Arms Control *see* Disarmament

Arms, General: 92, 152, 214, 264, 275, 302, 345

Army Museum, Halifax, N.S.: 113, 155, 218

Arnhem, 1944: 249

Artillery: 113, 114, 126, 135, 156, 219

Ashbury College, Ottawa, Ont.: 67, 155, 305

Asia, Canadians in: 97, 227, 229, 324, 341

Atlantic, Battle of: 79-84, 86-93, 95, 97

Aviation medicine *see* Medicine, Aviation

Aviation, Naval: 68, 71, 74, 81, 86, 87, 89, 95, 102, 105-108, 110, 111, 310, 311, 327, 331, 336, 337, 340, 358, 360, 362, 364, 366-368, 376, 382, 384, 389, 396, 405

Badges: 156, 175, 205 *see also* Heraldry

Baldur, Man.: 54

Ballistics: 156, 219

Bands *see* Music, bands and song

Bank of Montreal: 67, 76, 156, 219, 305, 318

Bases, Abandoned: 50

Batoche, 1885: 121, 123

Battalions *see* Units, services, branches and formations

Batteries *see* Units, services, branches and formations

Battle fatigue *see* Medicine, Military

Battle of Britain *see* Britain, Battle of

Battle of the Atlantic *see* Atlantic, Battle of

Battlefields: 132, 133, 243

Supermarine Seafire: 108, 366
Supermarine Spitfire: 319
Affaire Guibord, 1869-1875: 128
Affiches de guerre: 2, 25
Aide au pouvoir civil: 44, 123, 124, 128, 131, 391, 395
Alberta: 32, 84, 243, 331
Aldershot (N.-É.): 132, 218, 291, 389
Aléoutiennes, Campagne des *voir* Campagne des Aléoutiennes
Alexandria (Ont.): 169
Alpha Delta Phi *voir* Université McGill
Américains dans les forces armées canadiennes: 84, 105, 180, 243, 291, 332, 390
Amiens, 1918: 186, 190, 193
Amiraux *voir* Officiers généraux
Anecdotes militaires: 73, 94, 151, 173, 210, 273, 302, 348
Angleterre, Bataille d', 1940: 319, 322, 338
Architecture militaire: 26
Archives nationales du Canada: 2, 3
Arctique canadien: 10, 11, 27, 31, 33-35, 38, 46-48, 52, 59, 259, 367
Argot: 311, 338, 363, 394
Armée britannique: 3, 116, 149, 150
Armée du Salut: 97, 279, 352
Armes militaires – Général: 92, 152, 214, 264, 275, 302, 345
Armes portatives: 43, 194
Arnhem, 1944: 249
Arsenal de Québec: 15, 113, 130, 155, 176, 219, 239
Art héraldique
    Aérien: 85, 212, 307, 311, 312, 314, 326, 334, 335, 341, 348, 361, 368
    Militaire: 30, 140, 196, 212, 223, 235, 241, 248, 249, 257, 265, 273, 274, 290, 292, 295, 300, 302, 384, 387, 391, 404, 406
    Naval: 63, 67, 74, 76, 80, 85, 95, 98, 100, 108, 110, 371, 406
    Unifié: 382
Artillerie: 113, 114, 126, 135, 156, 219
Ashbury College, Ottawa (Ont.): 67, 155, 305
Asie, Canadiens en: 97, 227, 229, 324, 341
Association canadienne de préparation industrielle: 10
Association canadienne des fantassins et des mitrailleurs *voir* Association de l'Infanterie canadienne
Association canadienne du service du matériel: 10
Association de la Cavalerie canadienne: 126, 169, 233, 286
Association de la Force aérienne du Canada: 317, 353
Association de l'Artillerie royale canadienne: 125, 142, 169, 232, 233
Association de l'Infanterie canadienne: 126, 170, 233, 287
Association des équipages aériens du Canada: 329
Association des officiers de milice du Canada: 143
Association des pilotes de chasse du Canada: 337, 347, 368

Bayonets: 140, 196, 257, 295
Beaumont-Hamel, 1916: 165
Beaver Club: 93, 269, 347
Belgium: 254, 270
Bilingualism: 7, 44, 50, 51, 381
Blacks in Canada: 206
Boer War *see* South African War
Bosnia-Hercegovina *see* Yugoslavia
Bramshott, England: 181
Branches *see* Units, services, branches and formations
Brant County, Ont.: 77, 222, 319
Bren Gun: 21, 232
Brigades *see* Units, services, branches and formations
Britain, Battle of, 1940: 319, 322, 338
British Army: 3, 116, 149, 150
British Columbia: 7, 9, 64, 181
British Columbia Land Surveyors: 69, 174, 308
British Commonwealth Air Training Plan: 5, 30, 39, 50, 58, 317-321, 328-330, 335,
    338, 343, 344, 347, 348, 351
Bruce County, Ont.: 190
Burford, Que.: 129
Business Council of Canada: 10

Caen, 1944: 237, 256, 257, 262, 277
Calgary, Alta.: 129, 175, 238, 239, 386
Canada-United States Permanent Joint Board on Defence: 11, 51
Canadair Ltd.: 344, 401
Canadian Aeroplanes Ltd.: 314
Canadian Armoured Association *see* Canadian Cavalry Association
Canadian Artillery Association: 125, 142, 169, 232, 233
Canadian Bank of Commerce: 68, 81, 149, 233, 306, 325
Canadian Broadcasting Corporation: 22, 81, 233, 262, 272, 326
Canadian Cavalry Association: 126, 169, 233, 286
Canadian Coast Guard: 63, 67, 76, 98
Canadian Defence League: 22
Canadian Fighter Pilots Association: 337, 347, 368
Canadian Hydrofoil Project *see* Hydrofoil Project
Canadian Industrial Preparedness Association: 10
Canadian Infantry Association: 126, 170, 233, 287
Canadian Institute of International Affairs: 5, 32
Canadian Jews: 81, 233, 240, 290, 326
Canadian Legion *see* Royal Canadian Legion
Canadian Machine Gun Corps Association *see* Canadian Infantry Association
Canadian Ordnance Association: 10
Canadian Pacific Railway: 170, 306

Association du Corps blindé canadien *voir* Association de la Cavalerie canadienne
Association du Corps de mitrailleurs canadien *voir* Association de l'Infanterie
    canadienne
Atlantique, Bataille de l': 79-84, 86-93, 95, 97
Aumôniers: 66, 73, 94, 96, 109, 153, 161, 165, 174, 178, 199, 201, 204, 209, 215,
    223, 228, 260, 265, 269, 271, 277, 296, 301, 326, 335, 348, 358
Aviation civile: 325

Baie d'Hudson: 25
Baïonnettes: 140, 196, 257, 295
Baldur (Man.): 54
Balistique: 156, 219
Banque canadienne de commerce: 68, 81, 169, 233, 306, 325
Banque de Montréal: 67, 76, 156, 219, 305, 318
Barreau de l'Ontario: 72, 202, 313
Bases abandonnées: 50
Bataille d'Angleterre *voir* Angleterre, Bataille d'
Bataille de l'Atlantique *voir* Atlantique, Bataille de l'
Bataillons *voir* Unités, services, branches et formations supérieures
Batoche, 1885: 121, 123
Batteries *voir* Unités, services, branches et formations supérieures
Beaumont-Hamel, 1916: 165
Beaver Club: 93, 269, 347
Belgique: 254, 270
Bilinguisme: 7, 44, 50, 51, 381
Bois de Moreuil, 1918: 187
Bosnie-Herzégovine *voir* Yougoslavie
Bramshott (Angleterre): 181
Branches *voir* Unités, services, branches et formations supérieures
Bravoure et le mépris (Émission de télévision): 21, 220, 276, 318, 350
Brigades *voir* Unités, services, branches et formations supérieures
British Columbia Land Surveyors: 69, 174, 308
Burford (Qué.): 129

Caen, 1944: 237, 256, 257, 262, 277
Calgary (Alb.): 129, 175, 238, 289, 386
Campagne de Normandie, 1944: 77, 79, 82, 84, 89, 95, 220, 221, 224, 229, 235,
    237-239, 241-243, 246, 249, 255-257, 262, 264, 266, 268-271, 273, 277, 278,
    318, 324, 325, 327, 329, 331, 339, 348
Campagne des Aléoutiennes, 1942-1943: 235, 236, 334
Campagne du Nord-Ouest, 1885: 113-116, 118, 120-124, 127-133, 135-139, 141,
    143-148, 150, 151, 153, 154
Canadair Ltée.: 344, 401
Canadian Aeroplanes Ltd.: 314
Canadien Pacifique (Chemin de fer): 170, 306

Canadian Patrol Frigate Program: 379
Canadian Red Cross: 198
Canadian War Museum: 24, 25
CANLOAN: 253, 269
Canol Pipeline: 31, 49
Canteens: 232, 286, 325, 357
Caribou Hut: 81, 83, 240, 330
Carleton Place, Ont.: 308
Cartoons: 83, 180, 238, 257, 265, 393
Casa Berardi, 1943: 235
Casualties, Canadian: 166, 172, 176, 181, 242, 255, 318
Catholic Army Huts *see* Knights of Columbus
Cavalry: 118, 126, 149, 187, 199
Censorship: 26, 39, 191
Chaplains: 66, 73, 94, 96, 109, 153, 161, 165, 174, 178, 199, 201, 204, 209, 215,
    223, 228, 260, 265, 269, 271, 277, 296, 301, 326, 335, 348, 358
Chattan Club (Toronto): 172
Chemical and biological warfare: 52
Chinese Canadians: 97, 278, 351
Chronology: 306, 309, 310, 322, 332, 334, 360, 361
Civil aviation: 325
Civil defence: 14, 62
Clothing *see* Dress
Coast Guard *see* Canadian Coast Guard
Cobourg, Ont.: 26, 173
Commonwealth War Graves Commission: 62, 82, 173, 236, 247, 248 *see also*
    Imperial War Graves Commission
Communist Party of Canada: 10, 38, 39, 53, 253
Companies *see* Units, services, branches and formations
Conference of Defence Associations: 26, 32, 48, 60, 384, 389, 407
Conscientious objectors: 211
Conscription: 6, 8, 9, 12, 27, 46, 47, 52, 54, 55, 162, 192, 197
Construction and maintenance: 329, 359, 386
Cooperative Commonwealth Federation: 27 *see also* New Democratic Party
Cornwall, Ont.: 169
Corps *see* Units, services, branches and formations
Corvettes: 87, 88
Cosmos 954 *see* Operation Morning Light
Courcelette, 1916: 155, 193
Croatia *see* Yugoslavia
Crow's Nest Club: 83, 92, 104, 105, 109, 238, 329, 403
Cuban Missile Crisis, 1962: 36, 106, 361
Customs and traditions: 54, 63, 67, 76, 98, 371, 386
Cyprus: 371, 372, 378, 389, 394, 396, 397

Canadiens d'origine chinoise: 97, 278, 351
Canadiens d'origine japonaise: 37, 38, 54, 190, 252, 266
Canadiens d'origine ukrainienne: 28, 38, 39, 42, 50, 52, 191, 193, 274, 349
Canadiens français: 6, 7, 22, 35, 47, 50, 51, 54, 55, 57, 108, 115, 151, 158, 168, 221, 281, 296, 366, 382
CANLOAN: 253, 269
Cantines: 232, 286, 325, 357
Caribou Hut: 81, 83, 240, 330
Caricatures: 83, 180, 238, 257, 265, 393
Carleton Place (Ont.): 308
Casa Berardi, 1943: 235
Cavalerie: 118, 126, 149, 187, 199
Censure: 26, 39, 191
Cents jours, 1918: 190, 193, 195, 208
Champs de bataille: 132, 133, 243
Chansons *voir* Musique, fanfares et chansons
Chemins de fer: 24
Chevaliers de Colomb: 176, 190, 235, 254
Chevaux: 211
Chronologie: 306, 309, 310, 322, 332, 334, 360, 361
Chypre: 371, 372, 378, 389, 394, 396, 397
Club Chattan (Toronto): 172
Club Crows' Nest: 83, 92, 104, 105, 109, 238, 329, 403
Cobourg (Ont.): 26, 173
Collection aéronautique nationale: 343
Collège d'agriculture de l'Ontario, Guelph (Ont.): 72, 201, 313
Colombie-Britannique: 7, 9, 64, 181
Comique: 81, 90, 257, 335, 341, 361
Commandement de la Défense aérospatiale de l'Amérique du Nord (NORAD): 20, 27-30, 34, 36, 38, 47, 362, 387
Commission de l'air: 36, 320, 336
Commission des ressources en munitions: 14
Commission des sépultures de guerre du Commonwealth: 62, 82, 173, 236 *voir aussi* Commission impériale des sépultures de guerre
Commission impériale des munitions: 314
Commission impériale des sépultures de guerre: 62, 70, 71, 82, 85, 182-186, 246-248 *voir aussi* Commission des sépultures de guerre du Commonwealth
Commission internationale de contrôle et de surveillance *voir* Conflit du Viêt-nam
Commission permanente canado-américaine de Défense: 11, 51
Compagnies *voir* Unités, services, branches et formations supérieures
Composition ethnique des forces armées canadiennes: 36, 59
Comté de Brant (Ont.): 77, 222, 319
Comté de Bruce (Ont.): 190
Comté de Durham (Ont.): 128, 172, 235
Comté de Huntingdon (Qué.): 139

D-Day *see* Normandy Campaign, 1944
Decorations *see* Medals and decorations
Defence Construction Limited: 11
Defence production: 11, 12, 31, 53
Defensively Equipped Merchant Ships *see* Merchant marine
Delta Upsilon *see* McGill University
Demobilization and rehabilitation: 47, 164, 168, 227
Department of Munitions and Supply: 39
Department of Public Works: 127
Dependents, Military: 47
Deserters: 164
Dictionaries (Military history): 7
Dieppe, 1942: 11, 33, 96, 218, 219, 221, 224, 230, 238, 240, 245, 248, 249, 251, 254, 256, 258, 263-265, 267, 273, 275-277, 333, 350
Disarmament: 5, 7, 10, 15, 17, 22, 26, 37, 52, 53, 55, 56, 60
Distant Early Warning Line: 47
Divisions *see* Units, services, branches and formations
Dress
    Air: 321
    Military: 3, 56, 118, 134, 146, 151, 152, 154, 210-212, 216, 228, 229, 235, 272, 273, 278, 282, 283, 301-303, 405-407
    Naval: 68, 101
    Unified: 379, 382
Drummondville, Que.: 58, 95, 273, 348
Dunwich, Ont.: 95, 274, 349
Durham County, Ont.: 128, 172, 235
Dutton, Ont.: 274, 349

Edmonton, Alta.: 87, 312, 342
Edmonton Military Institute: 253, 337
Ellesmere Island, N.W.T.: 35
Emergency planning *see* Civil defence
Entertainments: 94, 197, 221, 271, 347
Escape and evasion *see* Prisoners of war and internment operations
Espionage *see* Intelligence
Ethnic composition (Canadian Forces): 36, 59
Exercise Eskimo: 231
Exercise Musk Ox: 282, 356

Falaise, 1944: 237, 242, 243, 246, 255, 278
Fenian Raids: 11, 13, 113, 115, 117, 118, 121, 132, 139, 141, 143, 146, 148, 151
Ferrying of aircraft: 327, 333, 340, 344, 350, 352
Fishermen's Reserve: 91
Formations *see* Units, services, branches and formations
Fort Henry, Kingston, Ont.: 44, 193

Comté de Lennox et Addington (Ont.): 71, 188, 311
Comté de Missisquoi (Qué.): 141
Comté de Peel (Ont.): 116, 160, 223
Comté de Pictou (N.-É.): 116, 161, 224, 282
Comté de Waterloo (Ont.): 73, 202, 313
Conférence des Associations de la Défense: 26, 32, 48, 60, 384, 389, 407
Conférence d'Ottawa sur l'entraînement aérien, 1942: 343
Conflit du Viêt-nam, 1957-1973: 28, 32, 44, 58, 291, 373, 390, 393
Conscription: 6, 8, 9, 12, 27, 46, 47, 52, 54, 55, 162, 192, 197
Conseil canadien des chefs d'entreprises: 10
Conseil de la Milice: 119
Conseil du service social du Canada: 208
Conseil nationale de recherches: 33, 90, 258, 325, 330, 341
Construction de Défense Ltée.: 11
Construction et entretien: 329, 359, 386
Contrôle des armes *voir* Désarmement
Convoyage des aéronefs: 327, 333, 340, 344, 350, 352
Cooperative Commonwealth Federation: 27 *voir aussi* Nouveau Parti démocratique
Corée *voir* Guerre de Corée
Cornwall (Ont.): 169
Corps *voir* Unités, services, branches et formations supérieures
Corvettes: 87, 88
Cosmos 954 *voir* Opération Morning Light
Courcelette, 1916: 155, 193
Coutumes et traditions: 54, 63, 67, 76, 98, 371, 386
Crise des missiles cubains, 1962: 36, 106, 361
Crise d'octobre, 1970: 44, 391, 395
Crise d'Oka, 1990: 37, 387, 390, 392, 396, 407
Croatie *voir* Yougoslavie
Croix de Georges: 58
Croix de Victoria: 8, 46, 58, 171, 307
Croix-rouge *voir* Société canadienne de la Croix-rouge

Décorations *voir* Médailles et décorations
Défense civile: 14, 62
Défense impériale: 5, 8, 9, 15, 17, 27, 29, 31, 51, 52, 55, 57, 61, 65, 73, 124, 125, 131, 145
Delta Epsilon, *voir* Université McGill
Démobilisation et réintégration: 47, 164, 168, 227
Désarmement: 5, 7, 10, 15, 17, 22, 26, 37, 52, 53, 55, 56, 60
Déserteurs: 164
Détection lointaine avancée: 47
Développement nucléaire: 31, 44
Dictionnaires d'histoire militaire: 7

Fortifications: 17, 121
French Canadians: 6, 7, 22, 35, 47, 50, 51, 54, 55, 57, 108, 115, 151, 158, 168, 221, 281, 296, 366, 382
Frigates: 396
Frog Lake, Alta.: 116, 136
Front de la libération du Québec *see* October Crisis, 1970

Gallipoli, 1915: 174, 180
Gas, poison: 195 *see also* Ypres, 1915
General officers: 8, 35, 48, 52, 188, 241, 246, 249, 390
George Cross: 58
Gimli, Man.: 373
Grand Trunk Railway: 123, 124
Great Britain, Canadians in: 94, 96, 227, 235, 269, 271, 278, 347, 351
Guibord Affair, 1869-1875: 128
Gulf War *see* Persian Gulf War, 1990-1991

Habbakuk Project: 33
Halifax, N.S.: 35, 65, 66, 69, 70, 73, 81, 94, 109, 121, 131, 133, 164, 235, 258, 309, 405
    Explosion, 1917: 25, 67, 69, 72, 197
    Riots, 1945: 81, 92, 232, 264, 325, 345
Hamilton, Ont.: 161, 224, 274, 282, 373
Hartney, Man.: 150, 305
Hawkesbury, Ont.: 169
Headley, England: 269
Heraldry
    Air: 85, 212, 307, 311, 312, 314, 326, 334, 335, 341, 348, 361, 368
    Military: 30, 140, 196, 212, 223, 235, 241, 248, 249, 257, 265, 273, 274, 290, 292, 295, 300, 302, 384, 387, 391, 404, 406
    Naval: 63, 67, 74, 76, 80, 85, 95, 98, 100, 108, 110, 371, 406
    Unified: 382
Hindenburg Line, 1918: 195, 211
Hodgson, Man.: 43
Holland *see* Netherlands
Hong Kong, 1941: 92, 218, 224, 230, 232, 242, 244, 255, 263, 275
Honours and awards *see* Medals and decorations
Horses: 211
Hudson Bay: 25
Hudson Straits Expedition, 1927-1928: 340
Humour: 81, 90, 257, 335, 341, 361
Hundred Days, 1918: 190, 193, 195, 208
Huntingdon County, Que.: 139
Hydrofoil Project: 107, 395

Dieppe, 1942: 11, 33, 96, 218, 219, 221, 224, 230, 238, 240, 245, 248, 249, 251, 254, 256, 258, 263-265, 267, 273, 275-277, 333, 350
Divertissements: 94, 197, 221, 271, 347
Divisions *voir* Unités, services, branches et formations supérieures
Droit militaire: 78, 99, 140, 164, 227, 228, 232, 235, 269, 279, 284, 379
Drummondville (Qué.): 58, 95, 273, 348
Dunwich (Ont.): 95, 274, 349
Dutton (Ont.): 274, 349

Écussons *voir* Insignes
Edmonton (Alb.): 87, 312, 342
Edmonton Military Institute: 253, 337
Émeutes: 81, 92, 232, 264, 325, 345
Enquêtes sur les accidents aériens: 360, 388
Entraînement: 35, 100-102, 118, 119, 123-125, 135, 188, 249
Entretien *voir* Construction et entretien
Épouses militaires: 385, 392
Épuisement au combat *voir* Médecine militaire
Escadres *voir* Unités, services, branches et formations supérieures
Escadrilles *voir* Unités, services, branches et formations supérieures
Escadrons *voir* Unités, services, branches et formations supérieures
Escaut, 1944: 218, 243, 259, 273, 277
Espagne *voir* Guerre civile d'Espagne
Espionnage *voir* Renseignement militaire
Evasions *voir* Prisonniers de guerre et opérations d'internement
Expédition à la Rivière Rouge, 1869-1870: 113, 114, 124, 125, 130, 133-137, 140, 142, 143, 145, 150-153
Expédition vers le détroit d'Hudson, 1927-1928: 340
Exercice Eskimo: 231
Exercice Musk Ox: 282, 356

Falaise, 1944: 237, 242, 243, 246, 255, 278
Familles des militaires: 47
Fanfares *voir* Musique, fanfares et chansons
Femmes: 10, 36, 51, 77, 79, 84-86, 95, 96, 101, 218, 221-223, 241, 245, 251, 262, 265, 273, 277, 278, 320, 330, 333, 336, 345, 349, 350, 352, 359, 368, 369
Féniens *voir* Raids des Féniens
Forces aéroportées: 25, 235, 248, 249, 260, 278, 288, 291, 292, 374, 384, 388, 391
Forces polonaises: 170, 234, 326
Formations *voir* Unités, services, branches et formations supérieures
Fort Henry, Kingston (Ont.): 44, 193
Fortifications: 17, 121
Foyer Rideau pour les Anciens combattants, Ottawa (Ont.): 86, 189, 251, 293, 311, 337
Foyers d'accueil pour les soldats de religion catholique *voir* Chevaliers de Colomb

Imperial defence: 5, 8, 9, 15, 17, 27, 29, 31, 51, 52, 55, 57, 61, 65, 73, 124, 125, 131, 145

Imperial Munitions Board: 314

Imperial War Graves Commission: 62, 70, 71, 82, 85, 182-186, 246-248, 309, 310
    see also Commonwealth War Graves Commission

Infantry and Machine Gun Association of Canada *see* Canadian Infantry Association

Insignia *see* Heraldry

Intelligence, Military: 10, 37, 38, 57, 68, 77, 128, 131, 132, 139, 178, 187, 223, 230, 241, 256, 287, 290, 393

International Commission of Control and Supervision *see* Vietnamese Conflict

Internment operations *see* Prisoners of war and internment operations

Irish Canadians: 205

Italy, 1943-1945: 228, 231, 233-236, 238, 240, 242, 244, 259, 261, 268, 272

Japanese Canadians: 37, 38, 54, 190, 252, 266

Jews *see* Canadian Jews

Kangaroo *see* Armoured Fighting Vehicles

Kapyong, 1951: 295

Kingston, Ont.: 44, 66, 73, 94, 150, 193, 209, 271, 301

Kinmel Park, Wales: 203

Knights of Columbus: 176, 190, 235, 254

Korean War, 1950-1953: 12, 14, 57, 62, 84, 100, 105, 108, 110, 282, 284, 285, 291, 292, 295, 296, 301, 303, 357, 360

Law, military: 78, 99, 140, 164, 227, 228, 232, 235, 269, 279, 284, 379

Lennox and Addington County, Ont.: 71, 188, 311

Liberal Party of Canada: 31, 49

Liphook, England: 181

Little Blitz: 334

Little Norway: 343

London, Ont.: 148, 174

Lower Fort Garry, Man.: 153

Loyola High School and College, Montreal, Que.: 69, 83, 177, 240, 289, 308, 330

McGill University, Montreal, Que.: 70-72, 74, 84, 89, 95, 178, 189, 194, 215, 242, 256, 286, 311, 315, 340, 350

McKee Trophy: 348, 368, 406

Machine Gun Association of Canada *see* Canadian Infantry Association

Maintenance *see* Construction and maintenance

Malta: 318

Manitoba: 151, 210, 211, 272, 273, 302

Maple Leaf (Newspaper): 265

Maple Leaf Services: 295

Frégates: 396
Frog Lake (Alb.): 116, 136
Front de libération du Québec *voir* Crise d'octobre, 1970
Frontière non-défendue: 52, 54, 57
Fusil Ross: 15, 17, 144, 145, 167, 202

Gallipoli, 1915: 174, 180
Garde côtière canadienne: 63, 67, 76, 98
Gaz toxique: 195 *voir aussi* Ypres, 1915
Généraux *voir* Officiers généraux
Gimli (Man.): 373
Grand-Tronc (Chemin de fer): 123, 124
Grande-Bretagne, Canadiens en: 94, 96, 227, 235, 269, 271, 278, 347, 351
Guerre chimique et biologique: 52
Guerre civile d'Espagne, 1936-1939: 220, 249, 251, 253
Guerre de Corée, 1950-1953: 12, 14, 57, 62, 84, 100, 105, 108, 110, 282, 284, 285, 291, 292, 295, 296, 301, 303, 357, 360
Guerre du golfe Persique, 1990-1991: 383, 386, 398, 403
Guerre des Boers, 1899-1902: 15, 17, 31, 47, 50, 55, 115, 116, 118, 121-126, 131, 135-142, 144-150
Guerre des tranchées: 204
Guibord *voir* Affaire Guibord

Halifax (N.-É.): 35, 36, 65, 66, 69, 70, 73, 81, 94, 109, 121, 131, 133, 164, 235, 258, 309, 405
    Émeutes, 1945: 81, 92, 232, 264, 325, 345
    Explosion, 1917: 25, 67, 69, 72, 197
Hamilton (Ont.): 161, 224, 274, 282, 373
Hartney (Man.): 150, 305
Hawkesbury (Ont.): 169
Headley (Angleterre): 269
Hodgson (Man.): 43
Hollande *voir* Pays-Bas
Hong Kong, 1941: 92, 218, 224, 230, 232, 242, 244, 255, 263, 275
Hydroptères *voir* Projet des hydroptères

Île de Ellesmere (T.N.-O.): 35
Île-du-Prince-Édouard: 145, 199
Infirmières: 43, 143, 160, 173, 200, 216, 254, 259, 296, 399
Insignes: 156, 175, 205 *voir aussi* Art héraldique
Insignes de service de guerre: 38
Institut canadien des Affaires internationales: 5, 32
Intervention alliée en Russie *voir* Russie
Italie, 1943-1945: 228, 231, 233-236, 238, 240, 242, 244, 259, 261, 268, 272

Maritime Museum of Canada: 65, 72, 90, 108

Medals and decorations: 8, 10, 24, 30, 37, 63, 64, 67, 76, 91, 98, 115, 124, 143, 144, 153-155, 158, 167, 171, 202, 204, 205, 216, 221, 222, 232, 243, 261, 278, 281, 303, 305, 318, 319, 325, 331, 353, 400, 407

Medicine, Aviation: 3, 325, 330, 338

Medicine, Military: 80, 84, 139, 232, 237, 241, 330

Memorials *see* War memorials

Merchant marine: 36, 82, 84, 86, 91, 92, 96

Middle East: 10, 281

Military intelligence *see* Intelligence, Military

Military lands: 121, 164

Military photography *see* Photography, Military

Military wives *see* Wives, Military

Militia Council: 119

Milton, Ont.: 43, 87, 254, 338

Miquelon *see* St. Pierre and Miquelon

Missisquoi County, Que.: 141

Mobilization: 14, 51, 52, 58, 118, 179, 258, 263, 340

Montreal, Que.: 26, 145, 148, 161

Moreuil Wood, 1918: 187

Motorcycles: 161, 224, 281, 373

Mount Sorrel, 1916: 216

Munitions: 14, 22, 24, 25, 49, 53, 61

Munitions Resources Commission: 14

Music, bands and song: 26, 86, 91, 97, 108, 193, 241, 251, 290, 336, 392, 398

National Aeronautical Collection: 343

National Archives of Canada: 2, 3

National Aviation Museum: 312, 313, 341, 342, 365, 398, 399

National Research Council: 33, 90, 258, 325, 330, 341

Naval aviation *see* Aviation, Naval

Netherlands: 230, 251, 253, 254, 257, 260, 261, 275, 276

Neutrality: 55

New Brunswick: 86, 249, 335

New Brunswick Museum: 146

New Democratic Party: 49 *see also* Cooperative Commonwealth Federation

Newfoundland: 45, 81, 83, 91, 96, 102, 143, 165, 200, 202, 234, 235, 240, 260, 326, 330, 342

    Naval reserves: 64, 66, 74, 94, 110

Niagara district, Ont.: 129, 315, 351

Nile Voyageurs: 137, 139, 149, 153

Normandy Campaign, 1944: 77, 79, 82, 84, 89, 95, 220, 221, 224, 229, 235, 237-239, 241-243, 246, 249, 255-257, 262, 264, 266, 268-271, 273, 277, 278, 318, 324, 325, 327, 329, 331, 339, 348

North American Aerospace Defence Command: 20, 27-30, 34, 36, 38, 47, 362, 387

Jour de la Victoire en Europe *voir* Halifax (N.-É.) – Émeutes, 1945
Jour J *voir* Campagne de Normandie, 1944
Juifs – Canada: 81, 233, 240, 290, 326

Kangaroo *voir* Véhicules de combat blindés
Kapyong, 1951: 295
Kingston (Ont.): 44, 66, 73, 94, 150, 193, 209, 271, 301
Kinmel Park (Pays de Galles): 203

Langues officielles *voir* Bilinguisme
Légion royale canadienne: 54, 77, 81, 98, 221, 233, 281, 319, 326, 354
Ligne Hindenburg, 1918: 195, 211
Ligne Pinetree: 394
Ligue de la défense du Canada: 22
Liphook (Angleterre): 181
"Little Norway" (Ont.): 343
London (Ont.): 148, 174
Lower Fort Garry (Man.): 153
Loyola College, Montréal (Qué.): 69, 83, 177, 240, 289, 308, 330

Maintien de la paix: 2, 9, 11, 16, 18-20, 31, 32, 36, 39, 43, 48, 53, 55, 58, 62, 106,
    291, 292, 294-296, 298, 302, 360, 361, 372, 390, 391, 397, 398, 400
Malte: 318
Manitoba: 151, 210, 211, 272, 273, 302
Maple Leaf (Journal): 265
Marché des grains de Winnipeg: 216
Marine marchande: 36, 82, 84, 86, 91, 92, 96
Médailles et décorations: 8, 10, 24, 30, 37, 63, 64, 67, 76, 91, 98, 115, 124, 143,
    144, 153-155, 158, 167, 171, 202, 204, 205, 216, 221, 222, 232, 243, 261,
    278, 281, 303, 305, 318, 319, 325, 331, 353, 400, 407
Médecine aérienne: 3, 325, 330, 338
Médecine militaire: 80, 84, 139, 232, 237, 241, 330
Mesures de guerre: 21, 38, 52 *voir aussi* Crise d'octobre, 1970
Milton (Ont.): 43, 87, 254, 338
Ministère des Munitions et Approvisionnements: 39
Ministère des Travaux publics: 127
Miquelon *voir* Saint-Pierre et Miquelon
Mitrailleuse Bren: 21, 232
Mobilisation: 14, 51, 52, 58, 118, 179, 258, 263, 340
Mont Sorrel, 1916: 216
Montréal (Qué.): 26, 145, 148, 161
Monuments commémoratifs: 9, 62, 69, 70, 74, 75, 97, 127, 165, 168, 169, 172,
    178, 180, 181, 192, 196, 200, 212, 216, 255, 260, 278, 294, 307-309, 312,
    314, 315, 351, 400 *voir aussi* Commission des sépultures de guerre du
    Commonwealth; Commission impériale des sépultures de guerre *et* Tour de
    la Paix

North Atlantic Treaty Organization: 12, 14, 19, 31, 32, 37, 39, 44, 45, 50, 53, 54, 58, 60, 363, 364
North Bay, Ont.: 34, 248
Northwest Campaign, 1885: 113-116, 118, 120-124, 127-133, 135-139, 141, 143-146, 148, 150, 151, 153, 154
Northwest Highway System: 296
Norwegian Air Force *see* Little Norway
Nova Scotia: 3, 37, 91, 189, 260, 343
Nuclear development: 31, 44
Nurses: 43, 143, 160, 173, 200, 216, 254, 259, 296, 399

October Crisis, 1970: 44, 391, 395
Officers Association of the Militia of Canada: 143
Official languages *see* Bilingualism
Ogdensburg Agreement, 1940: 56
Oka Crisis, 1990: 37, 387, 390, 392, 396, 407
Ontario: 37, 62, 189, 216
Ontario Agricultural College, Guelph, Ont.: 72, 201, 313
Ontario Bar Association: 72, 202, 313
Ontario teachers: 72, 201, 313
Operation Cavalier: 378
Operation Harmony: 378
Operation Morning Light: 392, 398, 407
Operational research: 31, 33, 49, 58, 90, 98, 257, 280, 314, 347, 353, 372, 379-381, 397, 403
Ortona, 1943: 243, 244, 261
Ottawa Air Training Conference, 1942: 343
Ottawa, Ont.: 137, 144, 187, 190, 252, 293

Pacifism: 56, 59
Papal Zouaves *see* Zouaves pontificaux
Parkdale Collegiate Institute, Toronto, Ont.: 72, 73, 202, 313
Passchendaele, 1917: 176
Pay and allowances: 68, 79, 118-120, 122, 163, 164, 167, 227, 228, 231, 255, 284, 321, 324
Peace Tower: 69, 70, 72, 74, 172, 180, 196, 212, 307, 309, 312, 314
Peacekeeping: 2, 9, 11, 16, 18-20, 31, 32, 36, 39, 43, 48, 53, 55, 58, 62, 106, 291, 292, 294-296, 298, 302, 360, 361, 372, 390, 391, 397, 398, 400
Peel County, Ont.: 116, 160, 223
Permanent Joint Board on Defence *see* Canada-United States Permanent Joint Board on Defence
Persian Gulf War, 1990-1991: 383, 386, 398, 403
Photography, Military: 90, 92, 109, 146, 170, 171, 205, 265, 298, 345, 367
Pictou County, N.S.: 116, 161, 224, 282
Pinetree Line: 394

426

Motocyclettes: 161, 224, 281, 373
Moyen-Orient: 10, 281
Munitions: 14, 22, 24, 25, 49, 53, 61
Musée canadien de la guerre: 24, 25
Musée de l'Armée, Halifax (N.-É.): 113, 155, 218
Musée du Nouveau-Brunswick: 146
Musée maritime du Canada: 65, 72, 90, 108
Musée national de l'aviation: 312, 313, 341, 342, 365, 398, 399
Musique, fanfares et chansons: 26, 86, 91, 97, 108, 193, 241, 251, 290, 336, 392, 398

Navires – Histoires collectives: 65, 72, 88-90, 106, 107, 396
Navires marchands armés *voir* Marine marchande
Neutralité: 55
Niagara, Région de (Ont.): 129, 315, 351
Noirs – Canada: 206
Nord-Ouest, Campagne du *voir* Campagne du Nord-Ouest
Normandie, Campagne de *voir* Campagne de Normandie
North Bay (Ont.): 34, 248
Norvège – Aviation *voir* "Little Norway" (Ont.)
Nouveau-Brunswick: 86, 249, 335
Nouveau Parti démocratique: 49 *voir aussi* Cooperative Commonwealth Federation
Nouvelle-Écosse: 3, 37, 91, 189, 260, 343

Objecteurs de conscience: 211
Oeuvres d'art de guerre: 6, 35, 59, 65, 67-70, 75, 80, 82, 88, 89, 91, 92, 97, 155, 168, 170, 171, 187, 197, 200, 205, 212, 216, 219, 221, 232, 234, 236, 254, 258, 259, 265, 278, 305, 306, 309, 311, 314, 315, 321, 325, 326, 328, 339, 342, 345, 351, 359, 385, 407
Officiers généraux: 8, 35, 48, 52, 188, 241, 246, 249, 390
Ontario: 37, 62, 189, 216
Opération Cavalier: 378
Opération Harmony: 378
Opération Morning Light: 392, 398, 407
Opérations d'internement *voir* Prisonners de guerre et opérations d'internement
Opinion publique: 55
Organisation du Traité de l'Atlantique Nord: 12, 14, 19, 31, 32, 37, 39, 44, 45, 50, 53, 54, 58, 60, 363, 364
Ortona, 1943: 243, 244, 261
Ottawa (Ont.): 137, 144, 187, 190, 252, 293

Pacifisme: 56, 59
Parkdale Collegiate Institute, Toronto (Ont.): 72, 73, 202, 313
Parti communiste du Canada: 10, 38, 39, 53, 253
Parti Libéral du Canada: 31, 49

Polish forces: 170, 234, 326
Postal service: 6, 37, 147
Posters, War: 2, 25
Prince Edward Island: 145, 199
Prince Rupert, B.C.: 77, 221, 319
Prisoners of war and internment operations: 7, 25, 42, 44, 60, 61, 78, 83, 86, 94, 155, 159, 171, 177, 180, 189, 192-195, 199, 202, 205, 207, 210, 212, 214, 218-220, 224, 227, 234, 239, 249, 253, 254, 256, 257, 263, 266, 271, 272, 275-277, 279, 320, 324, 329, 335, 336, 339, 346-348, 351 *see also* Japanese Canadians
Public opinion: 55
Public relations: 239, 240, 289

Quebec: 6, 34, 42, 52, 133, 179, 192
Quebec Arsenal: 15, 113, 130, 155, 176, 219, 239
Quebec, Que.: 7, 34, 47
Queen's University, Kingston, Ont.: 73, 115, 158, 204, 221, 281, 313

Radar: 47, 77, 90, 258, 333, 343, 345
Radio: 93, 268, 272, 346 *see also* Canadian Broadcasting Corporation
Railways: 24
Raleighites: 91
Red Cross *see* Canadian Red Cross
Red River Expedition, 1869-1870: 113, 114, 124, 125, 130, 133-137, 140, 142, 143, 145, 150-153
Red Triangle Club *see* Young Men's Christian Associations
Rehabilitation *see* Demobilization and rehabilitation
Reserve forces: 9, 13, 19, 372, 386, 390, 407
Rhineland, 1945: 264, 277
Rideau Veterans Home, Ottawa, Ont.: 86, 189, 251, 293, 311, 337
Ridgeway, 1866: 143
Riots: 81, 92, 232, 264, 325, 345
Ross Rifle: 15, 17, 144, 145, 167, 202
Royal Air Force, Canadians in: 318
Royal Canadian Air Force Association: 317, 353
Royal Canadian Armoured Corps (Cavalry) Association *see* Canadian Cavalry Association
Royal Canadian Legion: 54, 77, 81, 98, 221, 233, 281, 319, 326, 354
Royal Canadian Military Institute: 7, 54, 206, 314, 392
Russia, Allied intervention, 1918-1922: 58, 195, 196, 208, 211, 212, 220, 256, 257, 259, 269, 273, 274, 314, 340, 346

Saint John, N.B.: 154, 217, 279, 351
St. Pierre and Miquelon: 6
Salonika: 195

Passchendaele, 1917: 176
Pays-Bas: 230, 251, 253, 254, 257, 260, 261, 275, 276
Pertes militaires canadiennes: 166, 172, 176, 181, 242, 255, 318
Petit Blitz: 334
Photographie militaire: 90, 92, 109, 146, 170, 171, 205, 265, 298, 345, 367
Pipeline Canol: 31, 49
Plan d'entraînement aérien du Commonwealth britannique: 5, 30, 39, 50, 58, 317-
    321, 328-330, 335, 338, 343, 344, 347, 348, 351
Planification d'urgence *voir* Défense civile
Pologne *voir* Forces polonaises
Prince Rupert (C.-B.): 77, 221, 319
Prisonners de guerre et opérations d'internement: 7, 25, 42, 44, 60, 61, 78, 83, 86,
    94, 155, 159, 171, 177, 180, 189, 192-195, 199, 202, 205, 207, 210, 212,
    214, 218-220, 224, 227, 234, 239, 249, 253, 254, 256, 257, 263, 266, 271,
    272, 275-277, 279, 320, 324, 329, 335, 336, 339, 346-348, 351 *voir aussi*
    Canadiens d'origine japonaise.
Production de défense: 11, 12, 31, 53
Professeurs de l'Ontario: 72, 201, 313
Projet de la Frégate canadienne de patrouille: 379
Projet des hydroptères: 107, 395
Projet Habbakuk: 33

Québec: 6, 34, 42, 52, 133, 179, 192
Québec (Qué.): 7, 34, 47

Radar: 47, 77, 90, 258, 333, 343, 345
Radio: 93, 268, 272, 346
Radio-Canada *voir* Société Radio-Canada
Raids des Féniens: 11, 13, 113, 115, 117, 118, 121, 132, 139, 141, 143, 146, 148,
    151
Raleighites: 91
Recherche opérationnelle: 31, 33, 49, 58, 90, 98, 257, 280, 314, 347, 353, 372,
    379-381, 397, 403
Recherche et sauvetage: 354, 365, 368, 395, 405
Red Triangle *voir* Young Men's Christian Associations
Réintégration *voir* Démobilisation et réintégration
Relations publiques: 239, 240, 289
Renseignement militaire: 10, 37, 38, 57, 68, 77, 128, 131, 132, 139, 178, 187, 223,
    230, 241, 256, 287, 290, 393
Réserve des pêcheurs: 91
Rhénanie, 1945: 264, 277
Ridgeway, 1866: 143
Rivière Rouge *voir* Expédition à la Rivière Rouge
Route de l'Alaska: 5, 26, 33, 43, 60, 218, 222, 236, 268, 272, 274, 288, 296, 333,
    346, 349

Salvation Army: 97, 279, 352
Sarajevo *see* Yugoslavia
Sarnia, Ont.: 174, 308
Saskatchewan: 154, 189, 216, 251, 278, 303, 407
Scheldt, 1944: 218, 243, 259, 273, 277
Search and Rescue: 354, 365, 368, 395, 405
Services *see* Units, services, branches and formations
Ships – collective histories: 65, 72, 88-90, 106, 107, 396
Sicily, 1943: 228, 231, 240, 259, 268, 272
Slang: 311, 338, 363, 394
Small arms: 43, 194
Snowbirds: 366, 372, 388, 398, 400, 404
Social Service Council of Canada: 208
Song *see* Music, bands and song
South African War, 1899-1902: 15, 17, 31, 47, 50, 55, 115, 116, 118, 121-126,
        131, 135-142, 144-150
Spanish Civil War, 1936-1939: 220, 249, 251, 253
Spies *see* Intelligence, Military
Squadrons *see* Units, services, branches and formations
Stratford, Ont.: 174, 308
Submarines: 19, 67, 69, 73, 84, 105, 388
Sudan *see* Nile Voyaguers

Toronto, Ont.: 69, 76, 176, 187, 212, 218, 308, 310, 317
Tournaments, Military: 132, 274
Traditions *see* Customs and traditions
Training: 35, 100-102, 118, 119, 123-125, 135, 188, 249
Trench warfare: 204
Trinity College School, Port Hope, Ont.: 95, 274, 349
Trinity College, Toronto, Ont.: 75, 217, 274, 316
Trinity Methodist Church, Toronto, Ont.: 74, 213, 314

Ukranian Canadians: 28, 38, 39, 42, 50, 52, 191, 193, 274, 349
Undefended border: 52, 54, 57
Unification of the Armed Forces: 3, 8, 36, 42, 55, 372
Uniforms *see* Dress
Units, services, branches and formations
        Australia
                462 Squadron: 350
        Canada
                Unified and tri-service branches and establishments
                        Aerospace Engineering Test Establishment: 373
                        Canadian Forces Base Baden-Soellingen, Germany: 372
                        Canadian Forces Base Bagotville, Que.: 319, 354, 373, 380
                        Canadian Forces Base Borden, Ont.: 374

Royal Air Force, Canadiens dans la: 318
Royal Canadian Military Institute: 7, 54, 206, 314, 392
Russie, Intervention des forces alliées, 1918-1922: 58, 195, 196, 208, 211, 212, 220, 256, 257, 259, 269, 273, 274, 314, 340, 346

Saint-Jean (N.-B.): 154, 217, 279, 351
Saint-Pierre et Miquelon: 6
Salonique: 195
Sarajevo *voir* Yougoslavie
Sarnia (Ont.): 174, 308
Saskatchewan: 154, 189, 216, 251, 278, 303, 407
Sépultures de guerre *voir* Commission des sépultures de guerre du Commonwealth *et* Commission impériale des sépultures de guerre
Service postal: 6, 37, 147
Services *voir* Unités, services, branches et formations supérieures
Services de la Feuille d'érable (MLS): 295
Sicile, 1943: 228, 231, 240, 259, 268, 272
Snowbirds: 366, 372, 388, 398, 400, 404
Société canadienne de la Croix-rouge: 198
Société Radio-Canada: 22, 81, 233, 262, 272, 326
Soldats autochtones: 84, 94, 110, 137, 180, 210, 243, 272, 291, 332, 348
Solde et indemnités: 68, 79, 118-120, 122, 163, 164, 167, 227, 228, 231, 255, 284, 321, 324
Soudan *voir* Voyageurs sur le Nil
Sous-marins: 19, 67, 69, 73, 84, 105, 388
Stratford (Ont.): 174, 308
Système routier du Nord-Ouest: 296

Tenue
    Aérienne: 321
    Militaire: 3, 56, 118, 134, 146, 151, 152, 154, 210-212, 216, 228, 229, 235, 272, 273, 278, 282, 283, 301-303, 405-407
    Navale: 68, 101
    Unifiée: 379, 382
Terre-Neuve: 45, 81, 83, 91, 96, 102, 143, 165, 200, 202, 234, 235, 240, 260, 326, 330, 342
    Réserves navales: 64, 66, 74, 94, 110
Terres militaires: 121, 164
Toronto (Ont.): 69, 76, 176, 187, 212, 218, 308, 310, 317
Tour de la Paix: 69, 70, 72, 74, 172, 180, 196, 212, 307, 309, 312, 314
Tournois militaires: 132, 274
Traditions *voir* Coutumes et traditions
Trinity College School, Port Hope (Ont.): 95, 274, 349
Trinity College, Toronto (Ont.): 75, 217, 274, 316
Trinity Methodist Church, Toronto (Ont.): 74, 213, 314

Canadian Forces Base Calgary, Alta.: 374, 395
Canadian Forces Base Chatham, N.B.: 374, 395
Canadian Forces Base Chilliwack, B.C.: 374
Canadian Forces Base Cold Lake, Alta.: 374, 400, 404
Canadian Forces Base Comox, B.C.: 391, 392
Canadian Forces Base Edmonton, Alta.: 392
Canadian Forces Base Esquimalt, B.C.: 374
Canadian Forces Base Gimli, Man.: 373
Canadian Forces Base Greenwood, N.S.: 375
Canadian Forces Base Kingston, Ont.: 375
Canadian Forces Base Lahr, Germany: 399
Canadian Forces Base Montreal, Que.: 126, 234, 287, 327, 358, 380, 384
Canadian Forces Base Moose Jaw, Sask.: 375
Canadian Forces Base North Bay, Ont.: 375
Canadian Forces Base Ottawa, Ont.: 375
Canadian Forces Base Penhold, Alta.: 386, 387
Canadian Forces Base Petawawa, Ont.: 375
Canadian Forces Base Portage la Prairie, Man.: 375
Canadian Forces Base Saint-Jean, Que.: 380
Canadian Forces Base Shearwater, N.S.: 376
Canadian Forces Base Shilo, Man.: 376
Canadian Forces Base Summerside, P.E.I.: 376
Canadian Forces Base Toronto, Ont.: 376
Canadian Forces Base Trenton, Ont.: 337, 362, 376, 390, 393
Canadian Forces Base Valcartier, Que.: 380
Canadian Forces Base Winnipeg, Man.: 376
Canadian Forces College, Toronto, Ont.: 383
Canadian Forces Dental Service: 286, 383
Canadian Forces Medical Service: 284, 356, 382
Canadian Forces Personnel Applied Research Unit: 3
Canadian Forces School of Administration and Logistics: 400
Canadian Forces Station Barrington, N.S.: 363, 394
Canadian Forces Station Beausejour, Man.: 394
Canadian Forces Station Chibougamau, Que.: 357, 381
Canadian Forces Station Falconbridge, Ont.: 394
Canadian Forces Station Gypsumville, Man.: 362, 393
Canadian Forces Station Holberg, B.C.: 355, 376
Canadian Forces Station Lac St. Denis, Que.: 395
Canadian Forces Station Moisie, Que.: 363, 365, 395
Canadian Forces Station St. John's, Nfld.: 86, 106, 249, 292, 336, 362, 392
Canadian Forces Station Senneterre, Que.: 362, 392
Canadian Forces Station Sioux Lookout, Ont.: 359, 362, 387, 393
Canadian Forces Station Sydney, N.S.: 360, 389

Trophée McKee: 348, 368, 406
Trophées de guerre: 171, 307
Troupes de réserve: 9, 13, 19, 372, 386, 390, 407

Unification des forces armées: 3, 8, 36, 42, 55, 372
Uniformes *voir* Tenue
Unités, services, branches et formations supérieures
    Australie
        462e Escadron: 350
    Canada
        Services et établissements interarmes
            Base des Forces canadiennes de Baden-Soellingen (Allemagne): 372
            Base des Forces canadiennes de Bagotville (Qué.): 319, 354, 373, 380
            Base des Forces canadiennes de Borden (Ont.): 374
            Base des Forces canadiennes de Calgary (Alb.): 374, 395
            Base des Forces canadiennes de Chatham (N.-B.): 374, 395
            Base des Forces canadiennes de Chilliwack (C.-B.): 374
            Base des Forces canadiennes de Cold Lake (Alb.): 374, 400, 404
            Base des Forces canadiennes de Comox (C.-B.): 391, 392
            Base des Forces canadiennes d'Edmonton (Alb.): 392
            Base des Forces canadiennes d'Esquimalt (C.-B.): 374
            Base des Forces canadiennes de Gimli (Man.): 373
            Base des Forces canadiennes de Greenwood (N.-É.): 375
            Base des Forces canadiennes de Kingston (Ont.): 375
            Base des Forces canadiennes de Lahr (Allemagne): 399
            Base des Forces canadiennes de Montréal (Qué.): 126, 234, 287, 327, 358, 380, 384
            Base des Forces canadiennes de Moose Jaw (Sask.): 375
            Base des Forces canadiennes de North Bay (Ont.): 375
            Base des Forces canadiennes d'Ottawa (Ont.): 375
            Base des Forces canadiennes de Penhold (Alb.): 386, 387
            Base des Forces canadiennes de Petawawa (Ont.): 375
            Base des Forces canadiennes de Portage-la-Prairie (Man.): 375
            Base des Forces canadiennes de Saint-Jean (Qué.): 380
            Base des Forces canadiennes de Shearwater (N.-É.): 376
            Base des Forces canadiennes de Shilo (Man.): 376
            Base des Forces canadiennes de Summerside (Î.-P.-É.): 376
            Base des Forces canadiennes de Toronto (Ont.): 376
            Base des Forces canadiennes de Trenton (Ont.): 337, 362, 376, 390, 393
            Base des Forces canadiennes de Valcartier (Qué.): 380
            Base des Forces canadiennes de Winnipeg (Man.): 376
            Branche de la logistique: 378

Canadian Forces Station Yorkton, Sask.: 395
Canadian Forces Technical School: 380
Canadian Joint Air Training Centre: 294, 363
Canadian Services Colleges: 99, 100, 102, 287, 358
    Collège militaire royal de Saint-Jean: 102, 104, 105, 107,
       287-289, 295, 358, 359, 383, 384, 397
    Royal Military College of Canada: 56, 77, 91, 93, 109,
       120, 123, 125, 145, 147, 203, 206, 222, 262, 266,
       267, 297-299, 320, 344-346, 367, 402, 404
    Royal Roads Military College: 83, 88, 105, 107, 290, 294,
       359, 363, 387, 395, 403
Communication Command: 393
Communications and Electronics Branch: 383
Defence Research Board: 35, 99, 100, 106, 284, 285, 292, 356,
    361, 379
Defence Research Establishment, Ottawa: 49, 380, 386
Defence Research Establishment, Suffield: 386
Defence Research Establishment, Valcartier: 379
Fort Churchill, Man.: 105, 290, 360
Land Electrical and Mechanical Engineering Branch: 387
Logistics Branch: 378
Mapping and Charting Establishment: 378
Operational Research and Analysis Establishment: 390, 397
Physical Education and Recreation Branch: 400
Research and Development Branch: 379
Naval forces
    Branches and services
       Medical Assistant Branch: 65, 73, 92, 109
       Royal Canadian Fleet Reserve: 78
       Royal Canadian Naval Reserve: 78, 79
       Royal Canadian Naval Volunteer Reserve: 65, 72, 79, 89,
          107, 396
       Royal Canadian Sea Cadets: 101
       Sick Berth Branch *see* Medical Assistant Branch
       University Naval Training Divisions: 101, 102, 111
       Women's Royal Canadian Naval Service: 79, 85, 95, 101
    Formations
       1st Canadian Minesweeping Squadron: 105
       3rd Canadian Escort Squadron: 110
       29th Canadian Motor Torpedo Boat Flotilla: 76
       Maritime Command Atlantic: 100, 102, 378
       Maritime Command Pacific: 101, 102

Branche de l'éducation physique et loisirs: 400
Branche des communications et de l'électronique: 383
Branche du génie électrique et mécanique terrestre: 387
Bureau de recherche de developpement: 379

Centre d'analyse et de recherche opérationnelle: 390, 397
Centre de recherches pour la Défense Ottawa: 49, 380, 386
Centre de recherches pour la Défense Suffield: 386
Centre de rechereche pour la Défense Valcartier: 379
Centre d'entraînement aérien interarmes: 294, 363
Centre d'essais techniques (Aérospatiale): 373
Collège des Forces canadiennes, Toronto (Ont.): 383
Collèges militaires canadiens: 99, 100, 102, 287, 358
     Collège militaire royal de Saint-Jean: 102, 104, 105, 107,
        287-289, 295, 358, 359, 383, 384, 397
     Collège militaire royal du Canada, 56, 77, 91, 93, 109, 120,
        123, 125, 145, 147, 203, 206, 222, 262, 266, 267,
        297-299, 320, 344-346, 367, 402, 404
     Royal Roads Military College: 83, 88, 105, 107, 290, 294,
        359, 363, 387, 395, 403
Commandement des communications: 393
Conseil de recherches pour la Défense: 35, 99, 100, 106, 284,
    285, 292, 356, 361, 379
École d'administration et de logistique des Forces canadiennes:
    400
École technique des Forces canadiennes: 380
Fort Churchill (Man.): 105, 290, 360
Service de cartographie: 378
Service de santé des Forces canadiennes: 284, 356, 382
Service dentaire des Forces canadiennes: 286, 383
Station des Forces canadiennes Barrington (N.-É.): 363, 394
Station des Forces canadiennes Beauséjour (Man.): 394
Station des Forces canadiennes Chibougamau (Qué.): 357, 381
Station des Forces canadiennes Falconbridge (Ont.): 394
Station des Forces canadiennes Gysumville (Man.): 362, 393
Station des Forces canadiennes Holberg (C.-B.): 355, 376
Station des Forces canadiennes Lac St. Denis (Qué.): 395
Station des Forces canadiennes Moisie (Qué.): 363, 365, 395
Station des Forces canadiennes St. John's (T.-N.): 86, 106, 249,
    292, 336, 362, 392
Station des Forces canadiennes Senneterre (Qué.): 362, 392
Station des Forces canadiennes Sioux Lookout (Ont.): 359, 362,
    387, 393
Station des Forces canadiennes Sydney (N.-É.): 360, 389
Station des Forces canadiennes Yorkton (Sask.): 395
Unité des recherches psychotechniques des Forces canadiennes: 3

Ships

CC 1: 67, 73
CC 2: 67, 73
CNAV Endeavour: 98
HMCS Agassiz: 89
HMCS Algonquin, second of name: 385
HMCS Annapolis, second of name: 103
HMCS Anticosti: 385
HMCS Assiniboine, second of name: 103
HMCS Athabaskan, first of name: 77
HMCS Athabaskan, second of name: 99, 100, 111
HMCS Athabaskan, third of name: 385
HMCS Bonaventure: 109, 405
HMCS Bras d'Or, second of name: 107, 395
HMCS Chaudière, second of name: 103
HMCS Cobourg: 76
HMCS Columbia, second of name: 103
HMCS Cormorant, second of name: 385
HMCS Crescent: 99, 100
HMCS Fraser, second of name: 103
HMCS Gatineau, second of name: 103
HMCS Grilse, second of name: 103
HMCS Haida: 77, 93, 98
HMCS Huron, second of name: 399
HMCS Iroquois, first of name: 96, 111, 407
HMCS Iroquois, second of name: 96, 111, 399, 407
HMCS Kootenay, second of name: 103
HMCS Labrador: 106
HMCS Mackenzie: 103
HMCS Magnificent: 99, 100
HMCS Margaree, second of name: 103
HMCS Moresby: 385
HMCS Nene: 85, 91
HMCS Nipigon, second of name: 108
HMCS Ojibwa: 103
HMCS Onondaga: 103
HMCS Ottawa, third of name: 103
HMCS Preserver, second of name: 385
HMCS Prince Robert: 87
HMCS Protecteur: 385
HMCS Provider, second of name: 104, 403
HMCS Qu'Appelle, second of name: 98, 104, 377
HMCS Quebec: 106
HMCS Restigouche, second of name: 104
HMCS Saguenay, second of name: 104

Forces navales
Services
Branche de l'assistance médicale: 65, 73, 92, 109
Cadets de la Marine royale du Canada: 101
Divisions universitaires d'entraînement naval: 101, 102, 111
Réserve de la Marine royale du Canada: 78, 79
Réserve volontaire de la Marine royale du Canada: 65, 72,
79, 89, 107, 396
Royal Canadian Fleet Reserve: 78
Service féminin de la Marine royale du Canada: 79, 85, 95,
101
Sick Berth Branch *voir* Branche de l'assistance médicale
Formations
1er Escadron canadien des dragueurs de mines: 105
3e Escadre d'escorte du Canada: 110
29e Flotille canadienne de vedettes-torpilleurs: 76
Commandement maritime, Atlantique: 100, 102, 378
Commandement maritime, Pacifique: 101, 102
Navires
CC1: 67, 73
CC2: 67, 73
L'Agassiz: 89
L'Algonquin, deuxième du nom: 385
L'Annapolis, deuxième du nom: 103
L'Anticosti: 385
L'Assiniboine, deuxième du nom: 103
L'Athabaskan, premier du nom: 77
L'Athabaskan, deuxième du nom: 99, 100, 111
L'Athabaskan, troisième du nom: 385
Le Bonaventure: 109, 405
Le Bras d'Or, deuxième du nom: 107, 395
Le Chaudière, deuxième du nom: 103
Le Cobourg: 76
Le Columbia, deuxième du nom: 103
Le Cormorant, deuxième du nom: 385
Le Crescent: 99, 100
Le Fraser, deuxième du nom: 103
Le Gatineau, deuxième du nom: 103
Le Grilse, deuxième du nom: 103
Le Haïda: 77, 93, 98
Le Huron, deuxième du nom: 399
L'Iroquois, premier du nom: 96, 111, 407
L'Iroquois, deuxième du nom: 96, 111, 399, 407
Le Kootenay, deuxième du nom: 103
Le Labrador: 106

HMCS St. Croix, second of name: 104
HMCS St. Laurent, second of name: 104
HMCS Saskatchewan, second of name: 104
HMCS Skeena, first of name: 87
HMCS Skeena, second of name: 104
HMCS Swansea: 89
HMCS Terra Nova: 104
HMCS Trentonian: 85
HMCS Uganda: 85, 95, 110 *see also* HMCS Quebec
HMCS Ville de Québec, second of name: 402
HMCS Warrior: 103
HMCS Yukon: 104
Bases and static units
Esquimalt Naval Base: 65, 66, 71, 75, 88, 96, 111, 371, 407
HMCS Cornwallis, N.S.: 85, 93, 105, 106
HMCS Discovery, Vancouver, B.C.: 75, 95, 96, 110, 111, 406, 407
HMCS Donnacona, Montreal, Que.: 85, 106, 390
HMCS Griffon, Thunder Bay, Ont.: 95, 110, 406
HMCS Montcalm, Quebec, Que.: 380
HMCS Naden, Esquimalt, B.C.: 85, 91, 106, 108, 398
HMCS Prevost, London, Ont.: 91, 108
HMCS Scotian, Halifax, N.S.: 86, 106, 392
HMCS Tecumseh, Calgary, Alta.: 82, 104
HMCS Unicorn, Saskatoon, Sask.: 78, 99, 377
HMCS Venture, Esquimalt, B.C.: 111
Halifax Naval Base: 66, 73, 75, 81, 90, 92, 94, 109, 392, 405
Naval Research Establishment, Halifax, N.S.: 88, 106
RCSCC Exeter, Lac La Biche, Alta.: 89, 107
RCSCC Rainbow, Victoria, B.C.: 102
Royal Naval College of Canada: 73, 93
Land forces
Branches and corps
Armour Branch: 371
Cadet Services of Canada: 164, 229, 231, 284, 285, 373
Canadian Forestry Corps: 158, 188, 197, 217, 278
Canadian Intelligence Corps: 131, 178, 187, 223, 241, 290, 393
Canadian Machine Gun Corps: 181, 194, 230, 233, 246
Canadian Officers' Training Corps: 164, 170, 212, 228, 273, 283, 302
Canadian Provost Corps: 233, 287
Canadian Women's Army Corps: 218, 225, 228, 231, 237, 241, 245, 251, 265, 273, 278

Le Mackenzie: 103

Le Magnificent: 99, 100

Le Margaree, deuxième du nom: 103

Le Moresby: 385

Le Nene: 85, 91

Le Nipigon, deuxième du nom: 108

L'Ojibwa: 103

L'Onondaga: 103

L'Ottawa, troisième du nom: 103

Le Preserver, deuxième du nom: 385

Le Prince Robert: 87

Le Protecteur: 385

Le Provider, deuxième du nom: 104, 403

Le Qu'Appelle, deuxième du nom: 98, 104, 377

Le Québec: 106

Le Restigouche, deuxième du nom: 104

Le Saguenay, deuxième du nom: 104

Le St-Laurent, deuxième du nom: 104

Le Ste-Croix, deuxième du nom: 104

Le Saskatchewan, deuxième du nom: 104

Le Skeena, premier du nom: 87

Le Skeena, deuxième du nom: 104

Le Swansea: 89

Le Terra Nova: 104

Le Trentonian: 85

L'Uganda: 85, 95, 110 *voir aussi* Le Québec

Le Ville de Québec, deuxième du nom: 402

Le Warrior: 103

Le Yukon: 104

NAMC Endeavour: 98

Bases et unités sédentaires

Base navale Esquimalt: 65, 66, 71, 75, 88, 96, 111, 371, 407

Base navale Halifax: 66, 73, 75, 81, 90, 92, 94, 109, 392, 405

École navale royale du Canada: 73, 93

Établissement canadien de recherches navales, Halifax (N.-É.): 88, 106

Le CCRMC Exeter, Lac La Biche (Alb.): 89, 107

Le CCRMC Rainbow, Victoria (C.-B.): 102

Le Cornwallis (N.-É.): 85, 93, 105, 106

Le Discovery, Vancouver (C.-B.): 75, 95, 96, 110, 111, 406, 407

Le Donnacona, Montréal (Qué.): 85, 106, 390

Le Griffon, Thunder Bay (Ont.): 95, 110, 406

Le Montcalm, Québec (Qué.): 380

Corps of Canadian Railway Troops: 190, 201, 215
Corps of Guides: 120
Infantry Branch: 118, 393
Logistics Branch: 378
Military Engineering Branch: 406
Royal Canadian Armoured Corps: 174, 205, 214, 237, 242,
        266, 267, 273, 276, 280, 286, 289, 290, 298, 299,
        371, 388
Royal Canadian Army Cadets: 34, 116, 120, 160, 223, 281,
        284, 285, 373
Royal Canadian Army Chaplain Corps: 209, 228, 271, 301
Royal Canadian Army Medical Corps: 120, 121, 128, 143,
        147, 160, 164, 195, 200, 206, 208, 216, 228, 229,
        237, 260, 266, 284, 289, 296, 373, 397
Royal Canadian Army Pay Corps: 118, 119, 147, 163, 164,
        228, 255, 266, 284, 299
Royal Canadian Army Service Corps: 115, 117, 119-121,
        147, 153, 162, 190, 203, 206, 215, 266, 276, 283,
        299, 303
Royal Canadian Army Veterinary Corps: 119, 120, 164, 264
Royal Canadian Corps of Signals: 141, 198, 258, 269, 296,
        299, 300
Royal Canadian Dental Corps: 190, 252, 261, 293
Royal Canadian Elecrical and Mechanical Engineers: 242,
        256, 290, 293, 296, 298, 387, 388, 393
Royal Canadian Engineers: 120, 129, 137, 174, 178, 190,
        191, 228, 238, 244, 252, 291, 293, 294
Royal Canadian Ordnance Corps: 120, 121, 145, 147, 173,
        204, 206, 264, 266, 283, 285, 298, 299
Royal Canadian Postal Corps: 6, 7, 147
Royal Regiment of Canadian Artillery: 91, 113, 114, 118,
        125, 126, 137-139, 141, 143, 147, 149, 156, 190,
        198, 200, 206, 219, 226, 241, 252, 260, 266, 280,
        283, 286, 293, 295, 296, 298, 358, 378, 398, 399
Supply, Transport and Barrack Service *see* Royal Canadian
        Army Service Corps
Veterans Guard of Canada: 236, 276
Formations
    1st Canadian Army: 220, 225, 239, 240, 270, 278
    Canadian Expeditionary Force: 164-167, 196, 200, 201,
        216, 227
    1st Canadian Contingent, CEF: 161, 165, 170, 203, 212
    2nd Canadian Contingent, CEF: 207, 212
    1st Canadian Corps: 258
    2nd Canadian Corps: 246

Le Naden, Equimault (C.-B.): 85, 91, 106, 108, 398

Le Prevost, London (Ont.): 91, 108

Le Scotian, Halifax (N.-É.): 86, 106, 392

Le Tecumseh, Calgary (Alb.): 82, 104

L'Unicorn, Saskatoon (Sask.): 78, 99, 377

Le Venture, Esquimalt (C.-B.): 111

Forces terrestres

Branches et corps

Branche de la logistique: 378

Branche de l'infanterie: 118, 393

Branche des blindés: 371

Branche du génie militaire: 406

Cadets royaux de l'Armée canadienne: 34, 116, 120, 160, 281, 284, 285, 373

Corps blindé royal canadien: 174, 205, 214, 237, 242, 266, 267, 273, 276, 280, 286, 289, 290, 298, 299, 371, 388

Corps canadien de la prévôté: 233, 287

Corps canadien des mitrailleuses: 181, 194, 230, 233, 246

Corps de Guides: 120

Corps de santé royal canadien: 120, 121, 128, 143, 147, 160, 164, 195, 200, 206, 208, 216, 228, 229, 237, 260, 266, 284, 289, 296, 299, 373, 397

Corps dentaire royal canadien: 190, 252, 261, 293

Corps des transmissions royal canadien: 141, 198, 258, 269, 296, 299, 300

Corps des troupes ferroviaires canadiennes: 190, 201, 215

Corps féminin de l'Armée canadienne: 218, 225, 228, 231, 237, 241, 245, 251, 265, 273, 278

Corps forestier canadien: 158, 188, 197, 217, 278

Corps postal royal canadien: 6, 7, 147

Corps royal canadien du génie électrique et mécanique: 242, 256, 290, 293, 296, 298, 387, 388, 393

Corps royal canadien des magasins militaires: 120, 121, 145, 147, 173, 204, 206, 264, 266, 283, 285, 298, 299

Corps royal de l'aumônerie de l'Armée canadienne: 209, 228, 271, 301

Corps vétérinaire royal canadien: 119, 120, 164, 264

Corps-école des officiers canadiens: 164, 170, 212, 228, 273, 283, 302

Garde des Vétérans du Canada: 236, 276

Génie royal canadien: 120, 129, 137, 174, 178, 190, 191, 228, 238, 244, 252, 291, 293, 294

3rd Canadian Contingent, CEF: 212
Canadian Corps: 170, 175, 181
Mobile Command: 393
1st Canadian Division: 162, 166, 175, 179, 225, 227, 259,
    282, 284
2nd Canadian Division: 203
3rd Canadian Division: 208
4th Canadian Division: 179, 193, 197, 265
5th Canadian Armoured Division: 250
1st Canadian Armoured Brigade: 260
1st Canadian Infantry Brigade: 162, 175, 225, 226
1st Special Service Force: 218, 223, 261
4th Canadian Armoured Brigade: 218, 223
4th Canadian Infantry Brigade: 173
4th Canadian Mechanized Brigade Group: 291, 389, 397
5th Canadian Infantry Brigade: 237
8th Canadian Infantry Brigade: 264
10th Canadian Infantry Brigade: 261
38th Reserve Brigade: 222
Alberta Field Force: 131, 137
Canadian Cavalry Brigade: 187, 197, 199
Canadian Siberian Expeditionary Force: 269, 274
Montreal Militia Brigade: 117
Nova Scotia Overseas Highland Brigade: 207
Yukon Field Force: 134
Units
Armoured and cavalry
    1st Battalion, Canadian Tank Corps: 211
    1st Canadian Armoured Carrier Regiment: 225
    1st Hussars: 148, 250, 293, 297, 388
    4th Princess Louise Dragoon Guards: 136, 190, 352
    8th Canadian Hussars (Princess Louise's): 129, 135,
        175, 189, 238, 251, 282, 289, 293, 301, 376,
        386
    9th Mississauga Horse: 200
    12e Régiment blindé du Canada 398, 406 *see also*
        Régiment de Trois-Rivières
    12th Manitoba Dragoons: 151, 211, 249, 264, 273,
        302
    14th Canadian Hussars: 278
    17th Duke of York's Royal Canadian Hussars: 150,
        209, 261, 271
    26th Stanstead Dragoons: 117, 140
    31st British Columbia Horse: 132, 179
    British Columbia Dragoons: 147, 205, 266, 299

442

Intendance royale canadienne: 115, 117, 119-121, 147, 153, 162, 190, 203, 206, 215, 266, 276, 283, 299, 303

Régiment royal de l'Artillerie canadienne: 91, 113, 114, 118, 125, 126, 137-139, 141, 143, 147, 149, 156, 190, 198, 200, 206, 219, 226, 241, 252, 260, 266, 280, 283, 286, 293, 295, 296, 298, 358, 378, 398, 399

Service canadien du renseignement: 131, 178, 187, 223, 241, 290, 393

Service des cadets du Canada: 164, 229, 231, 284, 285, 373

Trésorerie royale canadienne: 118, 119, 147, 163, 164, 228, 255, 266, 284, 299

Formations

1ère Armée canadienne: 220, 225, 239, 240, 270, 278

Corps expéditionnaire canadien: 164-167, 196, 200, 201, 216, 227

1er Contingent canadien, CEC: 161, 165, 170, 203, 212

1er Corps canadien: 258

2e Contingent canadien, CEC: 207, 212

2e Corps canadien: 246

3e Contingent canadien, CEC: 212

Corps canadien: 170, 181, 175

Force mobile: 393

1ère Division canadienne: 162, 166, 175, 179, 225, 227, 259, 282, 284

2e Division canadienne: 203

3e Division canadienne: 208

4e Division canadienne: 179, 193, 197, 265

5e Division blindée canadienne: 250

1ère Brigade blindée canadienne: 260

1ère Brigade d'infanterie canadienne: 162, 175, 225, 226

1ère Force d'opérations spéciales: 218, 223, 261

4e Brigade blindée canadienne: 218, 223

4e Brigade d'infanterie canadienne: 173

4e Groupe-brigade mécanisé du Canada: 291, 389, 397

5e Brigade d'infanterie canadienne: 237

8e Brigade d'infanterie canadienne: 264

10e Brigade d'infanterie canadienne: 261

38e Brigade de réserve: 222

Brigade de cavalerie canadienne: 187, 197, 199

Brigade de milice de Montréal: 117

Brigade Highland de la Nouvelle-Écosse (Service outre-mer): 207

Corps expéditionnaire canadien de Sibérie: 269, 274

British Columbia Regiment (Duke of Connaught's Own): 134, 148, 188, 198, 208, 249, 269, 292, 300, 391 *see also* 6th Regiment, The Duke of Connaught's Own Rifles

Elgin Regiment: 129, 179, 238, 289, 386

Fort Garry Horse: 148, 165, 207, 243, 268, 275, 281, 300, 404

Governor General's Horse Guards: 127, 130, 140, 245, 251, 292, 293

Halifax Rifles: 145, 147, 204, 206, 263, 267, 298, 299 *see also* 63rd Halifax Battalion of Rifles

King's Own Calgary Regiment: 224, 256, 276

Lord Strathcona's Horse (Royal Canadians): 129, 130, 132, 152, 175, 180, 194, 210, 214, 216, 238, 243, 255, 256, 272, 275, 291, 294, 301, 302, 389, 395, 396, 405, 407

Ontario Regiment: 148, 207, 268, 269, 297, 299

Queen's Own Canadian Hussars: 130

Queen's York Rangers (1st American Regiment): 115, 116, 159, 160, 222, 223, 279, 281, 373 *see also* 12th Regiment, York Rangers

Régiment de Hull: 263, 298, 402

Régiment de Trois-Rivières: 133, 182, 246, 253, 292, 391 *see also* 12e Régiment blindé du Canada

Royal Canadian Dragoons: 121, 132, 134, 154, 178, 186, 191, 217, 242, 248, 266, 270, 279, 292, 301, 303, 391, 405

Sherbrooke Hussars: 137, 190, 252, 293, 297

Sherbrooke Regiment *see* Sherbrooke Hussars

South Alberta Light Horse: 256, 300

Windsor Regiment: 303

Artillery

Canadian Reserve Artillery: 157

Royal Canadian Horse Artillery: 141, 198, 258, 295, 398

4th Brigade, Canadian Field Artillery: 194

16th Brigade, Canadian Field Artillery: 199, 259

1st Anti-Tank Regiment: 250, 258

1st Medium Regiment: 276

1st Regiment, Royal Canadian Horse Artillery: 147, 206, 266, 299, 403

1st Survey Regiment: 244

2nd Field Regiment: 250

2nd Heavy Anti-Aircraft Regiment: 278

2nd Medium Regiment: 261

Corps expéditionnaire du Yukon: 134
Force de campagne de l'Alberta: 131, 137
Unités
Unités blindées et cavalerie
1er Bataillon, Corps des chars d'assaut canadien: 211
1st Hussars: 148, 250, 293, 297, 388
1er Régiment canadien de transport blindé: 225
4th Princess Louise Dragoon Guards: 136, 190, 352
8th Canadian Hussars (Princess Louise's): 129, 135, 175, 189, 238, 251, 282, 289, 293, 301, 376, 386
9th Mississauga Horse: 200
12e Régiment blindé du Canada: 398, 406 *voir aussi* Régiment de Trois-Rivières
12th Manitoba Dragoons: 151, 211, 249, 264, 273, 302
14th Canadian Hussars: 278
17th Duke of York's Royal Canadian Hussars: 150, 209, 261, 271
26th Stanstead Dragoons: 117, 140
31st British Columbia Horse: 132, 179
British Colombia Dragoons: 147, 205, 266, 299
British Columbia Regiment (Duke of Connaught's Own): 134, 148, 188, 198, 208, 249, 269, 292, 300, 391 *voir aussi* 6e Régiment, The Duke of Connaught's Own Rifles
Elgin Regiment: 129, 179, 238, 289, 386
Fort Garry Horse: 148, 165, 207, 243, 268, 275, 281, 300, 404
Governor General's Horse Guards: 127, 130, 140, 245, 251, 292, 293
Halifax Rifles: 145, 147, 204, 206, 263, 267, 298, 299 *voir aussi* 63e Bataillon de fusiliers, Halifax
King's Own Calgary Regiment: 224, 256, 276
Lord Strathcona's Horse (Royal Canadians): 129, 130, 132, 152, 175, 180, 194, 210, 214, 216, 238, 243, 255, 256, 272, 275, 291, 294, 301, 302, 389, 395, 396, 405, 407
Ontario Regiment: 148, 207, 268, 269, 297, 299
Queen's Own Canadian Hussars: 130
Queen's York Rangers (1st American Regiment): 115, 116, 159, 160, 222, 223, 279, 281, 373 *voir aussi* 12e Régiment, York Rangers
Régiment de Hull: 263, 298, 402
Régiment de Trois-Rivières: 133, 182, 246, 253, 292, 391 *voir aussi* 12e Régiment blindé canadien

3rd Light Anti-Aircraft Regiment: 250

3rd Regiment, Royal Canadian Horse Artillery: 282, 378

4th Medium Regiment: 244, 245

5e Régiment d'artillerie légère: 128, 383, 391, 397

5th Anti-Tank Regiment: 268

5th British Columbia Regiment: 146, 205, 264

5th Light Anti-Aircraft Regiment: 260

6th Anti-Tank Regiment: 250

6th Field Regiment: 128, 173, 235, 253, 288

7th Anti-Tank Regiment: 250

7th Medium Regiment: 250, 255

7th Toronto Regiment: 117, 161, 224, 282

8th Light Anti-Aircraft Regiment: 250

11th Field Regiment: 127, 172, 234, 288

12th Field Regiment: 220

13th Field Regiment: 219

14th Field Regiment: 267

15th Field Regiment: 270

17th Field Regiment: 250, 265

19th Army Field Regiment: 226

23rd Field Regiment: 269, 274, 275

30th Field Artillery Regiment: 137, 190, 252, 293

New Brunswick Regiment, Canadian Artillery: 114

"A" Battery: 138

1st Heavy Battery: 190

1st Siege Battery: 178

2nd Heavy Battery: 155

3rd (Montreal) Field Battery: 127

4th Anti-Tank Battery: 266

4th Field Battery: 182

6th Field Battery: 179

6th Siege Battery: 186

7th Siege Battery: 194

10th Siege Battery: 173

11th Field Battery: 179

13th Field Battery: 140, 196, 208, 256, 295, 397

18th Field Battery: 202

23rd Howitzer Battery: 150, 195, 213

26th Field Battery: 213

27th Field Battery: 196

39th Field Battery: 189, 251

43rd Howitzer Battery: 180, 191

55th Field Battery: 193

57th Battery: 128, 173, 235, 288

Royal Canadian Dragoons: 121, 132, 134, 154, 178,
    186, 191, 217, 242, 248, 266, 270, 279, 292,
    301, 303, 391, 405
Sherbrooke Hussars: 137, 190, 252, 293, 297
Sherbrooke Regiment *voir* Sherbrooke Hussars
South Alberta Light Horse: 256, 300
Windsor Regiment: 303
Artillerie
    Artillerie à cheval royale canadienne: 141, 198, 258,
        295, 398
    Artillerie canadienne de réserve: 157
    4e Brigade, artillerie de campagne canadienne: 194
    16e Brigade, artillerie de campagne canadienne: 199,
        259
    1er Régiment d'artillerie antichars: 250, 258
    1er Régiment, artillerie à cheval royale canadienne:
        147, 206, 266, 299, 403
    1er Régiment d'artillerie moyenne: 276
    1er Régiment du service topographique: 244
    2e Régiment d'artillerie moyenne: 261
    2e Régiment de campagne: 250
    2e Régiment de DCA (Artillerie lourde): 278
    3e Régiment, artillerie à cheval royale canadienne:
        282, 378
    3e Régiment de DCA (Artillerie légère): 250
    4e Régiment d'artillerie moyenne: 244, 245
    5e Régiment (Colombie-Britannique): 146, 205, 264
    5e Régiment d'artillerie antichars: 268
    5e Régiment d'artillerie légère: 128, 383, 391, 397
    5e Régiment de DCA (Artillerie légère): 260
    6e Régiment d'artillerie antichars: 250
    6e Régiment de campagne: 128, 173, 235, 253, 288
    7e Régiment d'artillerie antichars: 250
    7e Régiment d'artillerie moyenne: 250, 255
    7e Régiment de Toronto: 117, 161, 224, 282
    8e Régiment de DCA (Artillerie légère): 250
    11e Régiment de campagne: 127, 172, 234, 288
    12e Régiment de campagne: 220
    13e Régiment de campagne: 219
    14e Régiment de campagne: 267
    15e Régiment de campagne: 270
    17e Régiment de campagne: 250, 265
    19e Régiment d'armée de campagne: 226
    23e Régiment de campagne: 269, 274, 275
    30e Régiment de campagne: 137, 190, 252, 293

60th Field Battery: 208
61st Battery: 176
65th Anti-Tank Battery: 250
66th Field Battery: 210
67th Field Battery: 199, 259
68th Field Battery: 199, 259
69th Light Anti-Aircraft Battery: 272
London Field Battery: 148
2nd Divisional Ammunition Column: 173
Engineers, railway troops and construction:
    1st Battalion, Canadian Railway Troops: 215
    1st Combat Engineer Regiment: 378
    1 Construction Engineering Unit: 329, 359, 386
    No. 1 Railway Operating Group: 257
    2nd Battalion: 226
    2nd Battalion, Canadian Railway Troops: 190
    2nd Construction Battalion: 206
    2nd Pioneer Battalion: 155
    6th Battalion: 215
    7th Battalion, Canadian Railway Troops: 201
    67th Pioneer Battalion: 173
    1st Field (Air) Survey Company: 226
    3rd Field (Reproduction) Survey Company: 226
    4th Field Survey Company: 226
    6th Field Company: 178, 215, 242
    8th Field Squadron: 253
    10th Field Company: 213
    23rd Field Company: 226
Signals
    1st Canadian Special Wireless Group: 236
    2nd Armoured Brigade Signals: 263
    4th Divisional Signal Company: 216
Infantry
    Militia battalions, 1867-1900
        2nd Battalion, Queen's Own Rifles of Canada:
            115, 122, 135, 136, 149
        6th Battalion Fusiliers: 134
        7th Battalion Fusiliers: 126, 138, 150, 170, 233
        9th Battalion, Voltigeurs de Québec: 114, 153
        10th Battalion, Royal Grenadiers: 128
        13th Battalion of Infantry: 129, 142, 148, 150
        17th Lévis Battalion of Infantry: 130
        26th Middlesex Battalion of Light Infantry: 113
        27th Lambton Battalion of Infantry: 136

New Brunswick Regiment, Artillerie canadienne: 114
Batterie "A": 138
1ère Batterie de siège: 178
1ère Batterie lourde: 190
2e Batterie lourde: 155
3e Batterie de campagne (Montréal): 127
4e Batterie antichars: 266
4e Batterie de campagne: 182
6e Batterie de campagne: 179
6e Batterie de siège: 186
7e Batterie de siège: 194
10e Batterie de siège: 173
11e Batterie de campagne: 179
13e Batterie de campagne: 140, 196, 208, 256, 295, 397
18e Batterie de campagne: 202
23e Batterie d'obusiers: 150, 195, 213
26e Batterie de campagne: 213
27e Batterie de campagne: 196
39e Batterie de campagne: 189, 251
43e Batterie d'obusiers: 180, 191
55e Batterie de campagne: 193
57e Batterie: 128, 173, 235, 288
60e Batterie de campagne: 208
61e Batterie: 176
65e Batterie antichars: 250
66e Batterie de campagne: 210
67e Batterie de campagne: 199, 259
68e Batterie de campagne: 199, 259
69e Batterie de DCA (Artillerie légère): 272
London Field Battery: 148
2e Section divisionnaire des munitions: 173
Le génie, les troupes ferroviaires et la construction
1er Bataillon, troupes ferroviaires du Canada: 215
1er Régiment de génie: 378
No 1 Groupe de sapeurs de chemin de fer: 257
1re Unité du génie construction: 329, 359, 386
2e Bataillon: 226
2e Bataillon de construction: 206
2e Bataillon de pionniers: 155
2e Bataillon, troupes ferroviaires du Canada: 190
6e Bataillon: 215
7e Bataillon, troupes ferroviaires du Canada: 201
67e Bataillon de pionniers: 173
1ère Compagnie du service topographique de campagne (aérienne): 226

38th Battalion Dufferin Rifles of Canada: 148, 150

43rd Ottawa and Carleton Battalion of Rifles: 149

48th Battalion Highlanders: 114, 117, 132

62nd Saint John Fusiliers: 151

63rd Halifax Battalion of Rifles: 131

65th Battalion, Mont-Royal Rifles: 129

Halifax Provisional Battalion: 148

Infantry School Corps: 149

Militia regiments, 1900-1920

1st Regiment, Prince of Wales' Fusiliers: 127, 149

2nd Regiment, Queen's Own Rifles of Canada: 128, 131, 143

5th Regiment, Royal Highlanders of Canada: 129, 149, 222

6th Regiment, The Duke of Connaught's Own Rifles: 138

7th Regiment, Fusiliers: 153, 215

10th Regiment, Royal Grenadiers: 128

12th Regiment, York Rangers: 136

21st Regiment, Essex Fusiliers: 113

43rd Regiment, The Duke of Cornwall's Own Rifles: 127

55th Regiment, Irish-Canadian Rangers: 190

58th Regiment, Westmount Rifles: 179

65e Régiment, Carabiniers Mont-Royal: 127

79th Regiment, Cameron Highlanders of Canada: 209

90th Regiment, Winnipeg Rifles: 117, 127, 197

91st Regiment, Canadian Highlanders: 116, 160

97th Regiment, Algonquin Rifles: 153

101st Regiment, Edmonton Fusiliers: 137

Canadian Expeditionary Force battalions and regiments, 1914-1918

1st Battalion: 194

2nd Battalion: 199

3rd Battalion: 156, 159, 222

4th Battalion: 180

7th Battalion: 189, 193, 198, 205

8th Battalion: 159, 216

10th Battalion: 175, 188

13th Battalion: 178, 196

14th Battalion: 159, 178, 179, 242

3e Compagnie du service topographique de campagne (Reproduction): 226

4e Compagnie du service topographique de campagne: 226

6e Compagnie de campagne: 178, 215, 242

8e Escadron de campagne: 253

10e Compagnie de campagne: 213

23e Compagnie de campagne: 226

Transmissions et communications

1er Groupe spécial de TSF: 236

2e Brigade blindée de transmissions: 263

4e Compagnie divisionnaire des transmissions: 216

Infanterie

Bataillons de la Milice, 1867-1900

2e Bataillon, Queen's Own Rifles of Canada: 115, 135, 136, 149

6e Bataillon de fusiliers: 134

7e Bataillon de fusiliers: 126, 138, 150, 170, 233

9e Bataillon, Voltigeurs de Québec: 114, 153

10e Bataillon, Royal Grenadiers: 128

13e Bataillon d'infanterie: 129, 142, 148, 150

17e Bataillon d'infanterie de Lévis: 130

26e Bataillon d'infanterie légère Middlesex: 113

27e Bataillon d'infanterie de Lambton: 136

38e Bataillon, Dufferin Rifles of Canada: 148, 150

43e Bataillon de fusiliers, Ottawa et Carleton: 149

48e Bataillon Highlanders: 114, 117, 132

62e Bataillon, St. John Fusiliers: 151

63e Bataillon de fusiliers, Halifax: 131

65e Bataillon, Fusiliers Mont-Royal: 129

Bataillon provisoire de Halifax: 148

Corps-école d'infanterie: 149

Régiments de la Milice, 1900-1920

1er Régiment, Prince of Wales' Fusiliers: 127, 149

2e Régiment, Queen's Own Rifles of Canada: 128, 131, 143

5e Régiment, Royal Highlanders of Canada: 129, 149, 222

6e Régiment, The Duke of Connaught's Own Rifles: 138

7e Régiment de fusiliers: 153, 215

16th Battalion: 159, 204, 214
20th Battalion: 174
21st Battalion: 188
22nd Battalion: 155, 172-174, 180, 203
24th Battalion: 159, 179, 214
25th Battalion: 193, 194
26th Battalion: 181, 194
27th Battalion: 211
28th Battalion: 161, 188
29th Battalion: 173, 195, 214
31st Battalion: 208
41st Battalion: 179
42nd Battalion: 212
44th Battalion: 206
46th Battalion: 195
47th Battalion: 179
49th Battalion: 179, 196
50th Battalion: 209, 215
52nd Battalion: 159, 198
54th Battalion: 156
60th Battalion: 208
64th Battalion: 195, 213
72nd Battalion: 149, 198, 209
73rd Battalion: 208
75th Battalion: 207, 208
76th Battalion: 158
77th Battalion: 188, 207
78th Battalion: 207
85th Battalion: 188, 193, 207
87th Battalion: 196
101st Battalion: 201
102nd Battalion: 181
104th Battalion: 191
106th Battalion: 207
116th Battalion: 155, 201
120th Battalion: 200
127th Battalion: 190
131st Battalion: 192
137th Battalion: 156
140th Battalion: 177
144th Battalion: 197, 198
158th Battalion: 114, 157
160th Battalion: 190
161st Battalion: 199
163rd Battalion: 209

10e Régiment, Royal Grenadiers: 128
12e Régiment, York Rangers: 136
21e Régiment, Essex Fusiliers: 113
43e Régiment, The Duke of Cornwall's Own
  Rifles: 127
55e Régiment, Irish-Canadian Rangers: 190
58e Régiment, Westmount Rifles: 179
65e Régiment, Carabiniers Mont-Royal: 127
79e Régiment, Cameron Highlanders of
  Canada: 209
90e Régiment, Winnipeg Rifles: 117, 127, 197
91e Régiment, Canadian Highlanders: 116, 160
97e Régiment, Algonquin Rifles: 153
101e Régiment, Edmonton Fusiliers: 137
Bataillons et régiments du Corps expéditionnaire
  canadien
1er Bataillon: 194
2e Bataillon: 199
3e Bataillon: 156, 159, 222
4e Bataillon: 180
7e Bataillon: 189, 193, 198, 205
8e Bataillon: 159, 216
10e Bataillon: 175, 188
13e Bataillon: 178, 196
14e Bataillon: 159 178, 179, 242
16e Bataillon: 159, 204, 214
20e Bataillon: 174
21e Bataillon: 188
22e Bataillon: 155, 172-174, 180, 203
24e Bataillon: 159, 179, 214
25e Bataillon: 193, 194
26e Bataillon: 181, 194
27e Bataillon: 211
28e Bataillon: 161, 188
29e Bataillon: 173, 195, 214
31e Bataillon: 208
41e Bataillon: 179
42e Bataillon: 212
44e Bataillon: 206
46e Bataillon: 195
47e Bataillon: 179
49e Bataillon: 179, 196
50e Bataillon: 209, 215
52e Bataillon: 159, 198
54e Bataillon: 156

165th Battalion: 155
193rd Battalion: 207
196th Battalion: 214
199th Battalion: 177, 190
207th Battalion: 202
219th Battalion: 207
226th Battalion: 213
231st Battalion: 209
241st Battalion: 187
2nd Canadian Mounted Rifles: 191
4th Canadian Mounted Rifles: 155, 157
5th Canadian Mounted Rifles: 167, 175
2nd Quebec Regiment: 175
Canadian Corps Cyclist Battalion: 178
Infantry regiments since 1920
1st Canadian Parachute Battalion: 248, 260,
    278, 292
48th Highlanders of Canada: 114, 157, 161,
    219, 220, 224, 280, 297, 372, 376 *see
    also* 48th Battalion Highlanders
Algonquin Regiment: 234 *see also* 97th
    Regiment, Algonquin Rifles
Argyll and Sutherland Highlanders of Canada
    (Princess Louise's): 116, 160, 223, 252,
    293, 297 *see also* 91st Regiment,
    Canadian Highlanders
Black Watch (Royal Highland Regiment) of
    Canada: 136, 147, 189, 206, 222, 236,
    252, 262, 283, 293 *see also* 5th
    Regiment, Royal Highlanders of Canada
Brockville Rifles: 153, 215, 276, 303
Calgary Highlanders: 220, 241, 290
Cameron Highlanders of Ottawa: 116, 161,
    224, 265, 297 *see also* 43rd Ottawa and
    Carleton Battalion of Rifles *and* 43rd
    Regiment, Duke of Cornwall's Own
    Rifles
Canadian Airborne Regiment: 248, 288, 292,
    374, 388, 389, 396 *see also* 1st Canadian
    Parachute Battalion
Canadian Fusiliers (City of London Regiment):
    126, 170, 233 *see also* 7th Battalion
    Fusiliers *and* 7th Regiment, Fusiliers

60e Bataillon: 208
64e Bataillon: 195, 213
72e Bataillon: 194, 198, 209
73e Bataillon: 208
75e Bataillon: 207, 208
76e Bataillon: 158
77e Bataillon: 188, 207
78e Bataillon: 207
85e Bataillon: 188, 193, 207
87e Bataillon: 196
101e Bataillon: 201
102e Bataillon: 181
104e Bataillon: 191
106e Bataillon: 207
116e Bataillon: 155, 201
120e Bataillon: 200
127e Bataillon: 190
131e Bataillon: 192
137e Bataillon: 156
140e Bataillon: 177
144e Bataillon: 197, 198
158e Bataillon: 114, 157
160e Bataillon: 190
161e Bataillon: 199
163e Bataillon: 209
165e Bataillon: 155
193e Bataillon: 207
196e Bataillon: 214
199e Bataillon: 177, 190
207e Bataillon: 202
219e Bataillon: 207
226e Bataillon: 213
231e Bataillon: 209
241e Bataillon: 187
2e Bataillon, Canadian Mounted Rifles: 191
4e Bataillon, Canadian Mounted Rifles: 155, 157
5e Bataillon, Canadian Mounted Rifles: 167, 175
2e Régiment du Québec: 175
Bataillon cycliste du Corps canadien: 178
Régiments d'infanterie depuis 1920
1er Bataillon de parachutistes canadiens: 248, 260, 278, 292
48th Highlanders of Canada: 114, 157, 161, 219, 220, 224, 280, 297, 372, 376 *voir aussi* 48e Bataillon Highlanders

Canadian Grenadier Guards: 121, 131, 159, 165, 177, 196, 240, 290, 297 *see also* 1st Regiment, Prince of Wales' Fusiliers *and* 6th Battalion Fusiliers

Canadian Guards: 283, 286, 297

Canadian Scottish Regiment (Princess Mary's): 126, 159, 161, 170, 204, 222, 225, 233, 242, 266, 281, 287, 299

Cape Breton Highlanders: 259

Carleton and York Regiment: 262, 274 *see also* 62nd St. John Fusiliers

Durham Regiment: 128, 172, 235 *see also* Hastings and Prince Edward Regiment

Essex Scottish: 257, 268 *see also* 21st Regiment, Essex Fusiliers

Fusiliers de Sherbrooke: 146, 205, 264, 298, 403

Fusiliers du St-Laurent: 131, 138, 177, 192, 239, 254, 289, 387, 388

Fusiliers Mont-Royal: 126, 155, 172, 234, 287, 387 *see also* 65th Battalion, Mont-Royal Rifles and 65e Régiment, Carabiniers Mont-Royal

Governor General's Foot Guards: 114, 133, 145, 157, 181, 204, 220, 245, 400

Grey and Simcoe Foresters: 116, 148, 152, 160, 206, 212, 223, 267, 273, 281, 299, 302, 373, 404, 406

Hastings and Prince Edward Regiment: 153, 215, 222, 234, 259, 269, 277, 287, 300, 303, 402, 407 *see also* Durham Regiment

Highland Light Infantry of Canada: 219, 269, 297

Irish Regiment of Canada: 244, 252, 265, 278

Lake Superior Scottish Regiment: 117, 150, 161, 209, 255, 271, 282, 301, 377

Lincoln and Welland Regiment: 146, 205, 249, 265

Lorne Scots (Peel, Dufferin and Halton Regiment): 115, 138, 159, 193, 222, 255, 283, 294

Loyal Edmonton Regiment: 210, 251, 255, 262, 271, 297 *see also* 101st Regiment, Edmonton Fusiliers

North Nova Scotia Highlanders: 221, 243

Algonquin Regiment: 234 *voir aussi* 97e Régiment, Algonquin Rifles

Argyll and Sutherland Highlanders of Canada (Princess Louise's): 116, 160, 223, 252, 293, 297 *voir aussi* 91e Régiment, Canadian Highlanders

Black Watch (Royal Highland Regiment) of Canada: 136, 147, 189, 206, 222, 236, 252, 262, 283, 293 *voir aussi* 5e Régiment, Royal Highlanders of Canada

Brockville Rifles: 153, 215, 276, 303

Calgary Highlanders: 220, 241, 290

Cameron Highlanders of Ottawa: 116, 161, 224, 265, 297 *voir aussi* 43e Bataillon de fusiliers, Ottawa et Carleton *et* 43e Régiment, Duke of Cornwall's Own Rifles

Canadian Fusiliers (City of London Regiment): 126, 170, 233 *voir aussi* 7e Bataillon de fusiliers *et* 7e Régiment de fusiliers

Canadian Grenadier Guards: 121, 131, 159, 165, 177, 196, 240, 290, 297 *voir aussi* 1er Régiment, Prince of Wales' Fusiliers *et* 6e Bataillon de fusiliers

Canadian Guards: 283, 286, 297

Canadian Scottish Regiment (Princess Mary's): 126, 159, 161, 170, 204, 222, 225, 233, 242, 266, 281, 287, 299

Cape Breton Highlanders: 259

Carleton and York Regiment: 262, 274 *voir aussi* 62e Bataillon, St. John Fusiliers

Durham Regiment: 128, 172, 235 *voir aussi* Hastings and Prince Edward Regiment

Essex Scottish: 257, 268 *voir aussi* 21e Régiment, Essex Fusiliers

Fusiliers de Sherbrooke: 146, 205, 264, 298, 403

Fusiliers du St-Laurent: 131, 138, 177, 192, 239, 254, 289, 387, 388

Fusiliers Mont-Royal: 126, 155, 172, 234, 287, 387 *voir aussi* 65e Bataillon, Fusiliers Mont-Royal *et* 65e Régiment, Carabiniers Mont-Royal

Governor General's Foot Guards: 114, 133, 145, 157, 181, 204, 220, 245, 400

North Saskatchewan Regiment: 401 *see also*
Saskatoon Light Infantry
North Shore (New Brunswick) Regiment: 115,
158, 221, 281
Nova Scotia Highlanders *see* Cape Breton
Highlanders *and* North Nova Scotia
Highlanders
Oxford Rifles: 128, 141, 173, 198, 237, 258,
288, 295, 385
Perth Regiment: 128, 137, 173, 191, 237, 252,
288, 293, 297, 385
Princess Louise Fusiliers: 402
Princess of Wales' Own Regiment: 126, 139,
172, 195, 234, 256, 288, 294
Princess Patricia's Canadian Light Infantry:
188, 193, 199, 202-204, 215, 243, 251,
261, 271, 278, 283, 290, 293, 296, 303,
378, 400, 401, 404, 406
Queen's Own Cameron Highlanders of Canada:
148, 152, 208, 213, 263, 265, 269, 274,
298, 302, 406 *see also* 79th Regiment,
Cameron Highlanders of Canada
Queen's Own Rifles of Canada: 113, 115, 117,
122, 123, 131, 135, 136, 143, 145, 149,
156, 162, 177, 201, 203, 219, 226, 260,
261, 263, 280, 283, 297, 298, 401 *see
also* 2nd Battalion, Queen's Own Rifles
of Canada *and* 2nd Regiment, Queen's
Own Rifles of Canada
Régiment de la Chaudière: 117, 126, 162, 225,
234, 265, 282, 287, 384, 403
Régiment de Lévis: 140, 196, 257, 295 *see
also* 17th Lévis Battalion of Infantry
Régiment de Maisonneuve: 133, 155, 181, 243,
245, 257, 292, 298, 390, 403
Régiment de Montmagny: 138, 192, 254
Régiment du Saguenay: 403
Regina Rifle Regiment: 255
Rocky Mountain Rangers: 146, 152, 205, 214,
242, 265, 275, 403
Royal Canadian Regiment: 114, 116, 132, 135,
136, 149, 157, 178, 179, 220, 236, 242,
244, 271, 280, 288, 290, 297, 298, 378,
385, 394, 401 *see also* Infantry School
Corps

Grey and Simcoe Foresters: 116, 148, 152, 160, 206, 212, 223, 267, 273, 281, 299, 302, 373, 404, 406

Hastings and Prince Edward Regiment: 153, 215, 222, 234, 259, 269, 277, 287, 300, 303, 402, 407 *voir aussi* Durham Regiment

Highland Light Infantry of Canada: 219, 269, 297

Irish Regiment of Canada: 244, 252, 265, 278

Lake Superior Scottish Regiment: 117, 150, 161, 209, 255, 271, 282, 301, 377

Lincoln and Welland Regiment: 146, 205, 249, 265

Lorne Scots (Peel, Dufferin and Halton, Regiment): 115, 138, 159, 193, 222, 255, 283, 294

Loyal Edmonton Regiment: 210, 251, 255, 262, 271, 297 *voir aussi* 101e Régiment, Edmonton Fusiliers

North Nova Scotia Highlanders: 221, 243

North Saskatchewan Regiment: 401 *voir aussi* Saskatoon Light Infantry

North Shore (New Brunswick) Regiment: 115, 158, 221, 281

Nova Scotia Highlanders *voir* Cape Breton Highlanders *et* North Nova Scotia Highlanders

Oxford Rifles: 128, 141, 173, 198, 237, 258, 288, 295, 385

Perth Regiment: 128, 137, 173, 191, 237, 252, 288, 293, 297, 385

Princess Louise Fusiliers: 402

Princess of Wales' Own Regiment: 126, 139, 172, 195, 234, 256, 288, 294

Princess Patricia's Canadian Light Infantry: 188, 193, 199, 202-204, 215, 243, 251, 261, 271, 278, 283, 290, 293, 296, 303, 378, 400, 401, 404, 406

Queen's Own Cameron Highlanders of Canada: 148, 152, 208, 213, 263, 265, 269, 274, 298, 302, 406 *voir aussi* 79e Régiment, Cameron Highlanders of Canada

Royal Hamilton Light Infantry (Wentworth Regiment): 134, 186, 248, 292, 297, 391 *see also* 13th Battalion of Infantry

Royal Montreal Regiment: 159, 178, 242 *see also* 58th Regiment, Westmount Rifles

Royal Newfoundland Regiment: 165, 174, 180, 200, 202

Royal Regiment of Canada: 115, 133, 159, 181, 222, 238, 245, 262, 281, 291 *see also* 10th Battalion Royal Grenadiers; 10th Regiment, Royal Grenadiers *and* Toronto Regiment

Royal Rifles of Canada: 144, 147, 202, 206, 224, 244, 261, 267, 296

Royal 22e Régiment: 155, 172-174, 180, 203, 218, 221, 238, 241, 253, 262, 267, 280, 287-290, 294, 299, 371, 372, 381, 384, 386, 388, 389, 394, 397, 402-404

Royal Winnipeg Rifles: 117, 151, 154, 162, 211, 216, 226, 273, 278, 283, 302, 406 *see also* 90th Regiment, Winnipeg Rifles

Saskatoon Light Infantry: 242, 258, 262, 276, 401 *see also* North Saskatchewan Regiment

Seaforth Highlanders of Canada: 198, 252, 266, 299

South Saskatchewan Regiment: 223, 262, 270

Stormont, Dundas and Glengarry Highlanders: 115, 159, 221, 272, 281, 372

Toronto Regiment: 156, 159, 222 *see also* Royal Regiment of Canada

Toronto Scottish Regiment: 162, 166, 195, 226, 246, 256, 262, 283, 295, 302, 396

Victoria Rifles of Canada: 152, 153, 159, 179, 214, 226, 275, 302

Voltigeurs de Québec: 126, 153, 171, 214, 234, 276, 282, 287, 303, 384 *see also* 9th Battalion, Voltigeurs de Québec

West Nova Scotia Regiment: 263, 407

Westminster Regiment: 147, 206, 260, 267, 299, 404

Winnipeg Grenadiers: 135, 189, 251, 293

York Rangers: 279 *see also* 12th Regiment, York Rangers *and* Queen's York Rangers (1st American Regiment)

Queen's Own Rifles of Canada: 113, 115, 117, 122, 123, 131, 135, 136, 143, 145, 149, 156, 162, 177, 201, 203, 219, 226, 260, 261, 263, 280, 283, 297, 298, 401 *voir aussi* 2e Bataillon, Queen's Own Rifles of Canada *et* 2e Régiment, Queen's Own Rifles of Canada

Régiment aéroporté du Canada: 248, 288, 292, 374, 388, 389, 396 *voir aussi* 1er Bataillon de parachutistes canadiens

Régiment de la Chaudière: 117, 126, 162, 225, 234, 265, 282, 287, 384, 403

Régiment de Lévis: 140, 196, 257, 295 *voir aussi* 17e Bataillon d'infanterie de Lévis

Régiment de Maisonneuve: 133, 155, 181, 243, 245, 257, 292, 298, 390, 403

Régiment de Montmagny: 138, 192, 254

Régiment du Saguenay: 403

Regina Rifle Regiment: 255

Rocky Mountain Rangers: 146, 152, 205, 214, 242, 265, 275, 403

Royal Canadian Regiment: 114, 116, 132, 135, 136, 149, 157, 178, 179, 220, 236, 242, 244, 271, 280, 288, 290, 297, 298, 378, 385, 394, 401 *voir aussi* Corps-école d'infanterie

Royal Hamilton Light Infantry (Wentworth Regiment): 134, 186, 248, 292, 297, 391 *voir aussi* 13e Bataillon d'infanterie

Royal Montreal Regiment: 159, 178, 242 *voir aussi* 58e Régiment, Westmount Rifles

Royal Newfoundland Regiment: 165, 174, 180, 200, 202

Royal Regiment of Canada: 115, 133, 159, 181, 222, 238, 245, 262, 281 *voir aussi* 10e Bataillon Royal Grenadiers; 10e Régiment, Royal Grenadiers *et* Toronto Regiment

Royal Rifles of Canada: 144, 147, 202, 206, 224, 244, 261, 267, 296

Royal 22e Régiment: 155, 172-174, 180, 203, 218, 221, 238, 241, 253, 262, 267, 280, 287-290, 294, 299, 371, 372, 381, 384, 386, 388, 389, 394, 397, 402-404

Miscellaneous units, bases and schools
A-7 Canadian Signal Training Centre: 233
A-14 Canadian Infantry Training Centre: 218
A-15 Canadian Infantry Training Centre: 218
1st Canadian Motor Machine Gun Brigade: 193, 214
No. 1 General Hospital: 161
No. 1 Provost Company: 260
2nd Dvisional Train: 203
No. 3 Canadian Public Relations Group: 226
3rd Divisional Mechanical Transport Company: 209
No. 3 General Hospital: 178, 203
4 Canadian Armoured Troops Workshop: 242
No. 4 Field Ambulance: 161, 224, 282, 376
No. 4 General Hospital: 195
4 Service Battalion: 389, 395
5 Light Anti-Aircraft Workshop: 255
No. 7 General Hospital: 188
No. 8 Field Ambulance: 187
No. 8 General Hospital: 254
No. 11 Field Ambulance: 165
No. 24 Field Ambulance: 245
42nd Infantry Reserve Company, Veterans Guard of
    Canada: 236
No. 54 District, Canadian Forestry Corps: 188
No. 62 Royal Canadian Army Cadet Corps: 274
No. 65 Tank Transporter Company: 239
80th Infantry Reserve Company, Veterans Guard of
    Canada: 276
85 Bridge Company: 264
100th Canadian Army (Basic) Training Centre: 234
103rd Canadian Army (Basic) Training Centre: 267
No. 1390 Royal Canadian Army Cadet Corps: 133,
    180, 244, 390
Aldershot, Camp, N.S.: 218, 291, 389
Borden, Camp, Ont.: 172, 307
Canadian Convalescent Hospital (Bear Wood): 189
Canadian Land Forces Command and Staff College,
    Kingston, Ont.: 56, 110, 300, 368, 405
Canadian Ordnance Training Centre: 274
Canadian Special Air Service Company: 291
Carleton University Contingent, COTC: 283
District Depot, Military District No. 3: 268
Dominion Orthopaedic Hospital: 174
Fort Chippewa, North Bay, Ont.: 248
Gagetown, Camp, N.B.: 393

Royal Winnipeg Rifles: 117, 151, 154, 162, 211, 216, 226, 273, 278, 283, 302, 406 *voir aussi* 90e Régiment, Winnipeg Rifles

Saskatoon Light Infantry: 242, 258, 262, 276, 401 *voir aussi* North Saskatchewan Regiment

Seaforth Highlanders of Canada: 198, 252, 266, 299

South Saskatchewan Regiment: 223, 262, 270

Stormont, Dundas and Glengarry Highlanders: 115, 159, 221, 272, 281, 372

Toronto Regiment: 156, 159, 222 *voir aussi* Royal Regiment of Canada

Toronto Scottish Regiment: 162, 166, 195, 226, 246, 256, 262, 283, 295, 302, 396

Victoria Rifles of Canada: 152, 153, 159, 179, 214, 226, 275, 302

Voltigeurs de Québec: 126, 153, 171, 214, 234, 276, 282, 287, 303, 384 *voir aussi* 9e Bataillon, Voltigeurs de Québec

West Nova Scotia Regiment: 263, 407

Westminster Regiment: 147, 206, 260, 267, 299, 404

Winnipeg Grenadiers: 135, 189, 251, 293

York Rangers: 279 *voir aussi* 12e Régiment, York Rangers *et* Queen's York Rangers (1st American Regiment)

Unités, bases et écoles diverses

1ère Brigade canadienne motorisée de mitrailleuses: 193, 214

1ère Compagnie de la prévoté: 260

1er Hôpital général: 161

2e Dépôt d'entraînement, Service de Santé de l'Armée canadienne: 160

2e Train divisionnaire: 203

3e Compagnie divisionnaire de transport motorisé: 209

3e Groupe canadien de relations publiques: 226

3e Hôpital général: 178, 203

4e Ambulance de campagne: 161, 224, 282, 376

4e Atelier des troupes blindés: 242

4e Bataillon des services: 389, 395

4e Hôpital général: 195

5e Atelier des réparations (Armes antiaériennes légères): 255

7e Hôpital général: 188

8e Ambulance de campagne: 187

Hughes, Camp, Man.: 204
Military District No. 10: 207, 261
Montreal Highland Cadets: 127
Niagara, Camp, Ont.: 129, 143
Officers' Training Centre, Brockville, Ont.: 219
Pacific Coast Militia Rangers: 264
Petawawa, Camp, Ont.: 144
Royal Canadian Armoured Corps School, Camp Borden, Ont.: 291
Saint John Fortress, N.B.: 97, 154, 217, 351
Sewell, Camp, Man.: 209
Sussex, Camp, N.B.: 268
Takhini, Camp, Yukon: 296
Training Depot No. 2, Canadian Army Medical Corps: 160
University of Ottawa Contingent, COTC: 220, 280
University of Toronto Contingent, COTC: 170, 233
University of Western Ontario Contingent, COTC: 212, 273
Valcartier, Camp, Que.: 117, 161, 209, 224
Air forces
  Branches and headquarters
    Air Cadet League of Canada: 325, 353, 358
    Air Command: 364, 371, 374, 397
    Chaplaincy Service (Roman Catholic): 307, 326, 358
    Directorate of Manning, Air Force Headquarters: 340
    Ground Observer Corps: 354, 356
    Women's Division: 330, 337, 345, 352, 359, 369
  Groups and Wings
    6 Group: 326, 330
    1 Wing: 353, 354, 368
    4 Wing: 360, 367
    16 Wing: 384
    22 Wing: 344, 366, 400
    35 Wing: 324
    39 Wing: 321
    126 Wing: 318
    143 Wing: 334, 341
  Squadrons and flying units
    1 Squadron see 401 Squadron
    16 Squadron: 326, 358, 384
    18 Squadron see 438 Squadron
    32 Squadron: 323, 355, 376
    111 Squadron see 440 Squadron
    118 Squadron see 438 Squadron

8e Hôpital général: 254

10e District militaire: 207, 261

11e Ambulance de campagne: 165

24e Ambulance de campagne: 245

42e Compagnie d'infanterie de réserve, La garde des Vétérans du Canada: 236

54e District, Corps forestier du Canada: 188

62e Corps, Cadets royaux de l'Armée canadienne: 274

65e Compagnie de transporteurs de chars: 239

80e Compagnie d'infanterie de réserve, La garde des Vétérans du Canada: 276

85e Compagnie de pontage: 264

1390e Corps, Cadets royaux de l'Armée canadienne: 133, 180, 244, 390

Cadets Highland de Montréal: 127

Camp Aldershot (N.-É.): 218, 291, 389

Camp Borden (Ont.): 172, 307

Camp Gagetown (N.-B.): 393

Camp Hughes (Man.): 204

Camp Niagara (Ont.): 129, 143

Camp Petawawa (Ont.): 144

Camp Sewell (Man.): 209

Camp Sussex (N.-B.): 268

Camp Takhini (Yukon): 296

Camp Valcartier (Qué.): 117, 161, 209, 224

Canadian Special Air Service Company: 291

Centre d'instruction A-7 du Corps canadien des transmissions: 233

Centre d'instruction A-14 de l'infanterie canadienne: 218

Centre d'instruction A-15 de l'infanterie canadienne: 218

Centre d'instruction des officiers, Brockville (Ont.): 219

Centre d'instruction du Corps canadien des magasins militaires: 274

Centre d'instruction (élémentaire) no 100 de l'Armée canadienne: 234

Centre d'instruction (élémentaire) no 103 de l'Armée canadienne: 267

Collège de commandement et d'état-major des forces terrestres canadiennes, Kingston (Ont.): 56, 110, 300, 368, 405

Contingent de l'Université Carleton, CEOC: 283

Contingent de l'Université de Toronto, CEOC: 170, 233

400 Squadron: 323, 356, 377
401 Squadron: 323, 334, 340, 355, 377
402 Squadron: 327, 331, 358, 360, 384
404 Squadron: 323, 343, 355, 366, 377
406 Squadron: 323, 355, 376
407 Squadron: 317, 319, 331, 359, 386
408 Squadron: 323, 341, 348, 355, 377, 368, 406
409 Squadron: 321, 323, 355, 377
410 Squadron: 341, 364, 397
411 Squadron: 329, 339, 359, 363, 387, 396
412 Squadron: 343, 365, 399
413 Squadron: 318
414 Squadron: 317, 353, 371
415 Squadron: 323, 327, 340, 355, 377
416 Squadron: 331, 337, 360, 362, 392
417 Squadron: 331, 360, 389
418 Squadron: 297, 317, 337, 340, 349, 367, 369, 407
419 Squadron: 331, 342, 343, 360, 366, 389
420 Squadron: 340
421 Squadron: 331, 360, 389, 407
422 Squadron: 331, 360, 389
423 Squadron: 323, 355, 376
424 Squadron: 319, 342, 354, 365, 372, 398, 402
425 Squadron: 323, 348, 356, 377
426 Squadron: 327, 337, 341, 361, 362, 393
427 Squadron: 331, 360, 389, 401
429 Squadron: 377
430 Squadron: 323, 355, 366, 372, 377, 388, 398, 400, 404
431 Squadron: 398
433 Squadron: 323, 335, 355, 377
434 Squadron: 323, 356, 377
435 Squadron: 321
436 Squadron: 321
437 Squadron: 323, 356, 377, 402
438 Squadron: 327, 358, 384
439 Squadron: 407
440 Squadron: 329, 331, 360, 389
441 Squadron: 407
442 Squadron: 364, 396
443 Squadron: 323, 355, 376
447 Squadron: 359, 388
450 Squadron: 402
666 Squadron: 321
880 Squadron: 323, 355, 376, 401
103 Rescue Unit: 368, 405

Contingent de l'Université d'Ottawa, CEOC: 220, 280
Contingent de l'Université Western Ontario, CEOC: 212, 273
Dépôt du District, District militaire no 3: 268
École du Corps blindé royal canadien, Camp Borden (Ont.): 291
Fort Chippewa, North Bay (Ont.): 248
Forteresse de Saint-Jean (N.-B.): 97, 154, 217, 351
Hôpital canadien de convalescence (Bear Wood): 189
Hôpital orthopédique du Dominion: 174
Rangers de la côte du Pacifique: 264

Aviation
    Divisions et quartiers généraux
        Commandement aérien: 364, 371, 374, 397
        Corps des observateurs terrestres: 354, 356
        Direction de l'effectif, Quartier général de l'Aviation: 340
        Division féminine: 330, 337, 345, 352, 359, 369
        Ligue des cadets de l'air du Canada: 325, 353, 358
        Service d'aumônerie (Catholique): 307, 326, 358
    Groupes et escadres
        6e Groupe: 326, 330
        1ère Escadre: 353, 354, 368
        4e Escadre: 360, 367
        16e Escadre: 384
        22e Escadre: 344, 366, 400
        35e Escadre: 324
        39e Escadre: 321
        126e Escadre: 318
        143e Escadre: 334, 341
    Escadrons et unités de vol
        1er Escadron *voir* 401e Escadron
        16e Escadron: 326, 358, 384
        18e Escadron *voir* 438e Escadron
        32e Escadron: 323, 355, 376
        111e Escadron *voir* 440e Escadron
        118e Escadron *voir* 438e Escadron
        400e Escadron: 323, 356, 377
        401e Escadron: 323, 334, 340, 355, 377
        402e Escadron: 327, 331, 358, 360, 384
        404e Escadron: 323, 343, 355, 366, 377
        406e Escadron: 323, 355, 376
        407e Escadron: 317, 319, 331, 359, 386
        408e Escadron: 323, 341, 348, 355, 377, 368, 406
        409e Escadron: 321, 323, 355, 377
        410e Escadron: 341, 364, 397
        411e Escadron: 329, 339, 359, 363, 387, 396

Bases, schools and static units
No. 1 Bombing and Gunnery School: 331
No. 1 Central Navigation School: 339
1 Construction Engineering Unit: 329, 359, 386
No. 1 Naval Air Gunners' School: 92, 345
No. 1 Operational Training Unit *see* Bagotville, RCAF Station, Que.
No. 1 Technical Training School: 317, 322
No. 1 Wireless School: 318
No. 2 Bombing and Gunnery School: 322, 328
2 Canadian Forces Flying Training School: 311, 336, 363, 392
No. 2 Initial Training School: 322
No. 3 Bombing and Gunnery School: 349
No. 3 Manning Depot: 335
No. 3 Service Flying Training School: 331
No. 4 Air Observer School: 339
No. 4 Initial Training School: 322
No. 4 Repair Depot: 349
No. 4 Wireless School: 347
No. 5 Air Observer School: 330
No. 5 Bombing and Gunnery School: 322, 329
No. 5 Elementary Flying Training School: 336
No. 6 Repair Depot: 337, 362, 394
No. 7 Air Observer School: 322, 345
No. 7 Bombing and Gunnery School: 344
No. 8 Air Observer School: 321
No. 8 Bombing and Gunnery School: 327
No. 8 Repair Depot: 343
No. 9 Bombing and Gunnery School: 329, 342
No. 9 Repair Depot: 345
No. 9 Service Flying Training School: 343
No. 11 Service Flying Training School: 351
No. 12 Service Flying Training School: 317
No. 15 Elementary Flying Training School: 345
No. 15 Service Flying Training School: 351
No. 19 Elementary Flying Training School: 350
No. 19 Service Flying Training School: 343
No. 20 Elementary Flying Training School: 343
No. 24 Elementary Flying Training School: 322
No. 30 Air Materiel Base: 363
No. 31 Air Navigation School: 345
No. 31 Bombing and Gunnery School: 351
No. 31 Elementary Flying Training School: 327
No. 31 Operational Training Unit: 344

412e Escadron: 343, 365, 399
413e Escadron: 318
414e Escadron: 317, 353, 371
415e Escadron: 323, 327, 340, 355, 377
416e Escadron: 331, 337, 360, 362, 392
417e Escadron: 331, 360, 389
418e Escadron: 297, 317, 337, 340, 349, 367, 369, 407
419e Escadron: 331, 342, 343, 360, 366, 389
420e Escadron: 340
421e Escadron: 331, 360, 389, 407
422e Escadron: 331, 360, 389
423e Escadron: 323, 355, 376
424e Escadron: 319, 342, 354, 365, 372, 398, 402
425e Escadron: 323, 348, 356, 377
426e Escadron: 327, 337, 341, 361, 362, 393
427e Escadron: 331, 360, 389, 401
429e Escadron: 377
430e Escadron: 323, 355, 366, 372, 377, 388, 398, 400, 404
431e Escadron: 398
433e Escadron: 323, 335, 355, 377
434e Escadron: 323, 356, 377
435e Escadron: 321
436e Escadron: 321
437e Escadron: 323, 356, 377, 402
438e Escadron: 327, 358, 384
439e Escadron: 407
440e Escadron: 329, 331, 360, 389
441e Escadron: 407
442e Escadron: 364, 396
443e Escadron: 323, 355, 376
447e Escadron: 359, 388
450e Escadron: 402
666e Escadron: 321
880e Escadron: 323, 355, 376, 401
103e Unité de sauvetage: 368, 405
Bases, écoles et unités sédentaires
1re Unité du génie construction: 329, 359, 386
1ère École centrale de navigation: 339
1ère École de bombardement et de tir: 331
1ère École de radionavigants: 318
1ère École de tir de l'aéronavale: 92, 345
1ère École d'instruction technique: 317, 322
1ère Unité d'entraînement opérationnel *voir* Station de l'ARC
     Bagotville (Qué.)
2e École de bombardement et de tir: 322, 328
2e École de pilotage des Forces canadiennes: 311, 336, 363, 392

No. 31 Service Flying Training School: 344
No. 32 Radio Unit: 346
No. 32 Service Flying Training School: 344
No. 33 Air Navigation School: 342
No. 33 Elementary Flying Training School: 343
No. 35 Elementary Flying Training School: 333
No. 36 Service Flying Training School: 344
No. 37 Service Flying Training School: 320
No. 39 Service Flying Training School: 348
No. 41 Service Flying Training School: 331
No. 211 Aircraft Warning Squadron: 365
No. 419 Repair and Salvage Unit: 347
No. 2416 Aircraft Control and Warning Squadron: 359
Air Force College: 98, 280, 353
Aylmer, RCAF Station, Ont.: 353
Borden, Camp, RCAF Station, Ont.: 351, 374
Chatham, RCAF Station, N.B.: 358, 363, 374, 395, 399
Clinton, RCAF Station, Ont.: 358
Cold Lake, RCAF Station, Alta.: 366, 374, 400, 404
Dartmouth, RCAF Station, N.S.: 349
Greenwood, RCAF Station, N.S.: 323, 355, 374
Lincoln Park, RCAF Station, Alta.: 363
Moisie, RCAF Station, Que.: 363, 365, 395
Pennfield Ridge, RCAF Station, N.B.: 343
Portage la Prairie, RCAF Station, Man.: 323, 355, 375
Senneterre, RCAF Station, Que.: 362, 392
Sioux Lookout, RCAF Station, Ont.: 359, 362, 387, 393
Summerside, RCAF Station, P.E.I.: 323, 355, 376
Sydney, RCAF Station, N.S.: 360
Torbay, RCAF Station, Nfld.: 344
Trenton, RCAF Station, Ont.: 328, 337, 346, 362, 390
Ucluelet, RCAF Station, B.C.: 347
Uplands, RCAF Station, Ont.: 369
France
Foreign Legion: 262
Surcouf, submarine: 62, 97
Great Britain
Royal Navy
Fleet Air Arm: 336
HMS Nabob: 96
HMS Orion: 88
HMS Puncher: 91
Royal Naval Reserve Newfoundland: 64, 66, 73, 94, 110

2e École préparatoire d'aviation: 322
3e Dépôt des effectifs: 335
3e École de bombardement et de tir: 349
3e École de pilotage militaire: 331
4e Dépôt de réparations: 349
4e École de radionavigants: 347
4e École d'observation aérienne: 339
4e École preparatoire d'aviation: 322
5e École de bombardement et de tir: 322, 329
5e École d'observation aérienne: 330
5e École élémentaire de pilotage: 336
6e Dépôt de réparations: 337, 362, 394
7e École de bombardement et de tir: 344
7e École d'observation aérienne: 322, 345
8e Dépôt de réparations: 343
8e École de bombardement et de tir: 327
8e École d'observation aérienne: 321
9e Dépôt de réparations: 345
9e École de bombardement et de tir: 329, 342
9e École de pilotage militaire: 343
11e École de pilotage militaire: 351
12e École de pilotage militaire: 317
15e École de pilotage militaire: 351
15e École élémentaire de pilotage: 345
19e École de pilotage militaire: 343
19e École élémentaire de pilotage: 350
20e École élémentaire de pilotage: 343
24e École élémentaire de pilotage: 322
30e Base de matériel aéronautique: 363
31e École de bombardement et de tir: 351
31e École de navigation aérienne: 345
31e École de pilotage militaire: 344
31e École élémentaire de pilotage: 327
31e Unité d'entraînement opérationnel: 344
32e École de pilotage militaire: 344
32e Unité radio: 346
33e École de navigation aérienne: 342
33e École élémentaire de pilotage: 343
35e École élémentaire de pilotage: 333
36e École de pilotage militaire: 344
37e École de pilotage militaire: 320
39e École de pilotage militaire: 348
41e École de pilotage militaire: 331
211e Escadron d'avertissement anti-avions: 365
419e Unité de réparations et de récupération: 347
2416e Escadron d'alerte et de contrôle aérien: 359

British Army
    21 Army Group: 239, 246
    100th (The Prince of Wales' Royal Canadian) Regiment of Foot:
        115
    166th (Newfoundland) Field Regiment, Royal Artillery: 235, 254
Royal Air Force
    10 Squadron: 346, 350
    No. 31 Depot, Moncton, N.B.: 337
    109 Squadron: 350
    215 Squadron: 332
    242 Squadron: 334
    356 Squadron: 332
    657 Squadron: 318
    Beamsville, RAF Station, Ont.: 307
    Ferry Command: 327, 340, 344, 350, 352
    Greenwood, RAF Station, N.S.: 343
    Linton-on-Ouse, RAF Station, England: 341
    Long Branch, RAF Station, Ont.: 305
    Patricia Bay, RAF Station, B.C.: 343
    Pennfield, RAF Station, N.B.: 317
    Royal Air Force Canada: 305, 307, 314
    Transport Command: 333
International Formations and Units
    25th NORAD Region: 367
    International Commission of Control and Supervision: 393
    Mackenzie-Papineau Battalion: 220, 249, 251, 253
    United Nations Emergency Force: 43, 53, 298
Norway
    Royal Norwegian Air Force: 343
United States
    13th Regiment, National Guard, State of New York: 137
University of Alberta: 95, 275, 349
University of British Columbia: 74, 76, 213, 221, 315, 319
University of Manitoba: 74, 213, 315
University of Toronto: 74, 75, 95, 213, 214, 217, 274, 275, 315, 316, 349
University of Western Ontario: 212
Upper Canada College, Toronto, Ont.: 217

V-E Day *see* Halifax, N.S. - Riots, 1945
Valour and the Horror (Television programme): 21, 220, 276, 318, 350
Vancouver, B.C.: 142, 187, 198, 258, 296
Vankleek Hill, Ont.: 169
Vehicles: 85, 225, 227, 244, 248, 332 *see also* Armoured fighting vehicles
Victoria College *see* University of Toronto
Victoria Cross: 8, 46, 58, 171, 307

Collège de l'Aviation: 98, 280, 353
Station de l'ARC, Aylmer (Ont.): 353
Station de l'ARC, Camp Borden (Ont.): 351, 374
Station de l'ARC, Chatham (N.-B.): 358, 363, 374, 395, 399
Station de l'ARC, Clinton (Ont.): 358
Station de l'ARC, Cold Lake (Alb.): 366, 374, 400, 404
Station de l'ARC, Dartmouth (N.-É.): 349
Station de l'ARC, Greenwood (N.-É.): 323, 343, 355, 374
Station de l'ARC, Lincoln Park (Alb.): 363
Station de l'ARC, Moisie (Qué.): 363, 365, 395
Station de l'ARC, Pennfield Ridge (N.-B.): 343
Station de l'ARC, Portage la Prairie (Man.): 323, 355, 375
Station de l'ARC, Senneterre (Qué.): 362, 392
Station de l'ARC, Sioux Lookout (Ont.): 359, 362, 387, 393, 362
Station de l'ARC, Summerside (Î.-P.-É.): 323, 355, 376
Station de l'ARC, Sydney (N.-É.): 360
Station de l'ARC, Torbay (T.-N.): 344
Station de l'ARC, Trenton (Ont.): 328, 337, 346, 362, 390
Station de l'ARC, Ucluelet (C.-B.): 347
Station de l'ARC, Uplands (Ont.): 369
États-Unis
13th Regiment, National Guard, State of New York: 137
Formations et unités internationales
25e Région de NORAD: 367
Bataillon Mackenzie-Papineau: 220, 249, 251, 25
Commission internationale de contrôle et de surveillance au Viêt-nam:
393
Force d'urgence des Nations unies: 43, 53, 298
France
Le Surcouf, sous-marin: 62, 97
Légion étrangère: 262
Grande-Bretagne
Royal Navy
Fleet Air Arm: 336
HMS Nabob: 96
HMS Orion: 88
HMS Puncher: 91
Royal Naval Reserve Newfoundland: 64, 66, 73, 94, 110
Armée britannique
21e Groupe d'armée: 239, 246
100th (The Prince of Wales' Royal Canadian) Regiment of Foot:
115
166th (Newfoundland) Field Regiment, Royal Artillery: 235, 254
Royal Air Force
10e Escadron: 346, 350
31e Dépôt, Moncton (N.-B.): 337

Vietnamese Conflict, 1957-1973: 28, 32, 44, 58, 291, 373, 390, 393
Vimy, 1917: 158, 165, 187, 189, 194, 195, 199, 204, 216

War art: 6, 35, 59, 65, 67-70, 75, 80, 82, 88, 89, 91, 92, 97, 155, 168, 170, 171,
    187, 197, 200, 205, 212, 216, 219, 221, 232, 234, 236, 254, 258, 259, 265,
    278, 305, 306, 309, 311, 314, 315, 321, 325, 326, 328, 339, 342, 345, 351,
    359, 385, 407
War graves *see* Commonwealth War Graves Commission *and* Imperial War Graves
    Commission
War Measures Act: 21, 38, 52 *see also* October Crisis, 1970
War memorials: 9, 62, 69, 70, 74, 75, 97, 127, 165, 168, 169, 172, 178, 180, 181,
    192, 196, 200, 212, 216, 255, 260, 278, 294, 307-309, 312, 314, 315, 351,
    400 *see also* Commonwealth War Graves Commission; Imperial War Graves
    Commission *and* Peace Tower
War posters *see* Posters, War
War service badges: 38
War trophies: 171, 307
Waterloo County, Ont.: 73, 202, 313
Wellington, P.E.I.: 75, 96, 111, 215, 277, 303, 350
Windsor, Ont.: 174, 308
Wings *see* Units, services, branches and formations
Winnipeg, Man.: 87, 254, 338
Winnipeg Grain Exchange: 216
Wives, Military: 385, 392
Women: 10, 36, 51, 77, 79, 84-86, 95, 96, 101, 218, 221-223, 241, 245, 251, 262,
    265, 273, 277, 278, 320, 330, 333, 336, 345, 349, 350, 352, 359, 368, 369

Yarmouth, N.S.: 137, 192, 212, 294
Young Men's Christian Associations: 37, 97, 158, 217, 279, 352
Ypres, 1915: 166, 171, 173, 195, 213
Yugoslavia: 253, 272, 294, 378, 386, 396, 404
Yukon: 134

Zouaves pontificaux: 114, 131, 134, 137, 138, 140, 143, 146, 149, 154

109e Escadron: 350
215e Escadron: 332
242e Escadron: 334
356e Escadron: 332
657e Escadron: 318
Ferry Command: 327, 340, 344, 350, 352
Station de la RAF, Beamsville (Ont.): 307
Station de la RAF, Greenwood (N.-É.): 343
Station de la RAF, Linton-on-Ouse (Angleterre): 341
Station de la RAF, Long Branch (Ont.): 305
Station de la RAF, Patricia Bay (C.-B.): 343
Station de la RAF, Pennfield (N.-B.): 317
Royal Air Force Canada: 305, 307, 314
Transport Command: 333

Norvège
Aviation royale norvégienne: 343
Université de l'Alberta: 95, 275, 349
Université de la Colombie-Britannique: 74, 76, 213, 221, 315, 319
Université de Toronto: 74, 75, 95, 213, 214, 217, 274, 275, 315, 316, 349
Université du Manitoba: 74, 213, 315
Unversité McGill, Montréal (Qué.): 70-72, 74, 84, 89, 95, 178, 189, 194, 215, 242, 256, 286, 311, 315, 340, 350
Université Queen's, Kingston (Ont.): 73, 115, 158, 204, 221, 281, 313
Université Western Ontario: 212
Upper Canada College, Toronto (Ont.): 217

Vancouver (C.-B.): 142, 187, 198, 258, 296
Vankleek Hill (Ont.): 169
Véhicules: 85, 225, 227, 244, 248, 332
Véhicules de combat blindés: 225, 241
Vêtements voir Tenue
Victoria College voir Université de Toronto
Viêt-nam, Conflit du voir Conflit du Viêt-nam
Vimy, 1917: 158, 165, 187, 189, 194, 195, 199, 204, 216
Voyageurs sur le Nil: 137, 139, 149, 153

Wellington (Î.-P.-É.): 75, 96, 111, 215, 277, 303, 350
Windsor (Ont.): 174, 308
Winnipeg (Man.): 87, 254, 338

Yarmouth (N.-É.): 137, 192, 212, 294
Young Men's Christian Associations: 37, 97, 158, 217, 279, 352
Yougoslavie: 253, 272, 294, 378, 386, 396, 404
Ypres, 1915: 166, 171, 173, 195, 213
Yukon: 134

Zouaves pontificaux: 114, 131, 134, 137, 138, 140, 143, 146, 149, 154

PERSONS — LES PERSONNES

Abautret, René: 218
Abbey, Edwin Austin: 155
Abbink, Cindy, *see/voir* Abbink, Harry
Abbink, Harry: 155
Abbot, Kim: 317
Adam, G. Mercer: 113
Adami, George: 155
Adams, E.G.: 5
Adams, James: 280, 353, 371
Adelberg, Philip: 317, 353, 371
Adleman, Robert H.: 218
Aernoudts, Karel: 213
Aitchison, J.H.: 5
Aitken, William Maxwell, *see/voir* Beaverbrook, William Maxwell Aitken, baron
Alcorn, Douglas: 317
Alexander, Anne: 1
Alexander, G.M.: 218
Alford R.A.: 371
Allard, Jean V.: 5, 218, 280, 371
Allen, E.P.S.: 155
Allison, Les: 318
Allister, William: 218
Amery, L.S.: 5
Amey, Ada: 218
Anderson, Frank: 113
Anderson, P.: 155
Andrew, G.C.: 6
Angers, François-Albert: 6
Anglin, Douglas G.: 6
Annis, Clare: 318, 353
Appleton, Thomas E.: 63, 67, 76, 98
Arbuckle, Graeme: 63, 67, 76, 98, 371
Argo, J.A.: 155
Armit, W.B.: 113, 155, 218
Armstrong, Elizabeth H.: 6
Aronsen, Lawrence, *see/voir* McKercher, B.J.C.
Arora, Ved Parkash: 3
Ashton, Martin: 318
Asselin, Olivar: 6
Aston, William H.: 113
Atherton, W.H.: 6
Atkin, Ronald: 219
Atkins, Emily: 55 *see also/voir aussi* St. Denis, Thomas

Attwood, Peter Hinds: 113
Audet, Pierre: 371
Austin, A.B.: 219

Babin, Lenard L.: 156
Babin, Ronald, *see/voir* Shragge, Eric
Bagley, Fred: 156
Baglow, Bob: 353
Bagnall, F.W.: 156
Bagshaw, M.E.: 156
Bailey, John Beswick: 156
Bailey, W.J.: 6, 7
Bainbridge, Charles G., *see/voir* Paquette, Edward R.
Baker, George Harold: 167, 175
Baldwin, Harold: 156
Baldwin, J.R.: 43
Baraton, Jean Pierre: 372
Barker, James, *see/voir* Lucas, James S.
Barker, William George: 312
Barlow, Maude: 7
Barnard, Leslie G.: 156
Barnard, W.T.: 113, 156, 219, 280
Barnes, C.H.: 113, 156, 219
Barnes, Leslie W.C.S.: 113, 114, 156, 157, 219, 280
Barnholder, Michael: 131
Barnett, Donald C.: 114
Barrass, J.R.: 219, 318
Barratt, Glynn: 7
Barrett, W.W.: 219
Barris, Alex, *see/voir* Barris, Ted
Barris, Ted: 7, 76, 219, 318
Barry, A.L.: 157
Bartlett, E.H.: 76
Bartlett, Jack Fortune: 219
Barton, William H.: 98, 280, 353, 372
Bashow, David L.: 353, 373
Bassett, John: 114, 157
Bates, Maxwell: 219
Batten, Jack: 219, 280, 373
Baxter, John Babington Macauley: 114
Baylay, George Taylor: 114, 157, 220
Bayley, G.H.U.: 318
Beach, Thomas Miller: 114, 128
Beal, Bob: 114 *see also/voir aussi* Wiebe, Rudy
Beattie, Kim: 114, 157, 220, 280

Beatty, David Pierce: 157

Beaudoin, Emile, *see/voir* Burrow, Len

Beauregard, Claude: 22, 55, 168, 382 *see also/voir aussi* Comeau, Paul-André

Beauregard, George: 114

Beaverbrook, William Maxwell Aitken, baron: 157

Beck, Norman Edward: 114, 157

Beckles, Gordon [*pseud.*], *see/voir* Willson, Gordon Beckles

Beeching, William C.: 220

Begg, Alexander: 114

Bélanger, Yves: 7

Belhameur, Charles: 145

Bell, F. McKelvey: 157, 169

Bell, J. Mackintosh: 220

Bell, K.: 7, 114, 157, 220, 280

Bell, Ralph: 157

Bell, Sandra: 2

Bell, T.J.: 220

Bell-Irving, Duncan: 313

Bellefeuille, E. Lef. de: 114

Belton, James: 157

Bennett, Chris: 382

Bennett, Robert L., *see/voir* Campbell, Ian J.

Bennett, S.G.: 157

Benson, Winslow, *see/voir* Glazebrook, G. de T.

Bercuson, David J.: 7, 76, 158, 220, 281, 318 *see also/voir aussi* Granatstein, J.L., *and/et* Wise, S.F.

Berger, Monty: 318

Bergeron, Caroline, *see/voir* Bernard, Yves

Bernage, Georges: 220

Bernard, Yves: 7, 220

Bernier, Robert: 318

Bernier, Serge: 7 *see also/voir aussi* Allard, Jean V.; Haycock, Ronald G; Pariseau, Jean *and/et* Stanley, George F.G.

Berton, Pierre: 158

Beurling, George F.: 318, 343

Bezeau, M.V.: 220, 281

Bidwell, R.E.S.: 67, 76, 98

Big Bear: 116, 133

Biggar, E.B.: 115

Biggar, J.H.: 43

Biggar, J. Lyons: 119

Biggs, E.R.J.: 158

Bindon, Kathryn M.: 115, 158, 221, 281

Bird, C.W.: 158

Bird, Michael J.: 67

Bird, Will R.: 115, 159, 221, 281
Birney, Earle: 76, 221, 319
Bishop, Charles W.: 158
Bishop, William Arthur: 8, 63, 67, 76, 98, 115, 158, 221 281, 305, 319, 353
Bishop, William Avery: 7, 305, 306, 311, 312, 319
Bittner, Jean-François: 332
Black, Don: 319
Black, Edgar C.: 325
Black, Ernest G.: 158
Blackburn, George G.: 221
Blair, Stephenie A., *see/voir* Morrison, W. Alexander
Blais, Pierre: 372
Blakely, Tom: 76
Bland, Douglas: 8, 372
Blanchette, Richard V.: 403
Blatchford, Derek, *see/voir* McClenaghan, John
Blatherwick, F.J.: 8, 63, 67, 76, 98, 319, 353
Blay, Cecil E.: 158, 305
Bobak, Molly Lamb: 221
Boissonnault, Charles-Marie: 115, 158, 221, 281
Booker, A.: 143
Borden, Henry: 8
Borden, (Sir) Robert Laird: 8, 23
Borthwick, J.B.: 76
Boss, W.: 115, 159, 221, 281, 372
Bothwell, Robert, *see/voir* Cross, Michael
Bottomley, Nora: 319, 354, 372
Boulton, Charles Arkoll: 115, 154
Bourassa, Henri: 8-9, 50, 54, 56, 63, 76
Boutilier, James A.: 63, 67, 77, 98
Bow, Malcolm N., *see/voir* Holmes, John W.
Bowering, Clifford H.: 77, 98, 221, 281, 319, 354
Bowman, Bob: 221
Bowman, Phylis: 77, 221, 319
Boxendale, Michael S., *see/voir* MacLaine, Craig
Boyd, John: 9
Boyd, William: 159
Boyle, Joseph Whiteside: 205, 211
Bracken, Robert: 319
Bradford, R.C.: 222
Brault, Lucien, *see/voir* Gouin, Jacques
Brebner, Phyllis Lee: 222
Breckon, Fred: 159
Bremner, Charles: 151
Brewin, Andrew: 9

479

Bricker, Calvin: 9, 372
Brillant, Jean: 171
Brindle, W.: 160
Brisson, Pierre: 319, 354, 373
Broadfoot, Barry: 77, 222, 320
Brock, Jeffry V.: 77, 98, 101
Brock, Thomas Leith: 77, 222, 320
Brockington, Leonard W.: 77
Brodeur, Louis Philippe: 49, 65
Brodsky, G.W. Stephen: 223
Brooker, Chris: 223
Brophy, John Bernard: 310
Brough, H. Bruce: 115
Brouillette, Benoît: 9
Brown, Arthur Roy: 308
Brown, Brian A.: 116, 152, 223, 281, 373
Brown, Elizabeth: 77, 320
Brown, George: 320
Brown, George A.: 10
Brown, H.E.: 95, 275, 349
Brown, Kingsley: 320 *see also/voir aussi* Greenhous, Brereton
Brown, Stanley McKeown: 116, 140
Brown, W.J.: 116, 160, 223, 281, 373
Brown, Walter: 160
Brown Family/Famille Brown: 77, 320
Bruce, Constance: 160
Bruce, Herbert A.: 160
Bruce, Jean: 10, 77, 223, 320
Bruce, Walter: 116, 160, 223
Bryden, John: 10, 77, 223
Buchan, John, *see/voir* Tweedsmuir, John Buchan, baron
Buchan, Lawrence: 116
Buchan, Susan Charlotte (Grosvenor), *see/voir* Tweedsmuir, Susan Charlotte
    (Grosvenor) Buchan, baroness
Buchanan, G.B.: 223
Buchner, W.R.: 10
Buck, Tim: 10
Buckham, Robert: 320
Buckingham, N.A.: 223
Buker, Peter Edward: 373
Bull, Gerald: 280, 353, 371
Bull, Stewart H.: 116, 160, 223, 281, 373
Bull, William Perkins: 116, 160, 223
Burhans, R.D.: 223
Burch, E.T.: 223

Burgess, John, *see/voir* Macpherson, K.R.
Burnham, John Hampden: 116
Burns, E.L.M.: 10, 160, 224, 281
Burns, Max: 161, 224, 281, 373
Burrow, Len: 77
Burton, E.F.: 77
Buswell, Leslie: 161
Butcher, Alan D.: 77, 98
Butler, Vernon Bartlett Graves: 336
Butler, (Sir) W.F.: 116
Butson, A.R.C.: 161, 224, 282, 373
Butt, Bob: 320, 354, 373
Byers, R.B.: 11

Cadenhead, J.F.: 161
Calder, Donald George Scott: 161
Caldwell, Nathaniel French: 11
Callan, John J.: 161
Callan, Les: 224
Cambon, Ken: 224
Cameron, Ian, *see/voir* Cole, David E.
Cameron, James M.: 78, 116, 161, 224, 282
Cameron, Kenneth: 161
Cameron, William Bleasdale: 116
Camp, A.D.: 117, 161, 224, 282
Campagna, Palmiro: 11, 354
Campbell, (Sir) Alexander: 124, 125
Campbell, Francis Wayland: 117
Campbell, Ian J.: 224
Campbell, John P.: 11, 224
Campbell, Len: 161
Canfield, H.S., *see/voir* Miller, James Martin
Capon, Alan R.: 25, 126, 171, 234, 287
Cardin, P.J.A.: 58 *see also/voir aussi* King, William Lyon Mackenzie
Cardin, Rejean: 319, 354, 373
Cardoulis, John N.: 81, 102, 234, 326, 358, 383
Carisella, P.J.: 307
Carlson, Don: 326
Carnegie, David: 25
Caron, (Sir) Adolphe P.: 47, 118, 141
Caron, Serge: 25
Carr, William Guy: 69, 81, 307, 326
Carrel, Frank: 171
Carroll, Warren: 307, 326
Carter, David J.: 25, 171, 234

Carter, G.: 25

Carter, H. Dyson: 25

Carter, William S.: 326 *see also/voir aussi* Dunmore, Spencer

Cartier, (Sir) George: 55, 149

Casey, D.A. *see/voir* Daniel, I.J.E.

Casey, Douglas E.: 102

Cash, Gwen: 234

Cassar, George: 171

Cassells, Richard Scougill: 139

Cassidy, G.L.: 234

Castonguay, Jacques: 102, 126, 171, 234, 287, 307. 326, 358, 383, 384 *see also/voir aussi* Stone, J.R.

Catley, Harry: 81

Cave, Joy B.: 172

Cederburg, Fred: 234

Chaballe, Joseph: 172

Chadwick, J., *see/voir* Phillips, Roger

Chafe, Edward W.: 235

Chajkowsky, William E.: 172, 307

Chamberlain, Peter, *see/voir* Ellis, Chris.

Chambers, Ernest J.: 127, 128

Chambers, Robert W: 81, 235

Champion, Thomas Edward: 128

Chandler, C.M.: 128, 172, 235

Chaplin, Philip: 80, 101

Chapman, Harry: 25, 69

Chapman, J.K.: 327

Chappell, Mike: 128, 172, 235, 288

Charles, Jennifer: 172

Charlton, Peter: 81, 102, 327, 358, 384

Charters, David A.: 25, 288, 384

Chartrand, René: 128 *see also/voir aussi* Summers, Jack

Chase-Casgrain, T.: 25

Chassé, Noël: 25, 172

Châtillon, Claude: 235

Chevrier, Jacques: 318

Childerhose, Chick: 358

Chirol, J.-M.: 327

Choko, Marc: 25

Chrétien, Guy: 82, 235, 327

Christie, Carl A.: 327

Christie, N.M.: 172

Churchill, (Sir) Winston Leonard Spencer: 25, 59, 61, 350

Chute, Arthur Hunt: 172

Clancy, Timothy Fergus: 158

Clark, Don: 307
Clark, Gregory: 173, 235
Clark, H.D.: 173
Clark, Lovell C.: 128
Clark, Thomas: 235, 288, 384
Clarke, D.G., *see/voir* Holland, J.A. Kent
Claude-Laboissière, Alphonse: 235
Claxton, Brooke: 7, 158, 173, 235
Claxton, John P.: 268
Clegg, Howard: 235
Cliche, Yvan, *see/voir* Coulon, Jocelyn
Climo, Percy L.: 26, 173
Cline, Andrew, *see/voir* Rankin-Lowe, Jeff
Clink, William L.: 114
Clint, H.C.: 128, 173, 235, 288
Clyne, Henry Randolph Notman: 173
Coale, Griffith: 82
Coates, Kenneth A.: 26, 235, 236, 288 *see also/voir aussi* Morrison, William R.
Cochin, Louis: 128
Code, David E.: 26
Coffin, W.F.: 26, 128
Cohen, Morris Abraham "Two Gun": 177, 240
Cohen, Stan: 236, 327
Coldwell, M.J.: 27
Cole, David E.: 394
Cole, J.A.: 128
Coleman, Frederick: 173
Collier, Dianne: 385
Collins, Robert: 327
Collishaw, Raymond: 307, 327
Colombo, John Robert: 26
Colton, E. Bert: 236
Colville, Alex: 258
Comeau, Paul-André: 26
Comeau, Robert: 22, 168, 382
Comfort, Charles F.: 236
Conant, Melvin: 27
Conn: K.B.: 339
Conn, Stetson: 27
Connolly, Don: 328, 359, 385
Conrad, Peter C.: 328
Conrod, W. Hugh: 237
Cook, E.D.: 129
Cooper, J.A.: 173
Copp, Terry: 82, 237, 328

Corbet, E.: 82, 104
Corfield, William E.: 128, 173, 237, 288, 385
Cormier, Moise: 146
Cormier, Ronald: 237
Cornelius, J.R.: 237
Corneloup, Claudius: 173
Corrigall, D.J.: 174
Corrigan, Cecil Edwin: 238
Corriveau, Paul: 174, 238, 289, 386
Cosgrove, Edmund: 308, 328
Cosgrove, L. Moore: 174
Costello, W. Brian: 308
Cotton, C.A.: 386
Couffon, Claude: 238
Coughlin, Bing: 238
Coughlin, Tom: 328
Coulon, Jocelyn: 27, 386
Countryman, Barry: 328
Coursaget, A.C.: 238
Couture, Claude-Paul: 238
Cowan, John Scott: 27
Cowan, Stewart F.: 347
Cowling, Bill: 82
Cox, David: 27, 28 *see also/voir aussi* Taylor, Alastair
Coyne, F.W.: 174
Cramm, Richard: 174
Crandall, Max E.: 329
Crane, Brian A.: 2, 23, 28
Cranston, Bobby: 69, 82, 104, 386
Cras, Hervé: 238
Crebolder, Gerjan *see/voir* Van de Weerd, Evert
Creed, Catherine: 69, 174, 308
Creighton, (Sir) Kenelm: 82
Crerar, Duff: 174
Cresswell, C.E.: 174, 308
Crickard, Fred W.: 28, 386 *see also/voir aussi* Datta, Shabnam K.; Jones, David
    R., *and/et* Robinson, David A.
Critchley, A.: 174, 329
Croak, John B.: 172
Crook, E.D.: 129, 175, 238, 289, 386
Cross, Michael: 2, 28, 129, 175, 289
Cross, W.K.: 175
Crow, Rita, *see/voir* Norman, Jim.
Cruikshank, E.A.: 129
Cuff, R.D.: 28 *see also/voir aussi* Granatstein, J.L.

Culhane, Claire: 28
Cumming, William D. *see/voir* Page, Ron D.
Cunliffe, J.W.: 175
Cunliffe, M., *see/voir* Darby, H.
Cunniffe, Dick: 129, 175, 238, 289, 386
Cunningham-Dunlop, C.J.A.: 129
Curchin, Leonard A.: 129, 179, 238, 289, 386
Currie, (Sir) Arthur: 152, 175, 176, 189, 207, 214, 275
Currie, J.A.: 175
Curry, Frank: 83
Curry, Frederic C.: 175
Cushnie, J.E.: 386
Cuthbertson, Brian: 28
Cuthbertson-Muir, R. Major: 129
Cyr, Joseph C.[*pseud.*], *see/voir* Demara, Ferdinand Waldo

Dafoe, Colin Scott: 272
Dafoe, John W.: 28, 175
Daly-Gingras, L.J.: 175
Dancocks, Daniel G.: 83, 175, 176, 238, 239, 329
Daniel, I.J.E.: 176
Daoust, Charles R.: 129
Darby, H.: 239
Datta, Shabnam K.: 28
David, J.: 360, 389
Davidson, (Sir) Charles: 21, 22, 168
Davidson, William McCartney: 129
Davies, Raymond Arthur: 28
Davin, Nicholas Flood: 130
Davis, Eldon S.: 239
Davis, Henry Hague: 21, 232
Davis, Robert H.: 130
Davison, Stan: 83, 105
Dawson, Coningsby: 176
Dawson, R. MacGregor: 28
Dawson, S.J.: 124, 130
De Cruyenaere, Albert Joseph Michael: 336
Deere, David N.: 386
Deller, K.M.: 329, 359, 386
De Malijay, Paul: 28, 130
Demara, Ferdinand Waldo, "The Great Imposter": 104
de Montigny, B.A.T. *see/voir* Ouimet, Adolphe
Denby, Edward E., *see/voir* Irwin, Ross W., *and/et* Roncetti, Gary A.
Denison, Frederick C.: 130
Denison, George T.: 29, 130

485

Denison, S.A.: 130
Denison Family/Famille Denison: 133
de Repentigny, Yvon: 50
de Saint-Jullien, Paul: 158
Deschamps, Gaston: 29
Desjardins, L.G.: 29, 130
Desjardins, Maurice: 239
Desmares, Joseph: 329
Desquesnes, Rémy: 83, 176, 239, 329
Desruisseaux, Pierre: 154
De Trémaudan, Auguste-Henri: 130
De Verneuil, Marcel: 176
Dewar, Jane: 95, 213, 274, 302, 349
DeWitt, David B.: 29
De Wolfe, J.H.: 29, 176
Dhand, H.L. Hunt: 2
Dick, William: 387
Dickie, J.B., *see/voir* Ruffee, G.E.M.
Dillon, G.M.: 29, 105, 387
Dinesen, Thomas: 176
Dingman, Isabel, *see/voir* Ellis, Jean M.
Diubaldo, R.J.: 29
Dixon, F.E.: 130
Dodds, Ronald V.: 308 *see also/voir aussi* Collishaw, Raymond
Donneur, André: 29
Donoghue, Jack: 239, 289
Dornbusch, C.E.: 2, 130, 131, 177, 239
Dornier, François: 131, 177, 239, 289, 329, 389
Dorosh, Michael A.: 239
D'Orsonnens, L.G. d'Odet: 29, 130, 131
Dorward, David M.: 240
Dosé, Daniel: 30, 387
Douglas, Archibald C.: 64
Douglas, (Sir) Archibald Lucius: 64
Douglas, J. Harvey: 177
Douglas, W.A.B.: 30, 64, 83, 105, 329, 240, 330, 387
Dow, Gene: 177
Dow, James: 29, 359
Doward, Norman R.: 131, 177
Dowe, Francis: 30
Drage, Charles: 177, 240
Drew, George: 308
Drolet, "Gil": 83, 177, 240, 289, 308, 330
Drolet, Gustave A.: 131
Drouin, Marc: 387

Drysdale, A.M.: 177
Dubé, Timothy D.: 3
Duchaîne, Jean-François: 387
Dudley-Mathiesen, V.: 330, 359
Duff, (Sir) Lyman P.: 227, 232
Duffin, W.K.G.: 330
Duffy, Angus: 269, 300
Dugas, Jean-Guy: 83
Duguid, Archer Fortescue: 69, 72, 131, 172, 177, 196, 240, 290, 307, 308, 312
Duley, Margaret: 83, 240, 330
Dumais, Lucien A.: 240
Dumont, Gabriel: 131, 139, 144, 154
Dunbar, Francis J.: 30
Duncan, Donald Albert: 240
Duncan, Harvey Daniel, *see/voir* Bagley, Fred
Duncan-Clark: S.J., 69, 178, 308
Dundonald, Douglas Mackinnon Baillie Hamilton Cochrane, 12th/12e earl: 15, 17, 30, 44, 123, 124, 131, 138
Dunkelman, Ben: 240, 290
Dunlevie, Horace G.: 131
Dunmore, Spencer: 30, 330
Dunn, Jack: 131
Dunnett, Peter J.S.: 83, 105, 290, 359, 387
Dunwoody, James M.: 178, 240
Dupuis, F., *see/voir* Phillips, Roger
Duthie, William Smith: 161
Dutton, E.E., *see/voir* Gunn, J.N.
Dyer, Gwynne: 30, 131, 178, 240
Dziuban, Stanley W.: 30

Eagles, Douglas Eaton: 316
Eagles, Elizabeth Joan (Yates): 316
Easton, Allan: 83
Eayrs, James: 31
Edelstein, H.: 241
Edgar, Alistair D.: 31
Edwards, B.A.: 359, 387
Edwards, Charles A.: 241, 290, 387
Edwards, E.W.: 178
Edwards, J.F. "Stocky": 339
Egan, Thomas J.: 131
Eggleston, Wilfred: 31
Ehrhart, Hans-Georg: 31
Elliot, S.R.: 131, 178, 241, 290
Elliott, Ron: 105

Ellis, Chris: 241
Ellis, Frank: 309, 330, 359
Ellis, Jean M.: 241
Ellis, L. Gregory: 152
Ellis, W.D.: 178
Emmott, Norman: 330, 359
England, Robert: 178
English, John A.: 241
Epps, Ken: 31
Essex, James W.: 84
Estoriak, E., *see/voir* Shea, A.A.
Ettenger, G.H.: 84, 241, 330
Eustace, Marilyn: 31
Evans, George H.: 84
Evans, Jack, *see/voir* McMullen, Fred
Evans, John: 140
Evans, L.J.: 388
Evans, W. Sanford: 31, 131
Everard, Hedley: 330
Evonic, I.N.: 3
Ewart, John S.: 31

Fairchild, Byron, *see/voir* Conn, Stetson
Fairweather, Jack L.: 221
Faiseur d'enclos: 114, 128
Falardeau, Victor: 241, 290, 388
Falconer, D.W.: 241
Fallis, George O.: 178, 241
Fancy, Margaret: 3
Farran, Roy: 241, 290
Farrel, J.C.: 242
Fast, Beverley G.: 388
Feasby, W.R.: 242
Ferguson, Frank Byron: 178
Ferguson, Julie H.: 69, 84, 105, 388
Ferguson, Ted: 242
Ferguson, William Kennedy: 329
Fetherstonhaugh, R.C.: 84, 132, 133, 178, 179, 242, 290, 309, 331
Field, Peter: 331
Filteau, Gérard: 179
Finlay, A.H., *see/voir* McEvoy, Bernard
Finnie, Richard: 31
Firth, L.M.: 179
Fitzgerald, Edward: 277
Flahaut, Jean: 179

Flatt, S.A.: 242
Fletcher, David C.: 331, 359
Fletcher, Henry Charles: 32, 132
Flick, C.L.: 132, 179
Florentin, Eddy: 242, 243
Forbes, D.F.: 243
Forbes, J. Charles: 243, 290
Fortin, Marc: 389
Fortmann, Michel: 32
Foster, Charles Lyons: 161
Foster, J.A.: 64, 70, 84, 105, 132, 179, 273, 290, 309, 331, 360, 389
Foulds, Glen: 331, 360, 389
Foulkes, Charles: 32
Fournier, Jean-Pierre: 44
Fournier, Pierre, *see/voir* Bélanger, Yves
Fowler, T. Robert: 84, 243, 331
Fox, Brent: 132, 291, 389
Fox, Henry L.: 179
Franklin, B.A.J.: 291
Fraser, Alexander: 132
Fraser, Dan: 360, 389
Fraser, Donald: 180
Fraser, W.B.: 132, 180, 243, 291, 389
Frayne, R.M.: 335, 361
Frazer, W.W.: 332
French, John Pinkstone French, 1st/1er earl: 32, 132, 138
Frise, Jimmy: 180
Frost, C. Sydney: 243
Frost, Leslie: 180
Fryer, Mary Beacock: 132, 133, 243
Fuller, G.A.: 309, 332, 360

Gaffen, Fred: 32, 84, 105, 180, 243, 244, 291, 332, 360, 390 *see also/voir aussi* Swettenham, John
Gagan, David: 133
Gagnon, Jean-Paul: 244
Gagnon, Jean-Pierre: 22, 169, 180, 382
Gagnon, Réginald: 390
Gallant, A.M.: 133, 180, 244, 291, 390
Gallishaw, John: 180
Galloway, G. Gordon: 213
Galloway, Strome: 244
Gardam, John: 32, 84, 105, 180, 244, 291, 309, 332, 360, 390
Gardiner, John J., *see/voir* MacDonald, F.B.
Gareau, Noah J.: 169

Gariépy, Léo: 267
Garneau, Grant S.: 244
Garvin, Amelia Beers (Warnock): 70, 180, 309
Gault, William Hamilton: 153, 215, 278
Gauvin, Michel, *see/voir* Ross, Armand
Gavin, T.M.: 244
Gellner, John: 32, 33
Geneja, Stephen Conrad: 85
German, Tony: 64, 70, 85, 105
Gesell, Christine, *see/voir* Kasoff, Mark J.
Gian, M.S.: 390
Giangrande, Carole: 33
Gibbons, Arthur: 180
Gibson, Colin: 33, 332, 360
Gibson, George Herbert Rae: 180
Gibson, W.L.: 180
Giesler, Patricia: 85, 181, 245, 291, 332
Giles, L.C.: 181, 245
Gillis, Clarence: 33
Gilman, William: 332
Gilmore, Iris, *see/voir* Talmadge, Marion
Gilmour, Blair, *see/voir* Whitcombe, Fred
Glashan, Keith: 85, 106, 390
Glazebrook, G. de T.: 33
Gludish, M.S.: 390
Godenrath, Percy F.: 70, 181, 309
Godsell, Philip H.: 33, 333
Goetze, Bernard: 390
Goguen, Léandre: 146
Gold, Lorne W.: 33
Golden, Aubrey E., *see/voir* Haggart, Ron
Golden, L.L.L.: 33
Goldie, Mary L.: 33
Gomiratto, Paul: 90, 257, 341
Good, Mabel Tinkiss: 33
Goodfellow, T.H.: 390
Goodleaf, Donna: 390
Goodspeed, Donald J.: 11, 14, 106, 133, 181, 245, 291, 292, 361
Goodwin, V.E.: 157
Goossen, G.: 85, 106
Gordon, David A.: 245
Gordon, John: 309, 333, 361
Goshawk, L., *see/voir* Dhand, H.L. Hunt
Gossage, Carolyn: 85, 221, 245, 333
Gough, Barry M.: 109

Gouin, Jacques: 54, 133, 181, 245, 292, 341, 390 *see also/voir aussi*
Swettenham, John
Gould, L. McLeod: 181
Gould, R.W.: 181
Gowanlock, Theresa: 133
Grafton, C.S.: 181, 246
Graham, Dominick: 246, 292
Graham, Howard: 181, 246, 292
Grahame, Fred B.: 333 *see also/voir aussi* Robinson, J.R.
Granatstein, J.L.: 33, 34, 85, 106, 133, 182, 246, 292, 333, 391 *see also/voir aussi* Bercuson, David J.; Cuff, R.D.; Morton, Desmond, *and/et* Taylor, Alastair
Grand ours: 116, 133
Grant, D.W.: 246
Grant, Reginald: 182
Grant, Shelagh D.: 34
Gravel, Jean-Yves: 34, 133, 182, 246, 292, 391
Graves, Donald E.: 3 *see also/voir aussi* McAndrew, William J.
Graves, Sandham: 309
Gray, Colin S.: 34, 391 *see also/voir aussi* Byers, R.B.
Gray, Edwin: 333
Green, F.G: 186
Greenhous, Brereton: 34, 83, 134, 186, 187, 248, 292, 310, 333, 334, 391 *see also/voir aussi* Douglas, W.A.B.
Greer, Rosamond "Fiddy": 85
Gregg, William: 248
Gregorovich, J.B.: 39
Gregory, James W.: 391
Gregory, Walter: 85
Gregory, William T.: 187
Griesbach, W.A.: 134, 187
Griffin, D.F.: 334
Griffin, Frederick: 134, 187, 248
Griffin, John A.: 334, 361, 334, 361, 391 *see also/voir aussi* Fuller, G.A., *and/et* Kostenuk, Samuel
Griffin, Justin A.: 134
Grimshaw, Louis E.: 248, 292, 391
Grodzinski, J.R.: 187
Grogan, John Patrick: 248
Gronbeck-Jones: D.A., 391
Groves, Hubert: 187, 310
Guiou, Norman Miles: 187
Gundy, W.T., *see/voir* Kembar, A.K.
Gunn, J.N.: 187
Gunning, C.: 34, 248
Gwyn, Sandra: 187

Hacking, N.R.: 85, 106

Haddow, Robert: 34

Hadley, Michael L.: 65, 71

Hagedorn, Hermann: 334

Haggart, Ron: 391

Haglund, David G.: 34 *see also/voir aussi* Edgar, Alastair D., *and/et* Ehrhart, Hans-Georg

Hahn, E.: 187

Hale, Kathleen [*pseud.*] *see/voir* Garvin, Amelia Beers (Warnock)

Halford, Robert G.: 86

Hall, Beverly, *see/voir* Robinson, Maurice

Hall, H. Duncan: 34

Hallam, T. Douglas: 71, 310

Halliday, H.A.: 35, 187, 310, 311, 334, 361 *see also/voir aussi* Milberry, Larry

Halstead, John: 35 *see also/voir aussi* Holmes, John W.

Halton, Matthew: 249

Hamel, Hélène: 51

Hamilton, C. Frederick: 140

Hamilton, Fred J.: 134

Hamilton, (Sir) Ian: 134

Hamilton, J.H.: 187

Hamilton, Mary Riter: 200

Hammond, H.R.L.: 334, 361

Hampson, Bill: 311, 335, 361, 391

Hamre, John, *see/voir* Byers, R.B.

Hannon, Leslie: 35

Hansen, W.J.: 335

Harbottle, Colin Clarke: 113, 156, 219

Harbron, John D.: 86

Harding, John: 335

Hardy, René: 134

Harker, Douglas E.: 134, 188, 249, 292, 391

Harland, John, *see/voir* McKay, John

Harley, George E.: 188

Harman, S. Bruce: 135

Harper, Joseph H., *see/voir* Dunbar, Francis J.

Harrington, Don A.: 392

Harris, John Norman: 311

Harris, Stephen: 35, 135, 188, 249 *see also/voir aussi* Greenhous, Brereton.

Harrison, Deborah: 392

Harrison, W.E.C.: 35

Harsh, George: 335

Hart-McHarg, William: 135

Hartney, Harold E.: 311

Harvey, J. Douglas: 335, 361
Harvey, Jean-Charles: 35
Harvie, John D.: 335
Hasek, John: 35
Hatch, Fred J.: 335 *see also/voir aussi* Christie, Carl A.
Hattersley-Smith, G.: 35
Hawkins, Ronald F.: 86, 249, 335
Haycock, Ronald G., 35, 135, 188 *see also/voir aussi* Hunt, B.D.
Haydon, Peter T.: 36, 106, 361 *see also/voir aussi* Crickard, Fred W.
Haydon, Walter: 36
Hayes Geoffrey: 249
Hayes, Joseph: 188
Hayward, Daniel: 36
Hayward, Harry, *see/voir* Allison, Les
Heal, S.C.: 36, 86
Heaps, Leo: 249, 392
Hearn, Owen: 335
Heckbert, Harry M., *see/voir* MacGowan, S. Douglas
Hellyer, Paul: 36
Hempenstall, Robert: 292
Henderson, Peter A.: 86, 106, 336, 362, 392
Henderson, R.J., *see/voir* Madsen, C.M.V.
Henderson, Thomas: 392
Henry, C.E.: 249
Henry, Hugh G.: 249
Henry, Jacques: 249
Hermann, J. Douglas: 86, 249, 336
Herrington, Walter S.: 71, 188, 311
Hertzman, Lewis: 36
Hewitt, G.E.: 188
Hezzelwood, Oliver: 74, 213, 314
Hibbert, Joyce: 86, 250, 356
Hickey, R.M.: 250
Hicks, Bob: 36
Hildebrandt, Walter: 135
Hill, B. Kirkbride: 86
Hill, Roger: 36
Hillmer, Norman: 36
Hillsman, John Burwell: 250
Hinse, Jean-Robert: 362, 392
Hitchins, F.H.: 36, 336 *see also/voir aussi* Stacey, C.P.
Hitsman, J. MacKay: 36, 86, 135 *see also/voir aussi* Granatstein, J.L.
Hoar, Victor: 251
Hoare, John: 86, 336

Hobbs, Charlie: 336
Hobson, Sharon: 106, 392 *see also/voir aussi* Miller, Duncan "Dusty" E.
Hockin, Thomas A., *see/voir* Hertzman, Lewis
Hodder-Williams, Ralph: 188, 251, 293
Hodgins, J. Herbert: 36, 86, 251, 336
Holberton, Fred G.: 251
Holland, J.A.: 188
Holland, J.A. Kent: 392
Holliday, Joe: 336
Holloway, Ian: 86, 106, 392
Holman, R.F.: 311, 336, 363, 392
Holmes, J.G.: 135
Holmes, John W.: 37
Holodwisky, T., *see/voir* Gronbeck-Jones, D.A.
Holyoak, F.G.: 189
Hopkins, Anthony: 86, 251, 336
Hopkins, J. Castell: 37, 189
Horn, Michiel, *see/voir* Kaufman, David
Hornung, Rick: 37, 392
Horrocks, William: 86, 189, 251, 293, 311, 337
Houghton, C.F.: 135
Houghton, F.L.: 87
Houghton, J.G.: 135
Hovey, H. Richard: 337, 362, 392
How, Douglas: 87, 135, 189, 251, 293
Howard, Fred: 189
Howard, Gordon L.: 189, 251
Howard, Joseph Kinsey: 135
Howard, Victor, *see/voir* Hoar, Victor
Howland, Harry: 189
Hubbell, E.L.: 135, 189, 251, 293
Hubel, J.R.M.: 392
Hubly, Russell C.: 136
Hughes, G.W.: 136, 189, 251, 293, 393
Hughes, J. Paul: 37
Hughes, Robbie, *see/voir* MacFarlane, John
Hughes, (Sir) Sam: 23, 25, 35, 125, 126, 135, 154, 171, 188, 216
Hughes, Stuart: 136
Huizinga, M.H.: 251
Humby, P.A.: 362, 393
Humphrey, James McGivern: 189, 251
Hundeby, Irv: 337
Hundevad, John: 189
Hunt, B.D.: 37
Hunt, L., *see/voir* Dhand, H.

494

Hunt, Lloyd: 337
Hunt, M.S.: 37, 189
Hunter, A.T.: 136
Hunter, T. Murray: 251
Hurst, Alan M.: 37
Hurt, Percy: 8
Hutchison, Paul P.: 136, 189, 252, 293
Hutton, (Sir) Edward Thomas Henry: 125
Huyshe, G.L.: 136
Hyatt, A.M.J.: 189
Hyde, H. Montgomery: 37

Inches, C.F.: 190
Ing, Stanley: 37
Irvine, M. Bell: 136
Irvine, T.A.: 106
Irwin, Ross W.: 37 *see also/voir aussi* Neale, Graham H.
Ito, Roy: 37, 190, 252
Iverach, John A.: 337

Jackman, S.W.: 65
Jackson, Fred: 337
Jackson, H.M.: 37, 136, 137, 190, 252, 293
Jackson, Louis: 137
Jackson, W.H.: 120, 122
Jacobson, Ray: 337, 362, 393
James, F. Cyril: 37
James, F. Treve: 190
James, Fred: 190
Jamieson, F.C.: 137
Jarvis, T.E.: 220
Jarymowycz, Roman Johann: 393
Jeffrey, R.A.: 190
Jellicoe, John Rushworth Jellicoe, 1st/1er earl: 9, 38, 76, 87
Jennings, Cedric: 190
Jenson, L.B.: 88
Jockel, Joseph T.: 38, 362 *see also/voir aussi* Sokolsky, Joel J.
Johnson, Bill: 89
Johnson, Bill, *see/voir* Philp, O.B.
Johnson, Charles Monroe: 252
Johnson, E.A. "Rick": 337, 362, 393
Johnson, J.E.: 337
Johnson, Leonard V.: 38, 362, 393
Johnson, Robbie: 38
Johnson, Sara E.: 337

Johnston, G. Chalmers: 191
Johnston, Mac: 87
Johnston, Murray: 252, 293, 393
Johnston, Stafford: 137, 191, 252, 293
Johnston, Thos., *see/voir* James, F. Treve
Johnston, Wilf: 362, 393
Jones, Athur: 97, 279, 352
Jones, D.C.: 336
Jones, David R.: 38
Jones, G.C.: 191
Jones, Gwilym: 253
Jones, Ted: 253
Jones, William: 253
Jones, William R.: 191
Joos, Gerhard, 362 *see also/voir aussi* Ward, Richard
Jouan, R.: 265
Joubert, Marie-Claude: 38, 394 *see also/voir aussi* Dornier, François
Joy, Edward H.: 253
Juteau, Maurice "Pipo": 253, 294

Kardash, William: 38, 39, 253
Karkut, E.T.: 337, 362, 394
Karpan, Arelene: 137
Karpan, Robin, *see/voir* Karpan, Arlene
Kasoff, Mark J.: 39
Kaufman, David: 253
Kay, Hugh R.: 191
Kaye, G.D., *see/voir* Mayne, J.W.
Kaye, V.J.: 39, 191
Kealy, J.D.F.: 71, 87, 106, 311, 337, 362
Keating, Tom: 39
Keene, Louis: 191
Kellett, N.A.: 394
Kellock, R.L.: 81, 232, 325
Kelly, Arthur J.: 253
Kelly, Elizabeth: 253
Kembar, A.K.: 253
Kemp, A.E.: 22
Kemp, Hugh: 338
Kennedy, H.G.: 137
Kennedy, Howard Angus: 137
Kennedy, I.F.: 338
Kennedy, J.A.: 338
Kennedy, J. de N.: 39
Kenney, Paul, *see/voir* Murphy, Tony

Kent, J.A.: 338
Kerr, Ashton L.: 253
Kerr, John: 253
Kerr, W.K.: 3, 338
Kerr, Wilfred Brenton: 3, 191
Kerry, A.J.: 137, 191, 252, 294
Keshen, Jeffrey A.: 39, 191
Kilgour, Robert W.: 106
Kimball, Harold G.: 191
Kimble, George H.T.: 39
King, Horatio C.: 137
King, W.D.: 137, 192, 254, 294
King, William Lyon Mackenzie: 32, 33, 39-42, 49, 55, 58, 59, 61, 338
Kirkconnell, Watson: 42
Kirkwood, W.A., *see/voir* Young, A.H.
Kitching, George: 254, 294
Knap, Jerome K., *see/voir* Phillips, Roger
Knight, Eric: 42
Konowal, Filip: 193
Kordan, Bohdan S.: 192 *see also/voir aussi* Hillmer, Norman
Kostenuk, Samuel: 338, 363
Krawchuk, Peter: 42, 254
Krepps, Rex G.: 254
Kreutzweiser, Erwin E.: 137
Kronenburg, Vernon J.: 42
Kvas, Peter: 363, 394

Labat, Gaston P.: 137
Labelle, Placide: 277
Lachance, François: 137
Lacroix, D.J.: 394
Laflamme, Jean: 42, 192
Lafrance, Norman: 239
Laidlaw, Alexander: 138
Laing, Gertrude: 87, 254, 338
Laird, Donald Harry: 192
Lake, (Sir) P.H.N.: 43, 138
Laliberté, Lucie, *see/voir* Harrison, Deborah
Lamb, James B.: 87, 138 *see also/voir aussi* Lynch, Thomas G.
Lamb, Ken: 43, 87, 254, 338
Lamontagne, Léopold: 138, 192, 254
Lanctôt, François: 154
Lanctot, Gustav: 43
Landells, E.A.: 43, 254
Langenfeld, Michael J.: 241, 290, 387

Langeste, Tom: 311, 338, 363, 394
Langford, R.J.S., *see/voir* Singer, Burrell M.
Langille, Howard Peter: 43
Langstaff, J.M.: 196
Lanks, Herbert R.: 43
Lannoy, Danny: 254
Lapointe, Arthur J.: 192
Lapointe, Ernest: 43, 59
Large, W.S.: 339
Lash, Z.A.: 43
Laurendeau, André: 43
Laurie, J.L.: 121, 122
Laurie, R.C.: 138
Laurier, (Sir) Wilfrid: 23, 49, 65
Lauterpacht, E.: 43
Lavender, Douglas, *see/voir* Granatstein, J.L.
Lavender, Emerson: 339
Lavigne, J.P.A. Michel: 339 *see also/voir aussi* Brown, George
Lavoie, Joseph A.: 138, 192, 254
Law, C. Anthony: 87
Law, Clive: 43
Lawrence, Hal: 88
Lawrence, W.H.C.: 43
Lay, H. Nelson: 88, 106
Leacock, Stephen: 43, 88
Lean, Cheryl, *see/voir* Metson, Graham
Leash, Homer E.: 192
Leasor, James: 254
LeBreton, Marcel: 394, 395
Le Caron, Henri [*pseud.*], *see/voir* Beach, Thomas Miller
Lee, A.M.: 339, 363, 395
Lee, Robert Mason: 395
Lee, William M.: 43
Lefebvre, Florent: 43
Lefroy, Donald A.L.: 102, 287, 358, 384
Legge, Walter R.: 254
Leggett, Henry Furniss: 88, 106
Leigh, Z. Lewis: 339, 363
LeMaistre, Susan: 192, 255, 294
Leonard, R.W.: 138
Leroux, Gérard: 249
Leshchenko, L.O.: 43
Letellier, Armand: 44
Létourneau, Paul: 44
Lett, Sherwood: 205, 266

Levant, Victor: 44
Lévesque, Thérèse: 88, 255, 339
Lewis, R.: 193
Leyton-Brown, David, *see/voir* DeWitt, David B.
Lind, Francis Thomas: 193
Lindsay, Oliver: 255
Lindsey, C.B.: 193
Lindsey, G.R.: 13, 29, 105, 387 *see also/voir aussi* Byers, R.B.
Little, C.H.: 65, 88
Littler, John Caldecott: 88, 107
Livesay, J.F.B.: 193
Lockwood, A.M.: 255
Lodolini, Ello: 138
Logan, H.T.: 193
Logan, J.D.: 193
Londerville, J.D.: 255
Longair, A.K.: 44
Longard, John R.: 88, 106
Longstaff, F.V.: 65, 71, 88
Loomis, Dan G.: 44, 395
Lotz, Jim: 44
Lovell, D.W.: 395
Lower, A.R.M.: 44
Lucas, James S.: 255
Luciuk, Lubomyr Y.: 44, 50, 193 *see also/voir aussi* Hillmer, Norman
Luxton, E.C.: 255
Lycan, J.A.: 395
Lyman, Tom: 255
Lynch, Alex: 193
Lynch, John William: 193
Lynch, Mack: 88
Lynch, Thomas G.: 88, 107, 395
Lyons, Herbert H.: 138
Lyzum, Jim: 363, 395

McAlister, Alec: 339
McAndrew, William J.: 89, 255, 339 *see also/voir aussi* Copp, Terry
MacArthur, D.C.: 193
Macartney-Filgate, Terence: 96, 277, 350
McAvity, J.M.: 255
Macaw, H.B.: 363, 395
Macbeth, Jack: 89, 107
Macbeth, John Douglas: 256
McBride, Herbert W.: 194
McCaffery, Dan: 311, 339, 363

McClenaghan, John: 339, 363, 396
McClintock, Alexander: 194
McClung, Nellie L., *see/voir* Simmons, Mervin C.
MacCormac, John: 44
McCormick, A.S.: 138
McCourt, Edward: 139
McCracken, George W.: 107, 294, 364
McCrae, John: 114, 145, 157, 172, 203
MacDermot, H.E.: 139
MacDermot, T.W.L.: 194
McDill, W.A., *see/voir* Kerry, A.J.
Macdonald, Angus L.: 45, 89
Macdonald, B.J.S.: 256
MacDonald, Brian: 45 *see also/voir aussi* Tugwell, Maurice
MacDonald, F.B.: 194
MacDonald, Frank: 194
MacDonald, G.H.: 282, 376
Macdonald, Grant: 89, 93, 256, 340
MacDonald, Grant: 340, 364, 396
MacDonald, J.A.: 194
MacDonald, J.D.: 396
Macdonald, John A.: 139
Macdonald, William Balfour: 65, 71
McDougall, Barbara: 45
Macdougall, G.L.: 256
McElheran, Brock: 89
McEvoy, Bernard: 194
MacFarlane, J. Douglas, *see/voir* Rowland, Barry D.
MacFarlane, John: 89, 107, 340, 364, 396
Macfie, Arthur: 194
Macfie, John: 194
Macfie, Roy: 194
McGee, Robert: 139
MacGowan, S. Douglas: 194
McGrane, J.E.: 89, 107
McGregor, F.: 130, 194, 256, 294, 396
Machum, George C.: 46, 195
McInnis, Edgar: 45
McIntosh, Dave: 340
McIntyre, Bob: 364, 396
Macintyre, D.E.: 194
McKay, John: 89
McKay, Russell: 340
McKean, G.B.: 195
McKee, Alexander: 195, 256

McKee, Fraser M.: 65, 72, 89, 107, 396
McKee, Sandra Lynn: 139
McKenna, Brian: 220, 276, 318
McKenna, Terence: 220, 276, 318
Mackenzie, C.J.: 59
McKenzie, F.A.: 195
Mackenzie, G.L.B.: 201
Mackenzie, J.J.: 195
Mackenzie, Kathleen Cuffe: 195
MacKenzie, Lewis: 294, 396
McKenzie, Thomas: 139
Mackenzie-Naughton, J.D.: 139, 195, 256, 294
McKeown, J.D.: 195
McKeown, Michael G.: 295
McKercher, B.J.C.: 45
McKillican, D.R.: 195, 256, 295, 396
MacKinnon, Hedley V.: 139
McKinsey, Lauren: 45
Macksey, Kenneth: 195, 397
MacLaine, Craig: 396
MacLaren, Roy: 139, 195, 256, 340
Maclean, John P., *see/voir* Vokes, Chris
McLean, N.B.: 340
MacLennan, F.A., *see/voir* Kay, Hugh R.
MacLeod, Anne E., *see/voir* Graves, Donald E.
MacLeod, Elizabeth: 139
MacLeod, John N.: 195
Macleod, Malcolm: 45
MacLeod, R.C.: 139
Macleod, Rod, *see/voir* Beal, Bob
McLin, Jon B.: 45
McMahon, J.S.: 256
McMicken, Gilbert: 139, 151
MacMillan, D.A.: 340
MacMillan, James: 364, 396
Macmillan, Margaret O.: 45
McMullen, Fred: 195
MacNachtan, F.: 139
McNaught, Kenneth *see/voir* Brewin, Andrew
McNaughton, Andrew George Latta: 58, 59, 211, 273
McNeil, Bill: 45, 89, 256, 340
McNichol, D., *see/voir* Slinger, J.E.
MacPhail, (Sir) Andrew: 195
MacPhail, Doug, *see/voir* Fletcher, David C.
Macpherson, K.R.: 65, 72, 90, 107, 396

MacPherson, Pennington: 140
McQuarrie, John: 397
McQuiston, John H.: 340
McRoberts, B.G.: 397
MacShane, J.R.: 140
McVicar, Don: 340
McWilliams, James L.: 195
Madill, D.S.: 397
Madsen, C.M.V.: 256
Magee, George, *see/voir* Kay, Hugh R.
Magee, John Gillespie: 334
Magnacca, Stephen A.: 140, 196, 256, 295, 397
Maguire, E.: 256
Main, J.R.K.: 312, 340, 364
Mainprize, R.B., *see/voir* Hodder-Williams, Ralph
Major, J.C.: 140
Malone, Dick: 46, 256
Maltby, R.G.: 256
Manarey, R. Barrie: 140, 196, 257, 295
Mandar, Allin J.: 257
Manion, R.J.: 40, 196, 338
Mansikka, Eric: 90, 257, 341
Marchand, Gérard: 257
Marcotte, Jean-Marie: 257
Marcoux, Jules: 107, 295, 364, 397
Marquis, G.E.: 140, 196, 257 295
Marquis, Roland: 266
Marquis, T.G.: 140
Marraro, Howard R.: 140
Marrion, R.J., *see/voir* Summers, Jack L.
Marsters, J.H.: 321
Marteinson, John K.: 140, 196, 257 295, 397 *see also/voir aussi* Crook, E.D.;
    Service, G.T., *and/et* Tugwell, Maurice
Martin, Charles Cromwell: 257
Martin, Paul: 46, 295
Martin, Peter, *see/voir* Rosen, Albert
Martin, Stuart: 196
Massey, Hector J.: 46
Massey, Raymond: 196, 257
Massey, Vincent: 46
Mathieson, William D.: 196, 312
Maule, Henry: 257
Maxwell, George A.: 196
Mayne, J.W.: 90, 257, 341, 397
Mazéas, Daniel: 140, 196, 257, 295, 312, 341, 364

Meanwell, R.W.: 257

Meek, John F.: 196

Meighen, F.S.: 196

Melady, John: 108, 257, 295, 364

Mellish, Anne Elizabeth: 140

Mellor, John: 258

Melnycky, Peter, *see/voir* Kordan, Bohdan S.

Melnyk, T.W.: 341

Melrose, William: 140

Menzies, J.H.: 46, 197

Meredith, D.L.: 46

Merrick, Bob: 341, 364, 397

Merritt, William Hamilton: 46, 140, 197

Messenger, Ken, *see/voir* Burns, Max

Metson, Graham: 72, 90, 197, 258

Meyer, Kurt: 243, 256

Meyers, Edward C.: 108

Michalos, Alex C.: 46

Michel, Jacques [*pseud.*], *see/voir* Poisson, Camille

Middlemiss, Danford William: 46

Middleton, (Sir) Fred: 135, 141

Middleton, W.E. Knowles: 90, 258

Mika, Helma, *see/voir* Mika, Nick

Mika, Nick: 141

Milberry, Larry: 312, 341, 364, 365, 397, 398 *see also/voir aussi* Halliday, H.A.,
    and/et Pickler, Ron

Millar, W.C.: 198

Miller, Carman: 47, 141

Miller, Duncan "Dusty" E.: 398

Miller, James Martin: 72, 198, 312

Mills, Carl: 108, 365

Milne, Gilbert A.: 90

Milne, Ramsay H.: 341

Milner, Marc: 47, 90 *see also/voir aussi* Macpherson, K.R.

Milnes, Herbert: 141, 198, 258, 295

Milsom, H.G.: 198

Mimms, John A.: 258

Minifie, James M.: 47

Minto, Gilbert John Elliot, 4th/4e earl: 60, 152

Mirtle, Jack: 91, 108, 398

Mitchell, Donald G., *see/voir* Riddle, David K.

Mitchell, G.D.: 141, 198, 258, 295, 398

Mitchell, Howard: 258

Mitchell, Michael: 141, 198, 258, 296, 398

Mitchell, Steve: 258

Miville-Deschênes, Charles: 258, 341
Mohr, Merilyn Simonds, *see/voir* Weisbord, Merrily
Moir, J.S.: 141, 198, 258, 296
Mokler, R.J.: 365
Molson, K.M.: 312, 341, 342, 365, 398 *see also/voir aussi* Fuller, G.A.
Monaghan, Hugh B.: 198, 312
Monk, F.D.: 47
Monnon, Ernest F.: 341
Monnon, Mary Ann: 72 *see also/voir aussi* Monnon, Ernest F.
Montague-Marsden, M.: 198
Montizambert, C.E.: 142
Moogk, Peter: 142, 198, 258, 296
Moore, Alexander Huggins: 142
Moore, Mary Macleod: 198
Mordal, Jacques [*pseud.*], *see/voir* Cras, Hervé
Morenus, Richard: 57
Morgan, Len: 342
Morice, A.G.: 142
Morin, René: 47
Morley, A.W.: 198
Morneault, J.C.: 342, 365, 398
Morris, David: 142, 199, 259, 296, 398
Morris, Jerrold: 342
Morris, Leslie: 48
Morrison, C.A.: 398
Morrison, E.W.B.: 142
Morrison, J. Clinton: 199
Morrison, W. Alexander: 47, 259, 296, 365, 398
Morrison, William R.: 48, 259 *see also/voir aussi* Coates, Kenneth A.
Morton, Desmond, 48, 49, 142, 199, 259 *see also/voir aussi* Bell, K., *and/et* Granatstein, J.L.
Morton, W.L.: 28, 114
Mottistone, John Edward Bernard Seely, baron: 199
Moule, Dick: 342
Moulton, J.L.: 259
Mowat, Farley: 91, 259
Mulvaney, Charles Pelham: 142
Mummery, Robert: 398
Munn, Edwidge: 55 *see also/voir aussi* Comeau, Paul-André
Munnings, (Sir) Alfred James: 197
Munro, Iain R.: 49
Munro, Ross: 259
Munroe, Jack: 199
Murdie, R.: 199
Murdoch, B.J.: 199

504

Murphy, Tony: 91
Murray, Howard: 49
Murray, Joan: 91, 259, 342
Murray, L.W.: 78
Murray, W.W.: 199
Musciano, Walter: 312
Myers, C.V.: 49
Myles, Eugenie: 312, 342
Mynarski, Andrew Charles: 343, 366

Naismith, George Gallie: 49, 200
Neale, Graham H.: 143
Neary, Peter, *see/voir* Granatstein, J.L.
Needler, G.H.: 141, 143 *see also/voir aussi* Middleton, (Sir) Fred
Nelson, H.S.: 143
Newman, Peter C.: 49
Niblett, Mollie Glen: 150
Nicholson, G.W.L.: 91, 143, 200, 259, 260, 296, 399
Nicholson, L.H.: 260
Nicks, D.A.: 399
Nielson, Richard, *see/voir* Copp, Terry
Nieuwenhuys, Jan: 260
Nightingale, Geoff, *see/voir* Wilkinson, William Arthur
Nikerk, J., *see/voir* Phillips, Norman
Nixon, Rod: 399
Noblston, Allen: 260
Nolan, Brian: 49, 91, 343
Nord, Max: 260
Norman, Jim: 49
Norris, Armine: 201
Nossal, Kim Richard, *see/voir* McKinsey, Lauren
Novak, Marie: 319, 354, 373
Noyes, Frederick: 201

Obodiac, Stanlee: 343
O'Brien, Jack: 201
O'Brien, Jerome W.: 3
O'Connor, Edward: 91
O'Dea, Agnes C.: 1
Odell, E.G., *see/voir* Belton, James
Ogilvie, William G.: 201
Ogle, Robert J.: 201, 260, 296
O'Gorman, J.R.: 201
O'Gorman, John J.: 49
O'Kiely, Elizabeth: 313

Oldfield, J.E.: 260

O'Leary, Byron E., *see/voir* MacGowan, S. Douglas, *and/et* Wright, Harold E.

Ollivant, Simon: 49

Olmsted, Bill: 343

Olson, Theodore: 50 *see also/voir aussi* Ing, Stanley

O'Malley, David, *see/voir* McQuarrie, John

O'Neill, E.C.: 91

O'Neill, John: 143

Oppen, William A.: 144

Ord, Lewis Redman: 139, 144

Organ, Richard: 366

Ørvik, Nils: 50

Osbaldeston, Gordon F.: 50

Osgoode, William B.: 127

Osler, John G.: 261

Oswald, W.R.: 144

Otter, (Sir) William D.: 142, 144, 199, 259

Oughton, J.D., *see/voir* Vincent, Carl

Ouimet, Adolphe: 144

Outerbridge, L.M.: 91

Oval, E.I. [*pseud.*], *see/voir* Lavoie, Joseph A.

Owram, Douglas: 1

Ozorak, Paul: 50

P.I.X. [*pseud.*] *see/voir* Hallam, T. Douglas

Page, Bette: 343, 366

Page, Robert: 50

Page, Ron D.: 343, 366, 400

Pallas, S.M.: 144, 202, 261, 400

Panchuk, Bohden: 50

Panet Family/Famille Panet: 133, 147, 245

Papineau, Talbot: 50

Paquette, Edward R.: 91

Paré, Lorenzo: 108, 296, 366

Parent, Jean, *see/voir* Falardeau, Victor

Pariseau, Jean, 50, 51 *see also/voir aussi* Bernier, Serge; Donneur, André;
    Douglas, W.A.B.; Gaffen, Fred, *and/et* Summers, Jack L.

Parker, Mike: 91

Parkinson, F.J., *see/voir* Lower, A.R.M.

Parrot, D.F.: 261

Parsons, W. David: 202

Paterson, R.A.: 261

Patterson, Tom: 261

Patterson, W.J., *see/voir* Boss, W.

Pavey, Walter G.: 261

Peacock, Robert S.: 296
Pearce, Donald: 261
Pearcy, Arthur: 344, 366
Pearkes, George R.: 54, 205, 266
Pearson, George: 202
Pearson, John A.: 70, 180, 309
Pearson, Lester Bowles: 48
Peat, Harold R.: 202
Peat, Louisa: 51
Peck, Sydney: 2, 23
Peden, Murray: 51, 344, 366
Pedley, James H.: 202
Peebles, A.A., *see/voir* Singer, H.C.
Pellatt, (Sir) Henry Mill: 134, 187, 248
Pellatt, Reginald: 261
Pelletier, Oscar C.: 144
Penlington, Norman: 51
Pennefather, John P.: 144
Penny, Arthur G.: 144, 202, 261, 296
Pepin, J.C.: 261
Peppard, Herb: 261
Perkins, Dave: 73
Perkins, Roger: 1
Perry, Hattie A., *see/voir* Kvas, Peter
Peterson, W.G.: 202
Peterson, (Sir) William: 202
Pettipas, Leo: 108, 366
Phillips, Norman: 261
Phillips, Roger: 144, 145, 202
Phillips-Wolley, Clive: 51
Philp, O.B.: 366, 400
Phipps, Brian: 366, 400
Pickett, James: 344, 366, 400
Pickler, Ron: 344, 366, 401
Pieroth, Doris H.: 212, 274
Pierson, Ruth Roach: 51, 262
Pigott, Peter: 313, 344
Pike, Stephen: 177
Pindera, Loreen, *see/voir* York, Geoffrey
Pipet, Albert: 262
Pirie, Alexander Howard: 203
Pittman, Richard: 172
Plewman, W.R., *see/voir* Duncan-Clark, S.J., *and/et* Miller, James Martin
Plumptre, A.F.W.: 51
Plummer, Mary: 203

Poisson, Camille: 51
Polumin, Nicholas: 367
Pontifex, Bryan: 203
Pook, Ronald: 203
Pope, Maurice A.: 52, 203, 262
Pope, R.H.: 52
Popham, Hugh, *see/voir* Dumais, Lucien A.
Popp, Carol: 91
Porter, Gerald: 52
Poulin, J.G.: 262
Pouliot, Ghislain: 135
Poundmaker: 114, 128
Powell, Griffith: 344
Power, Charles Gavin: 52
Powley, A.E.: 262
Pratt, Larry, *see/voir* Keating, Tom
Préfontaine, Renaud, *see/voir* Holland, J.A. Kent
Prescott, John F.: 145, 203
Preston, Richard A.: 52, 65, 73, 91, 109, 145, 203, 262, 297, 298, 344, 367, 402
    see also/voir aussi Stanley, George F.G.
Price, Harold: 310
Price, Paul, *see/voir* Robinson, Maurice
Prince, Thomas George "Tommy": 268, 300
Prokop, Pat: 42, 254
Proud, Edward B.: 7
Proulx, Benjamin A.: 92, 263
Prouse, A. Robert: 263
Provencher, Jean: 52
Prymak, Thomas M.: 52
Puddester, J.: 92, 109, 403
Pugh, Harry, *see/voir* Clark, Thomas
Pugsley, William H.: 92, 109
Purver, Ronald G.: 52
Putkowski, Julien: 203

Queen-Hughes, R.W.: 263, 298
Quigley, John Gordon: 145, 204, 263, 298

Rabjohn, R.H.: 204
Racette, Calvin: 145
Racette, Sherry Farrell: 145
Raddall, Thomas H.: 263
Rae, Herbert [*pseud.*], *see/voir* Gibson, George Herbert Rae
Ralphson, George H.: 204
Ralston, J.L.: 52, 263

508

Ranger, Robin: 52
Rankin-Lowe, Jeff: 403
Rannie, William P.: 145, 204, 264, 298
Rawling, Bill: 204, 264 *see also/voir aussi* McAndrew, William J.
Rawlinson, James H.: 204
Ray, Anna Chapin: 192
Read, Daphne: 34, 186
Redman, Stanley R.: 92, 264, 345
Reed, R.H.: 92, 345
Reford, Robert: 53
Regehr, Ernie: 53
Reid, Brian A.: 145 *see also/voir aussi* Mitchell, G.D.
Reid, Gordon: 204
Reid, Max: 92
Rempel, W. Kim: 83, 105, 290, 359, 387
Renison, Robert John, 53 *see also/voir aussi* Hopkins, J. Castell
Revely, Henry: 92
Reville, F. Douglas: 145
Reyburn, Wallace: 264
Reynolds, Mac, *see/voir* Hoar, Victor
Reynolds, Quentin: 264
Richard, Béatrice: 55
Richards, R.: 204
Richards, S.T.: 65, 73, 92, 109
Richardson, Michael, *see/voir* Colombo, John Robert
Richthofen, Manfred Albrecht, Freiherr von: 307, 308, 314
Ricketts, Thomas R.: 172
Riddle, David K.: 204, 205, 313
Riel, Louis: 2, 3, 129, 143, 145
Rioux, Denise: 146, 205, 264, 298, 403
Ritchie, Mary Christine: 146
Rivac, Richard: 345
Roberts, Charles G.D., *see/voir* Beaverbrook, William Maxwell Aitken, baron
Roberts, James Alan: 264
Roberts, Leslie: 313, 345, 367 *see also/voir aussi* Beurling, George F., *and/et* Leacock, Stephen
Robertson, F.A.: 146, 205, 264
Robertson, Heather: 92, 115, 205, 265, 314, 345
Robertson, Peter: 92, 109, 146, 205, 265, 298, 345, 367
Robertson, Terence: 265
Robertson, William Scot: 53
Robinson, C.W.: 53
Robinson, David A.: 53
Robinson, J. Alex.: 193
Robinson, J.R.: 345

Robinson, Maurice: 403
Rockett, Melanie E.: 403
Roddick, (Sir) Thomas: 139
Rodney, William: 205
Roe, Kathleen Robson: 265
Rogers, Betty: 345
Rogers, John: 127
Rogers, Norman M.: 53
Rogers, R.L.: 146, 205, 265
Rollason, Bryan: 44, 193
Rollifson, M.O.: 265
Roncetti, Gary A.: 146
Roodman, H.S.: 265
Rosen, Albert: 205
Rosenblum, Simon, *see/voir* Regehr, Ernie
Rosner, Gabriella: 53, 298
Ross, Alexander: 161
Ross, Alexander M.: 265
Ross, Armand: 265 *see also/voir aussi* Castonguay, Jacques
Ross, (Sir) Charles: 144, 145, 202
Ross, D.A.: 403
Ross, David: 146
Ross, Douglas Alan: 54 *see also/voir aussi* Crickard, Fred W., *and/et* Goldie,
    Mary L.
Ross, Hendrie Drury: 54
Ross, Richard: 265
Rossiter, Ivan: 205
Rouillard, Jacques: 1
Rouleau, C.-E.: 146
Rousseau, Claude, *see/voir* Gordon, John
Roux, E.: 54
Rowe, Kenneth: 147
Rowland, Barry D.: 265 *see also/voir aussi* Rowland, David Parsons
Rowland, David Parsons: 265
Roy, Ferdinand: 54
Roy, Patricia: 54, 266
Roy, Pierre-Georges: 147
Roy, R.H.: 54, 147, 180, 205, 266, 299 *see also/voir aussi* Morton, Desmond
Ruck, Calvin W.: 206
Rudbach, N.E.: 147, 206, 267, 299
Rudler, Raymond: 267
Rudmin, Floyd W.: 54
Ruffee, G.E.M.: 267
Rumilly, R.: 54
Rundle, Edwin G.: 148

510

Rusden, Harold Penryn: 139

Russell, E.C.: 54, 93 *see also/voir aussi* Kealy, J.D.F., *and/et* Thorgrimsson, Thor

Russenholt, E.S.: 206

Rutherford, T.H.: 267

Rutherford, Tom: 148, 206, 267, 299

Rutledge, Stanley: 207

Ryan, James W., *see/voir* Carisella, P.J.

Rycquart, Barbara: 404

Ryerson, George Sterling: 148, 207

Rylaarsdom, P.A., *see/voir* Roodman, H.S.

Sabourin, J. Armand: 267

Saillant, François, *see/voir* Drouin, Marc

St. Denis, Thomas: 55, 404 *see also/voir aussi* Yost, William J.

Saint-Jacques, Fabien: 187

Saint-Pierre, Marjolaine: 267

Sallans, G.H.: 93, 267

Sanders, Helen: 77, 222, 319

Sanders, Wilfred: 55

Sanderson, Marie, *see/voir* Sanderson, Robert Miles

Sanderson, Robert Miles: 268

Sandwell, A.H.: 314, 346

Sandwell, B.K.: 55

Santor, Donald M.: 55, 207, 314

Sargent, W. William: 346

Sarty, Roger, *see/voir* Hadley, Michael L.

Savage, J.M.: 268

Savard, Adjutor: 93, 268, 346

Savard, Claude: 404

Savill, Mervyn: 242

Scheinberg, S.J., *see/voir* Diubaldo, R.J.

Schmidt, John: 268, 346

Schragg, Lex: 148, 207, 268, 299

Schull, Joseph: 93

Scislowski, Stanley: 268

Sclater, William: 93

Scoble, T.C.: 55, 148

Scollins, Rick: 146

Scott, Frederic George: 207

Scudamore, T.V.: 207

Sealey, D. Bruce: 268, 300

Seely, J.E.B., *see/voir* Mottistone, John Edward Bernard Seely, baron

Segal, Jean Brown: 346

Selin, Shannon: 37, 55 *see also/voir aussi* Barlow, Maude

Senior, Elinor Kyte: 148
Senior, Hereward: 148
Service, G.T.: 148, 207, 268, 300, 404
Sévigny, Pierre: 268
Sexton, Donal J.: 268, 300, 404
Shadwick, Martin W.: 55
Shapiro, L.S.B.: 268
Sharpe, Robert J.: 207
Shaw, E.K.: 55, 367
Shaw, Robbie: 404
Shea, A.A.: 93, 268, 346
Sheffe, Norman, *see/voir* Lavender, Emerson
Sheffield, E.F.: 93
Sheldon-Williams, Inglis: 207
Sheldon-Williams, Ralfe Frederic Landry: 207
Sherlock, Robert A.: 148
Sherman, Michael E.: 55
Shields, Thomas Todhunter: 55
Shores, Christopher: 314, 346, 405
Shragge, Eric: 55
Shrive, Frank J.: 314, 346
Shrive, Norman, *see/voir* Shrive, Frank J.
Siddall, C.G.: 81, 233, 325
Siegfried, André: 51
Sifton, C.: 208
Sigler, John: 55
Silver, A.I.: 148
Silver, L. Ray: 346
Sim, Brian D., *see/voir* Curchin, Leonard A.
Simcock, W., *see/voir* Mitchell, G.D.
Sime, J.G.: 208
Simmons, Mervin C.: 208
Simonds, Guy: 246, 256, 269, 292
Simonds, Peter: 269
Simonski, S.C.: 140
Simpson, Allan: 346, 368
Sinclair, J.D.: 148, 208, 269
Singer, Burrell M.: 279
Singer, H.C.: 208
Skelding, William: 347
Skrypnyk, Mary: 42
Skuce, J.E.: 208, 269
Slack, Michael, *see/voir* Byers, R.B.
Slaney, Ted, *see/voir* Morrison, W. Alexander
Slater, James: 149

Slinger, J.E.: 269

Sloan, T.J.H., *see/voir* Barrass, J.R.

Smith, Doug: 269

Smith, Fred: 56, 368

Smith, G. Oswald: 74, 214, 315

Smith, G.Y.: 368, 405

Smith, Gaddis: 73

Smith, Goldwin: 56

Smith, Gordon S.: 2

Smith, I. Norman: 347

Smith, John Owen: 269

Smith, Joseph S.: 208

Smith, Kenneth B.: 269, 300

Smith, Lawrence N.: 269

Smith, Marilyn Gurney: 66, 73, 94, 109, 405

Smith, R. Guy C.: 56

Smith, S.K., *see/voir* Gould, R.W.

Smith, Sidney E.: 56

Smith, W. Richmond: 140

Smith, Waldo E.L.: 66, 73, 94, 109, 269

Smith, Wilfred: 269

Smye, Fred: 56, 368

Smylie, Eric: 56

Snell, A.E.: 208

Snowie, J. Allan: 109, 269, 405

Socknat, Thomas Paul: 56

Sokolosky, Joel: 56 *see also/voir aussi* Haglund, David G.; Jockel, Joseph T., *and/et* Middlemiss, Danford William

Sorenson, David S., *see/voir* Macmillan, Margaret O.

Sorobey, Ron, *see/voir* Luciuk, Lubomyr Y.

Souster, Raymond, *see/voir* Alcorn, Douglas

Soward, Stuart E.: 110, 368, 405

Speaight, Robert: 209, 270

Spencer, R.A.: 270

Spittael, George E.: 270

Spremo, Boris: 292, 391

Squair, J.: 54

Squires, Clinton H.: 347

Stacey, C.P.: 2, 28, 56, 57, 94, 110, 117, 129, 149, 162, 175, 225, 226, 270, 271, 289, 300, 347, 368 *see also/voir aussi* Bell, K.

Stafford, David: 57

Stailing, Libby: 405

Stairs, Denis: 57

Stalmann, Reinhart: 347

Stanley, George F.G.: 3, 66, 73, 94, 150, 209, 271, 300, 301, 405

Stead, Gordon W.: 94
Stedman, Ernest W.: 314, 347
Steele, Harwood: 150, 209, 271
Steele, R. James, *see/voir* McWilliams, James L.
Steele, (Sir) Samuel Benfield: 150
Stefaniuk, M.E.: 301
Stephens, W. Ray: 94, 271, 347
Stephenson, (Sir) William: 37, 57
Steven, Walter T.: 209, 271, 301
Stevens, G.R.: 57, 210, 271, 301 *see also/voir aussi* Fetherstonhaugh, R.C.,
     and/et Hodder-Williams, Ralph
Stevenson, Michael A.: 23
Stevenson, R.V., *see/voir* Moogk, Peter
Stevenson, William: 57
Stewart, Charles Henry: 210, 272
Stewart, Charles Herbert: 3, 150
Stewart, Grieg: 57, 368
Stewart, Larry R.: 57
Stirling, John: 150
Stobie, Margaret: 151
Stofer, Eric: 347
Stofer, Ken: 347
Stone, J.R.: 301
Strachan, Tony: 94, 210, 272, 347
Strange, Thomas Bland: 56, 138, 139, 151
Strange, William: 57, 94 *see also/voir aussi* Stacey, C.P.
Street, Brian Jeffrey, 272 *see also/voir aussi* Berger, Monty, *and/et* Nolan, Brian
Strocel, Terry, *see/voir* MacDonald, Grant
Stuart, (Sir) Campbell: 151, 210, 272, 301
Stubbs, Roy St. George: 151, 210, 272
Sturdee, E.T.: 151
Stursberg, Peter: 272
Sullivan, Alan: 314
Sulte, Benjamin: 151
Summerby, Janice: 94, 110, 210, 272, 301, 348
Summers, Jack L.: 151, 210, 272, 301, 405
Sutherland, Alice Gibson: 348, 368, 406
Sutherland-Brown, A.: 348
Suthren, Victor: 73, 94, 151, 210, 273, 302, 348
Swain, Hector: 66, 74, 94, 110
Swalm, E.J.: 211
Swan, Minto: 348
Swanston, Victor N.: 211
Sweanor, George: 348

Swettenham, John: 58, 95, 211, 273, 314, 348 *see also/voir aussi* Wood, Herbert Fairlie
Syrett, Victor Edward "Candy": 347

Taché, Alexandre Antonin: 151
Tackaberry, R.B.: 58, 302
Tait, Stewart: 348, 368, 406
Talmadge, Marion: 58
Tamblyn, D.S.: 211
Tardif, H.P.: 58, 302
Taschereau, Gabriel: 348
Tascona, Bruce: 151, 211, 273, 302, 406
Tassie, W.T.: 152
Taylor, Alistair: 58
Taylor, Charles: 58
Taylor, H.A., *see/voir* Molson, K.M.
Taylor, Leonard W.: 211
Taylor, M. Brook: 1
Telford, Murray M.: 152, 212, 273, 302, 406
Tennant, Joseph F.: 152
Thakur, Ramesh: 58
Thibault, Jean: 58, 95, 273, 348
Thiessen, M., *see/voir* LeBreton, Marcel
Thistle, Mel: 59
Thomas, Hartley Munro: 212, 273
Thomas, Jim, *see/voir* Witt, Eugene
Thomas, Robert H.: 59
Thompson, Brad: 95, 110, 406
Thompson, John Herd: 59
Thompson, R.W.: 273
Thompson, Roy J.C.: 74, 95, 110, 152, 212, 273, 302, 314, 348, 406
Thompson, Walter R.: 348
Thorburn, Ella M.: 74, 212, 314
Thorgrimsson, Thor: 110
Thorn, J.C.: 212
Thornton, J.M.: 95, 110, 406
Thurston, Arthur: 212, 349
Ticehurst, Michael, *see/voir* Gregory, Walter
Tierney, Ruth: 273
Tippett, Maria: 59, 212
Titler, Dale: 314
Toews, J.A.: 59
Tolton, Gordon E.: 152
Tompkins, Stuart Ramsay: 212, 274
Tooley, Edwyn R.: 118

Tooley, Robert: 274
Toop, E.R., *see/voir* Bailey, W.J.
Topp, C. Beresford: 212
Torontow, Cy: 349, 368
Tracy, Nicholas: 59, 406
Treddenick, J.M., *see/voir* Meredith, D.L.
Tremblay, Jeanne-D'Arc: 59
Tremblay Family/Famille Tremblay: 59
Tricoche, George Nestler: 152
Tripp, F.R.: 274
Trotter, Reginald G.: 60
Tucker, A.B.: 60, 213
Tucker, Gilbert Norman: 66, 74, 95
Tugwell, Maurice: 60
Tupper, Reginald H.: 213
Tupper, Victor Gordon: 213
Turner, Arthur C.: 60
Turner, H.S.: 213
Turner, James Alexander: 160
Turner, T.H.: 274
Tweedsmuir, John Buchan, baron: 60, 152
Tweedsmuir, Susan Charlotte (Grosvenor) Buchan, baroness: 60
Twichell, Heath: 60, 274, 349
Twining, (Sir) Geoffrey: 146
Tyler, G.C.A.: 152, 213, 274, 302, 406
Tyler, Grant, *see/voir* Ross, David

Ulanoff, Stanley M.: 311
Upton, Terence B.: 152, 214, 275
Urquhart, Hugh M.: 153, 214, 275
Ursulak, Caroline, *see/voir* Code, David E.

Vachon, Stanislas: 60
Vaillancourt, Emile: 60
Vaillancourt, Jean-Guy, *see/voir* Shragge, Eric
Valleur, Marie-France, *see/voir* Silver, A.I.
Vallée, Pierre: 275
Vance, Jonathan F.: 60
Van Der Schee, W.: 152, 214, 275, 302, 407
Van der Smissen, William Henry Victor: 156
Van Der Velde, B.J.: 265
Van de Vyvere, Peter, *see/voir* Sealey, D. Bruce
Van de Weerd, Evert: 276 *see also/voir aussi* Veldheer, Peter A.
Vanier, Georges-P.: 209, 270, 275
Vano, Gerard S.: 60

Vaughan, Arnold P.: 349, 369, 407
Vaughan, H.H.: 61
Veldheer, Peter A.: 275 *see also/voir aussi* Van de Weerd, Evert
Velleman, Alexander: 349
Veness, Jack M.: 221
Vennat, Pierre: 275
Verrault, Georges: 275
Viljoen, Tina, *see/voir* Dyer, Gwynne
Vincent, Carl: 275, 349, 350, 369
Vincent, E., *see/voir* Vincent, Carl
Vogel, Robert, *see/voir* Copp, Terry
Vokes, Chris: 275
Vondette, H.W.: 111

Wagner, D.P.: 81, 233, 325
Wagner, Gordon: 350
Waiser, Bill: 61, 214, 276
Walker, D.E.: 276
Walker, William K.: 214
Wallace, John F.: 214, 276
Wallace, N. Willoughby: 153
Wallace, O.C.S.: 215
Wallace, W.S., *see/voir* Duncan-Clark, S.J.
Walmsley, R.Y.: 276
Walton, George, *see/voir* Adleman, Robert H.
Wamper, Hans: 276
Ward, Richard: 369
Ware, Frances B.: 153, 215
Warnock, John W.: 61 *see also/voir aussi* Hertzman, Lewis
Warren, Arnold: 153, 215, 276, 303
Warren, Falkland: 61
Warrilow, Betty: 96
Waters, John: 96
Watson, Robert: 153
Watson, W.S.: 153, 215, 276, 303
Watt, Frederick B.: 96
Watt, Sholto: 350
Watton, J.F.: 279
Watts, E.M.: 276
Watts, Jack: 350
Weatherbe, K.: 215
Weisbord, Merrily: 276, 350
Wells, Clifford Almon: 215
Wells, Eric, *see/voir* Tascona, Bruce
Wells, George Anderson: 96, 153, 215, 277

Wells, Herb: 96, 277, 350
Wells, Jeanne Carden, *see/voir* Wells, George Anderson
Wentzel, Fritz: 277
Werra, Franz von: 277
West, Bruce: 350
West, Christopher: 61
Whalley, B.J.P., *see/voir* Walmsley, R.Y.
Whalley, Peter: 264
Wheeler, Victor W.: 215
Wheeler, William J.: 407
Whitaker, W. Denis: 277
Whitaker, Shelagh, *see/voir* Whitaker, W. Denis
Whitby, Michael J.: 96, 111, 407 *see also/voir aussi* Charlton, Peter, *and/et* McAndrew, William J.
Whitcombe, Fred: 277
Whitehead, William: 96, 277, 350
Whitsed, Roy, *see/voir* Martin, Charles Cromwell
Whitton, Charlotte: 96, 277, 350 *see also/voir aussi* Thorburn, Ella M.
Wickett, Tom: 2, 23
Wickham, H.J.: 61, 66
Wicksteed, R.J.: 153
Wiebe, Rudy: 153
Wile, Frederic William: 175
Wilkes, R.O. "Rusty": 223
Wilkinson, Alta R.: 277
Wilkinson, Arthur Campbell: 277
Wilkinson, (Sir) George Henry: 61
Wilkinson, J.W.: 61
Wilkinson, William Arthur: 96, 111
Will, J.S.: 51
Willcocks, K.D.H.: 153, 215, 277, 303, 407
Willes, John A.: 278
Willett, J.C.: 407
Williams, C.D.: 278
Williams, Jack: 315, 351
Williams, James N.: 351
Williams, Jeffery: 153, 215, 278, 303
Williams, Jon D.: 407
Williams, S.H.: 216
Williams-Taylor, (Sir) Frederick: 61
Willms, A.M.: 27
Willson, Gordon Beckles: 76, 96, 216, 278, 351
Willson, (Sir) John: 61
Wilson, A.J., *see/voir* Herrington, Walter S.
Wilson, Andy, *see/voir* Johnston, Wilf

Wilson, Barbara M.: 62, 153, 216 *see also/voir aussi* Stacey, C.P.
Wilson, J.A.: 315, 351, 369
Wilson, J.E.: 278
Wilson, Keith: 154
Wilson, Peter: 215
Wilson-Simmie, Katherine M.: 216
Windsor, John: 278
Winnington-Ingram, Arthur F.: 216
Winter, Charles F.: 154, 216
Winters, B.A.: 66, 75, 96, 111, 407
Winton, Maurice V.: 154, 216, 278, 303, 407
Wise, S.F.: 315 *see also/voir aussi* Bercuson, David J.
Witol Gregory L., *see/voir* Crickard, Fred W.
Witt, Eugene: 66, 75, 96, 111, 407
Wodehouse, R.F.: 75, 97, 216, 278, 315, 351
Wonders, William C.: 278
Wong, Marjorie: 97, 278, 351
Wood, Gordon: 278
Wood, Herbert Fairlie: 62, 154, 216, 303
Wood, J.E.R.: 279
Wood, William: 62
Woodcock, George: 154
Woodend, S.H., *see/voir* Gian, M.S.
Woods, N.G., *see/voir* Pallas, S.M.
Woodward, Vernon C.: 334
Woolley, H.W.: 351
Worthington, F.F.: 62, 217, 279, 304
Worthington, Larry: 154, 216, 217, 279, 303, 304
Wouk, Jonathan: 29, 105, 387
Wright, Glenn T., *see/voir* Morton, Desmond, *and/et* O'Brien, Jerome
Wright, Harold E.: 97, 154, 217, 279, 351
Wright, J.: 97
Würtele, A.G.G.: 147, 154
Würtele, Ernest F.: 147
Wyatt, Bernie: 352
Wynn, Edgar J.: 352

X., P.I., [*pseud.*] *see/voir* Hallam, T. Douglas

Yates, Harry A.: 316
Yates, Todd R., *see/voir* Jones, David R.
York, Geoffrey: 407
Yorston, Frederic: 198
Yost, William J.: 62
Young, A.H.: 75, 217, 316

Young, Albert Charles: 97, 217, 279, 316, 352
Young, C.R.: 279
Young, George: 62, 97
Young, Scott: 97, 279, 352

Zarn, George: 97
Zepeda Turcios, Roberto: 279
Ziegler, Mary: 352, 369
Zimmerman, David: 97
Zink, Lubor J.: 62